Oswald Cockayne

Leechdoms, Wortcunning and Starcraft of early England

Oswald Cockayne

Leechdoms, Wortcunning and Starcraft of early England

ISBN/EAN: 9783741194658

Manufactured in Europe, USA, Canada, Australia, Japa

Cover: Foto ©Thomas Meinert / pixelio.de

Manufactured and distributed by brebook publishing software
(www.brebook.com)

Oswald Cockayne

Leechdoms, Wortcunning and Starcraft of early England

LEECHDOMS, WORTCUNNING,

AND

STARCRAFT

OF

EARLY ENGLAND.

BEING

A COLLECTION OF DOCUMENTS, FOR THE MOST PART NEVER BEFORE PRINTED,

ILLUSTRATING

THE HISTORY OF SCIENCE IN THIS COUNTRY BEFORE THE NORMAN CONQUEST.

COLLECTED AND EDITED

BY THE

REV. OSWALD COCKAYNE, M.A. CANTAB.

VOL. II.

PUBLISHED BY THE AUTHORITY OF THE LORDS COMMISSIONERS OF HER MAJESTY'S
TREASURY, UNDER THE DIRECTION OF THE MASTER OF THE ROLLS.

LONDON:
LONGMAN, GREEN, LONGMAN, ROBERTS, AND GREEN.

1865.

CONTENTS.

PREFACE.

PREFACE.

No historical records are complete without the usual
chapter on Manners and Customs; and the true scholar
never feels himself well in possession of the requisite
knowledge of the past age, till he has so learnt its
time honoured tale, as to apprehend in a human and
practical sense those feelings which made its super-
stitions plausible, its heathenism social, its public
institutions tend, in the end, to the general welfare.

The Saxons have not been more fortunate than others
in their appreciation by us, self satisfied moderns. They
have been, and still are, I believe, commonly regarded
as mangy dogs, whose success against the Keltic race
in this country was owing chiefly to their starved
condition and ravening hunger. The children protest
that, positively, as they know from their most reliable
handbooks, these roving savages stuffed their bellies
with acorns, and the enlightened *literati* and *dilettanti*
begrudge them any feeling of respect for their queens
and ladies, or any arts such as befit our " Albion's
" glorious isle " under an English king.

The work now published for the first time, and
from a unique manuscript, will, if duly studied, afford
a large store of information to a very different effect,
and show us that the inhabitants of this land in
Saxon times were able to extract a very fair share
of comfortable food, and healing medicines, and savoury
drinks directly or indirectly from it. Many readers

will be glad to see drawn together into one the scattered notices which occur most plentifully here, and
occasionally elsewhere, upon this matter.

At his noon meat or dinner, at the *hora nona*, or
ninth hour of the day,[1] for the word noon has now
changed its sense, the Saxon spread his table duly
and suitably with a table cloth.[2] He could place on
it for the entertainment of his family and household,
the flesh of neat cattle,[3] now Normanized, as Sir Walter
Scott has made familiar to all, into beef, the flesh of
sheep,[4] now called mutton, of pig, of goat,[5] of calf,[5] of
deer, especially the noble hart,[6] of wild boar,[6] the peacock, swan, duck,[7] culver or pigeon,[8] waterfowl, barn-
door fowl,[9] geese,[10] and a great variety of wild fowl,
which the fowler caught with net, noose, birdlime,
birdcalls, hawks, and traps;[11] salmon, eels, hake, pil-
chards, eelpouts,[12] trout, lampreys, herrings, sturgeon,
oysters, crabs, periwinkles, plaice, lobsters, sprats,[13]
and so on.[14]

The cookery of these viands was not wholly contemptible. It was entrusted to professors of that admired
art,[15] who could, though their accomplishments have
been neglected by the annalists, put on the board
oyster patties,[16] and fowls stuffed with bread and such
worts as parsley.[17] Weaker stomachs could have light

---

[1] Hom. II. 256. Also Seo sunne
aþystꞃobe.ꝼꞃam mibbæᵹe oð non,
M.H. 158 a, *The sun was darkened
from midday till noon.* Even here
our dictionaries blunder.

[2] Beobclað, Æ.G. 8, line 31. Myꞃe
hꞃæᵹel, Lye.

[3] Lb. II. vii., etc.

[4] Coll. Monasticon, p. 20.

[5] Lb. II. xvi.

[6] Coll. Mon. p. 22.

[7] Lb. II. xvi.

[8] Lb. II. xxx. 2.

[9] DD. 504 ; Lb. II. xvi. 2.

[10] Lb. II. xvi. 2.

[11] Coll. Mon. p. 25.

[12] Young eels (Kersey).

[13] Sprottas not in the dictionaries.
Besides two passages in which it
occurs, reserved for reasons which
readers of the Shrine will understand, it occurs Coll. Mon. p. 23.
See French Celerin, Selerin ; the
MS. has Salin.

[14] Coll. Mon. pp. 23, 24.

[15] Coll. Mon. p. 29.

[16] Lb. II. xxiii.

[17] Lb. III. xii.

food, chickens,[1] giblets, pigs trotters,[2] eggs, broth, various preparations of milk, some of the nature of junkets.[3]

From some of their drawings, their cookery of meat seems to have been more Homeric[4] than Roman or modern English, for we see portions of meat brought up on small spits, all hot, to the table. All food that required it was sweetened with honey, before men had betaken themselves to sugar. For fruits, we know they had sweet apples,[5] which are not indigenous to England, pears, peaches,[6] medlars, plums, and cherries.

Saxons, thus well provided with eatables, could satisfy thirst with not a few good and savoury drinks; with beer, with strong beer, with ale, with strong ale, with clear ale, with foreign ale, and with what they called twybrowen, that is, double brewed ale, a luxury, now rare, and rare too then probably.[7] These ales and beers were, of course, to deserve the name, and as we learn from many passages of the present publication, made of malt, and some of them, not all probably, were hopped.[8] I have sufficiently, in the Glossary,[9] established that the hop plant and its use were known to the Saxons, and that they called it by a name, after which I have inquired in vain among hop growers and hop pickers in Worcestershire and Kent, the Hymele.[10] The hop grows wild in our hedges, male and female, and the Saxons in this state called it the hedge hymele; a good valid presumption that they knew it in its fertility. Three of the Saxon legal deeds

---

[1] As before.
[2] Lb. II. i.
[3] Gl. ꝼlecan.
[4] Καὶ ἀμφ' ὀβέλοισιν ἔθηκαν.
[5] Mylsce æppla, Lb. II. xvi.
[6] Persocas, Lb. p. 176 ; Lacn. 89 ; Διδαξ. 31.
[7] Lb. I. xlvii. 3.

[8] Hb. lxviii.
[9] See also Preface, Vol. I. p. lv.
[10] I find Ymele, fem., gen -an, for a roll, scroll, volumen. The Hymele is in glossaries frequently Volubilis; and the two suggest a derivation for either from Ymbe = 'Αμφί, so that Hymele means coiler.

extant refer[1] to a hide of land at Hymel-tun in Worcestershire, the land of the garden hop, and as tun means an enclosure, there can be not much doubt that this was a hop farm. The bounds of it ran down to the hymel brook, or hop plant brook, a name which occurs about the Severn and the Worcestershire Avon in other deeds. One of the unpublished glossaries affords the Saxon word Hopu, Hops,[2] and Hopwood in Worcestershire doubtless is thence named. Perhaps, to explain some testimonies to a more recent importation of hops, it may be suggested that, as land or sea carriage of pockets of hops from Worcestershire to London or the southern ports was difficult, the use of the hop was long confined to that their natural soil, while the Kentish hops may be a gift from Germany.

A table is well enough furnished where the flagons are filled with good malt liquor; it is flat heresy, they say, to discover mischief in University " particular :" but, notwithstanding, the Saxons drank also mead, an exhilarating beverage, which from its sweetness must have been better suited to the palates of the ladies, and which was of an antiquity far anterior to written or legendary history. They had also great store of wines, which they distinguished by their qualities, as clear, austere, sweet, rather than by their provinces or birth. They made up also artificial drinks, oxymel, hydromel, mulled wines, and a Clear drink, or Claret,[3] of the nature of those beverages which are now called cup.

Salt, which is an indispensable condiment to civilized man, they obtained from Cheshire and Worcestershire, where they had furnaces for the evaporation of the

---

[1] C.D. 209, 680, 1066.
[2] " Lygistra hopu," Gl. Cleop. f. 57 a. Ligustra, though known to every ear, by the line Alba ligustra cadunt, were long doubtful ; we believe them to be the blossoms of privet.
[3] See the Glossary in þlæccop ꝺþenc.

brine.[1] Salt for salted meats,[2] which also were quite
familiar to them, might be got from the saltpans on
the sea shore.

The dishes, on which their meats were served, were
sometimes of silver,[3] nor was this esteemed a high
distinction.[4] The vessels from which they drank were
sometimes of glass ;[5] and those they had also transpa-
rent in quality.[6] The supply upon the tables of a chief-
tain, who had many retainers, was abundant, and not
over studious of luxury and refinement.[7] When not
engaged in war or hunting, the princes thought a good
deal of their gormandize.[8] Festive assemblies were more
frequent than among other races of men ; they were
duly ordered, and attended by gleemen, from whose
lips the honeysweets of song flowed readily and freely,
and whose reward came from the munificence of the
prince. The feasts not rarely lasted through the
night.[9]

In the monastic colloquy, an exercise for students,
who were to be "bilingues," capable of conversing in
their own language and in that of Rome, which is,
therefore, quite destitute of artifice or ambition, a boy
is asked what he has to eat. His reply is, worts (that
is, kitchen herbs), fish, cheese, butter, beans, and flesh
meats. He drinks ale, and, if he cannot get that, water,
for he cannot afford wine. This is the daily diet of
a boy under education in a monastery.

Altogether, if the comfortable prejudices of modernism
do not shut out trustworthy and contemporary testi-

---

[1] C.D. 451.
[2] Lb. p. 234, etc.
[3] Discus argenteus regalibus
epulis refertus, Beda, III. vi.
[4] Est videre apud illos argenteæ
vasa, legatis et principibus eorum
muneri datæ, non in alia vilitate
quam quæ humo finguntur. Tacitus,
Germ. 5.

[5] Calicem is translated glæppæc,
Beda, p. 618, line 12.
[6] C.E. 78, ult.
[7] Epulæ et, quanquam incompti,
largi tamen adparatus, Tacit. Germ.
14.
[8] Dediti somno ciboque, Tacit.
Germ. 15.
[9] Tacit. Germ. 22.

mony the Saxons must be concluded to be very far
removed from that pasturage upon the herb of the
field which was the regale of human innocence, and
that feeding upon grass which was the doom of an
arrogant Oriental king. They seem to dine like Eng-
lishmen.

The Saxon imported purple palls, and silk, precious
gems, gold, rare vestments, drugs, wine, oil, ivory, ori-
chalchum (a very fine mixed metal of gold and silver),
brass, brimstone, glass, and many more such articles.[1]
Tin came by water from Cornwall. Their enterprise by
sea was distinguished ; they pursued the dangerous
whale, and were known for their adventurous hostile
landings upon the Gallic coasts before they had settled
in this country.[2]

When the Saxons got possession of Britain, they
found it, not such as Julius Cæsar describes it, but
cultivated and improved by all that the Romans knew
of agriculture and gardening. Hence rue, hyssop, fennel,
mustard, elecampane, southernwood, celandine, radish,
cummin, onion,[3] lupin, chervil, flower de luce, flax
probably, rosemary, savory, lovage, parsley, coriander,
olusatrum, savine, were found in their gardens and
available for their medicines. Among the foreign drugs,
or the like, which are mentioned in this volume, we find
mastich, pepper, galbanum, scamony, gutta ammoniaca,
cinnamon, vermilion, aloes, pumice, quicksilver, brimstone, myrrh, frankincense, petroleum,[4] ginger.

The Saxons and Engle for the supply of their tables,
thus, as we have seen, abundantly supplied, kept herds
of cattle. The agriculture was in great measure, with
alterations adapted to the moister climate, and with
improvements from lapse of time and from other coun-

[1] Col. Mon. p. 27.
[2] Ammianus Marcellinus, xxviii.
5.

[3] Ynneleac has for its first element a Latinism, unionem, *onion*.
[4] Lb. pp. 53, 57, 61, 101, 125
289, 297.

tries, Roman. Among them arable land was excellently cared for, much on the same method as we observe on the downs of Kent, the garden of England. By throwing a thousand small allotments into one great field, they were well rid of the encumbrance, the weeds, the birds, the boys going a birdnesting, and the repair of hedges or other fences. But the pasture land was not so well managed. The Romans, who had an elaborate machinery of aqueducts and irrigation, grew hay in their prata, or meadows, which were artificially supplied with water, and to get two crops a year, or three or four,[1] gave a large flow of that element to the soil. This, of course, had its inconveniences, herbs that thrive in wet came up stronger than the grass, especially horsetail, and a "nummulus" with pods. They had an awkward inefficient way of cutting the grass with a hook, held in the right hand only, and this was followed by a second operation, called sickling,[2] to cut what the hooks had left. They tedded the hay, as is done now, by hand, with forks,[3] took care it should be dry enough not to ferment, leaving it in cocks,[4] and when ready carried it off to the farm,[5] and stored it in a loft.[6]

Our forefathers here were able, from the frequent Hay. rains, to dispense for the most part with irrigation. They cut the hay with sithes,[7] the pattern of which was probably borrowed from the continental Kelts,[8] and, most naturally, by the subdued British before the settlement of the English, since they were relatives, spoke

---

[1] Interamnæ in Umbria quater anno secantur etiam non rigua, Plin. xviii. 67 = 28.
[2] Sicilire; Plin. as above, Varro, R.R. i. 19.
[3] Furcillis.
[4] Metæ.
[5] Villa.
[6] In tabulato. Sub tecto, Columella, II. xix.

[7] Hom. II. p. 162. Also a Saxon drawing in MS. Cott. Tiber. B. v., where the painter has given straight handles to the sithes ; and has certainly committed an error in drawing haymaking for August, and reaping for June.
[8] Galliarum latifundia maioris compendii, Plin. as above.

the language, and were in frequent communication with Gaul. They stored the hay in ricks [1] and mows,[2] where it was less likely to get mouldy than in the half close lofts of the Romans.

But according to the Roman system little hay was prepared thus, there were legal impediments to extending widely the formation of inclosed pasturages, and we read often enough of feeding the cattle upon leaves, or rather on foliage.[3] The man employed in procuring small boughs for his cattle was called Frondator.[4] The greater part, by far, of Italian pasture land was common, overspread by bushes and trees, where the employment of herdsmen and shepherds was indispensable, and improvement was almost impossible.

Cattle thieves.   In the same way, in early England, a grass field[5] is rarely heard of, while the law books are full of precautions against cattle thieves, whose bad business was made easy by the threading commons and wide moors, along which a stolen herd could be driven, picking up subsistence on its way, and evading observation by keeping off the great roads. So much were the farmers pestered with cattle thefts, that the legislature required responsible witnesses to the transfer of such property, and would have it transacted in open market; it also invented a team; that is to say, when Z, who has lost his oxen, found them and identified them in possession of A, the said A was bound by trustworthy witnesses to show that he had them lawfully from B; B was then compelled to go through the same process, and to

---

[1] This word is not in the Saxon dictionaries, and I will not at present indicate the passage where it is to be found.

[2] Mugan, Exodus xxii. 6.

[3] " Quid maiora sequar ? Salices " humilesque genistæ

" Aut illæ pecori frondem aut " pastoribus umbram " Sufficiunt."
          Virgil. Georgic. II. 434.
" Hic ubi densas agricolæ strin- " gunt frondes."
          Id. Ecl. ix. 60.
[4] Virgil. Ecl. I. 57.
[5] Gærrtun.

show that he gave honest money for them to C; thus
a team or row of successive owners was unravelled till
it ended in P, who had neglected to secure credible
witnesses to his bargain ; or in Q, who bought them
at a risky price from the actual thief. Then Z recovered
his cattle or their value.[1] Under this legislation the
chief difficulty of a loser was to trace the direction in
which his cattle had been driven off, and the skill of
the hunter in tracking the slot of the deer, helped to
follow the foot prints of horse or sheep or ox.[2] The
less fertile parts of England are still patched by strips
of common, or ways with grassy wastes skirting them,
and the wanderer may often ramble by hedgerow elms
mid hillocks green, among the primroses and violets,
by ups and downs, through quagmires and over gates,
from his furthest point for the day, till he nears the
town and his inn. Elwes, the famous miser, could ride
seventy miles out of London without paying turnpike.
The Saxon herdsman watched the livelong night.[3]

The Saxons also, like the Romans, fed their cattle, Cattle fed on
sometimes, so as to make the notion familiar, with the leaves.
foliage of trees. In his life of St. Cuðberht, the venerable
Beda gives an account of a worthy Hadwald (Eadwald),
a faithful servant of Ælflæd, abbess of Whitby, who was
killed by falling from a tree.[4] Ælfric three hundred
years afterwards telling the same story, gives us either
from some collateral tradition, by writing may be, may
be by word, or from his judgment of what was naturally
the mans business at tree climbing, an account that this
tree was an oak, and that he was feeding the cattle
with the foliage, so that he was killed in discharge
of his duty as herdsman.[5] In the summer of 1864 this

[1] DD. in many passages.
[2] Hoꞃpec, Foꞇꞃpoꞃ.
[3] Coll. Mon. p. 20. Tota nocte
sto super eos vigilando propter
fures.

[4] Incautius in arborem ascen-
dens deciderat deorsum, Beda, 256,
22.
[5] Hom. II. 150.

poor resource is said to have been used in some counties
of England, notwithstanding the "great strides science
"has made."

Sheep.   Sheep were driven to pasture by their shepherd with
his dogs, and at night were taken back home and folded.[1]
With goats, sheep provided most part of the milk and
cheese consumed in early times; cow butter is frequently named in this volume by way of distinction;
these smaller beasts were robbed of their milk from the
teats between the hind legs. A Saxon calendar heads
the month of May with a painting representing sheep and
goats under the shepherds care.

Swine.   Swine were entrusted to the swineherd, who pastured
them in his masters woods, or on a customary per-
centage of the stock,[2] in the woods of some other pro-
prietor. He had a perquisite, a sty pig out of the farrow,
with another for his comrade or deputy, besides the
usual dues of servitors.[3]

Boar hunting.   A drawing of a purely Saxon type, in a Saxon manuscript, represents the hunting of the wild boar; a thane,
or as we say gentleman, on foot, has some wild pigs,
bristly and yellowish brown, in view; he carries a long
boar spear, and his left hand rests on the hilt of his
sword, which is to save his life, if the boar charges;
he is followed by an unarmed attendant, with a pair
of dogs in a leash, and a hunting horn. The painter
has probably assigned this drawing to the wrong
month.[4]

Hawking.   The same artist has drawn a Saxon gentleman out
a hawking on horseback, with an attendant on foot,
each provided with a hawk; the wild fowl, ducks or
teal, are in the picture, these the hawk dispatched

---

[1] Coll. Mon. 20.
[2] One third of very fat ones, one
fourth, and one fifth of less fat.
DD. p. 58.
[3] DD. p. 187.

[4] September. To say this painting
represents herding swine is a strange
inaccuracy. No hand is raised to
shake down mast.

quickly, splitting their skulls with a stroke of his beak.
A large bird, perhaps a heron, is introduced into the
scene.

Feather beds, with bolsters and pillows, were in use
in Saxon times. [1]

It seemed necessary to pave the way for an examina- England
tion of the work now published by some such remarks civilized.
as these, which are not all trite or matters of course ;
in order that the minds of readers not very familiar
with these early times might give the rest of our facts
a readier acceptance. The entire scope and tenor of
all that we possess in the way of home literature, laws,
deeds, histories, poems, regarding these Angles and
Saxons, implies a tolerable degree of civilization ; and
many modern writers have persistently misrepresented
their customs, and pretended to unloose the very bonds
of society among them. I take leave to touch on one
or two points, tending still to prepare us for the facts
on the face of the present volume.

Tacitus says that the German races were well pleased Coins.
with Roman money, and that such coins as were of
approved value, the milled edged, and the pair horse
chariot stamped,[2] had currency among them. In England the kings, great and small, learned to imitate on
their own account the currency of Rome. Writers on
the subject dwell upon this, and we are, in our mended
age, ourselves guilty of this want of originality. Saxon
pennies are common enough, but the numismatists say
that they coined no gold, because no gold coins have
been turned up. Saxon gold mancuses are mentioned
in twenty different passages of manuscripts : they were
not money of account, for we read of mancuses by
weight ; and a will, now in the hands of a zealous
editor, settles the question by the following words :
" Then let twenty hundred mancuses of gold be taken

---

[1] Gl. Somn. p. 60 b, line 40. | [2] Serratos bigatosque.

" and coined into mancuses ;" [1] that is, there was a gold coin of a determinate weight called a mancus, and coined in England. Suppose when the document is fairly before us that this will turn out suspect; suppose it be pronounced a forgery; still we have Saxon authority for coining gold mancuses, and at home. All works that touch the subject, know that there were in those times royal mints and royal moneyers.

Herbalist learning.

The Glossary appended to this work exhibits, from among a still wider list, a large number of names of herbs; and materials exist for determining most of these to full conviction. The change of residence produced doubtless some confusion, by depriving the Saxons of specimens of the trees and plants answering to their names. The Germanic races had not before their arrival here pushed down upon the Mediterranean shores, but we all know historically that they had not been confined to cold climates, and one very curious proof exists that in some instances the name they fixed on a plant was appropriate only to its aspect in warmer countries. [2] It is true that the oak, beech, birch, hawthorn, sloethorn, bore native names, but elm, [3] walnut, maple, holly, [4] are equally native names; and, except the walnut, native trees. The cherry was brought to Italy by Lucullus, from Κερασοῦς, Cerasus, a city of Cappadocia, where it was plentiful, and it has ever borne the same name. The students of nature learn that many species of its Fauna, and also, though less so, of its Flora, can be traced to a single spot. Thus the peach, peβroc,

---

[1] þanne minpe (read nime) man trentiʒ hunð mancufa golber ⁊ gemynetiʒe to mancuṛan, HID. fol. 21 a. The transcript is not by any means cotemporary.

[2] I regret I cannot here explain this fully.

[3] Not a Latinism.

[4] Holen, which is originally an adjective, Holeʒn, Holeʒen, and even now so applied to Holn Wood on the banks of the Dart, near Ashburton. Holeʒ, Holly, is the original substantive, C.E. 437, line 19. The old Latin name is Aquifolius : the Ilex was glandiferous, the evergreen oak.

Malum Persicum, was from Persia; there is no other
name for it but "the Persian apple." For such as these
it was impossible to have any other name; they were
fruit trees foreign to all but their own countrymen.
The plum is a better sloe ; can be raised only by graft-
ing, for seedlings are found to degenerate; which is
also the case with the pear, having its native equivalent
in the *Pirus domestica*, of Bewdley Forest. The syca-
more, which has been alleged to prove the Latinism
of the Saxons, is merely a maple. Yet the great
influence which a Latin education, and scarce any instruction in old English, has upon ourselves, is traceable even among the Saxons : the true signification of
some native names was passing away, and the plants
supposed once to have borne them began to be known
by some Roman denomination. For so common a plant
as mint, seen in every running ditch, on every watery
marge, there seems to be no name but that which is
Hellenic, and Latin. The Germanic races, on the con-
trary, were the original patrons of hemp [1] and flax,[2]
as against wool. It is, however, with their reach over
the material world, and their proficiency in the arts
which turn it to mans convenience, after, and not
before, their arrival in England, that we are now deal-
ing; and we maintain that a great part of what the
Roman could teach, the Saxons, their successors, had
learnt.

The most cursory examination of the work now Book learning.
before us will show that we are reading of a civilization such as the above details would lead us to ex-
pect. Here a leech calmly sits down to compose a
not unlearned book, treating of many serious diseases,
and assigning for them something he hopes will cure
them. In the Preface to the first volume it was ad-

[1] Vol. I. p. x. note.
[2] Feminæ sæpius lineis amictibus utuntur. Tacitus, Germ. 17.

mitted that Saxon leeches fell short of the daring skill of Hellas, or the wondrous success of the leading medical men of either branch in London or Paris. Notwithstanding that this is a learned book, it sometimes sinks to mere driveling, The author almost always rejects the Greek recipes, and doctors as an herborist. It will give any one who has the heart of a man in him a thrill of horror to compare the Saxon dose of brooklime and pennyroyal twice a day, for a mother whose child is dead within her,[1] with the chapter in Celsus devoted to this subject, in which we read, as in his inmost soul, an anxious courageous care, and a sense of responsibility mixed with determination to do his utmost, which is, even to a reader, agitating.[2]

The manuscript. The volume consists of two parts; a treatise on medicine in two books, with its proper colophon at the end, and a third of a somewhat more monkish character. The book itself probably once belonged to the abbey of Glastonbury, for a catalogue of the books of that foundation, cited by Wanley,[3] contains the entry " Medicinale Anglicum," which is rightly interpreted, " Saxonice scriptum ;" and this book, rebound in 1757, has preserved on one of the fly leaves an old almost illegible inscription, " Medicinale Anglicum." Search has been made for any record of the books, which, on the dissolution of the monasteries, might have found their way from Glastonbury to the Royal Library, but in vain.

An earlier, the first, owner is pointed out in the colophon.[4]

Bald habet hunc librum, Cild quem conscribere iussit.

---

[1] Lb. p. 331.
[2] Adhibenda curatio est, quæ numerari inter difficillimas potest. Nam et summam prudentiam moderationemque desiderat, et maxi- mum periculum affert. Celsus, VII. xxix.
[3] Hickes, Thesaur. Vol. II. Præf. ad Catalogum.
[4] P. 298.

In this doggrel, Bald is the owner of the book; we
have no right to improve him into Æðelbald; Cild is, ·
probably, the scribe; some will contend, the author.
In classical Latin no doubt would exist, conscribere
would at once denote the composing of the work :
but in these later days, when millions of foreigners
learnt the Latin language as a means of interchange of
thoughts, occasionally intruding their own Gothic words,
all such niceties of the ear went for nothing; Cild
might well be the mere penman. But then the marginal tokens, and private memoranda, show that the
work so written had passed either through the hands
of the author, which from the use of private marks
is probable, or through those of another leech, who was
able to discover the sources of the authors information.
Bald anywise may have been the author himself.

Let us give a few touches to the, as yet, bare outline Cild.
of the penman Cild. The famous Durham book is a
charming work of ancient Saxon art ; those who cannot
inspect the original may see a copy of a piece of the
ornamentation in the Gospel of St. Matthew, edited
by the Rev. Joseph Stevenson, and published by the
Surtees society. According to an entry of a later age
in the book itself, not of doubtful authenticity, this
exquisite piece of pattern work, which is a part of
the writing, was the performance of EadfriÞ, bishop
of Lindisfarne, who occupied that see from 698 to 721.
It is of Irish tone, and like many other dignitaries this
prelate had, very likely, completed his Christian education in the Isle of Saints. Cild was certainly not of the
make and metal of a bishop, for the words " conscribere
" iussit " forbid it ; Dunstan forefend ! It would be
somewhat speculative to say, that in Northumbria,
A.D. 700, the art of writing was at a higher premium
than afterwards. I will not venture to say it, but
proceed upon surer data. One of the poems in the
Exeter book, of uncertain date, but before the end

of the tenth century, mentions as a valued accomplish-
ment the art of writing in fair characters.[1]

One can cunningly
word speech write.

Ælfric also himself in a sermon on Midlent Sunday,—
" Oft one seeth fair letters awritten; then extolleth he
" the writer and the letters, and wotteth not what they
" mean. He who kenneth the difference of the letters,
" he extolleth the fairness, and readeth the letters,
" and understandeth what they mean." The honour
remained to beautiful writing, but the writer did not
stalk in so lofty a station. On the top margin of a
page [2] of the Oxford copy of the Herd Book, or Liber
Pastoralis, of King Ælfred may be read these words,—

pillimot ppit þuf oððe bet,

that is, *Willimot, write thus or better.* A little further
on,[3]

ppit þuf oððe bet oððe þine hybe foplet,

Write thus or better, or bid good bye to thy hide, that
is, get a good hiding. In an Harleian MS.[4] there is
a bit of nonsense, but the same idea of a hiding is
uppermost;

ppit þuf oððe bet þibe apeg.

ælfnæppattafox þu þilt rpinʒan ælfpic cilb;

*Write thus or better; ride away; Ælfnærpattafox; thou
wilt swinge child Ælfric.* From these marginal
scribblings it is plain that the penman had descended
from his episcopal throne, to be a tipsy drudge, kept
in order by the whip. Cild, " quem Bald conscribere
" iussit," was nearer the whip than the crooked staff.

Bald.
The owner of the book, Bald, may be fairly presumed
to have been a medical practicioner, for to no other

---

[1] " Sum mæg reapolice,
    " popb cpibe ppizan."
                    C.E. 42, 14.

[2] Fol. 53 a.
[3] Fol. 55 b.
[4] Harl. 55, fol. 4 b.

could such a book as this have had, at that time, much
interest. We see then a Saxon leech here at his studies;
the book, in a literary sense, is learned; in a professional
view not so, for it does not really advance mans knowledge of disease or of cures. It may have seemed by
the solemn elaboration of its diagnoses to do so, but I
dare not assert there is real substance in it. Bald,
however, may have got some good out of it, he may
have learned to think, have begun to discriminate, to
take less for granted. Thus we see him in his study,
among his books becoming, for his day, a more ac-
complished physician; and he speaks with a genuine
philosophs zeal about those his books. "nulla mihi tam
" cara est optima gaza Quam cari libri:" fees and stored
wealth he loved not so well as his precious volumes.
If Bald was at once a physician. and a reader of learned
books on therapeutics, his example implies a school of
medicine among the Saxons. And the volume itself
bears out the presumption. We read in two cases [1] that
" Oxa taught this leechdom;" in another [2] that " Dun
"' taught it;" in another " some teach us;" [3] in another
an impossible prescription being quoted; [4] the author, or
possibly Cild, the reedsman, indulges in a little facetious
comment, that compliance was not easy. I assume that
Oxa and Dun were natives, either of this country or
of some land inhabited by a kindred people. Any way,
we make out, undoubtedly, a bookish study of medicine;
the Saxon writers, who directly from the Greek, or
through the medium of a Latin translation studied
Trallianus, Paulus of Ægina, and Philagrios, were men
of learning not contemptible, in letters, that is, not to
say in pathology. Some of the simpler treatment is
reasonable enough; the cure of hair lip [5] contains a true

---

[1] Lb. p. 120.
[2] Lb. p. 292.
[3] Lb. p. 114.
[4] Ibid.
[5] Lb. L xiii.

element; the application of vinegar with prussic acid[1] for
head ache is practical; the great fondness for elecampane,
Inula helenium, is parallel to the frequent employment,
at the present day, of Arnica. But it would be vain to
defend the prescriptions, some are altogether blunders,
and the fashion of medical treatment changes so much
that the prescriptions of Meade and Radcliffe are now
condemned as absurd. It suffices that Saxon leeches
endeavoured by searching the medical records of foreign
languages to qualify themselves for their profession.

Age.

The character of the writing fixes, as far as I venture
on an opinion, this copy of the work to the former half
of the tenth century; some learned in MSS., who have
favoured me with an opinion, say the latter half, 960
to 980. My own judgment is chiefly based upon comparison with books we know to have been written about
900.

King Ælfred.

The inquisitiveness of men at that period about the
methods in medicine pursued in foreign countries is
illustrated by the very curious and interesting citation
from Helias, patriarch of Jerusalem.[2] The account given
has strong marks of genuineness. We will assume that
King Ælfred had sent to Jerusalem requesting from
the patriarch some good recipes ; for it would be not
in the manner of mens ordinary dealings for the head
of the church in the Holy Land to obtrude upon a
distant king any drugs or advice of the kind. He
returns then a recommendation of scamony, which is the
juice_ of a Syrian convolvulus, of gutta ammoniaca, a
sort of liquid volatile salts, of spices, of gum dragon,
of aloes, of galbanum, of balsam, of petroleum, of the
famous Greek compound preparation called θηριακή, and
of the magic virtues of alabaster.[3] These drugs are good
in themselves, and such as a resident in Syria would
naturally recommend to others. The present author

---

[1] Lb. I. i. 10 and 12.   [2] On the Phœnician origin of this
[3] Lb. p. 290.   word, see SSpp. p. 285.

drew his information, we may fairly suppose, from that
handbook which the king himself kept, in which were
entered " flowers, culled from what masters soever,"
" without method,"[1] " according as opportunity arose,"
and which at length grew to the size of a psalter; whence
also most likely came in due time the voyage of Oth-
here. It is very much the custom of the present swarm
of critics to drag up every old author to their modern
standard of truth, to peer into dates, to sift, and weigh,
and measure, and in short, to put an old tale teller into
the witness box of a modern court of justice, and there
teaze and browbeat him because they cannot half understand his simple talk, nor apprehend how small matters, in a truthful story, the exact day of the week
and the twentieth part of a mile become. When one
writer of the Middle Ages copies another there commonly arises a want of clearness in marking the transitions from the text of the old author to the words
of him who cites him. But in this case all seems smooth ;
the man named was patriarch of Jerusalem ; he was
contemporaneous with King Ælfred, and the drugs he
recommended were sold in the Syrian drug shops, or
apothekæ. I am, therefore, well pleased to claim for
this volume the publication in type of a new fact
about the inquiring watchfulness of that illustrious
ruler.

Thus, Oxa, Dun, perhaps some others of the same Many sources.
sort, and Helias, patriarch of Jerusalem, are sources
of some of the teaching in this book. To these we
may add a mixture of the Hibernian,[2] and of the
Scandinavian.[3] Some of the recipes occur again in the
Lacnunga and in Plinius Valerianus, who, from his
mention[4] of the physician Constantinus, was later than

---

[1] Flosculos undecunque collectos
a quibuslibet magitris, et in corpore
unius libelli, mixtim quamvis, sicut
tunc suppetebat redigere, Asser. p. 57.

[2] Lb. p. 10, I. xlv. 5.
[3] Lb. I. xlvi., I. lxx. lxxi., III.
lviii.
[4] Fol. 14 b. 15 a.

this work. Large extracts and selections are made
from the Greek writers.   It is not to be expected that
many will soon travel over the field of research which
the present edition required, and it will be but fair to
those who are examining the facts, to present them with
at least one passage as a specimen.

Περὶ λυγμῶν. Ὁ λυγμὸς γίνεται ἢ διὰ πλήρωσιν, ἢ διὰ κένωσιν, ἢ
δριμέων χυμῶν δακνόντων τὸν στόμαχον. ὧν ἐμεθέντων παύεται. πολλοὶ δὲ
καὶ τὸ διὰ τῶν τριῶν πεπέρεων μόνον λαβόντες, ἐὰν εὐθέως ἐπιπίωσιν
οἶνον λύζουσιν. ὅτι δὲ καὶ διαφθείροντές τινες τροφὴν λύζουσιν τῶν
γινωσκομένων ἐστί. καὶ ῥιγώσαντες δὲ πολλοὶ λύζουσιν. ἔμετον μὲν οὖν
εὑρήσομεν αὔταρκες ἴαμα τῶν διὰ πλῆθος ἢ δῆξιν λυζόντων. θερμασίαν
δὲ τῶν διὰ ψύξιν. ὅταν δὲ ὑπὸ πληρώσεως ὑγρῶν γένηται λυγμός,
βιαίας δεῖται κενώσεως. τοῦτο δὲ ὁ πταρμὸς ἐργάζεται. τοὺς δὲ ἐπὶ
κενώσει λυγμοὺς οὐκ ἰᾶται πταρμός. Διδόναι δὲ τοῖς λύζουσιν πήγανον
μετ᾽ οἴνου ἢ νίτρον ἐν μελικράτῳ, ἢ σέσελι ἢ δαῦκον ἢ κύμινον ἢ
ζιγγίβερ ἢ καλαμίνθην ἢ νάρδον κελτικήν. ταῦτα τῶν ἐπὶ διαφθορᾷ
σιτίων ἢ ἐπὶ ψύξεσιν ἢ ἐπὶ πληρώσει βοηθήματα. τοῖς δὲ ὑπὸ πλήθους
λύζουσιν ἐπὶ ψυχροῖς καὶ γλίσχροις χυμοῖς καστόριον τριωβόλου δίδου
πίνειν δ᾽ ὀξυκράτου, κ.τ.λ.   Paulus Ægin. lib. ii. cap. 56.

TRANSLATION.

Of hiccupings.   Hiccup comes on either by reason of repletion, or of emptiness, or of austere juices biting upon the
stomach, and when these are vomited forth it ceases.   Many
also by only taking the medicine called " by the three
" peppers," if immediately on that they swallow wine, hiccup.
It is also a recognized fact, that some turning their food sour,
hiccup ; and many also hiccup after shivering.   We shall find
then that a vomit is a sufficient cure for those who hiccup
from repletion or irritation ; and the application of warmth
for those that do so from chill.   But when the hiccup comes
on by fulness of moistures, it needs a violent evacuation ;
and this sneezing produces ; but sneezing does not cure the
hiccups which depend on emptiness.   Give the sufferer from
hiccup rue with wine, or nitre in sweetened wine, or seseli, or
carrot, or cummin, or ginger, or calamintha, or Keltic valerian.
These are proper for the cases in which food turns sour on
the stomach, or for chill, or for emptiness.   But for those that
suffer by repletion with cold and viscid humours, give cas-
toreum, three obols worth, and to drink some oxymel, etc.

This is to be compared with Lb. I. xviii. The correspondence is so close as to leave no doubt but that the work before us drew from Paulus, or from one of the Greek authors, from whom he compiled his work. The number of passages the Saxon thus draws from the Greek is great; they would make perhaps one fourth of the first two books, and the question of course occurs strongly to the mind whether they came direct from the study of Greek manuscripts.

At first sight a passage[1] which says that the ficus in the eyes is called "on læben" chymosis, may seem to resolve the question as that this author copied Latin works. So it may have been; but the place is not conclusive, those words may come from Oxa, Dun, or other writers of the native school of medicine; or læben, leben, may be used as it often is in a loose sense for *language*,[2] *foreign language*. It is not at this point, that it will repay our trouble to stay for consideration: we shall much more profitably form an opinion whether the Saxon leeches in general had access to the sense of the Greek authors, than whether in particular the author of these books knew anything of them. If the best men among our leeches of the tenth century could avail themselves of what Paulus of Ægina, Alexander of Tralles, and Philagrios wrote, that will suffice to raise our estimate of that day into approbation. *Internal testimony.*

M. Brechillet Jourdain[3] has shewn that in those early days, before the invention of printing, the wise men of the middle ages possessed Latin translations of Aristoteles. There was therefore no reason for their not possessing other authors. Some among them were able to translate, some to speak Greek. The Byzantine authors in our own hands come down to a late date. *Greek learning.*

---

[1] Lb. p. 38.
[2] Ealle hiꞅ ꞃppecaꝺ an lyben, Genesis xi. 6.

[3] Recherches critiques sur l'âge et origine des traductions Latines. d'Aristote. Paris. 1819.

Now if an Italian or a Frenchman could acquire Greek, and translate into Latin, a Saxon might do the same. Beda[1] tells of Theodorus the archbishop, and abbot Hadrianus, that they collected pupils, taught them versification, astronomy, and the ecclesiastical arithmetic of the computus, and some remained while Beda wrote who were acquainted with the Greek and Latin languages as well as with their own.[2] Further on[3] Beda gives an example of one of these disciples, Albinus, who understood Latin not less than his own language, English, with not a little Greek. Of Tobias, bishop of Rochester, another of these pupils, he says[4] that he knew the Greek and Latin languages as familiarly as his own.

King Ælfred and Ælfric both lament the decay of learning consequent upon the invasions of the Danes. Of the works translated from the Latin, by order of Ælfred and by his confidential servants or by himself, some are, in scattered passages, turned rather literally than correctly; some are executed with great spirit, and even improved in the version. Ælfric himself is a very pleasing translator, he kept his own faculties alive in the execution of his tasks; thus he translates dactyli, *dates*, as finger apples, plainly shewing that Greek words were known to him; it is also striking to find him correcting Bedas error, "lutræ,"[5] *otters*, the quadrupeds out of the sea, which came and warmed St. Cuðberhts feet with their breath, into "seals."[6]

I have shown, by the curious pieces published in the preface to the first volume of the Leechdoms, that in

---

[1] Beda, Hist. Eccl. IV. ii.

[2] Latinam Græcamque linguam æque ut propriam in qua nati sunt norunt. The Saxon interpreter gives a full emphasis to æque ut ; that will bear softening down in this late Latin.

[3] Beda, V. xx., p. 209, line 11.

[4] Beda V. xxiii. Ita Græcam quoque cum Latina didicit linguam, ut tam notas ac familiares sibi eas, quam nativitatis suæ loquelam haberet.

[5] Beda, p. 237.

[6] Hom. I. 138.

a fair practical sense, for the purpose they had in view, pupils in old England received instruction in Greek, and though learning decayed in times of distress, still there existed some who wished to acquire this knowledge, and some who were willing to give it. Some day the monstrous compounds, and the absurd spellings of our scientific nomenclature, pretending to be Greek, and a dozen other weak points of the day on this subject, will be regarded as proofs of barbarism.

It appears, therefore, that the leeches of the Angles and Saxons had the means, by personal industry or by the aid of others, of arriving at a competent knowledge of the contents of the works of the Greek medical writers. Here, in this volume, the results are visible. They keep, for the most part, to the diagnosis and the theory; they go back in the prescriptions to the easier remedies; for whether in Galenos or others three was a chapter on the εὐπόριστα, the "parabilia," the resources of country practitioners, and of course, even now, expensive medicines are not prescribed for poor patients.

On the margin of the pages are some private marks, *Private marks.* such as may be observed on the facsimile page. The purport of these marks is evident at fol. 56 a., chap. lxxv., which has something near a H with "totum"; again, at lxxvi. with "totum," at fol. 56 b., chap. lxxx., the figure in the middle of the facsimile margin with "totum," fol. 57 a., top line of lxxxiii. an I. nearly, with "totum." These were plainly memoranda secretly indicating the author from whom the passages so marked were taken, and "totum" means that the whole article was taken from that source. The token nearly an I. occurs at fol. 9 b., at the beginning of ii.; again at fol. 31 a., at the end of the folio; again at I. lxxxiii. with "totum" and the Roman numeral xviii. twice; again at fol. 94 b., line 8, eþt to milte feocum men; again at fol. 126 b., to chapter lxvii. These references

contain a problem, which, in our imperfect knowledge
of the works of the physicians of the lower empire, is,
it seems, beyond solution. If the prescription of celandine for the eyes, Lb. I. ii. be supposed to have been
derived from Marcellus 272 g., then the other passages
cannot, as far as, after repeated examination I see, be
discovered in that author. A mark which comes near
to F. is set, in the MS., over against the words Þɪð
eaʒna mifte, fol. 10 b., line 3, and it does not occur
again; compare Marcellus 272 b. It adds to the difficulty of the investigation, that recipes became a tradition passing from one author to another. A cypher
rather differing from H., which I will call h., occurs at
fol. 10 b. at the words Eþc pið ðon ɪlcan celeþonɪan:
nearly the same on the same folio, towards the end, at
Eþc pɪnoleþ. That this prescription is found in Plinius
Valerianus does not help us. Another like a plummet
line, sometimes as in the facsimile, and at fol. 30 b.
for angnail, with a ring at top, sometimes with a cross
line, as at fol. 30 b., line 4. ʒɪþ næʒl fie, is so much
like that called I., that it may be meant for the same
name. There is another like F. reversed, occurring at
ol. 11 a. Eþc pyþlaþ, also at fol. 32 a., towards the
end of the leaf, þonne þu þyp, at fol. 55 b. as in the
facsimile, twice with a slight difference, at fol 56 b. top
line, with another small variation, at fol. 57 b. at last
line but one; at fol. 94 a., eþc ʒenɪm ɪþɪeþ leaþ; at fol.
125 b., by the third line of chapter lxiiii., with these
words, "quia omni potu et omni medicinæ maleficia-
"torum et demoniacorum a[d]miscenda est aqua bene-
"dicta, et psalmis et orationibus vacandum est, sicut
"in hoc capitulo plene docetur." At fol 31 b. by the
word eallunʒa is a mark with a blot, meant probably
for I. At fol. 55 b. ʒɪþ þu pɪlle, at 55 b., as in facsimile, at 56 a., chapter lxxv. lxxvi, is a sign like H.,
with legs of varied length, thus running into reversed F. At folio 56 b., chapter lxxxii., is an orna-

mented cross; this occurs but once. At fol. 94 a., chapter
xli., the mark I. is three times repeated III. The
marginal ꝺimitte, fol. 108 b., means that the scribe was
getting his task done: he was not aware of the additional book III. If these signs refer to native treatises,
unknown to us, and now irrecoverable, they go to illus-
trate the existence of an English school of teaching
medicines; as do the expressions " as leeches ken," not
of rare occurrence.

Besides these marks and signs as given above, we More cypher.
find at fol. 30 b. by the end of the sentence, bo flytan
to, etc., in chapter xxxiv., some writing in cypher,
thus:—

[cypher symbols]

and again at fol. 89 b., chapter xxxiv., thus:—

[cypher symbols]

The key to writing of this sort has never been published, and now for those who are skilled in such
matters an account of it shall be given,

The letters were divided into groups, and these, of The law of this
course, were at the discretion of every man severally, cypher.
as regarded their number and how many letters they
might contain. The groups, first, second, third, and so
on were commonly denoted by dots; the upstrokes
shewed by their number what place in the group each
letter held. Thus, to spell Oxa, if the first group
began at A, and contained six letters, then the second
would begin at H, and if it contained eight letters,
omitting J as not ancient, then the third group would
begin at Q, and might go on, combining U and V, to
the end; so that Oxa would be thus spelt:—

[cypher symbols]

and Dun would be thus :—

$$ \cdot\ ////\ \vdots\ /////\ \vdots\ ////// $$

Some of the first letters in the specimens before us
have no dot, and may perhaps be reckoned from the
beginning, A.

Another method employed a line of dots instead of
upstrokes, so that Oxa appeared, if the groups of
letters remained the same, thus :—

and Dun thus :—

In his Thesaurus, Hickes and his associate Wanley give
other methods employed by the Saxons, of which a
common one was to employ the next following letter
to that meant, so that Oxa would be Pyb, and Dun,
Ewo. These devices, which have in them something
of the quality of riddles and conundrums, were as
amusing to the idle mind in old times as they are
now. When among the varied accomplishments with
which men are gifted, we read in the Codex Exoniensis,

ᚠum biþ lift henbiᵹ ᴄo aᴘᴘicanne ᴘoᚿb ᵹeᚿᚠno,
One is cunning handy to awrite word mysteries,

we have an allusion to this art of secret writing, or
to its kindred riddle puzzles.

There is but little encouragement to unravel these
marginal marks of the Leechbook, since the two specimens afford us but a very scant basis for inductive
reasoning. But, doubtless, when laid before the inqui-
sitive eyes of restless men, they may naturally give
rise to some unhappy conjectures.

Norse element.   Perhaps in dissecting the curious mosaic work of
this Leechbook, we may be as much struck by the
Old Dansk, or as people now say, Norse element in
the words Torbegete, Rudniolin, Ons worm, and the

herb Fornets palm, as by its Irish admixture, or its
Greek and Latin basis, or its fragments from King
Ælfreds handbook.

The third book of the volume is a separate produc- Third book.
tion from the two former. This is evident by the
colophon at the end of the second, declaring who owned,
and who wrote the book, and by the word " dimitte" in
the margin of the last section, indicating the approach
of a close. This other book, then, is generally of the
same tone as the preceding ; a marginal mark, as mentioned above, is the same as stands by the side of some
recipes given earlier, and the monkish habit of saying
some good words over the sick is as ready to show
itself. We may therefore conclude it to be, at least, of
the same age ; possibly by the same hand as the other
two.

On the whole, this work brings into a clear strong light,
the plentiful supply of good English food for the brave
appetites of the AngulSeaxe, the large importation of
foreign wine and ale and plenteous brew of potent home
beer and ale and mead, the mulled and honeyed drinks
for weaker palates ; the colleges of leechcraft, the Greek
and Latin medical studies of the most eminent teachers,
the wide and far back traceable herboristic traditions,
the far and wide inquiries of King Ælfred and men
of his time like him, and it will prove every way a
most valuable work to the student of English antiquity.

In the preface to Vol. I. a few pages were devoted
to an examination of some points of grammar ; these
were, of course, to some extent a precaution against
idle cavils and ignorant criticism of the translation.
The same considerations make it desirable to set forth
a few more simple observations and to support them
by examples.

It seems clear enough that the modern system of Long vowels.
marking long vowels by an accent is not in harmony

with ancient authorities; a long syllable often gets the
accent, but a short vowel also is frequently found to
take one.[1] The manuscripts have a method unexcep-
tionable, and discriminative, of showing that a vowel
is long by writing that vowel twice, and in some words
that mode of spelling prevails now. They give us, occasionally, ʒooð, *good*, boom, *doom*, " aam, cautere,"[2]
(whence we may conclude that the cognate Oman, will
have O long,[3]) aac, *oak*, pus, *wise*,[4] and so forth. The
information contained in this device of our forefathers
has not yet attracted a due share of notice ; for example,
the word Sið, *a path*, deriving itself probably from the
same source as Semita, becomes in the Mœsogothic
Sinþ-, and has been supposed to exhibit a vowel
necessarily, as before two consonants, short by nature ;
thus producing a short I in the old English. But Sið
we know to have a long vowel by the spelling Siið.[5]
It is not true that a Teutonic or Old English vowel
before two consonants is necessarily short. Some glossaries throw the alphabet into confusion for the sake
of giving short A first, then long A. Mislead by
accentual marks, the compilers presume that the prefix
A must be long, whereas the tradition of our language,
as in Afraid, Abroad, Abased, and the short vowel of
the particles which it generally represents, prove that
in those instances it is short. Where A represents An,
one, as in Aɲæð for Anɲæð, *constant*, the case may be
different. In the parallel case of Un- the prefix, the
Greek Aν-, the Latin In-, the vowel is undoubtedly
short, but in pronunciation it has an accent, as in
Unknown, and it is frequently found accented in the
MSS. Nothing but a notion that the language of

---

[1] Vol. L pp. xciv., xcv.
[2] Gl. C.
[3] See also the Glossary.
[4] Beda, 547. 16.
[5] Beda, 571. 34. See Layamon,

25836, 25837. In Bir. Moritz,
Heyne has marked the vowel long,
rightly. We have also Gesuð, but
Gesiððas.

Ælfric and Ælfred is dead could encourage a foreigner
to such experiments.

It is said by those who had opportunities of know- Accents.
ing, that the painful accentual system devised by the
late J. M. Kemble was abandoned by him before his
death. It was, indeed, opposed to the elementary laws
of vocalization; for it is known to all, who have gone
fully into the subject, that a prefix, if accented itself,
affects the accentuation and the vocalization of any
word with which it is compounded. The subject might
be largely illustrated and its essential laws developed
from the Oriental languages; but I will confine myself to that which is now before us. There can be no
reasonable doubt but that Þilbe, *wild,* and Deoþ, *deer,*
were pronounced with the vowels long, and the ridiculous
theory that a vowel before two consonants is short
by nature, can mislead but few; it amounts to this,
that we never could say Beast, Least, but must pro-
nounce those words, Best, Lest. These two words Þilbe,
Deoþ, being compounded and formed into one, retained
the accent and full sound on the syllable most important to the sense, and may be found in the genitive
singular under the form Þilbþeɼ.[1] Thus the affix Deoþ
lost its proper accent because a more powerful claim-
ant had become it close neighbour. Another example
is found in Þican, *to reproach,* which, as appears from
Layamon,[2] had its vowel by nature long. This word
is often compounded with the preposition Æc, which
by defect of grammatical knowledge among the old
penmen commonly appears as eb–; Layamon[3] exhibits
the compound still retaining the long vowel; but the
Paris Psalter[4] spells ebþicc, where, according to the

---

[1] CE, 258, line 10.

[2] Layamon, 21311.

[3] Ofte heo heom on smiten,
    Ofte heo heom atwiten.
                    Layamon, 26584.

[4] Psalm cxviii. 39.

German way of talking, the second ᴛ is "inorganic,"
and serves only to mark the shortness of the vowel.
Under this form the word is our Twit.

Enough has been said to show that the length of
the vowels in Saxon English is a very wide subject,
and to justify the postponement of any decisions in
the Glossary.

Letters.   In our oldest manuscripts þoꞃn often occurs where
it is the custom to print T. Reꞃð, *bed*, *rest*, Luꞃð,
pleasure, lust, and a hundred others are examples :
the superlatives end in þoꞃn, as þ æðeleꞃðe mæðen,
the very noble maiden, the participles also. In the
Codex Exoniensis the editor removed these features
of antiquity ; they offended him ; and were not according to Rask.[1] If any such occur in the present
volume they are preserved ; they are not dialectic,
but archaic.

Genders.   In genders the glossaries are untrustworthy ; thus,
the most recent is found, as regards the few words
common to both, much wrong, when compared with
the citations in that at the end of this volume. It
is unsafe to trust compounds with ȝe-, for the genders of the simples, for Ge– being a form of Con–, and
collective, its compounds are found to have a tendency
to run into the neuter.[2] Simples cannot always be relied
on for the gender of the compound ; all moderns take
ꞃoþþyꞃð for a feminine, after pyꞃð, but in a wide scope
of unpublished materials I have always found it neuter.[3]
Occasionally a new principle comes in, and by attraction the article agrees with the former element in the
compound, instead of the latter ; hence pæꞇeꞃæðꞃe

---

[1] For example, Gebieꞃȝað, Geþel-
ȝað, p. 358; þeoð, p. 357. Abꞃe-
oþeð, p. 337 ; Blæð, p. 310.

[2] Thus Spꞃæc is feminine, Ge-
ꞃꞃꞃæc, neuter.

[3] Tꞃa cneopholen, Lb. I. xlvii. 3,
perhaps makes kneeholly neuter ;
or else Tꞃa, is *two parts.* This
remark should have appeared in the
Glossary.

appears as neuter; Sıðpæꞃc,[1] feminine. Hence the Codex Exoniensis prefers to write ꝥ ꝼlæꞅchoꞃꝺ.[2]

Numerals with a singular.

Numerals admit of a substantive in the singular, so that our traditional expressions, Twelvemonth, a Six foot rule, he weighs Twelve stone, are correct according to ancient usage.[3] Distinction must be drawn between masculines, which had a plural in s, and feminines, as Night in Fortnight, or neuters, as in Five pound note, Twelve horse power, for these had in ancient time no s in the plural. Thus xii. monaþ,[4] þꞃıe cucleꞃ,[5] did not require remark: similarly ꞇꝩeᵹen ꝼæꞇelꞅ ꝼull ealað,[6] nıᵹanꞇyne ꝩınꞇeꞃ ⁊ ꞇꝩeᵹen monaþ,[7] iv. monaþ,[8] and the MS. reading in Beowulf, 4342,[9] may stand.

Idiomatic apposition.

Examples are not very rare in other works beside this Leechbook, when of a set of words under one regimen, those that come last in order appear in the nominative, that is, in no regimen at all. Thus ꝼoꞃðꝼeꞃðum Deuꞅðeðıꞇ ꞅe Aꞃcebıꞅceop, *defuncto Deusdedit archiepiscopo.*[10] Feꞃðe þa ꞅıððan · ⁊ ᵹeꝼeꞇꞇe ænne mæꞅꞅeꝑꞃeoꞅꞇ polıcaꞃpuꞅ ᵹehaꞇen · halıᵹ ꝩeꞃ ⁊ ꞅnoꞇoꞃ,[11] which would be literally, *Deinde profectus attulit presbyterum, policarpus appellatus, vir sanctus atque prudens.* þa æꞇeoꝑðe ꞅebaꞅꞇıanuꞅ on ꞅꝩæꝼne anꞃe ꝩuðeꝑan · lucına ᵹecıᵹeð ꞅꝩıðe æꝑꝼæꞅꞇ man,[12] which would be equivalent to, *Tunc apparuit Sebastianus in somnio viduæ cuidam, Lucina nominata, homo valde religiosa.* This, when it comes to be acknowledged generally, may be called Idiomatic apposition.

Harsh transitions in pronouns from plurals to singulars, and back again, are not peculiar to this work;

---

[1] Lb. p. 260, line 1.
[2] CE, 373, line 3.
[3] So in German.
[4] Lib. III. xviii.
[5] Lb. I. xvi. 2. Tꝩyðæl, Lb. I. vi. 3, viii. 2, is a compound.
[6] OT, 256. 5.
[7] Beda, 539. 23.
[8] Beda, 564. 13.
[9] Thorpe, 4355.
[10] Beda, p. 563, line 6.
[11] MH. 32 a.

they are found in others of an earlier date, bearing
episcopal names for their authors.

I desire again to acknowledge many courtesies and
kindnesses at Cambridge, Oxford, the Corpus Library,
and that of the British Museum.

O. C.

December, 1864.

ADDITIONS AND CORRECTIONS.

Page 60, sect. xviii., line 2. *for* ɯcan *read* ɯlian.

Page 130, sect. lx., line 1. *for* ɼealɼe *read* ɼealɼe.

Page 174, line 24. *for* momᵹe *read* moniᵹe.

Page 194, line 11. *for* Taen *read* Tacn.

Page 210, line 18. *for* blobeɼɼ *read* blobeɼ.

Page 224, sect. xxviii., line 1. *for* uᵹeɼɼe *read* uɼeɼɼe.

Page 292, note 2. *add* " they are possibly a corrupt representation of " ἱερὰ βοτάνη."

Page 324, sect. xxx., line 4. ɼuðnɼeaxán is one word.

Page 349, line 29. ἅγιος.

Page 391, glossary, v. Þeaɼ. Cf. Ƿelanð ᵹeɼoɼc ne ᵹeɼɼiceð monna æniᵹum ðaɼa ðe mimminᵹ can heaɼne ᵹehealban. (Fragments printed by Prof. Stephens.) *The Wieland work will fail no man, who kenneth to wield biting Mimming,* where the editor reads heaɼne as *hoar.*

LEECH BOOK.

VOL. II.   A

[L Æ C E B O C.][1]

fol. 1 a.

.I. LÆCE DOMAS[2] ƿIÐ eallum untpymnerrum heaþðef ꝇ hpanan ealler ȝe healper heaþðef ece cume · ꝇ clæꝛnunȝa ꝇ fpilinȝ piÐ hꝛum ꝇ ȝillıftꝛum to heaþðeꝛ hælo · ꝇ hu mon ꝛcyle ȝebꝛoceneꝛ heaþðeꝛ tılıȝean ꝇ ȝıf þæt bꝛæȝen ut fıe. :·

.II. Læcebomaꝛ piÐ eallum tıebeꝛnerrum eaȝena · piÐ eaȝna mıfte ȝe ealbeꝛ ȝe ȝeonȝeꝛ manneꝛ ꝇ hpanan þ cume ꝇ piþ ꝛlıe ꝇ piÐ eaȝna teaꝛum ꝇ piÐ pemme on eaȝum · piÐ æꝛmælum · ꝇ ȝıf mon fuꝛeȝe ꝛıe · piÐ poccef on eaȝum ꝇ piÐ ȝeꝼıȝom ꝇ piþ pyꝛmum on eaȝum ꝇ eaȝꝛealꝼa ælcef cynneꝛ.

.III. Læcebomaꝼ piÐ eallum eaꝛena ece ꝇ faꝛe · piþ eaꝛena beaꝼe · ꝇ piÐ yꝼelꝛe[3] hlyfte · ꝇ ȝıf pyꝛmaꝛ on eaꝛan ꝛyn ꝇ piþ eaꝛpıcȝan[4] ꝇ ȝıf eaꝛan bynıen ꝇ eaꝛ ꝛealꝼe ælceꝛ cynneꝛ.

fol. 1 b.

.IIII. Læcecꝛæꝼtaꝛ piþ healꝛȝunbe ꝇ hu þu meaht ȝecunnıau hpæþeꝛ hıt healꝛȝunÐ fıe ꝇ þ fıo abl ıꝛ tpeȝea cynna oþeꝛ on þám ȝeaȝle oþeꝛ on þæꝛe Ðꝛotan pyꝛtÐꝛenc ꝇ realꝼ piþ þon · ꝇ piþ ceacena fpyle ꝇ piÐ fpeoꝛcoþe ꝇ ȝeaȝleꝛ fpyle.

---

[1] See II. xlii. contents.
[2] This first page of the MS. has suffered somewhat from time and use.
[3] This reading makes hlyꝛt feminine. See the text.

[4] Wanley reads eaꝛpıcȝaꝛ. The text seems to my eyes to be as I have given it; pıcȝȝan occurs I. lxi. 2.

LEECH BOOK.[1]

i. Leechdoms against all infirmities of the head, and whence comes ache of all or of the half[2] head,[3] and cleansings and swilling against filth and ratten to the health of the head; and how one must tend a broken head, and *how* if the brain be out.

ii. Leechdoms against all tendernesses of the eyes, against mist of the eyes, either of an old or of a young man, and whence that comes, and against white spot and against tears of eyes, and against speck on eyes, against imminutions, and if a man be bleareyed, against pocks on eyes, and against "figs,"[4] and against worms, *or insects;* and eye salves of every kind.

iii. Leechdoms against all ache and sore of ears, against deafness of ears, and against ill hearing, and if worms be in the ears, and against earwigs, and if the ears din, and ear salves of every kind.

iv. Leechcrafts against neck ratten,[5] and how thou mayest ascertain whether it be neck ratten, and that the disease is of two sorts, either in the jowl or in the throat, and a wort drink and a salve for that, and for swellings of the jaws and for quinsy, and for swelling of the jowl.

---

[1] See II. xlii. contents.
[2] Or megrim (ἡμικρανία).
[3] ἡμικράνιον.

[4] *A disease so called, sties, wisps.*
[5] Probably from scrofula.

A 2

.V. Læceðomaƒ ȝiƒ manneƒ muð ƿaþ ƿie ȝe tyðneð ⁊ piþ ȝebleȝnaðƿe tunȝan muþ fealƒ piþ þon ilcan. Þið fulſim oƿoðe · III. læceðomaƒ.

.VI. Læceðomaſ pið toþþæƿce · ⁊ ȝiƒ pyƿm toþ ete ⁊ toþƿealƒa · eƿt pið þam uƿeƿan toþ ece ⁊ pið þam niþeƿƿan.   :·

.VII. Læceðom ȝiƒ mon bloð hƿæce.   :·

.VIII. Læceðomaƒ pið blæce ón ꝺplitan ⁊ bƿip piþ þon ilcan ꝺ fealƒ ealƿa ƿeopeƿ.   :·

.VIIII. Læceðomaƒ ȝiƒ men yƿne bloð óƒ nebbe eƿt bloðƿetena ȝe ón to binðanne ȝe ón eaƿe to ðonne ȝe hoƿfe ȝe men ealƿa · X.   :·

.X. Læceðóm piþ ȝeſnote · ꝺ piþ ȝepoſſm.   :·

.XI. Læceðomaƒ piþ ƿaƿum peoloƿſm.   :·

.XII. Læceðóm pið peam¹ muþe ꝺ pið ceolan fpyle · þƿy læceðomaƒ.   :·

fol. 2 a.

.XIII. Læceðóm piþ hæƿƿceaƿbe.   :·

[XIV.] Læceðóm piþ ƿeaðan.²   :·

[XV.] Læceðomaƒ pið hpoftan hu he miƿƿenlice ón man becymð ꝺ hu hiƿ man tilian fcyle ꝺ pyƿtðƿencaƒ piþ hpoftan ꝺ piþ anȝbƿeofte ꝺ ðƿyȝum hpoftan enðleƿan cƿæƿtaƒ.   :·

[XVI.] .XIIII. Læceðomaſ pið bƿeoft pæƿce · IIII. cƿæƿtaſ.

[XVII.] .XV. Læceðomaƒ piþ heoƿtpæƿce · V. cƿæƿtaſ.   :·

[XVIII.] .XVI. Læceðomaƒ piþ þam miclan ȝicþan ꝺ hu he cymð oƒ acoloðum maȝan oþþe to fpiðe hatum oððe oƒ to micelƿe fylle oþþe læƿneƿƿe oþþe óƒ yƿelƿe pætan ſlitenðƿe ꝺ hu hiſ món tilian ƿcyle pið ælc þaƿa.   :·

---

¹ In text pouum, for pohum. | ² reaðan ; text.

---

[1] The *lomentum* of the Roman women, a paste of pulse, generally of lentils ; women used it to improve their complexions, and it was eatable though unsavoury.

[2] Colds in the head.

[3] See II. xxxix.

[4] Host, *cough*, pronounced with o short.

[5] Wark is *pain*.

[6] *Emptiness.*

[7] *Humour.*

[xix.] .xvii. Læcedomaꞅ ƿiþ ƿlætan tƿeᵹen æþele. :·

.xx. Læcedomaꞅ ƿiþ ꞅculdoꞃ ƿæꞃce · iii. cꞃæꝼtaſ.

.xxi. Læcedomaꞅ ƿið þæꞃe ſƿiðꞃan ꞅidan ſaꞃe ⁊ þæꞃe ƿineſtꞃan ꞅyx cꞃæꝼtaꞅ. :·

.xxii. Læcedomaꞅ ƿið lendenece ꝼeóƿeꞃ. :·

.xxiii. Læcedomaſ ƿiþ þeohece tƿeᵹen ⁊ an ƿiþ þon ᵹiꝼ þeoh ꞅlapan.

fol. 2 b. .xxiiii. Læcedomaꞅ ƿiþ cneoƿ ƿæꞃce ⁊ ᵹiꝼ cneoƿ ſaꞃ ſie. :·

.xxv. Læcedomaꞅ ƿiþ ſcancena ꞅaꞃe ⁊ ᵹiꝼ ſcancan ꝼoꞃade ſynd oþþe oþeꞃ lim ꝼeoƿeꞃ cꞃæꝼtaſ ⁊ hu mon ſƿelcean ꞅcyle. :·

[a] Read ſino. .xxvi. Læcedomaſ ᵹiꝼ ſina[a] ꞅcꞃince ⁊ æꝼteꞃ þam ſie ꞅaꞃ oððe ſƿelle oððe ᵹiꝼ monneꞅ ꝼót to hommum ſcꞃimme ⁊ ſcꞃince ⁊ ᵹiꝼ ſino clæppette ⁊ cꞃaciᵹe ealleꞅ ꝼeoƿeꞃ cꞃæꝼtaſ. :·

.xxvii. Læcedomaſ ƿiþ ꝼotece oþþe oþꞃeꞅ limeꞅ oþþe ꝼota ᵹeſƿelle ꝼoꞃ miclan ᵹanᵹe · vi. cꞃæꝼ[taꞅ]. :·

.xxviii. Lacædomaꞅ ƿiþ ban ece ⁊ ꞅealꝼ ⁊ dꞃenc þꞃy cꞃæꝼtaꞅ þæꞅ ꞅynd. :·

.xxviiii. Læcedomaſ ᵹiꝼ manneꞅ ᵹetapa beoþ ſaꞃe oþþe aþundene þꞃy cꞃæꝼtaꞅ. :·

.xxx. Læcedomaſ ƿiþ æcelman ⁊ ƿiþ ðon ðe men acale þæt ꝼel oꝼ þam ꝼotūm. :·

.xxxi. Læcedomaꞅ ƿiþ ælcum heaꞃdum þinᵹe oþþe ſƿyle oþþe ᵹeſƿelle ⁊ ƿiþ ælcꞃe yꝼelꞃe ſƿellendꞃe ƿætan ⁊ ƿiþinnan ᵹeƿyꞃſmedum ᵹeſƿelle þam þe ƿyꞃð oꝼ ꝼylle oððe oꝼ ꞅleᵹe oþþe oꝼ hꞃyꞅca[1] hƿilcum ⁊ ƿiþ ſƿiðe
fol. 3 a. ƿæꞃlicum ſƿylūm ⁊ ƿiþ deadum ſƿylum ⁊ ꞅealꝼæ ⁊ dꞃencaſ ⁊ ſƿeþinᵹe ⁊ bæþ ƿiþ eallum lichoman ſƿylūm ealꞃa læcedoma tƿam læꞅ þꞃitiᵹ. :·

[1] Text hꞃicꞅca: read hꞃicꞅa?

---

[1] Exactly. *incapable of muscular action.*　　[2] *Be drawn up.*

.XXXII. Læcebomaſ pɪð þám yꝼlan blæce hu man þa
fealꝼa ⁊ baþu ⁊ ðꝛencaſ pɪþ ðon pyꝛcean ꝛcyle ⁊ pɪþ
hꝛeoꝼum lɪce ⁊ pɪð aðeaðebum lɪce bæþ ⁊ fealꝼa pɪþ
þon • bæþ ⁊ ꝛealꝼa ⁊ ðꝛencaſ pɪþ þam mɪclan lɪce ⁊
ſpɪle ealleꝛ ꝛɪꝼtyne læcebomaſ.   :·

.XXXIII. Læcebomaꝛ ⁊ ðꝛencaſ ⁊ ꝛealꝼa ⁊ [on]leȝna
pɪþ ſpꝛɪnȝe ȝe aðeaðebum ȝe unðeaðeðum • VIII. cꝛæꝼ-
taſ.

.XXXIV. Læceðóm ȝɪꝼ næȝl ſy oꝼ hanða ⁊ pɪþ anȝ-
næȝle ⁊ pɪþ peaꝛȝbꝛæðan.   :·

.XXXV. Læcebomaꝛ mɪcle ⁊ æþele be aſpeaꝛtebum ⁊
aðeaðeðúm lɪce ⁊ hpanan ſɪo aðl cume ⁊ hu hɪꝛ[1] mon
tɪlɪan ꝛcyle ȝíꝼ þ̷ lɪc to þon ſpɪþe aðeaðɪȝe þ̷ þæꝛ
ȝeꝼelneꝛ on ne ſy • ⁊ hu mon þ̷ ðeaðe bloð apeȝ
penɪan ꝛcyle • ⁊ ȝɪꝼ hím món lím óꝛceoꝛꝼan ſcyle oððe
ꝼyꝛ onꝛettan hu þ̷ mon ðon scyle • bꝛɪpaꝛ ⁊ ðꝛenceaꝛ
⁊ ꝛealꝼa pɪþ þæꝛe aðle.   :·

.XXXVI. Læcebomaꝛ pɪð þæꝛe aðle þe mon hæt cɪꝛcul
aðl bꝛɪp ⁊ ðꝛencaſ ⁊ ꝛealꝼa þæt ɪꝛ ſpɪþe ꝼꝛeönu[2] aðl ⁊
heꝛ ꝛeȝþ hpɪlcne mete oþþe ðꝛɪncan món ſcyle on
þæꝛe aðle ꝼoꝛȝan.   :·

.XXXVII. Læcebomaꝛ pɪþ ðon ȝíꝼ mon ne mæȝe hɪꝛ
mɪcȝean ȝeðealðan ⁊ þæꝛe ȝepealð naȝe ⁊ ȝɪꝼ he ȝemɪȝan ne mæȝe ⁊ ȝɪꝼ he bloðe mɪȝe • ⁊ ȝíꝼ: ꝼíꝼ on þon
teðꝛe ſíe • XIIII. læcebomaſ.   :·

.XXXVIII. Læcecꝛæꝛtaꝛ ⁊ ðolȝꝛealꝼa ⁊ ðꝛencaſ pɪþ
eallum punðum ⁊ clænſunȝúm on ælce pɪꝛan ȝe pɪð
ealðꝛe punðe toðꝛocenꝛe ⁊ ȝɪꝼ ban bꝛyce ón heaꝼoðe
ſíe • ⁊ pɪð hunðeꝛ ꝛlɪte • ⁊ ðolȝꝼealꝼ pɪð lunȝen aðle ⁊
pɪþ ɪnnan punðe ꝛealꝼ • ⁊ ꝛealꝼ ȝɪꝼ þu ꝛaðe pɪlle lytle
punðe lacnɪan ⁊ ȝíꝼ món mɪð ɪꝛene ȝeꝼunðoð ſíe • oþþe
mɪð tꝛeope ȝeꝛleȝen • oþþe mɪð ſtane ⁊ eꝼt ſealꝼa ȝíꝼ

---

[1] hɪꝛ refers to lɪc. | [2] Read ꝛꝛecnu.

xxxii. Leechdoms against the evil blotch, how a man Contents. shall work salves and baths and drinks against it, and for a leprous body and for a deadened body, a bath and salves for them. Baths and salves and drinks for the mickle body, *elephantiasis*, and swelling. In all fifteen leechdoms.

xxxiii. Leechdoms and drinks and salves and applications for pustules, either deadened or undeadened. Eight receipts.

xxxiv. A leechdom if a nail be off a hand, and against angnails, and against warty eruptions.

xxxv. Leechdoms mickle and excellent for a swarthened and a deadened body, and whence the disease cometh, and how a man shall treat it, if the body be deadened to that degree that there be not feeling in it; and how a man shall wean the dead blood away, and if it be desired to cut off a limb from the sick man or apply fire,[1] how it shall be performed. Brewits[2] and drinks and salves for the disease.

xxxvi. Leechdoms for the disease which is called circle addle *or shingles;* brewit and drinks and salves. This is a very troublesome disease, and here saith (our book) what meat or drink a man shall in this disease forego.

xxxvii. Leechdoms in case a man may not retain his mie,[a] and have not command of it, and if he may not [a] Urine. mie, and if he mie blood; and if a wife (*woman*) be tender in that respect. Fourteen leechdoms.

xxxviii. Leechcrafts and wound salves and drinks for all wounds and *all* cleansings (*discharges*) in every wise, and for an old broken wound, and if there be bone breach on the head, and for a tear by a dog; and a wound salve for disease of the lungs, and a salve for an inward wound; and a salve if thou wilt cure a little wound quickly, and if a man be wounded with iron, or struck with wood, or with

---

[1] *The cautery.* | [2] See viii.

men ʃie lim oꝼ lime óꝼáꞃleᵹen ꞃinᵹeꞃ oþþe ꝼót oþþe
hanb · oððe ᵹíꝼ meaꞃh[1] ute ſie ⁊ ᵹiꝼ bolh ꝼuliᵹe ealꞃa
ꝼꞃam ꝼꞃuman ꞃeoꝑeꞃ ⁊ þꞃitiᵹ læceboma.   :·

fol. 4 a.
.XXXVIIII. Læcebomaſ pið ælceꞃ cynneꞃ omum ⁊
óꞃꝼeallum ⁊ bancoþúm · piþ ut ableᵹnebum omúm ⁊
piþ omena ᵹebeꞃſte · ⁊ pið omum oꝛeꞃ hatúm ⁊ pið
ꞃeonðúm omum þ̵ iſ ꝼíc · bꞃencaſ ⁊ ꞃealꝼa piþ eallum
omum ealꞃa tꝛám læꞃ þꞃitiᵹ.   :·

.XL. Læcebomaſ ⁊ bꞃencaſ ⁊ ꞃealꝼa piþ póc able ealꞃa
ꞃyxe.   :·
.XLI. Læcebomaꞃ þꞃy æþele piþ innan onꝼealle ⁊
omum.   :·
.XLII. Læcebomaſ piþ ðæꞃe ᵹeolpan able ⁊ ſtanbæþ
⁊ piþ ᵹeal able ſio cymð oꝛ þæꞃe ᵹeolpan able · ſio biþ
ꞃbla ꞃicuſt abiteꞃoð ꞃe lichoma eall ⁊ aᵹeolpaþ ſpa
ᵹob ᵹeolo ſeoluc.   :·

.XLIII. Læcebomaſ piþ pæteꞃ bollan.   :·
.XLIIII. Læcebomaſ pið canceꞃ able þæt iſ bite ⁊
ſmeꞃeneꞃꞃa ⁊ ꞃealꝼ ꞃeoꝑeꞃ cꞃæꝼtaꞃ.   :·
.XLV. Læcebomaſ ⁊ bꞃencaſ piþ ælcum attꞃe pið
næðꞃan ꞃleᵹe ⁊ bite ⁊ ꞃlite · ⁊ piþ þon ᵹíꝼ món atteꞃ
ᵹeþicᵹe · ⁊ þæꞃ halᵹan cꞃiſteꞃ þeᵹneꞃ Iobanneꞃ ᵹebeb
⁊ ᵹealboꞃ ⁊ eác oþeꞃ ſcyttiſc ᵹecoſt ᵹealboꝛ ᵹehꝛæþeꞃ
piþ ælcum attꞃe · piþ ꝼleoᵹenbum attꞃe ⁊ ſpyle ⁊
beopúm bolᵹum · ᵹiꝼ hꝛa ᵹebꞃince ꝑyꝛm ón pæteꞃe
fol. 4 b.
piþ þon læcebomaſ · ⁊ ᵹiꝼ món ꝼoꝛboꝑen ſie ꞇalleꞃ ·
XX. oꞃæꝼta pið attꞃe.   :·

.XLVI. Læcebomaſ ᵹiꝼ ana ꝑyꝛm on men peaxe ſealꝼ
bꞃeno ⁊ clam piþ þon · v. læcebomaſ þæꞃ ſint.   :·

---

[1] meah, MS.

---

¹ A stone bath was a vapour bath, water being thrown on heated stones.
² Reptile.

.XLVII. Læcedomas ⁊ drencas ⁊ sealfa wiþ þeoradlum moniȝes cynnes þa betstan wiþ þeorwyrme ōn fet. XII. ealra wiþ þeor adlūm. :·

.XLVIII. Læcedomas wiþ þam wyrmum þe innan eȝlað mōnnūm. ⁊ wiþ wyrmum þe on cilda innoþe beoþ ⁊ wið cilda innoð sare ealra cræfta. XII. wiþ þam. :·

.XLVIIII. Læcedom on sundron anlipiȝ wiþ þam smalan wyrme. :·

.L. Læcedomas wiþ hand wyrmum ⁊ deaw wyrmum ⁊ ȝif wyrm hand ete. weaxsealf wiþ hand wyrme syx cræftas ealra. IIII. wisan. :·

.LI. Læcedomas wiþ wyrmum þe monnes flæsc etaþ. :·

.LII. Læcedomas twegen wiþ lusūm. :·

.LIII. Læcedomas tweten wiþ smoeȝa wyrmum. :·

.LIIII. Læcedomas wið wyrmætum lice ⁊ cweldehtum. :·

.LV. Læcedōm wiþ asleȝenūm lice. :·

.LVI. Læcedomas wiþ aslawenūm[1] lice ⁊ bæþ sealf. :·

.LVII. Læcedomas ⁊ drencas ⁊ sealfa wiþ fice. :·

.LVIII. Læcedomas to wen sealfe. ⁊ to wen bylūm. :·

fol. 5 a. .LVIIII. Læcedomas wið waralisin ꝥ is on engliſc lyft adl ⁊ wiþ neuirsne þry. :·

.LX. Læcedomas wið bryne ⁊ sealfa. VIII. ealra. :·

.LXI. Læcedomas wiþ lið wærce ⁊ wið liþseawe ⁊ ȝif liþseaw sio[2] ⁊ lioþole ūtrynne ealra cræfta feowertyne. :·

.LXII. Læcedomas wiþ seferadle to hælanne drencas wið þan. wiþ þriddan dæȝes fære ⁊ feorþan dæȝes fære ⁊ wið ælces dæȝes fere ⁊ wiþ lencten adle ꝥ is sefer. ⁊ hu man sceal wiþ þære adle on husl disce þone halȝan

---

[1] The passage of the text has asleȝenum.

[2] For siohe, subjunctive.

---

[1] A sort of dry rot : see the glossary. Μαρασμός.

[2] Possibly νευρᾶν πίεσις ; a kind of παράλυσις.

ꝼ þone miclan ȝoðeꞅ naman ppitan ꝼ on þone ðꞃenc
mið haliȝpætꞃe ðꞃean ꝼ haliȝ ȝebeð ón uꞃan ꞅinȝan ꝼ
cꞃeðo ꝼ paꞇeꞃ noꞅꞇeꞃ • x. læceðomaꞅ. :•

.LXIII. Læceðomaꞅ pið ꞅeonð ꞃeoðum men ðꞃencaꞅ ꞇo
þon ꝼ hu món ꞅcyle mæꞃꞃan ꝼ ȝebeðu ꝼ ꞃealmaꞅ oꞃeꞃ
þone ðꞃenð ꞃinȝan ꝼ ðꝼ ciꞃiobellum ðꞃincan • ꝼ piþ
bꞃæcꞅeocum men • ꝼ piþ peðen heoꞃꞇe ꝼ pið þon eallum ꞅex cꞃæꝼꞇaꞅ. :•

.LXIIII. Læceðomaꞅ piþ ælcꞃe leoðꞃunan ꝼ ælꞃꞅiðenne
ꝥ iꞅ ꞃeꞅeꞃcynneꞅ ȝealðoꞃ ꝼ ðuꞅꞇ ꝼ ðꞃenoaꞅ ꝼ ꞃealꝼ ꝼ
ȝiꝼ ꞅío aðl neꞇnum ꞅie • ꝼ ȝiꝼ ꞅío aðl pyꞃðe mannan
oððe maꞃe ꞃiðe ꝼ pyꞃðe ꞅeoꞃon ealleꞅ cꞃæꝼꞇa. :•

.LXV. Læceðomaꞅ eꝼꞇ pið lenoꞇen aðle ꝼ þaꞃa ꞅeopeꞃ
ȝoðꞅpelleꞃa namán • ꝼ ȝeꞃꞃiꞇu ꝼ ȝebeðu ꝼ ꞅpiȝenðe
ꞅceal món ꞅum ȝeꞃꞃiꞇ ppitan • v. cꞃæꝼꞇaꞅ. :•
.LXVI. Læceðomaꞅ unȝemynðe ꝼ piþ ðyꞅiȝúm. :•
.LXVII. Læceðomaꞅ ꝼ ðꞃenoaꞅ pið ȝenumenum meꞇe
ꝼ ȝíꝼ eala ꞃie apeꞃð oþþe meolcen meꞇe þꞃy cꞃæꝼꞇaꞅ. :•
.LXVIII. Læceðomaꞅ piþ þon ȝiꝼ hunꞇa ȝebiꞇe man-
nán ꝥ ꞅpiðꞃe oþꞃe[1] naman ȝanȝelꞃeꞃꞃa ꞃex ðuȝenðe
cꞃæꝼꞇaꞅ.
.LXVIIII. Læceðomaꞅ piþ peðe hunðeꞅ ꞅliꞇe ꝼ pið
hunðeꞅ ðolȝe • VII. læceðomaꞅ. :•
.LXX. Læceðomaꞅ ȝíꝼ mon ꞅie ꞇo pꞃæne oþþe ꞇo
unpꞃæne. :•
.LXXI. Læceðomaꞅ piþ ꞃæȝe ꞃeoꞅan ꞅaꞃe ꝼ ȝiꝼ hoh
ꞅino ꞅoꞃoð ꞃie. :•
.LXXI. Læceðomaꞅ on hꞃilce ꞇið bloð ꞃie ꞇo ꞃoꞃȝanne
on hꞃilce ꞇo ꞃoꞃlæꞇenne ꝼ hu ꞅie aꞇꞇꞃeꞅ ꞃul ꞅio
lꝼꞃꞇ on hlaꞃmæꞃꞃe ꞇið • ꝼ be ðꞃenoúm ꝼ uꞇꞃoꞃúm
on þam monþe ꝼ ꝥꞇe pyꞃꞇa on þam monðe ꞅinð ꞇo
pyꞃcanne. :•

---

[1] Compare the chapter, and read ꝥ iꞅ ꞅꞃiðꞃe ꝼ oþeꞃ.

---

[1] Now *Salticus scenicus.* Aranea venatoria is American. But here the tarantula was meant.   [2] *Aranea viatica.*
[3] August 1.

Romane ꙡ eall fuð ꝼolc poꝛhton hím eoꝛþ huf pıð
þæꝛe unlyꝼce · ꙡ hu món ꝛcyle bloblæfe on þæꝛa ꝛex
ꝼıꝼa ælcon on þæꝛ monan elbo ꝼoꝛꝫan on þꝛıcıꝫúm[1]
nıhca ꙡ hꝛonne becfc co læcanne · ꙡ ꝫıꝼ blob bolꝫ
yꝼelıꝫe · ꙡ ꝫıꝼ þu ꝛılle ón fnıbe blob ꝼoꝛlæcan oþþe ón
æbꝛe · oððe ꝫıꝼ þu ne mæꝫe blob bolꝫ ápꝛıþan · oþþe
ꝫıꝼ þu ne mæꝫe ꝫeocenb ǽbꝛe apꝛıðan oððe ꝫıꝼ mon
on fınpe beꝛlea æc bloblæcan.   :·

.LXXIII. Læcebom ꝫıꝼ men hꝛılc lım cıne.   :·
.LXXIIII. Læcebóm pıð peaꝛcum ꙡ peaꝛꝛum on lıme.   :·

.LXXV. Læcebom pıþ ꝛcuꝛꝼebum næꝫle.   :·
.LXXVI. Læcebóm pıð ꝫıcþan.   :·
.LXXVII. Læcebóm ꝫıꝼ þu ꝛılle þ yꝼel fpyle ꙡ æteꝛno
pæce uc beꝛſce.   :·
.LXXVIII. Læcebom ꝫıꝼ men unluſc fıe ꝫecenꝫe.   :·
.LXXVIIII. Læcebom ꝫıꝼ món on lanꝫúm peꝫe ceoꝛıꝫe. :·
.LXXX. Læcebóm pıð þon þe mon hıne ꝼoꝛðꝛınce.   :·
.LXXXI. Læcebóm pıð mıclúm cyle.   :·
.LXXXII. Læcebóm ꝫıꝼ men fıe ꝼæꝛınꝫa co mıcel pæcæ
ꝫecenꝫe.   :·
.LXXXIII. Læcebóm co manneꝛ ſcemne.   :·
.LXXXIIII. Læcebom pıð þon ꝫıꝼ mon þunꝫ ece.   :·

.LXXXV. Læcebóm pıð þon þe mon ꝼunbıꝫe pıð luf
ꝼeonb co ꝫeꝼeohcanne.   :·
.XXXVI. Læcebóm pıþ mıclum ꝫanꝫe oꝼeꝛ lanb þy
læꝛ he ceoꝛıꝫe.   :·
.LXXXVII. Læcebóm ꝫıꝼ manneꝛ ꝼeax ꝼealle fealꝼ pıþ
þon ꙡ ꝫíꝼ man calu fıe.   ·.
.LXXXVIII. Læcebómaf pıþ hoꝛꝛeꝼ hꝛeoꝛle ꙡ ꝫıꝼ boꝛf
ꝫeallebe fıe · ꙡ ꝫıꝼ hoꝛf fıe óꝛfcocen oþþe oꝛeꝛ neac.

The Romans and all the people of the south wrought for themselves houses of earth against the ill air; and how a man shall forego bloodletting on each of the six fives[1] of the moons age in the thirty nights, and when best to let *blood,* and if the incision for bloodletting take an ill turn, and if thou will let blood on an incision or on a vein, or if thou may not staunch the bleeding incision, or if thou may not bind up the flowing vein, or if one, in bloodletting, cut down on a sinew.

---

[1] Though a sidereal revolution of the moon be but 27·321 days, yet the moon often attains the thirtieth day of her age.

Alex. Trall.
lib. L
On þıſſum æneſtan læcecnæſtum ᵹeppıtene ſınt læcedomaſ pıð eallum heaſðeſ untpymneſſúm.

fol. 7 a.

Cf. Galen.
vol. xiv. p. 500,
ed. 1827.
Κεφαλαλγία.
Ꝛunna hatte pynt ᵹeᵹnıð ón montene þte penınᵹ
ᵹepeᵹe · ðo ſteap ſulne pıneſ to poſe ſmyne þonne þ
heaſoð mıð ⁊ ðnınce on nıht neſtıᵹ. Ꝥıð heaſoð pænce
ᵹením nuðan ⁊ pennıoð ᵹecnupa ⁊ menᵹ pıþ eceð ⁊ ele
aſeoh þunh claở ſmıne mıð þ heaſoð · oðởe clam óſ
þám ılcan pync leᵹe on þ heaſoð ⁊ beſpeþe pel þonne þu
to neſte pılle.

Lacn. 1.

ª Plinius Vale-
rianus, de re
Medica,fol.14 b,
for clearing
the head.
ᵇ Seap is neuter.
Ꝥıð þon ılcan ᵹením betonıcan ⁊ pıpoſ ᵹeᵹnıð ſpıðe
toᵹæðene læt ane nıht hanᵹıan on claðe ſmıne mıð.
Ꝥıð heaſoð pænceª betan pynttnuman ᵹecnupa pıð
hunıᵹ apnınᵹ ðo þ ſeap ón neb ⁊ ónᵹean ſunnan up-
peanð lıcᵹe · ⁊ þæt heaſoð ho oſ ðune þ ſeᵇ ſeap mæᵹe
þ heaſoð ᵹeonð ynnan · hæbbe hím æn on muþe ele
oþþe butenan ⁊ þonne uplanᵹ aſıtte hnıᵹıe ſonð læte
ſlopan oſ þam nebbe þa ᵹıllıſtnan ðo ſpa ᵹelome oþþæt
hıt clæne ſie.   :·

Ꝥıð heaſoð pænce ᵹenım hámpynt nıþepeanðe ᵹecnupa leᵹe ón cealð pæten ᵹnıð ſpıðe oþþ eall ᵹelebneð
ſie beþe mıð þ heaſoð.   :·

Lacn. 1.

fol. 7 b.
Ꝥıþ heaſoð pænce ᵹením heah heoloþan ⁊ ᵹnunðe
ſpelᵹean ⁊ ſencenſan ⁊ ᵹıtnıſan pel ón pætene læt
neocan on þa eaᵹan þonne hıt hat ſie ⁊ ymb þa eaᵹan
ᵹnıð mıð þæm pyntum ſpa hatúm.   :·

Ꝥıð heaſoð ece ᵹením ſealh ⁊ ele ðo ahſan ᵹepync
þonne to ſlypan ðo to hymlıcan ⁊ eoſon þnotan ⁊
ða neaðan netlan ᵹecnupa ðo þonne on þone ſlıpan

i.

1. In these first leechcrafts are written leechdoms for all infirmities of the head.

2. A wort has been named murra,ᵃ rub it in a mortar as much as may make a pennyweight, add to the ooze a stoup full of wine, then smear the head with that and let *the patient* drink *this* at night fasting. For head wark, take rue and wormwood, pound them and mingle with vinegar and oil, strain through a cloth, smear the head with it; or work a paste of the same, lay it on the head and swathe it up well, when thou will to bed. *ᵃ Scandix odorata.*

3. For the same, take betony and pepper, rub *them* thoroughly together, let *them* hang one night in a cloth, smear with *them*. For head wark, pound some roots of beet with honey, wring them, apply the juice to the face, and let *the patient* lie supine against the sun, and hang the head adown that the juice may run all over the head. Let him hold before that in his mouth oil or butter, and then sit up *and* lean forward *and* let the matter flow off the face. Let him so do often till it be clean.

4. For head wark, take the lower part of homewort,ᵇ pound it, lay it in cold water, rub it hard till it be all in a lather, bathe the head with it. *ᵇ Sempervivum tectorum.*

5. For head wark, take elecampaneᶜ and groundselᵈ and fen cress¹ and gitrife,² boil them in water, make them steam upon the eyes, when it is hot, and rub about the eyes with the worts, so hot. *ᶜ Inula helenium. ᵈ Senecio vulgaris.*

6. For head ache, take willow³ and oil, reduce to ashes, work to a viscid substance, add to this hemlock⁴ and carline⁵ and the red nettle,⁶ pound them,

¹ *Nasturtium officinale.*
² *Agrostemma githago.*
³ *Salix.*
⁴ *Conium maculatum.*
⁵ *Carlina acaulis.*
⁶ *Lamium purpureum.*

B 2

beþe mið. Þıþ heaƒoð ece hunðeƀ heaƒoð ȝebæpn to
ahƀan ꝭ fnıð ꝥ heaƒoð leȝe ón.   :·

Þıð heaƒoð pænce ȝením eƀelaſtan ȝecnua on cealð
pæteƀ ȝnıð betƀeoh hanðum ꝭ ȝecnupa cluƀƀunȝ ðo
þænto beþe mıð. Þıþ heaƒoð ece ȝenım hoƀan ꝭ pín
ꝭ eceð ȝeſpet mıð hunıȝe ꝭ fmıƀe mıð.   :·

[1] Þıþ heaƒoð ece ȝením ðıleƀ bloſtman feoð on ele
fmıƀe þa þunpanȝan mıð. [2] Þıþ þon ılcan ȝením heonoteƀ
hoƀneƀ ahƀan menȝ pıð eceð ꝭ noſan feap bınð on ꝥ
pænȝe. Þıþ þon ılcan ȝením ƒæt ƒul ȝƀenƀe ƀuðan
leaƒa ꝭ ƀeneƀeƀ ƀæðeƀ cucleƀ ƀulne ȝeȝnıð toȝæðeƀe
ðo æȝeſ ꝥ hƀıte to cucleƀ ƀulne · ꝥ fıo ƀealƀ ƀıe
þıcce fmıƀe mıð ƀeþeƀe on þa healƀe þe ƀaƀ ne fıe.   :·

ᵃ 'Ημικρανία.

Þıþ healƀeƀ heaƀðeƀ[a] ece ȝením þa ƀeaðan netlan
anſtelebe ȝetƀıƀula menȝ pıð eceð ꝭ æȝeſ ꝥ hƀıte ðo
eall toȝæðeƀe fmıƀe mıð.   :·

fol. 8 a.

Þıþ healƀeƀ heaƀðeƀ ece lauƀeƀ cƀoppan ȝetƀıƀula ón
eceð mıð ele fmyƀe mıð þy ꝥ penȝe.   :·

Þıð þon ılcan ȝením ƀuðan ƀeap pƀınȝ on ꝥ næƀ-
þyƀel þe on þa ƀaƀan[s] healƀe bıð.   :·

Þıþ healƀeƀ heaƀðeƀ ece · ȝením lauƀeƀ cƀoppan ðuſt
ꝭ fenep menȝ toȝæðeƀe ȝeót eceð ón fmıƀe mıð þa
ƀaƀan healƀe mıð þy · oþþe menȝe pıð pín þæƀ lauƀeƀ
cƀoppan · oþþe ƀuðan fæð ȝnıð on eceð ðo beȝa emƀela
ȝnıð ðon[4] hneccan mıð þy.   :·

[5] Tácnu þæƀe aðle · fıo aðl cymð óƀ yƀelƀe pætan uƀan
ƀlopenðƀe oþþe æþme oþþe óƀ bám · Þonne ƀceal mon æƀeſt

[1] Plinius, xx. 73.
[2] Galenus, vol. xiv. p. 398, ed.
1827.
[s] maƀan, MS.

[4] Read ðone.
[s] Alex. Trall. lib. i. cap. 12,
partly word for word.

put them then on the viscid stuff, bathe therewith. Against head ache; burn a dogs head [1] to ashes, snip the head; lay on.

7. For a head wark, take everlasting,[2] pound it in cold water, rub ·it between the hands, and pound cloffing,[3] apply it thereto, bathe therewith. For head ache, take hove [4] and wine and vinegar; sweeten with honey, and smear therewith.

8. For head ache, take blossoms of ·dill,[5] seethe in oil, smear the temples therewith. For the same, take ashes of harts horn, mingle with vinegar and juice of rose, bind on the cheek. For the same, take a vessel full of leaves of green rue, and a spoon full of mustard seed, rub together, add the white of an egg, a spoon full, that the salve may be thick; smear with a feather on the side which is not sore.

9. For ache of half the head,[6] take the red nettle of one stalk, bruise it, mingle with vinegar and the white of an egg, put all together, anoint therewith.

10. For a half heads ache, bruise in vinegar with oil the clusters of the laurus, smear the cheek with that.

11. For the same, take juice of rue, wring on the nostril which is on the sore side.

12. For a half heads ache, take dust of the clusters of laurel, and mustard, mingle *them* together, pour vinegar upon them, smear with that the sore side. Or mix with wine the clusters of laurel. Or rub *fine* in vinegar the seed of rue,[7] put equal quantities of both, rub the back of the neck with that.

13. Tokens of the disease. The disease cometh of evil humour flowing[8] or *evil* vapour, or of both. Then

---

[1] That the plant called " houndshead " in Herb. lxxxviii. is meant, I do not think.
[2] *Gnaphalivm.*
[3] *Ranunculus sceleratus.*
[4] *Glechoma hederacea.*
[5] *Anethum graveolens.*

[6] *Megrim.*
[7] *Ruta graveolens.*
[8] I hesitate to believe that uran, can mean *from below upwards*; yet Alexandros says κατὰ συμπάθειαν τοῦ στομάχου. Uran means *from above*.

on ða able ꝼoꞃeꞃeaꞃðꞃe bloð lætan óꝼ æðꞃe · æꝼteꞃ
þon ꞃceal man pyꞃt ðꞃenc ꞃellan Ᵹ lacnian ꞃiþþan þa
ꞃaꞃan ꞃtopa · ȝiꝼ ꞃeo aðl ꞃie cumen óꝼ micelꞃe hæto
þonne ꞃceal man miɖ cealɖūm læceðomum lacnian ·
ȝiꝼ hio oꝼ cealɖum Intinȝan cymð · þonne ꞃceal món
miɖ hatum læceðomum lácnian ȝehꞃæþeꞃeꞃ ꞃceal mon
nyttian Ᵹ miꞃcian ꝥ þone líchoman hæle Ᵹ æꝼeꞃ mæȝen
hæbbe · ħim beah ꝥ him món on eaꞃe ðꞃype ȝeplæc-
ceðne ele miɖ oꞃꞃūm ȝoðūm pyꞃtūm.   :·

ȝením piþ tobꞃocenum heaꝼbe betonican ȝetꞃiꝼula
Ᵹ leȝe on ꝥ heaꝼoð uꞃan þonne ꞃamnað hio þa punðe
Ᵹ hælð. Eꝼt piþ þon ilcán ȝením tunceꞃꞃan ꞃio þe ꞃelꝼ
peaxeð Ᵹ món ne ꞃæpð ɖo In þa noꞃu ꝥ ꞃe ꞃtenc mæȝe
on ꝥ heaꝼoð Ᵹ þæt ꞃeap.   :·

Þiþ þon ilcan eꝼt ȝenim banpyꞃt Ᵹ attoꞃlaþan Ᵹ
ðolhꞃunan · Ᵹ puðumeꞃce Ᵹ bꞃunpyꞃt Ᵹ betonican · ɖo
ealle þa pyꞃta to pyꞃt ðꞃence Ᵹ menȝe þæꞃ pið þa
ꞃmalan cliꞃan Ᵹ centauꞃian Ᵹ peȝbꞃæban · ealꞃa ꞃpiþuꞃt
betonican Ᵹ ȝiꝼ ꝥ bꞃæȝen ūtꞃiȝe ȝením æȝeꞃ ꝥ ȝeo-
lupe Ᵹ menȝ lythpon[1] piɖ huniȝ Ᵹ aꝼyl ða punðe · Ᵹ
miɖ acumban beꞃpeðe Ᵹ ꞃoꞃlæt ꞃpa þonne · Ᵹ eꝼt ymb
þꞃy ɖaȝaꞃ ȝeꞃpæt þa punðe · Ᵹ ȝiꝼ ꞃe hala ꞃeꞃþe pille
habban ꞃeaðne hꞃinȝ ymb þa punðe pite þu þonne
ꝥ þu hie ne meaht ȝehælan.   Þið þon ilcan ȝením
puðuꞃoꞃan Ᵹ puðu meꞃce Ᵹ hoꞃan Ᵹ pel on buteꞃan Ᵹ

---

[1] Lyhpon, MS.

shall one first in the early disease let blood from a vein; after that shall be administered a wort drink, and the sore places shall be cured. If the disease be caused by mickle heat, then shall one cure it with cold leechdoms; if it cometh of cold causes, then shall one cure it with hot leechdoms, of either shall advantage be taken, and they shall be mixed, *into a mixture* that may heal the body and have an austere efficacy in it. It is well for him that one should drip for him in his ear oil made lukewarm with "other" good worts.

14. For broken head, take betony,[1] bruise it and lay it on the head above, then it unites the wound and healeth *it*. Again for the same, take garden cress,[2] that which waxeth of itself and is not sown,[3] introduce it into the nose[4] that the smell and the juice may get to the head.

15. For the same again, take wallflower[5] and attorlothe[6] and pellitory and wood marche[7] and brownwort[8] and betony, form all the worts into a wort drink, and mix therewith the small cleaver[9] and centaury[10] and waybroad,[11] of all most especially betony, and if the brain be exposed, take the yolk of an egg and mix a little with honey and fill the wound and swathe up with tow, and so let it alone; and again *after* about three days syringe the wound, and if the hale sound part[12] will have a red ring about the wound, know thou then that thou mayest not heal it. For the same, take woodroffe and wood-

---

[1] *Betonica officinalis.*

[2] *Lepidium sativum.*

[3] Self sown; but a garden cress still.

[4] Ἔῤῥινον, therefore; but these were used like cephalic snuff; and never for broken head. See Nicolaos Myreps. xv.

[5] *Cheiranthus cheiri.*

[6] See Herbarium, xlv., to which assent is not easily given.

[7] *Apium graveolens.*

[8] *Scrophularia aquatica:* see Herb. lvii.

[9] *Galium aparine.*

[10] *Erythræa centaureum.*

[11] *Plantago maior.*

[12] The sense of ʀᴇᴘᴘᴇ is doubtful; but see glossary.

reoh þuph hæpenne [1] claðð ðo on ꝥ heaꝼoð þonne ȝanȝaþ
þa ban ût.   :·

fol. 9 a.
ᵃ þa, MS., but
erase it.

Þiþ lanȝûm raꝵe þær heaꝵber oþþe ðaꝵa ēaꝵiena oðððe
þaꝵa toþa þaᵃ þuꝵh hoꝵh oðððe þuꝵh ꝵoꝵꝼl ût ateo ꝥ
þæꝵ eȝleþ · ȝeꝼeoþ cenꝼillan on pætejꝵe ꝵele bꝵincan
þonne atihð ꝥ þa yꝵelan pætan ut oþþe þuꝵh muð
oðððe þuꝵh noꝼu. Eꝼt þur þu ꝵcealt þa yꝵelau ôꝵꝼe-
tenan pætan utaðon þuꝵh ꝼpatl ꝵ hꝵæcean menȝ piꝵoꝵ
piþ hꝵit cpubu ꝼele to ceopanne · ꝵ pyꝵc him to ꝼpillanne þone ȝeaȝl .[2] ȝeꝼîm eceð ꝵ pætejꝵ ꝵ ꝼenep ꝵ huniȝ
pyl toȝæbejꝵe hîꝼtum · ꝵ aꝵeoh ðonne læt colian ꝵele
þonne ȝelome ꝥ ȝeaȝl to ꝼpillanne ꝥ he þy ꝵel mæȝe
ꝥ yꝵel utahꝵæcean.

Þyꝵc þur ꝼpilinȝe to heaꝵber clænꝼunȝe ȝeꝼîm eꝼt
ꝼenepeꝵ ꝵæðer ðæl ꝵ næpꝼæðeꝵ ꝵ cenꝼan ꝵæðeꝵ · ꝼume men
hatað lambeꝵ cenꝵan ꝵ mejꝵcer ꝼæð ꝵ .xx. piꝵoꝵcojꝵna ·
ȝeꝼamna eall mið eceðe ꝵ mið huniȝe · ȝehæt ôn pætejꝵe
ꝵ habbe ôn muþe lanȝe þonne yꝵnð ꝥ ȝillîꝼtejꝵ ût.
[3] Eꝼt oþꝵu ꝼpilinȝ ôn ꝼumejꝵe cæꝵeneꝵ ȝoðne bollan ꝼulne ·

fol. 9 b.

ꝵ eceðeꝵ meðmicelne ꝵ yꝵopum hatte pyꝵt hiꝵe leaꝼ ꝵ
bloꝼtman menȝ toȝæbejꝵe ꝵ læt ꝼtanban neahtejꝵne ꝵ
ôn moꝵȝen on cꝵoocan oꝵeꝵþylle ꝵ ꝼupe þlæc ꝵ ꝥ ȝeaȝl
ꝼpile ꝵ þþea hîꝵ muð. [4] To þon ilcan ôn piꝵtꝵa ꝼenepeꝼ
ðuꝼteꝵ cuclejꝵ ꝼulne ꝵ huniȝeꝼ healꝵne cuclejꝵ ȝebo on
calic menȝe þonne æꝼtejꝵ þon pið pætejꝵ ꝵ hæte ꝵ reoh
þuꝵh linenne claðð ꝵ ꝼpile mið ꝥ ȝeaȝl · æꝼtejꝵ þâm
læceðome ȝelome mið ele ꝼpille þa hꝵacan. [5] Eꝼt pið þon
ilcan ȝeꝼîm mealpan ȝeȝnið on þlæc þîn ꝵele to ꝼpillanne ꝥ ȝeaȝl. Pið tobꝵocenum heaꝵðe ꝵ ꝼaꝵûm ꝵuðe

---

[1] hæpenne suggests itself.
[2] ȝeaȝl below is neuter.
[3] Plinius Valerianus, de re Med.,
fol. 14 a.
[4] Ibid.
[5] Plin. Val., fol. 13 b.

marche and hove, and boil in butter and strain through a coloured cloth, apply it to the head, then the bones come out.

16. For chronic disorder of the head or of the ears or of the teeth through foulness or through mucus, extract that which aileth there, seethe chervil in water, give it to drink, then that draweth out the evil humours either through mouth or through nose. Again, thus thou shalt remove the evil misplaced humours by spittle and hreaking; mingle pepper with mastic, give it *the patient* to chew, and work him *a gargle* to swill his jowl; take vinegar and water and mustard and honey, boil together cleverly, and strain, then let cool, then give it him frequently to swill his jowl, that he by that may comfortably hreak out the ill *flegm*.

17. Work thus a swilling *or lotion* for cleansing of the head, take again a portion of mustard seed and of navew seed and of cress seed, some men call it lambs cress, and of marche seed, and twenty pepper corns, gather them all with vinegar and with honey, heat them in water and have them long in the mouth, then the flegm runneth out. Again, another swilling in summer; mingle together a good bowl full of wine boiled down with herbs and a moderate one of vinegar, and hyssop, so the wort hight, its leaves and blossoms, and let *the mixture* stand for a night, and in the morning boil it over *again* in a crock (*or earthen pot*), and let him sup it lukewarm and swill his jowl and wash his mouth. For the same in winter, put in a chalice a spoon full of the dust of mustard and half a spoon full of honey, then after that mingle *this* with water, and heat it and strain it through a linen cloth and swill the jowl with it; after that leechdom frequently swill the throat with oil. Again for the same; take mallows, rub them into lukewarm wine, give it *the patient* to swill the jowl. For a broken

ȝeꞇꝛꝛelaðu mið ꞃealꞇe ꝫ mið hunıȝe ꞅmıꞃe þ heaꝛoð
ꝼoꞃeþeaꞃð mıð þy ꞅe cuþeꝛꞇa læceðom bıþ þam þe heaꝛoð
ꝩylm ꝫ ꞅaꞃ þꞃopıað. Þıþ þon ılcan eꝛꞇ ȝeȝnıð ꝛuðan
ōn pın ꞃele ðꞃıncan ꝫ ȝemenȝ eceð pıþ ꝛuðan ꝫ ele
ðꞃype ōn þ heaꝛoð ꝫ ꞅmıꞃe mıð.

.I. (*read* .ii.)

Alex. Trall.
lib. ii.

fol. 10 a.

Cf. Marcell.
268 h.

Læceðomaꞅ pıþ eaȝna mıꞅꞇe ȝenīm celeþenıan ꞃeap
oþþe bloꞅꞇman ȝemenȝ pıð ðoꞃena hunıȝ ȝeðo ōn æꞃen
ꝼæꞇ plece lıꝼꞇūm ōn peaꞃmum ȝleðum oþþ hıꞇ ȝeꞅoðen
ꞅıe · þıꞅ bıð ȝoð læceðom pıþ eaȝna ðımneꞅꞅe. Þıþ
þon ılcan eꝛꞇ pılðꞃe ꝛuðan ȝeðeaꝛꞃe ꝫ ȝeꞇꝛꞃꝛulaðꞃe
ꞅeap · ȝemenȝ pıð aꞅeopneꞅ hunıȝeꞅ em mıcel ꞅmyꞃe
mıð þa eaȝan. Þıþ eaȝna mıꞅꞇe monıȝe men þy læꞃ
hıoꞃa eaȝan þa aðle þꞃopıan locıað on cealð pæꞇeꞃ ·
ꝫ þonne maȝon ꝛyꞃ ȝeꞅeon ne pyꞃꞇ þ þa ꞃeōn · ac
mıcel pın ȝeðꞃınc ꝫ oþꞃe ȝeꞅpeꞇꞇe ðꞃıncan ꝫ meꞇꞇaꞃ ·
ꝫ þa ꞅpıþoꞃꞇ þa ðe on ðæꞃe uꝛeꞃan pambe ȝeꞃunıað ꝫ
ne maȝon melꞇan · āc þæꞃ yꝛele pæꞇan pyꞃceað ꝫ
þıcce. Poꞃ ꝫ capel ꝫ eal þa þe ꞅyn ꞅpa aꝛeꞃ ꞅınð ꞇo
ꝛleoȝanne ꝫ þ þe mon on beðbe ðæȝeꞅ ūppeaꞃð ne
lıcȝe ꝫ cyle ꝫ pınð ꝫ ꞃec ꝫ ðuꞃꞇ · þaꞃ þınȝ ꝫ þıꞅum
ȝelıc ælce ðæȝe ꞅceþþað þām eaȝūm. [1] Þıþ eaȝna mıꞅꞇe
ȝenım ȝꞃenne ꝛınul ȝeðo on pæꞇeꞃ .xxx. nıhꞇa ōn
ænne cꞃoccan þone þe ꞅıe ȝepıcoð uꞇan ȝeꝛylle þonne
mıð ꞃen pæꞇeꞃe · æꝛꞇeꞃ þon āpeoꞃꞃe ōꞃ þone ꝛınul ꝫ
mıð þy pæꞇeꞃe ælce ðæȝe þþeað þa eaȝan ꝫ onꞇyne.

fol. 10 b.

[2] Eꝛꞇ ōꞃ homena æþme ꝫ ꞅꞇꞃeme ꝫ ōꞃ plæꞇan cymð

---

[1] Cf. Galen. vol. xiv. p. 499, ed.   [2] Plinius Valerianus, fol. 20 b. for
1827.   fourteen lines.

and sore head; bruised rue[1] with salt and honey; smear the forehead with it, the most approved leechdom is *this* for *him* whose head hath burning and painful throes. For the same again; rub rue in wine, give *it* to drink *to the sufferer*, and mingle vinegar with rue and oil; drip it on the head and smear therewith.

Book I.
Ch. i.

ii.

1. Leechdoms for mistiness of the eyes; take juice or blossoms of celandine, mingle with honey of dumbledores,[a] introduce it into a brazen vessel, half warm it neatly on warm gledes, till it be sodden. This is a good leechdom for dimness of eyes. For the same, mingle the juice of wild rue,[2] dewy and bruised, mingle with equally much of filtered honey, smear the eyes with *that*. For mistiness of eyes many men, lest their eyes should suffer the disease, look into cold water and then are able to see far; that harmeth not the vision, but much wine drinking and other sweetened drinks and meats, and those especially which remain in the upper region of the wamb and cannot digest, but there form evil humours and thick ones; leek and colewort and all that are so austere are to be avoided, and *care must be had* that a man lie not in bed in day time supine; and cold and wind and reek and dust, these things and the like to these every day are injurious to the eyes. For mistiness of eyes, take green fennel, put it into water for thirty days in a crock (*or earthen vessel*), one that is pitched on the outside, fill it then with rain water; after that throw off the fennel and with the water every day wash the eyes and open them. Again, from the vapour and

[a] Melle Attico, doubtless.

---

[1] The verbs are often suppressed.
[2] Wild rue is a Hellenism, πήγανον ἄγριον, Dioskor. iii. 59, ἁρμόζει πρὸς ἀμβλυωπίας, or ruta silvestris; Plinius, xx. 51. These are *peganum harmala.*

eaȝna miſt ⁊ ſio ſceappneſ ⁊ roȝoþa ꝥ ðeþ piþ þon iſ
þiſ to ðonne. Þið eaȝna miſte ȝenim cileþonian ſeapeſ
cucleſ ꝼulne oþeſne ꝼinoleſ · þꝛibðan apꝛotanan ſeapeſ ·
⁊ huniȝeſ teaſeſ tu cucleſ mæl menȝ to ȝæðeſe · ⁊
þonne mið ꝼeþeſe ȝeðo In þa eaȝan ón moꝛȝenne ⁊
þonne mibbæȝ ſie · ⁊ eſt ón æꝼen æꝼteſ þon þonne ꝥ
aþꝛuȝoð ſie ⁊ toȝoten ꝼoꝛ þæſe ſealꝼe ſceappneſſe ·
ȝeníim piſeſ meoluc þæſ þe cilð hæbbe ðo on þa
eaȝan.   :·

Eſt æþele cꝛæꝼt ȝeníim balſami ⁊ huniȝeſ teaſeſ
em micel ȝemenȝ toȝæðeſe ⁊ ſmiſe mið þy.

Eſt pið þon ilcan celeþonian ſeap ⁊ ſæpæteſ ſmiſe
mið þa eaȝan ⁊ beðe. biþ þonne ſeleſt ꝥ þu nime
þæſe celeþonian ſeap ⁊ mucȝpyꝛte ⁊ ꝼuban ealꝼa em
ſela ðo huniȝ to ⁊ balðſamum ȝíſ þu hæbbe · ȝeðo on
ꝥ ꝼæt þe þu hit mæȝe ón mið ȝeꝼoȝe ȝeſeoþan ⁊ nytta
pel þæt bet.   :·

[1]Þiþ eaȝna miſte ȝebæꝛned ſealt ⁊ ȝeȝniðen ⁊ piþ
ðoꝛena huniȝ ȝemenȝeð ſmiſe mið.   :·

fol. 11 a. [2]Eſt ꝼinoleſ ⁊ ꝛoſan ⁊ ꝛuban ſeap ⁊ ðoꝛan huniȝ ⁊
ticceneſ ȝeallan toȝæðeſe ȝemenȝeð ſmiſe mið þa
eaȝan. [3]Eſt ȝꝛene cellenðꝛe ȝeȝniðen ⁊ piþ piſeſ
meoluc ȝemenȝeð aleȝe oꝼeꝛ þa eaȝan.   :·

a Med. de Quad.
iv. 7.
b Marcellus,
272, e. a [4]Eſt haꝛan ȝeallan ȝenimc ⁊ ſmiſe mið.   :·
b Eſt cꝛicc[5] pine pinclan ȝebæꝛnðe to ahꝛan ⁊ þa
ahꝛan ȝemenȝe pið ðoꝛena huniȝ.   :·

[1] Plin. Val. fol. 20 b.   [5] For veras our author read
[2] Plin. Val. fol. 21 b.   vivas. Or Plinius Valerianus, fol.
[3] Plin. Valerianus, fol. 19 b.   21 b, where we read "Cochleæ
[4] Also Plinius Valerianus, fol.   vivæ."
20 b., 21 b.

steam of ill juices and from nausea cometh mist of eyes, and the sharpness and corrupt humour causes that, against which this is to be done. For mist of eyes, take of celandines juice a spoon full, another of fennels, a third of southernwoods juice, and two spoon measures of the tear of honey (*virgin honey that drops without pressure*), mingle *them* together, and then with a feather put *some* into the eyes in the morning and when it be midday, and again at evening after that, when it is dried up and spent; for sharpness of the salve, take milk of a woman who hath a child, apply it to the eyes.

2. Again, a noble craft. Take equal quantities of balsam and of virgin honey, mix together and smear with that.

3. Again for the same, juice of celandine and sea water; smear and bathe the eyes therewith. It is then most advisable that thou take juice of the celandine and of mugwort[1] and of rue, of all equal quantities, add honey to it, and balsam, if thou have it, put it then into such a vessel that thou may seethe it with glue[2] and make use of it. It does much good.

4. For mist of eyes, salt burnt and rubbed *fine* and mixed with dumbledores honey;[3] smear therewith.

5. Again, juice of fennel and of rose and of rue, and dumbledores honey,[3] and kids gall, mixed together; smear the eyes with *this*. Again, lay upon the eyes green coriander rubbed *fine* and mixed with womans milk.

6. Again, let him take a hares gall and smear with it.

7. Again, live perriwinkles burnt to ashes; and let him mix the ashes with dumbledores[3] honey.

---

[1] *Artemisia vulgaris.*

[2] Or some cement; the original author perhaps meant a covered vessel sealed up with cement.

[3] Doubtless from " melle Attico," read as melle attaci ; the dumbledore is *apis bombinatrix.*

ᵃ Plinius,
xxxii. 24.
Marcellus,
272, g.

ᵇ Marcellus,
272, b.

fol. 11 b.

ᶜ Marcellus,
272, a.

ᵈ Marcellus,
272, c.

ᵃƐft þyrlaþ ealþa ea rifca ón funnan ȝemylte ⁊ þiŏ huniȝ ȝemenȝde fmiþe miŏ.   :·

Þiŏ eaȝna mifte eft betonican þeap ȝebeatenþe miŏ hiþe pyþttþumán ⁊ aþþunȝenþe ⁊ ȝeaþpan þeap ⁊ celeþonian em micel ealþa menȝ toȝæŏeþe ŏo ón eaȝe.

ᵇƐft finolef pyþttþumán ȝecnuaŏne ȝemenȝ þiŏ huniȝeþ þeap¹ feoŏ þonne æt leohtum fyþe liftelice oþ huniȝeþ þicneþþe · ȝeŏo þonne ón æþene fmpullan ⁊ þonne þeaþf þie fmiþe miŏ þiþ toŏþiþþ þa eahmiftaþ þeah þe hie þicce fynŏ.   :·

Þiþ eaȝna mifte eft celeþonian þeap oþþe þaþa bloftmena ȝeþþinȝ ⁊ ȝemenȝ þiŏ ŏoþena huniȝ ȝeŏo ón æþen fæt plece þonne liftum ón peaþmum ȝleŏum oþþe ón ahþan oþ þ hit ȝeŏon þie · þ biŏ anfpilŏe lyb þiþ eaȝena ŏimneþþe.   :·

Sume þæþ þeapeþ anlipiȝef nyttiaŏ ⁊ þa eaȝan miŏ þy fmiþiaŏ. Þiþ eaȝena mifte eft eoþŏiþies feap ⁊ finoleþ þeap ȝeŏo beȝea em þela ón ampullan ŏþiȝe þonne on hatþe funnan ⁊ þa eaȝan innepeaþŏ miŏ þy fmiþe. ᶜÞiþ eaȝena mifte eft eoþŏȝeallan² þeap þ iþ hyþŏepyþt fmiþe on þa eaȝan fio þyn biþ þy þceaþþþe · ȝiþ þu huniȝ to ŏeft þ ŏeah · ȝenimᵈ þonne þæþe ilcan pyþte ȝoŏne ȝelm ȝeŏo ón ceac fulne þinef ⁊ ȝeþeoþ oþnete æþ þþy ŏaȝaf · ⁊ þonne hio ȝeroben fie aþþinȝ þa pyþt óþ ⁊ þæþ þoþef ȝefpetteþ miŏ huniȝe ȝeŏþinc ælce ŏæȝe neaht neþtiȝ bollan fulne.   :·

ᶠ Cf. Celsus,
VI. vi. 34 and
29.

ᵉƐalŏeþ manneþ eaȝan beoþ unfceaþþfyno þonne þceal he þa eaȝan peccan miŏ ȝniŏinȝum miŏ ȝonȝum · miŏ þaŏum oþþe miŏ þy þe hine mon beþe oþþe on pæne feþiȝe · ⁊ hy þculan nyttian lytlúm ⁊ foþhtlicúm metum ⁊ hioþa heaþoŏ cemban ⁊ peþmoŏ ŏþuncan æþ þon þe

---

¹ " Tantundem mellis optimi de-
spumati "   is turned   " juice of
honey."

² Cf. Alex. Trall. p. 46, line 31,
ed. 1548.

8. 'Again, the fatty parts of all river fishes melted in the sun and mingled with honey; smear with that.

9. For mist of eyes again, juice of betony beaten with its roots and wrung, and juice of yarrow[1] and of celandine, equally much of all, mingle together, apply to the eye. Again, mingle pounded root of fennel with the purest honey, then seethe at a light fire cleverly to the thickness of honey. Then put it into a brazen ampulla, and when need be, smear with it, this driveth away the eye mists, though they be thick.

10. For mist of eyes again, wring *out* juice of celandine or of the blossoms *of it*, and mingle with dumbledores honey, put it into a brazen vessel, then make it lukewarm cleverly on warm gledes, or on ashes, till it be done. That is a unique medicine for dimness of eyes.

11. Some avail themselves of the juice singly, and anoint the eyes with that. For mist of eyes again; juice of ground ivy and juice of fennel; set equal quantities of both in an ampulla, then dry in the hot sun, and smear the inward part of the eyes with that. For mist of eyes again, smear earthgalls[2] juice, that is herdwort,[2] on the eyes, the vision will be by it sharper. If thou addest honey thereto, that is of good effect. Further take a good bundle of the same wort, introduce it into a jug full of wine, and seethe three days in a close vessel; and when it is sodden, wring out the wort, and drink of the ooze sweetened with honey every day, after a nights fasting, a bowl full.

12. The eyes of an old man are not sharp of sight; than shall he wake up his eyes with rubbings, with walkings, with ridings, either so that a man bear him[3] or convey him in a wain. And they shall use little and careful meats, and comb their heads and

---

[1] *Achillea millefolium.*
Erythræa centaureum.

[3] In a litter.

fol. 12 a.
ᵃ Rather
ɼealteɼ.

lue mete þicჳean. Þúɼ món ɼceal unɼceaɲpſynűm ſealɼe
pyɲcean to eaჳuın · ჳenım pıpoɲ ⁊ ჳebeat ⁊ ſpeჳleɼ
æppel ⁊ lıpon ɼealtᵃ ⁊ pín þ̄ bıþ ჳoð ɼealɼ.   :·

Þıþ mıclum eaჳece manıჳ man hæɼþ mıcelne ece
on hıſ eaჳum. Þyɲc hím þonne ჳɲunðe ſpelჳean ⁊
bıɼceop pyɲc ⁊ ɼınol pyl þa pyɲta ealle on pætɲe ·
meoluc bıð ɼelɲe læt þ̄ ɲeocan on þa eaჳan. Eɼt
celeþonıan ⁊ puðubınðelſ¹ leaɼ ჳeaceɼ ſuɲe pıð pın
ჳemenჳe.   :·

ᵇ Gr. ἄργεμα ;
Lat. Albugo.
ᶜ auſan, MS.

Eɼt to mıclum eaჳece cɲopleac nıoþopeaɲð ⁊ pıt-
mæɲeɼ pyɲt nıoþopeaɲð cnua ón ɲıne læt ſtanðan tɲa
nıht. Þıð ɼlıeᵇ eaჳɼealɼ ჳenım bɲomeſ ahſanᶜ ⁊ bollan
ɼulne hateɼ pıneſ ჳeot þɲıpa lytlum on hate þa ahſau
⁊ ðo þonne ón æɲen ɼæt oððe cypeɲen ðo hunıჳeſ
hpon to ⁊ menჳ toჳæðeɲe ðo on þæɼ untɲuman manneſ eaჳan · ⁊ aþþeah eɼt þa eaჳan on clænűm pylle.
Þıþ ɼlıe haɲan ჳeallan ðo peaɲınne ón ymb tɲa nıht

ᵈ Slab, MS. not
ɼlan.

ɼlıhð óɼ þam eaჳum. Þıþ ɼlıe ჳením onpæɲe ɼlahᵈ
þ̄ ɼeap ⁊ pɲınჳ þuɲh clað on þ̄ eaჳe ɼona ჳæð on
þɲım ðaჳum óɼ ჳıɼ ſıo ɼlah bıþ ჳɲene. Þıþ ɼlıe eceð
⁊ ჳebæɲneð ſealt ⁊ beɲen mela ჳemenჳ toჳæðeɲe ðo
ón þ̄ eaჳe haɼa lanჳe hpıle þıne hanð on.   :·

ᵉ Read oþþe
þone.
fol. 12 b.

Þıþ ɼlıe eahɼealɼ celeþonıan ſæð ჳením on þamᵉ
pyɲttɲuman ჳnıð ón ealð pín ⁊ on hunıჳ ðo pıpoɲ to
læt ſtanðan neahteɲne be ɼyɲe nytta þonne þu ɼlapan
pılle. Þıþ ɼlıe oxan ɼlyppan nıþepeaɲðe ⁊ aloɲ ɲınðe
pylle on buteɲan.   :·

Χύμωσις,
Lippitudo.

Þıþ þon ðe eaჳan tyɲen ɲuðan ſeap ⁊ ჳate ჳeallan ⁊

---

¹ Read -bınðeſ.

drink wormwood before they take food. Then shall
a salve be wrought for unsharpsighted eyes; take
pepper and beat it, and beetle nut[1] and a somewhat
of salt, and wine; that will be a good salve.

13. For much eye ache. Many a man hath mickle
ache in his eyes. Work him then groundsel and
bishopwort[2] and fennel, boil all the worts in water,
milk is better, make that throw up a reek on the
eyes. Again, let him mingle with wine celandine and
woodbines leaves and *the herb* cuckoosour.[3]

14. Again, for much eye ache, pound in wine the
nether part of cropleek[4] and the nether part of
Wihtmars wort,[5] let it stand two days. For pearl, an
eye salve; take ashes of broom and a bowl full of hot
wine, pour *this* by a little at a time thrice on the hot
ashes, and put *that* then into a brass or a copper vessel,
add somewhat of honey and mix together, apply to
the infirm mans eyes, and again wash the eyes in a
clean wyll *spring*. For pearl on the eye, apply the gall
of a hare, warm, for about two days, *it* flieth from the
eyes. Against white spot, take an unripe sloe, and
wring the juice of it through a cloth on the eye, soon,
in three days *the spot* will disappear, if the sloe be
green. Against white spot, mingle together vinegar
and burnt salt[a] and barley meal, apply it to the eye,
hold thine hand a long while on it.

[a] A substitute
for "sal am-
moniacum."

15. For pearl, an eye salve; take seed of celandine
or the root of it, rub it into old wine and into honey,
add pepper, let it stand for a night by the fire, use it
when thou wilt sleep. Against white spot, boil in
butter the nether part of ox-slip[6] and alder[7] rind.

16. In case the eyes be tearful, juice of rue, and

[1] The evidence, such as it is, for
this rendering will be given in the
glossary.
[2] Herbar. i. *Betonica officinalis.*
[3] *Oxalis Acetosella.*
[4] *Allium sativum*, probably.
[5] *Cochlearia anglica*, perhaps.
[6] *Primula veris elatior.*
[7] *Alnus glutinosa.*

C

ðopan huniȝ ealpa em ꝼela. ȝiꝼ eaȝan[1] typen heoꞃoꞇeꝼ
hoꞃneꝼ abꞃan ðo on ȝeſpeꞇ ꝼín. Ƿyꞃc eaȝꞃealꝼe piþ
pænne ȝením cꞃopleac ꝶ ȝaꞃleác beȝea em ꝼela ȝecnupa
pel ꞇoſomne ȝením ꝼín ꝶ ꝼeaꞃꞃeſ ȝeallan beȝea em
ꝼela ȝemenȝ piþ þy leace ðo þonne on aꞃꝼæꞇ læꞇ ſꞇanðan niȝon nihꞇ on þam aꞃꝼaꞇe apꞃinȝ þuꞃh claþ ꝶ
ȝehlyꞇꞇꞃe pel ðo on hoꞃn • ꝶ ymb niht ðo mið ꝼeþeꞃe
on þ eaȝe ſe beꞇſꞇa læceðóm.   :·

Þiþ penne[2] ón eaȝon ȝením þa holan ceꞃſan ȝebꞃæð
ðo on þ eaȝe ſpa he haꞇoſꞇ mæȝe.   :·
Þiþ eaȝece ȝepyꞃce hím ȝꞃunðſpelȝean ꝶ biſceop pyꞃꞇ
ꝶ beopyꞃꞇ ꝶ ꝼinul pyl þa pyꞃꞇa ealle on pæꞇeꞃe meoluc
biþ beꞇeꞃe.   :·

fol. 13 a.
Þiþ eaȝna ece ȝenim þa ꞃeaban hoꞃan apyl on ſuꞃum
ſpaꞇum oþþe on ſuꞃúm ealað ꝶ beþe þa eaȝan on þam
baþe beꞇeꞃe ſpa óꞃꞇoꞃ.   :·

Þiþ eaȝece ȝenim piþoꞃinðan ꞇꞃiȝa ȝecnupa apylle
on buꞇeꞃan[3] ðo on þa eaȝan.   :·

Ƿyꞃc eaȝꞃealꝼe ȝením hnuꞇcyꞃnla ꝶ hpæꞇe coꞃn ȝnið
ꞇoȝæðeꞃe ðo piꞃ ꞇo aſeoh þuꞃh clað ðo þonne on þa
eaȝan. Þiþ eaȝna pæꞃce ꝶ ece hpiꞇeꞃ hlaꝼeꞃ cꞃuman
ꝶ piꞃoꞃ ꝶ eceð menȝ pel leȝe on clað binð on þa eaȝau
nihꞇeꞃne. Þuꞃ món ꞃceal eaȝꞃealꝼe pyꞃcean • ȝením
ſꞇꞃeapbeꞃian piſan moþoꞃeaꞃðe ꝶ piꞃoꞃ ȝecnupa pel ðo
on claþ bebinð ꝼæſꞇe leȝe on ȝeſpeꞇ ꝼín læꞇ ȝeðꞃeoꞃan
on þa eaȝan ænne ðꞃoꞃan. Ƿyꞃc eaȝſealꝼe puðubinðeꞃ·
leaꝼ puðumeꞃce ſꞇꞃeapbeꞃian piſan ſuþeꞃne peꞃmoð
oxna lyb celeþoꞃian ȝecnupa þa pyꞃꞇe ſpiðe menȝ piþ

---

[1] Galen, vol. xii. p. 335, ed. 1826.   [2] Τύλος.
Sextus, cap. i. 1, Lat.   [3] The MS. has biꞇeꞃan.

goats gall and dumbledores honey, of all equal quantities. If eyes be tearful, add to sweetened wine ashes of harts horn. Work an eye salve for a wen, take cropleek and garlic,[1] of both equal quantities, pound them well together, take wine and bullocks gall, of both equal quantities, mix with the leek, put *this* then into a brazen vessel, let it stand nine days in the brass vessel, wring out through a cloth and clear it well, put it into a horn, and about night time apply it with a feather to the eye ; the best leechdom.

17. For a wen[2] on the eye, take hollow cress,[3] roast it, apply it to the eye, as hot as possible.

18. For eye ache, let him work for himself groundsel and bishopwort[4] and beewort[5] and fennel, boil all the worts in water ; milk is better.

19. For ache of eyes, take the red hove,[6] boil it in sour beer or in sour ale, and bathe the eyes in the bath, the oftener the better.

20. For eye ache, take twigs of withewind,[7] pound them, boil them in butter, apply them to the eyes.

21. Work an eye salve *thus* ; take nut kernels and wheat grains, rub them together, add wine, strain through a cloth, then apply to the eyes. For acute pain and ache of eyes, mingle well crumbs of white bread and pepper and vinegar, lay *this* on a cloth, bind it on the eyes for a night. Thus shall a man work an eye salve, take the nether part of strawberry plants and pepper, pound them well, put them on a cloth, bind them fast, lay them in sweetened wine, make somebody drop one drop into the eyes. Work an eye salve *thus* ; leaves of woodbind,[8] woodmarche,[9] strawberry plants, southern wormwood,[10] green hellebore,

---

[1] *Allium oleraceum ?*
[2] Wisps or sties are called wuns in Devon.
[3] *Gentiana campestris.*
[4] In Herb. i. *Betonica officinalis.*
[5] *Acorus calamus.*

[6] *Glechoma hederacea.*
[7] *Convolvulus sepium.*
[8] *Convolvulus.*
[9] *Apium graveolens.*
[10] *Artemisia abrotanon.*

ƿín bo on cypeꞃen ꝼæꞇ oþþe ón æꞃenum ꝼaꞇe haꝼa
læꞇ ꞅꞇanban ꝛeoꝼon niht oþþe ma apꝛinȝe þa pyꞃꞇa
ꞅꝼiðe clæne ȝebo pipoꞃ ón ⁊ ȝeꞅꝼeꞇ ꞅꝼiþe leohꞇlice mið

fol. 13 b.
hunȝe bo ꝛiþþan on hoꞃn ⁊ mið ꝛeþeꞃe bo on þa eaȝan
ænne bꞃoꞃan. Ƿyꞃc eaȝꝛealꝼe bꞃiȝe · ȝenim ꞅpeȝleꞅ
æppel ⁊ ꞅpeꝛl cꞃeciꝛc aꞇꞇꞃum ⁊ ȝebæꞃneð ꝛealꞇ ⁊ pipoꞃeꝛ
mæꝛꞇ ȝeȝꞃinb eall ꞇo buꞅꞇe aꝛiꝛꞇ þuꝛh clað bo on
næꝛc hæbbe him ón þy læꝛ hiꞇ þine · bo meðmicel
on þa eaȝan mið ꞇoþ ȝaꞃe ȝeꞃeꞅꞇe him æꝛꞇeꞃ ⁊ ꝛlape
⁊ þonne aþpeah liꝛ eaȝan mið clæne pæꞇꞃe ⁊ on ꝥ
pæꞇeꞃ lociȝe. Ƿyꞃc eaȝꝛealꝼe cymen ⁊ ꞅꞇꞃeaꝛbeꞃȝeꞃn
piꞅe ȝecnupa ꞅꝼiðe pel ⁊ óꝼ ȝeoꞇ mið ȝeꞅꝼeꞇꞇe pine bo
In cypeꞃen ꝼæꞇ oððe ón æꞃen læꞇ ꞅꞇanban ꝛela nihꞇa
ón apꝛinȝ þa pyꞃꞇe þuꝛh clað ⁊ ahluꞇꞇꝛa ꞅꝼiþe pel bo
þonne on þa eaȝan þonne þu pille ꞃeꞅꞇan · ȝiꝛ ꞅio

Imminutiones.
ꝛealꝼ ꞅie ꞇo heaꝛ[1] ȝeꞅꝼeꞇ mið hunȝe. Þið æꝛmælum
ȝením aꞇꞇꞃum ȝemenȝ ꝛið ꞅpaꞇl þa[2] eaȝan uꞇepeaꝛb
nalæꝛ innan.

Þið æꝛmælum niþepeaꝛb[3] æꝛcþꞃoꞇu ȝecopen ón muþe
⁊ apꝛinȝen þuꝛh clað on eaȝe ȝebon punboꞃlice hælþ.
Ƿiþ þon þe mon ꞅuꞃeȝe ꞅie ȝenim aȝꞃimoꞃian pelle
ꞅꝼiþe oþ þꝛibban bæl þþeah ȝelome þa eaȝan mið þy.

Pustula.
fol. 14 a.
Ƿiþ pocce on eaȝum · ȝením pað ⁊ ꞃibban ⁊ hleomocan
pyl on meolce on buꞇeꞃan iꝛ beꞇeꞃe ⁊ pyꞃc beþinȝe ·
pyl hleomóc ⁊ ȝeaꞃpan ⁊ pubu ceaꝛꝛillan on meolcum.

---

[1] Heaꝛ MS. If any word closely
answering to Germ. Herbe, Lat.
Acerbus, occurs in Saxon, it has
not met my eyes; the context is our
guide here. See Gl.

[2] ꞅmiꞃe must be supplied.
[3] niþepeaꝛb, MS.

celandine, pound the worts much, mingle with wine, put into a copper vessel or keep in a brazen vat, let it stand seven days or more, wring the worts very clean, add pepper, and sweeten very lightly with honey, put subsequently into a horn, and with a feather put one drop into the eyes. Work a dry eye salve *thus;* take beetle nut (?) and sulfur, Greek olusatrum[1] and burnt salt, and of pepper most, grind all to dust, sift through a cloth, put it on a fawns skin, let him keep it about himself, lest it get moist. Introduce a small quantity into the eyes with a tooth pick; afterwards let him rest himself and sleep, and then wash his eyes with clean water, and let him look in the water, *that is, keep his eyes open under water.* Work eye salve *thus;* pound thoroughly cummin and a strawberry plant, and souse with sweetened wine, put into a copper vessel or into a brazen one, let it stand many nights, wring the wort through a cloth and clear *the liquid* thoroughly, then apply to the eyes when thou may wish to rest; if the salve be too biting, sweeten it with honey. For imminution of the eyes, take olusatrum, mingle with spittle, *anoint* the eyes outwardly not inwardly.

22. For imminutions, the nether part of *the herb* ashthroat[2] chewed in the mouth and wrung through a cloth, *and* applied to the eye, wonderfully healeth. In case a man be blear eyed, take agrimony, boil it thoroughly *down* to the third part, wash the eyes frequently with that. For a pock *or pustule* in the eyes, take woad[3] and ribwort[4] and brooklime,[5] boil in milk, in butter is better, and work a fomentation. Boil brooklime[5] and yarrow[6] and wood chervil[7] in milk.

---

[1] *Smyrnium olusatrum.*
[2] In Herb. iv. *Verbena officinalis,* but in the gll. *Ferula.*
[3] *Isatis tinctoria.*
[4] *Plantago lanceolata.*
[5] *Veronica beccabunga.*
[6] *Achillea millefolium.*
[7] *Anthriscus silvestris.*

Σύκωσις,
Ficus.

Ƿiþ ƿyrmum ón eaȝum ȝením beolonan fæb ꞃceað
ón ȝleða · ðo ꞇꞃa bleða ꞃulle pæꞇeꞃef ꞇo feꞇꞓ ón ꞇꞃa
healꞃe ꞇ fiꞇe þæꞃ oꞃeꞃ bꞃæð þonne ꝥ heaꞃoð hiðeꞃ ꞇ
ȝeonð oꞃeꞃ ꝥ ꞃyꞃ ꞇ þa bleða eáꞓ þonne ꞃceaðaþ þa
ƿyꞃmaꞃ on þæꞇ pæꞇeꞃ. Ƿiþ þeoꞃable ón eaȝúm þe
món ȝeꞃiȝo hæꞇ on læðen haꞇꞇe cimosiꞃ · hænne æȝeꞃ
ȝeolocan ꞇ meꞃceꞃ ꞃæð ꞇ aꞇꞇꞃum ꞇ ꞇunminꞇan. Eꞃꞇ
pið ȝeꞃiȝon fceapef hohfcancan unfoðenne ꞇobꞃec ȝeðo

* Πτίλωσις.

þæꞇ meaꞃh on þa eaȝan. Ƿiþ þiccum bꞃæpúm* ȝením
þꞃeo hanð ꞃulla mucꞃyꞃꞇe þꞃeo ꞃealꞇeꞃ · þꞃeo papan²
ꞃylle þonne oþ ꝥ fie ꞇꞃæðe beꞃylleð þæꞃ pofeꞃ healð þonne
on cypeꞃenum ꞃaꞇe. Þam men² þe habbað þicce bꞃæpaꞃ
ȝením cypeꞃen ꞃæꞇ ðo þæꞃón lybcoꞃn ꞇ ꞃealꞇ ȝemenȝ ·
ȝením celeþonian ꞇ bifceoppyꞃꞇ ꞇ ȝeaceꞃ ꞃuꞃan ꞇ aꞇ-

fol. 14 b.

ꞇoꞃlaþan ꞇ fpꞃinȝpyꞃꞇ ꞇ enȝlifce moꞃan · ꞇ hpon ꞃæðiceꞃ
ꞇ hꞃeꞃneꞃ ꞃoꞇ apæꞃc þonne ealle ȝeoꞇ þonne ꝉin ón ·
læꞇ fꞇanðan aꞃeoh eꞃꞇ on ꝥ cypeꞃene ꞃæꞇ · læꞇ þonne
fꞇanðan ꝼiꞃꞇyne nihꞇ ꞇ þa ðeꞃfꞇan beoþ ȝoðe · haꞃa þe
clæne ꞃleꞇan ðo on ꝥ ꞃæꞇ þe þa ðeꞃfꞇan on ꞃyn fpa
ꞃela fpa þaꞃa ꞃlieꞇna þæꞃ ón cliꞃian mæȝe · fcꞃeꞃ þonne
oꞃ þam ꞃæꞇe ꝥ biþ fpiðe ȝoð ꞃealꞃ þam men þe hæꞃð
þicce bꞃæpaꞃ.   :·

.III.

Alex. Trall.,
lib. iii.

Læceðomaꞃ pið eallum eaꞃena faꞃe ꞇ ece ꞇ pið eaꞃena aðeaꞃunȝe · ꞇ ȝíꞃ ƿyꞃmaꞃ ón eaꞃan fynð oþþe

---

¹ See the glossary on ꞃiȝ ; it is
συκῆ, σύκωσις, not χύμωσις ; this is
a misinterpretation of an Hellenic
word.

² Read ꞃapan.

³ þam̃, MS. Read þá m̃.

23. For worms[1] in eyes, take seed of henbane,[2] shed it on gledes, add two saucers full of water, set them on two sides of the man, and let him sit there over them, jerk the head hither and thither over the fire and the saucers also, then the worms shed *themselves* into the water. For " dry" disease in the eyes, which is called *the disease* fig, and in Latin is called χύμωσις[a] the yolk of a hens egg and seed of marche[3] and olusatrum and garden mint.[4] Again for *the disease* fig, break to pieces a hock shank unsodden of a sheep, apply the marrow to the eyes. For thick eyelids, take three handfuls of mugwort,[5] three of salt, three of soap, boil them till two parts out of three of the ooze be boiled away, then preserve in a copper vessel. For him who hath thick eyelids, take a copper vessel, put therein cathartic seeds and salt there among, take celandine and bishopwort and cuckoosour and attorlothe [6] and springwort[7] and English carrot, and a somewhat of radish, and ravens foot,[8] then wash them all, then pour wine on; let *it* stand, strain again into the copper vessel; then let it stand fifteen nights and the dregs will be good. Have with thee clean curds and introduce into the vessel on which the dregs are, as much of the curd as may cleave thereon. Then scrape *the scrapings* off the vessel, that will be a very good salve for the man who hath thick eyelids.

iii.

1. Leechdoms for all sore of ears and ache, and for deafness of ears, and if insects are in the ears or an

---

[1] Worms are all creeping things, here insects, acari : Celsus has a chapter "de pediculis palpebrarum," Lib. VI. vi. 15,—" sive etiam vermi- " culos (*oculi*) habeant aut brigan- " tes qui cilia arare et exulcerare " solent." Marcellus, 275, e. Cf. ibid. f. The disease in Hellenic was φθειρίασις, and by keen eyes the in- sects could be seen to move, Actuarios.

[2] *Hyoscyamus niger.*

[3] *Apium.*

[4] *Mentha sativa.*

[5] *Artemisia vulgaris.*

[6] Uncertain. See Herb. xlv. vol. I. Pref. lvi.

[7] *Euforbia lathyris.*

[8] *Ranunculus ficaria.*

40   LÆCE BOC.

eapꞃıcȝa · ꙺ ȝıꝼ eaꞃan ðynıen · ꙺ eaꞃꞃealꝼa ꝼıꝼtyne
cꞃæꝼtaꞃ.   :·

Marcellus,
285, f.
Þıþ eaꞃena ꞃaꞃe ꙺ ece betonıcan nıꞃan ȝeꞃoꞃhte þa
leaꝼ ꞃelꝼ [1] ȝecnupa on peaꞃmum pæteꞃe ðo hꞃon ȝeꞃo-
ꞃoðeꞃ eleꞃ to · ȝenım þ ꞃpa placu mıð þıcꞃe ꞃulle ðꞃype
on þ eaꞃe. Eꝼt pıþ þon ılcan ȝenım cıeꞃan ȝeꞃeoþ on
ele ðꞃype on þ eaꞃe þone ele. Þıþ eaꞃꞃæꞃce ꙺ pıð
ðeaꞃe hunðeꞃ tunȝe ꙺ ꞃenmınte ꙺ cellenðꞃe ȝecnupa on

fol. 15 a.

Marcellus,
286, d.

Sextus, cap.
xi. 1. Lat.
pın oþþe on eala aꞃeoh ðo on eaꞃe. Þıþ þon ılcan
ȝenım hænne ꞃyꞃele ȝemylte ꙺ þonne ȝeðo placo on
eaꞃe ȝeðꞃype on. Þıþ þon ılcan ȝenım ele · ȝenım eac
ȝoꞃe ꞃyꞃele ȝeot on þonne ȝepıt þ ꞃaꞃ apeȝ.   :·

Þıþ þon ılcan ȝenım beolonan ꞃeap ȝeplece ꙺ þonne
on eaꞃe ȝeðꞃyp · þonne þ ꞃaꞃ ȝeꞃtılð.   :·

Cf. Marcell.
284, e.

Marcellus,
287, d.

Marcellus,
285, b.

Cf. Alex. Trall.,
lib. iii. 1.
= p. 56, line 21,
ed. 1548.
Þıþ þon ılcan ȝenım ȝaꞃleac ꙺ cıpan ꙺ ȝoꞃe ꞃyꞃele
ȝemylte toȝæðeꞃe pꞃınȝ on eaꞃe.   :·
Þıð þon ılcan ȝenım æmetan æȝꞃu ȝetꞃıꞃula pꞃınȝ
on eaꞃe. Þıð eaꞃena ꞃaꞃe ȝenım ȝate ȝeallan ðꞃype
on þ eaꞃe · menȝ pıð cu meolꞃc ȝıꝼ þu ꞃılle. Þıð
eaꞃena ðeaꞃe · ȝenım hꞃyþeꞃeꞃ ȝeallan pıþ ȝæten hlanð
ȝemenȝeð ȝeðꞃype ȝepleceð on þ eaꞃe.   :·

Þıþ þon ılcan ȝıꝼ eaꞃan ꞃıllen aðeaꞃıan oþþe yꝼel
hlyꞃt ꞃıe · ȝenım eoꞃoꞃeꞃ ȝeallan ꞃeaꞃꞃeꞃ ȝeallan ·
buccan ȝeallan ȝemenȝ pıþ hunıȝ ealꞃa em ꞃela ðꞃype
on þ eaꞃe.   :·
Þıþ þon ılcan ȝıꝼ [2] yꝼelne hlyꞃt hæbbe ıꞃıeꞃ ꞃeap
þæꞃ þe be eoꞃþan ꞃlıhð þ clænoꞃte ꞃeap ȝemenȝ pıð
pın ðꞃype on eaꞃe.   :·

fol. 15 b.
Eꝼt ꞃıbban ꞃeap ꙺ ȝepleceðne ele toȝæðeꞃe ȝemenȝeð
ðꞃype on punðoꞃlıce hælð. Þıþ þon ılcan ȝenım ꞃam-

---

[1] Read ꞃelꝼe ? | [2] Add hꞃa, or mon.

earwig, and if the ears din, and ear salves. Fifteen receipts.

2. For sore and ache of ears, pound new wrought betony, the leaves themselves, in warm water, add a somewhat of rose oil, take that lukewarm with thick wool, drip it into the ear. Again for the same, take an onion, seethe it in oil, drip the oil on the ear. For ear wark and for deafness, pound *the herb* hounds tongue[1] and fenmint[2] and coriander in wine or in ale, strain it, apply to the ear. For the same, take hen grease, melt it, and then apply it lukewarm to the ear, drip it on it. For the same, take oil, take also goose grease, pour into *the ear*, then the sore departs.

3. For the same, take juice of henbane, make it lukewarm, and then drip it on the ear; then the sore stilleth.

4. For the same, take garlic and onion and goose fat, melt *them* together, squeeze *them* on the ear.

5. For the same, take emmets eggs, crush *them*, squeeze *them* on the ear. For sore of ears, take goats gall, drip it on the ear; mingle, if thou will, cows milk with *it*. For deafness of ears, take neats gall mixed with goats stale, drip it, when made lukewarm, on the ear.

6. For the same, if the ears have a tendency to grow deaf, or if the hearing be ill, take boars gall, bulls gall, bucks gall, mix equal quantities of all with honey, drip *this* on the ear.

7. For the same, if one have ill hearing, mingle juice of ivy, that which runneth by the earth, the cleanest juice, with wine; drip it into the ear.

8. Again, drip into *the ear* juice of ribwort and oil made lukewarm, mingled together, it wonderfully healeth. For the same, take rams gall, with urine *of*

---

[1] *Cynoglossum officinale.* | [2] *M. silvestris.*

meſ ʒeallan mib hiſ ſelſeſ nihtneſtiʒeſ miʒoþan ʒemenʒe piꝥ buteſan ʒeót on eaſe. Eſt piþ þon ilcan
hnutbeameſ ſinbe feap ʒeplecebe bſype ón eaſe.   :·

Cf. Marcell.
264, g.

Þiþ bon ilcan ʒenim celenbſan feap ʒſenſe menʒ
piþ piſeſ meoluc ⁊ huniʒeſ bſopan ⁊ pineſ ʒeplehtc

Cf. Marcell.
285, a.

toſamne. Viþ eaſena abeaſunʒe eſt ellencſoppan ʒc-
tſiſulab ꝥ feap pſinʒ on ꝥ eaſe. Eſt piþ þon ilcan
ʒeníim eoſoſeſ ʒeallan · ⁊ ſeaſſeſ ⁊ buccan menʒ piþ
huniʒ oþþe ón ele pſinʒ on eaſe.   :·

Marcellua,
282, d.

Eſt piꝥ þon ilcan ʒeníim ʒſenne æſcenne ſtæſ leʒe
on ſyſ ʒenim þonne ꝥ ſeap þe híim oſ ʒæþ bo on þa
ilcan pulle pſinʒ ón eaſe ⁊ mib þæſe ilcan pulle ſoſ-
ſtoppa þæt eaſe.   :·

Þiþ ꝥ ilce eſt ʒenim æmetan hoſſ ⁊ cſopleáo ⁊
neoþopeaſbe ellenſinbe oþþe beolonan ⁊ ele ʒecnupa to
Somne pyſme on fcille bo þonne on eaſe þaſa ſeabena

fol. 16 a.

æmetena hoſſ · ʒenim þonne ſæbic ⁊ ecebe cnupa to
Somne pſinʒ on ꝥ eaſe. ʒiſ pyſmaſ on eaſan ſyn
ʒeníim eoſꝥ ʒeallan ʒſeneſ feap · oþþe hunan ſeap ·
oþþe peſmobeſ ſeap ſpilc þaſa an ſpa þu pille ʒeot ꝥ
feap on ꝥ eaſe ꝥ tihꝺ þone pyſm út. Þyſc fealſe
ʒecnupa finſullan ⁊ leoþopyſt[1] ⁊ poꝛ ʒebo þonne on
ʒlæſ ſæt mib ecebe ⁊ þuſh clab aſſinʒ bſype on ꝥ
eaſe. Þiþ þon ʒiſ eaſan bynien · ʒeníim ele bo ón mib
eoſociʒſe pulle ⁊ ſoſbytte ꝥ eaſe mib þæſe pulle þonne
þu ſlapan pille ⁊ bo eſt óſ þonne þu onpæcne.   :·

---

[1] Read leaþoppyſt.

the patient himself after a nights fasting, mix with butter and pour into the ear. Again for the same, drip into the ear juice of the rind of a nut tree made lukewarm.

9. For the same, mix with womans milk juice of green coriander, and a drop of honey and of wine, warmed together. For deafening of the ears again, *try* alder[1] bunches triturated, wring *out* the juice into the ear. Again for the same, take boars gall and bullocks and bucks, mingle with honey or in oil, wring into the ear.

10. Again for the same, take a green ashen staff, lay it on the fire, then take the juice that issues from it, put it on the same wool, wring into the ear, and stop up the ear with the same wool.

11. For the same, take emmets horses[2] and cropleek[3] and the lower part of alder rind or henbane and oil, pound *them* together, warm in a shell, then introduce into the ear the red emmets horses; than take radish and vinegar, pound them together, *and* wring into the ear. If there be insects in ears, take juice of green earthgall,[4] or juice of *hor*ehound, or juice of wormwood, whatsoever of these thou mayest wish, pour the juice into the ear, that draweth the worm out. Work a salve *thus;* pound sinfull[5] and latherwort[6] and leek, then place *them* in a glass vessel with vinegar, and wring through a cloth, drip *the moisture* on the ear. In case that there is a dinning in the ears; take oil, apply it with ewes wool, and close up the ear with the wool, when thou wilt sleep, and remove it again when thou awakest.

---

[1] *Sambucus nigra.*

[2] This talk of "emmets horses" is merely a misunderstanding of the ἱπποὑρμηκες of Aristoteles. Hist. Anim. viii. 27. The translation by Plinius, "formicæ pennatæ," that is, *male ants,* is commonly ac-cepted as true, of course, but it is both philologically and physically unsatisfactory.

[3] *Allium sativum.*

[4] *Erythræa centaureum.*

[5] One of the *sedum* tribe, or all.

[6] *Saponaria officinalis.*

Ɛ̵ft ƿiþ þon ilcan peƿmoð ȝefoðenne on pætene on
niƿūm cytele ðo ō̵f heoƿðe læt ƿeccan þone ſtēam on
þ̵ eaƿe ꞇ foƿðytte mið þæƿe pyƿte ſiþþan hit inȝeȝan
ƿie. Ƿiþ eaƿƿicȝan · ȝenīm þ̵ micle ȝƿeace pinðel ſtƿeaƿ
tƿyecȝe þ̵ on poƿþium pixð ceop on þ̵ eaƿe he bið ō̵f
ƿona.

.IIII.

Alex. Trall.,
lib. iv.

[1] Læceðomaſ pið healfȝunðe ꞇ þæſ tacn hƿæþeƿ he
hit ſie · ꞇ eāc pið ȝealhſpile ꞇ þƿotan · ꞇ paƿenðe · ƿiþ
ſpeoƿcoþe · XIIII. cƿæſtaſ.　　　　　　:·

fol. 16 b.
Marcellus, 306, a.

Ƿiþ healſȝunðe þonne æƿeſt onȝinne ſe healſȝunð
peſan ſmiƿe hine ſona mið hƿyþeƿeſ oþþe ſpiðoſt mið
oxan ȝeallan þ̵ iſ acunnoð ymb ſeapa niht bið hal.

Marcellus, 306, b.

ȝiſ þu polðe pitan hƿæþeƿ þ̵ healſ ȝunð ſie · ȝenīm
anȝeltpæccean ȝehalne leȝe on þa ſtope þæƿ hit aþƿuten
ſie ꞇ beƿƿeoh ſæſte uƿan mið leaſūm · ȝiſ hit healſȝunð bið ſe pȳƿm pyƿð to eoƿþan · ȝiſ hit ne biþ he
biþ ȝehal. Ɛ̵ft ƿiþ healſ ȝunðe ȝenīm celenðeƿ ꞇ beana

Marcellus, 306, b.

toȝæðeƿe ȝefoðene ꞇ aleȝe ōn Sona toſeneþ. Ɛ̵ft læceðom ƿiþ þon ilcan ȝenīm pætenhæƿeƿn ȝebæƿneðne ꞇ
þonne ȝeȝniðen ſmale ꞇ ƿiþ huniȝ ȝemenȝeð ꞇ ōn ȝeðon

Marcellus, 306, a.

Sona bið ſel. Ƿiþ þon ilcan eſt ȝalbanum hatte
ſuþeƿne þyƿt leȝe þa ōn þone ſpeoƿpæƿc · þonne atihð
hio mið ealle þa yſelan pætan ūt ꞇ þone ȝunð.

Ƿiþ þon ilcan eſt beƿen melo ꞇ hluttoƿ pīc ꞇ peax ·
ꞇ ele menȝ toſomne ſeoþ ðo cnihteſ oþþe cilbeſ miȝe-

fol. 17 a.

þan to to onleȝene ðo on þone ȝunð. Ƿið healſ ȝunðe

---

[1] Cf. Galen, vol. x. p. 881, ed. 1825.

12. Again for the same, *try* wormwood sodden in water in a new kettle, remove it from the hearth, let the steam reek upon the ear, and when *the application*[1] has gone in, close up *the ear* with the wort. Against earwigs, take the mickle great windlestraw[2] with two edges, which waxeth in highways, chew it into the ear, he, *the insect*, will soon be off.

iv.

Leechdoms against a purulent humour in the neck, and tokens of it, whether it be such, and also for swellings in the jowl and throat and weasand, and against quinsy. Fourteen receipts.

2. Against a purulence[a] in the neck, when first the neck ratten begins to exist, smear it soon with gall of a beeve, or best of an ox; it is a tried *remedy;* in a few nights he will be whole. If thou wouldst know whether it be neck purulence,[b] take an earthworm entire, lay it on the place where the annoyance is, and wrap up fast above with leaves; if it be neck ratten the worm turneth to earth, if it be not, he, *the patient*, will be whole. Again for neck ratten, take coriander and beans sodden together, and lay on, soon it removes *the disease*. Again, a leechdom for the same, take a water crab burnt and then rubbed small and mingled with honey and done on, *or applied*, soon he will be well. For the same again, a southern wort has been called galbanum, lay it on the neck pain, then it draweth altogether out the evil wet *or humour* and the ratten.

[a] Struma, Marcellus.

[b] A strumous swelling.

3. For the same again, mingle together bere *or barley* meal and clear pitch[c] and wax and oil, seethe *this*, add a boys or a childs mie, *make* into an external application on the matter. For ratten in the

[c] Resin.

---

[1] It; the application, because *team is masculine.

[2] *Cynosurus cristatus,* some; *Agrostis spica venti,* some.

eſc þæꝑe ꝑeaðan netelan pyꝑccꝑuman ᵹeꝛoðenne on
eceðe ⁊ ᵹebeatenne ⁊ on peaxhlaꝛeꝼ pıꝛan ōn aleð · ᵹıꝼ
ꝛe ᵹunð bıþ þonne onᵹınnenðe ſıo ꝛealꝼ hıne toðꝛıꝼþ ·
ᵹıꝼ he bıþ ealð hıo hıne ontynð ⁊ ſpa aſcıhð ꝥ yꝼel
ūc oþ ꝥ he hal bıð.   :·

Eꝼc pıþ þon manıᵹꝛealð tacn ⁊ læceðom pıð healꝼ-
ᵹunðe oþþe ᵹeaᵹlſpıle¹ oððe þꝛotan oþþe paꝛenðe · Sıo
aðl īꝛ tpeᵹea cynna. Oþeꝑ ıf on þam ᵹeaᵹle ⁊ þonne
mon þone muþ ontynð bıþ ᵹehpæþeꝑ ᵹeſpollen ⁊ bıþ ꝑeað
ymb þa hꝛæccunᵹa · ⁊ ne mæᵹ ſe man eþelıce eþıan
ac bıþ aſmoꝛoð · ne mæᵹ eſc nahc ꝛoꝛſpelᵹan ne pel
ſpꝑecan ne ſtemne ꝓæꝛþ · ne bıð þeoꝛ aðl hpæþeꝑe to
ꝛꝑecne. Oþeꝑ īꝛ þonne on þæꝑe þꝛotan bıþ ſpyle ⁊
lyꝛſen ſe ne mæᵹ nahc ᵹecpeþan ⁊ bıð ꝛe ſpıle ᵹe on
þam ſpeoꝛan ᵹe on þæꝑe cunᵹan · ne mæᵹ ſe man pel
eþıan · ne þone ſpeoꝛan on ceꝑꝑan · ne hıꝛ heaꝛoð
ꝛoꝛð ōn hylðan ꝥ he hıſ naꝛolan ᵹeſeon mæᵹe · ⁊
butan hıꝛ man ꝑaþoꝑ cılıᵹe he bıþ ymb þꝛeo nıhc
ᵹeꝛaꝑen. ᵹıꝼ ſıe þæꝑe able bꝛyne Innan þæꝛ ſcꝛanᵹ
ꝥ mōn ne mæᵹe utan ᵹeſeon ſıo bıþ ðy ꝛꝑecenꝑe.
ᵹıꝼ þonne ſıe² on ᵹehpæþeꝑe healꝼe þa ceacan aſpollen
⁊ ſıo þꝛotu ⁊ þu þa tacn ᵹeſeo þonne ſona læc þu
hım bloð ōn æðꝑe · ᵹıꝼ þu ꝥ þuꝑhteon ne mæᵹe
ſceaꝑpa hīm þa ꝛcancan ꝥ hīm ðeah.   :·

Sele hīm ſceaꝑpne pyꝑcðꝛeno pyꝑne hım meteſ æꝛceꝑ
þon bepınð þone ſpeoꝛan ⁊ leᵹe ōn læceðomaſ þa þe
utteon þa yꝼelan pætan ⁊ þæt ſaꝑ þonne bıþ þæꝑ pyꝑpe
pen. Pyꝛc hım þa ꝛealꝼe ᵹenīm ſpıneꝛ ꝑyſle ᵹeſmyꝑe
ane bꝛaðe pannan Inneþeaꝑðe mıð þam ꝑyꝛele pyl þonne
peoꝛp ᵹoſe ſceaꝑn to on þa pannan ⁊ ᵹeplece ⁊ þonne
hıc ſy ᵹemylc ðo þonne on lınenne cla, leᵹe on ꝥ ꝛaꝑ ⁊
beſpeþe ðo ꝥ pel ōꝛc on on ðæᵹ · ⁊ bıþ ſpa beceꝑe ſpa

---

¹ ᵹeaᵹlſꝑıþe, MS. | ² Read ſien.

neck again, *use* a root of the red nettle sodden in
vinegar and beaten, laid on in the manner of a cake
of wax; if the matter be then beginning, the salve
driveth it away; if it be old it openeth it, and so the
evil riseth out till he be hale.

4. Again for that, a manifold token and a leechdom
for the neck ratten or jowl swelling or *swelling of the*
throat or weasand. The disease is of two kinds; the
one is in the jowl, and when one openeth the mouth
it is both swollen and is red about the uvula; and
the man can not easily breathe, but will be smothered;
he can not also swallow aught nor speak well, nor
hath he voice; this disorder, however, is not dangerous.
Another *sort* is when there is a swelling in the throat
and purulence, he, *the patient*, may not speak aught,
and the swelling is both on the neck and on the tongue;
the man can not well breathe, nor turn his neck nor
lean forward his head so that he may see his navel;
and except one attend to him somewhat speedily, in
about three days he will be deceased. If the burning
of the disease within be strong, yet there are no
external signs of it, it is so much the more dangerous.
If then on either side the jaws be swollen and the
throat, and thou see the tokens, then soon let thou
him blood on a vein; if thou may not carry that
through, scarify for him his shanks, that doth him
good.

5. Give him a sharp wort drink, warn him off meat,
after that bandage the neck, and lay on leechdoms
which may draw out the evil humour and the sore,
there will be then hope of recovery. Work him the
salve *thus;* take swines fat, smear the inside of a
broad pan with the fat, boil up, then cast goose sharn
into the pan, and make lukewarm, and when it be
melted then put it on a linen cloth, lay it on the
sore, and swathe up, apply that pretty often in a day,
and it will be the better the oftener thou renewest

þu oꝼtoꞃ eðnipaꞅt þa ꞃealꝼe ⁊ oꝼtoꞃ onleᵹeꞅt ꞅio tihð
þ yꝼel ut.   :·

Ƿiþ healꞅᵹunðe ᵹením peax ⁊ ele ᵹemenᵹ ƿiþ ꞃoꞃan
bloꞅtmán ⁊ ᵹemelt toᵹæðeꞃe ðo þæꞃ ón.   Ƿiþ ſpeoꞃ-

fol. 18 a.

coþe pyꞃc ón lécᵹenðe ꞃealꝼe · ᵹením ꝼeaꞃꞃeꞅ ᵹelynðo
⁊ beꞃan ſmeꞃu ⁊ peax ealꞃa em ꝼela pyꞃc to ſealꝼe

ᵃ Alex. Trall.,
p. 67, ed. 1548.
Paul. Ægin.
iii. 27.

ſmiꞃe mið. ᵃEꝼt ƿiþ þon ilcan ᵹíꝼ þu ꞃinðe hꝼitne
hunðeꞃ þoſt aðꞃiᵹe þone ⁊ ᵹeᵹnið ⁊ aꞅyꞃt ⁊ ᵹehealð þ
ƿiþ þæꞃe ſpeoꞃcoþe ⁊ þonne þeaꞃꝼ ꞃie menᵹ ƿiþ huniᵹ
ſmiꞃe þone ſpeoꞃan mið þ biþ ſtꞃanᵹ ꞃealꝼ ⁊ ᵹoð ƿið
ſpelcꞃe ablaꞃunᵹe ⁊ bꞃuneþan ⁊ ƿiþ þaꞃa ceacna ᵹeſpelle oððe aſmoꞃunᵹe · ſceal þeah ſe hunð ban ᵹnaᵹan
æꞃ · þy biþ ſe þoſt hꞃit ⁊ micel ᵹiꝼ þu hine nimeſt ⁊
ᵹaðeꞃaſt æt ꝼylne¹ þonne ne biþ he to unſpete to
ᵹeſtincanne · þonne ꞃceal món þone ᵹeaᵹl eác ſpillan
ᵹelome on þæꞃe aðle · ⁊ ſpolᵹettan eceð ƿiþ ꞃealt ᵹemenᵹeð. Eꝼt ꞃiꞃleaꞃan ſeaꞃeꞅ þꞃy bollan ꝼulle lytle
ꞃceal ꝼoꞃcuuolꝼtan. Ƿiþ ſpeoꞃcoðe eꝼt ᵹaꞃleac ᵹeᵹniðen
ón eceð þ þe ſie ƿiþ pæteꞃ ᵹemenᵹeð ſpille þone ᵹeaᵹl mið
þy.   Ƿiþ ſpeoꞃcoþe eꝼt ꞃiᵹeꞃ ſeoꞃoþa ſeoþ on ᵹeſpettum

fol. 18 b.

pæteꞃe ſpille þa ceolan mið þy ᵹiꝼ ꞃe ſpeoꞃa ꞃaꞃ ꞃie
ꞃyn eác þa ſpillinᵹa hꞃilum hate þonne iꞃ eác to þiꞃꞃe
aðle ᵹeꞃet þ món unðeꞃ þæꞃe tunᵹan læte bloð oþþe óꝼ
eaꞃme ⁊ on moꞃᵹen ón ſpꞃenᵹe · ᵹiꝼ hit þonne cniht
ſie læt on þam ſpeoꞃan · ⁊ on þæꞃe aðle iꞃ to ꝼoꞃ-
pyꞃꞃanne ꞃineꞃ ⁊ ꝼlæꞃceꞅ ſpiþoꞃt þy læꞃ ꞅio ceole ſie
aꞅpollen.   ·:·

.V.

Ƿiþ þon ᵹiꝼ manneꞅ muð ꞃaꞃ ſie ᵹením betonican ⁊
ᵹetꞃiꝼula leᵹe on þa peoloꞃe. To muð ꞃealꝼe ⁊ to

---

¹ Read ꝼylle. In Lye ꝼillen, *omentum*, is an error for ꝼylmen.

the salve and the oftener thou layest on. It will draw the evil out.

6. For matter in the neck, take wax and oil, mingle with rose blossoms and melt together, put *this* thereon. For swerecothe *or quinsy*, work an onlaying salve. Take suet of bull and grease of bear, and wax, even quantities of all, work to a salve, smear with it. Again for the same, if thou find a white thost [a] of hound, dry it and rub it, and sift it, and hold it against the swerecothe, and when need be mingle with honey, smear the neck with it, that is a strong salve and good for such upblowing *or inflation* and brunella,[1] and for swelling of the jaws, or smothering. The hound must gnaw a bone ere *he droppeth the thost*, then will the thost be white and mickle; if thou takest and gatherest it at the fall, then it is not too unsweet of smell; one shall further often also swill the jowl in this disease, and swallow vinegar mingled with salt. Again, he shall swallow down three bowls of the juice of cinquefoil, little ones. For swerecothe *or quinsy* again, *use* garlic rubbed in vinegar which be mingled with water, swill the jowl with that. For quinsy, again, seethe the siftings of rye on sweetened water, swill the gullet with it, if the swere be sore, let the swillings also be whilom hot. Besides it is also laid down for this disease, that blood be let under the tongue or from an arm, and on the morrow apply a clyster. Further if it be a boy, let (blood) on the neck; and in this disease it is well to warn off (the sick) from wine, and specially from flesh *meat*, lest the gullet be swollen.

[a] Album Græcum.

v.

In case that a mans mouth be sore, take betony and triturate it, lay it on the lips. For a mouth

---

[1] A disease resembling diphtheria ; otherwise, Pruna.

ȝebleȝenaðne tunȝan ſiſleaſe • ⁊ bnembel leaſ pyl on
pætene haſn lanȝe on muðe ⁊ ȝelome. ȝiſ monneſ
onað ſie ſul ȝenim beſen mela ȝoð • ⁊ clæne huniȝ ⁊
hpit ſealt ȝemenȝ eall toſomne ⁊ ȝnið þa teþ mið
ſpiðe ⁊ ȝelome.   :·

.VI.

Læceðomaſ piþ toð pænce ⁊ piþ pynmúm ȝe piþ þam
uſenan toðece ȝe piþ þam[1] niþenan.   :·

ᵃ Herbar.
Apul. i. 8.

Þiþ toþ pænce •ᵃ betonican ſeoð on pine oþ þnidðan
dæl ſpile þonne ȝeonð þone muð lanȝe hpile.   :·

fol. 19 a.

Þið toþ pænce ȝiſ pynm ete • ȝením ealb holen léaſ
⁊ heonot cnop neoþepeanðne ⁊ ſaluian uſepeanðe bepyl
tpy bæl on pætne ȝeot ón bollan ⁊ ȝeona ymb þonne
ſeallað þa pſnmaſ ón þone bollan. ȝiſ pynm ete þa
teð ȝenim oſeſ ȝeaſe holen ſinðe ⁊ eoſoſ þnotan
monan pel on ſpa hatum[2] haſa on muþe ſpa hat ſpa
þu hatoſt mæȝe. Þiþ toð pynmum ȝenim ſic mela ⁊
beolonan ſæb ⁊ peax ealna em ſela menȝ tosomne
pyne to peax canbelle • ⁊ bænn læt ſeocan on þone
muð do blæc hnæȝl unðen þonne ſeallaþ þa pynmaſ
ón.   :·

Þið toþ pænce ȝebænn hpit ſealt ⁊ ȝanleác beſec on
ȝlebum ȝebnæb ⁊ beſenð ⁊ pipoſ ⁊ ſtnælpynt ȝeȝnið
eal toſomne leȝe ón.   :

Þiþ toþ pænce hneſneſ ſot pel on pine neoþopeanðne
oððe on ecebe ſup ſpa ðu hatoſt mæȝe. Þiþ toðpænce

ſiþü, MS. | ² hatum pætne ?

salve and for a blained tongue, boil in water fiveleaf, *that is, cinquefoil,* and bramble leaves, have it long in the mouth and frequently. If a mans breath be foul, take good barley meal and clean honey and white salt,[1] mingle all together, and rub the teeth with *it* much and frequently.

vi.

1. Leechdoms for sharp pain in the teeth and for worms, either for the upper tooth ache or for the nether.

2. For tooth wark, seethe betony in wine to the third part, then swill the mouth thoroughly for a long while.

3. For tooth wark, if a worm eat *the tooth,* take an old holly leaf and one of the lower umbels of hart-wort,[2] and the upward *part of* sage, boil two doles[3] in water, pour into a bowl and yawn over it, then the worms shall fall into the bowl. If a worm eat the teeth, take holly rind over a year old, and root of carline thistle, boil in so hot *water?* hold in the mouth as hot as thou hottest may. For tooth worms, take acorn meal and henbane seed and wax, of all equally much, mingle *these* together, work into a wax candle, and burn it, let it reek into the mouth, put a black cloth under, then will the worms fall on it.

4. For tooth wark, burn white salt and garlic, make them smoke on gledes, roast and tear to pieces, and *add* pepper and clubmoss, rub all together and lay on.

5. For tooth wark, boil in wine or in vinegar the netherward part of ravens foot,[4] sup as thou hottest may. For tooth wark, bray together to dust rind

---

[1] That is, the best, purest salt.
[2] *Seseli;* perhaps, however, Hart-bramble, *Rhamnus,* may be meant.
[3] That is, two of worts to one of water.
[4] *Ranunculus ficaria.*

hnutbeamer ɲinde ⁊ þoɲn ɲinde ȝecnua to duſte adɲiȝ
on pannan ſnið utan þa teþ ɼceað on ȝelome.   :·

Ƿyɲc þuſ toþɼealɼe oɼeɲɼæpiſc ɲind ⁊ huniȝ ⁊ piɲoɲ
menȝ toſomne leȝe on· pyɲc eác ɼealɼe oɼ penpyɲte
on þa ilcan piɼan.   :·

fol. 19 b.
Ƿiþ þám uɼeɲan toþece ȝením piþoɲinban leaɼ apɲinȝ
on þa noſu. Ƿiþ þam niþeɲan toþece ɼlit mid þe
ɼoþoɲne oþ þæt hie bleðen.   :·

Eɼt ȝením elmeɼ ɲinde ȝebæɲn to ahſan ȝemenȝ þa
ahɼan piþ pæteɲ ⁊ aſeoh haɼa þæt pæteɲ lanȝe on
Marcellus, 296, h.
muþe. Eɼt ȝením ȝeaɲpan ceop ſpiþe.   :·

.VII.

Herbar. Apul. i. 13.
Ȝiɼ mon blode hɲæce ȝenim betonican ſpilce ſpa
.III. peneȝaſ ȝepeȝen ȝeȝnid on ȝæte meolc ɼele þɲy
daȝaſ þɲy bollan ɼulle to dɲincanne.   :·

.VIII.

Ƿiþ blæce on ꞡplitan ꝥyl to bæþe ɼencepſan ⁊ neo-
þopeaɲðne ſecȝ· æɼcɲinde eaɲɼan ꝥyl on pæteɲe lanȝe
beþe mid.   :·

To ɼealɼe piþ blæce on ꞡplitan· omþɲan neoþopeaɲðe
þa þe ſpimme do ɼealt to ⁊ ɼlietan ⁊ æȝ. bɲip piþ
blæce on ꞡplitan ȝemelte eald ſpic bɲip on þon· do
ȝeȝɲundenne piþoɲ on· ⁊ cɲopleác hpæteneɼ melpeɼ
tɲy dæl ſpilce þæɼ piþoɲeſ ápyl hɲæt hpeȝa·· ȝenim
fol. 20 a.
þæɼ þɲeo ſnæda ȝeɲeſt æɼteɲ peaɲime. Ƿið blæce
ȝením heoɲoteɼ hoɲn ȝebæɲn to ahɼan ⁊ ſpeɼl ⁊ ȝe-
bæɲned ɼealt ⁊ píc to ahſan ⁊ ſpa oſteɲ ɼcella ⁊ ȝecnupa omþɲan ſmale ⁊ ȝemenȝ eall to bɲipe ⁊ ſmiɲe

of nut tree and thorn rind, dry then in a pan, cut[1] the
teeth on the outside, shed on frequently.

6. Work a tooth salve thus, mingle together oversea
rind[2] and honey and pepper, lay on. Work also a
salve of wenwort in the same wise.

7. For the upper tooth ache, take leaves of withewind, wring *them* on the nose. For the nether tooth
ache, slit with the tenaculum, till they bleed.

8. Again, take elms rind, burn to ashes, mingle the
ashes with water and strain, hold the water long in
the mouth. Again, take yarrow, chew it much.

vii.

1. If a man break up blood, take as much betony
as three pennies weigh, rub in goats milk, give for three
days three bowls full to drink.

viii.

1. For a blotch on the face, boil for a bath fencress[3]
and the netherward *part of* sedge,[4] ash rind, tares,
boil long in water, bathe therewith.

2. For a salve against a blotch in the face, *use* the
netherward part of dock, which will swim,[5] add to it
salt and curds and egg. A brewit for a blotch on the
face, melt old lard, on that a brewit, add ground pepper, and cropleek,[6] two doles of wheaten meal as well
as of the pepper, boil a little, take of it three slices,
after that go to bed and get warm. For a blotch, take
harts horn, burn to ashes, and sulfur, and burnt salt
and pitch burnt to ashes, and so oyster shells, and
beat sorrel[7] small, and mingle all into a brewit, smear

---

[1] By Sect. 7, it appears by ᵗᵉþ is
meant the gums, toþꞁeoman.

[2] *Cinnamon.*

[3] *Nasturtium officinale.*

[4] *Carex.*

[5] This seems by Gerarde to be
duckweed, Lemna.

[6] *Allium sativum.*

[7] *Rumex Acetosa.*

mið. Efꞇ ꞃealf pel on aþyðum fceapeꞃ fmeꞃupe hæᵹ-
þoꞃneꞃ bloftman Ɡ þa fmalan finᵹꞃenan Ɡ puðuꞃoꞃan
menᵹ þonne hꝑꞇꞇcꞃuðu ꝑiþ Ɡ hꝑon buꞇeꞃan,   :·

.VIIII.

Cf. Marcell.
290, c.

Ᵹif men yꞃne bloð oꝛ nebbe ꞇo fꝑiðe ᵹeniïm ᵹꞃene
beꞇonican Ɡ ꞃuðan ᵹecnupa ón eceð ᵹeꝑꝑinᵹ ꞇofomne
fꝑilce ꞃie an ꞃlah fꞇinᵹ on þa nofu. bloð ꞃeꞇen bifceop
pyꝑꞇ nioþoꝛeaꝛðe eꞇe oððe on meolce ðꝛince. Bloð
feꞇen éfꞇ ᵹeniïm heᵹecliꞃan ᵹebinðe ón fꝑeoꞃan.   :·

bloð feꞇen efꞇ fꝑꝑinᵹ pyꝑꞇ ðo ón eaꞃe.

Bloð ꞃeꞇen efꞇ peᵹbꝛæðan ðo ón eaꞃe.   :·
bloð ꞃeꞇen efꞇ ᵹebal beꞃen eaꞃ befꞇinᵹe on eaꞃe
fꝑa he nyꞇe. Sume þiꞃ ꝑꞃiꞇað ✠ æᵹꝑyn · ꞇhon · fꞇꝛuꞇh ·

fol. 20 b.

ꝛola aꞃᵹꞃenn · ꞇaꝛꞇ · fꞇꝛuꞇh · on · ꞇꝛia · enn · piaꞇh ·
haꞇhu · moꞃꞃana · on hæl ✠ aꞃa · caꝛn · leou · ᵹꞃoꞇh ·
peoꝛn · ﬔ · fꝛil · cꞃonði · p · ⋈ · mꝛo · cꝛon · æꞃcꝛio ·
eꝛmio · aeꞃ · leNo · ᵹe hoꝛfe ᵹe men bloð feꞇen.   :·

.X.

Þiþ ᵹefnoꞇe Ɡ ᵹepofum · ᵹeniïm oxna lyb niþeꞃeaꞃð
ᵹecnupa pel pið ꝛæꞇꝛe · ᵹiꞃ hio fie ᵹꞃene ne ðo þu
þæꞃ ꝛæꞇeꞃ ꞇo ꝑꞃinᵹ þonne on ꝥ neb.   :·

.XI.

Marcellas,
291, e.

Þiþ ꞃaꞃum peoloꞃuïm ᵹefmiꞃe mið huniᵹe þa peoloꝛaꞃ
geniïm þonne æᵹeꞃꝛelman beꞃceað mið piꝛoꝛe leᵹe on. :·

.XII.

[1]Þiþ pouum muþe ᵹeniïm omꝛꞃan Ɡ ealðne fꝑinef
ꞃyꞃle pyꝑc ꞇo ꞃealꞃe feꞇe on þone pon[2] ðæl. Þiþ ceolan

---

[1] Κυνικὸς σπασμός.
[2] pon, here is a contraction of pohan, poᵹan.

therewith. Again, a salve, boil in pressed sheeps grease, hawthorns blossoms, and the small stonecrop and woodroffe, then mingle mastic therewith and a little butter.

ix.

1. If blood run from a mans nose too much, take green betony and rue, pound them in vinegar, twist them together like as it might be a sloe, poke it into the nose. A blood stopper; eat the netherward part of bishopwort or drink it in milk. To stop blood again, take hedge cleavers, bind it on the neck.

. 2. As a blood stancher again, put springwort[1] into the ear.

3. To stop blood again, put waybroad[2] into the ear.

4. To stop blood again, poke into the ear a whole ear of bere *or barley;* so he be unaware of it. Some write this: . . . . either for horse or man, a blood stancher.

x.

For snot and poses *or catarrhs;* take the netherward part of stinking hellebore,[3] pound it well with water ; if it be green do not apply water to it, then wring on the nose.

xi.

For sore lips, smear the lips with honey, then take film of egg, scatter it with pepper, and lay on.

xii.

For distorted mouth, take dock and old swines grease, work to a salve, set on the wry part. For swelling of gullet, for that, everfern[4] also shall *come*

---

[1] *Euforbia lathyris.*
[2] *Plantago maior.*
[3] *Helleborus viridis.*
[4] *Polypodium vulgare.*

ſpile piþ þon ꝼceal eoꝼonꝼcaꝼin eac ſpa Ᵹ ᵹyþꝼiꝼan pyl
on meolce ſup þonne Ᵹ ᵹebeþe miꝺ. Þiþ ceolan ſpile
biꝼceop pynꞇ aꞇenlaꝺe niꝺepeanꝺe Ᵹ claꞇan pyl on
ealaꝺ.   :·

.XIII.

Þiꝺ hæn ꝼceanꝺe hpiꞇ cpuꝺu ᵹecnupa ſpiꝺe ſmale
ꝺo æᵹeꝼ ꝥ hpiꞇe ꞇo Ᵹ menᵹ ſpa þu ꝺeſꞇ ꞇeaꝼon ón-
ſniꝺ miꝺ ꝼeaxſe ſeopa miꝺ ſeolce ꝼæſꞇc ſmine miꝺ þonne
miꝺ þæne ꝼealꝼe uꞇan Ᵹ innan æn ꝼe ſeolóc noꞇiᵹe·
ᵹiꝼ ꞇoſomne ꞇeo nece miꝺ hanꝺa ſmine eꝼꞇ ꝼona.   :·

.XIIII.

Þiþ ꝼeaꝺan · necelꝼ lyꞇel ſpeꝼl ſpeᵹleſ æppel peax
ᵹinᵹiꝼen þunh honn ꝺnince· hunan haꝼócꝼynꞇ on
hluꞇꞇnúm ealoꝺ.   :·

.XV.

[1]Þiþ hpoſꞇan hu he minꝼenlice ón mon becume Ᵹ hu
hiſ mon ꞇilian ſcyle. Se hpoſꞇa hæꝼꝺ maniᵹꝼealóne
ꞇocyme ſpa þa ſpaꞇl beoꝺ minꝼenlicu· hpilum cymꝺ
óꝼ unᵹemeꞇꝼænꞇne hæꞇo· hpilum oꝼ unᵹemeꞇꝼænꞇum
cyle· Ꝺpilum oꝼ unᵹemeꞇlicne ꝺniᵹneꝼꝼe.

Þync ꝺnenc piþ hpoſꞇan· ᵹenim inucᵹꝼynꞇ ſeoþ on
cypenenum ciꞇele Ᵹ pyl oþ ꝥ hio[2] ſie ſpiþe þicce· Ᵹ hio[2]
ſie óꝼ hpæꞇenum mealꞇe ᵹenonhꞇ ᵹenim þonne eoꝼon-
ꝼeannes mænꞇ biſceop pynꞇ· hinꝺ heoloꝺan· ꝺpeonᵹe
ꝺpoſꞇlan ſinᵹnenan ꝺo ꞇo eall on ꝼæꞇ ſele ꝺnincan miꝺ-

ꝺelbaᵹum Ᵹ ꝼonᵹa ꝼun Ᵹ ſealꞇeꝼ ᵹehpæꞇ.   Þiþ hpoſꞇan

---

[1] Bɫ. | [2] Read he.

into use, and boil cockle in milk, them sup *some* and bathe with it. For swelling of gullet, boil in ale bishopwort, the netherward part of attorlothe, and burdock.

xiii.

For hair lip, pound mastic very small, add the white of an egg, and mingle as thou dost vermillion, cut with a knife *the false edges of the lip*, sew fast with silk, then smear without and within with the salve, ere the silk rot. If it draw together, arrange it with the hand; anoint again soon.

xiv.

For watery congestions[1] called κλύδωνες, a little incense, some sulfur, beetle nut, wax, ginger; let *the patient* drink through a horn *hore*hound and hawkwort[2] in clear ale.

xv.

For host *or cough*, how variously it comes upon a man, and how a man should treat it. The host hath a manifold access, as the spittles are various. Whilom it cometh of immoderate heat, whilom of immoderate cold, whilom of immoderate dryness.

2. Work *thus* a drink against cough. Take mugwort,[3] seethe it in a copper kettle, and boil till it[4] be very thick, and let it[4] be wrought of wheaten malt; then take of everfern most, bishopwort, water agrimony,[5] pennyroyal,[6] singreen,[7] set all in a vat, give to drink at the middays, and forego *what is* sour and every-

---

[1] Βρογχοκήλη, perhaps.
[2] *Hieracium.*
[3] *Artemisia vulgaris.*
[4] The gender of the pronoun makes it refer to the wort, whereas

the process seems to require a masculine, referring to the potion.
[5] *Eupatorium cannabinum.*
[6] *Mentha pulegium.*
[7] *Sempervivum tectorum.*

eft· ᵹenim hunan feoð on pætene fele fpa peapme dpincan. :·

Eft ᵹenim clippynt fume men hatað poxep clipe fume eapynt· ⁊ hio py ᵹepopht opep mibne fumop feoþ þa ón pætene oþ þ dpibban¹ dæl þæp pofep óp fie pele dpincan þpipa on dæᵹ. :·

Þið hpoftan eft ᵹenim fæmintan pyl on ealaþ pele dpincan. Eft ᵹenim fppacen bepindpeb pyl ón ealað pele dpincan. :·

Eft ᵹen[i]m hopan ᵹeappan peabe netelan pyl ón meolce. Eft ᵹenim piþ hpoftan ⁊ piþ anᵹbpeofte plapian ᵹobne dæl bo bollan pulne pinep to bepyl þpibban dæl on þa pynte fupe on niht neptiᵹ. :·

Eft ᵹenim mapubian pyl on ealað bo pipop on. Eft piþ anᵹbpeofte ᵹip men fie dpiᵹe hpofta· ᵹenim fpicep fnæbe þynne leᵹe on hatne ftan fceað cymeb ón fete hopn ón dpince þonne fmic. :·

Þiþ dpiᵹum hpoftan eft ᵹenim eolonan ⁊ ᵹalluc ete on huniᵹep teape. :·

fol. 22 a.   .XVI.

Þiþ bpeoft pæpce ᵹenim þa lytlan culmillan ⁊ cymeb pyl on hluttpúm ealaþ fupe ⁊ dpince. Eft ᵹenim dpeopᵹe dpoftlan ⁊ ᵹyþpipan kyncean pelle on hluttpum ealað dpince fcenc pulne ón neaht neptiᵹ. :·

Pyl ón ealað piþ þon ilcan pinul mapubian betonican ⁊ dpince. Þiþ bpeoft pæpce ᵹenim puban· hunan ⁊

---

¹ Read ðpibban = ðpibba.

thing salt. Again for host, take horehound, seethe in water, administer it so warm to drink.

3. Again, take cliffwort,[1] some men call it foxes cliff, some riverwort, and let it be wrought past midsummer, seethe it in water till the third part of the wash be off, give it thrice a day to be drunk.

4. For host again, take sea mint, boil it in ale, give to drink. Again, take black alder rendered *and purified*, boil *it* in ale, give *it* to be drunk.

5. Again, take hove,[2] yarrow, red nettle,[3] boil *them* in milk. Again, take against host and against breast anguish,[4] a good portion of slary,[5] add a bowl full of wine, boil away a third part on the wort; let *the patient* sup it at night fasting.

6. Again, take marrubium, boil it in ale, add pepper. Again, for breast anguish, if a man have a dry host, take a thin slice of lard, lay it on a hot stone, shed cummin on it, set it on a horn,[6] let *the patient* drink in the smoke.

7. For a dry cough again, take elecampane and comfrey; let *the patient* eat them in virgin honey.

xvi.

1. For acute pain in the breast, take the little centaury and cummin, boil in clear ale, let *the patient* sip and drink. Again, take pennyroyal and cockle, artichoke, let him boil in clear ale, let him drink a cup full at night fasting.

2. Boil in ale for the same, fennel, marrubium, betony, and let *the patient* drink. For pain in the breast, take rue, *hore*hound and abrotanon,[7] rub to-

---

[1] *Arctium lappa.*
[2] *Glechoma hederacea.*
[3] *Lamium purpureum.*
[4] *Angina pectoris* seems too limited.

[5] *Salvia sclarea.*
[6] Lye understands cymeb as χαμαιδρύς, *germander*, going by the syllables.
[7] *Artemisia abrotanon.*

apnotanan ӡeӡniꝺ toSomne fmæle on moptene menӡ
piꝺ huniӡ ⁊ þny ꝺaӡaf ælce ꝺæӡ æp mete þpie cuclep
fulle ӡeþicӡe.

.XVII.

Þiþ heopt pæpce puꝺan ӡelm feoþ on ele ⁊ ꝺo alpan
ane yntfan to fmipe miꝺ þy ꝥ ftilꝺ þam fape. Þiþ
heopt ece ӡif him on Innan heapꝺ heopt pæpc fie
þonne him pyxþ pinꝺ on þæpe heoptan ⁊ hine þeӡeꝺ
þupft ⁊ biþ unmehtiӡlic.   ;.
Þypc him þonne ftan bæꝺ ⁊ on þam ete fuþepne
pæꝺic miꝺ fealte þy mæӡ pefan fio punꝺ ӡehæleꝺ.

Þiþ heopot ece eft ӡenim ӡiþpifan feoþ on meolce pele
ꝺpincan . vi. ꝺaӡaf.   :.
Eft nioþepeapꝺ efoppeapin ӡyþpifan . peӡbpæ[ꝺan]
pyl toromne pele ꝺpincan. Þiꝺ hiopot ece eft ӡenim
pipop . ⁊ cymen . ⁊ coft ӡeӡniꝺ on beoӡ oþþe on
pætpe pele ꝺpincan.   :.

.XVIII.

Ꝺponan pe micla ӡeoxa cume oþþe hu hif mon
tican pcule. Se cymꝺ of þam fpiꝺe acoloꝺan maӡan .
oþþe of þam to fpiꝺe ahatoꝺan . oꝺꝺe of to micelpe
fylle . oþþe of to micelpe læpnepfe . oꝺꝺe of yfelum
pætan . plitenꝺum ⁊ fceoppenꝺum þone maӡan . ӡif
þonne fe peoca man þuph fpipeꝺpenc afpipꝺ þone yfelan
bitenꝺan pætan on peӡ . þonne fopiftent pe ӡeohfa . fpipe
þa ꝺeah þam monnum þe foӡ fylle ӡihfa plihꝺ oꝺꝺe
fopþon þe hie Innán pcypfꝺ ⁊ eác pe ӡeohfa pe þe of
þæp yfelan pætan micelnyppe cymꝺ hæfꝺ þeapfe fpip-
ꝺpincef . pe pypcꝺ micelne fnopan eác ⁊ fe hine bet .
Þonne pe ӡeohfa of þæpe iblan pambe cymꝺ ⁊ of þæpe

gether small·in a mortar, mingle with honey, and for three days, every day before meat, let *the patient* take three spoons full.

xvii.

For pain in the heart, seethe a handful of rue in oil, and add an ounce of aloes, rub *the body* with that, it stilleth the sore. For heart ache, if there be to him within, a hard heart wark, then wind waxeth in the heart for him, and thirst vexes him and he is languid.

2. Work him then a stone bath, and in that let him eat southern radish[1] with salt, by that the wound may be healed. For heart ache again, take githrife, seethe it in milk, give to drink for six days.

3. Again, boil together the netherward part of ever-fern, githrife, and waybroad ; give to drink. For heart ache again, take pepper and cummin and costmary, rub them into beer, or into water, administer to drink.

xviii.

We here explain whence the mickle hicket[2] cometh, and how a man should treat it. It cometh from the very chilled maw, or from the too much heated *maw*, or from too mickle fulness, or of too mickle leerness, *that is emptiness*, or of evil wet *or humour* rending and scarifying the maw. If then the sick man by a spew drink speweth away the evil biting wet, then the hicket abateth. A spew then is good for the men whom hicket teareth for fulness, or in case it scarifieth them within ; and also the hicket which cometh of the mickleness of the evil wet *or humour*, hath need of a spew drink, which eke worketh mickle sneezing, and amendeth *the sick*. When the hicket cometh of the

---

[1] *Rhafanus sativa.*
[2] Holland and old writers spell Hicket, the moderns "hiccup," "hic-
"cough."

fol. 23 a. ȝelæpan ne bet þone ſe ꝼnopa. ȝiꝼ ſe ȝeohſa óꝼ cile
cume þonne ſceal món miƀ pypmenƀum þinȝum lacnian
ſpile ſpa pipo�12 íꞃ ꝯ oþꞃa peꞃmenƀa pyꞃta oþþe ꝲuƀan
ȝeȝniƀe món opín [1] ꞃelle ƀꞃincan · oþþe meꞃceſ ꞃæƀ
miƀ ꞃine [2] oþþe eceƀ [2] ꞃelle ƀꞃincan oƀƀe míntan bꞃoƀ

Correct cymen, from the Hellenic. oþþe moꞃan · oƀƀe cymeneſ oþþe ȝinȝiꝼꞃan hpilum an-
lepiȝ ſpa ȝeꞃenoƀe · hpilum þa pyꞃta toȝæƀeꞃe ȝeƀon
ón þ poſ ꞃelle ƀꞃincan · ȝiꝼ oꝼ hatum pætan yꝼelum
on þone maȝon geſamnoƀum ſe ȝeohſa cume ꝯ he ȝeꝼele
þ ſe hine innan ſceopꝼe on þone maȝan · ꞃele hím þonne
placu pæteꞃ ƀꞃincan ſpiþe hat · ȝeƀo þonne ꝼeþeꞃe ón
ele ſtinȝe him ȝelome on þa hꞃacan þ he maȝe ſpipan ·
ꞃele hím piþ ȝeohſan cealƀ pæteꞃ ꝯ eceƀ ƀꞃincan ꝯ
apꞃotanan ȝeȝniƀene on ꞃine.

Cf. Paul.
Æginet.
lib. iii. 37.
ed. Ald. fol.
43 a. line 35.
Naurta.
'Ανορεξία.
fol. 23 b.

.XVIIII.

Þiþ plættau þam men þe hine ne lyſt hiꞃ meteꞃ ne
liþeꞃ oƀƀe on maȝan úntꞃum ſie · oþþe biteꞃe hꞃæce ·
eoꞃƀ ȝeallan ꝯ pipoꞃ ƀꞃince on peaꞃmum pæteꞃe þny
bollan ꝼulle on niht neꞃtiȝ. Eꝼt piþ platunȝe ꞃuƀan
peꞃmoƀ biſceop pyꞃt maꞃubian pyl on ealaƀ ſpiþe ȝeſpet
miƀ huniȝe leohtlice · ȝeƀꞃinc ſpa hateꞃ ſpa þin bloƀ
ſie ſcenc ꝼulne ƀo ſpa þonne þe þeaꞃꝼ ꞃie.   :·

.XX.

Þiþ ꞃculƀoꞃ pæꞃce ealbeꞃ ſpineꞃ toꞃƀ þæꞃ þe ꝼelƀ-
ȝanȝenƀe ſie menȝ piƀ ealƀne ꝲyꞃele ȝepyꞃme leȝe ún
þ ƀeah piþ ꞃculƀoꞃ pæꞃce ȝe piƀ ꞃiƀ pæꞃce · piƀ breoſt
pæꞃce · ꝯ piþ lenƀenpæꞃce. Eꝼt pyl betonican ꝯ neꞃ-
tan on ealoƀ ꞃele ƀꞃincan ȝelome ꝯ ſimle æt ꝼyꞃe
ȝeſmiꞃe miƀ penpyꞃte. Eꝼt ȝenim ſpineꞃ ꞃceaꞃn þæꞃ þe
on ƀun lanƀe ꝯ pyꞃtum libbe mænȝ piþ ealƀne ꝲyꞃele

For on ꞃín. | [2] Not the same case.

foul wamb and of the leer *or empty* one, the sneezing
doth not amend it.   If the hicket come of chill, then
shall a man cure it with warming things, such as
pepper is, and other warming worts, or let one rub
rue and give it in wine to drink; or give seed of marche
with wine or vinegar, or broth of mint or carrot,[a] ᵃ Δαῦκον, Gr.
or cummin, or ginger, at times singly *and* so prepared. At whiles give to drink the worts together
put into the wash.   If the hicket come of hot evil
humours collected into the maw, and *the sick man*
feel that it scarifieth him within in the maw, give
him then lukewarm water to drink " very hot," then
put a feather in oil, poke him frequently in the throat
that he may spew ; give him against hicket cold water
and vinegar to drink, and abrotanon rubbed in wine.

xix.

Against loathing *or nausea*, for the man who hath
no lust for his meat nor for his cup, or be infirm in
the maw, or breaketh bitter, *as in heartburn*, let him
drink earthgall and pepper in warm water, three
bowls full at night fasting.   Again for loathing, boil
strongly in ale slightly sweetened with honey, rue,
wormwood, bishopwort, marrubium, drink of this as
hot as thy blood be, a cup full, do so when need be
to thee.

xx.

Against shoulder pain, mingle a tord of an old swine,
which be a fieldgoer, with old lard, warm it, lay it on,
that is good for shoulder pain or for side pain, for
breast wark and for loin wark.   Again, boil betony and
nepeta in ale, give to drink frequently, and always
at a fire smear with wenwort.   Again, take sharn of
swine, which liveth on the downland and on worts,
mingle with old lard, lay on, and let *the patient* drink

leȝe ōn ꞵ ᵭrinc[1] betonican on ȝefpettum pine • ȝıf
ꝼeꝼeꞧ habbe ᵭꞧınce on pætene.   :•

.XXI.

Πλευρῖτιϛ.

Ꝼıꝛ̈ riᵭan ꞧaꞧe ꝼ æꝛe ꝼpıꝛꝛan boȝen ꞏ ꝛeᵭıc ꞏ hꞧıte
clæꝼꞧan pyꞧc ᴛo clame ꞏ ᴛo ᵭꞧence. Ꝼıꝛ̈ ꝼæꞧe pıneꝼ-
ᴛꞧan ꝼıᵭan ꝼaꞧe puᵭuꞧıꝼan ȝecnupa on eceᵭ ꞏ pyꞧc ᴛo
clame ȝebınᵭ on ꝛa ꝼıᵭan. Eꝼᴛ beᴛonican ꝼpılc ꝼꞧa
ꝛꞧy peneȝaꝼ ȝepeȝen • ꞏ pıpoꞧeꝼ ꝼeoꞧon ꞏ xx. coꞧna ᴛo
Sōmne ȝeᴛꞧıꝼulaᵭ • ȝeōᴛ ealᵭeꝼ pıneꝼ ꝛꞧy bollan ꝼulle
ᴛo • ꞏ ȝeplece ꝛele nıhᴛneꝛᴛıȝūm ᵭꞧıncan. Eꝼᴛ pıᵭ
ꝼıᵭan ꞧaꞧe ꞧuᵭan pıᵭ ꞧyꞧele[2] ȝemenȝeᵭ ꞏ ȝebeaᴛen
lecȝe on ꝛa ꝼıᵭan ꝛ̈ beᴛ. Ꝼıꝛ̈ rıᵭan ꞧaꞧe eꝼᴛ lauꞧeꝼ
cꞧoꞧꞧan ȝebeaᴛe ᵭꞧınce on pætene ꞏ on ꝛa ꝼıᵭan
bınᵭe. [3]Ꝼıꝛ̈ ꝼıᵭan ꝼaꞧe eꝼᴛ cauleꝼ pyꞧᴛᴛꞧuman ȝebæꞧn
ᴛo • ahꝼan ꞏ pıꝛ̈ ealᵭne ꞧyꞧele ȝemenȝ ꞏ aleȝe on ꝛa
rıᵭan.

.XXII.

Cf. Herbar.
Apul. i. 10.

Ꝼıꝛ̈ lenᵭen ece ȝenım beᴛonican ꝼpılce ᴛꝛeȝen peneȝaꝼ
ȝepeȝeu ᵭo ꝛæꞧᴛo ꝼꞧeᴛeꝼ pıneꝼ ᴛꝛeȝen bollan ꝼulle menȝ
pıꝛ̈ haᴛ pæᴛeꞧ ꝛele nıhᴛneꝛᴛıȝ ᵭꞧıncan. Eꝼᴛ ȝenım

Cf. Marcell.
353, c.

ȝꞧunᵭe ꝼpelȝean ȝebeaᴛ ꞏ ꝛ̈ ꝼeap ꝛele ᵭꞧıncan nıhᴛ-
neꝛᴛıȝum.

Ꝼıꝛ̈ lenᵭen ece ealıꝼeꞧ haᴛᴛe pyꞧᴛ ȝnıᵭ on ealaꝛ̈ ꞏ
ᵭꞧınce ꝛa. Ꝼıꝛ̈ ꝛon ılcan hunᵭeꝼ ᴛunȝe haᴛᴛe pyꞧᴛ

fol. 24 b.

ȝenım ꝛa léaꝼ aᵭꞧıȝ ꞏ ȝeȝnıᵭ ᴛo meluꞧe ȝenım ꝛonne
beꞧen mela ȝemenȝ pıꝛ̈ ꝛa pyꞧᴛ ꞏ ȝebꞧınȝ ꝛonne ōn
meolce.

.XXIII.

Ιϲχιάϛ.

Ꝼıꝛ̈ ꝛeoh ece • ꝼmıce mıᵭ ꞧeaꞧne ꝼpıꝛ̈e ꝛa ꝛeoh. Eꝼᴛ
ᴛo ᵭꞧence • pıpoꞧ • pın • pealpyꞧᴛ • hunıȝ. Eāc ᴛo ꝛon

---

[1] Read ᵭꞧınce.
[2] Tῷ πηγανῷ, Paul. Æg. and Galen, *a preparation of rue*.
[3] Paul. Æginet., lib. iii. cap. 33.

betony in sweetened wine. If he have fever, let him drink it in water.

xxi.

For sore of the right side, work thyme and radish and white clover to a paste, and to a drink. For sore of the left side, pound woodroffe in vinegar, and work it to a paste, bind it on the side. Again, betony as much as three pennies weigh, and twenty-seven corns of pepper triturated together; pour in three bowls full of old wine, and make lukewarm, give *to the patient* after his nights fasting to drink. Again for sore of side, lay rue mingled with lard and beaten, on the side; that amendeth it. For sore of side again, let him beat bunches of laurel *flower*, let him drink them in water, and bind them on the side. For sore of side again, burn to ashes roots of colewort, and mingle with old lard, and lay on the side.

xxii.

For loin ache, take betony, as much as two pennies Lumbago. weigh, add thereto two bowls full of sweet wine, mingle with hot water, give it to drink after his nights fasting. Again, take groundsel, beat it, and give the juice to drink after his nights fasting.

2. For loin ache, a wort is called ealiver,[a] rub it in [a] *Erysimun* ale, and let *the patient* drink it. For the same, a wort *alliaria,* hight hounds tongue, take the leaves, dry them, and *Gerarde.* rub them to meal, then mingle with the wort barley meal, and then apply it in milk.

xxiii.

For thigh ache, smoke the thighs thoroughly with Sciatica. fern. Again, for a drink, pepper, wine, wallwort, honey;

apulðoꞃ · þoꞃn · æꞃc · cꞃicbeam · eoꞃoþþnote æꞃcþnote ·
elone · bıꞃceop pyꞃt · ıꞃıᵹ · betonıca · ꞃıbbe · ꞃæðıc ·
fpꞃacen · pıpoꞃ · hpıt cpuðu · coft · ᵹınᵹıꞃeꞃ · monıaca ·
netle · blınðe netle ꞃıꞃc þıꞃ to ðꞃence. ᵹıꞃ þeoh
ꞃlapan aðelꞃ nıoþopeaꞃðne ꞃécᵹ pyl on pæteꞃe læt
ꞃeocan ón þæt lím þte ꞃlape fmıꞃe mıð ꞃealꞃe þe
món þuꞃ pyꞃce. Oꞃ fꞃıneꞃ fmeꞃꞃe · ꞃceapeꞃ fmeꞃu ·
buteꞃe · fcıpteaꞃo · pıpoꞃ · hpıt cpuðu · fpeᵹleꞃ æppel ·
fpeꞃl · coft · eceð · ele · hpeꞃpette · ꞃæðıc · eolene ·
bıfceop pyꞃt · ꞃealt · æꞃc · apulðꞃe · ſc · þoꞃn.

.XXIIII.

Þıþ cneop pæꞃce · puðu peaxe · ꞃ heᵹeꞃıꞃe ᵹecnupa
þa toᵹæðeꞃe ꞃ bo ón ealu læt lıcᵹean neahteꞃne ꞃele
hım þ þonne ðꞃıncan beþe mıð ꞃ leᵹe ón. Þıþ þon ᵹıꞃ
fol. 25 a.
cneop ꞃaꞃ fıe · ᵹením pealpyꞃt ꞃ cluꞃþunᵹ · ꞃeaðe
netlan apyl ón pæteꞃe beþe mıð.

.XXV.

ᵹıꞃ ꞃcancan ꞃaꞃe fynð ᵹením ᵹıþꞃıꞃan ꞃ ðolᵹꞃunan ·
ꞃ hamoꞃ pyꞃt · ꞃ betonıcan ꞃ ban pyꞃt · ꞃ lıꞃpyꞃt ꞃ
puðu meꞃce · ꞃ eoꞃðᵹeallan · ꞃ bꞃunpyꞃt ꞃeoþ on
buteꞃan fmıꞃe mıð :·
Gıꞃ[1] fcancan ꞃynð ꞃoꞃoðe ním banpyꞃt ᵹecnupa ᵹeot
æᵹeꞃ þ hꞃıte menᵹ toꞃomne fcancꞃoꞃeðum men. Þıð
ꞃoꞃeðum lıme leᵹe þaꞃ ꞃealꞃe on þ ꞃoꞃoðe lím ꞃ ꞃoꞃ-
leᵹe mıð elmꞃınðe ðo fpılc to · eꞃt fımle nıpa oþþ
ᵹehaloð fıe ᵹeꞃenðꞃıa elm ꞃınðe ꞃ apyl fpıðe ðo þonne
oꞃ þa ꞃınðe ᵹením lınꞃæð ᵹeᵹꞃınð bꞃıpe pıð þam elmeꞃ
ðꞃænce þ bıð ᵹoð ꞃealꞃ ꞃoꞃeðum lıme.

' Lıꞃ, MS.

also in addition, apple tree, thorn, ash, quickbeam, **Book I.** everthroat, ashthroat, helenium, bishopwort, ivy, betony, **Ch. xxiv.** ribwort, radish, spraken,[a] pepper, mastic, costmary, [a] *Rhamnus* ginger, sal ammoniac, nettle, blind nettle, work this *frangula.* to a drink. If thighs be paralyzed, delve up the netherward *part of* sedge, boil it in water, make it reek on the limb that is helpless, smear with a salve, which a man may thus work; from swines grease, sheeps grease, butter, ship tar,[1] pepper, mastic, beetle nut, sulfur, costmary, vinegar, oil, cucumber, radish, helenium, bishopwort, salt, ash, apple tree, oak, thorn.

xxiv.

For knee pain; pound together woodwax[2] and hedgerife, and put into ale; let it lie for a night, give him then that to drink, bathe with it, and lay it on. In case that a knee be sore, take wallwort and cloffing, and red nettle, boil in water, bathe therewith.

xxv.

1. If the shanks be sore, take githrife and pellitory and hammerwort and betony and bonewort and flaxwort and wild marche and earth gall and brownwort, seethe in butter, smear therewith.

2. If shanks be broken, take bonewort, pound it, pour the white of an egg *out*, mingle these together for the shank broken man. For a broken limb, lay this salve on the broken limb, and overlay with elm rind,[3] apply a splint, again, always renew *these* till the limb be healed; clean some elm rind, and boil it thoroughly, then remove the rind, *and* take linseed, grind it for a brewit *or paste* with the elms drink; that shall be a good salve for a broken limb.

---

[1] Pix navalis is frequent in Latin medicine of the time.

[2] *Genista tinctoria.*

[3] Cf. Aetius. I. i. v. πτελέα.

.XXVI.

Αγκύλωσις.
Marcellus,
403, d.

fol. 25 b.

Ᵹir fino ᵹeſcpince ⁊ eſt · æſten þon ſpelle ᵹením ᵹate topð ᵹemenᵹ pið eceð ſmit ón ᵹona halað. Ꝺoneᵹum men ᵹeſcpincað hiᵹ ſet to hiᵹ homme pync baþo ðo eanban to ⁊ cenſan ⁊ ſmale netelan ⁊ beopync ðo on tnoh hate ſtanaᵹ pel ᵹehætte ᵹebeþe þa hamma mið þam ſtan bað þonne hie ſien ᵹeſpate þonne necce he þa ban ſpa he ſpiþoſt mæᵹe ðo ſpelc to ⁊ betene ſpa mon oᵹton mið þy beþiᵹe. ᵹiſ fino clæppette mucᵹpync ᵹebeatenu ⁊ piþ ele ᵹemenᵹeð ⁊ ón aleð. Ꝺycᵹpynte ſeap pið ᵹenoſoðne ele ᵹemenᵹed ſmine mið þy ſona biþ ætſtilleð fio cpacunᵹ.

.XXVII.

Ποδάγρα.

Apul. Herb.
ii. 17.

Cf. Marcellus,
405, f. g.

fol. 26 a.

Þiþ ſót ece betonican · ᵹeonmenleaᵹ · ſinul · nibban · ealna emſela ᵹemenᵹe meoluc piþ pæten ⁊ þ toſpollene lím ſnam þæne uſennan healſe beþe þy læᵹ ſe ſpile Inᵹepite · ᵹenime þonne ᵹalluc ᵹeſobenne leᵹe ón. Þið ſota ſaᴙe oþþe ᵹeſpelle ſnam miclum ᵹanᵹe peᵹbnæðe ᵹetniſulað ⁊ pið eceð ᵹemenᵹeð. Þiþ þon ðeah ᵹnunðe ſpelᵹe ᵹebeatenu ⁊ pið nyſele ᵹemenᵹeð. ⁚·

Þiþ ſótece ᵹiſ ſe ſót ace inᵹeſpice ᵹením mucᵹpynte ſynſnuman menᵹ piþ ele ſele etan. Við ſót ece eſt hunán ſeap piþ ele ᵹemenᵹeð ſmine þa ſanan ſet mið. ⁚·

Þiþ ſotece ᵹením ellener leaᵹ · ⁊ peᵹbnæðan ⁊ mucᵹpynt ᵹecnupa leᵹe on ⁊ ᵹebinð ón.

.XXVIII.

Þiþ ban ece tuninᵹpynt ·[1] beolone · pealpynt ealðe ᵹnut ⁊ eceð · heopoteſ ſmena oþþe ᵹate · oþþe ᵹoſe

---

[1] Tunninᵹ pynt, Herbarium, cxxxviii. So read.

xxvi.

If a sinew shrink,[a] and again after that swell, take a she goats tord, mingle with vinegar, smudge *it* on, soon *the sinew* healeth. In the case of many a man, his feet shrink up to his hams, work baths, add tares and cress and small nettle and beewort,[1] put hot stones well heated in a trough, warm the hams with the stone bath, when they are in a sweat, then let him, *the patient*, duly arrange the bones as well as he can, apply a splint, and it is so much the better the oftener a man bathes with the *preparation*. If a sinew have pulsation, mugwort beaten and mingled with oil, and laid on *is good*. Juice of mugwort mingled with rose oil, smear with that, soon will the quaking be stilled.

[a] That is, when a leg is broken.

xxvii.

1. For foot ache, betony, germen leaves, *that is* Ποδάγρα. *mallow*, fennel, ribwort, of all equal quantities; mingle milk with water, and bathe the swollen limb, from the upper part of it, with that, lest the swelling go inwards; then take sodden comfrey, lay it on. For sore of feet or swelling from much walking, waybread triturated and mingled with vinegar. For that *disorder*, groundsel beaten and mingled with lard is good.

2. For foot ache; if the foot ache go inwards, take mugworts roots, mingle with oil, give to eat. For foot ache again, juice of *hore*hound mingled with oil, smear the sore feet with it.

3. For foot ache, take leaves of elder and waybroad and mugwort, pound, lay on, and bind on.

xxviii.

For leg ache, white hellebore, henbane, wallwort, old groats and vinegar, harts or she goats or goose

---

¹ *Acorus calamus.*

menȝ tofomne leȝe þonne ón. Þiþ banece eft to ðpence
elene · cneopholen · pealpypt · hune · clufþunȝ ȝecnupa
ðo ón pætep þ ofep ypne beþe to fype fpiðe þone
ece þpea mið þy pætepe ðo þ þpipa ón ðæȝ · pypc
þonne fealfe óf tun[i]nȝ pypte óf eolonan · of þunȝe ·
óf pepmoðe ðo ealpa empela pylle fpiðe.

. XXVIIII.

Ȝif mannef ȝetapa beoþ fape oððe áþunðene betonican ȝetpifula ón pine beþe þa fapan ftopa ꝺ þa
aþunðenan mið þy. Eft ȝif hie ðylftihte fien oððe
ȝebopiftene ȝením faluian feoð on pætepe beþe mið þa
ȝetapa.

Eft ðile ȝebæpneð ȝemenȝ pið ahfan huniȝ[1] pypc to
fealfe aþpeah þonne ꝺ ȝebeþe þa punða æpeft mið
hate pætepe æftep þon mið peapme ele ȝe fmipe on
þam þe pæpe pip ȝefoðen leȝe þonne þa fealfe on.

. XXX.

Þif fceal pið æcelman ꝺ pið þon þe men ácale þ fel
of þam fotum · ȝenime neoþopeapðe meðopypt ꝺ luft-
mocan · ꝺ acpinðe ȝecnua eall to ðufte ȝemenȝ pið
huniȝ lacna mið þy.

. XXXI.

V;þ ælcum heapðum fpile oððe ȝefpelle aðpiȝe beana
ꝺ ȝefeoþ butan fealte menȝ þonne pið huniȝ leȝe on.
Þiþ þon ilcan ȝením bepen melo feoþ on ecebe ðo ón

---

[1] Read ȝemenȝ þa ahfan pið huniȝ.

grease, mingle together, then lay on. For leg ache again, for a draught, helenium, kneeholly, *or butchers broom,* wallwort, *or dwarf elder, hore*hound, cloffing,[1] pound these, put them in water, so that it run over, warm at the fire thoroughly, wash the ache *or aching part* with the water, do that three times a day; then work up a salve of white hellebore, of helenium, of thung *or wolfs bane,* of wormwood, put equal quantities of them all, boil thoroughly.

xxix.

1. If a mans instrumenta genitalia be sore or puffed out, triturate betony in wine, bathe with that the sore and puffed up places. Again, if they be mucous, or in eruption, take sage,[1] seethe in water, bathe with that the instrumenta.

2. Again, *take* dill burnt, mingle the ashes with honey, work up to a salve, then wash and bathe the wounds first with hot water, after that with warm oil or grease, on which myrtle has been sodden, then lay the salve on.

xxx.

This shall *be good* for chilblain and in case that the skin of a mans feet come off by cold,[2] let him take the netherward part of meadowwort and lustmock and oak rind, pound all to dust, mingle with honey, effect a cure with that.

Pernio.

xxxi.

1. For every hard tumour or swelling, dry beans and seethe them without salt, than mingle with honey, lay on. For the same, take barley meal, seethe in

---

1 *Ranunculus sceleratus.*
2 Cf. Myreps. xlvii. 10.

2 Oꝼ þam ꝼotum, *off the feet,* not *of.*

Eft ƿiþ þon belenan menȝ ƿið nyrele leȝe ón. Ðið
fpile eft ȝebeat hunan menȝ ƿiþ nyrele leȝe ón oððe
ȝate honn ȝebænneð ꝳ ƿiþ pæteƿ ȝemenȝeð. Eft
ƿyrele oþþe ȝelynðo ƿiþ ȝanleác ȝemenȝeð ꝳ ón aleð
bone fpile þþænþ.

Ðiþ fpile eft cennille ȝecnupað mið nyrele ꝳ on
ȝemelt peax ȝeðon ꝳ ón aleð bet.   :·

Við fpile eft ȝate flærc ȝebænneð to ahfan mið

pætene ón ȝefmiten ealne þone fpile tofeneþ. Eft
iuniperu þ ir ȝonft þ ræð ȝecnupa ꝳ reoþ on pætene.
Eft rinrulle ƿiþ nyrele ȝemenȝeð ꝳ ƿiþ hlaf ꝳ ƿiþ
celenðnan æt · romne ȝemenȝeð. Ðiþ yrlum pætan ꝳ
fpile ȝením heonoter rceafoþan óf þám honne oþþe
þær honner melo menȝ ƿiþ pæteƿ fmit ón eal þ ponmf
ꝳ þone yrelan pætan apeȝ beþ ꝳ aðnifþ.   :·

Ðiþ fpile ȝením ȝate typblu on rceanpum ecebe
ȝeroben ꝳ ón relfe pifan ón ȝeðon.

Ðiþ ælcum yrlum pætan mucȝpynte þa ȝnenan leaf
ȝetnirulað ꝳ ƿiþ nyrele ȝeȝniðen toȝæðene fmine an
ȝe þeoh þæn ðylftan on fynð þ ðeah þiþ þan · ȝe þ
ðeah eác ƿiþ rota ȝefpelle. Ðiþ innan ȝepynfmeðum
ȝefpelle þam þe pynð of rylle oþþe óf rleȝe oððe óf
hnicrca hpilcúm · þa pynt þe hatte fírleafe · ȝením ꝳ
ȝebeat ꝳ leȝe on ȝelome oþ þte open fie re fpile lacna
þonne þa punða fpa oþne punða. Ðið fpile eft hlutton

píc ȝením ðo ahfan to feoð ætȝæðene ȝeleȝe þonne
þone fpile mið þy ȝelome. Ðiþ fpile eft ȝate typblu
ðniȝe ȝeȝnið ꝳ afirte þunh fmæl fire ðo þonne nyrle

vinegar, put on. Again for that, mingle henbane with lard, lay on. For a swelling again, beat *hore*hound, mingle with lard, lay on, or goats horn burnt and mingled with water. Again, lard or suet mingled with garlic, and onlaid, dwindleth the swelling.

2. For swelling again, chervil pounded with lard and added to melted wax, and laid on, is to boot *or amend.*

3. For a swelling again, goats flesh burnt to ashes, smudged on with water, removes all the swelling. Again, pound the seed of juniper, that is gorse,[1] and seethe in water. Again, houseleek mingled with lard and with bread and with coriander, mingled together. Against ill humours and swelling, take shavings off the horn of a hart, or meal of the horn, mingle with water, smudge it on, it doth away and driveth off all that ratten and the evil wet.

4. Against swelling, take goats treadles sodden in sharp vinegar, and applied in the same manner.

5. For every evil humour,[2] mugwort, the green leaves *of it,* triturated, and rubbed together with lard, both smear on the thighs on which the mucus is, that is good for them ; and that is good also for swelling of the feet. For a swelling purulent within, such as cometh of a fall or of a blow or of any crick, take the wort that hight fiveleaf *or cinquefoil,* and beat it and lay it on frequently till that the swelling be open, then tend the wounds as other wounds. For a swelling again, take "clear pitch,"[3] add ashes, seethe together, then overlay the swelling with that frequently. For swelling again, dry goats treadles, grate and sift them through a small sieve, then add lard, as much as

φλέγμα and χυμός.

. [1] Some verb must be supplied to form a sentence, as frequently happens. And of course iuniperus is not gorse.

[2] Pituita molesta, of Horatius.

[3] Probably resin, as solid. See Blæctepu, *pale tar*, in Lye.

to ſpa ſpa ɽyn tɽa punb ⁊ ealbeſ pineɽ ſpa mɪcel ſpa
þe þɪnce pyɲc to ſealɽe.

Eft ȝebæɲneb ɽealc ȝeȝnɪb pel on ȝeplecceb pæteɲ
oþ þ hɪc ſie ſpa þɪcce ſpa hunɪȝeſ ceaɲ leȝe ón þone
ſpɪle oɽeɲ leȝe mɪb claðe ⁊ mɪb eopcɪȝɲe pulle bɪnb
ón. Þɪþ ɽæɲlɪcum ſaɲe ⁊ ȝeſpelle nɪm peax ⁊ hemlɪc
ȝecɽuɽula pyɲc ſpa peaɲm to ɽealɽe bɪnb on þ ɽaɲɪ. :·

Þɪþ ɽæɲ ſpɪle · nɪm hunan ȝebeac ⁊ ȝemenȝ pɪþ
ɲyɽele leȝe ón. Eft maɲe cpynɪhte ȝɲuc mealceɽ
ſmeðma · ceɲſan · æȝeɽ þ hpɪce bɪſceop pyɲc · elene ·
oncɽe · elehcɲe · ſɪȝſonce · ȝalluc menȝ coſomne leȝe
ón. Þɪþ beabum ſpɪle · Nɪm ȝɽunbeſpelȝean leȝe ou
ȝleba ⁊ ȝepyɲme ⁊ leȝe þonne ſpa peaɲme on þone ſpɪle
⁊ bebɪnb mɪb claðe læc beon nɪhceɲɪne ón ȝɪɽ hɪɽ þeaɲɽ
ſie. Uɪð beabum ſpɪle áȝɲɪmonɪan ȝebeac menȝ pɪð pɪn
⁊ pɪþ ɽealc bo on þone ſpɪle ɽona ȝepɪc apeȝ. Þɪþ ſpɪle
accoɲlaðan ȝecnupa leȝe on þone ſpɪle leȝe læſc ón þ
bolh ɽelɽ. Ðɲenc pɪþ beabum ſpɪle þ he ucɽlea eoɽoɲ-
þɲoce · eolone · ȝocɽoðe · cɽa penpyɲca bo ón ealu
bɲɪnce. Þɪþ beabum ſpɪle ȝenɪm ſpane pyɲc ȝecnupa
pel ȝemenȝ pɪð ɽeɲſcɲe buceɲan leȝe on þone ſpɪle oþ
þ ȝelacnob ſie. Þɪþ ſpɪle cunɪlle · ſpɲɪnȝ pyɲc clace
pyl ón buceɲan ⁊ on hunɪȝe leȝe on þa pyɲca ȝemenȝ
pɪð æȝeɽ þ hpɪce. Speþɪnȝ pɪþ ſpɪle · ban pyɲc uɽe-
peaɲbe ȝecnupa ſmæle þa pyɲce ȝemenȝ pɪð æȝeɽ þ
hpɪce beclæm þ lɪm mɪb þe ɽe ſpɪle on ſie.

Pyɲc þ bæþ óɽ þam ɪlcum pyɲcum on cealbum pylle
pæcɲe ȝecnupa þa pɽɲca ſpɪþe pel leȝe ón þ pæceɲ
laɽa on þone ſpɪle. :·

Vɪð ſpɪle cnupa nɪðepeaɲbe hamoɲ pyɲc ⁊ ɽecȝ bɪnb
on.

two pounds, and as much of old wine as to thee may seem good, work to a salve.

6. Again, rub burnt salt well in water made luke-warm, till that it be as thick as a tear of honey, lay on the swelling, overlay with a cloth, and with wool of ewe, bind on. For sudden sore and swelling, take wax and hemlock, triturate, work this so warm into a salve, bind on the sore.

7. Against a sudden swelling, take *hore*hound, beat and mingle it with lard, lay on. Again, mingle to-gether the cottony potentilla, *commonly called silver-weed*, groats of malt, smede *or fine flour*, cress, the white of an egg, bishopwort, helenium, ontre, lupins, " sigsonte," comfrey, lay on. For a dead* swelling, take groundsel, lay it on gledes and warm it, and lay it so warm on the swelling, and bind on with a cloth, let it be on for a night, if need be for that. For a dead swelling, beat agrimony, mix with wine and with salt, apply it to the swelling, *which* soon will depart away. For swelling, pound attorlothe, lay on the swelling, lay least on "the wound" itself. A draught for a dead swelling, that it may break out, put carlina, helenium, goutweed, the two wenworts into an ale drink. For a dead swelling, take " swanwort," pound it well, mingle with fresh butter, lay on the swelling till that it be healed. For a swelling, boil cunila, springwort,[1] clote, in butter and in honey, lay the worts on, mingle with them the white of an egg. A swathing for a swelling, pound small the upper part of bonewort, mingle with the wort the white of an egg, plaster the limb on which the swelling may be, with that.

* Without feeling.

8. Work the bath of the same worts in cold well water, pound the worts very well, lay on, leave the water on the swelling.

9. For a swelling, pound the netherward part of hammerwort and sedge ; bind on.

---

[1] *Euforbia lathyris.*

.XXXII.

Læcedomaſ ƿiþ blæce ⁊ bæþ fiftyne ealƿa.

Þel eolenan niþereaƿðe ⁊ mintan ón[1] fealteſ ƿyniaɴ
þ hit ſie þicce ſƿa bƿiƿ ʒemenʒ toʒædeƿe ſmiƿe miᶁ.
Þiþ blæce ním eolonan niþereaƿðe ⁊ ompƿan eác ſƿa
ſio þe ſƿimme ⁊ ontƿan ⁊ biſceop ƿyƿt ⁊ æſcƿinðe
feoþ on buteƿan aƿeoh þuƿh claᶁ menʒ þonne ƿiᶁ piƿoƿ
⁊ ƿiþ teoƿan ʒeʒƿinᶁ ſmiƿe miᶁ.   Þiþ blæce ƿyl eolonan on buteƿan menʒ ƿiþ ƿote fealt · teoƿo · huniʒ ·
ealᶁ ƿape ſmiƿe miᶁ. Þiᶁ blæce ʒením ʒoƿe ſmeƿo ⁊
niþereaƿðe elenan ⁊ haƿan ſpƿecel biſceop ƿyƿt ⁊
heʒƿiſan þa feopeƿ ƿyƿta cnupa toſomne ƿel apƿinʒ
ᶁo þæƿón ealᶁƿe ſapan cucleƿ fulne ʒiſ þu hæbbe
lytel eleſ menʒ ƿiþ ſƿiþe ⁊ ón niht alyþƿe.   Sceaƿpa
þone ſpeoƿan ofeƿ ſunnan ſetlʒanʒe ʒeot ſpiʒenðe þ
bloᶁ ón yƿnenðe pæteƿ ſpiƿ þƿiƿa æſteƿ · cƿeþ þonne
haƿa þu þaſ unhæle · ⁊ ʒepit apeʒ miᶁ ʒanʒe eſt ón
clænne peʒ to huſe ⁊ ʒehƿæþeƿne ʒánʒ ſpiʒenðe. bæþ
ƿiᶁ blæce aƿyl tyn ƿiþum þa ƿyƿte on hƿeƿe ⁊ ſynᶁ-
ƿiʒea betonican · neſtan maƿubian[2] aʒƿimonian · ʒeapƿe·
minte ehheoloþe hinᶁheoloþe · cuƿmealle · eopᶁ ʒealla ·
ᶁile · meƿce · finul ealƿa emſela ʒepyƿc þonne ſtol of
þƿim tƿeopum niþan ᶁyƿele ſite ón bydene ⁊ þe ofeƿ-
hƿeſ uſan miᶁ hƿitle þy læſ ſe æþm ut · ʒeót unðeƿ
þone ſtol on þa bydene læt ƿeocan ón · ſƿa þu meaht
on þam ƿyƿtum þƿiƿa ᶁon · ⁊ unðeƿ niþan ſtype miᶁ
ſticcan ʒiſ þu hattƿe ƿille · ⁊ æƿ þam bæþe ſmiƿe
þone lichoman ⁊ þone yþlitan miᶁ ʒeſpette pætƿe ⁊
ʒehƿeƿ tƿa æʒƿu on hatum pæteƿe ʒeſmiƿe ealne
þone lichoman miᶁ.

---

[1] ón ón, MS. | [2] maƿubian, MS.

xxxii.

1. Leechdoms for blotch and baths. Fifteen in all.

2. Boil the netherward part of helenium and mint in the runnings of salt, that it be as thick as brewit, mingle together, smear therewith. Against blotch, take the netherward part of helenium, and so also of dock (that which will swim), and ontre, and bishopwort, and ash rind, seethe in butter, strain through a cloth, then mingle with pepper and with tar, grind *these*, smear therewith. For blotch, boil helenium in butter, mingle with soot, salt, tar, honey, old soap, smear therewith. For blotch, take goose grease and the netherward part of helenium and vipers bugloss, bishopwort and hayrife, pound the four worts together well, wring them, add thereto of old soap a spoon full, if thou have it, mingle a little oil with them thoroughly, and at night lather on. Scarify the neck after the setting of the sun, pour in silence the blood into running water, after that spit three times, then say, " Have thou this unheal, and depart away with it ;" go again on a clean way to the house, and go either way in silence. A bath[1] for blotch, boil ten times the worts in a basin and separately betony, nepeta, marrubium, agrimony, yarrow, mint, horseheal,[a] hindheal,[b] churmel,[c] earthgall,[d] dill, marche, fennel, of all equally much, work then a stool of three pieces of wood, with a hole below, sit on a bucket,[2] and robe thee over from above with a garment lest the vapour escape ; pour *the prepared hot liquor* under the stool into the bucket, let it reek on thee. So thou mayst do thrice with the worts, and underneath stir with a stick if thou wilt *have it* hotter ; and before the bath smear the body and the forehead with sweetened water, and shake up two eggs in hot water, smear the whole body therewith.

[a] *Inula helenium.*
[b] *Eupatorium cannabinum.*
[c] *Chlora perfoliata.*
[d] *Erythræa centaureum.*

---

[1] Πυρίη. Hippokr. | [2] Byden, now Bidet.

Læcedom ƿiþ hneoƀum lice · aðelƀe omppan ꝺ ȝeloð-
pyƿt ȝecnupa · pyl þonne on butepan ðo hpon ƀealteƀ
to.   Þiþ ðeaðum lice ſtæþpyƿt mepce ȝnið ón ealoð
ƀele ðpincan.   Þið hpeoƀle pell ón hlonðe cpicpinðe [1] ·
ellenpinðe niþepeapðe · æƀc ƀinðe · ꝺ pað · elm ƀinðe ·
hemlic ðo þonne butepan on ꝺ huniȝ.   Þiþ hpeoƀle
peȝbpæðe læcepyƈt · leac · minte · maȝþa · eolone ·
ſpeƀl ȝecnupa piþ ƀyſle ðo þæƀ ſ[p]eƀleƀ ſpilcan þapa
pyƈta tpæðe.

fol. 29 b.   Þiþ hpeoƀle eƀt ȝením hopƀeƀ ƀyƀele ȝemen[ȝ] ſpiþe
piþ ſealte ſmiƀe mið.   bæþ piþ hpeoƀle · pyl ón pætepe
æƀcpinðe · cpicbeam ƀinðe · holen ƀinðe · ƀulanbeameƀ ·
ananbeameſ · féoȝ · þeopƀyƈt · heȝeƀiƀe · maƀubian ·
beþe mið · ꝺ ꝥ lic ȝnið mið þæƀe heȝeƀiƀan.   Þyƈc
ƀealƀe óƀ maƀubian on butepan · óƀ pyƈm melupe · óƀ
hapan ſpƀecele · heȝeƀiƀan · ȝením healƀe þa ƀealƀe
ȝemenȝ piþ ȝecnupaðe elenan ſmiƀe oþ ꝥ batiȝe · riþþan
mið þæƀe oþeƀƀe.   bæþ piþ þam miclan lice eolone
bƀóm · iƀiȝ · mucpyƈt ælƀþone · beolone · cottuc · eƀelaſtan pyl ón pætepe ſpiþe ȝeót on byðene ꝺ ƀitte ón.
ðƀince þiƀne ðƀenc piþ þon · betonican · cupmille hoƀe ·
aȝƀimonia · ſpƀinȝpyƈt · ƀeaðe netle · elehtpe · Saluie ·
ſinȝpene· alexanðƀia · ſie ȝepoƀht óƀ pihiſóúm ealað
ðƀince on þam baþe ꝺ ne læte ón þone eþm.   Sealƀ piþ
þam miclan lice · elene · þúnȝ omppe · ȝpunðeſpelȝe ·
hole cepſan · peȝbpæðe · eƀelaſte · óntƀe · hoƀe · ȝallúc ·
fol. 30 a.   celeþonian · cottúc pel on butepan eal toȝæðeƀe healƀ

---

[1] Read opicbeamƀinðe.

3. A leechdom for a leprous body, delve up dock and silverweed, pound them, then boil them in butter, add a trifle of salt. For deadness of the body, rub in ale staithwort, marche, give *to the patient* to drink. For a leper, boil in urine[1] rind of quickbeam, the netherward part of elder rind, ash rind, and woad, elm rind, hemlock, then add butter and honey. For a leper, pound with lard waybroad, leechwort, leek, mint, maythe, helenium, sulfur, put of the sulfur two parts to one of the worts.

4. For a leper again, take fat of a horse, mingle thoroughly with salt, smear with that. A bath for a leper, boil in water ash rind, quickbeam rind, holly rind, the foultree *or black alder rind*, rind of spindle tree, sedge, ploughmans spikenard, hayrife, marrubium, bathe therewith, and rub the body with the hayrife. Work a salve of marrubium in butter, of worm[2] meal, of vipers bugloss, hayrife, take half the salve, mingle with pounded helenium, smear till it get better, then *smear* with the other half. A bath for the mickle body *or elphantiasis*, boil in water thoroughly helenium, broom, ivy, mugwort, enchanters nightshade (?), henbane, mallow, everlasting, pour into a byden, and let *the patient* sit upon it. Let a man drink against that *disorder* this drink; betony, churmel, hove, agrimony, springwort, red nettle, lupin, sage, singreen, alexanders, let it be wrought out of foreign ale, let *the sick* man drink it in the bath, and let him not allow the vapour to reach it. A salve for the mickle *leprous* body, helenium, wolfsbane, dock, groundsel, field gentian, waybroad, everlasting, ontre, hove, comfrey, celandine, mallow, boil all in butter together, let half *the salve*

---

[1] Cf. Aetius. L ii. 108.

[2] Thus in later times : "Fair large Earthworms gathered in May when they couple ; put them into a Pail of Water at night till the next morning, so will they have cleansed themselves, then dry them before the fire, or in an Oven, which when through dry, beat into Ponder." Salmon's English Physician, p. 697, ed. 1693. He adds the cures.

ſie ſpineſ ɲyɼele oððe hoɲɼeɼ ſmeɲu · ſmıɲe þonne mıð.
Þıð ſpıle ȝenĩm peȝbɲæban nıoþopeaɲðe ȝecnupæ ɲıþ
ɲyɼele leȝe Ᵹ ȝebınð ōn þone ſpıle.

.XXXIII.

Dɲencaſ Ᵹ ɼealɼa ɲıþ ſpɲınȝe · ſpɲınȝpyɲıt ɲeabe hoɼe ·
peȝbɲæbe · ɼeɼeɲ ɼuȝe · apɲotane · maȝeþe · pıpoɲ ·
ɲĩn · ȝıɼ he ōn eaɲan ſie ȝebeate peȝbɲæban · Ᵹ ɼeɼeɲ
ɼuȝean Ᵹ pıpoɲ · pɲınȝ ōn þ eaɲe. To ɼealɼe pıð
ſpɲınȝe · nĩm bolhɲunan · peȝbɲæban maȝeþan · þone
bɲaban capel nıoþopeaɲðne · ȝeoɲmenleaɼ nıþepeaɲð ·
ðocce nıþepeɲð · ɲeabe hoɼe · buteɲe Ᵹ hunıȝ. Sealɼ
eɼt meðopyɲt · acumban · hınð hıoloðe · ȝeaɲpe · cneopholen · æþelɼeɲðınȝ pyɲt · aȝɲımonıa.

Þıþ beaðum ſpɲınȝe. Þyl on buteɲan ſelɼætan
æɼteɲ þam[1]· Ᵹ ſpɲınȝpyɲıt. Þıþ ſpɲınȝe maȝeþa · pubu
meɲce · pyɲc to ɼealɼe ðɲınce ȝobe pyɲta. Uıþ ſpɲınȝe ·
nım elehtɲan ȝecnupa ōn hunıȝ menȝ to ſomne leȝe

on þone ſpıle oþþæt hal ɲıe. Þıð ſpɲınȝe ſpɲınȝpyɲıt
ceɲɼıllan Ᵹ hunıȝ Ᵹ ȝoɼe ſmeɲa ȝecnupa pyl to ɼomne
leȝe on ðone ſpɲınȝ.

.XXXIIΓ.

ȝıɼ næȝl ſie oɼ hanða Ᵹ ɲıþ peaɲhbɲæban nĩm hɲæte
coɲn menȝ pıð hunıȝ leȝe on þone ɼınȝeɲ. Þıð anȝnæȝle
aɲȝeſpeoɲɼ Ᵹ ealbe ɼapan Ᵹ ele ȝıɼ þu hæbbe ȝıɼ þu
næbbe bo ɼlytan to menȝ toſomne leȝe ōn.[2]   :·

Þıþ peaɲhbɲæban · maȝoþan cɲoppan pyl on buteɲan
Ᵹ ſealt ſmıɲe mıð.

---

be swines fat or horse grease; then smear therewith. Against swelling, take the netherward part of waybroad, pound with grease, lay and bind on the swelling.

xxxiii.

1. Drinks and salves against pustule; springwort, red hove, waybroad, feverfuge, abrotanon, maythe, pepper, wine. If it, *the pustule*, be on an ear, beat waybroad and feverfuge and pepper, wring *them* into the ear. For a salve against a pustule, take pellitory, waybroad, maythe, the netherward part of the broad colewort, the netherward part of mallow, the netherward part of dock, red hove, butter, and honey. A salve again, meadow wort, tow,[1] water agrimony, yarrow, butchers broom, stichwort, agrimony.

2. For a dead pustule; boil in butter the herb wild oat, æferth, and springwort. For a pustule, maythe, wood marche, work *these* into a salve, let him drink good worts. For a pustule, take lupin, pound in honey, mingle together, lay on the swelling till it be hole. For a pustule, pound springwort, chervil, and honey and goose grease, heat them together, lay this on the pustule.

xxxiv.

1. If a nail be off the hand, and against a warty eruption,[a] take wheat corn, mingle with honey, lay on the finger. For an angnail,[b] brass filings and old soap, and oil if thou have it, if thou have it not, add cream, mingle together, lay on.

2. For warty eruption, heat in butter bunches of maythe and salt, smear therewith.

[a] Πτερύγιον, probably.
[b] Παρωνυχία.

---

[1] Understand, in ashes. "Linteorum lanugo e velis navium maritimarum maxime, in magno usu medicinæ est; et cinis spodii (*ivory filings*) vim habet." Plinius, xix. 4.

.XXXV.

Μελανία.
Μελασμός.
Cf. Galenum de
Simpl. Med.
lib. viii. 43,
ed. 1826.

Be afpeaɲtebum ꞇ abeabebum lioe fio abl cymð oɲꞇoſꞇ
oꝼ omum æꝼꞇeɲ able pelme ón peʒ ʒepiꞇenɲe peoɲþeð
hpilum lic afpeaɲꞇoð· þonne oꝼ þam ꝼɲum pelme fio
abl mib cealbum þinʒum biþ ꞇo celanne ꞇ ꞇo lacnianne·
ꞇ þonne fio abl cymð uꞇan buꞇan fpeoꞇolúm ꞇacne·
þonne ɲoealꞇ þu æɲeɲꞇ þa hæꞇo celan mib cellenbɲe
ʒeꞇɲiꝼulabɲe mib hlaꝼeſ cɲuman oꝼþenbum mib cealb
pæꞇɲe oþþe mib þy ɲelꝼan feape þæɲe cellenbɲe· oþþe

fol. 31 a.

mib æʒeɲ þy hɲiꞇe oþþe mib ɲine oþþe mib oþɲum
þinʒum þam þe ꝥ ilce mæʒen hæbbe· þonne ꝼe þelma
ꞇ fio hæꞇo fie apeʒ ʒepiꞇen ꞇ ꝼe bæl þæꝼ lichoman
fie ʒepenbeð hpon oðбe blæc oþþe pón oþþe ſpilceɲ
hpæꞇ ɲceaɲɲa þonne þa ſꞇope þonne beꞇſꞇ þu ða· ꞇ
bɲiʒe mib ónleʒene fpa fpa món on peax hlaꝼe ꞇ oꝼ
peaɲmum beɲe· ꞇ oꝼ fpeloum þinʒum pyɲcð.[1] Niꝼ him
bloð ꞇo lætanne ón æbɲe ac ma hiɲa man ɲoeal ꞇilian
mib pyɲꞇbɲencúm uꞇyɲinenbum oþþe fpiɲlum oþþe miʒo-
lúm mib þy þu meahꞇ clænſian ꝥ ómcyn ꞇ þæꝼ ʒeallan-
coðe þa ɲeaban· ʒe þeah ꝥ yꝼel cumen ne fie oꝼ þaɲa
omena pelme fpa þeah beah fpilcum mannum ꝼe ɲceaɲɲa
pyɲꞇbɲenc. ʒiꝼ þa omihꞇan pannan þinʒ oþþe þa ɲeaban
fyn uꞇan cumen oꝼ punbum oþþe óꝼ fniþinʒum oðбe
oꝼ ɲleʒúm fona þu þa þinʒ lácna mib ɲoeaɲɲinʒe ꞇ
ónleʒena beɲeſ æꝼꞇeɲ þæɲe piſan þe læcaſ cunnan pel
þu hiꞇ beꞇſꞇ. ʒiꝼ ꝥ afpeaɲiꞇobe lic ꞇo þon fpiþe abeabiʒe

fol. 31 b.

ꝥ þæɲ nan ʒeꝼelneꝼ ón ne fie þonne ɲoealꞇ þu ɲona
eal ꝥ beabe ꞇ ꝥ unʒeꝼelbe óꝼ afniþan oþ ꝥ cpice lic·
ꝥ þæɲ na mihꞇ þæꝼ beaban liceſ ꞇo laꝼe ne fie ꝥæſ þe
æɲ ne iɲen ne ꝼyɲ ʒeꝼelbe. Æꝼꞇeɲ þon lacniʒe món
þa bolh fpa þu þone bæl þe þonne ʒíꞇ hpilce hpeʒa

---

[1] pyɲe, MS.

XXXV.

Of swarthened and deadened body. The disease
cometh oftenest of corrupt humours after the inflammation of the disease which has passed away, the body
whilom becometh swarthy. Then, from the original
inflammation, the disease is to be cooled and to be
tended with cold appliances. And when the disease
cometh from without, without a manifest token *of its
cause*, then shalt thou first cool the heat with triturated
coriander, with crumbs of bread moistened with cold
water or with the juice itself of the coriander, or with the
white of egg, or with wine, or with other things which
have the same virtue. When the inflammation and the
heat are gone away and the part of the body is turned
somewhat *to be* either pale or livid or somewhat such,
then scarify the place, thou wilt then better it; and
dry it with an application such as a man works of
wax cake and warm beer and of such things. He is
not to be let blood on a vein, but rather *the symptoms*
shall be tended with wort drinks, of a perfluent
nature, either emetic or diuretic, with which thou
mayest cleanse the corrupt humour and its red gall-
sickness. Yea, though the evil be not come of the
inflammation of the corrupt humours, yet for such men
the sharp wort drink is beneficial. If the pituitous
livid or red symptoms be come from without, from
wounds or from cuttings or from blows, soon do thou
heal those matters with scarifying and onlayings[a] of   [a] Ἐπιθέματα.
barley, after the manner which leeches well know;
thou shalt amend it. If the swarthened body be to
that high degree deadened that no feeling be thereon,
than must thou soon cut away all the dead and the
unfeeling *flesh*, as far as the quick, so that there be
nought remaining of the dead flesh, which ere felt
neither iron nor fire. After that one shall heal the
wounds, as thou wouldst the part which as yet may

F 2

ȝeƀelneffe hæbbe · ⁊ eallunȝa ðeaðe ne fynð.[1] þu ſcealt
mið ȝelomlicne ſceaſpunȝe hƿilûm mið miclum· hƿilum
mið ſeapûm þene ⁊ teoh[2] ꝥ bloð ſſam þæſe aðeaðeðan
ſtope lácna ða ſceaſpan þuſ· ȝenim bean mela oþþe
ætena· oððe beſeſ· oþþe ſpilceſ meluþeſ ſpa þe þince
ꝥ hit ônniman ſille ðo eceð to ⁊ huniȝ ſeoþ ætȝæðeſe
⁊ leȝe ôn ⁊ binð on þa ſaſan ſtopa. ȝif þu polðe ꝥ
ſio ſealf ſſiðſe ſie ðo lytel ſealteſ to ôn binð hƿilum ⁊
þþeah mið eceðe oþþe mið ſine. ȝif þeanſ ſie ſele
hƿilûm pyſtðſenc· ⁊ ȝeſceapa ſimle þonne þu þa ſtſanȝan læceðomaſ ðo hƿilc ꝥ mæȝen ſie ⁊ ſio ȝecynð þæſ
lichoman· hƿæþeſ hio ſie ſtſanȝ þe heaſð ⁊ eaþelice
mæȝe þa ſtſanȝan læceðomaſ abeſan þe hio ſie hneſce
⁊ meaſþe ⁊ þynne ⁊ ne mæȝe abeſan þa læceðomaſ.
ðo þu ða læceðomaſ ſpilce þu þa lichoman ȝeſie· ſoſ
þon ðe micel ȝeðal îſ on pæpneðeſ ⁊ piſeſ ⁊ cilðeſ
lichoman· ⁊ on þam mæȝene þæſ ðæȝhƿamlican
pyſhtan ⁊ þæſ iðlan þæſ ealðan ⁊ þæſ ȝeonȝan ⁊
þæſ þe ſie ȝepin[3] þſopunȝum· ⁊ þæſ þe ſie unȝe-
puna ſpelcum þinȝum· ȝe þa hƿitan lichoman beoð
meaſuſſan ⁊ teðſan þonne þa blacan· ⁊ þa ſeaðan.
ȝif þu ſille lîm aceoſſan oððe aſniðan oſ lichoman
þonne ȝeſceapa þu hƿilc ſio ſtop ſie· ⁊ þæſe ſtope
mæȝen· ſoſ þon ðe þaſa ſtopa ſum ſaþe ſotaþ ȝif
hiſe môn ȝimeleaſlice tilað· ſume latoſ ſelað þaſa
læceðoma ſume ſaþoſ· ȝif þu ſcyle aceoſſan oððe
aſniþan unhal lim oſ halum lice þonne[4] ceoſf þu ꝥ on
þam ȝemæſe þæſ halan liceſ· âc micle ſpiþoſ ſniÐ oððe
ceoſf on ꝥ hale ⁊ ꝥ cſice lic ſpa þu hit ſel ⁊ ſaþoſ
ȝelacnoſt. Þonne þu ſyſ ſette ôn mannan þonne nim
þu meſþeſ poſſeſ leaſ ⁊ ȝeȝniðen ſealt oſeſ leȝe þa

---

have some feeling, and be not altogether dead. Thou shalt with frequent scarifying, whilom with mickle, whilom with slight, wean and draw the blood from the deadened place. Cure the scarifyings thus; take bean or oat or barley meal, or some of such meal as to thee seemeth good, so that it will serve, add vinegar and honey, seethe together and lay on, and bind upon the sore places. If thou shouldst wish that the salve be stronger, add a little salt, bind on at whiles and wash with vinegar or with wine. If need be, give at whiles a wort drink, and observe always when thou art applying the strong leechdoms, what the power be, and what the nature of the body *of the patient;* whether it be strong and hardy, and easily may bear the strong leechdoms, or whether it be nice and tender and thin, and may not bear the leechdoms. Apply the leechdoms according as thou seest *the state of* the body. For a mickle difference is there, in the bodies of a man, a woman, and a child; and in the main *or constitution* of a daily wright *or labourer* and of the idle, of the old and of the young, of him who is accustomed to endurances, and him who is unaccustomed to such things. Yea, the white bodies be tenderer and weaker than the black and the red. If thou wilt carve off or cut off a limb from a body, then view thou of what sort the place be, and the strength of the place, since some *or one* of the places readily rotteth if one carelessly tendeth it: some feel the leechdoms later, some earlier. If thou must carve off or cut off an unhealthy limb off from a healthy body, then carve thou not it on the limit of the healthy body; but much more cut or carve in on the hole and quick body; so thou shalt better and readier cure it. When thou settest fire on a man, then take thou leaves of tender leek and grated salt, overlay the places, then shall be by that the more readily the heat of the fire drawn

ſtope þonne bið þy þe naþon þær ſyneſ hæto apeȝ
atoȝen · ꝥ ilce biþ nyttol iceſ ſlite oþþe hundeſ ȝiſ
hit man ſona to deð · ꝥ eſt ymb þreo niht ſmiꝛe
mið huniȝe ꝥ þy þe naþon ſio hꝛyſinȝ oſ ꝛealle.

. XXXVI.

[1]Ƿiþ þæꝛe adle þe mon hæt cincul adl ȝenim cꝛicbeam
ꝛinde · ꝺ æpſan · ꝺ apuldoꝛ · mapuldoꝛ · ellen · piþiȝ ·
ꝛealh · piꝛ · ꝛice · ac · ꝛlahþoꝛn · biꝛcean · elebeam ·
ȝatetꝛeoꝧ · æꝛceſ ꝛceal mæꝛt · ꝺ ælceſ tꝛeoꝛeſ dæl
þe man beȝitan mæȝ · butan hæȝþoꝛne ꝺ aloꝛe þaꝛa
tꝛeoꝛa mæꝛt þe heꝛ aꝛꝛiten ꝛynd ꝺ eac ȝaȝel ꝺ cneoꝛ
holen · ſinȝꝛenan eolonan · ꝛedic pealꝛyꝛt · þa ȝꝛeatan
netlan · peꝛmod eoꝛþ ȝeallan. ȝenim þonne tynam-
beꝛne cetel do þꝛiddan dæl þaꝛa ꝛinda ꝺ þa pyꝛta
pylle ſꝛiþe on maxꝛyꝛte ȝiſ þu hæbbe · ȝiſ þu næbbe
pyl on pætꝛe ſꝛiþe · do þonne oſ þa ꝛinda ꝺ do niꝛe on
innan ꝥ ilce poſ do ſpa þꝛiꝛa aſeoh þonne clæne ſpa
hatne þone dꝛenc ꝺ do þonne mele ſulne buteꝛan on
ſpa hatne ꝺ ȝehꝛeꝛe toȝædeꝛe læt ſtandan tꝛa niht
oþþe þꝛeo · abo þonne oſ þa buteꝛan ꝺ ȝenim þonne
ȝaȝel cꝛoppan · ꝺ iꝛiȝ cꝛoppan · helban · ꝺ betonican
eolonan · ꝛedic · banꝛyꝛt · eoꝛð miſtel ȝebeat toȝædeꝛe pylle on þæꝛe buteꝛan abo þonne þa buteꝛan
clæne oſ þam ꝛyꝛtum þær þe mon mæȝe · ȝenim þonne
ſmæl beꝛen mela ꝺ ȝebæꝛned ꝛealt bꝛiꝛe þonne on

---

[1] Zώνη, or Ζωστήρ.

away. The same *process* is advantageous for frogs[1] or hounds bite, if one soon applieth it. And again, for about three nights, smear with honey, that thereby the more readily the scab or crust may fall off.

xxxvi.

Against the disease which is hight circle addle[2] *or shingles*, take quickbeam rind, and aspen and apple tree, maple tree, elder, withy, sallow, myrtle, wich elm, oak, sloe thorn, birch, olive tree, the lotus tree,[3] of ash there shall be most, and a part of each tree which a man can get at (except hawthorn and alder), the largest quantity of the trees which are here written, and also gale and knee holly, *that is, butchers broom*, singreen, *that is, house leek*, helenium, radish, wallwort, the great nettle, wormwood, earthgall.[4] Take then a kettle holding ten ambers, put *therein* a third part of the rinds and the worts, boil strongly in mashwort, *that is, the unfermented wort of beer*, if thou have it, if thou have it not, boil strong in water, t hen remothe rinds, and put new *rinds* into that same decoction, do so three times, then strain out clean the drink so hot, and then add a basin full of butter so hot, and shake *them up* together : let *this* stand two nights or three, then remove the butter, and then take catkins of gale, berry branches of ivy, tansy, and betony, helenium, radish, bonewort, basil, beat together, boil in the butter, then remove the butter clean off the worts, as far as a man may : then take fine barley meal and burnt salt,

---

[1] No doubt *frog*, Cod. Ex. p. 426–9. Dioskorides Alexifarm. 31. has a chapter on the Φρύνη, or *toad*, and the Βάτραχος ἕλειος, or "marsh frog," as poisonous.

[2] In Plinius Valerianus, Circinus.

"Vesicae si hominem cinxerint occidunt."

[3] Are we to suppose Carpinus was read as Caprinus, and say hornbeam for lotus ?

[4] *Erythræa centaureum*.

þæɲe buteɲan ꞇ hɲeɲe þonne ſpiþe butan fyɲe ꞇ ðo
piþoɲ to ete þonne æɲeſt þone bɲip on neaht neɲtiȝ.
ðɲince þonne æ̀fteɲ þone ðɲenc ꞇ nanne oþeɲne pætan
tyn nihtum þɲitiȝ ȝif he mæȝe · ȝením þonne acmiſtel
ȝebeat ſmæle ꞇ aðɲiȝe ꞇ ȝeȝnið to melupe áþeh þonne
piþ ænne peninȝ ðo þ̷ on þ̷ bètſte ſín.   ðɲinc ſpa
niȝon ðaȝaſ ꞇ ne ete nipne ciſe ne feɲrce ȝoſ · ne
feɲrcne æl · ne fe[ɲ]rc ſpin · ne naht þæɲ þe of
fol. 33 b. moɲoðe cume · ne fixaſ · ûnɲcellebte · ne flohtenfote
fuȝelaſ · ȝif he hpilc þiɲſa ete ſie þ̷ fealt ꞇ nane
þinȝa beoɲ ne ðɲince ꞇ ȝemetlice ſín ꞇ eala · ȝif mon
þiſûm læceðome befyliȝð þonne biþ ſe man hal ; Þiþ
ciɲcul aðle ȝením ðoccan þa þe ſpimman pille ȝebeat
ſpiþe ſmale apylle on ealðum moɲoðe ȝoðe hanð fulle
ðo þonne þa pyɲta óf ðo eft oþɲe hanð fulle þæɲe
ilcan pyɲte pylle eft ſpiðe ȝeðo þonne þa pyɲta óf
ȝenim þonne ſpefl ȝebeat ſpiþe ſmale ȝeðo þonne on
þa fealfe þ̷ hio ſie ſpa picce ſpa bɲip ſmiɲe þonne þa
ſpeccan mið þæɲe ſealfe oþ þ̷ him fel ſie.

.XXXVII.

Marcellus,
362, d.   Þiþ þon þe mon ne mæȝe hiɲ micȝean ȝehealban ꞇ
þæɲe ȝepealð naȝe eoɲoɲeɲ clapa oþþe oþɲeɲ ſpineɲ ȝebæɲn to ahſan rceað þonne þa ahſan on þæɲ reocan
Marcellus,
362, d. e. manneſ ðɲincan.   Éft ſpineſ blæðɲan untyðɲenðeɲ þ̷ iſ
ȝylte ȝebæɲn to ahɲan ðo on ſín ſele ðɲincan. Þiþ
þon ilcan eft ȝate blæðɲe ahyɲſte ɲele etan · ſume ſpa
fol. 34 a. ȝebyɲſte ȝeȝniðaþ to ðuſte ſceað on ſín ɲellað ðɲincan
ȝif hie beoð butan ferɲie.   ȝif mon ne mæȝe ȝemiȝan
eft cymeneſ ȝenim ſpa micel ſpa ðu mið þɲim finȝɲum

next make a brewit of them in the butter, and shake it well up without fire, and add pepper, then let *the patient* eat first the brewit at night fasting. Further after that let him drink the draught and none other liquid for ten nights, for thirty if he can *endure it ;* then take mistletoe of the oak, beat it small and dry it, and rub down to meal, then weigh it against one penny, put that into the best wine; let *the sufferer* drink *this* accordingly for nine days, and let him eat neither new cheese, nor fresh goose, nor fresh eel, nor fresh pig, nor aught of that which cometh of a decoction, nor fishes without shells, nor web footed fowls ; if he eat any of these, let it be salted, and by no means let him drink beer, and wine and ale moderately. If this leechdom be followed then shall the man be hole. Against circle addle *or shingles*, take dock that will swim, beat it very small, boil in old inspissated wine a good handful, then remove the worts, afterwards add another handful of the same wort, boil again thoroughly, then remove the worts ; then take brimstone, beat it very small, then apply the salve, so that it may be as thick as brewit, then smear the specks with the salve till it be well with him, *the patient.*

xxxvii.

In case that a man may not retain his urine and have not control over it, burn to ashes claws of a boar or of another swine, then shed the ashes on the sick mans drink. Again, burn to ashes the bladder of an unprolific, that is a gelt, swine, put it into wine, administer it to drink. For the same, fry a goats bladder, give it *to the man* to eat; some, when so fried, reduce it to dust, and *when shed* into wine, give it *to the men* to drink, if they be without fever. Again, if a man may not pass water, take of cummin as much as thou mayst lift with three fingers, triturate it, and add

úp ahebban mæʒe ʒeꞇꞃuꝼula ꞇ ʒebo ꞇo pineꞃ ꞇpeʒen
bollan ꝼulle · ꞇ oþꞃe ꞇpeʒen pæꞇeneꝼ ꞃele bꞃuncan nihꞇ-
neꞃꞇiʒum. Eꝼꞇ ʒiꝼ mon ne mæʒe ʒemiʒan bꞃince ʒyþꞃiꝼan on pæꞇꞃe ʒeʒnibene. Eꝼꞇ ʒenime eác ʒeaꞃpan ꞇ
peʒbꞃæban pyl on pine ꞃele bꞃuncan. Eꝼꞇ ꞃammeꞃ

Marcellus,
358, g.

Marcellus,
362, d.

blæðꞃe ʒeꝼobene þicʒe he. ʒením ꝼinoleꝼ pyꞃꞇꞇꞃuman
eꝼꞇ · ꞇ þa pyꞃꞇ ꞃelꝼe ʒebeaꞇ ꞇ ʒeʒnib ón pin oꞃþæne
pel ꞇ aꞃeoh ꞃele bꞃuncan. Eꝼꞇ ʒoꝼa ꞇunʒan ʒebꞃæbbe
ꞇ ʒeþicʒe. Eꝼꞇ ʒiꝼ þu ꞃinbe ꞃiꝼc on oþꞃum ꞃiꝼoe
innan ʒením þone ꞇ ʒebꞃæb ꝼpiþe ꞇ ʒebꞃyꞇe on bꞃuncan ꞇ ꞃele þam ꞃeocan men bꞃuncan ꝼpa he nyꞇe ꝼpa
þu ꞃcealꞇ þa oþꞃe æꞇaꞃ ꞇ bꞃuncan ꞃellan. ʒiꝼ món ne
mæʒe ʒemiʒan bꞃince he hlian pyꞃꞇꞇꞃuman apylleðne
on pine oððe on ealað. ʒiꝼ he þonne ꞇo ꝼpiðe miʒe

fol. 34 b.

bꞃince ʒyþꞃiꝼan on pæꞇeꞃe ʒeʒnibene. ʒiꝼ món blobe
miʒe ʒením pubu ꞃoꞃan ꝼeoþ on pæꞇꞃe oððe on ealað
ꞃele bꞃuncan.

Gíꝼ ꝼíꝼ ne mæʒe ʒemiʒan nim ꞇunceꞃꞃan ꝼæb ꝼeoð
on pæꞇꞃe ꞃele bꞃuncan. ʒiꝼ món ne mæʒe ʒemiʒan
ʒecnupa luꝼeꝼꞇice ꞇ ellenꞃinbe ꞇ oleaꝼꞇꞃum þ íꞃ pilbe
elebeám ʒemenʒ pið ꝼuꞃum hluꞇꞇꞃum ealað ꞃele
bꞃuncan.

. XXXVIII.

Deꞃ ꝼinbon bolh ꞃealꝼa ꞇo eallum punbúm ꞇ bꞃencaꞃ
ꞇ clænꞃunʒa[1] on ʒehpilce ꞃiꝼan ʒe uꞇan ʒe on þam
innoþúm. Peʒbꞃæbe ʒebeaꞇen pið ealbne ꞃyꞃele ʒemenʒeb ꝼeꞃꞃc ne nyꞇ biþ.

[2]Eꝼꞇ bolhꞃealꝼ ʒením peʒbꞃæban ꝼæb ʒeꞇꞃiꝼula ꝼmale
ꞃceab on þa punbe ꞃona bið ꞃelꞃe.

---

thereto two bowls full of wine and two others of water,
give it *to the sick* to drink after his nights fasting.
Again, if a man cannot mie, let him drink githrife,
rubbed *fine* in water. Again, take also yarrow and
waybroad, boil *them* in wine, give *them* to be drunk.
Again, let him eat a rams bladder sodden. Again, take
roots of fennel and the wort itself, beat it and rub it
fine into wine, moisten well and strain *it, and* administer *it* to drink. Again, let him roast[1] and partake
of the tongues of geese. Again, if thou find a fish
within another fish, take and roast it thoroughly, and
break it to bits into a draught, and give it to the sick
man to drink in such a manner that he know it not.
So shalt thou give the other meats and drinks. If
a man may not pass water, let him drink a root of
a lily boiled in wine or in ale. If he then mie too
strongly, let him drink githrife in water, rubbed to
dust. If a man mie blood, take dog roses, seethe them
in water or in ale, administer them to drink.

If a woman may not pass water, take seed of garden
cress, seethe it in water and give it her to drink. If
one may not pass water, pound lovage and elder rind
and oleaster, that is wild olive tree, mix *this* with
sour clear ale, *and* give to drink.

Book I.
Ch. xxxvii.

xxxviii.

1. Here are wound salves for all wounds and drinks
and cleansings of every sort, whether without or in
the inwards. Waybroad beaten, mixed with old lard;
the fresh is not of use.

2. Again, a wound salve; take seed of waybroad,
bray it small, shed it on the wound, soon it will be
better.

---

[1] Our Saxon has not been careful   is set down in Marcellus as restrain-
in the selection of his recipes ; this   ing "profluvium urinae."

Þiþ ealdne punde tobnocenne ȝnundefpelȝe þiþ ealdne
nyrele ȝemenȝed ꝛ on aled lacna fpilce punda. To
punde clænrunȝe ·¹ ȝenim clæne huniȝ ȝepynme to
ryne ȝedo þonne on clæne ræt do realt to ꝛ hnepc oþ
þ hit hæbbe bnipej þicnejje fmine þa punde mid þonne

fol. 35 a.

fullað hio. ȝir banbnice on heafde fie maȝeþan ꝛ
ȝotpoþan ȝecnupa pel on huniȝe do þonne butenan on
þ bið ȝod dolhrealr. Eft pið þon eac biþ ȝod luft-
mocan cnop to lecȝanne on ȝebnocen heafod ꝛ ȝir
hund rlite. Þiþ hundej rlite ȝenim þa neaban netlan
ꝛ attonlaþan ꝛ fpicej ælcej emrela feoð on butenan
pync to realre rona beoð þa unnyttan ban ute.

dolh realr pið lunȝen able · hleomoce hatte pynt fio
peaxeð on bnoce ȝepync þa on monȝenne þonne hio
ȝebeap fie fume beoð unbeape ꝛ ȝofe fceapn þonne
hio ne ete · ȝecnupa þa hleomocan menȝ piþ þam ȝofe
rceapne · do læj þæj fceapnej pyl on butenan apninȝ
þ biþ ȝod realr. Sealr hapan fpnecel nim on ealduni
lande ꝛ lunȝenpync feo biþ ȝeolu urepeanð ꝛ æȝef
dydnin mid þy real mon lacnian þone man þe biþ
lunȝenne pund. Þiþ innan punde realr · fin ele ·

fol. 35 b.

ȝalluc · huniȝ. dolhrealr ȝyþnire ꝛ ȝelod pynt ꝛ þa
bnunan pynt bnablearan fio peaxeþ on puda ꝛ luft-
moce cnoppan · ȝecnupa þa ealle ꝛ pyl ænefl on butenan healre ꝛ apninȝ.

dolh realr ert ȝnunde fpelȝe þa ðe peaxað on ponþi-
ȝum fio biþ ȝod to dolhrealre ꝛ nibbe ꝛ ȝeanre ꝛ ȝiþ-
nire ȝecnupa þa pynta ealle pyl on butenan ꝛ apninȝ.
Eft dolhrealr ȝod acnind abnuȝe þa nunde ꝛ fpiðe fmale
ȝecnupa ꝛ adelr niþepeanðne rlah ðonn ærcar þa yte-

¹ clærnunȝe, MS.

3. For an old bruised wound, groundsel mingled
with old lard, and laid on : tend such wounds *thus.*
For cleansing of a wound ; take clean honey, warm it
at the fire, put it then into a clean vessel, add salt,
and shake it till it have the thickness of brewit, smear
the wound therewith, when it turneth foul. If there
be a bone breach in the head, pound maýthe and
goutweed well in honey, then add butter, that is
a good wound salve. Again for that, a bunch of
" lustmock " is good to lay on a broken head, and *also*
if a hound tear *a man.* For tearing by a hound, take
the red nettle and attorlothe and some lard, of each
an equal quantity, seethe in butter, work to a salve,
soon the useless bones will be out.

4. A wound salve for lung disease. A wort is called
hlemock, which waxeth in brooks, *and is now brooklime,* work it, *that is, deal with it* in a morning when
it is dewy, (some *plants of it* are undewy), and sharn
of goose *dropped* when the goose eats not ; pound the
brooklime, mingle with the dung of goose, put in less
of the sharn *than of the wort,* boil in butter, wring
through a cloth, that will be a good salve. A salve :
take vipers bugloss, *grown* on an old tilth, and golden
lungwort,[a] and a yolk of egg, with this shall one tend
a man who is wounded in the lung. For an inward
wound, a salve : wine, oil, comfrey, honey. A wound
salve : githrife and silver weed, and the broadleaved
brownwort which waxeth in woods, and a bunch of
the flowers of " lustmock "; pound all these and boil
first in a half proportion of butter, and wring *through
a cloth.*

5. Again, a wound salve: the groundsel which waxeth
in highways, that is good for a wound salve, and ribwort, and yarrow, and githrife ;[b] pound all the worts,
boil in butter, and squeeze *through a cloth.* Again, a
good wound salve : oak rind; dry the rind and pound
it very small, and delve up the nethermost *part of a*

[a] *Hieracium murorum* and *pulmonarium.*

[b] *Agrostemma githago.*

meſtan ꞃinbe ꞇ ſpiðe ſmale ӡecnupa aꞃiꞇ ſmale þuꞃh
ſmæl ſiꞃe bo beӡea emꞃela ꝥ mela biÐ ӡob on ꞇo
ſceabenne. Ӡiꞃ þu ꞃaðe ꞃille lyꞇle punbe ӡelacnian
eacꞇꞃſan ӡeꞇꞃꞃula oÐðe ӡeſeoÐ on buꞇeꞃan pyꞃc ꞇo
ꞃealꞃe ſmiꞃe miÐ. ðolh ꞃealꞃ · ӡeaꞃꞃan · ӡyþꞃꞃan ·
ſinӡꞃenan · ӡoꞇꞃoþan læſꞇ ӡecnupa piÐ buꞇeꞃan ſpiðe
pel leӡe neahꞇeꞃne ſpa ӡeoneben · bo þonne ón pannan
pyl ſpiðe bo ꝥ ꞃam óꞃ clæne aꞃeoh þuꞃh claÐ bo on hꞃiꞇ
ꞃealꞇ hꞃeꞃ ſpiðe oþ ꝥ ӡeſꞇanben ſie. ðolhꞃealꞃ meꞃſc
hoꞃe æþelꞃeꞃðinӡpyꞃꞇ ꞇ ӡyþꞃꞃan ꞇ ſinӡꞃenan on þa
fol. 36 a. ilcan piſan pꞃꞃce. ðolhꞃealꞃ ӡenim pabeſ cꞃoppan ꞇ
neꞇelan eác ӡecnupa pel · pyl on buꞇeꞃan aſeoh þuꞃh
claÐ bo hꞃiꞇ ſealꞇ ón hꞃeꞃe ſpiðe.

ðolhꞃealꞃ ácꞃinb · æꞃeꞃðe · meoðopyꞃꞇ abꞃiӡe ealle
ꞇ ӡecnupa ſmale aꞃiꞇ þuꞃh ꞃiꞃe menӡ piþ huniӡe ꞇ
æӡeꞇ ꝥ hꞃiꞇe. ðolhꞃealꞃ ӡiꞃ mon ſie miÐ iꞃene ӡe-
punðob · puðuꞃoꞃe · ſinӡꞃene · ӡeloðpyꞃꞇ ſpꞃinӡ pyꞃꞇ ·
ӡyþꞃꞃe · ӡꞃunbeſpelӡe · maӡoðe pyꞃm pyꞃꞇ nioþoꞃeaꞃb
ӡeonua pel ꞇoſomne ealle menӡ piÐ buꞇeꞃan pyl þa
pꞃꞃꞇa on þæꞃe buꞇeꞃan ſpiðe aꞃleoꞇ ꝥ ꞃam oꞃ clæne
aſeoh þuꞃh claÐ bo on bleðe hꞃeꞃ piÐ oþ ꝥ ӡeſꞇanben
ſie.

Ӡiꞃ mon miÐ ꞇꞃeope ӡeꞃleӡen ſie oÐðe miÐ ſꞇane
oþþe byl on men ӡebeꞃſꞇeÐ · ꞇo þon ðolhꞃealꞃ · ӡyþꞃꞃe · onꞇꞃe · ӡeloðpyꞃꞇ · ꞃiӡelhpeoꞃꞃa · ӡecnupa þa
pyꞃꞇa ſpiþe ӡemenӡ pel piÐ buꞇeꞃan ꞇ on þa ilcan
piſan ӡeꞃena þe ic æꞃ cpæþ.

Ӡiꞃ men ſie lim óꞃ aꞃleӡen · ꞃinӡeꞃ oÐðe ꞃóꞇ oþþe
hanð ӡiꞃ ꝥ mæaꞃh uꞇe ſie · ӡenim ꞃoeapeꞃ mæaꞃh ӡe-

blackthorn, shave off the outermost *part of the* rind
and pound it very small, sift it small through a small
sieve, put *together* equal quantities of both, the meal is
good to shed on *a wound*. If thou wilt quickly cure
a little wound, bruise or seethe in butter water cress,
work it into a salve, smear therewith. A salve for
wounds : pound very well with butter, yarrow, cockle,
singreen, *or houseleek*, of goutweed the least, lay them
by for a night so bruised, then put them into a pan, boil
thoroughly, remove the foam clean off, strain through
a cloth, add white salt,[1] shake it well up till it
be got firm. A wound salve; work *up* in the same
wise marsh hove, stichwort, and cockle, and singreen.
A wound salve; take heads of woad and of nettle,
also pound them well, boil in butter, strain through a
cloth, add white salt, shake thoroughly.

6. A wound salve : oak rind, " æferthe," meadowwort;
dry all *these* and pound them small, sift *the dust*
through a sieve, mingle with honey and the white of
an egg. A wound salve, if a man be wounded with
iron : woodroffe, singreen, silverweed, springwort,[a] gith-   [a] *Euforbia*
rife, groundsel, maythe, the lower part of wormwort,   *lathyris.*
pound them all well together, mingle with butter, boil
the worts in the butter thoroughly, skim the foam
off clean, strain through a cloth, put *it* on a saucer,
shake it till it be concrete.

7. If a man be smitten with wood or with stone,
or if a boil bursteth on a man, for this a wound salve :
cockle, " ontre," silverweed, turnsole, pound the worts
thoroughly, mingle well with butter, and prepare in
the same wise which before I quoth.

8. If a limb be smitten off a man, a finger, or a foot,
or a hand, if the marrow be out, take sodden sheeps

---

[1] Salt not quite pure is not white ;
much comes red from the pits ;
much dirty from the saltpans. Sal
ammoniacum is often prescribed in
the Latin and Greek authors ; perhaps this is an evasion of that
drug.

ꝛoben leᵹe on ꝥ oþeꞃ meaꞃh · apꞃıþ ſpıðe pel neahteꞃne. ðolh ꞃealꝼ · hæꞃleſ ꞃaᵹu Ᵹ holen ꞃınðe nıþepeaꞃðe · Ᵹ ᵹyþꞃıꝼan ᵹecnun ſpıðe pel þa pꝼꞃta ᵹemenᵹ pıð buteꞃan ſeoð ſpıðe ꝼleot oꝼ ꝥ ꞃam aſeoh þuꞃh cla ſpıþe clæne ᵹıꝼ þæꞃ ðolᵹeꞃ oꝼꞃaꞃ ſynð to hea ymb ſtꞃıc mıð hate ıꞃene ſpıðe leohtlıce ꝥ ꝥ ꝼel hꞃıtıᵹe.

ðolhꞃealꝼ ᵹŏtꞃoþan ᵹecnuꞃa ſpıðe pel meᵹ pıð buteꞃan ſeoð ſpıðe Ᵹ pyll Ᵹ apꞃınᵹ þuꞃh clað ꝼleot ꝥ ꞃam ŏꝼ ᵹeꝼelt ſpıðe pel · ᵹıꝼ ðolh ꝼulıᵹe ceop ſtꞃæl pyꞃt ŏn Ᵹ ᵹeaꞃpan. ðolhꞃealꝼ ᵹenım ꞃıbban · Ᵹ ᵹeaꞃpan · Ᵹ ðolhꞃunan nıoþopeaꞃðe · Ᵹ ðoccan Ᵹ ᵹoꞃe ꞃœaꞃn Ᵹ pıceſ lytel · Ᵹ hunıᵹ pylle on buteꞃan ðo on ꝥ ðolh þonne clænſað hıt Ᵹ halað. ðolhꞃealꝼ ᵹenĩm ᵹeaꞃpan Ᵹ læce pyꞃt pyl on buteꞃan.

Sealꝼ pıþ þon ꝥ ðolh ne ꝼulıᵹe ᵹenım bꞃeꞃ þe hıopan on peaxaþ ceop þa ꞃınðe on ꝥ ðolh ne ꝼulaþ hıt. ðolhꞃealꝼ meðopyꞃt nıoþepeaꞃð · luſtmoce · hoꝛe · eoꝛoꞃ ꝼeaꞃn · pyl on hunıᵹe ðo þıcce maxpyꞃt on ᵹemanᵹ. ðolhðꞃenc · eoꝛoꞃþꞃote nıoþopeaꞃð Ᵹ meðopyꞃt eác ſpa aᵹꞃımonıa nıoþopeaꞃð Ᵹ uꝼepeaꞃð pyl ŏn ealaþ þa pyꞃta ᵹebıꞃm mıð ᵹıſte ꝼele ðꞃıncan.

ðolhðꞃenc ᵹeaceꞃ ſuꞃan puðu cunılle ᵹıþꞃıꝼe · eoꝛoꞃþꞃote nıþepeaꞃðe æꞃcþꞃote cnupa ſmale ðo ŏn cealb pæteꞃ ᵹnıð betꞃeoh hanðum aſeoh þuꞃh clað ꝼele

marrow, lay it on the other marrow, bind it well up for a night. A wound salve : the lichen of hazel, and the netherward part of holly rind and githrife, pound the worts very well, mingle with butter, seethe thoroughly, skim off the foam, strain through a cloth very clean ; if the edges of the wound are too high,[1] run them round with a hot iron very lightly, so that the skin may whiten.

9. A wound salve: pound very thoroughly, gout-weed, mingle with butter, seethe thoroughly, and boil, and wring through a cloth, skim off the foam, salt it very well; if the wound get foul, chew strailwort up-on it and yarrow. A wound salve: take ribwort and yarrow, and the netherward part of pellitory, and dock, and goose dung, and a little pitch, and honey, boil in butter, apply it to the wound, then it cleanseth and healeth. A wound salve : take yarrow and leechwort, boil in butter.

10. A salve to the end that a wound may not foul : take briar, on which hips wax, *that is, dog rose,* chew the rind *and let it drop* on the wound, *then* it will not foul. A wound salve : the netherward part of meadow wort, lustmock, hove, everfern, boil in honey, add thick mashwort among *them.* A drink for wounds : the netherward part of everthroat, *that is, carline thistle,* and meadow sweet, so also the nether and up-ward part of agrimony, boil the worts in ale, barm them with yeast, *that is, introduce fermentation with yeast,* administer to drink.

11. A wound drink : pound small, cuckoo sour, wild cunila,[2] cockle, the netherward part of carline thistle, ashthroat, put them into cold water, rub be-tween the hands, strain through a cloth, administer to

---

[1] Probably, if the edges are likely to coalesce, before the parts that lie deeper.
[2] Plinius, xx. 63.

ðpuncan ſcenc ɼulne neahtneɾtiȝ. ðolhðpenc pibbe
nioþepeaɼıð ꝼ uɼepeaɼð · eoɼopþpotan · ꝼ æɾc þpotan
nioþopeapðe cnupa ſmale ðo on peallenðe pætep ȝnið
betpeoh hanðūm ꝼ aɾeoh þuph clað ɼele ðpıncan. To
ælcum ðolȝe ɼealꝼ · ȝeſomna cue meſa cu mıȝoþa ȝe-
pypce to ꝼlynan þa ſpa mon ſapan pypcð mıcelne cıtel
ɼulne · nım̄ þonne apulðop pınðe ꝼ æɾc pınðe ɼlahþopn
pınðe · ꝼ pıp pınðe · ꝼ elm pınðe · ꝼ holen pınðe · ꝼ
pıþıȝ pınðe ꝼ ȝeonȝpe aoe · ɼealh pınðe · ðo þa ealle on mıcelne cıtel ȝeot þa ꝼlynan ðn pyl ſpıþe lanȝe · ðo þonne
oꝼ þa pınða pyl þa ꝼlenan ꝥ hıo ſıe þıcce ðo ſımle ðn

læɼpan cıtel ſpa hıo læɾɾe ſıe · ȝeðt on ɼæt þonne hıo
ȝenoh þıcce ſıe · ȝeæl þonne cealcſtan ſpıðe ꝼ ȝeſamna
ɼðt ꝼ aſıꝼt þuph clað ꝼ þonc cealcſtan eác on þa
ꝼlynan ſmıpe mıð ꝥ ðollı. Eꝼt pıþ þon ılcan ȝenım
hoꝼan ꝼ ȝeloðpypt ꝼ bpune pypt ꝼ luꝼtmocan cpop ꝼ
hapan ſppeoel pyl on butepan ꝼ ppınȝ þonne oꝼ þa
pypta ðo oþpe ðn · pıbban · bıɼceoppypt ȝeappan attoplaþan ðo þa on þa ılcan butepan pyl eꝼt ſpıðe
appınȝ þa ðꝼ ꝥ bıþ ȝoð ðolhɼealꝼ.

.XXXVIIII.

Þeꝛ ſınt læceðomaſ pıþ æloeɾ cynneſ om̄um ꝼ ðn-
ɼeallum ꝼ bancoþūm eahta ꝼ tpentıȝ.

Nım ȝpeneɼ meɼceſ leaꝼ ȝeȝnıð oþþe ȝetpıɼula pıð
eoeðeɼ ðepſtan ſmıpe mıð þy þa ɼapan ſtopa. Þıþ
omum utableȝneðum nım̄ ſup molcen pypo to oealpe ꝼ
beþ mıð þy cealpe. Uıð omum eꝼt ȝenım beopðpæſta ꝼ

drink a full draught *to the sick* after his nights fasting.[1]
A wound drink: pound small the netherward and upward part of ribwort, carline thistle, and the netherward
part of ashthroat, put them into boiling water, rub
between the hands, and strain through a cloth, administer to drink. A salve for every wound: collect
cow dung, cow stale, work up a large kettle full into
a batter as a man worketh soap, then take appletree
rind, and ash rind, sloethorn rind, and myrtle rind,
and elm rind, and holly rind, and withy rind, and the
rind of a young oak, sallow rind, put them all in a
mickle kettle, pour the batter upon *them*, boil very
long, then remove the rinds, boil the batter so that it
be thick, put it ever into a less kettle as it groweth
less, pour it, when it is thick enough, into a vessel,
heat then a calcareous stone thoroughly, and collect
some soot, and sift it through a cloth with the quick-
lime also into the batter, smear the wound therewith.
Again for the same, take hove and silverweed and brownwort, and a bunch of the flowers of "lustmock," and
vipers bugloss, boil in butter and wring the worts off,
and put others in, ribwort, bishopwort, yarrow, atterlothe, put them into the same butter, boil again strongly,
wring these off; that will be a good wound salve.

Book I.
Ch. xxxviii.

xxxix.

1. Here are leechdoms for erysipelatous inflammations
of every sort, and fellons, and leg diseases of every
sort; eight and twenty *in number*.

2. Take leaves of green marche, rub or bruise them
with the lees of vinegar, smear with that the sore
places. For erysipelas which hath broken into blains,
take sour curds, work them to a chalder, and foment with
the chalder. For erysipelatous inflammations again, take

---

[1] Neptig must be understood as neptigum.

fapan Ᵹ æꝥeſ ꝥ hpıce Ᵹ ealðe ꝣꝛuc leꝣe on pıꝥ omena
ꝣeſpelle. Þıꝥ omena ꝣebenſce Sıcce on cealðum pæcene

fol. 38 a.

oꝥ ꝥ hıc aðeaðoð ſıe ceoh ꝥonne ûp ſleah ꝥonne ꝛeoꝥeꝛ
ſceaꝛpan ymb ꝥa poccaſ ucan Ᵹ læc yꝛnan ꝥ ſcıcce ꝥe
hıc pılle; pyꝛc ꝥe ꝛealꝛe ꝥuꝛ · Nım bꝛune pyꝛc Ᵹ menſc
meaꝛ ꝣeallan Ᵹ ꝛeaðe neclan pyl on bucenan Ᵹ ſmıꝛe
mıð Ᵹ beꝥe mıð ꝥam ılcum pyꝛcum.

[1] Þıꝥ ꝥon ılcan ꝣenım anꝣolcpæccean ꝣeꝣnıð ſpıꝥe ðo
eceð co Ᵹ on bınð Ᵹ ſmıꝛe mıð. Þıꝥ ꝥon ılcan ꝣenîm
ſaꝛınan ꝣnıð co ðuſce Ᵹ menꝣ pıꝥ hunıꝣ Ᵹ ſmıꝛe mıð.
Uıð ꝥon ılcan ꝣenım ꝣebꝛæðde æꝣꝛu menꝣ pıð ele
leꝣe ôn Ᵹ beꝥe ſpıðe mıð becan leaꝛum. Eꝛc ꝣenîm
cealꝛeꝛ ſceaꝛn oꝥꝥe ealbeꝛ hꝛyꝥeꝛeſ peaꝛn Ᵹ leꝣe ôn.
Eꝛc pıꝥ ꝥon ꝣenîm heoꝛoceꝛ ſceaꝛoꝥan oꝛ ꝛelle aſcaꝛen
mıð pumıce Ᵹ peſe mıð eceðe Ᵹ ſmıꝛe mıð. Eꝛc ꝣenım
eoꝛoꝥeꝛ ꝣeallan ꝣıꝛ ꝥu næbbe nım oꝥꝛeꝛ ſpıneꝛ ꝣeꝣnıð
Ᵹ ſmıꝛe mıð ꝥy ꝥæꝛ hıc ſaꝛ ſıe. Þıꝥ ꝥon ılcan ꝣenîm
ſpealpan neſc bꝛec mıð ealle apeꝣ Ᵹ ꝣebæꝛn mıð ſceaꝛne
mıð ealle Ᵹ ꝣnıð co ðuſce menꝣ pıꝥ eceð Ᵹ ſmıꝛe mıð.

fol. 38 b.

Þıð ꝥon ılcan ꝣehæc cealð pæceꝛ mıð hacan ıꝛene Ᵹ beꝥe
ꝣelome mıð ꝥy. Þıꝥ hacum omum · nîm beconıcan Ᵹ
peꝛmoð Ᵹ ꝛınul ꝣnıð ôn eala Ᵹ ꝛeðıc ꝛele hîm ðꝛıncan.
Þıꝥ hacum omum nîm ꝛen omꝥꝛan Ᵹ ꝥa ſmalan clacan
pyl on ꝣace meolce Ᵹ ſupe. Þıꝥ hacum omum nîm

---

[1] Plinius Valerianus, fol. 76, d, for eight lines.

dregs of beer, and soap, and the white of an egg, and old groats, lay *this* on against erysipelatous swellings. Against bursting of erysipelatous inflammations, let the man sit in cold water till the sore becometh numbed, then get him up, then strike four scarifying slashes about the pocks on the outside, and let the lymph run as it will. Work thyself a salve thus: take brownwort, and marsh gall, *or marsh gentian*, and red nettle, boil in butter, and smear and bathe with the same worts.

3. For the same, take an earthworm,[1] rub it thoroughly *fine*, add vinegar to it, bind it on and smear therewith. For the same, take savine, rub to dust, and mingle with honey and smear therewith. For the same, take roasted eggs, mingle with oil, lay on, and foment freely with leaves of beet. Again, take a calfs sharn, *that is dung*, or an old bullocks, *still* warm, and lay it on. Again for this *same*, take harts shavings, shaven off the fell or skin with pumice, and wash, *that is macerate*, with vinegar and smear therewith. Again, take a boars gall, if thou have not *that*, take *gall* of another swine, rub and smear with that where it is sore. For that ilk, take a swallows nest, break it away altogether, and burn it with *its* dung and all, and rub it to dust, mingle with vinegar and smear therewith. For the same, heat cold water with a hot iron, and bathe frequently with that. For hot erysipelatous humours, take betony, and wormwood, and fennel, rub them into ale, and radish *with them*, give *the mixture to the sick man* to drink. For hot erysipelatous humours, take fen ompre, *that is water dock*, and the small clote, *that is, cleavers*, boil in goats milk and sup. Against hot erysipelatous humours,

---

[1] Bjorn Haldorson mentions this treatment: the earthworm is called A'mumadkr (read ma'ŏkr), because erysipelas is usually cured by it ; "his lumbricis probari et curari "soleat, cum applicati marcescant "et moriantur." (On A'mumadkr.) A'ma is the Ome of the text.

hunan Ᵹ eꝼelaſtan Ᵹ alexanðꝛian Ᵹ betonican Ᵹ celeþonian Ᵹ cenlicej ꞃæð ðꝛince on pine. Sealꝼ nī́m
ellenef bloſtman Ᵹ þone cꝛop ƿyl on buteꞃan Ᵹ ſmiꞃe
mið · ȝiꝼ hit pille pynſman ſmiꞃe mið æȝeſ ȝeolcan oꝼeꞃ
ſmiꞃe mið þy Ᵹ ðꝛiȝe to ȝleðum oþ þ hit heanð ſie
þpeah þonne apeȝ Ᵹ ſmiꞃe eꝼt mið þæꞃe ꞃealꝼe. Ƿiþ
hatum omum nim pineſ ðꞃæſtan menȝ piþ hꞃeap æȝꞃu
Ᵹ mið ꝼeþeꞃe ſmit ón Ᵹ ne þpeah æꞃ hit hal ſie.
Ƿiþ ſeonðū́m omum nim cneopholen micle æꞃ oðꞃum
mete ðæȝhpam to þam ðolȝe · Ᵹ hꝛyþeꞃeſ ȝeallan
huniȝ ſot · bo toſomne lacna mið. Ƿiþ þon iloan þ iſ·
ꝼic · luſtmoce þa cꝛoppihtan nī́m to baþe Ᵹ ȝebæꞃne
to ꞃealꝼe pulꝼeſ ceacan þa pineſtꝛan Ᵹ þa teþ ſunðoꝛ
menȝ pið huniȝe Ᵹ ſmiꞃe mið Ᵹ ꝼeꝛꞃcne cyꝛe ón leȝe
menȝ þ oþeꝛ pið meoluce ſupe þꝛy moꝛȝenaſ niȝon
ſupan. Ƿiþ bancoþe þ iſ oman nī́m niȝontyne ſhæða
eolonan Ᵹ nyȝon ontꝛan Ᵹ enðleꞃan ꞃeaðeꞃ ſecȝeſ ðo
on eala Ᵹ ðꝛinc micle æꞃ þonne þu ete · Ᵹ þa eolonán
ane ſeoð oþ þ hio meþþe ſie cnupa toſomne ſmiꞃe mið
þæꞃ ut ꞃlea. ðꝛenc piþ onꝼeallum cymeð · pipoꝛ · coſt ·
meꝛceꝛ ꞃæð · ceaſteꝛ pyꝛte ſæð cnua pel ðo on eala.
ðꝛenc piþ onꝼeallum · cnua ón eala oþþe ȝeſeoð celeþonian Ᵹ heah hioloþan biſceop pyꝛt ȝyþꝛiꝼan. ðꝛenc
piþ onꝼeallum · ſiȝꝛonte · cipe · leac · peȝbꝛæðe nioþo-
peaꝛð · ƿyl ealle on pætꞃe Ᵹ ȝeſpet mið huniȝe. ðꝛenc
piþ þon nim þa ſmalan clæꝛeꞃ pyꝛt nioþopeaꝛðe ƿyl on
ealoþ oððe ón beoꝛe. ðꝛenc piþ onꝼealle ƿyl ón ealoð

fol. 39 a.

take horehound, and everlasting, and alexanders, and
betony, and celandine, and charlock seed, drink them
in wine. A salve : take blooms of elder, and the crop,
or bunch or umbel, boil them in butter, and smear
therewith ; if it will, *that is, if it shew a tendency* to
form ratten *or purulent matter,* smear with yolk of
egg; smear over with that, and dry it by gledes, *or hot
coals,* till that it be hard, then wash away and smear
again with the salve. For hot erysipelatous eruptions,
take dregs of wine, mingle with raw eggs, and with a
feather smudge it on, and wash not till *the place* be
hole. For oozing erysipelatous blains, take knee holly,
that is, butchers broom, much ere other meat, daily
for the wound, and put together bullocks gall, honey,
soot; cure therewith. For the same, that is, for *the
disease called* fig, take for a bath *that sort of* "lustmock" which beareth crops *or flower bunches,* and
for a salve, burn a wolfs jaw, the left one, and the
teeth apart, mingle with honey and smear therewith,
and lay on fresh cheese, mingle the other *ingredient*[1]
with milk, sup for three mornings nine sips. For leg
disease, that is hot red blains, take nineteen snips of
helenium, and nine of "ontre," and eleven of red sedge,
put them in ale and drink much ere than thou eat; and
seethe the helenium alone till that it be tender, pound
together, smear therewith where *the disease* may be
striking out. A drink for fellons; cummin, pepper,
costmary, seed of marche, seed of black hellebore, pound
well, put into ale. A drink *or potion* for fellons;
pound in ale or seethe celandine, and elecampane,
bishop wort, githrife. A drink for fellons; sigsonte,
onion, leek, the netherward part of waybroad, boil all
in water and sweeten with honey. A drink for that;
take the netherward part of the small cloverwort, boil
in ale or in beer. A drink for fellons; boil in ale

---

[1] What other ingredient is not clear by the grammatical construction.

ꝼinuꞇlan biꞅceoppiꞃꞇ heah hioloþe. ꝺꞃenc piþ onꝼealle
ꝼyl on ealaꝺ ꞅpꞃinꞡ pyꞃꞇ oþþe on beoꞃe. ꝺꞃenc eꝼꞇ piꝺ
onꝼealle pyl on ealaþ cꞃopleac ꝺpeoꞃꞡe ꝺpoꞅꞇlan pyꞃm
pyꞃꞇ. ꝺꞃenc piþ onꝼealle meꞃꞇe aꞇꞇoꞃlaþe · beꞇoce ·¹
ꞃuꝺe · ꞅecꞡ · onꞇꞃe · claꞇe · biꞅceop pyꞃꞇ ꞡepyꞃꞷ on
ealaꝺ. Eꝼꞇ piþ onꝼealle ꞡeniꞓm æꞇ ꝼꞃuman hæꞃlenne
ꝼꞇiccan oþþe ellenne pꞃiꞇ þinne naman ón aꞃleah þꞃy
ꞃceaꞃpan ón ꞡeꝼylle miꝺ þy blobe þone naman peoꞃp
oꝼeꞃ eaxle oþþe beꞇpeoh þeoh on yꞃꞃenꝺe pæꞇeꞃ ꞡ
ꞅꞇanꝺ oꝼeꞃ þone man þa ꞃceaꞃpan aꞃlea ꞡ þ̶ eall ꞅpi-
ꞡinꝺe ꞡeꝺo.

Piꝺ ónꝼealle ꞡeꝼoh ꝼox aꞃleah óꝼ cucum þone ꞇuxl
læꞇ hleapan apeꞡ binꝺ on næꝼce haꝼa þe ón.

.XL.

Piþ póc aꝺle · onꞃeb hampyꞃꞇ · moþopeaꞃꝺ · ꝼelꝺmoꞃe
niþepeaꞃꝺ onꞃeꝺeꞅ emꝼela ꞡ þaꞃa oþeꞃꞃa ꞇꞃeꞡea ꝼelꝺ-
moꞃan healꝼe læꞃꝼe þonne hampyꞃꞇe cnupa ꞅpiꝺe ꞇo
ꝼomne ꝺo hluꞇꞇoꞃ ealu þ̶ þa pyꞃꞇa oꝼeꞃꞅꞇiꞡe · læꞇ ꞅꞇanꝺan þꞃeo nihꞇ ꝼele ꞃcenc ꝼulne ón moꞃꞡen. ꝺꞃenc piꝺ
ꞃoc aꝺle pyl pæꞇeꞃ ón cꞃoccan ꝺo huniꞡ ón ꝼleoꞇ ꞅimle

þ̶ ꝼám óꝼ oþ þ̶ hiꞇ nelle ma ꝼæman · ꞅup þonne ꞡ ꝺꞃinc
óꝼꞇ ꞡ ꞡelome ꞅpa þu haꞇoꞅꞇ mæꞡe ꞡ miꝺ þꝼ huniꞡe
ꞅmiꞃe þæꞃ hiꞇ uꞇꞃlea on þone póc ne biþ ꞃona nán
ꞇeona. Sealꝼ piþ póc aꝺle pyl on buꞇeꞃan ꞅinꞡꞃenan ·
ꞡeaꞃꞃe · ꞡyþꞃiꝼe ꞃeaꝺꞃe neꞇelan cꞃop. ꝺꞃenc piþ poccum

---

¹ Read beꞇonice.

fennel, bishop wort, elecampane. A drink for a fellon;
boil in ale or in beer springwort. A drink again for
a fellon ; boil in ale cropleek, penny royal, wormwort.
A drink for fellons; marche, attorlothe, betony, rue,
sedge, "ontre," clote, bishop wort, work *them up* in
ale. Again for fellons, take, to begin, a hazel or an
elder stick or spoon, write thy name thereon, cut three
scores on *the place,* fill the name with the blood, throw
it over thy shoulder or between thy thighs into running water and stand over the man. Strike the scores,
and do all that in silence.

For fellon, catch a fox, strike off from him *while*
quick, *that is alive,* the tusk, *or canine tooth,* let *the
fox* run away, bind it in a fawns skin, have it upon
thee.

xl.

For pock disease,[1] *use* "onred," houseleek, the nether
part of it, fieldmore, the nether *part of it;* of "onred"
an equal quantity, and of the two others by half less
of the fieldmore *or carrot* than of the houseleek,
pound them thoroughly together, add so much clear
ale as may mount above the worts ; let them stand
three nights, administer in the morning a cup full.
A drink for pock disease; boil water in a crock, add
honey, skim continually the foam away till it will
foam no more ; then sip and drink oft and whilom
as thou hottest may, and smear with the honey where
it may be breaking out into the pock, soon there will
be no mischief. A salve for pock disease ; boil in
butter singreen, yarrow, githrife, the crop, *or flower
head,* of red nettle. A drink against pocks; bishop

---

[1] *Small pox.* The disease was unknown in classical medicine ; it
appeared in France in 565, A.D.,
and in Arabia in 572, A.D. The
Arabic physician Razi treats of it
in a separate monograf about 923,
A.D., not long before this copy of
the Leech Book was written out.

biſceop pypt · attoplaþan · ſppinȝpypt · olatan moþepeapðe on ealað ȝepoph. Þiþ poccum ſpiðe ſœal món bloð lætan ȝ ðpincan amylte butepan bollan fulne · ȝif hie utylean ælcne man ſœall apeȝ abelfan mið þopne · ȝ þonne pin oððe alop[1] ðpenc ðpype on innan þonne ne beoð hy ȝeſyne.

Þiþ poccum ȝenim ȝloffypt apyl on butepan ȝ ſmipe mið.

.XLI.

Þiþ innan onfealle næȝlæp[2] hatte pypt ſuþepno ſio bið ȝob to etanne piþ innan ónfelle on niht nejtiȝ. Þiþ innan onfealle pyl elonan eluhtpan ón ealað ðpinc hateſ bollan fulne. Eft pypttðpenc óf pepmode betonican · of þæpe pupan peȝbpæðan ðpince fela nihta. Þiþ þæpe ȝeolpan able · hune · biſceop pypt · helbe · hofe menȝe þa toȝæðepie ðo ælcpe ȝoðe hanð fulle maxpypte ðo to pofe ambep fulne ȝ to ſtanbæþe ðyþhoman · hune pepmoð. Stanbæþ[3] ðpince ðpenc óf omppan óf pine ȝ of pætpe · ȝeſpete ſpiðe.

fol. 40 b.

.XLII.

[4]Of ȝeal able ſio biþ of þæpe ȝeolpan · cymeþ ȝpeat yfel ſio biþ ealpa abla picuſt · þonne ȝepeaxeð on innan unȝemet pætan þiſ fint tacn · þ him ſe lichoma eall abitepað ȝ aȝeolpað ſpa ȝoð feoluc · ȝ him beoð unðep tunȝan tulȝe ſpeapte æðpa ȝ yfele ȝ him bið micȝe ȝeolu · læt him of lunȝen æðpe blod fele him óft ſtypȝenðne ðpenc ſtanbaðu ȝelome. [5]Þypc him ðonne

---

[1] Alop, *alnus glutinosa*, has no medical properties. Probably the Alnus nigra, now *Rhamnus frangula*, Sppaeen, was meant by the Latin author copied.

[2] Read cunæȝlæffe, *cynoglossum*.
[3] By Stanbæþ understand Stanbæþðpieno, or amend thus.
[4] 'Iктεроς.
[5] Cf. Plinius Valerianus, fol. 61 d.

wort, attorlothe, springwort, the netherward part of clote, *or burdock,* worked up in ale. Against pocks, a man shall freely employ bloodletting and drink melted butter, a bowl full *of it :* if they break out one must delve away each one *of them* with a thorn ; and then let him drip wine or alder drink within them, then they will not be seen, *or no traces will remain.*

Against pocks : take glovewort, boil in butter, and smear therewith.

xli.

For inward fellon, there is a southern wort hight cynoglosson, which is good to eat against inward fellon, at night fasting. Against inward fellon, boil helenium *and* lupins in ale, drink a bowl full of the hot *infusion.* Again, a wort drink from wormwood *and* betony, *and* from the rough waybroad *or plaintain,* let him drink it many nights. For the yellow disorder, *or jaundice, hore*hound, bishop wort, tansy, earth ivy, mingle them together, of each employ a good handful, add of mash-wort, for an infusion an amber full, and for a stone bath *use* dithhomar, *or papyrus,* horehound, *and* wormwood. A stone bath; *that must be, to use with a stone bath ;* let *the man* drink a drink from ompre *or sorrel,* from wine and from water; sweeten thoroughly.

xlii.

From gall disease, that is from the yellow *jaundice,* cometh great evil; it is of all diseases most powerful, when there wax within *a man,* unmeasured humours; these are the tokens : that *the patients* body all becometh bitter and as yellow as good silk ; and under the root of his tongue there be swart veins and pernicious, and his urine is yellow. Let him blood from the lung vein, give him often a stirring drink, stone baths

ftilne ðpenc óf omppan on pine Ᵹ on pætpe Ᵹ ón þam
baðe ȝehpilce monȝene ðpince mylfce ðpincan fio ȝebet
þa bitepneppe þæf ȝeallan.

.XLIII.

fol. 41 a.

[1] Þiþ pæcep bollan betonican fpilce anef peninȝef ȝe-
pæȝe on peapmum pætepe ȝuiðe ðpince þny ðaȝaf ælce
ðæȝ ȝoðne bollan fulne. Eft ȝením ærchpotan oþþe
pealpypte pyttpuman þæf feapef feopen cuclepaf fulle
ȝeðo on bollan fulne pinef fele ðpincan.

.XLIIII.

Þiþ cancep aðle þ if bite · fupe · fealt · pibbe ·
æȝ · fót · ȝebæpneð lam · hpætef fmeðma menȝ pið
æȝpu meðopypt æfepþe acpunð · apulðop pinð · flah
þupn pinðe · ȝif fe bite peaxe on men ȝepipc nipne
cealpe Ᵹ leȝe ón clænfa[2] þa punðe mið.

Þiþ cancepe ón cypepenum fæte ȝebæpn fpefl ȝeȝnið to ðufte fpa þu fmaloft mæȝe Ᵹ afift þuph cla ð
menȝ pið ealðe fapan Ᵹ fie fpefl picpa ðo huniȝef
teapef meðmicel to[3] fceape · ȝif to ftið fie þrem mið þf
huniȝe leȝe on ȝeopmen leaf þonne hit haliȝe pyl on
butepan ȝeacef fupan Ᵹ finȝpenan Ᵹ puðupopan fmipe
mið þa offaf þæp hit peaðiȝe læt þa oðpe fealfe clæn-
fian þ ðolh ne ðo nan pætep to. Sealf piþ cancpe ·
ȝením cu meoluc butan pætepe læt peopþan to fletum
ȝeþþep to butepan ne pæpc on pætpe. Ním fiȝel-
hpeoppan þa fmalan unpæpcene ðo clæne cnua fpiðe
ȝemenȝ pel pið þæpe butepan ðo on pannan ofep fyp
apyl fpiðe afeoh pel þuph cla ð lacna mið þy. Þiþ cancep
aðle · ác pinð ón nopþan tpeope be eopþan · Ᵹ meðo-

fol. 41 b.

[1] "Tðpeнψ.
[2] clæna, MS.

[3] Supply a point after to, not in
MS. Read þæn.

often. Work him then a composing drink of sorrel in wine and in water, and in the bath, every morning, let him drink a mulled draught; it will amend the bitterness of the gall.

xliii.

For dropsy, rub betony, as much as a penny weight, in warm water, let *the patient* drink for three days, each day, a good bowl full. Again, take of the juice of the roots of ashthroat or of dwarf elder four spoons full, put them into a bowl full of wine, give them to drink *to the patient.*

xliv.

1. Against the disease cancer, that is, bite: sorrel, salt, ribwort, egg, soot, burnt loam, smede *or fine flour* of wheat; mingle with eggs, meadow sweet, "referth," oak rind, appletree rind, sloethorn rind: if the cancer wax on a man, work up some new chalder and lay on; cleanse the wound therewith.

2. Against cancer; burn sulfur in a copper vessel, rub it to dust, as small as thou may, and sift through a cloth, mingle with old soap, and let the sulfur predominate, add a moderate quantity of virgin honey; see if it be too stiff, moisten it with the honey; lay on a mallow leaf; when it healeth, boil in butter cuckoo sour and singreen and woodroffe, smear therewith the borders, where it is red; make the other salve cleanse the wound, put no water. A salve for cancer; take cows milk, without water, make it become cream, turn it to butter, wash it not in water. Take the small turnsole unwashen, make it clean, pound it thoroughly, mix it well with the butter, put it into a pan over the fire, boil it thoroughly, strain well through a cloth, cure therewith. Against disease of cancer: oak rind on the north side of the tree by the earth, and the

pypꞇ nioþepeapð · æꝼeꞃðe niþepeapþ · ouneglæꝼꝼe nio-
þopeapþ · ðo ealpa emꝼela ᵹecnua ꞇo ðuꝼꞇe · ðo henne
æᵹeꝼ ꝥ hpiꞇe ꞇo · Ᵹ huniᵹ ðo beᵹea emꝼela ᵹemenᵹ
pið þam ðuꝼꞇûm clæm on ðone cancep ne ðo nan
pæꞇep ꞇo.

.XLV.

Þiþ aꞇꞇpe ðpencaꝼ Ᵹ læceðomaꝼ · beꞇonican mepce ·
pepmoð · ꝼinul · ꝛeðic · cnua on ealað ꝛele ðpincan.
Þið aꞇꞇpe beꞇonican Ᵹ þa ꝼmalan aꞇꞇoꝛlaþan ðo on
haliᵹ pæꞇep ðpinc ꝥ pæꞇep Ᵹ eꞇ þa pypꞇa. Uið ælcum
aꞇꞇpe · ꝛeðic Ᵹ claꞇe eꞇe æp ne mæᵹ þe nan man aꞇꞇpe
apypðan. Þið ælcum aꞇꞇpe biꝛceoppypꞇ niþepeapð Ᵹ
elehꞇpe · Ᵹ ꝼppinᵹ pypꞇ nioþepeapð eoꝛopþpoꞇan · Ᵹ
claꞇan · apyl on ealað ꝛele ðpincan ᵹelome. Ᵹiꝼ næð-
ðpe ꝛlea man þone blacan ꝼneᵹl apæꝛc on haliᵹ pæꞇpe
ꝛele ðpincan oþþe hpæꞇ hpeᵹa ꝡæꝛ þe ꝼpam ꝼcoꞇꞇum
come. Eꝼꞇ peᵹbpæðan ᵹeᵹnið ꝼpiþe ðꞃínc on pine.
Þiþ næðpan biꞇe beꞇonican ꝥꞇe þꝛy peneᵹaꝼ ᵹepeᵹe ðo
on þꝛy bollan ꝛulle pineꝼ ꝛele ðpincan.

Þiþ næðpan biꞇe eꝼꞇ ꝼíꝛleaꝛe appunᵹenu Ᵹ piþ ꝼín
ᵹemenᵹeð ᵹoð biþ ꞇo ðpincanne. Viþ næðpan biꞇe eꝼꞇ
celeþonie ᵹeꞇpiꝼulaðe ðpince ón neahꞇ neꝛꞇiᵹ · III.
bollan ꝛulle. Þiþ næðpan ꝛleᵹe ꝼppinᵹpypꞇ · aꞇoꝛlaþan ·
eoꝛopþpoꞇan · biꝛceoppypꞇ pypc ꞇo ðpence.

Þiþ þon þe môn þicᵹe aꞇop · ᵹenim þa hapan hunan
ᵹepypc micelne ðæl Ᵹ næðeppypꞇe cnua ꞇoᵹæðepe · Ᵹ
ppinᵹ ꝥ ꝛeap ðo pineꝼ þꝛie mel ón Ᵹ ꝛele ðpincan.
Þiþ næðpan ꝛliꞇe nîm peᵹbpæðan · Ᵹ aᵹpimonian · Ᵹ
næððep pypꞇ ꝛele ᵹeᵹniðene ón pine ðpincan · Ᵹ pypc
ꝛealꝼe oꝛ þâm ilcum pypꞇum · Ᵹ nîm þa aᵹpimonian

netherward part of meadow sweet, the netherward part of " æferthe," the netherward part of cynoglosson, employ of all equal quantities, pound to dust, add thereto the white of a hens egg, and honey, employ equal quantities of the two, mingle with the dusts, clam *or make it cling* on the cancer, put no water to it.

xlv.

1. Drinks *or potions* and leechdoms against poison. Pound in ale betony, marche, wormwood, fennel, radish; administer *this* to drink. Against poison; put in holy water betony and the small atterlothe, drink the water and eat the worts. Against any poison ; eat ere *the danger cometh* radish and clote ; no man may *then* do thee a mischief with poison. Against any poison ; boil the netherward part of bishopwort and lupin, and the netherward part of springwort, everthroat, and clote in ale ; give to drink frequently. If an adder strike a man, or *for* whatever of that which cometh of shots, wash the black snail in holy water, give *to the sick* to drink. Again, rub waybroad thoroughly *fine*, drink it in wine. For bite of snake, put so much of betony as may weigh three pennies into three bowls full of wine, give it *the man* to drink.

2. For bite of snake again ; cinqfoil wrung and mingled with wine is good to drink. For bite of snake again; celandine bruised, at night fasting, let *the man* drink three bowls full. For adders wound, work euforbia, attorlothe, stemless carline, ammi, into a drink.

3. In case a man swallow poison, take then horehound, work up a mickle deal of it, and adderwort, pound them together and wring the juice, pour thereon three measures of wine and give this *to the poisoned man* to drink. For hurt from snake ; take waybroad, and agrimony, and adderwort, administer them rubbed *up* in wine to be drunk ; and work *up* a salve of the

ᵹepypc anne hᴘinᵹ ymb þone ꞅlice utan ne oꞅepꞅtihð
hit ꞅuꞃþoꞃ · ⁊ binð þa pyᴘce eꞅt oꞅeᴘ þ̵ bolh.   Þiþ
næbᴘan ꞅleᵹe ðo oꞅ þinū̄m eaᴘan þ̵ teoᴘo ⁊ ꞅmiᴘe mið
ymb ⁊ ꞅinᵹ þᴘiᴘa þæꞅ halᵹan Scē Iohanneꞅ ᵹebeð ⁊
ᵹealðoᴘ.

<table>
<tr><td>

From the
legendary
Assumptio nc̄i
Iohannis
apostoli.

* phalangius AL

fol. 43 a.

</td><td>

ðeuꞅ meuꞅ et paceᴘ et ꞅiliuꞅ et ꞅpiᴘicuꞅ Sanccuꞅ.
Cui ōmnia ꞅubiecta ꞅunt.   Cui omniꞅ cᴘeatuᴘa be-
Seᴘuic et omniꞅ poceꞅtaꞅ ꞅubiecta eSt et mecuic et
expaueꞅcic et ðᴘaco ꞅuᵹic et ꞅilic uiᴘeᴘa et ᴘubeta
illa que ðicicuᴘ ᴘana quieta toᴘᴘeꞅcic et ꞅcoᴘᴘiuS ex-
cinᵹuicuᴘ et ᴘeᵹuluꞅ uincicuᴘ et ꞅpelaiuꞅ * nihil noxium
oᴘeᴘacuᴘ et omnia ueuenata et aðhuc ꞅeᴘocioᴘa ᴘepen-
cia¹ et animalia noxia te ueᴘencuᴘ² et omneꞅ aðueᴘꞅe
Saluci³ humane ᴘaðioeꞅ aᴘeꞅcunt.   Tu ðomine excinᵹue
hōc uenenatum uiᴘuꞅ excinᵹue oᴘeᴘatjoneꞅ eiuꞅ moᴘci-
ꞅeᴘaꞅ et uiᴘeꞅ quaꞅ In ꞅe habet euacua et ða In con-
ꞅpeccu tuo ōmnibuꞅ quoꞅ tu cᴘeaꞅtᴊ · oculoꞅ ut uiðeant
auᴘeꞅ ut auðiant coᴘ ut maᵹnicuðinem tuām Incelle·
ᵹant ·⁴ et cum hōc ðixiꞅꞅet totum ꞅemet ᴊᴘꞅum ꞅiᵹno
cᴘuciꞅ aᴘmauit et bibic totum quoð eᴘat In calice ·
peᴘ ᴘiᵹnum Sancte cᴘuciꞅ · et peᴘ te xᴘ̄e ihū et⁵
ðeo ꞅū̄mmo patᴘe uiuiS ꞅaluatoᴘ munði In unicate
ꞅpiᴘicuꞅ Sancti peᴘ omnia Sæcula Sæculoᴘum amen ;

</td></tr>
</table>

Þiþ ꞅleoᵹenðum atᴘe ⁊ ælcum æteᴘnum ꞅpile · on
ꞅᴘiᵹeðæᵹe aþþeᴘ buteᴘan þe ꞅie ᵹemolcen oꞅ aneꞅ bleoꞅ
nytne oððe hinðe · ⁊ ne ꞅie ᴘiþ pætᴘe ᵹemenᵹeð ·
aꞅinᵹ oꞅeᴘ niᵹon ꞅiþū̄m lecania · ⁊ niᵹon ᴘiþum pateᴘ
noꞅteᴘ · ⁊ niᵹon ꞅiþum þiꞅ ᵹealðoᴘ. Acᴘæ · æᴘcᴘæ ·
æᴘnem · naðᴘe · æᴘcuna hel · æᴘnem · niþæᴘn · æᴘ ·
aꞅan · buiþine · aðcᴘice · æᴘnem · meoðᴘe · æᴘnem ·
æþeᴘn · æᴘnem · allū · honoᴘ · ucuꞅ · iðaᴘ · aðceᴘc ·
cunolaᴘi · ᴘaticamo · helæ · icaꞅ xᴘica · hæle · toðæᴘc ·
teᴘa · ꞅueli · cuꞅ · ᴘoðateᴘ · plana · uili · þ̵ ðeah to

---

¹ ᴘepentᴊe, MS.
² tenebantuᴘ, MS.
³ aðueᴘꞅe Salutis, MSS.

⁴ -ᵹunt, MS.
⁵ Supply cum. This doxology is
an addition, not in the legend.

same worts, and then take agrimony, form a ring around
the incision on the outside, *the mischief* will proceed no
further, and bind the wort also over the sore. For
stroke of viper, remove from thine ears the wax and
smear around therewith, and say thrice the prayer
of Saint John.

4. Dominus meus et pater et filius et spiritus sanctus;
cui omnia subiecta sunt; cui omnis creatura deservit
et omnis potestas subiecta est et metuit et expavescit;
et draco fugit, et silet vipera, et rubeta illa quæ dicitur
rana quieta torpescit, et scorpius extinguitur et regulus
the basilisc vincitur et σπήλαιος[a] nihil noxium opera-
tur, et omnia venenata et adhuc ferociora, repentia et
animalia noxia, te verentur; et omnes adversæ saluti
humanæ radices arescunt; tu, domine, extingue hoc ve-
nenatum virus, extingue operationes eius mortiferas, et
vires, quas in se habet, evacua, et da in conspectu tuo
omnibus quos tu creasti, oculos ut videant, aures ut au-
diant, cor ut magnitudinem tuam intelligant. Et cum
hoc dixisset, totum semet ipsum signo crucis armavit,
et bibit totum quod erat in calice: per signum sanctæ
crucis, et per te Christe Iesu, *qui cum* domino summo
patre vivis, salvator mundi, in unitate Spiritus Sancti,
per omnia secula seculorum. Amen.

[a] The tarantula lies hid in a hole watching for prey.

5. For flying venom and every venomous swelling,
on a Friday churn butter, which has been milked from
a neat or hind *all* of one colour; and let it not be
mingled with water, sing over it nine times a litany,
and nine times the Pater noster, and nine times this
incantation. *The charm is said in the table of contents
to be Scottish, that is Gaelic,[1] but the words themselves
seem to belong to no known language.* That is valid

---

[1] Or Gadhelic, or Irish. An early
instance of the mention of Ireland,
as not Scotland, occurs in Ælfrics
Homilies, vol. ii. p. 346.

ælcũm ꞇ huꞃu to beopum bolȝꞇm.　Sume an ꞃoꞃð ꝥ
næbꞃan bιte læꞃað to cꞃeþenne ꝥ ιꞅ ꞅaul ne mæȝ lĩm
beꞃꞃan.　Þιð næbꞃan ꞅlιte ȝιꞅ he beȝet ꞇ yt ꞃꞇnbe ꞅιo
þe cymð oꞃ neoꞃxna ponȝe ne beꞃeð hꞇm nan aꞇꞇeꞃ·

þonne cꞃæþ ꞃe þe þaꞃ boc ꞃꞃaꞇ ꝥ hꞇo pæꞃe toꞃ
beȝete.

Ȝιꞅ hꞃa bꞃꞇnce ꞃyꞃm on pæꞇeꞃe óꞅ ꞅnιðe ꞅceap ꞃaðe
bꞃꞇnce haꞇ ꝥ ꞃceapeꞃ blob·　ȝιꞅ mon ꞅιe ꞃyꞃꞇum ꞃoꞃ-
boꞃen ꞃele ꞅpꞃꞇnȝpyꞃꞇ ꝥ he eꞇe ꞇ halιȝ pæꞇeꞃ ꞃupe.
Þιþ þon þe mon ꞅιe ꞃoꞃboꞃen·　ȝιꞅ he hæꞃþ on hꞇm
ꞅcyꞇꞇιꞅc peax·　þa ꞅmalan aꞇꞇoꞃlaðan oððe ón aꞃylbum
ealað bꞃꞇnce ne mæȝ hꞇne pyꞃꞇum ꞃoꞃbeꞃan.

.XLVI.

Ȝιꞅ ana pyꞃm on men peaxe·　ꞅmꞇꞃe mιb þæꞃe blacan
ꞃealꞃe ȝιꞅ he uꞇ þuꞃh eꞇe ꞇ þyꞃel ȝepyꞃce·　ȝeꞃĩm
hunιȝeꞃ bꞃoꞃan bꞃype on þæꞇ þyꞃel·　haꞃa þonne ȝe-
bꞃꞇocen ȝlæꞃ ȝeaꞃa ȝeȝꞃunden ꞅceab on ꝥ þyꞃel þonne
ꞃona ꞅpa he þæꞃ onbιꞃιȝð þonne ꞅpιlꞇ he.　Sealꞃ pιð
anapyꞃme·　þuꞅ món ꞃceal pyꞃcean.　ȝeꞃĩm quinque-
ꞃoꞃ꞉an ꝥ ιꞅ ꞃιꞃleaꞃc·　ꞃuban pyl on buꞇeꞃan ȝeꞅpeꞇ mιb
hunιȝe.

bꞃenc quinqueꞃoꞃ꞉an ꝥ ιꞅ ꞃιꞃleaꞃe ꞃele ón ealað bꞃꞇn-
can þꞃιꞇιȝ nιhta.　bꞃenc pιð þon ꞃæbιceꞅ ꞅæb ꞇ cauleꞃ
ȝꞃιb ón eala oþþe on ꞃín bꞃꞇnce pιþ anapyꞃme lanȝe ꞇ
ȝelome oþ ꝥ ꞃel ꞅιe.　Clam pιþ þon þa ꞃeaban ꞇιȝelan
ȝecꞃupa to buꞅꞇe ȝemenȝ pιð ȝꞃuꞇ abꞃæb cιcel leȝe ón

ꝥ bolh pyꞃc oþeꞃꞃe ȝιꞅ þeaꞃꞅ ꞅιe.

for every, even for deep wounds. Some teach *us* against bite of adder *to* speak one word, that is, Faul;[1] it may not hurt him. Against bite of snake, if *the man* procures and eateth rind, which cometh out of paradise, no venom will damage him. Then said he that wrote this book, that *the rind* was hard gotten.

6. If one drink a creeping thing in water, let him cut into a sheep instantly, let him drink the sheeps blood hot. If a man be "restrained" with worts,[2] give him springwort for him to eat, and let him sup up holy water. In case that a man be "withheld;" if he hath on him Scottish wax, *and* the small atterlothe; or let him drink it in boiled ale, he may not be "restrained" by worts.

xlvi.

1. If Ons worm[a] grow in a man, smear with the black salve. If *the worm* eat through to the outside and make a hole, take a drop of honey, drop it on the hole, then have broken glass ready ground, shed it on the hole, then as soon as *the worm* tastes of this he will die. A salve against an Ons worm, thus shall a man work it : take cinquefoil, that is five leaved grass, and rue, boil *them* in butter, sweeten with honey. [a See Glossary.]

2. A drink; administer in ale cinquefoil, that is five leaved grass, *or potentilla,* to drink for thirty nights. A drink for that; rub *down* into ale or into wine seed of radish and of colewort, let *the man* drink that long and frequently against Ons worm, till that *his* case be bettered. A plaster for the same : pound to dust a red tile *or brick,* mingle with groats, bake a cake, lay it on the wound ; work another *plaster* if need be.

---

[1] Cf. "Duo," to drive away scorpions, Plinius, lib. xxviii. 5.

[2] From hæmebþinȝ. See ȝoþbeþan in Glossary.

H 2

. XLVII.

Læcebomaſ pið þeoparðlum · æꞃcꞃinð · æꞃpan ꞃinð · elin ꞃinð · cꞃicꞃinð · ſio micle poꞃþiȝ netle nioþopeaꞃð · peꞃmoð · hinðhioloðe · beſoꞃeaða þa ꞃinða ealle utan ꝼ ȝecnua ſpiꞃe pyl toſomne · ðo ealꞃa emꞃela oꝼ ȝeot mið hluttꞃe ealoþ læt ſtanðan þone ðꞃenc nihteꞃnc ón ꝼate æꞃi món hine ðꞃincan ꞃille · ðꞃince ón moꞃ-ȝenne ſcenc ꝼulne þiꞃeꞃ ðꞃenceꞃ · to mibbeꞃ meꞃȝeneſ ſtanðe eaſt peaꞃð ꝼ bebeoðe hine ȝoðe ȝeoꞃnlice ꝼ hine ȝeꞃeniȝe cyꞃꞃe hine funȝonȝeꞃ ymb æꝼteꞃi þam ðꞃence ȝanȝe ꞃiþþan ꝼ ſtanðe ſume hpile æꞃi he hine ꞃeſte ȝeote ſpa micel ón ſpa he ꞃæꞃi oꝼ ðo · ðꞃince þiꞃne ðꞃenc niȝon niht ꝼ þicȝe ſpilcne mete ſpa he ꞃille. ðꞃenc ꞃiþ þeoꞃable · funð[1] ompꞃan ymb ðelꝼ ſinȝ þꞃiꞃa pateꞃ nꞃi · bꞃeð úp þonne þu cpeþe ſet[2] libeꞃa noſ a malo · ȝenim þæꞃe ꝼiꝼ ſnæða ꝼ ſeoꝼon piꞃoꞃi coꞃn ȝecnua toȝæðeꞃe ꝼ þonne þu þ pyꞃce ſinȝ .xii. ſiþum

fol. 44 b. þone ꞃealm · miꞃeꞃeꞃe mei ðeuſ · ꝼ ȝloꞃia In excelꞃiſ ðeo · ꝼ pateꞃi noꞃteꞃi · oꝼȝeot þonne mið pine þonne ðæȝ ꝼ niht ꞃcaðe[3] ðꞃince þonne þone ðꞃenc ꝼ beꞃꞃeoh ðe peaꞃme. ȝenim þonne hinð hioloþan ane[4] óꝼȝeot mið pæteꞃe ðꞃince oþꞃe mönȝne ſcenc ꝼulne þonne oþꞃe ꞃiþe ſeoꝼon ſnæða ꝼ niȝon piꞃoꞃicoꞃn · þꞃiðban ꞃiþe niȝon ſnæða ꝼ xi. piꞃoꞃicoꞃn. ðꞃinc ꞃiþþan ſpiðne ðꞃenc ꞃeþe ꞃille úp yꞃnan ꝼ óꝼ ðune · læt þonne bloð unðeꞃi ancleoꞃ. .

---

[1] Read ſuꞃe ?
[2] That is, feb ; the MSS. usually set.

[3] At morning twilight.
[4] Some words are here, it seems, omitted.

xlvii.

1. Leechdoms for "dry" diseases; ᵃ ash rind, aspen rind, elm rind, quickbeam rind, the netherward part of the mickle highway nettle, wormwood, hindheal, *that is, water agrimony,* empurple all the rinds on the outside, and pound them thoroughly, boil them together, apply equal quantities of all, souse them with clear ale, then let the drink stand for the space of a night in a vessel, before a man shall choose to drink it. Let him in the morning drink a cup full of this drink; in the middle of the morning hours,[1] let him stand towards the east, let him address himself to God earnestly, and let him sign himself with the sign of the cross, let him *also* turn himself about as the sun goeth *from east to south and west;* after the drink let him next go and stand some while ere he repose himself; let him pour as much *liquid into the vessel* as he removes from it : let him drink this potion for nine nights and eat what meat he will. A drink for the "dry" disease; delve about sour ompre, *that is, sorrel dock,* sing thrice the Pater noster, jerk it up, then while thou sayest sed libera nos a malo, take five slices of it and seven pepper corns, bray them together, and while thou be working it, sing twelve times the psalm Miserere mei, deus, and Gloria in excelsis deo, and the Pater noster, then pour *the stuff* all over with wine, when day and night divide, then drink the dose and wrap thyself up warm. Then take hindheal alone, souse it with water, drink the next morning a cup full, then the next time seven slices and nine pepper corns, the third time nine slices and eleven pepper corns; afterwards drink a strong potion which will run up and adown ;² then let blood below *the* ancle.

---

[1] This should be read as beginning the morning at dawn, and ending it at unbegun, our nine o'clock. The middle will be about seven on the average.

² Purgative and emetic.

ðꞃenc piþ þeoꞃaðle nime healf puðu ⁊ bulentꞃan þa
fmalan · þunoꞃ pyꞃt · puðupeaxan nioþoꞃeaꞃð · pealpyꞃt
nioþoꞃeaꞃðc ᵹecnua þonne ealle toꞃomne pyꞃce him to
ðꞃence ðo on pylifc ealo · oþþe on beoꞃ læt ftanðan
nihteꞃne · ðꞃince þonne fpilcne niᵹon moꞃᵹenaf · nime
þy teoþan moꞃᵹne þæꞃ ðꞃincef tꞃa bleða fulle · bepylle

fol. 45 a.

on ane ⁊ þa pyꞃta fien miß aꞃeoh þuꞃh claþ aꞃete
up þæꞃ hit eoꞃþan hꞃinan ne mæᵹe oþ þ hit mon
ðꞃincan mæᵹe ;¹ þonne þu hit² ᵹeðꞃuncen hæbbe be-
pꞃeoh þe peaꞃme liᵹe on þa fiðan þe he þonne ᵹetenᵹe
fie · ᵹif he³ on þam mnoþe bið þonne aðꞃifð hine þef
ðꞃinc ut. Sealf piþ þeoꞃe nim ᵹaꞃleac ⁊ ᵹꞃeate pyꞃt ·
peꞃmoð leaðe⁴ netlan ciß ᵹecnua fmale ⁊ hioꞃot fmeꞃu
ᵹemanᵹ þ hit fie fpilc fpa ðah ðo þonne on lmenne
claß pyꞃme þonne ᵹehpæþeꞃ ᵹe þ lic ᵹe þa ꞃealfe to
fyꞃe þonne þu hit fmyꞃian pille þæꞃ fio aðl fie fylᵹe
him miß þiꞃfe fealfe ⁊ miß þyꞃ⁵ ðꞃence. ðꞃenc piþ
þeoꞃaðle ðꞃiᵹe peꞃimoð · ꞃeðic pealpyꞃt ealꞃa þꞃeoꞃa
em ꞃela ðo on calu ᵹmiß pel læte æt æꞃeftan ftanðan
þꞃeo niht æꞃ þon he hine ðꞃince · ⁊ ꞃiþþan he hine
ðꞃince ymb feoꞃon niht ꞃoꞃlæte blod unðeꞃ þam ancleope ðꞃince ꞃoꞃþ þone ðꞃenc ꞃeoꞃeꞃtyne niht · læte
þonne eꞃt blod unðeꞃ þam oꞃꞃan ancleope. ðꞃince
ealleꞃ þone ðꞃenc þꞃitiᵹ nihta on unðeꞃn ᵹoðe bleðe
fulle oþꞃe þonne þu ꞃeftan pille. Þiþ þeoꞃpyꞃme on
ꞃet nim þa ꞃeaðan netlan ᵹecnua ðo pæteꞃ to leᵹe on
haꞇne ftan læt aꞃꞃeoþan binß on þone ꞃot nealhteꞃne.
Eꞃt ꞃealf ætan ᵹecnua leᵹe on. Þiþ þeoꞃe on ꞃet
ᵹeᵹniß pealpyꞃt on ᵹefpet pin · ⁊ hꞃitcpuðu ⁊ pipoꞃ
ðꞃince þ.

---

¹ næᵹe, MS.
² hꞇ, MS.
³ The only antecedent abl ought
to be followed by feminine pronouns.

⁴ This word seems corrupt ; perhaps ꞃeaðe ; red nettle, a plant
of it.
⁵ þyꞃ, MS., understand as þyꞃ um.

fol. 45 b.

2. A drink against the "dry" disease; take field balm[a] and the small bulentse, thunderwort,[b] the nether part of woodwax, the netherward part of wallwort, then pound all together, work it for him (*the patient*) for a drink, put it into foreign ale or beer, let it stand for the space of a night, then let him drink such *drink* for nine mornings, take on the tenth morning two cups full of the drink, boil them both in one, and let the worts be therewith, strain through a cloth, set it up where it may not touch the earth, till that a man may drink it; when thou have drunken it, wrap thee up warm; lie on the side to which the *pain* is incident, if it be in the inwards, then this drink will drive it out. A salve against the "dry" disease; take garlic and great wort, wormwood, a plant of nettle, pound small, and along with it harts grease, that it may be such as dough is, place it then on a linen cloth, then warm both the body and the salve at the fire; when thou wilt smear *the body or the spot* where the disease may be, follow up *the patient* with this salve and with this drink. A drink for the "dry" disease; dry wormwood, radish, wallwort,[c] of all these equal quantities, put into ale, rub *the herbs down* well, *the man* should have *the liquid* stand at first for three nights before he drink it, and subsequently let him drink it for about seven nights, let him let blood under the ancle, let him drink the drink straight on for fourteen nights; let him next let blood under the other ancle. Drink the dose for thirty nights in all, a good cup full at nine A.M. or when thou wilt go to bed. For a "dry" worm in the foot; take the red nettle, pound it, add water to it, lay it on a hot stone, make it froth, bind it on the foot for the space of a night. Again, a salve; pound oats, lay on. For the "dry" rot in the foot, triturate wallwort into sweetened wine, and mastic and pepper; let him drink that.

Book I.
Ch. xlvii.
[a] *Calamintha nepeta.*
[b] *Sempervivum tectorum.*
[c] *Sambucus ebulus.*

Oxa læpðe þifne læcebom · ʒenime pealpypt ꝉ cluf-
þunʒ ꝉ cneopholen ꝉ efelaftan ꝉ camecon ꝉ tunʒilfin-
pypt · VIIII. bjiune bifceop pypt · ꝉ attoplaþan ꝉ ꝓeaðe
netlan · ꝉ ꝓeaðe hofan ·ꝉ pepmoð ꝉ ʒeaꝓpan · ꝉ hunan
ꝉ ðolʒꝓunan · ꝉ ðpeoꝓʒe ðpoftlan ðo ealle þaf pypta
on pylifc ealo ꝉ ðꝓmce þonne niʒon ðaʒaf ꝉ bloð læte.
Þiþ þeoꝓ pæꝓce pypc to ðꝓence alexanðꝓe · finfulle
peꝓmoð · tpa cneopholen · faluian · fafine · pealmoꝓe ·
lufeftice · fefeꝓ fuʒe · meꝓce · coft · ʒaꝓleac · æjc-
þꝓotu · betonice · bifceop pypt · on tpybꝓopnúm ealað
ʒepyꝓce fpet mið huniʒe ðꝓmc niʒon moꝓʒenaf nanne
oþeꝓne pætan ðꝓmc æfteꝓ fpiþne ðꝓenc ꝉ læt bloð
oxa læꝓðe þifne læceðom. Þiþ þeoꝓe cneopholen niþe-
peaꝓð · acumba · cpið · ꝉ bꝓune pypt ealꝓa emfela ðo
ón pilifc ealu · bepyl oþ þꝓiððan ðæl ꝉ ðꝓmce þa hpile
þa he þuꝓfe · ꝉ þæꝓ fio aðl ʒefitte fylʒe him fimle
mið tiʒe hoꝓne oþ ꝥ hal fie.

.XLVIII.

[1] Þiþ þam pyꝓ mumþe innan eʒlað þam men · ʒenim
peʒbꝓæðan ʒetꝓifula ꝉ ꝥ feap fele on cuclepe fupan
ꝉ þa pypt felfe fpa ʒecnupaðe leʒe ón þone nafolan.
Þið cilba innoþef pypnium · ʒenim ʒꝓene mintan ænne
ʒelm ʒeðo ón pꝓy feftꝓaf pætcepef feoð oþ þꝓiððan ðæl
afeoh þonne fele ðꝓmcan. Þið cilba innoþ fape ðpeoꝓʒe
ðpoftle · ꝉ cymen ʒenim ʒebeat ʒemenʒe piþ pæteꝓ
leʒe ofeꝓ ðone nafolan fona bið hal. Við pypmum þe
innan eʒlað · ʒeælðef heoꝓtef hoꝓnef ahfan oððe ðuft

¹ Herb. Apul., ii. 10.

3. Oxa taught *us* this leechdom: take wallwort, and cloffing, and kneeholn, and everlasting, and cammock,[1] and white hellebore, in the proportion of nine to one, brownwort, bishopwort, and atterlothe, and red nettle, and red hove, and wormwood, and yarrow, and *horehound*, and pellitory, and pennyroyal, put all these worts into foreign ale, and then let *the man* drink for nine days and let blood. For the "dry" pain; make· into a drink, alexanders, sedum, wormwood, *the* two kneeholns,[2] sage, savine, carrot, lovage, feverfue, marche, costmary, garlic, ashthroat, betony, bishopwort, work them up into double brewed ale, sweeten with honey, drink for nine mornings no other liquid ; drink afterwards a strong potion, and let blood. Oxa taught this leechdom. Against "dry" rot; put into foreign ale, the netherward *part of* kneeholn, tow,[3] matricaria (?), and brownwort, of all equal quantities; boil down to one third part, and let *the patient* drink while he may require it; and where the disease has settled, follow him up ever with the drawing horn[4] till the place be hole.

xlviii.

Against the worms which ail men within; take waybroad, triturate it, and give the juice in a spoon to sup, and lay the wort itself, so pounded, on the navel. Against worms of the inwards of children ; take green mint, a handful of it, put it into three sextariuses of water, seethe it down to one third part, strain, then give to drink. For inward sore of children take pennyroyal and cummin, beat them up, mingle them with water, lay them over the navel, soon it will be whole. Against worms which ail *a man*

---

[1] *Peucedanum officinale.*
[2] Only *Ruscus aculeatus* grows wild in England. There are three others.

[3] Understand as reduced to ashes. See note on L. xxxiii. 1.
[4] Cupping glass.

ʒemenʒ pið huniʒ ʒefmıpe mıð þone bæcþeaꞃm ꞇ þone
naꞃolan mıb þy þonne ꞃeallað hıe. ¹ Ꝥıð pyꞃmum þe
ınnan ezlað ʒeꞇꞃıꞃolab² coſꞇ ꞇo bufꞇe · ʒebo ʒobne bæl
ın haꞇ pæꞇeꞃ ꞃele bꞃıncan.

³ Ꝥıþ pꞃꞃmum eꞃꞇ ʒaꞇe ꞇoꞃb hcaꞃb ꞇ ſꞃıðe bꞃıʒc ʒemenʒ ꞇ ʒeʒnıb pıþ hunıʒ ꞃele bꞃıncan þæꞇ abꞃıꞃþ hıe
apeʒ. Ꝥıð pyꞃmum þe ınnan ezlað eꞃꞇ ꞃebíc ſeoð on
pæꞇꞃe oþ þone þꞃıbban bæl menʒe pıþ ꞃín ꞃele bꞃıncan.
Eꞃꞇ pıþ þon ʒaꞇe ʒeallan ʒebo on pulle leʒe ꞇ bınb on
þone naꞃolan. Ꝥıþ þon ılcan · mínꞇan pel ʒeꞇꞃıꞃulabe
menʒ pıþ hunıʒ pyꞃc ꞇo lyꞇlum clıpene læꞇ ꞃóꞃſpelʒan.
Eꞃꞇ ele ꞇ ecebeꞃ em mıcel ʒemenʒeb ꞃele þꞃy baʒaꞃ
bꞃıncan. Eꞃꞇ eoꞃoꞃþꞃoꞇe · meꞃce · beꞇonıce · neꞃꞇe ·
ʒıðcoꞃn pyl on pıne. Ꝥıþ pyꞃmum þe ınnau ezlað
pyꞃꞇbꞃenc óꞃ onꞇꞃan · oꞃ ꞃelbmoꞃan ſcle bꞃıncan·
Sealꞃ · eꞇe cclebonıan · bꞃuncpyꞃꞇ apyllc on moꞃobe ·
bo þonne ſcıp ꞇeaꞃo ꞇ ſpeꞃl ꞇo ſmıꞃe mıð.

.XLVIIII.

Ꝥıþ þam ſmalan pyꞃme. Ꝥıþeꞃınban ꞇꞃıʒ ꞃoꞃepeaꞃb ·
ꞇ þa ꞃcalpan boccan næꞃ þa ꞃeaban · ꞇ þıſ ʒꞃeaꞇe
ꞃealꞇ ʒebcaꞇen ꞇoʒæbeꞃe ſꞃıðe ſmale ꞇ lyꞇcl buꞇeꞃan.

.L.

Vıþ honb pyꞃmum ꞇ beaꞃ pyꞃmuııı · ʒcnım boccan
oððe claꞇan þa þe ſpınman polbe þa pyꞃꞇꞇꞃumau menʒ
pıð ꞃleꞇan ꞇ pıð ꞃealꞇ læꞇ ſꞇanbau þꞃeo mıhꞇ ꞇ þy
ꞃeoꞃþan bæʒe ſmıꞃe mıb þa ꞃaꞃan ſꞇopa.

---

¹ Plinius Valerianus, ut infra.   ² Plinius Valerianus, fol. 44, c.
² Read ʒeꞇꞃıꞃola.

within; mingle with honey, ashes or dust of burnt harts horn, smear therewith the fundament and the navel, then they fall *away*. For worms which ail within; triturate costmary to dust, put a good deal into hot water, give to drink.

2. For worms again; mingle and rub up with honey a hard and very dry goats tord, administer it to be drunk, that will drive them away. Against worms which ail *a man* within, again; seethe in water radish to the third part, mingle with wine, give to drink. Again for that; put goats gall on wool, lay and bind it on the navel. For that ilk; mingle with honey, mint well triturated, work it into a little bolus, make him swallow it. Again, give for three days to drink oil and of vinegar an equal quantity. Again, everthroat,[1] marche, betony, nepeta, githcorn; boil *them* in wine; For worms which are troublesome within; give to drink a wort drink of "ontre" and of parsnip. A salve; let him eat celandine; let him boil brownwort in inspissated wine, then add thereto ship tar and sulfur; smear therewith.

xlix.

For the small worm; the forepart of a twig of withewind, and the fallow dock,[a] not the red one, and this coarse salt beaten together very small and a little butter.

l.

1. For hand worms[2] and dew worms; take dock or clote, such as would swim, mingle the roots with cream and with salt, let it stand for three nights, and on the fourth day smear therewith the sore places.

---

[1] *Carlina acaulis.*
[2] Some Gl. make gad flies the hand worms; are they rather here Κειρίαι = tæniæ ? *tape worms*, worms like ribands or tapes; read as χειρίαι.

ᵹɪꝼ pyꞃm hanb ete· ᵹením menꞅc meaꞃ ᵹeallan ꟁ
ꞃeaðe neꞇlan ꟁ ꞃeaðe boccan ꟁ ꞅmæle clɪꝼan ꞃyl on cu
buꞇeꞃan þonne ꞅio ꞃealꝼ ᵹeꞅoben ꞅɪe ꞃuꞃþum nɪm þonne
ꞃealꞇeꞃ þꞃy men ꞅceab ón hꞃeꞃ ꞇoꞅomne· ꟁ ꞅmɪꞃe mɪð·
lyþꞃe mɪð ꞅapan ymb nɪlꞇ ꞅmɪꞃe mɪð. Þɪþ beaꞃpyꞃme
ꞅꞇæppe on haꞇ col cele mɪð pæꞇꞃe ꞅꞇæppe ón ꞅpa haꞇ
ꞅpa he haꞇoꞅꞇ mæᵹe. Þɪð beaꞃpyꞃme· ꞅume nɪmað
ꞃeaꞃm cꞃeab monneꞅ þynne bɪnbað neahꞇeꞃne ón·
ꞅume ꞅpɪneꞅ lunᵹenne ꞃeaꞃme. Þɪþ honb pyꞃme ᴎɪm
ꞅcɪpꞇeaꞃo· ꟁ ꞅpeꞃl ꟁ pɪpoꞃ· ꟁ hꞃɪꞇ ꞃealꞇ menᵹ ꞇoSomne
ꞅmɪꞃe mɪð. Þeax ꞃealꝼ pɪþ pyꞃme· peax ꞃealꝼ· buꞇeꞃe
pɪpoꞃ hꝵíꞇ ꞃealꞇ menᵹ ꞇoꞅomne ꞅmɪꞃe mɪð.

.LI.

Þɪþ pyꞃmum[1] þe manneꞃ ꝼlæꞃc eꞇað ꞃám ᵹeallan
þone ꝼaᵹan cnua on nɪpe ealo æꞃ þon híꞇ aꞃɪpen ꞃɪe
ꞃele ꝥ oꝼeꞃ ꝼyllo bꞃɪncan þꞃeo nɪhꞇ. Eꝼꞇ ᵹením ᵹꞃunbe
ꞅpelᵹean þe ón eoꞃþan ꞃeaxeþ ꟁ ꞅceaꞃeꞃ ꞅmeꞃu menᵹ
ꞇoꞅomne ᵹelɪce ꞃela leᵹe ón. Eꝼꞇ ᵹenɪm beꞃen eaꞃ
beꞅenᵹ leᵹe ón ꞅpa haꞇ ꟁ haꞇ pæꞇeꞃ laꞃa ón. Þɪþ
ꝼlæꞃc pyꞃmum ᵹenɪm monneꞅ ꞅuꞃan ꞃa leaꝼ ᵹeꞃel
ꞇoᵹæbꞃe ᵹebꞃæb on ᵹæꞃꞅe ᵹecnua þonne leᵹe on ꞅpa
þu haꞇoꞅꞇ mæᵹe aꞃæꞃnan.

.LII.

Þɪþ luꞅúm acꞃɪnb ꟁ lɪpon peꞃɪnob ᵹecnua ón ealu
ꞃele bꞃɪncan. Uɪð luꞅuɪn cꝵíc ꞃeolꝼoꞃ ꟁ ealb buꞇeꞃe
an penɪnᵹ ꞃeolꝼꞃeꞃ· ꟁ ꞇu penɪnᵹ pæᵹe buꞇeꞃan menᵹ
on aꞃꝼæꞇ cal ꞇoSomne.

---

[1] Φθειρίασις ?

2. If a worm eat the hand; take marsh maregallBook I.
Ch. l.
Gentiana
pneumonanthe. and red nettle, and red dock, and *the* small bur, boil in cows butter; when the salve is sodden, then further take of salt three parts, shed thereupon, shake together, and smear therewith; lather with soap, about night *time* smear therewith. Against a dew worm; let *the man* step upon a hot coal, let him cool *the foot* with water; let him step upon it as hot as he hottest may. For a dew worm, some take warm thin ordure of man, they bind it on for the space of a night; some *take* a swines lung warm. Against a hand worm; take ship tar, and sulfur, and pepper, and white salt, mingle them together, smear therewith. A wax salve against a worm; a wax salve; butter, pepper, white salt, mingle *them* together, smear therewith.

li.

Against worms which eat a mans flesh; pound into new ale, before it be strained, the party coloured ram gall,[1] give the running over to drink for three nights. Again, take groundsel which waxeth on the earth, and sheeps grease, mingle *them* together, alike much *in quantity*, lay on. Again, take an ear of beer *or barley*, singe it, lay it on so hot, and hot water, leave it on. Against flesh worms; take mans sorrel, boil the leaves together, spread them out on the grass, then pound them, lay them on, as thou hottest may endure *them*.

lii.

Against lice; pound in ale oak rind and a little wormwood, give *to the lousy one* to drink. Against lice; quicksilver and old butter; one pennyweight of *quick*silver and two of butter; mingle all together in a brazen vessel.

---

[1] *Menyanthes trifoliata.*

.LIII.

Við ſmeʒa pynme nιpe cyſe ꝥ beobꞃeaƀ ꝥ hꞃætenne
hlaꝼ ete. Eꝼꞇ mónneꞃ heaꝼoƀ ban bæꞃn ꞇo ahꞃan ƀo
mιƀ pιpan on.

.LIIII.

Þιꝥ pyꞃmætſim lιce ꝥ cꝑelbehꞇum ſcꞃιnƀe ƀuſꞇ·
ꝏꞃcꞃιnƀe ƀuſꞇ· ellen ꞃιnƀe ƀuſꞇ on noꝥꝥan neoꝥan
ꝥam ꞇꞃeope· eolonan moꞃan ƀuſꞇ· ƀoccan moꞃan ƀuſꞇ·
pyꞃm ſcmeluꝑeꞃ ƀuſꞇ pιpoꞃeſ ƀuſꞇ ſιʒlan ƀuſꞇ· ſpeꞃleꞃ
ƀuſꞇ· ele· ꝥ hoꞃꞃeꞃ ſmeꞃu ꞇo poꞃe ꝥ ꞃcιꝑꞇeaꞃoſ læſꞇ·
ꝥꞃꞃa ealꞃa emꞃela ꝥ ꝥaꞃa ƀuſꞇa ealꞃa emꞃela ʒemenʒ
eal cealƀ ꞇoꞃomne ꝥ hιꞇ ꝼꞃam ꝥam poſum eal ꝑel
ſmιꞇenƀe ſmιꞃe mιƀ on nιhꞇ ꝥ on moꞃʒen aleꝥꞃe.

.LV.

Þιꝥ aꞃleʒenum lιce· bꞃom· ꝼelꞇeꞃe· ʒeaꞃꝑe· hoꞃe·
ꝑyl on buꞇeꞃan ꝥ on hun [1] ſmιꞃe mιƀ.

.LVI.

Vyꞃc bæꝥ pιꝥ aꞃleʒenum lιce· ʒenîm ꝥ mιcle ꝼeaꞃn
nιoꝥoꝑeaꞃƀ· ꝥ elm ꞃιnƀe ʒꞃene ʒecnua ꞇoſomne ꝥ meƀ-
ƀꞃoſna ƀo ꞇo pæꞇan ʒnιƀ ſꝑιƀe ꞇoſomne leʒe ôn lanʒe
hꞃιle oꝥ ꝥ he peaꞃm ſιe oꝥꝥe onſꞇæppe.

Þιꝥ aꞃleʒenum lιce ꞃealꝼ eolone ſꝑιƀe ʒeſoben ꝥ
nιƀeꞃeaꞃƀ homoꞃꞃécʒ ꝥ ealƀ ſpιc cnua eal ꞇoꞃomne
pyꞃm ꝥuꞃh claƀ ꞇo ꝼyꞃe ſmιꞃe mιƀ· ꞃceaꞃꝑa ꝥonne
ſιmle ymb· VII. nιhꞇ ꞃeꞇe hoꞃn on ꝥa openan ꞃceaꞃꝑan

fol. 48 a.

---

[1] Here an erasure occurs, as if huniʒe had been meant, but not filled in.

liii.

Against a boring worm ; let *the man* eat new cheese
and beebread and wheaten loaf.   Again, burn to ashes
a mans head bone *or skull*, put it on with a pipe.

liv.

For a wormeaten and mortified body; dust of oak
rind, dust of ash rind, dust of elder rind, taken on the
north of the tree, and the nether part, warm, dust
of the root of helenium, dust of root of dock, dust of
acorn meal, peppers dust, dust of rye, sulfurs dust, oil,
and horses grease for a liquid, and the least proportion of ship tar, of all these equal quantities, and of all
the dusts equally much; mingle all cold together, so
that by means of the liquids may be all well smudg-
ing, *or thoroughly unctuous*, smear therewith at night,
and in the morning lather.

lv.

For slain, *that is, stricken*, body, broom, fel terræ,[a] *Erythræa centuareum.*
yarrow, hove, boil *these* in butter and in honey, smear
therewith.

lvi.

1. Work a fomentation for a stricken body ; take
the mickle fern,[b] the netherward part, and elm rind *Aspidium filix.*
green, pound them together, and for a liquor add mead
dregs, rub them up thoroughly together, lay on for
a long while, till that *the sufferer* be warm or walk
about.

2. For a stricken body, a salve; helenium thoroughly
sodden, and the netherward part of hammersedge, and
old lard, pound all together, warm through a cloth
at the fire, smear therewith ; then scarify continually
about the bruise for seven nights, set a horn [1] upon

---

[1] A cupping horn.

fol. 48 b.   ſmıɲe mıð þæɲe blacan ɾealſe ſpa nıht ſpa ꞇpa ſpa
þeaɲſ ſie ꞊ hy opene ɾynð.

.LVII.

Ӿʋκꞃ.   Þıþ ſıce bɲenc ꞊ ɾealſ · pyɲm pyɲꞇ pylle on meolce
꞊ bɲınce.   Sealſ cnua ᵹlæɟ ꞇo buſꞇe bo hunıᵹeɟ ꞇeaɲ
ón lacna þ bolᵹ mıð.

.LVIII.

To penɾealſe ꞊ ɲen bylûm · pyɲc hıe óſ nıoꞇopeaɲbɲe
neꞇlan ꞊ óſ hemlıce ꞊ oſ þæɲe cluſıhꞇan penpyɲꞇe ꞊
oſ þæɲe ſmalan moɲpyɲꞇe pyl ealle ſeopeɲ ón buꞇeɲan
꞊ ón ɾceaɲeɟ ſmeɲpe oþþ ᵹenoh ɲıe ᵹecnua eɟꞇ þa
ılcan pyɲꞇa on þæɲe ɾealſe ꞊ ɾcıp ꞇeaɲo ꞊ ᵹaɲleác ꞊
cɲopleác ꞊ ɾecᵹleác ꞊ ɾealꞇ menᵹ pel bo on clað pyɲm
ꞇo ſyɲe ſpıðe[1] ſmıɲe mıð.

Þenɾealſ ónꞇɲe ceɲɲan ɲeaðe neꞇlan peɲmoð · ꞇpa
penpyɲꞇa · ellen ɲınðe · peᵹbɲæbe · ſuɲan · bıɾceop pyɲꞇ ·
buloꞇ nıðeɲeaɲð · ſmeɲe pyɲꞇ · ɾealꞇ · ɾcıpꞇeaɲo · ꞊
ɾceaɲen ſmeɲa.   Þıþ pen byle Nım cɲopleác · onꞇɲe ·
fol. 49 a.   eolone · cluɾehꞇe penpyɲꞇ · ᵹecnua ealle þa pſɲıꞇa ſpıþe
pel leᵹe ón.
Þenɾealſ hıoɲoꞇeſ meaɲh · ıſıᵹ ꞇeaɲo ꞊ ᵹebeaꞇen pıpoɲ
꞊ ſcıp ꞇeaɲo.
[2][Þıþ þa blacan bleᵹene ſýle þam men eꞇan ꞇɲeᵹen
cɲoppaſ oððe þɲý oſ þæɲe pýɲꞇe þe man on þɲeo pıſaɲ
haꞇeð mýxenplanꞇe.]

---

[1] ſpıð, MS.
In the margin, in a different and later hand.

the open scarifications, smear with the black salve, be
it for a night, be it for two, as need be, and as they
be open.

lvii.

For the disease called fig, a drink and a salve; let
him boil wormwort in milk and drink it. A salve ;
pound glass to dust, add a drop of honey, leech the
wound therewith.

lviii.

1. For a wen salve and for wen boils; work *the salve*
of the netherward part of nettle and of hemlock, and
of the wenwort which has cloves *or bulbed roots*,ᵃ and
of the small moorwort, boil all four in butter and in
sheeps grease till there be enough, pound again the
same worts in the salve, and ship tar, and garlic, and
cropleek, and sedgeleek,ᵇ and salt, mingle well, put
on a cloth, warm thoroughly at the fire, smear therewith.

ᵃ Probably
*Ranunculus
ficaria.*

ᵇ *Allium
schænoprasum.*

2. A salve for wens; ontre, cress, red nettle, wormwood, *the* two wenworts, elder rind, waybroad, sorrel,
bishopwort, the nether part of bulot, smearwort, salt,
ship tar,[1] and sheeps grease. For a wen boil; take
cropleek, ontre, helenium, the clove rooted wenwort,
pound all the worts thoroughly well, lay *the stuff* on.

3. A wen salve; harts marrow, ivy tar, and beaten
pepper, and ship tar.

4. [Against the black blain, give to the man to eat
two bunches or three off the wort, which is called in
three ways, *the* mixen plant.[2]]

---

[1] Pix navalis is occasionally prescribed by the medical authors, as
Nic. Myreps, 481, c., in the Medicæ Artis Principes.

[2] *Atropa belladonna.*

LVIIII.

¹ Ƿiþ lyft adle · nim ꞃcenc fulne þeallendes þæteneſ oþeꞃne eleſ · ⁊ hpiteꞃ ꞃealteꞃ ſpilc ſpa mæȝe mid ꝼeo-þeꞃ ꝼinȝꞃum ȝeniman · hꞃeꞃ toȝædeꞃe oþ þ hit eall on an ſie. Ðꞃinc eall be dꞃopan ꞃeſt hpile ſtinȝ ꝼinȝeꞃ on ciolan aſpip² eꝼt eall ⁊ ma ȝiꝼ þu mæȝe · þonne on moꞃȝen ꝼoꞃlæt blod oꝼ eaꞃme · oððe oꝼ ſpeoꞃan ſpa mæꞃſt aꞃæꝼnan mæȝe · ⁊ ꞃceaꞃþiȝe · ⁊ hpon onſette oꝼeꞃ eall ſmiꞃe þonne mid hatan ele ⁊ him æȝhpæt ꞃealteꞃ beoꞃȝe · bꞃuce ȝlædenan ⁊ eoꝼoꞃꝼeaꞃneſ uppe on tꞃeope ⁊ mid hneꞃce þulle oꝼeꞃ þꞃiðe ealle þa ſceaꞃþan þonne hie ſien ȝefmyꞃede. Ƿiþ neuꞃiꞃne danpyꞃt do on ſuꞃe fletan ⁊ on huniȝ æȝeꞃ ȝeola menȝ tofomne ſmiꞃe mid. Eꝼt ꞃenpyꞃmaſ cnua do on.

.LX.

Ƿið bꞃyne þyꞃc ꝼealꝼe · ȝenim ȝate topd ⁊ hpæte healm ȝebæꞃn to dufte ȝemenȝ butu þiþ buteꞃan do on pannan oꝼeꞃ ꝼyꞃ apyl ſpiðe þel aꝼeoh þuꞃh claþ ſmiꞃe mid.

Ƿiþ bꞃyne ȝenim ꝼinuleſ niþepeaꞃbeſ ȝebeat þið ealdne pyꞃele ⁊ leȝe on. Eꝼt ȝenim lilian ⁊ ȝeaꞃpan pyl on buteꞃan ſmiꞃe mid. Ƿiþ þon ilcan pylle ꞃibban on buteꞃan ⁊ ſmiꞃe mid.

Ƿiþ þon ilcan pylle ȝeaꞃpan on buteꞃan ſmiꞃe mid.

Ƿiþ þon ilcan pylle cottuc on ꞃceapeſ ſmeꞃþe ⁊ attoꞃlaþan ⁊ eoꝼoꞃꝼeaꞃn do on huniȝ oððe on peax. Ƿiþ þon do æȝeꞃ þ hpite on ȝelome.

---

¹ Παράλυσις. | ² aſpiþe, as third person better.

lix.

Against palsy; take a cup full of boiling water,
another of oil, and of white salt so much as one may
pick up with four fingers; shake together till that it
be all one: drink all this by drops, rest awhile, poke
thy finger into the gullet, spew up again all and more
if thou [1] may; then in the morning let blood from the
arm or from the neck, as much as he [1] may bear; and
scarify and let him put something on, then after all
smear with hot oil and let him taste a trifle of salt;
employ gladden and everfern *picked high* up on the
tree, and cover over with nesh wool all the scarifications when they have been smeared. Against "neu-
risn" put bonewort into sour cream, and into honey,
mingle together *with this* the yolk of an egg, smear
therewith. Again, pound up earthworms, apply them.

lx.

1. Against a burn work a salve; take goats tord and
halm of wheat, burn them to dust, mingle both with
butter, put into a pan over the fire, boil thoroughly
well, strain through a cloth, smear therewith.

2. For a burn, take some of the netherward part of
fennel, beat it up with old grease, and lay on. Again,
take lilly and yarrow, boil *them* in butter, smear
therewith. For the same, boil ribwort in butter and
smear therewith.

3. For that ilk, boil yarrow in butter, smear therewith.

4. For that ilk, boil mallow in sheeps grease, and
attorlothe, and everfern, put them into honey or into
wax. For that *same*, put the white of an egg on
frequently.

---

[1] The careless use of pronouns belongs to the text.

Þiþ bpyne paƀ ȝecnua pyl on butepan fmiþe miƀ.

.LXI.

[1]Þiþ liƀ pæpce cnua liƀ pypt piƀ huniȝe oþþe ceop ⁊ leȝe ón.   Ef't pulfep heafoƀ ban bæpn fpiƀe ⁊ ȝecnua fmale aȝyȝt þuph claƀ ƀo on þ̵ ƀolȝ.   Þiƀ liþ pæpce cnua pepmoƀ piþ teoppe ⁊ fencepfan appinȝ þ̵ feap óf menȝ tofomne clæm on þ̵ liƀ þe þæp fap pie ȝebinƀ fæpte ón.   Þiþ liƀ feape ȝeloƀ pypt · bpune pypt · ⁊ haþe pypt lytelu óftoft peaxeþ ón tune hæþ̵ hpite bloftman ȝecnua ƀa þpeo pypta ȝemenȝe þ̵ biþ ȝoƀ pealf.   Ⱳaneȝum men liƀ peau pyhƀ̵[2] ȝepþinȝ æpleȝ feap ón ⁊ hoþneȝ fceafoþan fpiƀe fmale ȝepceaȝ cpim on þ̵ ƀolh innán ƀo þ̵ óf ⁊ fimle nipe ón.   Þiþ liƀ feape liþþypt hunbeȝ heafoƀ ȝebæpne ⁊ ȝecnupiȝe ⁊ ȝebpæƀebne æppel · menȝ þ̵ eall tofomne ƀo þ̵ ón.   Efft ȝením fuþne æppel ȝebpæƀ ⁊ leȝe ón · ƀo ȝput ón ufan þone æppel   :·

Þiþ liƀ feape · ȝenim maȝeþan menȝ piƀ huniȝ ƀo on þ̵ ƀolȝ ⁊ binƀ fæfte.   Þiþ feape ȝenim ácpinƀe ⁊ ƀpiȝe ⁊ pipc to fmeƀman ⁊ flahþopn pinƀe nioþopeapƀe fyȝt

fol. 50 a.

---

[1] 'Ἀρθρῖτις.

[2] Subluvium. We find the out-flowing of the synovia an object of legal enactment. See Ælfreds

Dooms, p. 42. art. 53. "Si quis in " humero plagietur ut glutinum " compagum effluat:" Laws, Henry I., p. 265.

5. For a burn, pound up woad, boil it in butter, smear therewith.

lxi.

1. Against racking pain in the joints, pound lithwort with honey, or chew it and lay it on. Again, burn thoroughly the head bone *or skull* of a wolf and pound it small, sift it through a cloth, put it on the wound. Against pain in the joints, pound wormwood with tar and fen cress, wring out the juice, mingle together, stick *the residue* upon the joint where the sore is, bind it on fast. For the synovia of the joints, silverweed, brownwort, and the little harewort,[1] it oftenest waxeth in a garden, it hath white blossoms, pound the three worts, mingle them, that is a good salve. With many men the synovia of the joints oozeth out,[2] wring on *the spot* the juice of an apple, and shave very small some shavings of horn, crumble them on the wound within it, remove that and ever apply *the same* anew. For the synovia of the joints, burn lithwort,[a] houndshead, and pound them up with roasted apple; mingle all that together, apply it. Again, take a sour apple, roast and lay it on; apply groats over above the apple.

2. For the synovia of the joints, take maythe, mingle *it* with honey, apply it to the wound and bind it fast. For *the* secretion *of the joints*, take oak rind and dry it and work it to a fine *flour or* smede, and *further* sloethorn rind, the netherward part of it, sift them

[a] *Sambucus ebulus.*

[1] *Lepidium ?*
[2] " Tunc articuli tumentes inflau-
" tur, ac deinde durescunt et soli-
" dati saxeam faciunt qualitatem ;
" tum etiam nigriores efficiantur,
" atque contorti, ut in obliquas
" partes digiti vertantur, aut reflexi
" supinentur, aut vicinis adfixi in-
" cumbant, et aliquando humore
" purulento vel mucilento collecto,
" aut viscoso, generent poros, quos
" nos transitus dicere poterimus."—
Cælius Aurelianus, about A.D. 230,
Chron. lib. v. cap. 2.

þa þurh clað ⁊ sceað on ꝥ dolg. Ƿið lið seaƿe · genīm cetelhrūm ⁊ berenhealm gebærn ⁊ gnid togædere ⁊ sceað ón. gif liþule utyrne genīm merce niþoƿeardne ⁊ hunig ⁊ hƿætenes meluƿes smedman ⁊ ƿicggan Innel[1] begnid tosómne lege ón. Eft genīm medoƿyrte niþoƿearde gecnua smale meng ƿiþ hunige lege ón þæt gebatod sie.

fol. 50 b. Gif liþule útyrne genim eced ⁊ sure cruman berenes hlafes ⁊ renƿyrmas meng[2] toSomne bind ón ƿæt ꝥ liþ mid ecede oþþe mid suran ealað. gif liþule útyrne · genīm ƿermod ⁊ gecnua do ón teoro clæm ón ⁊ bind ón fæste.

.LXII.

[3] Ƿiþ fefer adle · elehtran · gyþrife · ƿegbræde gecnua ón ealu læt standan tƿa niht sele drincan. Ƿiþ fefre eft betonican drince sƿiðe · ⁊ ete þreo snæda. Eft drinc on hluttrum ealað ƿermod · gyþrifan · betonican · biscopƿyrt · fen minte · bogen · sio clufihte · ƿenƿyrt · marrubie · drince þritig daga. drenc ƿiþ þon · betonican · springƿyrt attorlaðe · berbine · eoforþrote · hundestunge · dƿeorge dƿostle · ƿermod. Ƿið þriddan dæges fefre ón ƿearmum ƿætre drince betonican tyn sopan þonne to ƿille. Ƿið feorþan dæges fefre drince ƿegbræðan seaƿ on sƿetum ƿætre tƿam tidum ær him se fefer to ƿille. Ƿiþ ælces dæges fefere drince ón cealdum ƿætere betonican dustes ꝥ ænne pening geƿege · oþer sƿilc ƿegbræðan.

fol. 51 a.

Ƿiþ fefre eft hylpð syndrigo marubie to drincanne. Ƿiþ lencten adle ƿermod eofor þrote · elehtre · ƿegbræde · ribbe · cerfille · attorlaðe · feferfuge · alexandre · biscopƿyrt · lufestice · Saluie · cassuc ƿyrt to

[1] Read Innelse ?
[2] men, MS.
[3] Πυρετός, Febris.

through a cloth, and shed that on the wound. For synovia of the joints, take kettle soot and barley halm, burn and rub them together, and shed on. If the synovia run out, take the netherward part of marche and honey, and the smede of wheaten meal, and the bowels of an *ear* wig, rub them together, and lay on. Again, take the netherward part of meadowwort, pound it small, mingle with honey, lay on till it be mended.

3. If the synovia run out, take vinegar and sour crumbs of a barley loaf, and earthworms, mingle together, and bind on ; wet the joint with vinegar or with sour ale. If the synovia run out, take wormwood and pound it, put it on tar, plaster it on, and bind it on fast.

lxii.

1. For fever disease ; pound in ale lupins, githrife, waybroad, let it stand for two nights, administer to drink. For fever again ; let him drink betony much, and eat three bits *of it*. Again, drink in clear ale wormwood, githrife, betony, bishopwort, fen mint, rosemary, the clove rooted wenwort, marrubium, drink for thirty days. A drink for that, betony, springwort, attorlothe, vervain, everthroat, houndstongue, dwarf dwosle, wormwood. For a tertian fever, let *the sick* drink in warm water ten sups of betony, when *the fever* is approaching. For a quartan fever, let him drink juice of waybroad in sweetened water two hours before the fever will to him. For a quotidian fever, let him drink in cold water so much of the dust of betony as may weigh a penny ; as much more of waybroad.

2. For fever again it helpeth, to drink marrubium alone. For lent addle, *or typhus fever*, work to a drink wormwood, everthroat, lupin, waybroad, ribwort, chervil, attorlothe, feverfue, alexanders, bishopwort, lovage,

ðɲence on pelſcum ealað ðo haliᵹ pæꞇeɲ ꞇo · ⁊ ſpɲinᵹ
ꞃyɲꞇ.
Þiſ món ꞃceal pɲiꞇan on huꞃlbiꞃce ⁊ on þone ðɲenc
inið haliᵹ pæꞇeɲe þpean ⁊ ꞃinᵹan on ·
+ + + Λ + + + + + C D + + + + + + + + +
In pɲincipio eɲaꞇ ueɲbum eꞇ ueɲbum eɲaꞇ apuꞇ
ðeum eꞇ ðeuꞃ eɲaꞇ ueɲbūm. Ꝺoc eɲaꞇ In pɲincipio
apuꞇ ðeum ómnia peɲ ipSūm ꝼácꞇa Sunꞇ. Þpeah þonne
ꝥ ᵹepɲiꞇ mið haliᵹ pæꞇꞃe oꝼ þam ðiſce on þone ðɲenc ·
ſinᵹ · þonne cɲeðo ⁊ paꞇeɲ noꞃꞇeɲ ⁊ þiſ leoþ. ꝺeaꞇi
Inmꜹculaꞇꝫ þone ſealm mið að ðominum þam . XII.
ᵹebeð ꞃealmūm. Aðiuro uoS ꝼɲiᵹoɲeſ¹ eꞇ ꞃebɲeS · peɲ
ðeum paꞇɲem ómnipoꞇenꞇem eꞇ peɲ eiuſ ꝼiliuᵐ ieꞃᵘm
cɲiſꞇum peɲ aꞃcenſum eꞇ ðiꞃcenſum² Saluaꞇoɲiſ noꞃꞇɲi
uꞇ ɲeceðaꞇiS ðe hóc ꝼamulo ðei · eꞇ ðe coɲɲuSculo
eiuſ quam³ ðominuꞃ noꞃꞇeɲ Inluminaɲe Inſꞇiꞇuiꞇ. Uinciꞇ uóꞃ leo ðe ꞇɲibu iuða ɲaðix ðauið. Uinciꞇ uóꞃ qui
uinci nón poꞇeSꞇ · + xp̄ꞃ naꞇuſ · + xp̄ꞃ paſſuꞃ · +
xp̄ꞃ uenꞇuɲuſ · + aiuꞃ ·⁴ + aiuꞃ · + aiuꞃ · + Scꞃ ·
+ Scꞃ · + Scꞃ · Jn ðieᵃ Saluꞇiꝼeɲiſ inceðenꞃ ᵹɲeꞃſibuꞃ
uɲbeꞃ · oppiða ꞃuɲa uicoſ caꞃꞇɲa caſꞇella peɲaᵹɲanſ.
Omnia ðepulꞃꞀꞃ ſanaðaꞇ coɲɲoɲa moɲbiꞃ ·⁵ ⁊ þɲiɲa þonne
onſupe þæꞃ pæꞇeɲeſ ſpelceſ ᵹehpæþeɲ þaɲa manna.

.LXIII.

Þiþ ꝼeonð ſeocūm men · þonne ðeoꝼol þone mónnan
ꝼeðe oððe hine innan ᵹepealðe mið aðle. Spipeðɲenc
eluhꞇɲe · biſceoppyɲꞇ · beolone cɲopleác ᵹecnua ꞇoSomne
ðo eala ꞇo pæꞇan læꞇ ſꞇanðan neahꞇeɲne ðo ꝼiꝼꞇiᵹ
lybcoɲna ón ⁊ haliᵹ pæꞇeɲ. ðɲenc piþ ꝼeonðſeocum
men oꝼ ciɲicbellan ꞇo ðɲincanne · ᵹyþɲiꝼe · ᵹlæꞃ ·⁶ ᵹeaɲpe ·
elehꞇɲe · beꞇonice · aꞇꞇoɲlaþe · caꞃꝽc · ꝼane · ɲinul ·

---

¹ Frigora.
² Descensum.
³ Quem.
⁴ aiuꞃ = ἄγιος.
⁵ Read Oppida, rura, casas, vicos,
castella   peragrans ;   Sedulius,
Carm. Pasch , Lib. III., 23. Inter-
woven in the text of Beda, III.
xxviii.
⁶ For neᵹlæꞃ, cynæᵹlæꞃꞃan ?

sage, cassock, in foreign ale; add holy water and Book I.
Ch. lxii.
springwort.

3. A man shall write this upon the sacramental An exorcism
of fever.
paten, and wash it off into the drink with holy water,
and sing over it . . . . In the beginning, etc. (John
i. 1.) Then wash the writing with holy water off the
dish into the drink, then sing the Credo, and the
Paternoster, and this lay, Beati immaculati, the psalm;[1]
with the twelve prayer psalms, I adjure you, etc. And
let each of the two[2] men then sip thrice of the water
so prepared.

> Inde salutiferis incedens gressibus urbes,
> Oppida, rura, casas, vicos, castella peragrans
> Omnia depulsis sanabat corpora morbis.
> SEDVLIVS.

lxiii.

For a fiend sick man, *or demoniac*, when a devil
possesses the man or controls him from within with
disease; a spew drink, *or emetic*, lupin, bishopwort,
henbane, cropleek; pound *these* together, add ale for
a liquid, let *it* stand for a night, add fifty libcorns,
or cathartic grains, and holy water. A drink for a
fiend sick man, to be drunk out of a church bell; Church bell.
githrife, cynoglossum, yarrow, lupin, betony, attorlothe,
cassock, flower de luce, fennel, church lichen, lichen, of

---

[1] Psalm, cxix.
[2] Two, the leech and the sick; two is in ᵹehpæþeꝑ.

ciριcραᵹu · cɲıſter mæleꞃ ꞃaᵹu · luꞃeſtıce · ᵹeꝑyꞃc þone
ðꞃenc óꞃ hluttꞃum ealað ᵹeſinᵹe ſeoꞃon mæꞃꞃan oꞃeꞃ
þám pyꞃtum ðo ᵹaꞃleác ꞇ halıᵹ pæteꞃ to ꞇ ðꞃype ón ælcne
ðꞃincan þone ðꞃenc þe he ðꞃincan pılle éꝛt · ꞇ ſinᵹe
þone ſealm · beatı Inmaculatı ꞇ exuꞃᵹát · ꞇ Saluum
me ꝼác ðeuꞃ · ꞇ þonne ðꞃınce þone ðꞃenc óꞃ cıꞃıcbellan ꞇ
ſe mæꞃꞃe pꞃeoſt hím ſinᵹe æꝛteꞃ þam ðꞃence þıſ oꞃeꞃ.
ðomıne Sancte pateꞃ omnıpotenſ. Þıþ bꞃæcſeocum
men · coſt · ᵹotꞃoþe · eluhtꞃe · betonıce · attoꞃlaðe ·
cꞃopleác · holeceꞃſan · hoꞃe · ꞃınul · aſinᵹe món mæꞃꞃan oꞃeꞃ pyꞃce óꞃ pylıſcum eáloð ꞇ oꞃ halıᵹ pæteꞃe.
ðꞃınce þıꞃne ðꞃenc æt æᵹhꞃılcum nıpe nıᵹon moꞃᵹenaſ
ꞇ nane oþꞃe pætan þ þıcoe ꞇ ſtılle ſıe · ꞇ sælmeꞃꞃan
ꞃelle ꞇ hím aꞃena ᵹoð ᵹeoꞃnlıce bıðbe. Þıð peðen
heoꞃte bıſceoppyꞃt · elehtꞃe · banpyꞃt · eoꞃoꞃꞃeaꞃn ·
ᵹıþꞃıꞃe · heahhıoloþe þonne bæᵹ ſcaðe [1] ꞇ nıht þonne
ſinᵹ þu ón cıꞃıcean letanıaſ þ ıꞃ þaꞃa halıᵹꞃa naman ·
ꞇ pateꞃ noꞃteꞃ mıð þy ſanᵹe þu ᵹa þ þu ſıe æt þam
pyꞃtum ꞇ þꞃıpa ymbᵹa ꞇ þonne þu hıe nıme ᵹanᵹ eꝛt
to cıꞃıcean mıð þy ılcan ꞃanᵹe · ꞇ ᵹeꞃınᵹ .xii. mæꞃꞃan oꞃeꞃ ꞇ oꞃeꞃ ealle þa ðꞃencan þe to þæꞃe aðle

belımpaþ ón peoꞃðmynðe þaꞃa tpelꞃa apoſtola.

.LXIIII.

Þıþ ælcꞃe yꞃelꞃe leoðꞃunan ꞇ pıð ælꞃꞃıðenne þıꞃ
ᵹeꞃꞃıt pꞃıt hím þıꞃ ᵹꞃecıſcum ſtaꞃúm · + + Λ + +
O + y° + ı ꝑ в у м ꟾꟾꟾꟾ :· в е ꝑ ꝑ N NIKNЕttANI.
Eꝛt · oþeꞃ ðuſt ꞇ ðꞃenc pıþ leoðꞃunan · ᵹením bꞃembel
æppel ꞇ elehtꞃan ꞇ polleᵹıan ᵹecnua · ſıꝛt þonne ðo on
pohhan leᵹe unðeꞃ peoꞃoð ſinᵹ nıᵹon mæꞃꞃan oꞃeꞃ ðo
ón meolóc þ ðuſt ðꞃyp þꞃıpa on halıᵹ pæteꞃeſ [2] ꞃele

---

[1] At morning twilight.
[2] A partitive genitive ; halıᵹ in halıᵹ pæteꞃ is commonly unde-
clined, or regarded as part of a compound.

Christs mark *or cross*, lovage ; work up the drink off
clear ale, sing seven masses over the worts, add garlic and
holy water, and drip the drink into every drink which
he will subsequently drink, and let him sing the psalm,
Beati immaculati, and Exurgat, and Salvum me fac, deus,
and then let him drink the drink out of a church bell,
and let the mass priest after the drink sing this over
him, Domine, sancte pater omnipotens.[1]   For a lunatic;
costmary, goutweed, lupin, betony, attorlothe, cropleek,
field gentian, hove, fennel; let masses be sung over,
let it be wrought of foreign ale and of holy water ;
let him drink this drink for nine mornings, at every
one fresh, and no other liquid that is thick and still,
and let him give alms, and earnestly pray God for his
mercies. For the phrenzied; bishopwort, lupin, bonewort,
everfern,[2] githrife, elecampane, when day and night divide, then sing thou in the church litanies, that is,
the names of the hallows *or saints*, and the Paternoster; with the song go thou, that thou mayest be
near the worts, and go thrice about them, and when
thou takest them go again to church with the same
song, and sing twelve masses over them, and over all
the drinks which belong to the disease, in honour of
the twelve apostles.

lxiv.

Against every evil rune lay,[3] and one full of elvish
tricks, write *for the bewitched man* this writing in
Greek letters: alfa, omega, IESVM (?) BERONIKH.[4]   Again, IXΘΥΣ ?
another dust *or powder* and drink against a rune lay ;
take a bramble apple,[a] and lupins, and pulegium, pound
them, then sift them, put them in a pouch, lay them
under the altar, sing nine masses over them, put the

---

[1] A formula of Benediction ;
several such are found in the
Missals.

[2] *Polypodium vulgare.*

[3] Heathen charm.

[4] Invoking the miraculous portrait of Christ on the kerchief of
St. Veronica.

•

ðpincan on þpeo tiða · on unðepn · on miððæʒ · on
nón · ʒiꝼ ꝼio aðl netnum ꝼie ʒeot mið haliʒ pætpe ón
muð þ̄ ilce ðuꝼt. Sealꝼ elehtpe heʒepiꝼe · biꝼceoppypt ·
þa peaðan maʒoþan · apmelu · cpopleac · pealt pyl on
butepan to fealꝼe fmipe ón þ̄ heaꝼoð ꝡ þa bpeoꝼt.
ðpenc hapan fppecel · alexanðpie · puðe · elehtpe
heʒepiꝼe · biꝼceoppypt · maʒoþe · cpopleác · apmelu ·
ꝼio cneoehte · penpypt ðo on haliʒ pætep. ʒiꝼ món
mape piðe · ʒenim elehtpan ꝡ ʒapleac · ꝡ betonican ·
ꝡ pecelf binð on næpce hæbbe him món ón ꝡ he
ʒanʒe in on þaꝼ pypte.

.LXV.

Eꝼt ðpenc pið lencten aðle ꝼeꝼepꝼuʒe · hpam ʒealla ·
ꝼinul · peʒbpæðe · ʒefinʒe mon ꝼela mæꝼꝼan oꝼep þæpe
pypte ·¹ oꝼʒeót mið ealað ðo haliʒ pætep ón pyl fpiþe
pel ðpince þonne fpa he hatoꝼt mæʒe micelne fcenc
ꝼulne æp þon ꝼio aðl to pille :· ꝼeopep ʒobfpellapa
numan ꝡ ʒealðop ꝡ ʒebeð · ⊞ . Matheuꝼ · + + + + +
MapcuS + + + + + · lucaS · ⊞ · Iohanneꝼ ⁺⁺₊₊₊₊ Intep-
ceðite ppo me · Tiecon · leleloth · patpon · aðiupo uoS.
Eꝼt ʒoðcunð ʒebeð · Jn nomine ðomini fit beneðic-

tum · beponice · beponicen · et habet In ueftimento et
In ꝼemope fuo · fcpiptum pex peʒum et ðominuꝼ ðomi-

nantjum * · Eꝼt ʒoðcunð ʒebeð. Jn nomine fit bene-
dictum · ᛗ ᛗ ᛗ ᚱ ᛗ þ · ᚾ ꝡ · þ ᛏ ᛗ ᛗ ᚱ ꝼ ᛈ ᚾ ꝡ · þ ᛏ ᚷ .²
Et ꝼceal mon fpiʒenðe þiꝼ ppitan ꝡ ðon þaꝼ popð
fpiʒenðe on þa pinftpan bpeoꝼt ꝡ ne ʒa he in ón
þ̄ ʒeppit ne in on bep · ꝡ eác fpiʒenðe þiꝼ on ðon ·
HAMMANyᵒEL · BPONice · NOyᵒePTAyᵒEPᚷ.

---

¹ This use of the singular is mere
carelessness.
² Read ᛗ ᛗ ᚱ ᛗ þ · ᚾ ꝡ · þ ᛏ ᛗ ·

ᛗᛗᚱᛗþ · ᚾꝡ · þᛏ ᚷ, and understand the ᛏ as an I.

dust into milk, drip thrice some holy water upon them,
administer *this* to drink at three hours, at undern, *or*
nine *in the morning*, at midday, at noon, *hora nona,
or three in the afternoon.*   If the disease be on cattle,
pour that ilk dust into the mouth with holy water.
A salve ; boil lupin, hedgerife, bishopwort, the red
maythe, harmala,ᵃ cropleek, salt, in butter to a salve,
smear it on the head and the breast.   A drink ; put
into holy water, vipers bugloss, alexanders, rue, lupins,
hedgerife, bishopwort, maythe, cropleek, harmala, the
wenwort which hath knees.ᵇ   If a mare ¹ or *hag* ride
a man, take lupins, and garlic, and betony, and frankincense, bind them on a fawns skin, let a man have
the worts on him, and let him go in *to his home.*

*Book I.
Ch. lxiv.*

ᵃ *Peganum har-
mala, Bot.*

ᵇ *Lolium
temulentum ?*

lxv.

1. Again, a drink against lent addle *or typhus ;*
feverfue, the herb rams gall,² fennel, waybroad ; let a
man sing many masses over the worts, souse them
with ale, add holy water, boil very thoroughly, let *the
man* drink a great cup full, as hot as he may, before
the disorder will be on him ; *say* the names of the
four gospellers, and a charm, and a prayer, etc.³   Again,
a divine prayer, etc., DEEREÞ· HAND· ÞIN· DEREÞ·
HAND· ÞIN· thine hand vexeth, thine hand vexeth.

Again, a man shall in silence write this, and silently
put these words on the left breast, and let him not
go in *doors* with that writing, nor bear it in *doors.*
And also in silence put this on, EMMANUEL, VERONICA.⁴

---

¹ As in night mare.
² *Menyanthes trifoliata.*
³ Leliloth is an Arabic idol.

(Freytag.) Cf. Alilat Herod. iii. 8.
⁴ The image on the kerchief.

fol 53 b.

Ðɪþ unʒemynðe ꝼ pɪð ðyꞃʒunʒe ðo ón ealo bɪꞃceop
pyꞃꞇ · elehꞇꞃan · beꞇonican þa ſuþeꞃnan ꞃɪnuʒlan ·
neꞃꞇan hɪnðhɪoloðan · ʒyþꞃɪꝼan · meꞃce · ðꞃɪnce þonne.
Ðɪþ unʒemynðe ꝼ bɪꞃʒunʒe ðo ón eala caꞃſiám · ꝼ elehꞇꞃan · bɪꞃceoppyꞃꞇ · alexanðꞃɪan · ʒɪþꞃɪꝼe · ꝼelðmoꞃan
ꝼ halɪʒ pæꞇeꞃ ðꞃɪnce þonne.

Vɪð ʒenumenum meꞇe · ʒením elehꞇꞃan leʒe unðeꞃ
peoꞃoð ſinʒ nɪʒon mæꞃꞃan oꝼeꞃ ꝥ ꞃceal pɪþ ʒenumenum meꞇe leʒe unðeꞃ ꝥ ꝼæꞇ · þe þu pɪlle ón melcan.[1]
Ʒɪꝼ ealo apeꞃð ſie · ʒenɪm þa elehꞇꞃan leʒe on þa
ꝼeoꞃeꞃ ꞃceaꞇꞇaꞃ þæꞃ æꞃneſ ꝼ oꝼeꞃ þa ðuꞃu ꝼ unðeꞃ
þone þeꞃꝺpolð ꝼ unðeꞃ ꝥ ealoꝼæꞇ ðo mɪð halɪʒ pæꞇꞃe
þa pyꞃꞇ on ꝥ eala ;

Ʒɪꝼ meꞇe ſy apyꞃð ꝼ unʒehꝓæðe mylcen oððe ꝼɪlð
oþþe bꞃyþen · halʒa þa pyꞃꞇe ðo ón ꝼ unðeꞃ ꝥ ꝼæꞇ ·
ꝼ unðeꞃ þa ðuꞃu · ðo elehꞇꞃan ꝼ clɪꝼan · ꝼ beꞇonican
ꝼ bɪꞃceoppyꞃꞇ.

fol. 54 a.

Ðɪþ þon ʒɪꝼ hunꞇa ʒebɪꞇe mannan ꝥ ɪꞃ ſpɪþꞃa ꞃleah
þꞃy ꞃceaꞃꞃan neah ꝼꞃompeaꞃðeſ læꞇ yꞃnan ꝥ bloð ón
ʒꞃennne ſꞇɪccan hæꞃlenne peoꞃꝓ þonne oꝼeꞃ ꝼeʒ apeʒ
þonne ne bɪþ nan yꝼel. Eꞇ aꞃleah ane ꞃceaꞃꞃan ou
þam ðolʒe ʒecnua læcepyꞃꞇ leʒe ón ne bɪþ hím nan
yꝼel. Ðɪþ ʒonʒelpæꞃꞃan bɪꞇe · nɪm æꞃeꞃþan nɪoþo-

---

[1] The Saxons used milk and preparations of milk for the food of the
churls family. Hence the churls
cow is called his Meat cow, DD.
187, 188.

lxvi.

Against mental vacancy and against folly; put into
ale bishopwort, lupins, betony, the southern *or Italian*
fennel, nepte, water agrimony, cockle, marche, then let
the man drink.　For idiotcy and folly, put into ale,
cassia, and lupins, bishopwort, alexanders, githrife, fieldmore, and holy water ; then let him drink.

lxvii.

1. For *the better digestion of* meat taken; take lupins, lay them under the altar, sing over them nine
masses, that shall avail for meat taken; lay it under
the vessel into which thou hast in mind to milk.　If
ale be spoilt, then take lupins, lay them on the four
quarters of the dwelling, and over the door, and under
the threshhold, and under the ale vat, put the wort
into the ale with holy water.

2. If meat be spoilt,[1] and a good quantity of milken
food, or a milking,[2] or brewing, hallow the worts,[3] put
them into and under the vat, and under the door ; use
lupins, and clifwort, and betony, and bishopwort.

See III. liii.

lxviii.

In case that a hunting spider[3] bite a man, that is
the stronger *spider*, strike three scarifications near, in
a direction from the bite, let the blood run into a
green spoon of hazel wood, then throw it over the road
away; then no harm will come of it.　Again, strike a
scarification on the wound; pound leechwort; lay it
on, no harm will happen to the man.　Against bite of
a weaving spider,[4] take the netherward part of æferthe,

---

[1] Cf. Luke xiv. 34.　Marshall.

[2] By one of the benisons in the
ecclesiastical Manuale.

[3] *Salticus scenicus* is now described by this name; but it is very
appropriate for the *Aranea tarantula*, the habits of which our
author had, doubtless, learnt.

[4] *Aranea viatica*.

peaɲðe Ᵹ ꞃlahþoꞃn · ꝺaȝe aðꞃiȝ ꞇo ꝺuꞇ ȝeþæn miꝺ
huniȝe lacna ꝥ ꝺolh miꝺ. Ꝡiþ hunꞇan biꞇe blace ꞅneȝlaꞃ
ón haꞇꞇꝼe pannan ȝehyꝼꞇe[1] Ᵹ ꞇo ꝺuꞇ ȝeȝniꝺene · Ᵹ
piꝓoꝼ · Ᵹ beꞇonican eꞇe ꝥ ꝺuꞇ Ᵹ ꝺꞃince Ᵹ ón lecȝe.
Ꝡiꝺ huuꞇan biꞇe Ním niþepeaɲðne[2] coꞇꞇuc leȝe on
ꝥ ꝺolh. Eꝼꞇ aꞃleah · v. ꞃceaꝼpan ane on þam biꞇe
Ᵹ ꞃeopeꞃ ymbuꞇan peoꝼꝓ miꝺ ꞅꞇiccan ꞅꝼȝenðe oꝼeꝼ
pænpeȝ.

Ꝡiþ peðe hunꝺeꞃ ꞃliꞇe aȝꝓimonian Ᵹ peȝbꝼæðan ȝemenȝe miꝺ huniȝe Ᵹ æȝeꞃ ꝥ hꝼiꞇe lacna þa punðe miꝺ
þy. Ꝡiþ hunꝺeꞃ ꝺolȝe ꞃoxeꞃ claꞇe · ȝꝓunðeꞅpelȝe pyl
on buꞇeꝼan ꞅmiꝼe miꝺ. Eꝼꞇ beꞇonican ȝeꞇꝼiꞃula leȝe
ón þone biꞇe. Eꝼꞇ peȝbꝼæðan ȝebeaꞇ leȝe ón. Eꝼꞇ
ꞇꝓa ciꝓan oððe þꝼeo ꞅeoþ ȝebꝼæð ón ahꞅan menȝ ꝓiꝺ
ꝓyꞃle Ᵹ huniȝe leȝe ón. Eꝼꞇ ȝebæꝼne ꞅꝼineꞅ ceacan
ꞇo ahꞅan ꞃceaꝺ ón. Eꝼꞇ ȝením peȝbꝼæðan moꝼan
ȝecnua[3] piþ ꝓyꞃle ꝺo on ꝥ ꝺolh þonne aꞅcꝓyꝓꝺ hio ꝥ
aꞇeꝼ apeȝ.

.LXX.

Ȝiꝼ mon ꞅie ꞇo pꝼæne pyl hinðheoloþan on piliꞅꞅ́im
ealaꝺ ꝺꝼince on neahꞇ neꝼꞇiȝ. Ǵiꝼ mon ꞅie ꞇo un-
pꝼæne pyl on meolce þa ilcan pyꝼꞇ þonne apꝼænꝼꞇ þu.
Ꝡyl ón eope meolce eꝼꞇ hinðhioloþan alexanðꝓian ꞃoꝼ-
neꞇeꞃ ꞃolm haꞇꞇe pyꝼꞇ þonne biþ hiꞇ ꞅpa híim leoꞃoꞅꞇ
biꝺ.

---

[1] For ȝehyꝼꞃꞇeðe.
[2] niþepeaɲðe corrected to the masculine, MS.
[3] ȝecna, MS.

and lichen from the blackthorn, dry it to dust, moisten
with honey, tend the wound therewith. Against bite
of hunting spider, black snails fried in a hot pan and
rubbed to dust, and pepper, and betony, let *the man*
eat the dust, and drink *it*, and lay it on. For bite of
hunting spider, take the netherward part of mallow,
lay it on the wound. Again, strike five scarifications,
one on the bite, and four round about it, throw *the
blood* with a spoon silently over a wagon way.

Book I.
Ch. xlviii.

lxix.

For bite of mad dog; mingle with honey agrimony
and waybroad, and the white of an egg, dress the
wound with that. For wound by a hound; foxes
clote,ᵃ groundsel, boil *these* in butter, smear therewith. ᵃ *Burdock.*
Again, triturate betony, lay it on the bite. Again,
beat waybroad, lay *it* on. Again, seethe two or three
onions, roast them on ashes, mingle with fat and
honey, lay on. Again, burn a swines cheek *or jaw* to
ashes, shed *this* on. Again, take more *or root* of waybroad, pound it, put it on the wound with lard, then
it will scrape the venom away.

lxx.

If a man be too salacious, boil water agrimony in
foreign ale, let *him* drink *thereof* at night fasting. If
a man be too slow ad venerem, boil that ilk wort in
milk, then thou givest him corage. Boil in ewes
milk, again, hindheal, alexanders, *the* wort *which* hight
Fornetsᶦ palm,ᵃ then it will be with him as he would ᵃ Unknown.
liefest have it be.

ᶦ For Fornet or Fornjot, see the index of names.

.LXXI.

Vıþ þæʒe ɲeoſan ɲuðan ſpa ʒɲene ſeoþ on ele Ᵹ on
peaxe ſmıɲe mıð þone ɲæʒeɲeoſan. Єſꞇ nı́m ʒaꞇe hæɲ
ſmec unðeɲ þa bɲec ɲıþ þæɼ ɲæʒe ɲeoſan. ʒı́ſ hoh
ſıno ſoɲað ſıe · nım ſoɲneꞇeſ ſolm ſeoð on pæꞇɲe
beþe mıð ꝥ lım Ᵹ þpeah mıð ꝥ lım Ᵹ pyɲce ſealſe
óſ buꞇeɲan ſmıɲe æſꞇeɲ baþe.

.LXXII.

On hpılce ꞇıð bloð ſıe ꞇo ſoɲʒanne on hpılce ꞇo
læꞇenne. bloðlæɼ ıſ ꞇo ſoɲʒanne ſı́ſꞇyne nıhꞇum æɲ
hlaſmæɼɼe Ᵹ æſꞇeɲ ſı́ſ Ᵹ þɲıꞇıʒ nıhꞇum ſoɲ þon þonne
ealle æꞇeɲno þınʒ ſleoʒaþ Ᵹ mannum ſpıðe ðeɲıað ·
læcaɼ læɲðon þa þe pıſoſꞇe pæɲon ꝥ nan man on þam
monþe ne ðɲenc ne ðɲunce ne ahpæɲ hıſ lıchoman panıʒe
buꞇan hı́ſ nyðþeaɲſ pæɲe · Ᵹ þonne on mıððelðaʒúm
ınne ʒepunoðe ſoɲ þon þe ſıo lyſꞇ bıþ þonne ſpıþoſꞇ ʒemenʒeð. Romane hım ſoɲþon Ᵹ ealle ſuð ſolc poɲhꞇon
eoɲþ huſ ſoɲ þæɲe lyſꞇe pylme Ᵹ æꞇeɲneɼɼe. Єác
ſecʒeað læcaɼ ꝥꞇe ʒeblopene pyɲꞇa þonne ſıen beꞇſꞇe
ꞇo pyɲcenne ʒe ꞇo ðɲencum ʒe ꞇo ſealſum ʒe ꞇo ðuſꞇe.
Ðu món ſcule bloðlæſe ón þaɲa ſıx ſıɼa ælcúm on
monðe ſoɲʒan Ᵹ hponne hıꞇ[1] beꞇſꞇ ſıe · læcaɼ læɲað
eác ꝥ nan mán on þon ſı́ſ nıhꞇa ealðne monan Ᵹ eſꞇ
x. nıhꞇa Ᵹ ſıſꞇyne Ᵹ ꞇpenꞇıʒeſ Ᵹ ſı́ſ Ᵹ ꞇpenꞇıʒeſ Ᵹ

---

[1] The idea is blóð ſoɲlæꞇan, for bloðlæſe is feminine.

lxxi.

For the dorsal muscle, seethe in oil and in wax, rue
so green, smear the dorsal muscle therewith. Again,
take goats hair, make it smoke under the breech up
against the dorsal muscle. If a heel sinew be broken,
take Fornets palm, seethe it in water, foment the limb
therewith, and wash the limb therewith ; and work a
salve of butter, smear after the fomentation.

lxxii.

On what season bloodletting is to be foregone, on
what to be practised. Bloodletting is to be foregone
fifteen nights ere Lammas,[1] and after it for five and
thirty nights, since then all venomous things fly and
much injure men.[2] Leeches who were wisest, have
taught, that in that month no man should either drink
a *potion* drink, nor anywhere weaken his body, except
there were a necessity for it ; and that in that case,
he during the middle of the day should remain within, since the lyft *or air* is then most mingled *and
impure.* The Romans for this reason, and all south
folk, wrought to themselves earth houses, for the boiling heat and venomousness of the lyft.[3] Also leeches
say that blossomed worts are then best to work, either
for drinks, or for salves, or for dust. *Here is set forth*
how a man shall forego bloodletting on each of the
six fives in the month, and when it is best. Leeches
teach that no man on the five nights old moon, and
again on the ten nights *old*, and fifteen *nights old*,
and twenty, and five and twenty, and on the thirty

---

[1] August 1.
[2] This refers to Italy and to its
plumbeus auster, Autumnusque
gravis, Libitinæ quæstus acerbæ.

[3] The Italian sirocco, per autum-
nos nocentem corporibus.

K 2

148 LÆCE BOC.

þriꞇigef nihꞇa ealðne monan ne læꞇe blob ac beꞇþeox
þaꝺa ꝛex ꝼiꝼa ælcúm · ꝺ nif nan bloblæꝛꞇið fpa ꝣob
fpa on ꝼoꝺiepeaꝺðne lencꞇen þonne þa yꝛelan pæꞇan

beoþ ꝣeꝣaðeꝺoðe þe on pinꞇꝛa ꝣebꝛuncene beoð ꝺ on
kalenðaf apꝛilif ealꝺa ꝛelefꞇ þonne ꞇꝛeop ꝺ pyꝛꞇa
æꝺefꞇ úp fꝛꝛyꞇꞇað þonne peaxeð fio yꝛele ꝣilleſꞇꝛe ꝺ
ꝥ yꝛele blob on þam holcum þæꝛ lichoman. ꝣíꝛ monneꝛ blob bolh yꝛeliꝣe ꝣením þonne ꝣeoꝛꝺmen leaꝛ apylle
on pæꞇꝛe ꝺ beþe mið · ꝺ ꝣecnua nioþoꝛeaꝺðe leꝣe ón.
ꝣíꝛ þu pille on fmibe blob ꝼoꝺlæꞇan · ním ceꞇelef hꝛum
ꝣeꝣnið ꞇo ðufꞇe ꝛceað ón þa punðe. ꝣením ꝛiꝣen healm
eꝼꞇ ꝺ beꝛen ꝣebæꝛn ꞇo ðufꞇe · ꝣiꝛ þu ne mæꝣe blob
ðolh apꝛiþan ꝣením hoꝛꝛeꝛ ꞇoꝛð nipe aðꝛiꝣe ón funnan
oððe be ꝼyꝛe ꝣeꝣnið ꞇo ðufꞇe fꝛiþe pel leꝣe ꝥ ðufꞇ
fꝛiþe þicce on linenne clað ꝛꝛꝛþ mið þy ꝥ bloððolh
neahꞇeꝛne. ꝣiꝛ þu ꝣeoꞇenð æðꝛie nc mæꝣe apꝛiþan
ꝣenim ꝥ ꝛelꝼe blob ꝼe oꝼyꝛꝛð ꝣebæꝛn ón haꞇum fꞇane
ꝺ ꝣeꝣnið ꞇo ðufꞇe leꝣe on þa æðꝛe ꝥ ðufꞇ ꝺ[1] apꝛꝛð
fꝛiðe. ꝣíꝛ mon æꞇ bloblæꞇan ón finpe beꝛlea menꝣ
ꞇoꝛomne peax ꝺ píc ꝺ fceapen fmeꝛa leꝣe on clað ꝺ
on ꝥ ðolh.

.LXXIII.

Ꝣiꝛ men cine hpilc lim ꝣením ꝛiꝣen mela ðo on ꝥ
lim ꝺ nane pæꞇan · ꝣiꝛ þu pæꞇan ðefꞇ ꞇo oþþe fmeꝛa
ꝛealꝛe ne meahꞇ þu hiꞇ ꝣelacnian ꝺ ꝛe man ꝛceal fꝛiþe
fꞇille beon þy þu ꝛcealꞇ hine halne ꝣeðon.

.LXXIIII.

Ꝥiþ peaꝛꞇum ꝺ peaꝛꝛium[1] ón lime · ꝣením finꝣꝛenan
ꝺ huniꝣef ꝛeap menꝣ ꞇoꝣæðeꝛe ðo on þa peaꝛꞇan ꝺ

---

[1] So in Latin Verrucæ are distinguished from Vari.

nights old moon should let blood, but betwixt each of
the six fives: and there is no time for bloodletting so
good as in early lent, when the evil humours are
gathered which be drunken in during winter, and
on the kalends of April best of all, when trees and
worts first up sprout, when ' the evil ratten waxeth,
and the evil blood, in the hulks *or hollow frame-
works* of the body. If a lancet wound grow corrupt
in a man, then take mallow leaves, boil them in water,
and bathe therewith, and pound the netherward part
of the wort; lay on. If thou wilt stop blood running
in an incision, take kettle soot, rub it to dust, shed it
on the wound. Again, take rye and barley halm, burn
it to dust; if thou may not stanch a blood*letting* wound,
take a new horses tord, dry it in the sun, or by the
fire, rub it to dust thoroughly well, lay the dust very
thick on a linen cloth, tie up for a night the blood-
letting wound with that. If thou may not stanch a
gushing vein, take that same blood which runneth out,
dry it on a hot stone and rub it to dust, lay the dust
on the vein, and tie up strong. If in bloodletting a
man cut upon a sinew, mingle together wax, and
pitch, and sheeps grease, lay on a cloth, and on the
cut.

lxxiii.

If for a man any limb *of his* become chinked *or
chopped,* take rye meal, apply it to the limb and no
wet; if thou puttest wet to it, or a grease salve, thou
mayest not cure it, and the man shall be very still, in
that way thou shalt make him hole.

lxxiv.

Against warts and callosities on a limb ; take singreen, and juice of honey, mingle together, apply to the

peaꞃꞃaſ. Eꝼꞇ cealꝼeꞅ ſceaꞃn ⁊ ahſan ȝemenȝ Ꝋið eceð
⁊ leȝe ón. Eꝼꞇ Ꝋiþieꞅ ꞃinðe ȝebæꞃn ꞇo ahſan Ꝋo eceð
ꞇo ꞇꞃiꝼula ſꝊiðe ⁊ leȝe ón.

. LXXV.

Ƿiþ ſcuꞃꝼeðum næȝle . nꝼm ȝecyꞃnaðne ſꞇiccan ꞃeꞇe
ón þone næȝl Ꝋið þa peaꞃꞇa ꞃleah þonne ꝥ ꝥ bloð
ſꝊꞃinȝe úꞇ . pyꞃc þonne þymel ꞇo ⁊ leȝe ealð ſꝊic ón
uꝼan þone næȝl healð þꞃiꞇiȝ nihꞇa Ꝋiþ pæꞇan . Nim
þonne hꝊæꞇen coꞃn ⁊ huniȝ menȝ ꞇoſomne leȝe on Ꝋo
ꝥ ꞇo oþ ꝥ hal ꞃie.

. LXXVI.

Ƿiþ ȝicþan ðoccau ⁊ pyꞃim melu ⁊ ꞃealꞇ[1] ealꝟa emꞃela
menȝ Ꝋið ſuꞃe ꞃleꞇan ⁊ ſmiꞃe mið þy. Ƿiþ ȝicþan
nꝼm ſciꝟꞇeaꞃo ⁊ iꞃiȝꞇeaꞃo ⁊ ele ȝꞃið ꞇoȝæðeꞃe Ꝋo
þꞃiððan ðæl ſealꞇeꞃ[2] ſmiꞃe mið þy.

fol. 56 b.

. LXXVII.

Ȝiꝼ þu Ꝋille ꝥ yꝼel ſꝊile ꞃaðe uꞇbeꞃſꞇe nim peax ⁊
hemlic haꞇꞇe pyꞃꞇ ȝebeaꞇ ȝepyꞃmeð ꞇoſomne pyꞃc ꞇo
ꞃealꝼe binð on þa ſꞇopa.

. LXXVIII.

Giꝼ men unluſꞇ ſie ȝeꞇenȝe . nime beꞇonican ꝥ Ꝋille
þꞃy peneȝaꞅ ȝepeȝan ðꞃꝼnc ón ſpeꞇꝊm pæꞇeꞃe.

[LXXVIIII.]

Ȝiꝼ món ꝼꞃam lonȝum peȝe ȝeꞇeoꞃoð ſie ðꞃince be-

---

[1] ȝebon in the margin of MS., by later hand ; ȝebo on was meant.
[2] After ſealꞇeꞃ add on.

warts and the callosities. Again, mingle with vinegar
calfs sharn and ashes, and lay on.   Again, burn to
ashes withys rind, add vinegar, triturate thoroughly,
and lay on.

lxxv.

For a scurfy nail;[1] take a granulated bit of wood,
set *it* on the nail against the warts, then strike, so that
the blood may spring out, then work a thumbstall for
it, and lay old lard above upon the nail, hold it for
thirty nights against wet, then take wheaten corn and
honey, mingle *these* together, lay on, apply that till
all be well.

lxxvi.

For itch, *take* dock and worms *reduced to* meal, and
salt, of all equally much, mingle with sour cream, and
smear with that.   Against itch, take ship tar, and ivy
tar, and oil, rub together, add a third part of salt,
smear with that.

lxxvii.

If thou shouldst desire that an evil swelling should
rathely burst, take wax and a wort hight hemlock,
beat them together when warmed, work to a salve,
bind on the places.

lxxviii.

If to a man loss of appetite happen, let him take
betony, so much as will weigh three *silver* pennies,
and drink it in sweetened water.

[lxxix.]

If a man is tired by a long journey, let him drink

---

[1] Thus, " Unguium scabritiem " ; Plin. xxx. 37.

tonican on þam suðrenan oxumelle · ꝥ[1] eced drenc þe ƿe ær beforan ƿriton ƿiþ þære healf deadan adle.

.LXXX.

Ƿiþ þon þe mon hine fordrince. drince betonican on ƿætre ær oþerne drincan. Eft ƿyl betonican ⁊ eorð geallan on hluttrum ealað oþþe ón sƿilcre ƿætan sƿa he drincan scyle drince simle ær mete. Eft genim sƿines lungenne gebræd ⁊ on neaht nestig genim fif snæda simle.

.LXXXI.

Ƿiþ miclan cele nim netelan seoþ ón ele smire ⁊ gnid ealne þinne lichoman mid se cyle gewit aweg.

.LXXXII.

Gif men sie micel ƿæce getenge popig gegnid ón ele smire þinne ⁊ ƿlitan mid ⁊ þone lichoman ealne ƿundorlice raþe him biþ sio ƿæcce gemetgod.

fol. 57 a.

.LXXXIII.

To monnes stemne nim cerfillan ⁊ ƿuducerfillan bisceopƿyrt ontran · grundesƿelgean ƿyrc to drence on hluttrum ealað · Nim þreo snæda buteran gemenge ƿið hƿæten mela ⁊ gesylte þige mid þy drence do sƿa nigon morgenas ma gif his þearf sie.

---

[1] drenc is masculine, ꝥ may have been written since eced, neuter, comes as the next word, and so seems most likely; or even as early as this, ꝥ may begin to stand for any gender.

betony in the southern drink, oxymel; the acid drink of which we before wrote in *treating* of the half dead disease.[1]

lxxx.

In case a man should overdrink himself; let him drink betony in water before his other drink. Again, boil betony and earthgall in clear ale, or in such drink as he, *the drunkard*, may have to drink, let him drink this always before meat. Again, take a swines lung,[a] roast it, and at night fasting take five slices always.

[a] Plin.xxx.51.

lxxxi.

Against mickle cold; take nettles,[b] seethe them in oil, smear and rub all thine body therewith: the cold will depart away.

[b] See Catullus, xliv.

lxxxii.

If to a man there betide much wakefulness, rub down a poppy in oil, smear thy forehead therewith, and all thy body, wonderfully soon the wakefulness will be moderated for him.[2]

lxxxiii.

For a mans voice; take chervil, and wood chervil, bishopwort, "ontre," groundsel, work *these* to a drink in clear ale. Take three slices of butter, mingle with wheaten meal, and salt it, swallow this with the *above* drink; do so for nine mornings, more if there be need of it.

---

[1] No such disease had been mentioned in this book; it is found, II. lix, with the receipt for oxymel.

[2] The change of pronouns is an error of the text.

.LXXXIIII.

Ȝɪf mon þunȝ ete aþeȝe buteɲan ⁊ dɲɪnce · ſe þunȝ
ȝepɪt on þa buteɲan. Efт pɪþ þon ſtande on heaɲbe
aɲlea hɪm mon ɲela ſceaɲpena ón þam ɲcancan þonne
ȝepɪt uт ꝥ atтeɲ þuɲh þa ɲceaɲɲan.

.LXXXV.

Gɪf mon ɲundɪȝe pɪþ hɪſ ɲeond тo ȝeɲeohтanne ſтæþ
ſpealpan bɲubbaſ ȝeſeoþe ón pɪne ete þonne æɲ · oþþe
ɲylle pæтɲe ſeoðe.

.LXXXVI.

Þɪþ mɪclum ȝonȝe oɲeɲ land þy læɲ he тeoɲɪȝe
mucȝpyɲт nɪme hɪm on hand oþþe bo on hɪɲ ɲoo þy
læɲ he meþɪȝe ⁊ þonne he nɪman pɪlle æɲ ɲunnan
upȝanȝe cpeþe þaſ poɲd æɲeſт. Tellam[1] тe aɲтemeɲɪa
ne laɲſuɲ ſúm[2] In uɪa · ȝeſena hɪe þonne þu up тeo : ·

fol. 57 b.

.LXXXVII.

Ȝɪf manneɲ ɲeax ɲealle pyɲc hɪm ɲealɲe ním þone
mɪclan þunȝ ⁊ haɲan ſpɲecel ⁊ eapyɲтe nɪoþopeaɲde ·
⁊ ɲeɲdpyɲт · pyɲc oɲ þæɲe pyɲтe ⁊ oɲ þɪſúm eallum
þa ɲealɲe ⁊ oɲ þæɲe buteɲan þe nan pæтeɲ on ne
come. ȝɪɲ ɲeax ɲealle apylle eoɲoɲɲeaɲɲ ⁊ beþe ꝥ heaɲod
mɪd þy ſpa peaɲme. Þɪþ þon ȝɪf man calu ſɪe · plɪnɪuɲ
ſe mɪcla læce ſeȝþ þɪɲne læcedom · ȝením deade beon
ȝebæɲne тo ahſan ⁊ lɪnſæd eác bo ele тo on ꝥ ſeoþe
ſpɪþe lanȝe oɲeɲ ȝledúm aſeoh þonne ⁊ apɲɪnȝe ⁊ nɪme
peɪɪeɲ leaɲ ȝecnupɪȝe ȝeoтe ón þone ele · pylle eɲт
hpɪle ón ȝledúm aſeoh þonne ſmɪɲe mɪd æɲтeɲ baþe.

Nowhere.

[1] Read Tollam. | [2] Read ſim.

lxxxiv.

If a man eat wolfs bane, let him eat and drink butter, the poison will go off in the butter. Again for
that, let him stand upon his head, let some one strike
him many scarifications on the shanks, then the venom
departs out through the incisions.

lxxxv.

If a man try to fight with his foe, let him seethe
staith swallow nestlings¹ in wine, then let him eat
them ere *the fight*, or seethe them in spring water.

lxxxvi.

For mickle travelling over land, lest he tire, let him
take mugwort ᵃ to him in hand, or put it into his shoe, Vol. I. xi. 1.
lest he should weary, and when he will pluck it, be-
fore the upgoing of the sun, let him say first these
words, " I will take thee, artemisia, lest I be weary on
the way," etc. Sign it with the sign of the cross,
when thou pullest it up.

lxxxvii.

1. If a mans hair fall off, work him a salve, take
the mickle wolfs bane, and vipers bugloss, and the
netherward part of burdock, and ferdwort, work the
salve out of that wort, and out of all these, and out
of that butter on which no water hath come. If hair
fall off, boil the polypody fern, and foment the head with
that, so warm. In case that a man be bald, Plinius,
the mickle leech, saith this leechdom: take dead bees,
burn them to ashes, and linseed also, add oil upon that,
seethe very long over gledes, then strain, wring out,
and take leaves of willow, pound them, pour *the juice*
into the oil, boil again for a while on gledes, strain
them, smear therewith after the bath.

---

¹ *Sand martins, hirundines ripariæ.*

Deapod bæþ pi∂ þon · peliʒer leaf pylle on ræteʃe
þpeah mi∂ þf æʃ þu lhc fmeʃiupe ꝺ þa leaf cnua fpa
ʒefoden ppiþ on niht ón oþ ꝥ hio fie¹ ðʃiʒe ꝥ þu mæʒe
fmeʃʃan æften mi∂ þæʃe fealfe ∂o fpa .xxx. nihta
lenʒ ʒif hif þeaʃf fie. Þiþ þon þe² hæʃ ne peaxe
æmettan æʒʃu ʒenim ʒni∂ fmit on þa ftope ne cym∂
þæʃ næfʃe æniʒ feax úp;

ʒif hæʃ to þicce fie ʒením fpealpan ʒebæʃn unðeʃ
tiʒelan to ahfan ꝺ læt fceadan þa ahʃan ón.

.LXXXVIII.

Þiþ hoʃʃef hʃeofle · nim þa³ haʃanpyʃt cnua pel
ʒemenʒ þonne pi∂ fepfcʃe buteʃan pyl fʃi∂e ón but-
ʃan ∂o on ꝥ hoʃf fpa hit hatoft mæʒe fmiʃe ælce
dæʒe ∂o fimle þa fealfe ón · ʒif fio hʃeofol fie micel
ʒením hlon∂ ʒehæt mi∂ ftanum þpeah mi∂ þy hlon∂c
fpa hatum ꝥ hoʃf · þonne hit ðʃiʒe fie fmiʃe mi∂
þæʃe fealfe lacna inne. Éft ʒením ʃyniaʃ fealt³
ʒehæt þpeah mi∂ þy · ꝺ ∂onne ðʃiʒe fie fmiʃe mi∂
fifcef fmeʃpe. ʒif hoʃf ʒeallede fie · nim æþelfeʃ∂inʒ
pyʃt ꝺ ʒotpoþan · ꝺ maʒeþan ʒecnua pel ∂o buteʃan
to pʃinʒ pætenðe þuʃh cla∂ ∂o hʃit fealt ón hʃeʃ
fpiþe lacna þone ʒeallan mi∂. Þiþ hoʃʃef ʒeallan ním
æʃcþʃotan ꝺ ʒotpoþan ufepeaʃ∂e ꝺ boʒen eac fpa cnua
tofomne pyl on ʃyfle ꝺ ón buteʃan afeoh þuʃh cla∂
fmiʃe mi∂.   :·

ʒif hoʃf fie ófcoten oþþe oʃeʃ neat ním ompʃan
fæ∂ ꝺ fcittifc peax ʒeʃinʒe món .XII. mæʃʃan oʃeʃ ꝺ
∂o haliʒ pæteʃ ón ꝥ hoʃf o∂∂e on fpa hʃilc néat fpa
hit fie hafa ∂e þa pyʃte fimle mi∂.

Þiþ þon ilcan ním tobʃeceʃʃe næ∂le eaʒe ftinʒe
hin∂an on þone byʃlan ne biþ nan teonа.   :·

---

¹ For fien.
² Read miþ þon ꝥ.
³ After þa a word appears wanting.

⁴ Read ʃyniaʃ fealteʃ, as before,
xxxii. 2. ?

2. A head bath for that; boil willow leaves in water, wash with that, ere thou smear it, and pound the leaves so sodden, bind on at night, till they be dry, that thou may after smear with the salve; do so for thirty nights, longer if need for it be. In order that the hair may not wax; take emmets eggs, rub *them up*, smudge on the place; never will any hair come up there.

3. If hair be too thick, take a swallow, burn it to ashes under a tile, and have the ashes shed on.

lxxxviii.

1. For a horses leprosy,[1] take the . . . . . harewort, pound it well, then mingle with fresh butter, boil thoroughly in butter, put it on the horse as hot as possible, smear every day, always apply the salve. If the leprosy be mickle, take piss, heat it with stones, wash the horse with the piss so hot; when it is dry, smear with the salve, apply *also* leechdoms inwardly. Again, take runnings of salt, heat them, wash with that, and when it is dry, smear with fishes grease. If a horse be galled, take stichwort, and goutweed, and maythe, pound well, add butter, wring it wetting it through a cloth, add white salt, shake thoroughly, leech the gall therewith. For a horses gall, take ashthroat, and the upward part of goutweed, and rosemary also, pound together, boil in fat and in butter, strain through a cloth, smear therewith.

2. If a horse or other neat be elf shot,[2] take sorrel seed and Scottish wax, let a man sing twelve masses over it, and put holy water on the horse, or on whatsoever neat it be, have the worts always with thee.

3. For the same; take an eye of a broken needle, give *the horse* a prick *with it* behind in the barrel, no harm shall come.

---

[1] Grease in the legs ?

[2] The Scottish phrase for this disease ; see the Glossary.

Book II.

.I. Þᴀs læceðomaſ belimpa𝛿 co eallſim innoþa met-
cꞃymneꞃꞃúm.   :·

.II. Læceðomaſ piþ maȝan ꞃaꞃe ealꞃa · x. ꞇ ȝiſ ſe
maȝa aþeneð ſie ꞇ hpæc he þicȝean ꞃcyle ón þæꞃe
able.   :·

.III. Læceðomaꞃ be ȝeſpelle ꞇ ꞃaꞃe þæꞃ maȝan hu
him món ſcyle bloð læcan.   :·

.IIII. Læceðomaꞃ piþ heaꞃðum ſpyle þæꞃ maȝan ꞇ
ſmeꞃeneꞃꞃa ꞇ hpæc he þicȝean ꞃcyle.   :·

.V. Læceðomaꞃ piþ maȝan aþunðeneꞃꞃe ꞇ hpæc he ón
þæꞃe able þicȝe.   :·

.VI. Læceðomaſ piþ unluſce ꞇ plæcan þe óꞃ maȝan
cymð ꞇ hpæc he þicȝean ſcyle · IIII. cꞃæꞃcaſ.   :·

.VII. Læceðomaſ pi𝛿 abeaboðum maȝan ꞇ ȝiſ he ꞃoꞃ-
ſoȝen ſie ꞇ cacn abeaboðeꞃ maȝan hu þ ne ȝemylc þ
he þiȝeþ · VI. læceðomaꞃ.   :·

.VIII. Læceðomaꞃ piþ ꞃaꞃe ꞇ unluſce þæꞃ maȝan ꞃe
þe ne mæȝ ne mið mece ne mið ðꞃincan beon ȝelacnoð
ꞇ biceꞃe hꞃæcecunȝe þꞃopað · IIII. cꞃæꞃcaꞃ.

.VIIII. Læceðomaſ piþ inpunðe maȝan.   :·

.X. Læceðóm pið plæccan ꞇ co hæcenne uncꞃumne
maȝan ;

.XI. Læceðóm piþ aþunðeneꞃꞃe maȝan pinðiȝꞃe ꞇ
eþunȝe.   :·

.XII. Læceðóm piþ ſpipþan ꞇ piþ þon ðe him mece
unðeꞃ ȝepunian nelle.   :·

.XIII. Læceðóm piþ maȝan ſpꞃinȝe.   :·

.XIIII. Læceðóm pið eallum maȝan uncꞃúmneꞃꞃúm. :·

.XV. Læceðóm piþ þæꞃ maȝan ſpꞃinȝe þonne þuꞃli
muþ biceꞃe hꞃæcð oþþe bealcec oþþe him on þam

Book II.

i. These leechdoms belong to all disorders of the inwards.

ii. Leechdoms for sore of the maw, in all ten, and if the maw be distended, and what the patient shall eat in that disorder.

iii. Leechdoms for swelling and sore of the maw, how one must let him, *the patient*, blood.

iv. Leechdoms for hard swelling of the maw, and smearings, *or unguents*, and what *the patients* diet shall be.

v. Leechdoms for puffing up of the maw, and what *the patient* shall partake of in this disorder.

vi. Leechdoms for want of appetite and for nausea, which cometh of the maw, and what *the patient* shall eat; four crafts, *or skilful recipes*.

vii. Leechdoms for deadened maw, and if it have bad lymph, and tokens of deadened maw, how that digests not, which it eateth; six leechdoms.

viii. Leechdoms for sore and want of appetite of the maw, which may be cured neither with meat nor drink, and suffereth bitter risings in the throat; four receipts.

ix. Leechdoms for an inward wound of the maw

x. A leechdom for nausea, and to heat an infirm maw.

xi. A leechdom for windy inflation of the maw, and for puffing up.

xii. A leechdom for spewing, and in case that *a mans* meat will not keep down.

xiii. A leechdom for flux of the maw.

xiv. A leechdom for all infirmities of the maw.

xv. A leechdom for irritation of the maw when there is a bitter heart burn in the mouth, or there is belching,

maȝan ʃe mete abıtepað ꝺ ʃyȝeþ¹ ꝺ hu ʃio ablapunȝ
þæʃ maȝan cymð oʃ þam blacum omum.   :·

.XVI. Læcebomaʃ ꝺ tacn þæʃ hatan omıhtan maȝan
unȝemet ʃæʃta ꝺ þæʃ unȝeʃceaðlıce cealban maȝan
tacn hu ʃe hata omıhta maȝa unȝemet þuʃʃt ꝺ ʃpol
þnopað ꝺ neaponeʃʃe ꝺ ȝeʃpoȝunȝa ꝺ ȝemoðeʃ tpeonunȝe
unluʃt ȝe plætta · ꝺ hu ðone cealban maȝan unȝelıc-
lıce mettaʃ lyʃte · læcebomaʃ to bæm mıcle ꝺ eþele ·
ꝺ be lattpe meltunȝe ʃumpa metta.

.XVII. Læcecpæʃtaʃ be lıʃpe mıʃSenlıce ȝecynðo ꝺ
ablũm ꝺ hu hıo on þa ʃpıðpan ʃıðan aþeneð bıþ oþ
þone nuʃeoþan · ꝺ hu hıo bıþ ʃıʃkeppeðu · ꝺ hu hıo ıʃ
blobeʃ tımbeþ ꝺ huʃ ꝺ þte ʃex þınȝ pyпceaþ lıʃeп-
pæпce ꝺ lácnunȝ þaпa ealпa ꝺ ʃpeotol tacn þaпa ealпa
ȝe be mıȝean ȝe be unluʃte · ȝe be lıʃ lıpe · ꝺ
oþпũm maneȝum tacnum.

.XVIII. Læcaʃ læпað þıʃne læcebõm pıþ lıʃпe ʃpyle ꝺ
aþunðeneʃʃe.   :·
.XVIIII. Læceaʃ ʃecȝeaþ þaʃ tacn be aʃpollenпe ꝺ
ȝepunðaðпe lıʃпe · ꝺ læcebomaʃ pıð þon · ꝺ be þæпe
lıʃпe heaпðunȝe.
.XX. Læcaʃ læпað þıʃ pıþ þæпe lıʃпe pınðe þonne
ʃe ʃpyle ȝe pyпmʃ tobyпʃt.   :·
.XXI. Læcebomaʃ ꝺ tacn aheaпðoðпe lıʃпe · ꝺ ũblap-
enпe õn manıȝʃealbe pıʃan ȝe on þãm læppum ȝe on
þãm uʃeпuın ȝe on þam ʃılınenum ȝe on þam holcum
þæпe lıʃпe.   :·
.XXII. Læcebomaʃ pıþ þæпe ȝeʃelan² heaпðneʃʃe þæпe

lıʃпe ꝺ ʃealʃa ꝺ pyпtðпencaʃ oþþe ȝıʃ hıo tobyпʃt ꝺ
nıþeп ȝeʃıt oððe úpaʃcıhð oþþe to lanȝʃum pyпð ʃio
unȝeʃele aheaпðunȝ þæпe lıʃпe ;

---

¹ The text has ʃaȝeð. | the full text we cannot alter to
² As the same reading occurs in | unȝeʃelan.

or if the meat turns bitter in the maw and he hickets, and how the upblowing of the maw cometh of black bile.

xvi. Leechdoms and tokens of the hot inflamed maw, immeasurably fast, *and not to be moved*, and of the unreasonably cold maw; tokens how the hot inflamed maw suffers infinite thirst, and swealing heat, and oppression, and swoonings, and vacillation of the mind, loss of appetite or nausea; and how variety of meats pleases the cold maw; leechdoms for both, mickle and noble; and of the late digestion of some meats.

xvii. Leechcrafts of the various nature and disorders of the liver, and how it is extended on the right side as far as the pit of the belly, and how it is five lobed, and how it is the material and home of blood; and that six things work acute pain in the liver, and the cure of all these, and a plain token of them all, either by the urine, or by loss of appetite, or by *the mans* complexion, and by many other tokens.

xviii. Leeches teach this leechdom for swelling and puffing up of the liver.

xix. Leeches speak of these tokens of a swollen and wounded liver; and leechdoms for that; and of hardening of the liver.

xx. Leeches teach this for wound of the liver, when the swelling or matter bursteth forth.

xxi. Leechdoms and tokens of a hardened and puffed up liver in manifold wise, either in the lobes, or in the margins, or in the membranes, or in the hollows, of the liver.

xxii. Leechdoms for the sense of hardness of the liver, and salves, and wort drinks, or if it burst and descend downwards or mounteth up upwards,[1] or if the insensibility and hardness of the liver become too prolonged.

---

[1] All the viscera were supposed to get out of place.

.XXIII. Læcebomaſ hpæt him ſie to ꝼonꜧanne on
liꝼen able hpæt him ſie to healbanne ꜧe on læcebomum ꜧe ón mete · ꞇ tacn þ̵ ꝛe ſpile þꝛinan ne mæꜧ
ne utyꝛnan ón þæꝛe liꝼꝛe.   :·

.XXIIII. Læcebomaſ ꞇ pyꝛtóꝛencaſ piþ eallum liꝼen
pæꝛcum ealꝛa þꝛeotyne ꞇ ꜧíꝛ liꝼeꝛ peaxe.   :·

.XXV. Læcaꝛ eac be eallum pambe coþum ꞇ ablúm
ſpeotol tacn ꝼunbon ꞇ læcebomaꝛ ꞇ hu món þa yꝼelan
pætan þæꝛe pambe lácnian ſcyle ꞇ þonne abl to þæꝛe
pambe pile ꝼoꝛ þæꝛe yꝼelan omihtan pætan cneoꝛ
hatiaᵭ¹ lenbenu heꝛeꜧiaᵭ ꝛaꝛiaᵭ þaꝛa lenbena liꝛan ·
toꜧeoteþ² betꝛeox ſculbꝛúm utꜧonꜧ ꜧemenꜧeb.

.XXVI. Læcebomaſ ꜧiꝛ ſio pamb punb biᵭ hu þ̵ món
ónꜧitan mæꜧe ꞇ ꜧelácnian · v. cꝛæꝛtaſ.   :·

.XXVII. Læcebomaꝛ be pambe miꝛSenlicꝛe ꜧecynbo
oþþe miꝛbynbo hu þ̵ món mæꜧe onꜧitan ꞇ ꜧelacnian
ꞇ be pambe hattꝛe ꜧecynbo · ꞇ be cealbꝛe ꞇ pætꝛe
ꜧecynbo ꞇ be hattꝛe ꞇ bꝛiꜧꝛe ꜧecynbo ꞇ þ̵ hæmeb þinꜧ
ne buꜧe · þyꝛꝛum lichoman ꞇ ne ſceþeþ hatum ne
pætum · ſeoꝛon cꝛæꝛtaꝛ ꞇ þ̵te hæmeb þinꜧ ſpiᵭoſt
eꜧlaᵭ þam ᵭe hoꝛn able habbaᵭ.   :·

.XXVIII. Læcebomaſ piþ þon þe monneꝛ þ̵ uꝛeꝛꝛe hꝛiꝛ
ſie ꜧeꝛylleb piᵭ yꝛelꝛe pætan ꞇ be ꝛínbiꜧꝛe pambe. :·

.XXVIIII. Læcebomaſ piþ þon þe mete untela mylte
ꞇ ciꝛꝛe ón ꝛule ꞇ yꝛle pætan oþþe ꝛcittan.   :·

---

¹ Read healtiaᵭ ? but hatiaᵭ is in
the full text.   ² Read toꜧetteþ from the full
                        text.

Book II.
Contents.

[1] The maw is the organ of digestion, the stomach; the wamb is the venter, whatever that may mean.

[2] The "hot and cold, wet and "dry" theory was an attempt of the "rationalis disciplina" of the Hellenes to arrive at scientific generalizations; it is traceable among the works attributed to Hippokrates and in Aristoteles.

L 2

.xxx. Læcebomaſ ʒiſ þu pille þ þin pamb ſie
ſimle ʒeſunð ⁊ be coðe ⁊ ſaſie be pambe coðe ⁊ innne-
ſaſian ſaſie ⁊ to pambe ʒemetlicunʒe ſyxtyne cſaſ-
taS.   :·

.xxxi. Læcebomaſ· ⁊ tacnunʒ on þam ſioppe ⁊ ſmæl
þeaſime ⁊ ōn utʒonʒe hu hie þſioſiað oſimætne þuſiſc·
⁊ unluſt· ⁊ be hioſia hiſie ⁊ þām naſolan ⁊ ſiæʒſieoſan
⁊ bæc þeaſime ⁊ niſieſeoþan ⁊ milte¹ ſcaſie ⁊ hu un-
lǣcaſ penað þ þ ſie lenðenaðl oþþe milt pæſic ⁊ hpæſi
]·a pamb ſeocan þa able þſioſien ⁊ hu hiin ſie· ⁊ hu

hioſia mon tilian ſcyle ſeoſieſi ſiſia.²   :·

.xxxii. Læcebomaſ hu mon ſpa ʒeſiaðne mān lacnian
ſcule· ʒe mið bloðlæſie ⁊ ſealſie ⁊ baðo ⁊ lācnūnʒ on
þ hſiiſ to Senðanne· ⁊ þaſ læcebomaſ maʒon pſð
lenðenece· ⁊ ʒiſ mōn ſonðe miʒe· ſiþ ut ſiæſice· ſið
maʒan ablum ⁊ claſiunʒa ⁊ ſiſia bedteſineſſum· ⁊ be
þæſie coðe hu man lyſte utʒan ⁊ ne mæʒ· ⁊ ʒiſ ſe
utʒanʒ ſie ſinðiʒ ⁊ ſiæteſiiʒ ⁊ bloðiʒ· XII. ſiſan.

.xxxiii. Læcebomaſ ſið þæſiſie ſiſiecnan coðe þæ ſe
mōn hiſi utʒanʒ þuſih ðone muð him ſſiām ſiyſiſið ⁊ ·
aſſiiſian ſceal· ⁊ ſið Innoðſiunðum ⁊ ſmæl þeaſima
ſaſie· ⁊ ſið tobſiocenum innoþūm ⁊ ſiþ ſoſitoʒeneſſie
innan· ⁊ ſið þæſie pambe þe late mylt ⁊ ſe þaſia læceðoma ne ʒimð þonne becymð him ōn ſiæteſi bolla liſieſi
pæſic milteſ ſiaſi micʒean ſoſihæſiðneſ pambe ablaſiunʒ
lenðenſiæſic ſonð ⁊ ſtaiaſ ōn blæðſian peaxað þſieotyne
cſiaſtaſ.   :·

¹ Read milte ⁊. | ² Before erasure, ſiſian.

xxx. Leechdoms if thou will that thy wamb be always sound, and of disease and sore; and of disease of the wamb and sore of the intestines, and for the moderation[1] of the wamb; sixteen receipts.

xxxi. Leechdoms and symptoms marking of the rope gut and small gut, and of the fæcal discharge; how they suffer unbounded thirst and loss of appetite; and of their *complexion or* hue, and of the navel, and the dorsal muscles, and rectum, and pit of the belly, and milt, and share *or pubes*, and how bad leeches ween that that is loin disease or milt wark, and where the wambsick suffer the disorder, and how it is with them, and how a man shall treat them: four methods.

xxxii. Leechdoms how a man shall cure one so afflicted, whether with bloodletting, and salve, and baths, and *how* to send curatives into the belly. And these leechdoms are efficacious against loin ache, if a man mie sand, for dysentery, for diseases of the maw, and gripings, and womens tendernesses, and of the disease where a man would evacuate and is not able (*tenesmus*), and if the discharge be windy, and watery, and bloody. Twelve methods.

xxxiii. Leechdoms for the perilous disease in which a man casteth from him and speweth, as they say, his excrement through the mouth; and for wounds of the inwards, and sore of the small guts, and for laceration of the inwards, and for inward spasm; and for the wamb which digests late, and the man who is not affected by the leechdoms; there cometh on him dropsy, pain in liver, sore of spleen, retention of urine, inflation of belly, pain in loins, sand and stones wax in the bladder. Thirteen receipts.

---

[1] The "tempcrics" and "commoderatio ventris," that it be neither too hot nor too cold.

fol. 61 b.

.XXXIIII. Læcebomaƿ ꞅ be þæƿ manneꞅ mihtum ꞅceal
mon þa læcebomaꞅ ƿellan þe þonne ȝeꝼoȝe ꞅynð · ȝe
heaƿðe · ȝe heoꞃtan · ꞅ ꝥambe · ꞅ blæðꞃan ꞅ ꞃoȝeþan·
ꞅ hu ȝcaꞃeꞅ hit ꞅie be hæto ꞅ cele ꞅ ꝥiþ lattꞃe meltunȝe · oððe ȝiꝼ ꝥamb ꝼoꞃꞃeaxen ꞅ ꝼoꞃꞃunðoð ꞅie·
ꞅ ȝiꝼ mon ꞅie innan ꝼoꞃblaꞃen · ꞅ ꝥið ꝥambe ꝥꞃinum[1]
ꞅ ȝicþûm · nyȝan ꝥiꞃan.   :·

.XXXV. Læcebomaꞅ be cilða oꝼeꞃꝼyllo ꞅ ꝥambe ꞅ ȝiꝼ
him mete tela ne mylte ꞅ him ꞅꝥat óꝼȝa ꞅ ꞅtince
ꝼulc.   -   :·

.XXXVI. Læcebomaꞅ be milte pæꞃce ꞅ ꝥ he bið on
þa pinꞃtꞃan[2] ꞅiðan ꞅ tacn ðæꞃe able hu hiȝeleaꞅe hi
beoð ꞅ hu lanȝ ꞅe milte ꞅie ꞅ be þæꞃ milteꞅ ꝼilmene
on þa pinꞅtꞃan healꝼe be hleahtꞃe þe óꝼ milte cymð·
hu ꞅe milte æȝhꝥæt þꞃoꝥað þæꞃ þe oþeꞃ limo ȝe hát
ȝe cealð · ꞅ be bæðe ꞅ hæmeð þinȝe ꞅ hꝥanan ꞅio
hæto cume ꞅ cele þæꞃ milteꞅ eahta cꞃæꝼtaꞅ. :·

fol. 62 a.

.XXXVII. Læcebomaꞅ hu món ꞅcyle þone mónnán
Innan ꞅ utan mið cealðum ꞅ hatum læcebomum lácnian ꞅ hꝥilc mete him ꞅie to þicȝenne ꞅ hꝥilc him ꞅie
to ꝼoꞃȝanne.   :·
.XXXVIII. Læcebomaꞅ hu mon ꞅceal þa pætan ꞅ pon-
ꞅceaꝼta utan lácnian ꞅ be þam pætum yꞃlum þæꞃ
milteꞅ ꞅ ꝥið ꞅliꞃunȝe pætan þæꞃ milteꞅ. · :·

.XXXVIIII. Læcebom ꝥiþ ꝥinðiȝꞃe aþunðeneꞅꞃe þæꞃ
milteꞅ ꞅio cymð oꝼ æpla æte ꞅ hnuta · ꞅ pyꞅena · ꞅ
huniȝeꞅ æte ꞅ þone ꞃoꝼ ꞅ inneꝼoꞃan ꞅ ꝥambe ꞅ

---

xxxiv. Leechdoms; and the leechdoms which are suitable to the case shall be administered according to the mans powers, whether in head, or heart, and of wamb, and bladder, and lymph;[1] and according as the time of year may be, in regard to heat and cold; and for late digestion, or if the wamb be overgrown and wounded; and if a man be blown out inwardly; and for prurience, and itchings of the wamb; nine methods.

xxxv. Leechdoms for the overfilling *or surfeit* of children, and for their wamb, and if their meat digest not well, and if sweat pass from them and stink foully.

xxxvi. Leechdoms of pain in the milt, and that *the milt* is on the left side, and tokens of the disease, how reckless *the sick* are, and how long the milt is, and of the film *or membrane* of the milt on the left side, and of *splenetic* laughter, which cometh of the milt, how the milt suffereth everything of that which other limbs *suffer* either hot or cold; and of the bath, and of sexual commerce, and whence the heat cometh and the cold of the milt: eight receipts.

xxxvii. Leechdoms how a man shall tend the man within and without with cold and hot leechdoms, and what meat he is to take, and what he is to forego.

xxxviii. Leechdoms how a man shall cure the humours and the livid complexion by external applications, and of the evil humours of the milt, and of the lubricity of the humours of the milt.

xxxix. A leechdom for a windy swollen state of the milt, which cometh of eating of apples, and of nuts, and of peas, and of honey, and which puffeth up throughout the rope gut, and the intestines, and the

---

[1] Gastric juice.

maȝan þa ȝeonð blapað · ⁊ pið roȝeþan ⁊ feaðan þe óf
milte cymð · ⁊ hu fio aðl ȝepent ón pæter bollan
ealler tyn cpæftar.   :·

.XL. Læceboniaf be ablapunȝe ⁊ aheapðunȝe þæf
blobef on ǀ am milte.   :·

.XLI. Læceðomaf piþ þæpe heapðnerre ⁊ fape milter
⁊ hu mon mæȝ fpiner blæðpan mið ecebe ȝefylðpc
ȝehnercan þa heapðnerre ⁊ piþ eallum inablum þny
cpæftaS.   :·

.XLII. Læceðomaf ȝíf omihtpe blob ⁊ yfele pætan
on þam milte ryn þinðenðe þonne rceal him món
blob lætan on þar piran þe þeor læceboc feȝþ · ⁊
be þar blober hipe.   .   :·

.XLIII. Læceðomar hpæt hím on þæpe able to þicȝenne fie hpæt to ropȝanne.   :·

.XLIIII. Læceboni eft re þe þ yfel uttihð of þam
milte fpiðe æþele · ⁊ re eác ðeah piþ maȝan ablapunȝe
⁊ Innoþa hinerceþ þa pambe þynnaþ þa oman · biteje
hpæcetunȝe apeȝ ðeþ ⁊ bjeoft coþe · ⁊ rið pæpc · ⁊
hifep able ⁊ milte pæpc · ⁊ pambe pinð eal þa liht. :·

.XLV. Læceðomar ⁊ fpiððrenc piþ afpollenum.   :·

.XLVI. Læceðomaf piþ ȝehpæþeppe fíðan rape ⁊ tacn
punðophcu hpanan fio cume ⁊ hu fio aðl topeapð fie ·
⁊ hu mon þapa tilian rcyle.   :·

.XLVII. Læceðomar þa ðe þynnunȝe hæbben ⁊ fmal-
unȝe mæȝen · þam lichoman þe þa hæto meðmicle
oþþe ftpanȝe þropien ⁊ hu món fcyle fpinef blæðpan
ón ðon.   :·

.XLVIII. Læceðomaf relpan ȝif þar oþpe helpe ne
fyn hu him món eác blob rcyle lætan.   :·

.XLVIIII. Læceðomaf ⁊ peax realfa ⁊ rceappunȝa piþ
fiðan rape ⁊ hpæt he þicȝean rcyle.   :·

fol 63 a.

.L. Læcebomaſ eꝼꞇ pıð ſıðan ꞃaпe. :·

.LI. Læcebomaꞃ pıð lunꞡen able ꞏ laþlıcu ꞇacn hꞃanan ſıo abl oume ꞏ hu môn lacnıan ſcyle · ðꞃencaꞃ ꞏ ꞃealꝼa ꞏ bꞃıpaſ ꞡe pıð lunꞡe punбe ꞏ ꞡıꝼ lunꞡen bꞃeoþe · ꞏ ꞡıꝼ lunꞡen ðꞃuꞡıꞡe an ꞏ ꞇꞃenꞇıꞡ oꞃæꝼꞇa. :·

.LII. Læcebomaſ ꞏ ſpıpeðꞃencaꞃ mannum ꞇo hæle ꞏ ꞡíꝼ man hıne oꝼeꞃ ꞡemeꞇ bꞃece ꞇo ſpıpanne ꞏ eꝼꞇ pece ðꞃenc oþþe ꞡıꝼ ðꞃenc ôꝼ men nelle eallef ꞇꞃenꞇıꞡ ðꞃencea. :·

.LIII. Læcebomaſ ꞏ leohꞇe ðꞃencaſ mannum ꞇo hælo ꞏ ûnſpıule ðꞃenceaꞃ pıþ unꞇꞃumum ınnoþum ealıꞇa cꞃæꝼꞇaſ. · :·

.LIIII. Læcebomaꞃ ꞏ ðꞃencaſ pıð ınſꞇıce ꞏ ꞡíꝼ ſꞇıce buꞇan ınnoþe ſıe. :·

.LV. Læcebomaſ ꞏ ðꞃencaſ ꞡıꝼ môn ınnan ꞃoꞃhæꝼð ſıe ꞏ pıþ ıncoþe ꞏ ꝼꞃeꞃ coþe. :·

.LVI. Læcebomaſ ꞡıꝼ mon ſıc ôn uꞇꞃæꞃce ꞏ ꞇacn be uꞇꞃıhꞇe ꞡe ôn þam uꝼeꞃꞃan hꞃıꝼe ꞡe ôn þam nıþeꞃꞃan ꞏ hꞃanan ſıo abl cume ꞏ hu môn hıe ꞃcyle lacnıan ꞏ hꞃæꞇ mon þıcꞡean ſcyle ꞏ eꝼꞇ pıþ þon ꞡıꝼ mon bloбe ane uꞇyꞃne ꞏ pıþ mıclum ꞃaꞃe ꞏ ablauneꞃꞃe þæꞃ ın-

fol. 63 b.

noþeꞃ oþþe ꞡíꝼ mon ꞃoꞃ ꞃoppeꞃ unꞇꞃumneꞃꞃe uꞇyꞃne oþþe ꞡıꝼ hꞃa bloðꞃyne þꞃoꞃıꞡe on þam nıþeꞃꞃan бælum hıꞃ lıchoman oþþe ꞡıꝼ hꞃam ꞃıe mıcꞡe on bloð ꞡıꝼ hıo ꞡehꞃyꞃꝼþ · oðбe ꞡıꝼ môn ûꞇꞡanꞡ næbbe ꞏ eꝼꞇ ûꞇ-yꞃnenбe bꞃıp ꝼíꝼ ꞏ hunб ſeoꝼonꞇıꞡ læcebomа. :·

.LVII. Læcebomaꞃ pıþ þeaꞃmeſ ûꞇꞡanꞡe ꞏ ꞡıꝼ men bılyhꞇe ſıe ymb þone þeaꞃm ꞏ pıð blæc[1] þeaꞃmeſ ûꞇꞡanꞡe nıꞡon pıꞃan. :·

---

[1] Read bꞃec.

[1] Cloudy.

.LVIII. Læceðomaſ be þæɲe aðle þe ſtanaʃ on men
Innan ȝepeaxen on þæɲe blæðɲan oððe elleʃ hþæɲ ꞽ
tacn þæɲe aðle be halɲa manna ꞽ unhalɲa micȝea
hꞽpum ꞽ hɲꞽlcne mete mõn þicȝean ſcyle oþþe ʃoɲȝan
tɲentꞽȝ cɲæʃta.   :·

.LVIIII. Læceðomaʃ pꞽþ þæɲe healʃðeaðan aðle ꞽ hpanũn
ſꞽo cume ꞽ hu mon lacnꞽan ‚ɲcyle ʃealʃa ꞽ onleȝena ꞽ
pyɲtðɲencaſ · oþþe ȝꞽʃ neb oþþe heaʃoð ſaɲ ſꞽe be baðe
ꞽ bloðlæʃe · ꞽ ꝥ ſꞽo aðl æɲ ʃeopeɲtꞽȝum oþþe ʃꞽʃtꞽȝum
pꞽntɲa on monnan ne becume · ꞽ be þam ʃuþeɲnan
pyɲteceððɲence an ꞽ tɲentꞽȝ cɲæʃta.   :·

   .LX. Læceðomaʃ pꞽþ pꞽʃa ȝecynðum ʃoɲſetenum ꞽ
eallum pꞽʃa tybeɲneʃʃum ȝĩʃ pꞽʃ beaɲn ne mæȝe ȝe-
beɲan oþþe ȝꞽʃ beaꞽn peoɲþe ðeað on pꞽʃeʃ Innoþe
oððe ȝꞽʃ hꞽo cennan ne mæȝe ðo on hꞽɲe ȝyɲðelʃ þaʃ
ȝebeðo ſpa on þꞽſum læceboc̃um ʃeȝþ ꞽ manꞽȝʃealð tacn
ꝥ mon mæȝe onȝꞽtan hɲæþeɲ hꞽt hyʃe cꞽlð þe mæðen
cꞽlð beon pꞽlle · ꞽ pꞽþ pꞽʃa aðle · ꞽ ȝĩʃ ᵱĩʃ mꞽȝan ne
mæȝe · ꞽ ȝĩʃ pꞽʃ ne mæȝe ꞽaðe beon ȝeclænʃoð ꞽ pꞽþ
pꞽʃa bloðʃꞽhtan · ꞽ ȝĩʃ pꞽʃ õʃ ȝemynðum ſꞽe ꞽ ȝĩʃ þu
pꞽlle ꝥ ᵱĩʃ cꞽlð hæbbe oþþe tꞽʃe hɲelp oþþe ȝꞽʃ men
cɲꞽð ʃꞽe ʃoɲpeaxen · oþþe ȝꞽʃ man Semnꞽnȝa ſpꞽȝꞽe · an
ꞽ ʃeopeɲtꞽȝ cɲæʃta.   :·

.LXI. Læceðõm pꞽþ þæɲe ȝeolpan aðlc ꞽ pꞽð þæm
mꞽclan lꞽce · ꞽ bolhðɲencaſ tɲeȝen ꞽ oþeɲ mæȝ pꞽþ
lunȝen punðe eac.   :·

.LXII. Læceðomaſ pꞽþ mꞽclum heaʃoð ece ꞽ pæɲce ꞽ
ʃealʃ to þon ꞽlcan · ꞽ leah ꞽ eaȝʃealʃa ꞽ ȝebeð to
eaȝũm.   :·

.LXIII. Læceðõm pꞽþ þeoɲaðle ꞽ pꞽþ lunȝenable ꞽ pꞽþ

fol. 64 b.

utpænce · ꝓ ᵹiꝼ mon bloðe ſpipe · ꝓ pɪþ blobꝓyne · ꝓ
ᵹɪꝼ lɪm ꝼæꝓɪnᵹa ace · ꝓ pɪþ blæce on ꝓplɪtan. :·

.LXIIII. Læcebóm ꝛe monɪan[1] pɪþ ɪnnoþeꝛ ꝼoꝛhæꝛb-
neꝛꝛe ꝓ ᵹutomon ·[2] pɪð mɪlte pæꝓce ꝓ ſtɪce ꝓ ſpɪcan
pɪþ utꝛɪhtan ꝓ ðꝛacontᴊan pɪþ ꝼule hoꝛaꝛ on men · ꝓ
alpan pɪþ untꝛymneꝛꝛum · ꝓ ᵹalbaneꝛ pɪþ neaꝛꝛúm
bꝛeoſtum · ꝓ balzaɪnan. ſmɪꝛɪnᵹ pɪþ eallúm untꝛúm-
neꝛꝛúm ꝓ petꝛaoleúm to ðꝛɪncanne anꝼealð pɪþ ɪnnan
tybeꝛneꝛꝛe ꝓ utan to ſmeꝛpanne · ꝓ tyꝛɪaca ɪꝛ ᵹob
ðꝛenc pɪþ ɪnnoþ tybeꝛneꝛꝛum · ꝓ ꝛe hꝛɪta ſtan pɪð
eallúm uncuþum bꝛocum. :·

.LXV. Læcebóm ᵹɪꝼ hoꝛſ ꝛɪe óꝛſcoten ꝓ pɪþ útpæꝓce ·
ꝓ ᵹíꝼ utᵹanᵹ ꝼoꝛſeten ꝛɪe · ꝓ pɪþ lencten able · eꝛt
pɪþ utpæꝓce ꝓ pɪþ unlybbum ꝓ pɪþ þæꝛe ᵹeolpan able
ꝓ ᵹɪꝼ men ſie ꝼæꝛlɪce yꝼele ꝓ to ᵹehealbanne lɪchoman
hælo ꝓ pɪþ ᵹɪcþan ꝓ ælue ꝓ pɪþ lonð able ꝓ ᵹonᵹel-
pæꝛꝛan bɪte · ꝓ pɪð utꝛɪhte ꝓ heaꝼoð ꝛealꝛa.

fol. 65 a.

.LXVI. be þam ſtane þe ᵹaᵹateꝛ hatte.

.LXVII. Be pæᵹe eleꝛ ꝓ oþeꝛꝛa mɪꝛSenlɪcꝛa þɪnᵹa. :·

[I.]

Alexander
Trallianus, lib.
vii. cap. ꝑ, ed.
R. Stephani,
1548.

þɪꝛ Sɪnt tacn aðlieꝛ maᵹan · æꝛeſt ᵹelome ſpætunᵹa
oððe hꝛæcunᵹa · cɪꝛneſ ꝓ ꝛe man hɪne ᵹelome to ſpɪ-
panne · ꝓ he óꝛꝛɪnðeþ ſpɪle ꝓ ꝥ þa oman beoð ɪnne
betynðe þuplɪ þa ablapunᵹe · ꝓ hɪm bɪð uneþe þuꝛſt
ᵹetenᵹe. Eúc oꝼ þæꝛ maᵹan able cumað momᵹe ꝓ
mɪꝛSenlɪca abla ᵹeboꝛſtena punða ꝓ hꝛamma ꝓ ꝼylle
pæꝛc ꝓ ꝛenða abl · ꝓ mɪcla muꝛnunᵹa ꝓ unꝛotneꝛꝛa
butan þeaꝛꝼe ꝓ oman ꝓ unᵹemetlɪca mete ꝛócna ꝓ
unᵹemetlɪce unluſtaſ ꝓ cɪꝛneꝛꝛa · ꝓ ſaꝛa ɪnable ón pɪꝼeꝛ

---

[1] Read ꝛeamonɪan, which is mentioned elsewhere in this book II. iii. 3.,
and is a strong purgative.

[2] Read ᵹut ammon.

blood, and for blood running ; and if a limb suddenly
ache, and for a blotch on the face.

lxiv. A leechdom ; scamony for constipation of
the inwards, and ammoniac drops for pain in the
milt, and stitch, and spices[1] for diarrhœa, and gum
dragon for foul disordered secretions on a man, and
aloes for infirmities, and galbanum for oppression in
the chest and balsam dressing for all infirmities, and
petroleum to drink simple for inward tenderness, and
to smear outwardly, and a tryacle, that is a good
drink, for inwards tendernesses, and the white stone,
lapis Alabastrites, for all strange griefs.

lxv. A leechdom if a horse be elf shot, and for pain
in evacuation of the fæces, and if the evacuation be
stopped, and for the "lent disease," *or typhus ;* again
for pain in evacuation, and for poisons, and for the
yellow disease *or jaundice*, and if sudden evils come
on a man ; and to preserve the bodys health, and
against itch and elf, and for "land disease" *or nostalgia*, and for bite of the gangway weaver, *spider*, and
for diarrhœa and head salves.

lxvi. Of the stone which agate hight.

lxvii. Of the weight of oil, and of other various
things.

i.

These are tokens of diseased maw ; first, frequent
spittings or breakings, choiceness *or a daintiness about
food*, and for the man to spew frequently ; and he will
have a sense of swelling, and that the hot inflamed
humours are shut up within him by the inflation ; and
an uneasy thirst is contingent upon him. Also from
disease of the maw come many and various diseases of
bursten wounds, and cramps, and epilepsy, and fiends
disease, and mickle murmurings and uneasiness without

---

[1] Cinnamon is much administered.

ȝecynbon ⁊ on foðum ⁊ blæbþan· ⁊ on unmoðe· ⁊
ou unȝemeð pæccûm¹ ⁊ unȝepiðlico popð· ꝛe maȝa biþ
neah þæꝛe heopðan ⁊ þæꝛe ȝeloðꝛ·² ⁊ ȝeaðopðenȝe þam
bꝛæȝ[en]e· oꝛ þam cumað þa abla ſpiꝛoſð oꝛ þæꝛ maȝan
inðinȝan ⁊ on³ yꝛlûm ꝛeapum pæðan aððeꝛbeꝛenðum·
þonne ða pæðan⁴ þa yꝛelan peopþaþ ȝeȝabeꝛobe on
þone maȝan· ⁊ þæꝛ ꝛixiað mið ꝛceaꝛꝛunȝa innan·

fol. 65 b.   ſpiþoſð on þam monnum þe habbað ſpiþe ȝeꝛelne ⁊
ſaꝛcꝛenne maȝan ſpa þ̄ hie ſume ſomnunȝa ſpelðaþ·
ne maȝon abeꝛan þa ſðꝛanȝan ꝛceaꝛꝛunȝa þæꝛa
æðeꝛna pæðena· hpilum pyꝛmaſ oꝛ þâm inþeꝛꝛan⁵
ðælûm ȝeꝛecað þa uꝛeꝛꝛan ðælaꝛ ðo þam maȝan· ⁊ eâc
heopðcoþe pyꝛceað· ⁊ anȝneꝛꝛa ⁊ ȝeſpopunȝa ſpa þðe
hpilum ſume men ꝛꝛam þaꝛa pyꝛma ꝛliðunȝe ſpelðað
⁊ ꝛoꝛpeopþað· ꝛoꝛ þon þæm mannûm beah þ him mon
on ꝛꝛuman þa meððaꝛ ȝiꝛe þe celunȝe ⁊ ſðꝛanȝunȝe
mæȝen hæbben ſpa ſpa⁶ beoþ æppla naleꝛ ðo ſpeðe
ealleꝛ âc ꝛuꝛmelſce ⁊ peꝛan ⁊ peꝛꝛucaꝛ ⁊ hlaꝛ ȝeðon
ôn cealð pæðeꝛ oþþe ôn hað be þæꝛe ȝelicunȝe þæꝛ
maȝan þe þa yꝛelan pæðan ſceoꝛꝛenban ⁊ ſceaꝛꝛan
hæꝛð· þiꝛ beah eâc ôn ꝛꝛuman þam ðe þa heopðcoðe
⁊ þ ȝeſceoꝛꝛ ðꝛopiað ælcꝛa ȝeꝛuſð þ him mon lyðluin
þa meððaꝛ ꝛelle þa þe laðe melðen· leax⁷ ⁊ þa ꝛixaꝛ
þa ðe laðe melðan ȝoꝛe inneꝛle⁸ ⁊ ſpineſ ꝛeð þa ðe
mæȝen piþ habban⁹ þam yꝛelan pæðan· ⁊ þonne him
ꝛel ſie þonne þicȝe he ſpeðꝛan meððaſ· ne biþ hîm

fol. 66 a.   nanpuhð ꝛelꝛe þonne he þa þicȝe þa þe laðe melðen¹⁰ ⁊

---

¹ The construction is faulty; it
should be ⁊ unmoð ⁊ unȝemeðꝛæcce.
² Read ȝeloðꝛe? See Lye in
ȝeloba. Also bꝛmæȝe, MS
³ Read oꝛ.
⁴ At this point our author skips
over seven folio pages and goes on
at lib. vii. cap. ιδ, p. 114, ed. 1548.
⁵ The interpreter omits οἱ τῆς ῥοᾶς
κόκκοι, the seeds of the pomegranate,
and ῥοδάκινα, nectarines, and ἡ αὐσ-
τηρὸν καὶ ψυχρὸν ἔχουσα σταφυλή,
grapes of a dry and cold flavour.

⁶ Read niþeꝛꝛan.
⁷ The interpreter takes ἰσικοί for
salmon, esoces, as was and is usual;
and he neatly escapes βοῦλβα,
στέρνιον, ἀσταχοί, cray fish, κτίνια,
scallops, κηρύκια, conch shell fish.
⁸ Read innelꝛe.
⁹ Read habban piþ.
¹⁰ Our interpreter here varies from
the printed text, which recommends
frequent snacks of food; very
wisely.

occasion, and erysipelatous eruptions, and immoderate
desires for meat, and immense want of appetite, and
daintinesses, and sore internal diseases in fœminæ natu-
ralibus, *that is, the uterus*, and in the feet, and in the
bladder, and despondency, and immoderately *long* wak-
ings, and witless words. The maw is near the heart and
the spine, and in communication with the brain, from
which the diseases come most violently, from the cir-
cumstances of the maw, and from evil juices, humours
venombearing. Then the evil humours get gathered
into the maw, and there they rule with excoriations
within; especially in the men who have a very
sensitive and soon sore maw, so that some of them
suddenly die; they are not able to bear the strong
excoriating effects of the venomous humours. At whiles
worms from the nether parts seek the upper parts, up
as far as the maw; and they also work heart disease,[1]
and oppressive sensations, and swoonings; so that sometimes some men by the gnawing of the worms die and
go to the dogs. Wherefore it is well for those men, that
at the first the meats be given them which have the
virtue of cooling and strengthening, such as be apples,
by no means too sweet, but by all means sourish, and
pears, and peaches, and loaf bread put into cold water or
into hot, according to the liking of the man which hath
the evil humours scarifying and sharp. This also is of
importance in the first place to them who suffer the
heart disease[2] and the abrasion; it is fitting that one
should give them by little *at a time* the meats which
tardily digest, as lax *or salmon*, and the fishes which
slowly digest, goose giblets, and swines feet, and such
as have a virtue against the evil humours; and when
he[3] is better, then let him partake of sweeter meats.

Contradicts
B. II. ch. xvi.

---

[1] The Saxon version misses the
meaning of καρδιακὰς διαθέσεις.

[2] Καρδιαλγίαν, *disease of the
digestive organ*, as the Hellenic
author had himself many times
said.

[3] The previous clauses were plural
unless ὄπομαν stand for ὄπομαν.

ſpa þeah ne fynð ſcitole · þicȝe to unðerneſ hlaf ȝe-
brocenne on hat ƿæteꝛ[1] oþþe æppla beꝛinðebe.[2] Eac
biþ ȝob fultum on ȝoðum pyꝛꝺꝛencum ſpa læcaſ
pyꝛcað· of ecebe ⁊ of ꝼinoleſ pyꝛꝺꝛuman ⁊ of ꝛinðe·
⁊ of alpan ⁊ of ðoꝛan huniȝe ·[3] ȝemenȝ þ ⁊ ꝛele þæꝛ
cucleꝛ fulne oþþe tꝛeȝen þonne hneꝛcað þ þa ꝛambe ⁊
tꝛymeþ· ⁊ þ ðeah piþ bꝛeoſt ꝛæꝛce ⁊ piþ heoꝛtcoþe ⁊
pið ꝼelleꝛæꝛce· ⁊ piþ þon þe mon ſie on þam maȝan
omiȝꝛe pætan ȝefylleð· ⁊ pið maneȝum ablum þ ðeah·
ða þe cumað of oꝛeꝛfyllo· ⁊ of miſꝛenlicum yꝛlum
pætum. ȝif hie cumen óf oꝛeꝛfyllo mið ſpipe þan[4]
hy mon ꝛceal lythan. ȝif hie þonne cumað óf oþꝛum
biteꝛúm ⁊ yꝼelum pætúm þa þe pyꝛceað oman þonne
beoþ þa elcꝛan to ſtillanne oþþ þe hie unſtꝛanȝꝛan
peoꝛþan· ſpiþoſt ȝif þa pætan beoð þicce ⁊ ꝛliꝛeȝꝛan.

Alex. Trall.,
cap. íγ., ed.
1548.

be ꝛambe coþe oþþe ȝif of þæꝛe ꝛambe anꝛe þa
yꝼelan pætan cumen ⁊ ne oꝛeꝛyꝛnen ealne þone lichoman þ món ꝛceall mið halpenðúm mettum anum lacnian ·[5] ȝif þonne ſio yꝼele pæte of þæꝛe ꝛambe oꝛeꝛ-
yꝛneþ ealne þone lichoman þæꝛ mon ꝛceal mið maꝛan
lácnunȝe tilian· hpilum hím mon ꝛceal óf æðꝛan blob
lætan ȝif þæꝛ blobeꝛ to ꝼela þince ⁊ þæꝛe yꝼlan pætan
⁊ eac pyꝛꝺꝛenc ꝛellan. Ac æꝛeſt mon ꝛceal blob
lætan æꝛteꝛ þon pyꝛꝺꝛenc ꝛellan.

fol. 66 b.

.II.

Þiþ ꝛaꝛúm ⁊ aþunðenum maȝan ȝenim ele ⁊ ȝebo
hꝛit cꝛuða ⁊ ðile ⁊ ſuþeꝛne peꝛmoð ón þone ele

---

[1] ὕδωρ ψυχρόν. Al. Trall.
[2] ἢ μῆλον ἢ κίτρον ἐκτὸς τοῦ λέτους
αὐτοῦ, A. T.
[3] μέλιτος ἀττικοῦ, A. T.
[4] Not very literally.
[5] Alex. Trall. has more words.

Naught is better for him than that he take those
which digest late, and are notwithstanding not purgative; let him eat at undern, or nine o'clock, loaf bread
broken into hot water, or apples peeled. There is also
good support in good wort drinks, as leeches work
them, of vinegar, and of fennels roots, and of its rind,
and of aloes, and of dumbledores[1] honey; mix that up
and administer a spoonful of it or two, then that
maketh the wamb nesh and firm; and it is efficacious
against breast wark, and heart disease, and epilepsy, and
in case that a man be filled with inflammatory humour in the maw, and that is valid against many disorders which come of surfeit and of various evil
humours. If they are come of surfeit with spewing, by
that *remedy* shall they be lessened. If however they
come of other bitter and evil humours, which work
inflammations, then are the latter to be stilled till that
they become less strong; chiefly if the humours be
thick and rather slippery.[2]

2. Of wamb disease, or if the evil humours come
from the wamb alone and do not overrun the whole
body, that *case* shall be treated with healing meats
alone. If moreover the evil humour from the wamb
overrunneth the whole body, this shall be dealt with
by means of the stronger remedies: at whiles one shall
let him blood from a vein, if there seems to be too
much of the blood and of the evil humour, and also
give a wort drink; but he shall first be let blood
and after that have the wort drink given him.

ii.

1. For a sore and swollen maw; take oil, and put
mastic, and dill, and southern wormwood into the oil,

---

[1] Attic. | [2] γλίσχροι.

M 2

læt ſtandan þɲeo niht ⁊ ȝebo þ̵ þa pyɲta ɲyn ȝe-
ɲobene on þam ele · ȝebo ðonne on hneɲce pulle
ſmiɲe þone maȝan mið. Eft piþ þon ilcan ȝenim
ealbne ɲyɲle ȝetɲiꝼula ón tɲeopenum moɲteɲe menȝ
pɪ̌ð æȝeſ þ̵ hpite bo on clǎð leȝe ón. Þiþ ɲaɲům
maȝan eft ȝebo ón peaɲmne ele þa pyɲt · þe hatte
ꝼenoȝɲecum ⁊ lauɲeɲ cɲoppan ⁊ ðile ſmiɲe þone
maȝan mið þy.   :·

fol. 67 a.   Þiþ ɲaɲum maȝan peȝbɲæban ɲcap ⁊ cceð bo on
clǎð leȝe ón. Eft ȝiꝼ ɲe maȝa aþunðen ſie oþþe aþeneð ·
ȝenim þæɲ ɲeleſtan pineſ ⁊ ȝɲeneſ eleɲ ſpilc healꝼ ſeoþ
peɲmoðeɲ cɲoppan bo on hneɲce pulle ſmiɲe mið. Selle
him þonne ꝼlæɲc etan lytelɲa puhta ſmælɲa ꝼuȝla ȝeɲo-
benɲa ⁊ ȝebɲæðɲa ⁊ maniȝꝼealð æppelcyn peɲɲan æpeɲin-
ȝaɲ · piSan oꝼþænða ⁊ ȝeſobena ón eceðe ⁊ on pætɲe ⁊ on
pine pel ſceaɲɲpum. Þiþ ɲaɲum maȝan · ɲoſan leaꝼa .v.
oþþe .vii. oððe niȝon ⁊ pipopeſ coɲna emꝼela ȝeȝnið
ſmale ⁊ on hatúin pæteɲe ɲele ðɲincan. Eft piþ þon
ilcan ȝením oꝼ pinhnyte .xx. ȝeclænſoðɲa cyɲnela ⁊
cymeneɲ ſpa micel ſpa þu mæȝe mið þɲum ꝼinȝɲum
ꝼoɲepeaɲðum ȝeniman ȝetɲiꝼula þoune bollan ꝼulne
pyl on moɲteɲe ȝebo cealðeſ pæteɲeɲ to .ii. ȝobe
bollan ꝼulle ɲele ðonne æɲeſt þ̵ healꝼ to dɲincanne.

fol. 67 b.   Eft iɲ onleȝen[1] to tɲymmanne þone maȝan ⁊ to
liinbanne æɲteɲ utɲihtan oþþe æɲteɲ pyɲtðɲence ȝe-
bæɲneðne hlaɲ clænue ſeoþ on ealðum pine ȝiꝼ þu
hæbbe · ȝiꝼ hit ſie ſumoɲ bo peɲmoðeſ ſæðeſ ðuɲt to
ſeoþ ætȝæbeɲe bo on clǎð oꝼeɲſmit mið ele leȝe ón
þone maȝan · ȝiꝼ hit ſie pinteɲ ne þeaɲꝼt þu þone
peɲmoð to bon.

.III.

Be ȝeſpelle ⁊ ɲaɲie þæɲ maȝan · ȝiꝼ ſe man þ̵ mæȝen
hæbbe læt him bloð æꝼteɲ þon mið þy ele ſmiɲe þe

_____

[1] 'Fɯίθεua.

let it stand three nights, and arrange that the worts be sodden in the oil, then put *that* upon nesh wool, smear the maw therewith. Again, for that ilk; take old lard, triturate it in a treen mortar, mingle therewith the white of an egg, put on a cloth and lay on. For a sore maw, again; put the wort into warm oil, which hight fenugreek, and bunches of laurel flowers, and dill; smear the maw with that.

2. For a sore maw; put on a cloth juice of waybroad and vinegar; lay on. Again, if the maw be swollen or distended; take some of the best wine, and of green oil half so much, seethe the heads of wormwood *therein*, put *this* on nesh wool, smear therewith. Then give him the flesh to eat of little creatures, as of small fowls, sodden and roasted, and manifold kinds of apples, pears, medlars, peas moistened and sodden in vinegar and in water, and in pretty sharp wine. For a sore maw; leaves of rose, five, or seven, or nine, and of pepper corns as many, rub them small, and administer in hot water to be drunk. Again, for that ilk; take twenty cleansed kernels of the nuts of the stone pine, and of cummin so much as thou mayest take up with the tips of three fingers, then triturate a bowl full, boil in a mortar, add of cold water two good bowls full, then give the half *thereof* in the first instance to be drunk.

3. Again, here is an onlay a *or application* to com- ᵃ ἐπίθεμα. fort the maw, and to bind it after the diarrhœa, or after a wort drink; seethe clean toasted bread in old wine, if thou have it; if it be summer, add dust of the seed of wormwood, seethe together, put on a cloth, smudge over with oil, lay on the maw; if it be winter, thou needst not apply the wormwood.

iii.

Of swelling and sore of the maw; if the man have the strength *to bear it*, let him blood; after that,

þa pypta fyn on ȝeȝobene þe pe æp nembon · æptep
þon mið hate huniȝe fmipe ⁊ opeppceaðe þonne mið
hpitep cpiðuep ⁊ alpan bufte ⁊ pipopep hpæt hpeȝa ·
opeplecȝe · þonne mið linene claðe oððe mið eopo-
ciȝpe pulle ⁊ pele peþmoð on peapmum pætepe tpam
nihtum æp opȝotenne þ pe þam omūm ftille · ⁊ pele
þonne ȝepipopoðne pyptðpenc · ⁊ ðonne pceal mōn þam
men mið ðpium hanðum on moþȝenne ⁊ on æpenne

þa hanða ⁊ þa pet ȝniðan fpiðe ⁊ þyn · ⁊ ȝip hit fie
ȝoð peðep he hīm on unbeppe ȝipe · ȝanȝe him ut
hpiðep hpeȝa fume hpile · ȝip hit ne fie peðep ȝanȝe
hīm in ȝeonð hip huf.

.IIII.

Piþ heapðum fpile þæp maȝan pele þu him pealte
mettap ⁊ hapan plærc ⁊ eopopef · puðan pypttpuman ·
⁊ ceppan · ⁊ pcip pīn · ⁊ eaðmelte mettap ⁊ onleȝena
utteonðe þone heapðan fpile · ⁊ bæð þenða fmeppunȝa
pypce op ele ⁊ op peþmoðe · ⁊ op hpitum cpiðue ⁊ pine ·
beþe ðonne fmipe mið þy · opleȝe þonne mið eopeciȝpe
pulle ⁊ befpeþe · ȝenim eāc milfce æppla ȝeðo neah-
tepne ōn pin ⁊ þonne ȝefeoð · ȝefpete þonne þ pōp
mið huniȝef teape ⁊ ȝepipepa mið .xx. copna pele
hīm þonne on moþȝenne lytelne bollan pullne oððe
cuclep pulne þup ȝepophtep ðpincan.

.V.

Læceðom piþ þæp maȝan aþunðenneppe · þæp mannep
pet ⁊ hanða man pceal fpiþe on moþȝentiðum þyn ·
⁊ hine mon pceal fpiðe hluðe hatan ȝpæðan oððe

smear with the oil on which the worts, which we ere
named, have been sodden; after that smear with hot
honey, and sprinkle over with dust of mastic and aloes,
and somewhat of pepper; then overlay *this* with a
linen cloth or with ewes wool, and give *him* wormwood in warm water, poured off *the wormwood* two
nights (*days*) previously, that it may still the inflammation,[1] and then administer a peppered wort drink;
and then one shall at morning and evening rub
smartly and squeeze the mans hands and feet with dry
hands, and if it be good weather let him at undern,
that is at nine in the morning, by Gods grace, go out
somewhither for a while; if it be not *fair* weather,
let him walk about within his house.

iv.

For a hard swelling of the maw; give *the sick* salt
meats, and hares and boars flesh, roots of rue, and
cresses, and sheer (*clear*) wine, and easily digested
meats, and applications drawing out the hard swelling,
and baths; work moist smearings, *that is, lotions,* of oil
and wormwood, and of mastic and wine; bathe *him,*
then smear with that, then overlay with ewes wool,
and swathe up; take also mild apples, put them for
the space of a night into wine and then seethe *them;*
then sweeten the wash *or infusion* with virgin honey,
and pepper it with twenty peppercorns; then give him
in the morning a little bowl full or a spoon full of
the thus wrought *potion* to drink.

v.

A leechdom for swelling of the maw; one shall in
the morning hours squeeze hard the mans feet and
hands, and one shall bid him cry or sing very loud,

---

[1] φλεγμονή, I suppose.

ſingan ⁊ hinc môn ꞃcel nealhtneꞃtiȝue¹ tylhtan ⁊ ȝꞃe-
nuan to ſꝑiꝑanne · ⁊ on moꞃȝen ſiniꝑcꝑan mið cle on
þam ðe ſie ȝeꞃoðen ꞃuðe ⁊ peꞃmoð ⁊ þa œꞃi ȝenemneðan mettaꞃ þicȝe.

.VI.

¹ Ꝥiþ unluſte ⁊ plættan þe óꞃ maȝan cymð ⁊ be hiꞃ
mete · ꞃele hîm neahtneſtiȝûm peꞃmoð oððe þꞃeo-
bꞃeað² ȝebon ón ꞃceaꝑp ꝑ́ia ꞃele nealhtneꞃtiȝum · ⁊
æꞃteꞃ þon ꞃealte mettaſ mið eceðe ȝeſꝑete · ⁊ ȝeꞃenoðne
ſenep ⁊ ꞃæðic þicȝen ⁊ ealle þa mettaſ ȝe ðꞃincan
þa þe habban hat mæȝen ⁊ ſceaꝑp ꞃele þicȝean · ⁊
ȝebeoꝑh Ꝥ hic unȝemeltneꞃꞃe ne þꞃoꝑian · ⁊ ȝoð ꝑín
ȝehæt ⁊ hluttoꞃ þicȝen ón nealht neꞃtiȝ · ⁊ neaht.
neꞃtiȝe laꝑien on huniȝ · ⁊ ꞃecen him b�ñc ón onꝑaðe ·
⁊ on pæne oððe ón þon þe hie a þꞃoꝑian mæȝen.
Eꞃt ꝑiþ meteꞃ unluſte · ȝenim ſuþeꝑne cymen oꞃþæne
mið eceðe abꞃiȝe ðonne · ⁊ ȝeȝnið ón moꞃteꞃe · ⁊
ꞃinoleſ ꞃæðeꞃ · ⁊ ðileꞃ þꞃeo cucleꝑ mæl ȝeȝnið eall
toȝæðeꞃe ȝeece ꝑiꝑoꝑeꞃ þꞃeo cucleꝑ mæl ⁊ ꞃuðan

leaꞃa .VII. cucleꝑ mæl ⁊ þæꞃ ſeleꞃtan huniȝeꞃ aſiꝑeneꞃ
an punð · ȝetꞃiꞃula eal toȝæðeꞃe · yce þonne mið
eceðe ſꝑa þe þuice Ꝥ hit ſie ón þa onlicneꞃꞃe ȝeꞃoꝑht
þe ſenoꝑ bið ȝetemꝑꞃoð to inꝑiſan · ȝeðo þonne on
ȝlæꞃ ꞃæt · ⁊ þonne mið hlaꞃe oððe mið ſꝑa hꝑilcum
mete ſꝑa þu ꝑille laꝑa ón ⁊ nytta ȝe þeah þu mið
cucleꝑe Ꝥ ſuꝑe þæt hylꝥ · þiꞃeꞃ þu nytta ȝe ón
æꞃenne · ȝe ón unðeꝑne · niꞃ Ꝥ ꝑiþ þam unluſte anuni
ȝoð þæꞃ maȝan · ãc eallum þam lichoman Ꝥ ðeah.

Ꝥiþ meteꞃ unluſte ðꝑeoꝑȝe ðꝑoꞃtlan on pætꞃe oꞃ-
þænðe · ȝeȝnið mið eceðe ꞃele ðꞃincan ꝑið plættan. Ꝥiþ

---

¹ neahteꞃtiȝne, MS.   lianus, lib. vii., cap. 7, pp. 108, 109
² 'Aνopεξla. In the first sentence   ed. 1548.
are some traces of Alexander Tral-   ³ beabꞃeað? πρόπολιs is one of the
     ingredients in A. I.

and one shall exhort him after his nights fast, and pro-
voke him to spew; and in the morning smear him
with oil on which has been sodden rue and wormwood, and let him diet on the before named meats.

vi.

Against want of appetite and nausea which cometh
from the maw, and from the mans meat; give him after
his nights fast wormwood or beebread, put into sharp
wine; give it him at night fasting, and after that salt
meats with sweetened vinegar, and prepared mustard,
and radish to eat, and make him eat all the meats
and drinks which have a hot and sharp quality; and
beware that "they" suffer not indigestion, and let
them take at night fasting good wine heated and clear;
and let them after the nights fast lap up honey; and let
them seek for themselves fatigue in riding on horseback, or in a wain, or such *conveyance* as they may
ever endure. Again, for want of appetite for meat;
take southern *or Italian* cummin, moisten it with
vinegar, then dry it and rub it to pieces in a mortar,
and of fennel seed, and of dill, three spoon measures,
rub all together, add of pepper three spoon measures,
and of leaves of rue seven spoon measures, and of the
best strained honey one pint; triturate all together;
eke it out then with vinegar as may seem fit to
thee, so that it may be wrought into the form in
which mustard is tempered for flavouring; put it then
into a glass vessel, and then with bread or with whatever meat thou choose, lap it up, and make use of it;
even though thou shouldst sup it up with a spoon, that
will help. This use thou either at even or at nine
o'clock. The *remedy* is not good for want of appetite
of the maw only, but it is valid for all the body.

For want of appetite for meat; rub up with vinegar
pennyroyal moistened in water, give it to be drunk
against nausea. For want of appetite again; give to

unluſte eſt míntan ⁊ pipoþeſ niȝan coþn ȝeȝniben ón
pine ſele ðþincan.

.VII.

Þiſ ſceal pið aðeaðoðum maȝan · ȝením huniȝeſ ⁊
eceð toȝæðeþe ȝemenȝeð ⁊ ȝebeatenne pipoþ ſele ón
moþȝenne cucleþ ſulne nealitneſtiȝum nyttiȝe ſceaþ-
peþa ðþincena· ⁊ metta· ⁊ æt baþe mið ſinope ȝnibe ⁊
ſmeþpe. Sele hím eác neahtneſtiȝum þiſ· ȝenim eceð
pið ȝlæðenan ȝemenȝeð hþæthpeȝa ⁊ lanȝeſ pipoþeſ .x.
coþn oþþe cþoppan ⁊ ſenep menȝe eall toȝæðeþe· ⁊
tþuſoliȝe ſele nihtneſtiȝúm an cucleþ mæl· ȝeþenc ðu
þonne hþæþþe þte ealle þa æþ ȝenemneðan læceðomaſ
⁊ þa æſteþ pputenan ne ſculon ón ane þþaȝe to lanȝe
beón to ȝeðone ác ſculon ſæc habban betþeonum ⁊
þeſte· hpilum tþeȝen ðaȝaſ hpilum þþy· ⁊ þonne him
món bloð læte ón æðþe ón þam ðaȝúm ne ðo hím mon
nanne oþeþne læceðóm to· nymþe ymb .v. niht oþþe
ma.   Þið ſoþſóȝenum maȝan oþþe aþunðenum· ȝením
hþyþeþen ſlæþc ȝeſoðen ón ecebe ⁊ mið ele ȝeþenoð
mið ſealte· ⁊ ðile· ⁊ poþ þicȝe þ ſeoſon niht þonne
liht þ þone ȝeſpenceðan maȝan· þiſ ſynð tacn aðea-
ðoðeſ maȝan þ he þiȝð ne ȝemylt þ· ác ſe ȝeþiȝeða
mete heſeȝaþ þone maȝan ⁊ he þone ſammeltan þuþh
ða pambe utſent.

.VIII.

Þið ſaþe ⁊ unluſte þæſ maȝan ſe þe ne mæȝ ne
mið mete ne mið ðþincan beon ȝelacnoð ⁊ biteþe
hþæcetunȝe · Ním centauþian þ iſ ſelteþþe ſume·
hata hyþðe pyþt· ſume eoþð ȝeallan ȝeȝnið ſn punð

drink mint and nine corns of pepper rubbed *small* in wine.

vii.

This shall apply for a deadened maw;[1] take some honey and vinegar mingled together, and pepper beaten up, give in the morning a spoon full *of it* to the man after his nights fast, let him employ sharp drinks and meats; and at the bath let him rub and smear himself with mustard. Give him also, after his nights fast, this : take vinegar mingled with somewhat of gladden, and of long pepper ten corns or clusters, and mustard ; mingle all together, and triturate; give him after a nights fasting, one spoon measure. Then consider thou, notwithstanding, that all the aforenamed leechdoms and the after written ones, shall not be to be done at one too long season, but must have space and rest between them, whilom two days, whilom three ; and when one lets him blood on a vein, on those days let none other leechdom be done to him, except about five days *later* or more. For a stomach troubled with hicket or puffed up, take beeves flesh sodden in vinegar and with oil, prepared with salt, and dill, and porrum, let *the sick* diet on that for seven days, then that relieves the labouring maw. These are tokens of a deadened maw ; what he taketh, that melteth *or digests* not, but the meat swallowed oppresseth the maw, and it sendeth out the half digested food through the wamb.

viii.

For soreness and loss of appetite in that maw, which may not be cured neither with meat nor with drink, and for the bitter hreaking *or retching* ; take centaury,[2] that is fel terræ, some call it herdsmans

---

[1] Now called a torpid liver. | [2] *Erythræa centaureum.*

ꝼ ȝeðo þæꝼon hatcꝼ pæteꝼeſ .IIII. bollan ꝼulle ꝼele
hím neaht neꝛtiȝum ðꝛincan þꝛy ðaȝaſ.

Eꝼt ȝením þa ꝛeaðe netlan uꝼepeaꝛðc hæbbenðe
ꝛæð aꝵꝵeah clæne � pyꝛ̈ce to ſupanne. Eꝼt ȝꝛeneſ
meꝛceꝛ· ȝetꝛiꝼulaðeꝛ ꝛeap � aꝵꝵunȝeneꝛ ꝛele ðꝛincan·
ꝼ on þa ilcan piꝛan ꝛele hím ðꝛincan hunan ꝛeap.
Eꝼt pꝛð maȝan ꝛaꝛe ꝛuðan ꝼ mintan· ðile · ðpeoꝛȝe
ðpoſtlan· aȝꝛimonian ſume hatað ȝaꝛcliꝛe· ꝼ cenꝼan
ȝecnua ealle ón pine oꝵꝵe on ealað ꝛele ælce ðæȝe to
ðꝛincanne.

. VIIII.

Þiꝵ Inꝛunðe maȝan· uím ȝate meoluc þonne hio
ꝛuꝵꝵúm amolcen ſie ꝛelc ðꝛincan· ſume peaꝛme copo
meoluc ðꝛincað piꝵ maȝau ſaꝛc· ſume þone ꝛeleſtan
ele ȝepyꝛmeðne· ſume piꝵ þa ȝate meoluc menȝað oꝵ
ꝥ hie ſꝛipað ꝥ hi ðe yꝵ ſꝛipan maȝon.

. X.

Viꝺ plattau ꝼ to hætanne maȝan· pꝛ̈teꝛ heꝛoben
ón peꝛmoðe· ꝼ ón ðile oꝵ þonc þꝛiððan ðæl ꝛelc ꝥ
ðꝛincan ꝥ pyꝛmꝺ ꝼ heaꝛðaꝵ þonc maȝan.

. XI.

ᵃ Πρὸς ἐμπνευ-
μάτωσιν. Alex.
Trall., lib. vii.
cap. 10; p. 112,
ed. 1548 ; but
the remedies
differ.

ᵃ Þiꝵ aꝵunðeneꝛꝛe ꝼ eꝵunȝe maȝan· ꝛinoleꝛ pyꝛttꝛu-
man ꝼ meꝛceſ óꝼ ȝeot mið ſciꝛe pine ealðe ꝼ oꝼ þon
ꝛele ðꝛincan nehtneꝛtiȝúm .II. bollan ꝼulle lytle. Þiꝵ
ꝛínðiȝꝛe aꝵunðeneꝛꝛe maȝan to pyꝛmanne þonc cealðan maȝan· ꝛuðan· ꝼ ðile· mintan· ꝼ meꝛce ſynð-
ꝛiȝe ꝛceaꝛaſ ȝeſeoð on þꝛím ceac² ꝼullum pꝛ̈teꝛeſ ꝥ
þæꝛ ne ſie butan an ꝼul ſele þonne ꝥ pꝛ̈teꝛ ðꝛincan.

---

¹ The method of Alex. Trallianus is, it seems, kept in view;
Περὶ τῶν δι' ἄμετρον ψῦξιν ἀνορεκ-

τούντων, lib. vii., cap. 7 ; p. 109, ed.
1548.
² ceacum ?

wort, some earth gall, rub *small* a pound of it, and apply thereto four bowls full of hot water; give it *to the sick* to drink for three days after his nights fasting. Again, take the upper part of the red nettle, while having seed, wash it clean, and work it up to sup. Again, administer to drink juice of green marche triturated and wrung out, and in the same wise, give him to drink juice of *hore*hound. Again, for sore of maw; rue and mint, dill, dwarf dwosle, agrimony, some call it garcliff, and cress, pound them all in wine or in ale, give *of this* each day to drink.

ix.

For an inward wound of the maw; take goats milk just when it is milked, administer to be drunk. Some drink for sore of maw warm ewe milk, some the best oil warmed, some mingle *that* with the goats milk till they spew, that they may spew the more easily.

x.

For nausea and to heat the maw; water sodden on wormwood and on dill, down to the third part, give *the man* that to drink; it warmeth and hardeneth the maw.

xi.

For puffing up and blowing of the maw; overpour roots of fennel and marche with clear old wine, and of that give *the sick* to drink after his nights fast two little bowls full. For a windy puffing up of the maw, to warm the maw, rue and dill, mint and marche; seethe bundles of them separate in three jugs full of water, and *continue seething* so that there be only one cup; then administer the water to be drunk.

.XII.

ᵃ Προς ἕμετον.

ᵃ Við ſpipþan ⁊ pið þon þe him mete unðeꞃ ne ᵹe-
puniᵹe · ᵹenim ſinꝼullan ᵹeᵹnið ón ſceaꞃp ꝼin ꞃele
bollan ꝼulne to ᵹeðꞃincanne æꝼteꞃ æꝼen ᵹepeoꞃce ·
ᵹenim piþ þon ilcan ꝼinoleꞃ ꞃeapeꞃ tpeᵹen bælaſ huniᵹeꞃ ænne ſeoþ oþ ꝥ ꝥ hæbbe huniᵹeſ þicneꞃꞃe ꞃele
þonne neaht neꝛtiᵹum cucleꞃ mæl ꝼull · ꝥ plættan
ᵹeſtipeð ꝥ lunᵹenne · bet ꝥ liꝼꞃe hælð. Við miclan
ſpipeþan ⁊ he ne mæᵹe nanne mete ᵹehabban · ᵹenim

fol. 71 a.

ðileꞃ ꞃæbeꞃ ane yntꝛan · piþoꞃeꞃ ꝼeopeꞃ · cymeneꞃ
þꞃeo ᵹeᵹnið ſpiþe ſmale · ðo þonne on pæteꞃ þe pæꞃe
minte ón ᵹeꞃoben ⁊ ſuꞃe æppla oððe pinᵹeaꞃðeꞃ tpiᵹu
uꝼepeaꞃð meꞃþe ᵹiꝼ ꝛe món ne ſie on ꝼeꝼꞃe yce mið
pine ⁊ ꞃele ðꞃincan þonne ne to ꝛeſte ᵹan pille · ⁊ leᵃ
utan ón þone maᵹan ᵹeſoðene puðu æpla ⁊ hlaꝼeꞃ
cꞃumán ⁊ ſpilce ónleᵹena.

.XIII.

ᵇ Ρευματισμός.

Þonne ꞃceal þiꝛ piþ þæꞃ maᵹan ſpꞃinᵹe Súm pyꝛe
cyn hatte lenticulaſ ete þaꞃa hunð teontiᵹ hꞃeaꞃꞃa.
Eꝼt ꞃceaꞃꞃeꝛ eceðeꞃ ᵹeſupe þꞃeo cucleꞃ mæl þonne he
ꝛlapan pille on æꝼen.

.XIIII.

Þiþ eallum maᵹan untꝛumneꝛꝛum · ᵹenim ꝼinoleꞃ
pyꝛttꞃuman utepeaꞃðꞃa ꝥ þæꞃ mæꞃꞃoſt ſie aðo oꝛ
þam ꝼinole ſpa micel ſpa oþeꞃ healꝼ punð ſie · ᵹeot

---

¹ The method of Alex. Trallianus   μαχον ἀπεμοῦντα τὴν τροφήν, p. 112.
is still preserved; he has a short   ed. 1548.
chapter, lib. vii. cap. 9, Πρὸς στό-   ² For leᵹe.

xii.

For spewing, and in case that *a mans* meat will
not keep down; take sinfulle, rub it *fine* into sharp
wine, give *the man* a bowl full to drink after evening
work. Take, for that ilk, two parts of juice of fennel,
one of honey, seethe *or boil down* till *the mixture*
have the thickness of honey, then give after a nights
fast a spoon measure full; that restraineth nausea,
that bettereth the lungs, that healeth the liver. For
mickle spewing, and *in case a man* may keep *in his*
stomach no meat; take one ounce of seed of dill, four of
pepper, three of cummin, rub very small; then put
into water in which mint has been sodden and sour
apples, or the tender upper part of the twigs of a vine;
if the man be not in a fever, eke it with wine, and
give *it him* to drink when he willeth to go to bed;
and lay outside on the maw sodden wood apples
(*crabs*), and crumbs of bread, and such applications.

xiii.

Besides, this shall be good for flux [1] of the maw;
one sort of peas hight lentils, let *the man* eat of them
raw one hundred. Again, let him sip three spoon
measures of sharp vinegar, when he willeth to sleep
at evening.

xiv.

For all infirmities of the maw; take of the out-
ward parts of the roots of fennel, what is there most
tender, remove from the fennel as much as may make

---

[1] For this translation I partly rely
on the guidance of Alexander
Trallianus, who has remedies πρὸς
στόμαχον ῥευματιζόμενον; lib. vii.,
cap. 8; p. 111, ed. 1548; p. 337, ed.
1556. Properly ῥευματισμὸς is of
the wamb, or venter, not of the
maw; and Aretæos says as much,
Chron. lib. ii., cap. 6. But other
authors have the same expression
as Alex. Trall; for instance Cælius
Aurelianus, Chron. lib. iii., cap. 2.

þonne ecebeʃ ón ʃpa oþeʃı healʃ ʃeʃceʃ ʃie læt þonne
þʃeo nıhc ʃtanðan ʃpa æcȝæðeʃıe · æʃceʃı þon oʃeʃıʃeoð
þa pyʃıccʃıuman hpæc hþeȝa ón þam ecebe ⁊ apʃıınȝ óʃ
fol. 71 b.
þam ecebe clæne · ȝebo þonne on þ eceb hunıȝeʃ mıð
þʃ ecebe · ȝebo þonne alpan ȝobne bæl þæʃı on þce
yncʃan ȝepeȝe oððe ma ⁊ oþeʃı ʃpılc hʃıceʃ cpeobopeʃ
⁊ ameoʃ hacce ʃuþeʃıne pyʃıc oþeʃı aʃaʃıu bo þaʃıa læʃ
ȝemenȝe hþæþeʃıe ealle coȝæðeʃıe ⁊ þonne ʃelle hım
þʃeo cucleʃı mæl.   ðo þıʃ pıð maȝan bʃıyne ⁊ þuʃıʃce
placo pæceʃı menȝe pıð þone ʃeleʃcan ele ʃele ðʃııncan
þ ʃcyʃð[1] þam þuʃıʃce.

.XV.

· Ὀξυρεγμία.
Þıþ þæʃ maȝan ʃpʃıınȝe þonne þuʃıh muð bıceʃıe
hʃæcð[a] oþþe bealcec oððe hım on þam maȝan ʃuȝeð ·
ȝeuım pıpoʃıeʃ ʃpılce an mynec ȝepeȝe · ðıleʃ ʃæðeʃ
ʃpılce .IIII. mynec ȝepeȝen · oþeʃı ʃpılc cymeneʃ ȝeȝnıð
eall ⁊ ʃele ón pıne cucleʃı mæl þonne he ʃlapan ȝan
pılle. Sıó aþenunȝ þæʃ maȝan ⁊ ʃıo ablapunȝe hæco
cymeð oʃ þam blacum omum · ac ȝenım þonne ʃpʃıun-
ȝean[2] ȝebo ón ʃceaʃıp eceb ȝepæce ʃpıðe leȝe oʃeʃı
þone maȝan þonne hıc ʃpılc ʃıe. Æʃceʃı þon ȝıʃ þæʃ
fol. 72 a.
ne ʃele leȝe oþʃıa onleȝena ón ʃcʃıenȝʃıan ⁊ aʃeʃıʃıau
ʃpa ʃpa íʃ ʃaʃı[3] óm pıð hunıȝ ȝemenȝeð ⁊ þon ȝelıc
ʃpa læcaʃ cunnon.

.XVI.

Þıʃ ʃınc cacn þæʃ hacan maȝan omıhcan unȝemec
ʃæʃclıcan · ⁊ þæʃ oʃeʃıcealðan · þæʃ hacan maȝan un-

---

[1] From ʃceopan. | the Hellenic. Alex. Trall., lib. vii.,
                                    | cap. 8; p. 110, foot, ed. 1548.
[2] Understand as ʃpoðȝean from | [3] Read ap. See the Glossary.

a pound and a half, then pour on of vinegar as much as be a sextarius and a half, then let these stand thus together for three nights; after that seethe the roots somewhat in the vinegar, and wring them clean from the vinegar. Then put into the vinegar some honey with the vinegar; then put a good deal of aloes therein, so much as may weigh an'ounce or more, and as much more of mastic and of ammi, as a foreign wort hight; or asarabacca; put in less of them, mingle, however, all together, and then give him three spoon measures. Do this against burning of the maw and thirst; mingle lukewarm water with the best oil, give to drink, that checketh the thirst.

xv.

For irritation of the maw when *the man* through the mouth has bitter hreaking or belching, or there is an ill lymph in his stomach; take of pepper as much as one coin may weigh, of seed of dill as much as may weigh four coin, as much besides of cummin, rub all fine and administer in wine a spoon full when *the man* willeth to go to sleep. The swelling of the maw and the heat of the puffing up cometh from the black flegms; but then take sponges, put them into sharp vinegar, wet it thoroughly, lay it over the maw, when it is such. After that, if it feel not this, *or be insensible to these remedies*, lay on some other applications, stronger and more austere, such as is copperas mingled with honey, and the like of that as leeches know.

xvi.

1. These are tokens of the hot flegmatic[1] maw, irretentive,[2] and of the overcold. Of the hot or irretentive

---

[1] Full of φλεγμονή.
[2] The diet is drawn from a passage thus headed; Θεραπεία τῆς διὰ θέρμην ἀσθενούσης δυνάμεως. Unχε- metχαρτ, unχemetχαρτlic are therefore the opposites of Καθεκτικός; and not what Somner supposed.

ʒemetꝼæꝼtan taon ſinðon þonne he bıð mıð omum
ʒeſpenceð þam men bıð þuꝼſt ʒetenʒe ꝼ neaꝶoneſ ꝼ
ʒeſpoʒunʒa ꝼ moðeꝼ tꝛeonunʒ ꝼ unluſt ꝼ plætta · hım
ıꝼ nyt[1] þ he hlaꝼ þıcʒen[2] on cealðum pætꝛe oððe on
eceðe[3] ꝼ ſꝛıðe ꝼæſte ʒeꝛoðen æʒꝶa oþþe ʒebꝶæððe to
unðeꝶneſ ꝼ pyꝶta · ꝼ lactucaſ þ ıꝼ leahtꝛıc ꝼ mealꝶan
ꝼ hænne ꝼlæꝛc næꝼ ſꝛıþe ʒeꝶoðen · ꝼ ʒoſe þa ytmeꝼ-
tan lımo · ꝼ ꝼıxaꝼ þa þe heaꝶð ꝼlæꝛc habban ·[4] ꝼ
pıne ꝶınclan · ꝼ oſtꝶan ꝼ oþꝶu pyꝼena cyn ꝼ mylſce
æppla ꝼ bæþ oꝼ ſꝛetum ꝼeꝶſcum pætꝛenum ſceal beon
ʒeꝶoꝶht hat bæþ hım ne beah.   Taen[5] þæꝼ oꝛeꝶceal-
ðan maʒan þ þa men ne þyꝶſt ne hı ſpol ʒeꝼelaþ on
maʒan ꝼ ne bıþ hım ænıʒ peaꝶm þꝶoꝶunʒ ʒetenʒe.

fol. 72 b.
Ac hy ʒıꝶnað metta ſꝛıþoꝶ þonne hít ʒelíchc ſıe ꝼ ʒıꝼ
hím oꝛſtonðeþ ón Innan ænıʒu cealð pæte þonne
ſꝛıꝶað hıe þ hoꝶh ꝼ þa mettaꝼ ʒehabban ne maʒon
þe hıe ʒeþıcʒeað · ꝼ æꝼteꝶ þam ſꝛıꝶað[6] ꝼona hím to
ʒıꝼanne bıðða · þa men þu ꝼcealt ſmeꝶꝶan mıð þy
ele þe mon peꝶmoð ón ſeoðe · ꝼ þa þıccan ʒeuꝶnen
ᵃ ꝼlıꝶıʒa ?
ón ꝼ þa ꝼlıꝶınʒa[a] pætan ón þam maʒan ꝼ þa acoloðan ·
ꝼ þ oꝼſtanðene þıcce ꝼlıꝶıʒe hoꝶh þu ꝼcealt mıð þám
æꝶ ʒenemneðan læceðomum pyꝶman ꝼ þynnıan. Þyꝶc
hím þonne pyꝶtðꝶenc oꝼ ꝼınoleſ pyꝶttꝶuman ꝶınðe ꝼ
meꝶꝶoſt ꝼıe þte ꝼıx yntſan ʒepeʒe ꝼ eceðeꝼ anne ꝼeꝼ-
teꝶ · ꝼ alpan þꝶeo yntſan · ꝼeoþ þonne on þam eceðe
þone ꝼınol oþ þ lıt ſıe pel ʒeꝼoðen aꝼꝶınʒ þonne þa
pyꝶta oꝼ þam eceðe ʒeðo þonne to þam eceðe clæneꝼ
hunıʒeſ punð ꝼeoþ þonne ætʒæðeꝶe oþ þ lıt ꝼıe ſpa
þıcce ſpa hunıʒ ſceað þonne þa alpan ón pel ʒeʒnıðene
fol. 73 a.
ꝼ ꝼele þꝶeo cucleꝶ mæl mıð pætꝛe þ beah pıþ heoꝶt
ece ꝼ pıþ ꝼelle pæꝶce.

---

[1] Alexander Trall., lib. vii., cap. 5 ;
p. 106, ed. 1548 ; cap. 3, p. 323, ed.
1556.
[2] Read þıcʒe.
[3] Gr. εἰς ἄκρατον, *dipped in wine
unmixed with water,* (as if brandy).

[4] ὀστρακοδέρμων, *shell fish.*
[5] From Alexander Trall., lib. vii.,
cap. 5; p. 105, ed. 1548 ; p. 319, ed.
1556, for a few lines only.
[6] Read ſpıþþan ?

maw are tokens, when it is vexed with inflammations, thirst is incident to the man, and oppression, and swoonings, and vacillation of mind, and loss of appetite, and nausea. It is beneficial for him that he should eat bread in cold water or in vinegar, and eggs very hard boiled or roasted, (at nine o'clock in the morning,) and worts, and lactucas, that is lettuces, and mallow, and hens flesh not much sodden, and the extremest parts of the limbs of goose, *that is giblets*, and fishes which have hard flesh, and periwinkles, and oysters, and others ; various sorts of peas, and mild apples, and a bath of sweet fresh waters shall be wrought; a hot bath will not suit him. Tokens of the overcold maw, that the men feel no thirst nor burning heat in the maw, nor is there any warm symptom incident upon them. But they yearn for meats more strongly than is proper, and if in their inwards there lodges any cold humour, then they spew up the filth and are not able to retain the meats which they swallow ; and after the spewing soon they pray that *somewhat* be given *them to eat*. Those men thou shalt smear with the oil on which wormwood has been sodden. And the thick coagulated and the viscid humours in the maw, and the chilled *humours*, and the intractable thick viscid foulness, thou shalt warm and thin with the afore named leechdoms. Work then *for the sick man* a wort drink of the rind of the root of fennel, and let it be very tender, *and such* that it may weigh six ounces, and one sextarius of vinegar, and three ounces of aloes ; then seethe the fennel in the vinegar till it be well sodden, then wring the worts off the vinegar, then add to the vinegar a pound of clean honey, then seethe *these* together, till it be as thick as honey, then shed the aloes into it, well rubbed up, and give three spoon measures with water ; that is good for heart ache and for epilepsy.

Alexander
Trallianus,
ibid.
Κυνώδης ὄρεξις.
Βούλιμος.

ƿe þæꞃe oꝼeꞃmiclan ꞃꝛclo þonne oꝼ þæꞃe ꞃelꝼan
cealban able þæꞃ maȝan cymð ꝥ ſio oꝼeꞃmiclo ꞃꝛclo
ꝓ ȝiꝼeꞃneꞃ aꝛꝛſt oꝼ þæꞃ hoꝛeꞃ pætan þe uꝼ þam maȝan
cymð ꝓ hie beoþ ſpipenbe ꝓ ſpa ſpa hunb eꝼt ꞃona
ſecað þa mettaꞃ • þam þu ꞃcealt ꞃellan clæne ꝓ hluttoꞃ ƿin¹ ꝓ ꞃeab ſpiðe ȝehæt ne ſie to ꞃceaꞃp • ne ꞃe
mete ne ſie to ꞃceaꞃp ne to ꞃuꞃ þe þu him ꞃelle •
āc ſmeþe ꝓ ꝛæt • ȝiꝛ² oꞃmæte hunȝoꞃ cymð oꝼ un-
ȝemetlicꞃe hæto þæꞃ maȝan ꝓ tybbeꞃneꞃꞃe ꝥ hie ꞃyn
ꞃona ȝeſpoȝene ȝiꝛ hie þone mete næbben. Ƿiþ oꞃmæ-
tum hunȝꞃe þonne ꞃcealt þu ꞃona þæꞃ mannes tilian
binb hiꞃ ytmeꞃtan limo mib bynbellum teoh him þa
loccaſ ꝓ pꞃinȝe þa caꞃan ꝓ þone panȝbeaꞃb tꞃicciȝe
þonne him ꞃel ꞃie ꞃele him ꞃona hlaꝼ ón pine ȝebꞃo-
cenne æꞃ he oþꞃe mettaꞃ þicȝe • ꞃele him þa mettaꞃ
þa þe ne ſien to ꞃaðe ȝemelte • late mylt hꞃyþeꞃ

fol. 73 b.

ꝼlæꞃc ȝæten • ꝓ hioꞃota • buccena íꞃ pyꞃꞃeſt ꝓ ꞃamma•
ꝓ ꞃeaꞃꞃa ꝓ þa þe ſpiðe ealbe beoð on ꞃeoþoꞃꝛotum
niecenum ꝓ ꞃuȝlaꞃ þa þe heaꞃb ꝼlæꞃc habbað • paꞃa •
ſpan • æneb þam ðe cealbe pambe habbað þu ſcealt
ꞃellan pel meltenbe mettaſ ꞃcellihte ꞃiſcaꞃ • ꝓ culꝼꞃena
bꞃibbaſ • hænne ꝼlæꞃc ꝓ ȝoꞃe ꞃiþꞃu ſpa beteꞃe ſꞃn
ꝼætꞃan ſien ꝓ ꝛeꞃſcꞃan þa ytmeꞃtan leomo • ſpina
beoð caðmelte ꝓ ȝeonȝ hꞃyþeꞃ ꝓ ticcenu • ꝓ ſpete
ƿin ꞃel mylt þonne ꝥ aꝛꞃe.

.XVII.

Ƿiþ eallum liꝼeꞃ ablūm ꝓ ȝecynbum ꝓ pꞃſtmūm ꝓ be
þam ꞃex þinȝum þe ðone liꝼeꞃ pæꞃc pyꞃceað ꝓ lacnunȝ
þaꞃa ealꞃa ꝓ ſpeotol tacn ȝe be micȝean ȝe be unluſte
ȝe hiꞃa liꞃe. Sio biþ on þa ſpiþꞃan ſiban āꞃeneb oþ þone

---

¹ τῷ ἀκράτῳ οἴνῳ καὶ τοῖς λιπαροῖς τῶν ἐδεσμάτων. Alex. Trall., who goes on to order legs of pheasants. Φασιανῶν μὲν τοὺς μηρούς.

² Alex. Trall., lib. vii, cap. 6 ; p. 106, ult. ed. 1548 ; p. 323, ed. 1556.

Book II.
Ch. xvi.

2. Of the overmickle appetite, when from the same cold disease of the maw it cometh that the overmickle appetite and greediness ariseth from the foul humour, which cometh from the maw, and *the sick* are spewing, and, as it were a hound, again soon seek the meats: to them thou shalt give clean and clear wine, and red, much heated; let it not be too sharp; nor let the meat be too sharp, nor too sour, which thou mayst give them, but smooth and fat. If extreme hunger cometh from immoderate heat and tenderness of the maw, so that they are soon in a swoon, if they have not the meat; then, for extreme hunger[1] thou shalt soon treat the man; bind the extremities of his limbs with ligatures, pull his locks for him, and wring his ears, and twitch his whisker, when he is better, give him soon some bread broken in wine, before he take other meats. Give him the meats which are not too soon digested. Beeves flesh, and goats, and harts digests late: bucks is worst, and rams, and bulls, and those of four footed neat which are very old, and fowls which have hard flesh; peacock, swan, duck. To those that have a cold wamb thou shalt give well digesting meats, shell fishes, and young of culvers, hens flesh, and gooses wings; they are the better as they are fatter and fresher. The extremities of the limbs of swine * are easy of digestion, and young beeves, and * Pigs trotters. kids; and sweet wine digests better than the rough.

xvii.

For all liver diseases, and of its nature, and increment, and of the six things which work the liver pain, and curing of all these, and plain tokens, either by the mie, or by the loss of appetite, or by the hue of *the*

---

[1] In Trallianus these appliances are meant for the fainting just mentioned, λειποθυμία.

nepeſeoþan ſio hæꝼð ꝼiꞃ læppan helꞇ þa lenðenbꞃæðan·
ſio iꞅ blobeꞃ ꞇimbeꞃ· ⁊ blobeꞃ huſ· ⁊ ꝼoꞅꞇoꞃ· þonne
þaꞃa meꞇꞇa melꞇunʒ biþ ⁊ þynneſ þa becumaþ on þa
liꝼeꞃ þonne penðaþ hie hioꞃa hiꞃ ⁊ ceꞃꞃað on blob·
⁊ þa unꞃeꝼeꞃneꞃꞃa þe þæꞃ beoþ hio apyꞃꞃþ uꞇ ⁊ þ
clæne blob ʒeſomnaþ ⁊ þuꞃh ꞃeopeꞃ æðꞃa ſꞃiþoſꞇ ón-
ꞃenꞇ ꞇo þæꞃe heoꞃꞇan ⁊ eắc ʒeonð ealne þone lichoman oþ þa yꞇmeꞃꞇan limo. þe ꞃex þinʒúm þe þone
liꝼeꞃꞃæꞃc pyꞃꞇceað æꞃeſꞇ ʒeſpel þ iꞅ aþunðeneꞃ þæꞃe
liꝼeꞃ.[1] Oþeꞃ iꞅ þæꞃ ʒeſpelleſ ꞇobeꞃꞅꞇunʒ. þꞃibbe íꞃ punð
þꞃoꞃe liꝼꞃe· ꝼeoꞃþe iꞅ pelmeꞃ hæꞇo mib ʒeꝼelneꞃꞃe ⁊ mib
ꞃaꞃe ʒeſpelle· ꝼiꝼꞇe iꞅ aheaꞃðunʒ þæꞃ maʒan mib ʒeꝼelneꞃꞃe ⁊ mib ꞃáꞃe. Sexꞇe iꞅ heaꞃðunʒ þæꞃe liꝼꞃe buꞇan
ʒeꝼelneꞃꞃe ⁊ buꞇan ſaꞃe. þæꞃe liꝼꞃe ʒeſpel oþþe aþun-
deneꞃꞃe þu meahꞇ þuꞃ onʒiꞇan· on þa ſꞃiðꞃan healꝼe
unðeꞃ þắm hneꞃcan[2] ꞃibbe biþ æꞃeſꞇ ꞃe ſpile ón þæꞃe
liꝼꞃe ⁊ ʒeꝼelð ſe món æꞃeſꞇ þæꞃ heꞃiʒneꞃꞃe ⁊ ꞃaꞃ ⁊
oꝼ þæꞃe ꞅꞇope oꝼeꞃ ealle þa ſiðan aſꞇihð oþ þ piþoban
⁊ oþ ðone ſpiþꞃan ꞃculðoꞃ þ ſaꞃ· ⁊ hiꞃ micʒʒe bið
blobꞃeað ſpilce hio blobiʒ ſie· biþ hím unluꞅꞇ ʒeꞇenʒe
⁊ hiꞃ hiꞃ blac ⁊ he biþ hꞃæꞇ hꞃeʒa hꞃiþenðe· ⁊ ſin-
ʒalne cyle þꞃoꞃaþ ⁊ cꞃacaþ ſpa món on lencꞇen aðle
deþ· ne mæʒ him meꞇe unðeꞃ ʒepunian þinꞇ ſio liꝼeꞃ
⁊ ne mæʒ þam ꞃaꞃe mib hanða ónbꞃinan bið ꞇo þon
ꞅꞇꞃanʒ ⁊ næꝼþ nanne ꞃ·læp þonne hiꞇ ꞅꞇꞃanʒoꞅꞇ biþ·
þonne ꞃe ſpile ꞇobyꞃſꞇ þonne bið ſeo micʒe lyꞃpen
ſpilce poꞃmꞅ· ʒiꝼ he uꞇyꞃnð þonne biþ þ ꞃaꞃ læꞃꞃe.

fol. 74 a.

fol. 74 b.

---

[1] Read liꝼꞃe. | [2] Read nexꞇan, last?

patients. The *liver* is extended on the right side as far as the pit of the belly, it hath five *lobes or* lappets, it has a hold on the false ribs, it is the material of the blood, and the house and the nourishment of the blood; when there is digestion and attenuation of the meats, they arrive at the liver, and then they change their hue, and turn into blood; and it casteth out the uncleannesses which be there, and collects the clean blood, and through four veins principally sendeth it to the heart, and also throughout all the body as far as the extremities of the limbs. Of the six things which work liver pain: first swelling, that is, puffing up of the liver; the second is the bursting of the swelling; the third is wound of the liver; the fourth is a burning heat with sensitiveness and with a sore swelling; the fifth is a hardening of the maw with sensitiveness and with soreness; the sixth is a hardening of the liver without sensitiveness and without soreness. Thou mayest thus understand swelling or puffing up of the liver; on the right side is under the nesh ᵃ rib first the swelling of the *Read last.* liver *observed,* and the *disordered* man there first feeleth heaviness and sore, and from that place the sore riseth over all the side as far as the collar bone, and as far as the right shoulder, and *the mans* mie is bloodred as if it were bloody; loss of appetite is incident unto him, and his hue is pale, and he is somewhat feverish, and he suffereth remarkable chill, and quaketh as a man doth in lent addle *or typhus fever;* his meat will not keep down, the liver enlarges, and he may not touch the sore with his hand, to that degree is it strong, and he hath no sleep when it is strongest. When the swelling bursteth then is the mie purulent, as ratten; if it runneth off then is the sore less.

.XVIII.

Vıþ þæıe lıꝼꝛc ꝼpıle oððe aþunðeneꝛꝛc ʒıꝼ ſe utʒanʒ ꝼoꝛſıtte hı́m ıſ on ꝼꝛuman bloð to ꝼoꝛlætenne ón æðꝛe on þa pıncſtꝛan healꝼe pyꝛc hı́m þonne beþınʒe þuꝛ ꝗ ꝛealꝼe oꝼ ele ꝗ ꝛuðan • ꝗ bıle ꝗ óꝼ meꝛceꝛ ſæðe ſpa mıcel ſpa þe þınce ꝛeoð eall mıð þy ele ꝗ þonne mıð hneꝛcꝛe pulle beþe mıð þy poꝛe lanʒe þa ſꝛıðꝛan ſıðan ꝗ þonne oꝼeꝛleʒe mıð pulle ꝗ beſpeþe ꝛæſte ymb .III. nıht pyꝛc hı́m eꝼt ónlecʒenðe ſealꝼe ꝗ beꝛen ʒꝛytte ʒeonð ʒotene mıð pıne ꝗ þonne ʒeꝛoðenc ꝗ ınıð ecebe ꝗ mıð hunıʒe call ʒetꝛıꝛulað ꝗ eꝼt ʒeꝛoðen leʒe ón þonc þıcceꝛtan claò oþðe on ꝼel ſpıðe¹ mıð ſpa peaꝛmıe ꝗ on þ́ ꝛaꝛ bınð ꝗ hꝛılum teoh mıð ʒlæſe oþþe ınıð hoꝛne. ʒıꝼ ꝛe utʒauʒ ꝼoꝛꝛıtte mıð pyꝛtðꝛencum ateoh hıne ut. Þyꝛc óꝼ peꝛmoðe • ꝗ oꝼ hıꝛðe pyꝛıte • ꝗ oꝼ ꝛuðan ꝛæðe • ðo aſeoponeꝛ hunıʒeꝛ ʒenoh to ꝛele neahtneꝛtıʒúm cucleꝛ ınæl.

.XVIIII.

Tacn be aſpollenꝛe ꝗ ʒepunðaðꝛe lıꝼꝛe læceðomaꝛ pıþ þon • ꝗ be þæꝛe lıꝼꝛe aheaꝛðunʒe. Se þe bıð ʒepunðoð þonne on þa lıꝼꝛe • ꝗ ʒıꝼ he ne bıþ þon ꝛaþoꝛ ʒelacnoð þonne becymð he ón þa aðle þe món poꝛmſe ſpıpeþ • ʒıꝼ ſe ʒeſpollena mon ón þæꝛe lıꝛꝛe oððe ꝛc aþunðena ſpa aſpollen ʒebıt oþ þone ꝼıꝼ ꝗ tpentıʒeþan ðıeʒ ſpa ꝛe ſpıle ne beꝛſteþ þonne ónʒınð ſıo lıꝼeꝛ heaꝛðıan ʒıꝼ huo ʒebyꝛſt þonne bıð þæꝛ pınð² ón þæꝛe lıꝼꝛe. þæꝛe punðe tacn ꝛınðon þonne ſıo punð

---

¹ Rather ſpeðc.
² Read pund, because þæꝛc punðe follows.

xviii.

For swelling or puffing up of the liver; if the outgoing [1] lodge, *the man* must first be let blood on a
vein, on the left side, then work him a bathing thus,
and a salve of oil, and rue, and of dill, and of marche
seed, as much as may seem good to thee, seethe all
with the oil, and then bathe with nesh wool with
the wash for a long time the right side, and then
overlay with wool, and swathe up fast for about
three nights; work him again an onlying salve, and
lay barley groats soused with wine, and then sodden,
and *this* all triturated with vinegar and with honey,
and sodden again, lay on the thickest cloth or on a
skin, swathe up therewith so warm, and bind upon
the sore, and at whiles draw with glass or horn, *as
with cupping glass.* If the secretion lodge, draw it
out with wort drinks; work *such* of wormwood and
of herdwort, and of seed of rue, add enough of strained
honey; give *the man* a spoon measure after his nightly
fast.

xix.

Tokens of a swollen and wounded liver; leechdoms
for that; and of the hardening of the liver. He who
is wounded in the liver, if he be not sooner cured, then
arriveth at the disorder in which a man speweth
purulent matter. If the man swollen in the liver, or
the bloated one, abideth so swollen until the five and
twentieth day, so as that the swelling bursteth not,
then beginneth the liver to harden; if it bursteth,
then is there a wound in the liver. Tokens of the

---

[1] Se utᵹanᵹ would be presumed
to be fæces, the outgoing of the
intestines; but, since this chapter
must be based on Alexander Trallianus, πρὸς ἐμφραξιν ἥπατος, the
writer ought to mean, the outgoing
of bile from the liver.

ȝebonſten biþ þonne biꝺ þuph þa þambe ſe utpyne
ſpilce blobiȝ pæten ⁊ biþ hiſ neb neaꝺ ⁊ aſpollen · ⁊
þonne þu him þine hanꝺ ꝛeteſt on þa liſne þonne ȝeſelþ
he ſpiþe micel¹ ſaꝛ ⁊ biþ ſe man ſpiꝺe meaꝛo · ⁊ oſ
þæꝛe able cymꝺ ſul oſt pæten bolla. Þiþ ȝeſpollenum
ſol. 75 b.   ſaꝛe. On ſꝛuman miꝺ onleȝenum ⁊ ꝛealſum ſceal
mon lacnian · ſio ꝛceal beon oſ beꝛenum ȝꝛyttum
on leaȝe ȝeſoꝺenum ⁊ oſ culſꝛena ꝛceaꝛine ȝeꝛopht miꝺ
huniȝe ⁊ þonne alecȝe mon þa ſealſe on hatne claꝺ
oþþe ſel oþþe captan beſpeþe miꝺ þonne hneꝛcaꝺ ꝛe
ſpile ſona ⁊ ȝebeꝛſteþ innan.   ꝺꝛince mulſa þ iſ ȝe-
milſcebe ꝺꝛincan ælce ꝺæȝe · ⁊ ȝate meoluc ȝeſobene
⁊ pæten on þam ſien ȝeſoꝺene ȝoꝺe pyꝛta.

.XX.

Læceꝺomaſ piþ þæꝛe liſne punꝺe þonne ſe ſpile ȝe-
pyꝛſmeꝺ tobyꝛſt · Nim ȝate meoluc ſpa peaꝛme niꝛan
ainolcene ꝛele ꝺꝛincan.   ꝺo eac to ꝺꝛence næꝺꝛan
ȝeꝛophte ſpa læcaſ cunnon ⁊ þonne hie ælcꝛa ꝺꝛincan
pillen ꝺꝛincan hie nemne pæteꝛ · æꝛ ȝeſoben oſ pyꝛ-
tum · on peꝛmobe ⁊ on oþꝛum ſpelcum ⁊ ſpilca onleȝena ſpa pe æꝛ pꝛiton.   Ac mon ꝛceal æꝛ miꝺ peaꝛ-
mum ſpꝛinȝum ⁊ hate pætꝛe beþian ⁊ þþean þa ſtope
⁊ on þam pætꝛe ſien ȝeꝛoꝺene lauꝛeſ cꝛoppan ⁊ hinꝺe-
ſol. 76 a.   pyꝛt þ iſ eoꝛꝺȝealla ⁊ peꝛmoꝺ miꝺ þy þu þa ſaꝛan
ſtopa lanȝe æꝛeſt beþe ⁊ læt ꝛeocan on · ȝiſ þonne
ꝛio punꝺ ſpiꝺe ꝛotiȝe þæꝛe liſne oþ þ he þ puꝛſm oſ
muꝺe hꝛæce · ȝepyꝛce him ȝemilſcaꝺe ꝺꝛincan · þ iſ
micel ꝺæl bepylleꝺeſ pæteneſ on huniȝeſ ȝoꝺum ꝺæle ·

¹ Micc, MS.

wound are *these;* when the wound is bursten out then the outrunning through the wamb is as it were bloody water, and *the mans* face is red and swollen; and when thou settest thine hand upon the liver then *the man* feeleth very much soreness, and the man is very tender, and from this disorder there cometh full oft a dropsy. For a swollen sore: at starting one shall cure with onlayings, *that is, external applications,* and salves; the *salve* shall be of barley groats sodden in ley, and of culvers sharn wrought with honey, and then let one lay the salve on a hot cloth, or on a skin, or on paper, beswathe with that, the swelling soon becometh nesh and bursteth within. Let *the man* drink "mulsum," that is, dulcet drinks, every day, and goats milk sodden, and water on which good worts have been sodden.

XX.

Leechdoms for the abscess of the liver, when the purulent swelling bursteth; take goats milk so warm, newly milked, give *the man that* to drink. Form also into a potion an adder, wrought so as leeches ken *how to work it,* and when *the sick* will to drink anything, let them drink nothing but water previously sodden with worts, on wormwood and on other such, and such onlayings as we before wrote of. But one shall previously bathe and wash the places with warm squirtings and with hot water, and on the water let there be sodden bunches of laurel *berries or flowers,* and herdwort, that is, earth gall, and wormwood; with these do thou long previously foment the sore places, and make *the reek* smoke them. If further the wound of the liver be very ratteny, so much as that *the man* hreaketh the ratten from his mouth, let him work himself a mulled drink, that is, a mickle deal of boiled water in a good deal of honey; from it shall the scum

oꝼ þam ſceal beón ꝥ ꞃoꞇ ʒelome adon ƿenden hiꞇ món ƿeld oþ[1] ꝥ þæꞃ nan ne ſie · læꞇ þonne colian ⁊ ſele þonne dꞃincan.[2]

.XXI.

Σκίρρωσις.

Ƿer ſinꞇ ꞇacn aheaꞃdodꞃe liꝼꞃe ʒe ón þam læppum ⁊ healocum ⁊ ꝼilmenum. Sío áheaꞃdunʒ íſ on ꞇƿa ƿiſan ʒeꞃad. Oþeꞃ biþ ón ꝼꞃuman æꞃ þon þe æniʒ oþeꞃ eaꞃꝼeþe ón liꝼꞃe becume · oþeꞃu æꝼꞇeꞃ oþꞃum eaꞃꝼeþum þæꞃe liꝼꞃe cymð · ſio biþ buꞇan ſaꞃe · ⁊ þonne ſe man meꞇe þiʒð þonne aƿyꞃpð he eꝼꞇ ⁊ ónƿendeþ hiſ hiƿ ⁊ hæꝼð unʒeƿealdene ƿambe ⁊ þa micʒean · ⁊ þonne þu ðine handa ſeꞇſꞇ uꝼan on þa liꝼꞃe þonne beoð ſƿa heꝼiʒe ſƿa ſꞇan ⁊ ne biþ ſaꞃ · ʒiꝼ ꝥ lanʒe ſƿa biþ þonne ʒehæꝼþ hiꞇ ón uneþelicne[3] ƿæꞇeꞃbollan.

fol. 76 b.

Ealle[4] þa blaƿunʒe ⁊ þa ƿelmaſ þa þe beoþ ʒehƿæꞃ ʒeond þone lichoman · þa cumað óꝼ haꞇum blode ⁊ ƿeallendum · ſƿa bið eác ſƿilce on ðæꞃe liꝼꞃe ꞇo ónʒiꞇanne hƿæþeꞃ ſio hæꞇo ⁊ ſío áblaƿunʒ ſie on þæꞃe liꝼꞃe ſelꝼꞃe on þám ꝼilmenum · ⁊ on þám þinʒum þe ymbuꞇan þa liꝼꞃe beoþ · ⁊ hƿæþeꞃ hio ſie on ðam liꝼeꞃbylum ⁊ læppum þe on þam liꝼeꞃholúm ⁊ healcum þe on þam dælum bæm. Þonne ſe læce ꝥ onʒiꞇ þonne mæʒ he þone læcedóm þe ꞃadoꞃ ꝼindan · Ƿiſ ſynd þa ꞇacn · ʒíꝼ ſio ablaƿunʒ ſio haꞇe biþ on þæꞃe liꝼꞃe oꝼꞃum oððe bylúm þonne biþ þæꞃ micel aþundeneſ ⁊ ꝼeꝼeꞃ mid ſƿeopunʒa[5] omena ⁊ ſꞇinʒende ſaꞃ oþ þa ƿiþoban oð ða eaxle ⁊ hƿoſꞇa ⁊ neaꞃoneſ bꞃeoſꞇa · ⁊ maꞃe heꝼiʒneſ þonne ſaꞃ · ⁊

[1] MS. has on.

[2] This passage may be from Philagrios on the preparation of ἀπόμελι, as preserved in Nikolaos Myrepsios, v. 3.

[3] For uneþeleacne.

[4] These words are found in Alexander Trallianus, vii. 19; p. 126, ed. 1548.

[5] Read ſpeolunʒa, from the words καὶ πυρετὸν ἐπιφέρει καυσώδη.

be frequently removed, while it is a boiling, till that
there be none there; then let it cool, and then give it
to be drunk.

xxi.

Here are tokens of a hardened liver, whether on the
lobes or the hulks, *that is, the hollows of it,* or the
films *and membranes.* The hardening occurs in two
ways; the one is in the outset before any other mischief cometh upon the liver; the second cometh after
other mischiefs of the liver; it is without sore, and
when the man taketh meat, then he casteth *it* up
again, and changeth his hue, and hath not under control his wamb and his mie; and when thou settest
thine hand from above upon the liver, then it is as
heavy as a stone and is not sore: if that continues
long so, then it involves a not easily cured dropsy.
All the *up*blowings and the burnings which be anywhere throughout the body, come of hot and boiling
blood. So also in like manner it is to be understood
of the liver, whether the heat and the upblowing be
on the liver itself, on the films, *that is, membranes,*[1]
and on the things[2] which be about the liver; and
whether they be on the liver prominences and lobes,
or in the liver holes and hulks,[3] or in both those
parts. When the leech understandeth that, then he
may the more easily find the leechdom. These are the
tokens; if the hot upblowing is on the margins or
prominences of the liver, then is there much distention
and fever with burning heats and a piercing soreness
as far as the collar bones, and as far as the shoulder, and
there is host, *or cough,* and oppression of the breast,

---

[1] χιτῶσιν, *tunics, coats,* Alex.
Trall.

[2] μυσί, *muscles,* id.

[3] Ζητεῖν ἆρά γε τὰ κυρτὰ πεπόνθασι

μᾶλλον, ἢ τὰ σιμά ἢ καὶ τὸ συναμφό-
τερον ; *the convexities or concavities,
or both at once.*

þonne ſio ablaþunʒ bi☼ ón þam ꞃilmenum ⁊ on þam
æðꞃúm þe ón ⁊ ymb þa liꝼꞃe beoð þonne biþ ꝥ ꞃaꞃ
ſceaꞃꞃꞃe þonne þæꞃ pelmeꞃ ꞃaꞃ þe on þæꞃe liꝼꞃe
ꞃelꝼꞃe beoð · ⁊ þu meaht be þon onʒitan ꝥ ſio abl
biþ þæꞃe liꝼꞃe læppum ⁊ oꝼꞃum. Ʒiꝼ þonne ſio liꝼꞃe

aheaꞃðunʒ ⁊ ꞃio abl ⁊ ꞃio ablaþunʒ biþ on þæꞃe liꝼꞃe
healcum ⁊ holocum ʒecenneð þonne þincþ him ſona ón
ꝼꞃuman ꝥ ſio pæte ſpiþoꞃ niþoꞃ ʒepite þonne hio
úpſtiʒe · ⁊ ſe món ʒeſpoʒunʒa þꞃopað ⁊ modeſ ʒeſpæ-
þꞃunʒa · ne mæʒ him ſe lichoma batian ác he bið
blác ⁊ þynne ⁊ acoloð ⁊ ꞃonþon ætꞃilð hím pæteꞃ-
bolla.

.XXII.

Ðiþ þæꞃe ʒeꝼelan heaꞃðneꞃꞃe þæꞃe liꝼꞃe ðonne iꞃ
ſio to beðianne mið hatan pætꞃe ón þám ſien ʒeſoðene pyꞃta. Ðeꞃmod · ⁊ pilðꞃe maʒþan pyꞃttꞃuman ·
ꞃenoʒꞃecum hatte pyꞃt · ⁊ eoꞃð ʒealla · þonne þu
ꞃien ealle ʒeſoðene beþe þonne mið miclum ſpꞃynʒum þa
ꞃaꞃan ſtope lanʒe · ꞃoꞃlæt ſpa .III. daʒaſ. Ðyꞃc þonne
ꞃealꝼe óꞃ hpætenum ʒꞃyttum ʒeꞃoꞃht oððe óꞃ bꞃuꞃe
óꞃ peꞃmode · ⁊ óꞃ pine · ⁊ óꞃ apꞃotanean ⁊ cymene ·
⁊ oꞃ lauꞃeꞃ cꞃoppan ðo huniʒeſ to ꝥ þu þyꞃꝼe ꞃele

him ꝥ þny daʒaſ · oþꞃe þꞃie ꞃete him hoꞃn ón oþþe
ʒlæꞃ teoh ut.   Sel þu lácnaſt ʒiꝼ þu ſeoþeſt ꞃuban
ón ele ⁊ ʒꞃenne peꞃmod oððe ðꞃiʒne · ⁊ hꞃit cpuðu
þy ealle beþe leʒe on uꞃan · læt beón ealne ðæʒ ⁊ eác
ꞃela ðaʒa þaꞃ þinʒ ſint to ðonne ⁊ þám monnum ſynð
to ꞃellanne miʒole ðꞃincan · þa pyꞃt peteꞃꞃilian · ⁊

and more heaviness than sore. And when the upblowing is on the films, and on the veins which be in and
about the liver, then is the sore sharper than the sore
of the inflammation which is on the liver itself, and
thou mayest by that understand that the disorder is
on the lobes and margins of the liver. If moreover
the liver hardening, and the disease, and the upblowing is kindled on the hulks and hollows of the liver,
then it soon seems to *the doctor* that the humour
descends downwards rather than ascends; and the man
suffers swoonings and failings of the mind;[1] his body
cannot amend, but it is pale, and thin, and chilled, and
hence there falleth upon him dropsy.

xxii

For the sensitive hardness of the liver; it is to be
bathed with hot water, on which worts have been
sodden, wormwood and roots of wild maythe, a wort
that hight fenugreek, and earth gall; when they are
all sodden, then bathe the sore places for a long time
with copious water fomentations;[2] leave it so for three
days; then work a salve wrought of wheaten groats
or of a brewit of wormwood, and of wine, and of
abrotanum, and of cummin, and of bunches of laurel
berries; add thereto as much honey as thou needest;
give *the man* that for three days; on other three set
on him *a cupping* horn or glass, draw out *by that,
what comes out.* Thou shalt treat *the sick* better if
thou settest rue in oil, and green or dry wormwood,
and gum mastic, with all that bathe *him,* also lay
it upon *him;* let it be for a whole day, and also for
many days these things are to be done, and to the
men must be given diuretic drinks; give thou him

---

[1] λειποθυμίας for the two.
[2] Medicated baths were well known, as to Oribasios.

dile · ⁊ mencer ræd oððe ƿyncトruman mid huniȝe ſele
þu him ælce dæȝe drincan · ȝif him feren ne ſie yc
ꝥ mid pine æfter þon oþre ƿyncdrencaſ ſculon riþþan
ꝥ ȝeſpel biþ ȝehpeled ⁊ cobynſt ⁊ ƿyrð unſanne ⁊
niþen ȝepic þurh ða pambe ⁊ ſe mán mihð ponmſe·
calaþ ꝥ he þonne hal ſie · þonne beoþ him co ſellanne

Aretæos,
Chron. i. 13.
ſpiþoſt þa miȝolan drincan ꝥce eall ꝥ yfel þurh ða
pambe ⁊ þurh þa micȝean peonðen¹ apeȝ adon · þy læſ
ſe mon peonþe þurh þone muþ ponmſ ſpipende ⁊ hine
hunu piþ bæð healde ⁊ piþ ȝncne æpla ȝif þonne ſe
ſpile ⁊ ꝥ ponmſ upſtihð co þon ꝥ þe þince ꝥ hic mon
ſniþan mæȝe ⁊ út foȝlætan · pync him þonne ſealfe
æneſt of culfran ſceapne ⁊ óf þam ȝelica · ⁊ æn mid
ſpryngum beþe þa ſtope mid þy pætre ⁊ pyncum þe
pe æn priton þonne þu onȝite ꝥ ꝥ ȝeſpel hneſciȝe ⁊

fol. 78 a.
Celsus, iv. 8.
ſpiþriȝe · þonne hrin ðu him mid þy ſmd iſene ⁊ ſnið
lyc hpon ⁊ hſtum ꝥ ꝥ blod mæȝe út funþum þylæſ
þiden in yfel poliha ȝeſiȝe · Ne fonlæt þu þæſ blodeſ

Aret. Acut. vi.
co fela ón ænne ſiþ · þyleſ ſe ſeoca mán co peniȝ
peonðe oððe ſpylce · ſc þonne þu hic coftinȝe oþþe
ſniþe þonne hafa þe linenne pætlan ȝeanone ꝥ þu ꝥ
dolh ſona mid fonþriðe · ⁊ þonne þu hic eft ma
lætan pille ceoh þone pætlan óf læt lytlum ſpa oþþ
hic adruȝie · ⁊ þonne ſio puñd ſie clæne · ȝenyme
þonne ꝥ ꝥ þyrel co neapo ne ſie · ſc þu hie ælce
dæȝe mid pipan ȝeond ſpæc · ⁊ aþƿeah mid þam þin-

---

¹ Read peonðe.

every day to drink the wort parsley, and dill, and seed
of marche or its roots with honey : if he hath no fever
eke that with wine. After that other wort drinks
are proper, when the swelling is become an abscess and
bursteth,[1] and is becoming more free from soreness, and
is passing off downwards through the wamb, and the
man pisseth ratten, reckoneth that he then may be
hole ;[2] then must be given him principally the diuretic drinks, in order that all the mischief through the
wamb and through the mie may be done away, lest
the man should take to spewing ratten through the
mouth ; and let him withhold himself somewhat from
the bath and from green apples. If however the
swelling and the ratten mounteth up to that degree
that it seem to thee that a man may cut *into* it and
let it out, then work him a salve first of culvers sharn
and the like of that, and previously bathe the places
with sousings, with the water, and with the worts
which are wrote of before. When thou understandeth
that the swelling is growing nesh and mild, then touch
thou it with the cutting iron,[3] and cut *in* a little,
and cleverly, even that the blood may come out, lest
an evil *sinus* or pouch descend in thither. Do not
let too much blood at one time, lest the sick man become too languid or die; but when thou dost prick or
cut it, then have for thyself a linen cloth ready that
therewith thou mayst soon bind up the cut ; and
when thou wilt again let more *blood* draw the cloth
off, let it *run* by a little at a time till it gets dry ;
and when the wound is clean, then enlarge it that the
thirl *or aperture* may not be too narrow ; but do
thou every day syringe through it with a tube, and

---

[1] The words are not from Trallianus, but he speaks in the same
order of ἀρχομένης πέττεσθαι τῆς
φλεγμονῆς καὶ γὰρ δι' οὔρων ὑποκλύτ-
τεται καὶ σμικρόνεται ὁ ὄγκος.

[2] τὰ τῆς πέψεως σημεῖα ἀσφα-
λέστερα. Trallianus, p. 128, ed.
1548.

[3] Cf. Aretæos ; chron. I. xiii.

ȝum ȳiþþan ófleȝe þe þa punðe clænȳien ·[1] ȝiȳ hio
fpiþoþ unfyȳne peoȳþe clænȳa[2] mið huniȝe Ᵹ ȝelæt eȳt
toȝæðeþe. Eȳt þonne feo unȝeȳelðe áheaȳðunȝ þæþe
liȳþe to lanȝfum pyȳð · þonne pyþcþ hio pæteþ bollan
þone þe mon ȝelacnian ne mæȝ. Ac món ȳceal ȳona
ón ȳþuman þa æþ ȝenemneban beþunȝa · ne ðȳince he
niȳeȳ nabt · Ᵹ ȝiȳ ȳe liȳeþfioca món blobeȳ to ȳela
hæbbe þonne ȳceal hím món æþ eallum oþþum læceðomum blob lætan oȳ þám fȳiðþan eaþme on þæþe
niþeþþan æðþe · ȝiȳ þa mon ne mæȝe eaþe ȝeþebian
þonne ȳceal món on þæþe miðbel æðþe blob lætan ·
þa þe þ̄ ne ðoþ on micel eaþȳeþum becumað.

.XXIII.[3]

Dþæt him fie to ȳoþȝanne ón liȳeþ able hþæt him
fie to healbanne ȝe on læceðomum ȝe on mete · ȳoþ·
þon iȳ þeaþȳ micel þ̄ món nauþeþ ne ȳealȳa ne baþu ·
ne ónleȝena æþ to nyðe · æþ him món blob læte þam
þe ȳela blobeȳȳ hæþ ·[4] æȳteþ þon þe ȳe lichoma fie
þuþh þa bloblæȳe ȝeclænȳað ·[5] þæf manneȳ bileoȳa[6]
iȳ to beȳceapianne · æþeft hím iȳ to ȳellanne þ̄
þone innoð ftille Ᵹ fmeþe · ne fie ȳceaþp ne to aȳoþ ·
ne ȳlitenðe · ne fþiȝene · ælc bþoþ iȳ to ȳoþȝanne
ȳoþ þon þe hit biþ þinbenðe Ᵹ yȳcle þætan pyþcþ ·
æȝþu fint to ȳoþȝanne ȳoþþonþe hiþa þæte bið ȳæt Ᵹ
inaþan hæto pyþcð · hlaȳeȳ cþuman ȝiȳ hie beoþ oȳ-
þæﬁbe oþþe ȝeȳobene fint to þicȝanne ác na to fþiðe ·
oþþe þætan[7] mete ȝeaþþa Ᵹ cócnunȝa ealle fint to
ȳoþbeoðanne · Ᵹ eal þa þætan þinȝ Ᵹ þa fmeþeþiȝan Ᵹ
oltephlaȳaf[8] Ᵹ eall fþete þinȝ þe pyþcað aþunðeneȳȳe ·
ȝe þa ȳceaþþan aȳþan þinȝ fint to ȳleonne · ȳoþþon þe

---

[1] clæȳnien, MS.
[2] clæþna, MS.
[3] Alexander Trallianus, p. 127, line 9, ed. 1548, by the general sense.
[4] Ei aima πλεονάζει.
[5] ȝeclæȳnað, MS.
[6] Alex. ut supra, line 17.
[7] Read hþætene ; τὰ δὲ ἀλλὰ πάντα σιτώδη.
[8] The Saxon leech skips four lines of Alexandros of Tralles.

wash it out by those means; after that, lay thereon what may cleanse the wound. If it turn off very impure, cleanse it with honey and draw it again come together. Again, when the insensible hardening of the liver is of too long duration, then it forms a dropsy which cannot be cured. But one must soon at the outset employ the before named fomentations; let him drink nothing new, and if the liversick man have too much blood, then one must, before all other leechdoms, let him blood from the right arm on the nether vein. If that may not easily be got at, then shall a man let blood upon the middle vein; they who do it not, come into mickle difficulties.

xxiii.

Here we treat of what *a man* must forego in liver disease, what he must hold by, whether in leechdoms or in diet. For as much as there is much need that for a man who has much blood one should employ neither salves, nor baths, nor external applications, ere he be let blood; after the body is cleansed through the bloodletting, the mans diet is to be examined: first must be given him what may still and soothe the inwards, *what* is neither sharp nor too austere, nor rending, nor caustic; all broth [1] must be foregone because it is inflating and worketh evil humours; eggs must be foregone because their liquor is fat and worketh more heat; crumbs of bread, if they be moistened or sodden, may be eaten, but not in excess; other wet [wheaten] meat-preparations, and cookings up must be forbidden, and all the moist things and greasy, and oyster patties, [2] and all sweet things which work inflation. Yea the sharp austere things [3] must be

---

[1] Ζέμα.
[2] ὀστρακόδερμα, *shell fish.*

[3] τὰ στύφοντα; but just above αχορ translated δριμύ.

þa fint ꝼonꞇynenꝺe þa innoþaꝼ · ꝡ ȝeꝼamnaꝺ þone ꝼpile
ꝡ unyþelice melꞇaꝺ · ꝼon ꝺonne æppla ·[1] ne ꝑin niꝼ ꞇo
ꝼellanne · ꝼon ꝺon þe hie habbaꝺ haꞇne bꝛæþ · þam iꝼ
ꞇo þicȝanne únꝼceaꝛp ꝑin · eác ꝛceal môn oxumellif[2]
ꝛellan þ̄ bıꝺ óꝼ ecebe ꝡ oꝼ huniȝe ȝeꝛoꝛhꞇ ꝺꝛenc
ꝼuþeꝛne · ꝡ þonne onȝinꝺ þꝛeꝛe hæꞇo pelm panian
ꝼpıþoꝼꞇ þuꝛh ꝺa micȝean · ꝡ hím iꝼ ꞇo ꝛellanne lác-
ꞇucaꝼ ·[3] ꝡ ꝼuþeꝛne popıȝ[4] innepeaꝛꝺ. Tacn[5] þ̄ ꝼe ꝼpile
þꝛinan ne mæȝ · ne uꞇyꝛnan on þꝛeꝛe liꝼꝛe · þ̄ ꝼe
môn hæꝼꝺ heꝼıȝ ꝼaꝛ ón niþepeaꝛbꝛe liꝼꝛe ꝺꝛlum ·
emne ꝼpa he ꝛıe mıꝺ hpilcꝛe hpeȝa byꝛþenne ȝeheꝼeȝoꝺ
ón þꝛe ꝼpıþꝛan healꝼe · ꝡ næꝼꝺ he ꝼeꝼꝛeꝼ hæꞇo ón
þam ꝺælum · þam men finꞇ ꞇo ꝛellanne þa ꝺꝛincan ꝡ
þa læceꝺomaꝼ þa ꝺe ꝛe læꝛꝺon þ̄ mon ꝺyꝺe ꞇo þꝛe
unȝeꝼelan heaꝛꝺneꝼꝛe onȝunnenꝛe on þꝛeꝛe liꝼꝛe ȝehn-
neꝛcıȝe mıꝺ þy þ̄ ꝼoꝛꝼeꞇene yꝼel · ȝiꝼ hꝛa þone lꝛce-
ꝺóm ꝺeþ ꞇo þe þa ꝼoꝛꝼeꞇꞇan þınȝ ónꞇyne ꝡ uꞇꞇeo aꝛꝛ
þon ꝺe he þone ꝛoꝛheaꝛbóꝺan ꝼpile ȝehneꝛce · peneþ þ̄
he hiꞇ beꞇe · ȝiꝼ þꝛeꝛ ahꞇ bıꝺ laꝛeꝺ þꝛaꝼ heaꝛꝺan · ne
heꞇ he hiꞇ ac pyꝛꞇ · ꝡ aꝺꝛıȝþ mıꝺ þy lꝛceꝺóme þꝛa
ꝛꝛꞇan ꝡ pıꝛꝺ ꝛe ꝼpile ꝼpa heaꝛꝺ ꝼpa ꝼꞇan · ꝡ ne mꝛȝ
hine môn ȝemelꞇan ne ȝehneꝛcian.[6]

.XXIIII.

Þyꝛꞇꝺꝛencaꝼ pıꝺ eallum liꝼeꝛ aꝺlum · pyꝛce môn
ꞇo ꝺꝛencum liꝼeꝛ ꝼeocum mannum · meꝛceꝼ[7] ꝛaꝺ ·
ꝺileꝼ · peꝛmoꝺeꝛ · þy ȝemeꞇe þe lꝛcaꝼ cunnon ȝnıꝺ ón
ꝛꝛꞇeꝛ ꝛele ꝺꝛincan. Eꝼꞇ[8] coꝼꞇeꝛ ꝡ pıꝛoꝛeꝼ ꝺuꝼꞇ ꝡ
oþꝛa pyꝛꞇa þiꝼum ȝelica ꝺꝛince .III. ꝺaȝaꝼ · ꝡ liȝe on

---

[1] For ποιαί, pomegranates.
[2] As before, foot of page ; missing four lines.
[3] For τὸ ἄσαρ, asarum Europæum,
and mæum, meum.
[4] For nardus keltica. Valeriana c.
The Saxon perhaps means Glaucium
luteum. Cf. Dioskorid. I. vii.
[5] The editions of Alex. Trall.

make a new chapter here, p. 127,
line 6, ed. 1548. The Saxon version is free.
[6] This passage ends at Alex.
TralL., p. 127, line 16, ed. 1548.
[7] From Alex. Trallianus. p. 129,
line 24, ed 1548, with omission of
asarabacca and almonds.
[8] Alex. Trall., p. 129, line 32.

avoided, inasmuch as they have a bad effect in closing
the inwards, and they collect the swelling, and it doth
not easily disperse,[1] hence neither apples nor wine
must be given, since they have a hot breath *or aroma.*
The man must take a not sharp wine; one must also
give him some oxymel, which is a southern *or Italian*
drink, wrought of vinegar and of honey : and when
the burning of the heat beginneth to wane away,
chiefly through the mie, he must have lettuces and
the inward part of southern poppy. Tokens that the
swelling in the liver may not abate, nor run off; that
that man hath a heavy sore in the parts of the nether
liver, even as if he were weighted with something of
a burden in the right side, and he hath not a heat of
fever in those parts. To such a man must be given
the drinks and the leechdoms, which we taught one
should use for the insensible hardness begun in the
liver ; with them let him make the obstructive mischief
nesh. If any one applieth the leechdom which unlocketh
and draweth out the obstinately lodged matters, before
he hath made nesh the badly hardened swelling, he
weeneth that he is amending it ; *but* if there be aught
left of the hard *matter*, he amendeth it not, but
harmeth, and with the leechdom he drieth the humours, and the swelling becometh as hard as a stone,
and it cannot be dissipated nor be made nesh.

xxiv.

Wort drinks for all liver diseases : let one work for
drinks for a liversick man, seed of marche, of dill,
of wormwood, rub *these fine* into water in the manner
in which leeches ken *how, and* give to drink. Again,
let *the patient* drink for three days dust of costmary,
and of pepper, and of other worts like these, and let
him lie on the right side for half an hour, and drink

---

[1] Τοὺς ὄγκους δυσφορήτους ἐργάζεται.

þa ſpiðnan ſiðan healƿe tib ⁊ ðjunce eƀt ón æƀenne ·
healðe hine þonne piþ eceð. Þiþ bæþ[1] piþ piſan ⁊
beana · ⁊ næpaſ · ⁊ piþ þa þinȝ þe pinðiȝne æþm ʻón men
pyjncen. Eƀt[2] coſt · ƀenum ȝjecum pipoj hajan typðlu
ealja emƀela · ȝebeat oþþe ȝeȝnið ⁊ ajiƀte · ȝeðo cuclej
ƀulne þæj ón pin jele ðjincan þam þe butan ƀeƀne

fol. 80 a.

ſie · þæm ðe ƀeƀej hæbbe þ ſj micel hæto ⁊ hjuð[3]
jele þám ón peajmum pætejie · ȝelicȝe þonne on þa
ſpiþjan ſiðan ⁊ alecȝe hij ſpiþjau hanð hĩm unðej
beajoð ajeahte healƿe tib.[4] Eƀt pyjtðjencaſ piþ lijej
able · clæƀjan ƀeapej . ii. lytle bollan ƀulle mið lytlc
hunȝe ȝemenȝðe · ðo peaji ƀulne ȝehætteƀ pineſ to
jele ðjincan þjy ðaȝaſ ȝiſ hpæt yƀlej on þæjeˢ[5] bið
ˢ Read julle.
ſie ðjenc lácnað. Eƀt pilðje mealpan ſeapej þjy lytle
bollan ƀullan ᵃ ȝemenȝðe piþ ſpilc tu pætejeſ jele ðjincan
cun . iiii. ðaȝaſ · ⁊ ȝiſ hĩm hjið abl ȝetenȝe bið þa
toðjiƀþ je pyjt ðjenc. Eƀt þín cymen ⁊ hunȝ
ȝeȝnið toSomne jele ðjincan. Eƀt ijiȝ cjoppena on
þam monðe ȝeȝaðejoð þe pe hatað ianuajiuj ón læben ·
⁊ on enȝliſc je æƀtejja ȝeola · ƀíƀ ⁊ xx. ⁊ pipojej eác
ſpa · ȝeȝnið þonne mið þy ſeleſtan pine · ⁊ ȝehæte jelc
þam ſeocan men neahtneſtiȝum ðjincan. Læceðóm pið

fol. 80 b.

lijej able eƀt caulej tpiȝu oþþe ſtelan mið þam cjop-
pum aðjiȝe clænlice bæjne to ahſan ȝehealð þa ahjan·
⁊ þonne þeajiƀ ſie ȝeðo þæje ahſan cuclej ƀulne mið
. xi. ȝeȝniðenjja pipoj cojna ón ealð ſpiþe hluttoj . .
. .[6] ȝehæt þonne jele ðjincan oþje jiþe niȝon cojn ·
þjiðban ſiðe ſeoƀon. Læceðom piþ lijƀe able eƀt laujej
cjoppan ⁊ pipojej cojna . xx. ȝeȝnið ſmale · ȝeðo ón
bollan ƀulne ealðej pinej · ⁊ ȝemenȝ toȝæðeje mið

---

[1] The text of Alex. Tra. 1528,
has **Baldewv**, but Albanus Torinus
" balneum."

[2] Alex. Trall., p. 130, line 3, ed.
1548.

[3] Otherwise found hjuð.

[4] This last clause, not in the text
of Alex. Tr., is in the Latin of
Albanus Torinus.

[5] Add lijne, omitted in MS.

[6] Some word, perhaps pin, is
here omitted by MS.

again in the evening. Let him withhold himself also
from vinegar, from the bath, from peas, and beans,
and navews, and from the things which work in a man
a windy vapour. Again, beat or rub up and sift
costmary, fenugreek, pepper, hares treadles, equal quantities of all; put a spoon full of this into wine, and
give it to him who is without fever, to drink. To
him who hath fever, that is mickle heat and fire,[1] give
it in warm water; then let him lie on the right side
and lay his right hand stretched out under his head, for
half an hour. Again, wortdrinks for liver disease: to
two little bowls full of juice of clover mingled with a
little honey, add a bowl full of heated wine; give this
to be drunk for three days, if anything of evil be on
the liver, the drink will cure it. Again, give to drink
for four days, three little bowls full of the juice of
wild mallow, mingled with two such of water: and if
fever disease be on him, the wort drink driveth it
away. Again, rub together wine, cummin, and honey,
give him *this* to drink. Again, five and twenty bunches
of ivy berries, gathered in the month which we hight
in Latin Januarius, and in English the second Yule,
and of pepper as much, rub *these up* with the best
wine, and heat it; give it to the sick man, after
his nights fasting, to drink. A leechdom again for
liver disease: dry clean some twigs or stalks of colewort with the flower heads, burn *them* to ashes, store
the ashes, and when occasion is, put a spoon full of
the ashes with eleven ground pepper corns into old
very clear *wine*, then heat it, give to be drunk the
next time nine corns, the third time seven. A leechdom again for liver disease: rub small a bunch of bay
berries and twenty pepper corns, put them into a bowl
full of old wine, and mingle them together with a glowing

---

[1] Properly *fever*; the Saxon seems to interpret Fever, as a
Latinism, by pure English words.

ȝlopenðe ɟɾene ɟele ðɾincan ⁊ ȝelicȝe ſtille. Þɪþ lɪɟɟe
aðluın ɟuðan ɾceaɟaɟ þɟy ȝeðo on pıne cɟoccan ⁊ þɟy
ınıcle bollan ɟulle pætepeſ oɟeɟpylle oþ þone þɟıðban
ðæl ⁊ ſpete ſpɪðe mɪð hunıȝe ⁊ þonne eɟt oɟeɟpylle
ɟele ðɾincan. Eɟt pıntɟeopeɟ þa ȝɟenan tpıȝu uɟe-
peaɟð ȝeȝnıð ón þ ɟeleſte pın ɟele ðɾincan. Eɟt heo-
ɟoteɟ lunȝena mıð þæɟe þɟotan aſpɟınðlað ⁊ aþeneð ⁊
aðɟıȝeð ón ɟece · ⁊ þonne hıe ɟul pel aðɟuȝoðe ſynð
ȝebɟɟte ⁊ ȝeȝnıð ⁊ þonne ȝeɟomna mıð hunıȝe ɟele
to etanne lıɟeɟ ɟeocum men þ ıɟ halpenðe læceðóm.
Ȝıɟ lıɟeɟ peaxe ðɾınce ſe man ſpıpolne ðɾenc. Ðɾınce
eɟt pucan æɟteɟ þon beón bɟoð ⁊ mænıȝe oþɟe pætan ·
oþɟe pucan ðɾınce peɟmoð ón maxpyɟte apylleðe · ⁊
nane oþɟe pætan ⁊ ealıɟeɟ hatte pyɟt apylle þa eác on
maxpyɟte ðɾınce þɟıðban pucan ⁊ nanne oþeɟne[1] pætaıı.
Ðɾınce æɟteɟ ſpeopolne ðɾenc ane ɟɟþe.

fol. 81 a.

<h4 style="text-align:center">.XXV.</h4>

DEꞧ ſınt tacn ſpeotol be pambe coþum ⁊ aðlúıı ⁊
hu ınón þa yɟelan pætan þæɟe pambe lacnıan ſcyle ·
þonne pamb aðl topeaɟð ſıe þonne beoþ þa tacıı.
Þent[2] hıe ſıo pamb ⁊ hɟyt ⁊ ȝeɟelð ɟaɟı þonne
ſe món ınete þıȝeð ⁊ punȝetunȝa ⁊ unluſt meteɟ.
Cneop hatıað[3] lenðenu heɟeȝıað ⁊ toȝetteþ betpeox
ſculðɟum ⁊ eall lıchoma ſtıcce mælum heɟeȝað ⁊ latıað
þa ɟet · ⁊ þa lıɟan þaɟa lenðena ɟaɟıað · þonne mou
þaɟ tacn onȝıte · þonne ıɟ ſe æɟeſta læceðóm ðæȝ-
ɟæſten þ ınon mıð þy þa pambe clænɟıȝe[4] þ hıo þy þe

---

[1] The change of gender is according to the MS.	tam : col. 376, B. in Medicæ Artis Principes, for five lines only.
[2] Diokles apud Paullum Ægine-	[3] Gravantur, Lat., healtıað ?
	[4] clæɟnıȝe, MS.

iron, give *to the patient* to drink, and let him lie still.
For liver diseases ; put three bundles of rue into wine in a crock, and three mickle bowls full of water, boil them down to the third part, and sweeten them thoroughly with honey, and then again boil off; give *this* to be drunk. Again, rub into the best wine the upper part of the green twigs of a pine tree ; administer this. Again, a harts lungs with the throat ripped up, and spread out, and dried in the reek; and when they are full well dried, break them and rub *them small* and then collect them with honey; give *this* to the liver-sick man to eat; it is a healing leechdom. If the liver wax *large,* let the man drink an emetic drink. Again, for a week after that let him drink bean broth and no other liquid, next week let him drink wormwood boiled in mashwort, and no other liquid, and there is a wort called ealiver,[1] boil that also in mashwort, let him drink that for the third week and no other liquid. Let him drink after *that* an emetic drink for one turn.

XXV.

Here are plain tokens of disorders and sicknesses of the wamb, and how a man shall cure the evil humours of the wamb. When wamb disease is present then the tokens are; the wamb turneth itself, and is fevered, and feeleth sore when the man eateth meat, and prickings, and loss of appetite for meat. The knees are slow, the loins are heavy, and there are spasms between the shoulders, and all the body by piece meal[2] is heavy, and the feet are tardy, and the muscles of the loins are sore; when a man observes these tokens, then the first leechdom is a days fasting, that with that he may cleanse the wamb, that it may be the lighter. Well,

---

[1] *Jack in the hedge; Erysimum alliaria.*

[2] *citra occasionem,*" the modern translation of the unprinted Greek.

leohtpe pie · ȝɪf fio abl fie þonne ȝɪt peaxenbe pæſtc
.ɪɪ. baȝaf toȝæbepe ȝɪf hɪm mæȝen ȝelæſte · ȝɪf he þ̄
ne mæȝe pelle hɪm mon leohtep hpæt hpeȝa to þɪc-
ȝanne fpa æȝpu beoð ꝡ ðon¹ ȝelɪc. Sume to þæpe

pambe clænpunȝa² feoþað netelán on pætpe ꝡ ón
pɪne · ꝡ on ele · fume þæpe peaban netlan tpɪȝu

fol. 81 b.

ȝpene · fume betan oþþe boccan³ on ȝefpettum pɪne
feoþað ꝡ pellað to þɪcȝenne · ꝡ ȝɪf fio abl mape pypð
ꝡ fe peocs man þ̄ mæȝen hæfð þonne feoþan hɪe hɪm
ftpenȝpan pypta ꝡ boþ hpæt hpeȝa pɪpep to ; Sceapɪȝc
món ȝeopne hpɪlc pe utȝanȝ fie þe mɪcel þe lytel þe þæp
nan ne fie · leopnɪȝe be þon pe læce hu hɪm þɪnce
hpæt món bon pcule · ȝɪf þ̄ fie omɪhte pæte ɪnnan
ónbupnenu tyhte hɪe món ut mɪb lɪþum mettum fɪn-
cenðum ꝡ ne læt ɪnne ȝefɪttan on þam lɪchoman ꝡ
pypð ȝeȝabepobu omɪȝ pæte ón þæpe pambe oððe
on þam fmælþeapme · ꝡ næfð þonne utȝanȝ fio ftop
nc bɪð apypbeb fio ftop ꝡ pe maȝa onpent ꝡ tóbpocen
ꝡ þ̄ heapob aþputen ꝡ pap · ꝡ þa Innoþap ablapene ꝡ
hate pefpap · ꝡ mɪcel þupft ꝡ eallep lichoman abla
peoppað apeahte. Sceal món lacnɪan fpɪlce able ȝɪf he
pepep næfð · mɪb cu meolcum oððe ȝate fpa nɪȝe mol-
cene bpɪnce. Eác hylpð ȝɪf món mɪb ea ftanum on-
bæpneðum · oþþe mɪb hatene ɪfene þa meolúc ȝepypð

fol. 82 a.

ꝡ pelþ bpɪncan · ꝡ ȝɪf þ̄ bɪþ ȝeonȝ man ꝡ þa tɪb hæfð
ꝡ mɪhte hɪm mon pceal óf eapme blob fpɪþe lætan
ꝡ ymb .ɪɪɪ. nɪht bpɪnce ept þa meoluc.

---

¹ ton, MS.
² clæpnunȝa, MS.

³ Paul. Ægin., as before.

if the disease be still on the increase, let *him* fast for two days together, if his strength will endure it ; if he be not able to do that, let him have somewhat light to eat, as eggs be and the like of them. Some, for the cleansing of the wamb, seethe nettle in water, and in wine, and in oil, some scethe in sweetened wine twigs of red nettle green, some beet or dock, and give *this* to be taken; and if the disease groweth stronger, and the sick man hath the strength *for it*, then they scethe stronger worts and add some little pepper. Let it be earnestly observed what the outgang, *or fœcal discharge,* is, whether mickle, or little, or whether there be none; let the leech learn by that how it seems to him a man should act. If there be an inflammatory flagrant humour within, let it be got out by gentle aperient diet, and let it not lodge within in the body, *for then* there will be gathered an inflammatory humour in the wamb, or in the small guts, and then the place has no passage out, but the spot is corrupted, and the maw is disturbed and upbroken, and the head is vexed and sore, and the inwards upblown ; and hot fevers, and mickle thirst, and diseases of all the body become awakened. Such a disease must be treated, if *the patient* have no fever, with cows milk, or let him drink goats milk newly milked. Also it helpeth if a man with water stones[1] put in the fire, or with heated iron, turneth the milk and *so* giveth it to be drunk ; and if it be a young man and he hath a suitable time *for it* and strength *to bear it,* he must be freely let blood from the arm, and let him drink the milk for about three days.

---

[1] Understand such stones as would bear to be heated and plunged in water.

.XXVI.

Be þambe coþum ꝼ ȝíꝼ hio mnan punð biþ hu
þ món onȝitan mæȝe ꝼ ȝelácnian · aꝑeꝼt ȝiꝼ hiꝑe
bið ón innan punð þonne biþ þæꝑ ꝼaꝑ ꝼ beotunȝa ꝼ
ȝeꝼceoꝼꝼ · ꝼ þonne hie mete þicȝeað ꝼ ðꝛuncað þonne
plataō hie ꝼ bið hioꝑa muð ꝼul ꝼ hꝛuðiað · ꝼ hꝛꝑa
utȝanȝ blobiȝ ꝼ ꝼtincð yꝼele · þam mannum ꝼceal man
ꝼellan æȝꝑa to ꝼupanne · beꝑen bꝛead clæne niꝑe
buteꝑan ꝼ niꝑe beꝑen mela oððe ȝꝛytta toȝæbꝛe
ȝebꝛiꝑeð ꝼpa cocaꝼ cunnon · ꝼelle mon neahtneꝛtiȝum.
Eꝼt pyꝼena ꝼeap ꝼ peȝbꝛæðan menȝe ꝑon pið aꝼeopen
huniȝ ꝼelle neahtneꝛtiȝum. Eác piþ þon bo man ȝobe
ꝼealꝑa[1] ónleȝena utan to þa þe þ yꝼel út ceon eað-
mylte mettaꝼ ꝼ ꝼciꝑ ꝼín ꝼ ꝼmeþe.

.XXVII.

Be þambe miꝛSenhiꝑe ȝecynbo oððe þæꝑe miꝛbyꝑðo
hu þ mon mæȝe ónȝitan. þonne[2] hio bið hatꝑe
ȝebyꝛbo ꝼ ȝecynbo · þonne mæȝ hiꝑe ꝼona lytel ðꝛinca
helpan · ȝíꝼ he maꝑa biþ ꝼe ðꝛinca ꝼona biþ ꝼeo pamb
ȝeheꝼeȝob ꝼ cloccet ꝼpa ꝼpa hit on cylle[3] ꝼlecȝete ꝼ ȝeꝼꝛhð ðꝛium mettum þonne ꝼio pæte pamb ne þꝛopað ꝼeo
þuꝑꝼt ꝼ ꝼio ꝼpiðe pæꝑꝑe ȝecynbo biþ ne þꝛopað ꝼeō þuꝑꝼt ne
heꝼiȝneꝼꝼe metta · ꝼ ȝeꝼꝛhð pætum mettum. be hatꝑe
ȝecynbo pambe · Sio pamb ꝼeo þe bið hatꝑe ȝecynbo
ꝼio melt mete pel ꝼꝑꝑoꝼt þa þe heaꝑbe beoð ꝼ úneað
mylte ꝼ ȝeꝼꝛhð peaꝑꝑꝛum mettum ꝼ ðꝛincum · ꝼ ne
biþ hiꝑe ȝeꝼceðeð ꝼꝛam cealbum mettum mib ȝemete
ȝeþꝛȝbum. Seo þe bið pæteꝛꝛȝꝛe ȝecynbo ꝼio hæꝼð
ȝobe ȝiꝑneꝼꝼe meteꝼ · hio næꝼð ȝobe meltunȝe ꝼꝑꝑoꝼt
ón þam mettúm þe uneaðe melte beoð · ȝeꝼꝛhð cealbum

---

¹ Read ꝼealꝑa ꝼ ?
² Twelve lines found in Actius
Tetrabibl. I. Seom. iv. capp. lxxii.,
lxxiii., lxxiv., consecutively; also in
Paulus of Ægina, lib. I. cap. lxiv.

³ By the printed books ꝼylle
would seem to be the true reading.
" Fluctuationes habeant, si id quod
" redundat, innatet."

xxvi.

Of sickness of the wamb, and if it be wounded
within, how a man may understand that and cure it.
First if there be a wound upon it within, then is there
sore, and grumblings, and irritation ; and when they
take meat and drink, then they have nausea, and their
mouth is foul, and they are fevered, and their discharge
is bloody and stinketh foully: to those men shall be
given eggs to sup up, barley bread, clean new butter,
and new barley meal or groats made into a brewit
together, as cooks ken *to do* ; let it be administered to
them after their nights fast. Again, let one mingle
juice of peas and waybroad with strained honey, and
give it after the nights fast. Again for that, let one
apply good salves, *and* external applications, such as
may draw out that evil, *also* easily digested meats, and
sheer and smooth wine.

xxvii.

Of the various nature of the wamb or of its caprice,
how a man may understand that. When it is of a
hot temper and nature, then a little drink may soon
help it. If the drink be more powerful soon the wamb
is oppressed and palpitates, as if in cold it were
beating, and it rejoiceth in dry meats. When the
wamb is moist it doth not suffer thirst, and it is of a
very moist nature ; it doth not suffer thirst nor heaviness from meats, and it rejoiceth in moist meats. Of
the hot nature of the wamb. The wamb, that *namely*
which is of a hot nature, digests meats well, especially
those which be hard and of difficult digestion, and
rejoices in warm meats and drinks, and it is not harmed
by cold meats, taken with moderation. That which
is of a watery nature hath a good appetite for meat ;
it hath not a good digestion, chiefly of the meats
which be of difficult digestion, it rejoices in cold meats.

mettum. þe cealðɲe ꝛ pætꞇɲe ȝecynðo pambe. Sio
pamb fio ðe bið cealðɲe oððe pætꞇe ȝecynðo oððe
miꝛbyɲðo · hím cymð bꞃæȝeneꝛ aðl ꝛ unȝepicꝼæꝛcneꝛ
him bið · ꝛ þonne fio ꝼoꝛðꞃuȝaðe ȝecynðo on þám
finum ꝛ on þam banum biþ · ᵽ þa ꝛyn ꝼoꝛþyꝛꝛoðe
þonne ne mæȝ món þa ȝelacnian · ȝiꝼ hio þonne biþ
innoꝛi on þam ꝼlæꝛcæhcum ſcopum mið fynðꞃiȝum
ſcopum ꝛ pæcinȝum ꝛ mectum ᵽ món mæȝ ȝelácnian
þenðen oꝼ þæꝛe liꝼɲe fio bloðꞃceapunȝ ȝeonð ȝec ealne
þone lichoman.   Seleſc læceðom iꝛ co fpilcum þinȝum
ᵽ món ȝelome nyccȝe piceꝛ[1] ꝛ þa pambe mið þy
ȝeꝛlea þonne hio ȝepyꝛimeðu fie ꝛ baþu oꝼ ɲen pæcepe
ꝛ niȝe molcen meoluc mið hunȝe ȝefmeþeð hím ðeah ·
baþȝe hine ȝelome ón ðæȝe ꝛ hꝛilum mið ele fmiꝛe.[1]
Dim hylpð eác ᵽ him ꝼæc cilð[1] æcꝛlape · ꝛ ᵽ he ᵽ
ȝeðo neah hiꝛ pambe fimle · him hylpð eác oꝼen bacen
hlaꝼ[1] ꝛ ꝛcellehce ꝼiꝛcaf ón pofe ·[1] ꝛ þone mece þe pel
mylcan pille. þe hacꝛe[1] ꝛ ðꞃiȝꝛe pambe ȝiꝼ ꝛio pamb
aðliȝ bið hac hꝛæc hꝛeȝa · eac þæꝛe ðꞃiȝneꝛꝛe · þonne
ne ꝛceal he hunȝeꝛ ónbican ác ealð ꝼín plæce mectaf ·
ȝiꝼ ꝛio yꝼle pæce co micel fie · þonne ðuȝon him
cealð pæceɲ ꝛ ꝛceaꝛꝛe mectaf bucan hæcu · hꝛilum
beoþ þa pæcan on þæꝛe pambe ꝼilmenum · þonne
ꝛceal món ᵽ piꝛlice fecean ꝛ pæꝛlice clænꝛian[2] mið
alpan · ꝛ mið fpelcum úcyꝛnenðum ðꞃencum aceon uc
þa hoꝛhehcan pæcan. þꝛæne mið þy æꝛieſc ꝛ þonne
pyꝛce leohce fpipole ðꞃencaꝛ oꝼ ꝛæðice fpa ᵽ læcaꝛ
cunnon. þe hæmeðþinȝum[3] eallúm þyꝛꝛum lichomum
hæmeðþinȝ ne ðuȝon ác fpiþoſc þyꝛꝛum ꝛ cealðum ·
ne ðeꝛeþ hic hacum ꝛ pæcum pyꝛꝛeſc bið þám cealðan hacan[4] fpiþoſc þam ðe hoꝛnable habbað. Spelcúm
mannum ðeah ᵽ hie hím ȝefpinc anȝefecen ꝛ hie ꝛelꝼe

¹ Oribaslus Synops., lib. V. liii.;   Paulus Ægineta, lib. I. cap. lxxi. in
also Paulus Ægineta, lib. I. lxxii.   Med. Art. Princ.
² clæꝛnan, MS.   ⁴ Read pæcan from the original.
³ Five or six lines found in

Of the cold and moist natured wamb. The wamb which is of a cold or moist nature or caprice; on *the man* cometh disease of the brain and loss of his senses; and when the desiccated nature is upon the sinews and on the bones, so that they are dried up, then they cannot be cured. Then if *this dryness* be more within on the fleshy parts, one may cure that with change of residence, and wettings, and meats, as long as from the liver the blood gushes through the whole body. The best leechdom for such things is, that a man should frequently make use of pitch, and strike the wamb with it, when it is warmed; and baths of rain water, and newly milked milk, softened with honey, is good for *the patient*. Let him bathe himself frequently in the day, and at whiles smear himself with oil. It is also helpful to him that a fat child should sleep by him, and that he should put it always near his wamb. Oven baked bread also helpeth him, and shell fishes in liquor, and (let him eat) the meat which will readily digest. Of the hot and dry wamb, if the diseased wamb be somewhat hot, besides, for the dryness; then shall *the patient* not taste of honey, but old wine and lukewarm meats. If the evil humour be too mickle, then are good for him cold water, and sharp meats without heat. At whiles the humours be on the membranes of the wamb; then shall a man wisely seek into that, and warily cleanse *them* with aloes, and draw out the turbid humours with such purging drinks: first clear *the wamb* with them, and then work light emetic drinks of radish, as leeches ken how to do it. Of venery: to all dry constitutions venery is not beneficial; but most to dry and cold ones; it harmeth not hot and wet ones; it is worst for the cold moist ones and them which have disorder of the gastric juices. To such men it is of benefit that they should seek to themselves exercise, and should dose themselves, without bath, and with

ðꝛencen[1] buꞇan baðe ⁊ miƀ ſmiꞃeneꞃꝛúm hie ſmeꞃꞃan.
ƀe cealðꞃe ȝecynƀo pambe. Se þe cealðꞃe ȝecynƀo ſie
nyꞇꞇiȝe ſe ȝemeꞇlicer yꞃeleꞃ ſꝑilce ꞃe þe ðꞃiȝꞃe oððe
pæꞇꞃe ſie. Se þe haꞇꞇꞃe ſie ſio ȝeȝaðꞃaþ óman · þa
món ꞃceal ȝiꞃ hie niþeꞃ beoð þuꞃh þa pambe uꞇꞃih-
ꞇan miƀ pyꞃꞇƀꞃence úꞇ aƀon · ȝíꞃ hie úpſꞇiȝen þuꞃh
ſꝑiꝑþan ꞃceal món aꞃeȝ aƀon.

.XXVIII.

Þiþ þon[2] þe manneꞃ þ uȝeꞃꞃe hꞃiꞃ ſie ȝeꞃylleð miƀ
yꞃelꞃe pæꞇan hoꞃhehꞇꞃe þ þám mannum ȝelimpð þe ón
miclum ȝeðꞃince pel ꞃeðenðe meꞇꞇaſ þicȝeað oþþe ſꝑipað
⁊ ſꝑiþuſꞇ æꝼꞇeꞃ meꞇe ⁊ him bið plæꞇꞇa ȝeꞇenȝe ·
beoð ȝeonð blaꝑene ⁊ bið ſio pamb aꝑeneð ⁊ hꞃæcꞇað
ȝelome. Ðam monnum ꞃceal[3] ꞃellan oxumelle miƀ
ꞃæbice þ iꞃ ſuþeꞃꞃe læceƀóm · ⁊ þonne ſꝑipað hie ꞃona
þone þiccan hoꞃh ⁊ him biþ ꞃel. Geꝑꞃꞃc[4] þe læceƀóm
þuꞃ óꞃ eceðe ⁊ óꞃ huniȝe · ȝením þ ꞃeleſꞇe huniȝ ðo
oꞃeꞃ heoꞃð aꞃeoþ þ peax ⁊ þ hꞃoꞇ óꞃ · ȝeðo ðonne ꞇo
þam huniȝe emꞃela eceðeſ þæꞃ ne ſie ſꝑiþe aꞃoꞃ ne ſꝑiðe
ſꝑeꞇe menȝ ꞇo ȝæðeꞃe ⁊ ðo ꞇo ꝼyꞃe ón cꞃoccan oꞃeꞃ
pylle on ȝoðum ȝleðum clænum ⁊ cꝑicum oþ þ hiꞇ ſie
ȝemenȝeð þ hiꞇ ſie án ⁊ hæbbe huniȝeꞃ þicneꞃꞃe ⁊ ne
ſie on benȝneꞃꞃe ꞇo ſꝑeoꞇol þæꞃ eceðeꞃ aꝼꞃe ꞃceaꞃpneꞃ ·
ȝiꞃ ſio pamb biþ ꝑinðeꞃ ꝼull þonne cymð þ oꞃ plácꞃe
pæꞇan · ſió cealðe pæꞇe ꝑyꞃcþ ꞃaꞃan. Þiþ þon ꞃceal món
ſeoþan cymen ón ele · ⁊ meꞃceꞃ ꞃæð · ⁊ moꞃan ſæð ·
⁊ ðileꞃ · ȝíꞃ ꞃe cyle ſie maꞃa ðo þonne ꞃuƀan ⁊ lauꞃeꞃ
bleƀe · ⁊ ꝼinoleꞃ ꞃæð ȝeꞃoðen ón ele · ȝiꞃ þonne ȝiꞇ
ſio aðl eȝle ȝeðꞃinȝe inne þuꞃh piꝑan oððe hoꞃn ſꝑa

---

[1] "Victus attenuans," Lat. version of P. Ægin.
[2] Nine lines found in Paulus Ægineta, lib. I. cap. xli.
[3] Read ꞃceal mon.

[4] Oribasius Med. Coll., lib. V., cap. xxiv. ; tom. i., p. 395, ed. Daremberg. Also Galenos, vol. VI. p. 271, ed. Kühn.

smearings smear themselves. Of the cold nature of the
wamb; he who is of a cold nature should avail himself of moderate discipline, as he who is of a dry or
moist nature. He who is of a hot nature, *with him*
the *wamb* gathereth inflammatory humours; these, if
they be low down, one must get rid of by wort drinks,
through purging of the wamb; if they mount up high
one must get rid of them by vomitings.

xxviii.

In case that the upper part of the belly is
filled with evil sordid humour, a thing which hap-
peneth to the men who in much continued drinking
take nutritious meats, or who spew, and chiefly after
meat, and who are subject to nausea, they are all
over blown *as with wind*, and the wamb is extended
and they frequently have hreakings. To these men
one must give oxymel with radish; that is a southern
leechdom: and then they soon spew up the thick corruption, and it is well with them. Work up the leechdom thus, from vinegar and from honey; take the
best honey, put it over the hearth, seethe away the
wax and the scum, then add to the honey as much
vinegar, so as that it may not be very austere nor
very sweet; mingle together, and set by the fire in a
crock, boil upon good gledes, clean and lively, till the
mixture be mingled, so that it may be one, and have
the thickness of honey, and on tasting it the austere
sharpness of the vinegar may not be too evident. If
the wamb is full of wind, that cometh from lukewarm humour; the cold humour worketh sores. For
that shall one seethe cummin in ale, and seed of
march, and seed of more *or carot*, and of dill. If
the chill be greater, then add rue, and leaf of laurel,
and seed of fennel sodden in oil. Then if the disease
still annoy, introduce this through a pipe or a horn, as

læcaſ cunnan þonne beþ þ þ ſaꞃ apeʒ. ʒıſ þonne ʒıꞇ
ſıo abl eʒle bo ſpaꞇl ꞇo ⁊ ʒelauꞃebne ele þ ıſ lauꞃeſ
ſeap oððe bloſꞇman ʒemenʒeð ⁊ eꞗc oþꞃu þınʒ ʒıꞃ
þeanꞃ ſıe ſece mon.

.XXVIIIL.

Ɖıþ þon þe men meꞇe unꞇela melꞇe ⁊ ʒecıꞃꞃe ón
yſele pæꞇan ⁊ ſcıꞇꞇan · þam monnum beah þ hıe ſpıꞃen ·
ʒıſ hım ꞇo uneaþe ne ſıe · ʒeʒꞃemme mıð pyꞃꞇbꞃence
þ he ſpıꞃe · þ he mıð ʒeſpeꞇꞇe pıne ʒepyꞃce ʒıſ þæſ
oꞃenþeanꞃ ſıe æꞃ meꞇe þ he ſpıꞃan mæʒe · ꞃleo þa
meꞇꞇaſ þa þe hım bylſꞇa ⁊ ꞃonbæꞃnunʒa ⁊ ſꞇıem on
Innan pyꞃoen ⁊ ꞇo hꞃæblıce melꞇan · þıcʒen þa ðe ʒob
ſeap pyꞃoen ⁊ pambe hneꞃoen. Ɖꞃılum hım beah þ
hım món ꞃelle leohꞇe pyꞃꞇbꞃencaſ ſꞃılce ſꞃa bıð pel
ʒeꞇeab alꞃe. Seo pæꞇe pyꞃoþ ʒıſ hıe món ne beþ apeʒ
uneaþlacna abla þ ıſ ꞃóꞇ pæꞃc · lıþ pæꞃc · lenben
pæꞃc ⁊ oſꞇ ſꞇꞃanʒ ꞃeſeꞃ becymð on þa men þe þa
able habbað.

.XXX.

Ʒıſ[1] þu ꞃılle þ þın pamb ꞃıe ſımle ʒeſunb þonne
ſcealꞇ u hıꞃe þuſ ꞇılıan ʒıſ þu pılꞇ · ʒeꞃceapa ꞗlce
bæʒe þ þın uꞇʒonʒ ⁊ mıcʒe ſıe ʒeſunblıc æſꞇeꞃ ꞃıhꞇe ·
ʒíſ ſıo mıcʒe ſıe lyꞇelu ſeoð meꞃoe ⁊ ꞃınul pyꞃc ʒob
bꞃoð · oððe ſeap[2] ⁊ oþꞃa ſpeꞇa pyꞃꞇa · ʒıſ ſe uꞇʒanʒ ſıe
læꞃſa[3] nım ða pyꞃꞇ þe haꞇꞇe on ſuþeꞃne ꞇeꞃebınꞇına ſpa
mıcel ſpa ele beꞃʒe · ꞃele þonne ꞇo ꞃeſꞇe ʒan pılle. þaſ
pyꞃꞇa ſınbon eꞗc becſꞇe ꞇo þon ⁊ eað beʒeaꞇꞃa · beꞇe · ⁊

---

[1] The substance is found in Paulus Æg., I. xliii.
[2] ſeap : the name of some wort is
omitted in MS. ; or strike out ⁊.

[3] Four lines occur in Paulus of
Ægina, lib. I., cap. xliii.

leeches ken to do it; then it removes the sore. If
however the disease still vex, add spittle and laurelled
oil, that is to say, juice or blossoms of laurel mingled
with oil, and if need be, let also other things be
sought out.

xxix.

In case a "mans" meat doth not well digest, and
turneth to evil humour and to excrement, it is good
for those "men" that "they" should spew, if it be
not too uneasy to "him," irritate him to spew by a
wort drink. If there be extreme need that he may
be able to spew before meat, let him manage that
with sweetened wine. Let him flee the meats which
work him mucus, and burnings, and heat in his inside,
and which too readily digest: let him take those
which work a good juice, and make the wamb nesh.
At whiles it is good for him that one should give
him light wort drinks, such as are aloes well prepared. The humour, if one doth not get rid of it,
worketh not easily cured diseases, that is to say, foot
pain, joint pain, loins pain; and often a strong fever
cometh on the men who have that disease.

xxx.

If thou wish that thy wamb be always sound, then
shalt thou thus treat it, if thou wilt. Look to it every
day that thy fæcal discharge, and thy mie, be of sound
aspect as right is. If the mie be little, seethe marche
and fennel, work a good broth, or *seethe* juice of
. . . and of other sweet worts. If the fæcal discharge
be too little, take the wort which in southern lands
hight turpentine tree, as much of it as the size of
an olive; give it *the sick* when he will go to bed.
These worts are also very good for that, and more

mealpe · Ᵹ bꞃaꞃꞃıca Ᵹ þıſum ȝelıca ȝeꞃobene œꞇȝæðꞃe
mıb ȝeonȝe ſpıneſ ꞃlæꞃce · þıcȝe ꝥ bꞃoð · Ᵹ eac bealꞧ¹
neꞇle ȝeſoben on pæꞇꞃe · Ᵹ ȝeꞃelꞇ ꞇo þıcȝanne · Ᵹ eac
elleneſ leaꞃ Ᵹ ꝥ bꞃoð on þa ılcan pıſan. Sume alpan
leaꞃ ꞃellað þonne mon pıle ꞃlapan ȝan · ſpelc ſpa bıð
þꞃeo beana² ælce bæȝe ꞇo ꞃoꞃſpelȝanne Ᵹ þıſum ȝelıce
bꞃencaſ Ᵹ ſpıðꞃan ȝıꝼ þeapꝼ ſıe ꞃynbon ꞇo ꞃellanne ·
ſpıðoſꞇ on ꞃoꞃepeaꞃbne lencꞇen æꞃ þon ſıo yꞃele pæꞇe ſe
þe on pınꞇꞃa ȝeSomnab bıð lıe ꞇoȝeoꞇe ȝeonð oþeꞃa
lıma. ꟼonıȝe³ men þæꞃ ne ȝymbon ne ne ȝymað
þonne becymð oꝼ þam yꝼlum pæꞇum · oððe ſıo healꝼ-
beabe abl oþþe ꝼylle pæꞃc oððe ſıo lꞇpıꞇe ꞃıeꝼþo þe
mon on ſuþeꞃne leppa hæꞇ oþðe ꞇeꞇꞃa oþþe ꞧeaꞃob
ꞧꞃıeꝼðo · oþþe oman. Foꞃþon ꞃceal mon æꞃ clænꞃıan⁴ þa
yꝼlan pæꞇan apeȝ æꞃ þon þa yꝼelan cuman Ᵹ ȝepeaxen
on pınꞇꞃa · Ᵹ þa lımo ȝeonð yꞃnen. Þıþ pambe coþe
Ᵹ ſaꞃe · lınſæbeꞃ ȝeȝnıben oððe ȝebeaꞇen bolla ꝼull ·
Ᵹ II. ꞃœaꞃþeꞃ eceðeꞃ oꞃeꞃpylle æꞇȝæbeꞃe ꞃele bꞃıncan
neahꞇneꞃꞇıȝum þam ſeocan men. Eꝼꞇ leȝe bꞃeoꞃȝe
bpoſꞇlan ȝecopene on þone naꞃolan ſona ȝeſꞇılleþ; Eꝼꞇ
bıleꞃ ſæbeꞃ lyꞇelne⁵ ȝeȝnıb on pæꞇeꞃ ꞃele bꞃıncan.
Þıþ pambe coðe Ᵹ pıþ ınneꞃoꞃan ſaꞃe. þonne ꞃoꞃ
mıclum cele pamb ſıe unȝepealben · bo ða þınȝ ꞇo þe þe
be uꞃan pꞃıꞇon. ȝıꝼ þæꞃ þonne ſıe þæꞃ hꞃıꝼeꞃ penbunȝ
oððe ȝeꞃceoꞃꝼ · ȝenim þꞃeo cꞃoppan lauꞃeſ bleba ȝeȝnıb
Ᵹ cymeneꞃ · Ᵹ peꞇeꞃꞃılıan ꞃynbꞃıȝe cucleꞃaꞃ ꝼulle · Ᵹ
pıpoꞃeꞃ .xx. coꞃna · ȝeȝnıb eall ꞇoȝæbeꞃe Ᵹ þꞃıe ꝼıl-
menna on bꞃıbba pambum abꞃıȝe · æꝼꞇeꞃ ðon ȝenim
pæꞇeꞃ ȝeȝnıb bıle on · Ᵹ þaꞃ þınȝ ȝehæꞇe ꞃele bꞃıncan · oþ ꝥ ꝥ ꞃaꞃ ȝeſꞇılleb ſıe. Þıþ þon ılcan ȝenim
hlaꞃ ȝeſeoð on ȝaꞇe meolce ꞃoppıȝe on ſuþeꞃne.⁶

fol. 85 b.

fol. 86 a.

---

¹ Four more lines found in V.
Æg. The Latin version, the original being unpublished, has *mercurialis* for *nettle*.

² The Latin gives, *aloes as big as
three vetches.*

³ Paulus Ægineta, lib. I: cap. c.;
cites Diokles to similar purport.
⁴ clœꞃnıan, MS.
⁵ Read lyꞇeloe bœl.
⁶ Read on ſuþeꞃne bꞃıenc.

easily procured, beet, and mallow, and-brassica *or cab-bage*, and the like to these, sodden together with young flesh of swine; let *the man* swallow the broth: and also nettle sodden in water and salted is good to swallow; and also leaves of elder and the broth in the same wise. Some give leaves of aloe, when a man willeth to go to sleep, as much as three beans, every day to be swallowed; and drinks like these, and more powerful ones, if need be, are to be administered; especially in early spring, before the evil humour, which is collected in winter, spread itself through the other limbs. Many men have not attended to this, no, nor do yet; then there cometh of the evil humours, either hemiplegia, or epilepsy, or the white roughness, which in the south hight leprosy, or tetter, or headroughness, or erysipelas. Hence one must cleanse away the evil humours before the mischiefs come and wax in the winter, and run through the limbs. For wamb sickness and sore; a bowl full of linseed, rubbed or beaten, and two bowls of sharp vinegar; boil together, give to the sick man to drink after his nights fast. Again, lay chewed pennyroyal on the navel, soon the pain will be still. Again, rub a small quantity of the seed of dill into water, give it to be drunk. For wamb sickness and sore of the bowels; when from much cold the wamb is not under control, do to it the things which we wrote above; then if there be a subversion or irritation of the stomach, take three bunches of laurel flowers, and separate spoons full of cummin and of parsley *seed* (?), and twenty pepper-corns, rub all together, and dry three membranes *which are* in the wambs of young birds; after that take water, rub dill into it, and heat these things; give *the man this* to drink till the sore is stilled. For the same, take bread and seethe it in goats milk, sop it in a southern *drink, such as hydromel, perhaps, or oxymel.*

Ƿiþ pambe coþe ſeoð ꞃuðan ón ele ⁊ þicᵹe on ele.
Eꝼꞇ pilðe culꝼꞃe ón eceðe ⁊ ón pæꞇꞃe ᵹeſoben ꞃele ꞇo
þicᵹenne. Ƿið pambe coðe eꝼꞇ lauꞃeſ leaꝼ ceope ⁊ ꝥ
ſeap ſpelᵹe ⁊ þa leaꝼ lecᵹe on hiſ naꞃolan. Eꝼꞇ heo-
ꞃoꞇeſ meaꞃh ᵹemylꞇ ꞃele ón haꞇum pæꞇꞃe ðꞃincan.
To pambe ᵹemeꞇlicunᵹe · ᵹenim beꞇan aðelꝼ ⁊ ahꞃiſe
ne þpeah þu hie ſc ſpa lanᵹe ſeoð ōu ceꞇele ⁊ pylle
oþ ꝥ hio ſie eal ꞇoꞃoben ⁊ þicᵹe¹ ᵹeuꞃnen · ðo þonne
lyꞇel ꞃealꞇeꞃ ꞇo ⁊ huniᵹeſ · v. cucleꞃ mæl · eleꞃ cucleꞃ
mæl ꞃele bollan ꝼulne. Eꝼꞇ heaꞃðehꞇeſ poꞃꞃeſ ᵹeꞃo-
ðeneſ² ꞃynðꞃiᵹne ꞃele þicᵹean. Eꝼꞇ þæꞃe ꞃeaðan neꞇlan ſæð ón hlaꝼ ꞃele þicᵹean. Eꝼꞇ byꞃiᵹbeꞃᵹena ſeap
ꞃelle ðꞃincan. Eꝼꞇ plum bleða eꞇe neahꞇneſꞇiᵹ. Eꝼꞇ
elneſ ꞃinðe ᵹebeaꞇene ꝥꞇe peninᵹᵹe peᵹe ón cealbeꞃ
pæꞇꞃeſ bollan ꝼullum ꞃele ðꞃincan.

³.XXXI.

fol. 86 b.

Be pambe coþum ⁊ ꞇacnum on ꞃoppe ⁊ ón ſmæl
þeaꞃmum. Sum cyn bið eac þæꞃe ilcan aðle on þæꞃe
pambe · ⁊ on þam ꞃoppe ⁊ ſmæl þeaꞃmum þe þiꞃ bið
ꞇo ꞇacne · ꝥ hie þꞃopiað oꞃmæꞇne þuꞃſꞇ · ⁊ meꞇeſ unluſꞇ ⁊ óꝼꞇ uꞇ yꞃꞃað ᵹemenᵹðe uꞇᵹanᵹe hꞃilum heaꞃð·
hꞃilum hꞃiꞇ · hꞃilūm óꝼꞇ on ðæᵹe úꞇᵹað ⁊ þonne lyꞇlum · hꞃilum æne · ⁊ þonne micel · hꞃilum hie⁴ pel
ᵹelyſꞇ uꞇᵹanᵹan · ⁊ him þa byþþenne ꝼꞃam apeoꞃꞃan·
⁊ ᵹeoꞃne ꞇilian ac ne maᵹon nabbað ꝥ mæᵹen þæꞃe
melꞇunᵹe ⁊ ðꞃopeꞇeð blod · ſpa þon ᵹelicoſꞇ þe ꞇoðꞃo-
cen ꝼæꞇ. be hioꞃa hipe ⁊ þam naꞃolan · ⁊ þam ꞃæᵹe-

¹ þicᵹe, that is þicce.
² Add cꞃoppan or the like.
³ Plainly a chapter περὶ κωλικῆς διαθέσεως.
⁴ Read hine.

2. For wamb sickness seethe rue in oil, and let *the sick* swallow it in oil. Again, give him to eat a wild pigeon sodden in vinegar and in water. For wamb sickness, again, let him chew leaves of laurel, and swallow the juice, and let him lay the leaves on his navel. Again, give melted harts marrow in hot water to drink. For moderating^a *the action of* the wamb; take beet, delve it up and shake *the mould off*, do not wash it, but seethe and boil it in a kettle so long, that it be all sodden to pieces, and run thick, then add a little salt, and of honey five spoon measures, of oil one spoon measure, give *the* man a bowl full. Again, give *to the sick* to eat, separate, the *top* of a sodden leek, having a head to it. Again, give him to eat some seed of the red nettle on bread. Again, give him to drink juice of mulberries. Again, let him eat after his nights fasting plum fruits. Again, give him to drink elder rind beaten, as much as may weigh a penny, in a bowl full of cold water.

xxxi.

Of wamb sicknesses, and of tokens in the colon and in the small guts. There is a kind of that ilk disease in the wamb, and in the colon, and small guts, of which this will be for a token; that *the sick* suffer immoderate thirst and loss of appetite for meat, and often they have a flux with a mingled fæcal discharge, at whiles hard, at whiles white, at whiles they discharge often in the day and then little at a time, at whiles once and then much; at whiles a desire is upon them to go to stool and to cast the burthen from them, and gladly would they attend to it, but they are not able,[1] they have not the power of digestion, and they drop blood, very much like a broken vessel. Of their hue, *or*

---

[1] Tenesmus.

ɲeoſan · ⁊ bæcþeaɲme ⁊ neƿeſeoþan · ⁊ mɪlꞇc[1] ſcaɲe ·
beoð æblæce ⁊ eal ſe lɪchoma āſcɪmoð · ⁊ yƿel ſꞇenc
nah hɪſ ɲelſeſ ȝeƿealð ⁊ bɪþ þ ſaɲ on ða ſƿɪðɲan
ſiðan · healſe[2] on þa ſcaɲe · ⁊ þa ƿambe ſƿɪþe ȝeneaɲ-
ƿoð · ⁊ eſꞇ ſɲam þam naſolan oþ þone mɪlꞇe · ⁊ on þa
ƿɪneſꞇɲan ſæȝeɲeoſan ⁊ ȝecymð æꞇ þam bæcþeaɲme ⁊
æꞇ þam neƿeſeoþan · ⁊ þa lenðenu beoð mɪð mɪcle ſaɲe

fol. 87 a.

beȝyɲðebu. Þenað unpɪſe læcaſ þ þ ſie lenðen aðl
oððe mɪlꞇe pæɲc · ac hɪꞇ ne bɪð ſpa · lenðen ſeoce
men mɪȝað bloðe ⁊ ſanðe þonne þam þe mɪlꞇe pæɲc
bɪð · þɪnðeþ hɪm ſe mɪlꞇ ⁊ bɪþ aheaɲðoð ón þam ƿɪneſꞇɲan bæle þæɲe ſiðan. þa ƿambſeocan men þɲoƿɪað
ón þam bæcþeaɲme ⁊ ón þám nɪþeɲɲan hɲɪſe ⁊ loſað
hɪm ſona ſio ſteſɲ ⁊ cele þɲoƿað ⁊ ſlæp oþꞇoȝen ⁊
ɲuɪhꞇ ⁊ ꞇɪlɪð ɪnnan þone ɲop ⁊ on þ ſmæl þeaɲme.

.XXXII.

Þɪſſe aðle ſɲuman mon mæȝ yþelɪce ȝelacnɪan · on
þa ɪlcan ƿɪſan þe þa uꞇyɲnenðan ⁊ æſꞇeɲ uneð · ȝɪſ
hɪo bɪð unƿɪſlɪce ꞇo lanȝe ſoɲlæꞇen. On ſɲuman món
ſceal bæȝ oððe .II. ꞇoȝæðeɲe ȝeſæɲꞇan ⁊ beþan þa
bɲeoſꞇ mɪð pɪne · ⁊ mɪð ele ⁊ ƿyɲcean ónleȝena oſ
ɲoſan ⁊ beɲenum melpe pɪð pɪn ȝemenȝeð ⁊ on hunɪȝe
ȝeſoðen ⁊ mɪð ele on moɲꞇeɲe ȝeſamnoð leȝe oƿeɲ þa
ſcaɲe oþ þone naſolan ⁊ oƿeɲ þa lenðeno oþ þone bæc-
þeaɲm ⁊ þæɲ hɪꞇ ſaɲ ſie · læꞇ hɪm bloð þuſ ⁊[3] ſeꞇe
ȝlæſ ón oððe hoɲn ⁊ ꞇeo þ bloð uꞇ ⁊ ſmeɲe mɪð ele

fol. 87 b.

⁊ beɲɲeoh hɪne ƿeaɲme ſoɲ þon þe cɪle bɪþ þæɲe aðle

---

[1] Add ⁊.
[2] The former of these synonyms should be erased.
[3] Omit ⁊.

complexion, and of the navel, and of the dorsal muscles, and of the back gut *or rectum*, and of the lower belly, and the milt, *and* the share ; they are horribly pale, and all the body is glazed, and an evil stench hath not control over itself,[a] and the sore is on the right side on the share, and on the wamb, much troubled[1] *by it*, and again from the navel to the spleen, and on the left dorsal muscle, and it reacheth to the anus, and to the lower belly, and the loins are girt about with much soreness. Unwise leeches ween, that it is loin disease, or milt wark : but it is not so ; loinsick men mie blood and sand ; on the other hand those, who have milt wark, the milt distendeth in them, and is hardened on the left part of the side. The wambsick men suffer in the back gut, and in the lower belly, and their voice soon is lost, and they suffer chill, and sleep is taken from them, and strength, and it draweth the colon from within and upon the small gut.

[a] Eufemiam.

xxxii.

One may easily cure the first stage of this disease in the same wise as the outrunning disease, *or relaxation of the bowels*, and afterwards less easily, if unwisely it be too long neglected. In the first instance a man must fast for a day or two, and foment the breast with wine, and with oil, and work poultices of roses and barley meal, mingled with wine, and sodden in honey, and gathered up with oil in a mortar, lay *these* over the share, as far as the navel, and over the loins as far as the back gut, and where it is sore. Let him blood thus ; set on him a *cupping* glass or horn, and draw the blood out, and smear with oil, and wrap him up warm, in as much as cold is an enemy in the

---

[1] It seems best to consider ᵹeneaᵹᵱoƀ as for ᵹeneaᵹᵱoƀe, with termination dropped.

feonð. Ƿyƿo him ƿealƿe þuf ƿiþ pambe coþûm ôƿ cƿicum
fpeƿle ꝥ ôƿ blacum piƿoƿe · ꝥ ôƿ ele ȝnibe môn fmæle
ꝥ menȝe toȝæbeƿe ꝥ peax ealƿa emƿela. Ƿeaxeƿ þeah
læft · ȝiƿ fio aðl fie to þon ftƿanȝ ꝥ þaƿ læcebomaf ne
onnime ȝiƿ fe mon fie ȝeonȝ ꝥ ftƿanȝ læt hîm bloð ôƿ
innan eaƿme oƿ þæƿe miclan æðƿe þæƿe mibbel æðƿe.

✝ Ƿyƿo þuƿ ƿealƿe ꝥ fmiƿe þa faƿan ftopa feoþ ƿuban
on ele ðo peteƿƿilian to ȝiƿ þu hæbbe ꝥ ƿicfa pyƿt-
tƿuman · ꝥ popiȝ fiþþan eal ȝeƿoben fie ðo þonne peax
ôn ꝥ ele ·¹ ꝥte ꝥ eall peoƿðe to hneƿcum peaxhlaƿe ꝥ
hit fie hƿæþƿe fpiþuft ȝeþuht ƿealƿ fmiƿe þa ftopa ꝥ
hit fie ƿaƿ mið þy · fpiþoft þone bæcþeaƿm baþo ƿiþ
pambe coþum · him oƿ ƿealtum pætƿum fint to pyƿc-
anne · ȝiƿ he þa næbbe ƿelte môn hioƿa mettaf. Ƿiþ
pambe coþum eƿt fpinef claƿe ȝebæƿnbe ꝥ to bufte
ȝeȝnibene ðo ôn fceaƿp fîn ƿele bƿincan. Ƿið pambe
coƿe ȝate liƿeƿ ȝebæƿneðu ꝥ hƿæt hƿeȝa ȝeȝnibeɴ ꝥ

ôn þa pambe aleb him biþ þe bet. Ƿiþ pambe coþum
eƿt lacnunȝ on ꝥ hƿiƿ to Senbanne · ȝenîm ȝaƿleaceƿ
þƿeo heaƿbu ꝥ ȝƿene ƿuban tƿa hanb ƿulle · ꝥ eleƿ
.IIII. punb oðð̆e fpa þe þince · ȝebeat ꝥ leâc ꝥ þa
ƿuban ȝeȝnib toȝæbeƿe apƿinȝ oðð̆e aƿeoh · ðo to þam
ele clænƿe buteƿan punb hlutƿef piceƿ ƿiftan healƿe
yntfan · ꝥ clæneƿ peaxeS .III. yntfan ȝemenȝe eal to-
ȝæbƿe ðo ôn ȝlæƿ ƿæt · clænƿa² þonne æƿeft þa pambe
mið bƿencef anƿealððƿe ônȝeotunȝe · ȝiƿ ꝥ ƿaƿ þonne
maƿe fie ðo maƿian ele to · ȝemenȝ þonne þa þinȝ þe
ic æƿ nembe ȝeplece ðo ôn. þaƿ þinȝ maȝon ȝe ƿiþ
lenben ece · þonne môn ƿonbe mihð̆ ȝe ƿið ƿoppeƿ ȝe
ƿið pambe ꝥ fmæl þeaƿmef ablum ꝥ ût pæƿce ȝe ƿiþ

---

¹ ele is usually masculine. | ² clærna, MS.

disease. Work him a salve thus, against wamb disorders; from live brimstone, and from black pepper,
and from oil; let them be rubbed small and mingled
together; and wax *also;* of all equal quantities, of
wax however least. If the disease be to that degree
strong that it will not accept these leechdoms, if the
man be young and strong, let him blood from the
inner arm, from (the mickle vein of) the middle vein.
Work a salve thus, and smear the sore places; seethe
rue in oil, add parsley, if thou have it, and roots of
rushes, and poppy; after all is sodden, then add wax
to the oil, in order that the whole may become a
nesh waxen cake,[a] that it may be however a highly • A cerote.
approved salve; smear the places, so that soreness
may come with it, especially the fundament. Baths
for wamb disorders; they must be wrought for them
of salt waters; if none can be had, let their (*the sick
mens*) meats be salted. For wamb disorders again;
put into sharp wine a swines claw burnt and rubbed
to dust; give *the man* this to drink. For wamb disorder; a goats liver burnt, and rubbed somewhat *small,*
and laid on the wamb, it will be the better for him.
For wamb disorders again; to send medicine into the
belly: take three heads of garlic, and green rue, two
handfuls *of it,* and four pints of oil, or as much as
seemeth good to thee; beat the leek and the rue, rub
together, wring out or strain, add to the oil a pound
of clean butter, and four ounces and a half of clear
pitch, *perhaps naphtha,* and three ounces of clean wax;
mingle all together, put into a glass vessel, then first
cleanse the wamb with the simple onpouring of a drink:
then if the sore be greater, add more oil, then mingle
the things which I before named; apply lukewarm.
These things are valid either against loin ache, when
a man pisseth sand, or for diseases and pain of the
long gut, or of the wamb, or of the small gut, and
for dysentery, or for diseases of the maw, and gripings,

magan adlum ⁊ clafunga · ⁊ wiþ wifa tedrum gecyn-
dum. Sum cofu is þære wambe ꝥ þone seocan mōnnan
lysteð utganges ⁊ ne mæg þonne he ute betyned
bið. Wiþ þon sceal mōn nædran æsmogu seoþan on
ele · oððe ōn buteran · oþþe on wine ōn tinum[1] fæte
⁊ smire þa wambe mid þy · gif se utgang sie windig ⁊
fol. 88 b. wætrig · ⁊ blodig beþige mon þone bæcþearm on gong-
stole mid fenugreco ⁊ merse mealwe · sume mid wice ⁊
smicað ⁊ beþiað. Sume of rigenum melwe wyrceað
briwas ⁊ cōcnunga mid sealte. Sume dreorge drostlan
geceowað ⁊ lecgeað on þone nafolan.

.XXXIII.

Be[2] þære frecnan cofe þe se mōn his utgang þurh
done muð him fram weorpe sceal aspiwan. He sceal
ōft bealcettan ⁊ eal se lichoma stinceð fule selle hīm
mon dile gesodenne ōn ele oððe ōn wætre to drincanne
⁊ hatne hlaf do on þone drincan. þisse adle eac wiþ-
standeþ tosnidenre hreaþemuse blod gesmiten on þæs
seocan mannes wambe. Wið Innoð wundum ⁊ wiþ smæl
þearma sare · ōn godne ele gesweтne do þone suþernan
wermod ꝥ is wrutene · ⁊ oþerne wermod ⁊ seoþ þicge
ꝥ swa hīm efost sie. Eft wiþ innoþ wundum heorotes
mearh gemylt on hatum wætre sele drincan. Wiþ
tobrocenum Innoþum ⁊ sarum wildre mintan dæl ge-
fol. 89 a. clænsa wel swa micel swa mōn mæge mid þrīm fingrūm
geniman do finoles sædes to ⁊ merces cucler mæl ·
do eall togædere gegnid smæle · gedo þonne ōn þæs
selestan wines .IIII. bollan fulle · hæte þonne oþ ꝥ hit
sie swa hat swa þin finger forberan mæge sele þonne
drincan · do swa þry dagas. Wiþ tobrocenum Inno-
ðum · cellendres sæd wel gegniden ⁊ lytel sealtes gedo
on sceapp wīn · gedo on ⁊ gewyrme mid hate glopende
isene sele drincan. Wiþ fortogenesse innān · heorotes

[1] Read tinenum.
[2] Five lines found in Oribasius Synops, lib. ix., cap. xvi, in M.A.P.

and for tenderness of the naturalia of women. There
is a disorder of the wamb, *such* that a desire cometh
upon the sick man for discharging his bowels, and he
is not able, when he is shut into the outhouse. For
that, one must seethe in oil, or in butter, or in wine,
the slough of a snake in a tin vessel, and let him
smear the wamb with that. If the discharge be windy,
and watery, and bloody, let one foment the back gut
on the gang stool, with fenugreek and marsh mallow:
some smoke and foment with pitch : some work brewits
from rye meal, and cookings with salt : some chew
pennyroyal and lay it on the navel.

Book II.
Ch. xxxii.

This prescrip-
tion is found
in Marcellus,
376 a.

xxxiii.

Of the dangerous disorder, in which a man, they
say, unnaturally speweth his fæces through the mouth.
He, they say, oft belcheth, and all the body stinketh
foully: let dill sodden in oil or in water be given him
to drink, and put a hot loaf of bread into the drink.
The blood of a reremouse *or bat* cut up, smudged on
the sick mans wamb, also withstandeth this disease.
For bowel wounds and sore of small guts ; into good oil
sweetened, put the southern wormwood, that is, abrotanum, and other wormwood, and seethe it ; let *the
man* take that as he most easily may. Again, for inwards wounds ; melt harts marrow in hot water, give
it to be drunk. For broken and sore inwards ; cleanse
part of wild mint well, as much as a man may take
up with three fingers, add a spoon measure of the
seed of fennel, and of marche, put all together, rub
small, then add four bowls full of the best wine, then
heat it so hot, as thy finger may bear, then give *it him*
to drink; do so for three days. For broken inwards ;
put into sharp wine, seed of coriander well rubbed,
and a little salt; put *these* in, and warm with an iron
glowing hot, give *it the man* to drink. For inward

hopn ʒebæpneð to ahfan ʒeʒniben ōn moptepe · ⁊
þonne apıſt ⁊ mıð hunıʒe ʒepealcen to fnæðum ſele
neahtneptıʒum to þıcʒanne. Gſt nīm þa betan þe
ʒehpæp peaxað ʒeſeoð on pætpeſ ʒoðum ðæle · ſele
þonne ðpıncan · .II. ʒoðe bollan ſulle ſcılðe hıne pıþ
cyle. þe latpe meltunʒe ınnan · nım ʒeappan ðpınce
on eceðe ꝥ ðeah eac pıð eallum blæðpan ablum. þe
latpe meltunʒe Innan puðan ræðeſ .VIIII. cypnelu ʒe-

fol. 89 b.
ʒnıbene .III. bollan ſulle ʒebo þa on eceðeſ ſeſtep
ſulne oſeppylle ſele þonne ðpıncan ōn fume pape nıʒon
baʒon. þe latpe meltunʒe nīm þæpe peaban netlan
ſpa mıcel ſpa mıð tpam hanðum mæʒe beſon · feoþe
ōn ſeſtep ſullūm pætpeſ ðpınc neaht neſtıʒ. Ræb
bıð ʒıſ he nımð mealpan mıð hıpe cıþum feoþe on
pætepe fele ðpıncan. þa þe þıſſa læceðoma ne ʒımað
on þıſſe able þonne becymð hīm ōn pætep bolla · lıſep
pæpc ⁊ mılteſ ſap oþþe ʒeſpel mıcʒean ſophæſðnıſ ·
pambe ablapunʒ lenðen pæpc on þæpe blæðpan ſtanaʒ
peaxað ⁊ Sonð.

.XXXIIII.[1]

Be þæſ monneſ mıhtum ſceal mōn þa læceðomaſ
ſellan þe þonne ʒeſoʒe fynð heapðe ⁊ heoptan pambe
⁊ blæðpan ⁊ hu ʒeapeſ hıt ſıe · ſe þe ne beſceapað
þıſ ſe hım ſceþeð ſpıþop þonne he hıne bete. Se ſceal
nyttıan ʒepoſoðeſ eleſ eceðeſ ⁊ pıneſ ⁊ mıntan leaſ
ʒeʒnıben on hunıʒ ⁊ þa unſmeþan tunʒan mıð þy
ʒnıban ⁊ ſmıpepan :·

fol. 90 a.
Pıþ latpe meltunʒe. Olıſatpum hatte pypt feo ðeah
to ðpıncanne. Gſt pyl on pætpe lılıan pypttpuman
ſele to ðpıncanne. ʒıſ pamb ſoʒpeaxe on men · ſınol ·
coſt · elehtpe · attoplaþe · ceplıceſ ræb · pypm melo

---

gripings; harts horn burned to ashes, rubbed *small*
in a mortar, and then sifted, and rolled up with honey
into morsels, give *to the sick* after his nights fast to
eat. Again, take the beet which groweth anywhere,
seethe it in a good deal of water, then *give of this to
the sick* two good bowls full to drink; let him shield
himself against cold. Of late digestion; let a man
drink in vinegar yarrow; that medicine is also good
for all diseases of the bladder. Of late digestion; nine
little grains of the seed of rue rubbed *small, with*
three bowls full of *water* (?), add these to a cup full
of vinegar, boil them, then administer to be drunk for
nine days, in succession. Of late digestion; take of
the red nettle, so much as with two hands thou
mayest grasp, seethe in a cup full of water, drink
after a nights fasting. It is advisable if he taketh
mallow with its sprouts; let him seethe them in water,
give this to be drunk. They who care not for these
leechdoms in this disease, on them then cometh dropsy,
liver pain, and sore or swelling of spleen, retention of
urine, inflation of the wamb, loin pain, stones wax in
the bladder, and sand.

xxxiv.

According to the mans powers one shall administer
the leechdoms which are suitable for the head and
heart, for the wamb and bladder, and according to
the time of the year; he who observeth not this,
doth him more scathe than boot. He shall employ
rose oil, vinegar, and wine, and mint leaves rubbed
into honey, and with that shall rub and smear the
unsmooth tongue.

For late digestion; a wort hight olusatrum, which
is good to drink. Again, boil in water roots of lilies,
give *that* to be drunk. If the wamb wax too great
on a man; fennel, costmary, lupin, attorlothe, char-

ón ealað ŗele bŗincan. ȝıŗ món ŗoŗŗunbod ſie · ꞃ pıð
bŗeoſt pæŗice · cuŗimealle ꞃ ðıle pyl on ealoð. Eŗt
ȝŗene ŗuðan lytlum oððe on hunıȝe þıȝe. ȝíŗ mon
ſıe ŗoŗiblapen ŗæ pınepınclan [1] ȝebæŗinðe ꞃ ȝeȝnıðene
ȝemenȝ pıþ æȝeŗ þ hŗıte ſinıŗie mıð. Þıþ pambe ȝıc-
þan · ðŗeoŗiȝe ðpoſtlan peoŗip on peallenðe pæteŗi læt
ŗocıan ón lanȝe oþ þ mon mæȝe ðŗıncan þ pæteŗi.
Þıþ pambe pyŗmum · [2] nım þa mıclan ſınŗullan pŗınȝ
þ ŗeap óŗ ŗeoŗieŗi lytle bollan ŗulle on pıneŗ anum
bollan ŗullum ſpa mıclum ŗele ðŗıncan þ ðeah pıþ
pambe pyŗimum. [2]

.XXXV.

Be cılba pambum ꞃ oŗeŗiŗylle ꞃ ȝıŗ hım mete tela
ne mylte · ꞃ ȝıŗ hım ſpat oŗȝa ꞃ ſtınce ŗule · þonne
mon þ onȝıte þonne ne ſceal hım mon anne mete
ȝebeoðan · ác mıŗSenlıce þ ŗeo nıopneŗ þaŗia metta
mæȝe hím ȝoðe beón · ȝıŗ hpa oŗeŗi ȝemet þıȝþ mete
þæŗ món tılað þe eaðelıcoŗi þe mon ŗiaþoȝ ȝeðo þ he
ſpıpe · ꞃ ȝelæŗi ſıe. ȝıŗ hıŗ món ȝetılað æt þæŗie
yŗelan pætan hım becumað ón mıŗSenlıca aðla · bŗeoſt
pæŗic · ſpeoŗicoþu cealŗ [3] aðl · heaŗbeŗ hŗıŗþo · healŗȝunð ·
cyŗinelu úneaðlacnu ꞃ þam ȝelıc · ȝıŗ hı ŗoŗi þıſûm ne
mæȝen ŗlapan ðonne ŗceal hım mon ŗellan hat pæteŗi
ðŗıncan þonne ſtılð þ ȝeŗceoŗiŗ ınnan ꞃ clænŗað [4] þa
pambe · Nyttıȝen baþeŗ meðmıclum · ꞃ mete þıcȝen ꞃ
mıð pætŗie ȝemenȝeðne ðŗıncan þıcȝen.

[1] pınepınclan. Somner, Gl., p. 60 a, line 32, also prints pıne; the Junian transcript of the lost MS. (Jun. 71, in the Bodleian) has pıne. The reprinter of the glossary [A.D. 1857] altered to pıne, erroneously, and silently. In the Colloquium Monasticon, the MS. has pınepınclan, torniculi, where the printed text [A.D. 1846, p. 24] gives pınepınclan, torniculos : the edition of 1857, pınepınclan, torniculi [p. 6]. Lye is quite correct. The present MS. has always w.

[2] pŗınum in the contents.
[3] Read ceaŗl.
[4] clæŗnað, MS.

lock seed ; worm meal in ale ; give *him that* to drink. If a man be badly wounded, and for pain in the breast; boil in ale, churmel and dill, Again, take green rue, a little at a time, or in honey. If a man be over much blown out, mingle with the white of an egg sea periwinkles, burnt and rubbed up, smear therewith. For hicket or hiccup of the wamb : throw dwarf dwostle into boiling water, let it soak therein long, till a man may drink the water. For worms of the wamb ; take the mickle sinful *or sedum*, wring out the juice, four little bowls full, in one bowl full of wine, as mickle *as the others ;* that is good for worms of wamb.

xxxv.

Of the wambs of children, and of overfilling, and if their meat do not well digest, and if sweat come from them, and stink foully. When a man understandeth that, then shall not a single meat be offered them, but various ones, that the newness *or novelty* of the meats may be good for them. If one eateth meat over measure, this *case* one tendeth the more easily, as one the sooner bringeth about that he spew, and be empty; if one tendeth him when troubled with the evil humour *arising from overeating*, then come on him various diseases, breast pain, neck disease, disease in the jowl, scurf of the head, purulence in the neck, churnels not easy to cure, and the like of those. If for these they may not sleep, then shall one give them hot water to drink, it will still the scour within, and will cleanse the wamb. Let them employ the bath moderately, and take meat and take drink mingled with water.

.XXXVI.[1]

Be milce pænce ⁊ þ he bið ón þæne pineſtpan
ſiban ⁊ tacn þæne aðle hu hipleaſe hie beoð ⁊ ðolh
uneaðlácno · þa men beoð mæʒpe ⁊ unpote · blace ón
onſyne þeah þe hie æp ſætte pæpon · ⁊ beoð hibep-
peapðe · ⁊ pamb únʒepealðen ⁊ unyþe micʒe biþ hal ·
ac hio biþ ſpeaptpe ⁊ ʒpenpe · ⁊ blacpe þonne hipe

piht ſie· ⁊ ſnæptiað ſpiþe beoþ ſoptoʒene · ʒiſ ſio aðl
biþ to lanʒSum · becymeþ þonne ón pætep bollan ne
mæʒ hine món þonne ʒelacnian tunʒe únʒepealðen ⁊
unſmeþe ⁊ þa ðolh beoþ uneaðlácnu þa þe on lichoman
beoð ⁊ hie beoð on þa pinſtpan ſiban mið ece ʒeſpen-
ceðe ⁊ ón ðone lið þæpa eaxla betpeox ʒeſculðpum biþ
micel ece ⁊ ón þám ʒehpeopſe þapa bana ón þam
ſpeopan habbað eac lipehte ſet cneop tpuciað. Ðu ſe
milce bið emlanʒ ⁊ ʒæbeptenʒe þæpe pambe hæſð
þynne ſilmene ſio hæſð ſætte ⁊ þicce æðpa · ⁊ ſio
ſilmen biþ þeccenðe ⁊ ppeonðe þa pambe ⁊ þa inno-
ſapan[2] ⁊ þa pypmð · ⁊ íſ aþeneð on þone pineſtpan
nepeſeoþan ⁊ iſ mið ſinehtum limum ʒehæſð · ⁊ iſ ón
oðpe healſe bpað ʒehpineð þæpe ſiban · ón oðpe íſ
ðam innoðe ʒetanʒ. Be hleahtpe þe óſ milce cymð
ſume ſecʒaþ þ ſe milce ðam ſinúm þeopiʒe ⁊ þte ſe
milce ón ſumum dælum þam monnum aðeaðiʒe oþþe

óſ ſie· ⁊ þ hi ſoпþon hlyhhan mæʒen. Soþlice on þa
ilcan piſan þe oþep limo þpopiað untpumneſſa ſe milce
þpopað on þa ilcan piſan. Oſ cele[3] unʒemethicum oſ
hæto ⁊ óſ ðpiʒneſſe oſ micelpe yſelpe pætan ſoпþon
pixþ ſe milce oſep ʒeſceap ⁊ ponað ⁊ heapðað ⁊ ſpiþoſt óſ
cele ⁊ oſ unʒemethicpe pætan · þonne cumað þa óſtoſt

---

[1] This chapter, and many more that
follow, seem to be from Philagrios,
as preserved in Trallianus. But such
symptoms as "tongue uncontrolled,"
and " muscular feet," are not to
be found in the Greek, as printed.

[2] The letter or letters between
inn and ſaſan have been cut off
from the margin of the MS.

[3] The words of Philagrios, in
Alex. Trall., book viii., chap. x.

xxxvi.

Of milt wark, *or acute pain in the spleen*, and that the milt is on the left side, and tokens of the disease, how colourless *the patients* are, and *there are* wounds not easy of cure. The men are meagre and uncomfortable, pale of aspect, though ere this they were fat, and still are *constitutionally disposed* that way; and the wamb is not under control, and scarcely *can it be that* the mie is healthy, but *rather* it will be swartish and greenish, and blacker than its right is to be, and the breathing is very hard drawn. If the disease is too longsome, then it turneth to dropsy, one may not then cure it; the tongue is uncontrolled and unsmooth, and the wounds which are upon the body are not easy of cure, and they are on the left side afflicted with ache, and in the joining of the shoulders, betwixt the shoulder blades, there is mickle ache, and in the turning about of the bones of the neck; they have also brawny feet, their knees fail *them.* *We tell* how the milt is alongside and adjacent to the wamb, it hath a thin film, which hath fat and thick veins, and the film covereth and embraceth the wamb and the inwards, and warmeth them; and it is extended on the left part of the lower abdomen, and it is held by sinewy attachments, and it is in the one quarter broad; it toucheth the side, on the other it is in contact with the viscera. Of the laughter which cometh from the spleen. Some say that the milt is the servant of the sinews, and that the milt in some parts is dead in men, or is wholly absent, and that for this reason they are able to laugh. In fact, in the same wise that other limbs suffer inconveniences, the milt in the same wise suffers. *We treat also* of immoderate cold, of heat, of dryness, of mickle evil wet, since the milt waxeth unnaturally, and diminishes, and hardeneth, and mostly of cold and immoderate wet; further,

óf mettum Ᵹ óf cealðum ðꞃincan ſpa ſpa ꞃinbon cealðc
oſꞇꞃan Ᵹ æpla Ᵹ miꞃSenlice pyꞃꞇa ſpiþoſꞇ on ſumeꞃa
þonne þa món þiȝð. bæþ him eȝleð ſpiðoſꞇ æꝼꞇeꞃ
meꞇe Ᵹ hæmeð þinȝ on oꝼeꞃꝼyllo. Sió unȝemeꞇlice
hæꞇo þæꞃ milꞇeꞃ cymð óf ꝼeꝼeꞃaðlum Ᵹ óf ꝼeꝼeꞃeſ [1]
ſpolle Ᵹ ón ylðo [1] ꝼoꞃ bloðe · bið aþeneð ꞃe milꞇe Ᵹ
aþunðen mið ȝeſpelle Ᵹ eac haꞇ lyꝼꞇ Ᵹ ſpolȝa bꞃinȝað
aðle ón ðam milꞇe · þonne ꞃe mon pyꞃð ꞇo ſpiþe ꝼoꞃ-
hæꞇ. Spa bið eác ón pinꞇꞃa ꝼoꞃ cyle Ᵹ ꝼoꞃ þaꞃa
peðꞃa [2] miꞃſenlicneꞃſe þ̷ ſe milꞇe pyꞃð ȝeleꝼeð. þ̷
maȝon piſe men ónȝiꞇan hꞃanan ꞃio aðl cume be miſ-
ȝeꞃiðeꞃum Ᵹ óf meꞇꞇa Ᵹ óf ðꞃincena þȝinȝe Ᵹ þuꞃh
þaꞃ þinȝ þa yꞃelan pæꞇan Ᵹ ꞃinðiȝo þinȝ beoþ acenneð
on þam milꞇe Ᵹ aðla peaxaþ :·

. XXXVII. [3]

Ꝺv món ꞃcyle þone monnan innan Ᵹ uꞇan lacnián
mið haꞇum Ᵹ cealðum innan mið lacꞇucan · Ᵹ claꞇan ·
Ᵹ cucuꞃbiꞇan ðꞃince on pine · baþiȝe hine on ſpeꞇum
pæꞇꞃe. Uꞇan he iſ ꞇo lacnianne mið ȝeꞃoſoðe ele Ᵹ
ꞇo ſmiꞃꞃanne · Ᵹ onleȝena ȝeꞃoꞃhꞇe óf pine Ᵹ ꞃinbeꞃ-
ȝum Ᵹ óꞃꞇ oꞃ buꞇꞃan · Ᵹ óf niꞃum peaxe Ᵹ óf yꞃoꞃo ·
Ᵹ óf ele onleȝen ȝeꞃoꞃhꞇ ; Ꝺenȝ ꞃiþ ȝoꞃe ſmeꞃu oðð̷e
ſpineꞃ ꞃyꞃle Ᵹ pꞃð ꞃecelꞃ · Ᵹ minꞇan · Ᵹ þonne [4] he hine
baþiȝe ſmiꞃe mið ele menȝ pꞃð cꞃoh. Ꝺeꞇꞇaſ him beoð
nyꞇꞇe þa þe ȝoð blóð pyꞃceað ſpa ſpa ſinꞇ ꞃcilꝼixaꞃ
ꞃinihꞇe Ᵹ ham [5] pilba hænna Ᵹ ealle þa ꝼuȝelaſ þe on

---

[1] The Saxon has misread his text.
[2] peðna., MS., with full stop.
[3] The words of Philagrios, as before.
[4] þon, MS.
[5] Insert Ᵹ.

these most often come of meats and of cold drinks,
such as are cold oysters, and apples, and various worts,
chiefly in summer, when one partaketh of such. Bathing is harmful to them *who are splenitic*, chiefly after
meat, and copulation *following* on surfeit. The unmeasured heat of the milt cometh from fevers and
from the swealing *or burning* of fever, and in old age
from *corruption of* the blood. The milt is extended
and distended with swelling, and also hot air and hot
weather bring disease upon the milt; when the man
becometh too much heated. So it is also in winter,
for the cold and for the variableness of the weather,
that the milt becometh corrupted. *We next treat* that
wise men may understand whence the disease cometh
by bad weather, and from partaking of *unholesome*
meats and drinks, and through these things the evil
humours and windy things are produced in the milt,
and diseases wax *therein.*

xxxvii.

We now explain how one must apply leechdoms to
the man, within and without, with hot and cold *treat-
ments;* within, with lettuce, and clote, and gourd; let
him drink them in wine; let him *also* bathe himself
in sweet water. Without, he is to be leeched and
smeared with oil of roses, and with onlayings *or
poultices made* of wine and grapes, and often must
an onlay be wrought of butter, and of new wax,
and of hyssop, and of oil; mingle with goose grease or
lard of swine, and with frankincense, and mint; and
when he bathes let him smear himself with oil ; mingle
it with saffron. Meats which work out good blood are
beneficial for him ; such as are shell fishes,[1] and those
that have fins,[1] and domestic and wild hens,[2] and all

---

[1] Not in the Greek. | [2] Wild hens are pheasants.

ðunum libbað · ꝺ pipionef þ beoð oulꝼnena bꞃubbaf ꝺ
healꝼealb ſpin · ꝺ ꝣate ꝼlæꞃc ꝺ pyſena ꞃeap mib huniꝣe ·
hpæc hpeꝣa ꝣepipeꞃob · ꝺ eal ðaꞃ pæcan þinꝣ bꞃeoſ-
cum ꝺ innoþum ne buꝣon ne þ ꝼin iꞃ co þicꝣenne þce
hæceþ ꝺ pæceþ þone Innoþ.

.XXXVIII.[1]

Ðu mán ꞃceal þa pæcan ꝺ þa ponꞃceaꝼcan ucan lacnián mib aꝼnum ꞃealꝼum. Pic ꝺ hlucon eceb ꝺ ꝣeno-
ſobne ele menꝣ coſomne leꝣe ucan ón. Þiþ þam pæcan
yꝼle þæꞃ milceꞃ · ním ꞃynbꞃiꝣ ꞃealc oððe pið peaxhlaꝼ
ſealꝼe ꝣemenꝣ · ꝺ ꝣepeꞃmeb ꝺ ón blæbꞃan ꝣebon þ
lacnað þone milce. Eꝼc nim ꞃealc ꝺ peax ꝺ eceb menꝣ
coꝣæbꞃe þ beah · Nim eꝼc ꞃiꝼleaꝼan[2] pyꞃccꞃuman · ꝺ
bꞃiꝣe peꝣbꞃæban ꝺ ꝣebæꞃneb ſealc ealꞃa emꝼela peſe
mib ecebe ꝺ ꝣeſomna bo bꞃiꝣe pic co · ꝺ peax · ꝺ ele
menꝣ eal coꝣæbeꞃe bo ón · Ne bið þ an þ þ bꞃiꝣe þa
pæcan ac þa aheaꞃboban ſpilaf þa ðe cumað óꝼ þiccum
pæcum ꞃlipeꝣꞃum bec ꝺ þþænð. Þiþ ꞃlipeꝣꞃum pæcum
þæꞃ milceꞃ · Nim acoꞃꝼeneꞃ ꞃealceꞃ[3] þ pæceꞃ þe þæꞃ
óꝼ ꝣæþ menꝣ pið þa æꞃ ꝣemenꝣneban[4] þinꝣ.

.XXXVIIII.[5]

Þiþ pinbiꝣꞃe aþunbeneꞃꞃe þæꞃ milceſ ꝼoꞃ æppla · ꝺ
hnuca ꝺ pyſena æce · ꞃoꞃ ꝺ ſmælþeaꞃme · pambe ꝺ
inneꝼoꞃan · ꝺ maꝣan þa ꝣeonb blapað. Þiþ þon beah
pipoꞃ ꝺ cymen · ꝺ huniꝣ · ꝺ ſealc menꝣe coꝣæbeꞃe.

---

¹ Philagrios, as before.
² Abridged from Philagrios ap.
Alexandr. Trallian., p. 477, ed.
Basil.
³ This is perhaps ἀλὴ καὶ ἄφρος
ἁλός, as above.
⁴ Read ꝣenemneban.
⁵ An adaptation from Philagrios
in Trallianus, lib. viii., cap. 11, p.
479, ed. Basil.

the fowls which live on downs, and pigeons, that is, the young chicks of culvers, and half grown swine and goats flesh, and juice of peas with honey, somewhat peppered: and all moist things are not beneficial to the breast and the inwards, nor is such wine to be taken as heateth and moisteneth the inwards.

xxxviii.

Here we explain, how one must treat the humours and the meagreness, on the outside, with sharp salves. Mingle together pitch, and clear vinegar, and oil of roses; lay on the outside. For the evil humours of the milt; take salt separately, or mingle it with a wax cake salve, *or cerote,* warmed and put upon *some* bladder; that healeth the milt. Again, take salt, and wax, and vinegar, mingle together, that is of benefit. Again, take a cinqfoil root, and dry waybroad, and burnt salt, of all equal quantities; soak them in vinegar, and collect them; add dry pitch, and wax, and oil; mingle all together *and* apply.   Not merely doth that *remedy* dry the humours, but it bettereth and softeneth the hardened swellings,[1] which come of thick slimy wets *or crass viscid humours.* For viscid humours of the milt, take the water of carved salt, *or rock salt,* that namely which passeth from it, mingle with the things before named.

xxxix.

For a windy distention of the milt from eating of apples, and of nuts, and of peas; they produce inflation through the long gut, and small guts, the wamb, and the inwards, and the maw; for that is useful pepper and cummin and salt, mingle them together.

---

[1] Scirrhous.

Ƿiþ foȝoþan ⁊ reaðan¹ ⁊ ȝeohſan þe ოf milte cymð · ȝitte hatte fuþeꞃne ꝼyꞃt ſio iſ ȝoð ón hlaꝼe to þicȝenne ⁊ meꞃceꞃ ſæð ⁊ cellenðꞃan ·³ ⁊ peteꞃꞃilian on hlaꝼ becneðen oþþe on pin ȝeȝniðen · ⁊ eac ჶ ðeah piþ ablaꝼunȝe þæꞃ milteꞃ · ȝiꝼ þonne ſio aþinðunȝ þæꞃ pinðeſ ſemninȝa cymð þonne ne maȝon þaſ þinȝ helpan · ꞃoꞃ þon ðe ჶ pile penðan on pæteꞃ bollan ·⁸ ȝiꝼ mon to þam þa pyꞃmenðan þinȝ ðeþ þonne ycþ món þa able.⁴ Ƿiþ milte ſeocum men hím món ꞃceal ꞃellan eceð on þam ſuþeꞃnan læceðome þe hatte oxumelle þe þe þꞃiton piþ þæꞃe healꞃðeaðan able ⁊ blæðꞃan able · Ním lauꞃeꞃ ꞃinðe · ⁊ ðꞃiȝe mintan ⁊ piꞃoꞃ ⁊ ꞃuðan ſæð ·⁵ coſt · ⁊ hunan · ⁊ centauꞃian · ჶ iſ hyꞃðepyꞃt oðꞃe naman eoꞃþȝealla ſpiþuſt þæꞃe ꞃeap · ðo þaſ pyꞃta on þone æꞃ nemðan læceðóm ón ჶ ꞃoꞃ þu meaht ȝeſeon æt þam æꞃ ȝenemðan aðlum hu þu ðone oxumelle pyꞃcean ꞃcealt.⁶ Aleꞃeſ⁷ ꞃinðe ſeoþ ón pætꞃe oþ ჶ þæꞃ pætꞃeꞃ ſie þꞃiððan bæl unbepelleð · ⁊ ꞃele þonne þæꞃ ȝoðne ceac ꝼulne to ðꞃincanne on þꞃy ſiþaſ læt ſimle ðæȝþeꞃne betꞃeonum. þíſ ilce ðeah lenðenꞃeocum men · eꝼt þæſ blacan iꞃiȝeꞃ⁸ cꞃoꞃpan æꞃeſt · þꞃeo · eꝼt .v. þonne .vii. þonne niȝon · þonne .xi. þonne .xiii. þonne .xv. þonne ſeoꞃantyne · þonne niȝantyne · þonne .xxi. ſele ſpa æꝼteꞃ ðaȝuni ðꞃincan ón pine. ȝiꝼ ſe mán hæbbe eác ꝼeꝼeꞃ ꞃele þu þa cyꞃnlu þæꞃ eoꞃþiꞃiȝeſ on hatum pætꞃe ðꞃincan · þiſ ilce ðeah piþ lenðenꞃeocum men. Eꝼt eoꞃðȝeallan ón pine ȝeſoðenne ꞃele ðꞃincan. Eꝼt betonican⁹ þyl ón pine ꞃele ðꞃincan. Sealꝼ ⁊ onleȝen piþ milte pæꞃce

---

¹ Κλύδωνας, *wavy movements,* much the same as βορβόρυγμα.
² ἄνισον, Al. Trall., p. 480.
³ Ταδε γὰρ προσήκει, εἰ ὁ ὑδερὸς οὐκ αὐτίκα ἐνθίνδε τυγχανει εἰ δὲ ἐξαίφνης γεγίνηται, τότε οὐδαμῶς ταὐτὰ συμφέρει.
⁴ From Alex. Trall., viii. 11, p. 481.
⁵ Many words are omitted, as

πευκίδανον: rue seed is πηγάνου ἀγρίον σπέρμα.
⁶ So far from Alex. Trallianus or Philagrios.
⁷ See Marcellus, col. 149 d. : *cyperus* for *ulnus.*
⁸ Marcellus, col. 349, A.
⁹ Marcellus, col. 348, H.

For ill juices and wavy movements and yoxing, *or hic-keting*, which cometh from the spleen. A southern wort hight gith, which is good to eat on bread, and seed of marche and of coriander and of parsley kneaded up into bread or rubbed *fine* into wine : and also that is beneficial for inflation of the milt. If however the distention from the wind cometh suddenly, then these things cannot help, since that will turn into dropsy. If one applieth the warming *leechdoms* to that, then one eketh *or augmenteth* the disease. For a miltsick man, one must give him vinegar in the southern leech-dom which hight oxymel, which we wrote of[1] against the half dead disease and disease of the bladder. Take rind of laurel, and dry mint, and pepper, and seed of rue, costmary, and *hore*hound, and centaury, that is herdwort, or by another name, earthgall, chiefly the juice of it, add these worts to the before named leech-dom into the ooze. Thou mayest see *where we have spoken* of the before named diseases, how thou shalt prepare the oxymel. Seethe in water rind of alder until there be of the water a third part unboiled away, and then give a good jug full of it to be drunk at three times ; leave always a days space between *the doses*. This same is beneficial for a loinsick man. Again, of the black ivy, first three berry bunches, next five, then seven, then nine, then eleven, then thirteen, then fif-teen, then seventeen, then nineteen, then twenty-one, give them so, according to the days, to be drunk in wine. If the man have fever also, give thou him the little grains of the ground ivy in hot water to drink. This same is good for a loinsick man. Again, give him to drink earthgall sodden in wine. Again, boil betony in wine, give *him that* to drink. A salve and a plaster for milt pain, work it up of honey and of

---

[1] As follows : II. lix.

ꝼyꞃc oꝼ huniȝe ꞇ oꝼ ecebe ꝺumelu[1] ꞇ linꞃæꝺ ꞇo ꞇ beꞃeꝼ
ȝꞃyꞇꞇa meꞃceꞃ ꝼæꝺ leȝe on ꞇ ꝼmiꞃe miꝺ þyꞃ. ꝺo eac
ꝺꞃiȝeꞃ peꞃmoꝺeꞃ bloꝼꞇmān ꞇo.

Eꝼꞇ þonne ꞃe milꞇe ablaꞃen ꝼyꞃꝺ ꝼona he ꞃile aheaꞃ-
bian ꞇ biþ þonne uneaþlæcne · þonne þ bloꝺ aheaꞃbaꝺ
on þam æꝺꞃūm þæꞃ milꞇeꞃ · lacna hine þonne miꝺ
þām æꞃ ȝenemban ꝼyꞃꞇum · menȝ þa ȝoꝺan ꝼyꞃꞇa
piꝺ oxumelli þone ꝼuþeꞃnan eceꝺ ꝺꞃenc · ꝺe ꝼe æꞃ
ꞃꞃiꞇon þa lācniaꝺ þone milꞇe ꞇ aꞃeȝ aboꝺ þ þicce ꞇ
liꝼꞃiȝe bloꝺ · ꞇ þa yꝼelan pæꞇan · næꞃ þuꞃh ꝺa micȝean ane āc eac þuꞃh oþeꞃne uꞇȝanȝ. Ꝺiꞃꝺeꝼyꞃꞇ ꝼeo
læꞃꞃe leȝe ȝebeaꞇene uꞇan · Nim eac clæꝼꞃan ꝼyꞃꞇ-
ꞇꞃuman ꝺo on eceꝺ ꞇ ȝaꞇe ꞇyꞃꝺlu[3] ꝼyꞃc þonne ꞇo ꞃcalꝼe
ꞇ beꞃen melo ꝺo þæꞃꞇo · ꞃele him þiꞃ eac on ꞃine
ꝺꞃincan.

Ꝥiþ þæꞃe heaꞃꝺneꞃꞃe ꞇ ꞃaꞃe þæꞃ milꞇeꞃ · ꝼꞃineꞃ
blæꝺꞃan nim ꝼꞃa niꞃe ȝeꝼyl miꝺ ꝼceaꞃꞃe ecebe aleȝe oꝼeꞃ
ꝺa heaꞃꝺneꞃꞃe þæꞃ milꞇeꞃ beꝼꞃeþe þonne þ hio aꞃeȝ ne
ȝliꝺe · āc ꞃy þꞃeo nihꞇ þæꞃon ꞃæꝼꞇe ȝebunꝺen · æꝼꞇeꞃ
þon onbinꝺ · þonne ꝼinꝺeꞃꞇ þu ȝiꝼ hiꞇ ꞇela biꝺ þa
blæꝺꞃan ȝelæꞃe ꞇ þ heaꞃꝺe ꞇohneꞃceꝺ ꞇ þ ꞃaꞃ ȝeꝼꞇilleꝺ.
Eꝼꞇ ȝenīm iꞃieꞃ leaꝼ ꝼeoꝺ on ecebe ꞇ oꝼeꞃꝼylle on
þam ꞃelꝼan ecebe ꝼiꞃeþan · ꝺo þonne on blæꝺꞃan binꝺ
on þ ꞃaꞃ · ꞃele þonne æꝼꞇeꞃ ꝼyꞃꞇꝺꞃenc ꝼona þuꞃ ȝe-
poꞃhꞇne ; Ꝥiþ heaꞃꝺneꞃꞃe milꞇeꞃ · ȝenim eoꞃꝺȝeallan
ȝebeaꞇ oþþe ȝeȝniꝺ ꞇo ꝺuꝼꞇe ꝼꞃa ꝼꞃa þꞃeo cucleꞃ mæl
ꝼien oꝺꝺe ma. ꝺo ꝼaꞃinan ꝺuꝼꞇeꞃ ꞇo cucleꞃ mæl þꞃeo ·

---

[1] Read ꝺo melu.

[2] Alexander Trallianus, book viii.,
chap. xii., p. 481, ed. Basil.

[3] Alex. Trall., p. 500, line 8,
ed. Basil; from Galenos.

[4] The next chapter of Alex. Tr.
is on the same subject ; but the
receipts are not his.

vinegar, add meal and linseed, and barley groats, and seed of marche; lay on and smear with this. Add also blossoms of dry wormwood.

xl.

Again, when the milt becometh upblown, soon it will harden, and then it is not easy to cure, when the blood hardeneth on the veins of the milt: then treat it with the before named worts, mingle the good worts with oxymel, the southern acid drink, which we before wrote of, they will cure the milt and will do away the thick and livery[1] blood, and the evil humours, not by the mie only, but also by the other *evacuation passage or* outgang. Lay on externally the lesser herdwort beaten up. Take also roots of clover, put them in vinegar, and goat treadles, then work them to a salve, and add thereto barley meal; give the man also this in wine to drink.

xli.

For the hardness and sore of the milt; take a swines bladder so new, fill it with sharp vinegar, lay it over the hardness of the milt, then swathe up, that it may not glide away, but may be thereon, fast bounden, for three nights. After that unbind; then thou wilt find, if it be good, the bladder clear, and the hard *part* made nesh, and the soreness stilled. Again, take leaves of ivy, seethe them in vinegar, and boil in the same vinegar some bran, then put this into a bladder, *and* bind upon the sore; then soon after give a wort drink thus wrought: for hardness of the milt; take earthgalls, beat or rub them to dust, so that there may be three or more spoon measures, add three spoon measures of dust of savine thereto, and three

[1] Such as flows through the liver.

ꝺ pcallenꝺeſ piceſ ꝺuſteſ þꝼeo cúclꞇ mæl · áꝼiꝼꞇe eall
ꝼele þonne on pinc neahꞇneꝼꞇiꝣum ꞇo ꝺꝼincanne cuclen
ꝼulne · ꝣiꝼ he ſie eác on ꝼeꝼꝼe ꝼele hím ón haꞇum
pæꞇꝼe ꝣepleceꝺum þa pꝼꝼꞇa ꝺꝼincan þy læſ ꝥ pic úꝼ·
ſꞇanꝺe miꝺ þy oþꝼe ꝺuſꞇe. Eꝼꞇ ꞇo milꞇe ſeocum men
ꝺ piþ eallum inaꝺlum · eceꝺ piþ ꝣlæꝺenan ꝣemenꝣeꝺ
pyꝼc þuꝼ ꝣlæꝺenán ꝼinꝺe lyꞇelꝼa ꝣeꝺo þꝼeo punꝺ on
ꝣlæſ ꝼæꞇ pel micel · ꝣeꝺo þonne þæꝼ ꝼceaꝼꝼeꝼꞇan pineſ
ꞇo ·v. ꝼeꝼꞇꝼaꝼ áꝼeꞇe þonne on haꞇe Sunnan on ſumeꝼa
ꝉonne þa haꞇoſꞇan peꝺeꝼ ſynꝺ · ꝺ þa ꝼciꝼan ꝺaꝣaꝼ
liꝼiꞇan þe pe ꝣepꝼiꞇene habbaꝺ · ꝥ hiꞇ ſiꝼiꝣe ꝺ ꝼociꝣe
.IIII. ꝺaꝣaꝼ oþþe ma · ꝼiþþan þæſ eceꝺeſ ꝼele þu milꞇe
ſeocum men cuclꞇ ꝼulne ꝺ ſona ꝣiꝼ hím æꝼꞇeꝼ þám
ꝺꝼincan · ꝼoꝣ þon þe ꝥ iꝼ ſpiþe ſꞇꝼanꝣ þam þe ꝥ napa
ꭉꝼ þiꝣꝺe. þonne ꝺeah þíꝼ piþ huniꝣe ꝣeyceꝺ ꝣe pꝼꝺ
milꞇe aꝺle · ꝣe piþ maꝣan · ꝣe pꝼꝺ hꝼean ꝣe piþ þon þe
món bloꝺe ſpipe· ꝣe piþ eallum innan aꝺlum· eác þón[1]
ꝼieꝼþo ꝺ ꝣicþa ſon apeꝣ ꝺeþ. þeꝼ læceꝺóm ꝺeah ꝣe
piþ hꝼieꝼꝺo ꝺ ꝣicþan· pyꝼc óꝼ eceꝺe peaxꝼealꝼe· ꝣením
ꭉꝼ eceꝺeſ ·v. cúclꞇ mæl ꝺo ón niꝼne cꝼoccan ꝺo
elcꝼ bollan ꝼulne ꞇo ſeoꝺ æꞇſomne ſceaꝺ niꝼeſ ſpeꝼleſ
ꝼíꝼ cúclꞇ mæl · ꝺ lyꞇel peaxeſ oꝼeꝼ pylle eꝼꞇ oþ ꝥ
þæꞇ ecꝺ ſie ꝼoꝼꝼeallen · ꝺo þonne óꝼ ꝼyꝼe ꝺ hꝼeꝼe ꝺ
ꝼiþþan ſmiꝼe miꝺ þy þa hꝼieꝼþo ꝺ þone ꝣicꝺan.

fol. 95 a.

.XLII.

Ꝣíꝼ omihꞇe bloꝺ ꝺ yꝼel pæꞇe on þam milꞇe ſie þin-
ꝺenꝺe þonne ꝼceal hím mon bloꝺ þuꝼ læꞇan. Giꝼ þe
·þince ꝥ þu oþeꝼne maꝼan læceꝺom ꝺon ne ꝺuꝼꝼe· ꝼoꝼ

---

[1] Read þoñ, that is, þonne.

spoon measures of the dust of "boiling pitch;"[1] sift all this, then give a spoon full in wine to the man after his nights fast to drink: if he be also in a fever, give him the worts to drink in "hot" water made "luke-warm," lest the pitch form a concrete with the other dust. Again, for a miltsick man, and for all inward disorders; vinegar mingled with gladden; work it thus: put three pound of little *bits of* rind of gladden in a good sized glass vessel, then add thereto of the sharpest wine, five sextarii, then set this in the hot sun, in sum-mer, when the hottest seasons are, and the clear white days of which we have written, that it may macerate and soak for four days and more; afterwards give thou to the sick man of the vinegar a spoon full, and after the dose soon, give him *something* to drink, since that is very strong for him who never before tasted it. Fur-ther, this eked out with honey is of benefit, either for milt disease, or for maw *disease,* or for rawness,[2] or in case a man spew blood, or for all inward diseases: it also further soon doth away roughness *of skin,* and itch. This leechdom is good either for roughness or itch: work of vinegar a wax salve, *or cerote*; take five spoon measures of the vinegar, put *it* into a new crock, add a bowl full of oil, seethe together, shed *therein* five spoon measures of new brimstone, and a little wax, boil it strongly "again," till the vinegar is boiled off, then remove from the fire, and shake, and after-wards smear therewith the roughness and the itch.

xlii.

If inflamed blood and evil humour be in the milt, distending it, then shall *the sick* be thus let blood. If it seem to thee, that thou dare not to do another

---

[1] Our Saxon has made some mis-take: the receipt is similar to one given by Marcellus, col. 348, n., where we read "ex picato mero vel "nigro tepefacto."

[2] Probably *cruditas, indigestion.*

unmihte þær manner oððe ꝼoꞃ unmeltunᵹe oþþe ꝼoꞃ
ylbe · oþþe ꝼoꞃ ᵹioᵹoðe · oþþe ꝼoꞃ unᵹeꞃiðeꞃum · oþþe
ꝼoꞃ ûtꞃihtan · ᵹebið þonne oþ þ̵ þu mæᵹe · oððe¹
ðyꞃꞃe · ᵹiꝼ hæto oþþe meht ne pyꞃne læt him blod
on þam pineꝼtꞃan eaꞃme oꝼ þæꞃe uꝼeꞃꞃan æðꞃe · ᵹiꝼ
þu þa ꝼinðan ne mæᵹe læt ôꝼ þæꞃe miðmeꞃtan æðꞃe ·
ᵹiꝼ þu þa ꝼinðan ne mæᵹe læt oꝼ þæꞃe heaꞃod æðꞃe.
þonne ᵹiꝼ mon þa ꝼinðan ne mæᵹe læt oꝼ þæꞃe pineꝼtꞃan hanða neah þam lytlan ꝼinᵹꞃe ôꝼ æðꞃe · ᵹiꝼ hit
fpꞃiðe ꞃeað ſie oþþe pon þonne bið hit þy þe ſpiþoꞃ to
lætanne · ᵹiꝼ hit clæne oþþe hluttoꞃ ſie læt þy þe
læꞃꞃe. Jſ hþæþeꞃe ſpa to lætanne ſpa þ̵ liꝼlice mæᵹen
ne aſpꞃinᵹe.

.XLIII.

þûꞃ² him môn ꞃceal þuꞃ mettaꞃ ſellan on þæꞃe
able ᵹeſeape pyſan ꝿ hlaꝼ on hatum pæteꞃe ꝿ oxumelle þe pe pꞃiton æn beꝼoꞃan piþ blæðꞃan able ſuþeꞃne eceð ðꞃenc · meꞃce on pætꞃe ᵹeſoðen ꝿ ſpilca
pyꞃta ꝿ miᵹole ðꞃincan ꝿ þynne ꝼín him iſ to ꞃellanne pel ſcip þ̵ bet þ̵ mæᵹen þæꞃ milteſ ꝿ ꞃcellihte
ꞃiſcaſ him ſint to þicᵹenne · ꝿ ꝼuᵹlaſ þa þe on ꝼen-
num ne ſien. þiꞃ him iſ to ꝼoꞃᵹanne · ne þicᵹen hie
ꝼen ꝼixaſ · ne ſæ ꝼixaſ þa þe habbað heaꞃð ꝼlæꞃc · ꝿ
þicᵹen hie þa æꞃ ᵹenemðan mettaſ · oſtꞃan · ꝿ pine-
pinclan ·³ ne þa mettaſ þa þe ablaꝼan monnan mæᵹen·
ne hꞃiþeꞃeſ ꝼlæꞃc · ne ſpineꞃ ne ſceapeſ ne þicᵹean
hie · ne ᵹate · ne ticceneſ · ne ðꞃince⁴ þicce ꝼín · ne
mete ne to fpꞃiðe hatne · ne eac to cealðne. Eꞃt⁵

fol. 95 b.

fol. 96 a.

¹ oðð, MS.

² þiꞃ, MS. With the text compare,
Ἐκόλυσα δὲ πάντα τὰ γλισχροὺς καὶ
παχεῖς χυμοὺς γεννῶντα, ὡσαύτως [δὲ]
καὶ τὰ κρέα [τὰ] βόεια, χοίρεια, προ-
βάτεια, αἴγεια καὶ ἐρίφεια, καὶ τῶν
ὀρνίθων τὰ ἐν λιμνώδεσιν ὕδασι διαιτώ-
μενα, καὶ τῶν ἰχθύων πάντας ἐλεώδεις
καὶ πελαγίους, ἄλλως τε [καὶ] τοὺς

σκληρὰς καὶ ταχεῖς.   Opp. Alex.
Tralliani, p. 496, ed. Basil.

³ p not p ; see note, p. 240.

⁴ ðꞃincan would be better.

⁵ Καὶ αὐτίκα κατ' ἀρχὴν τοῦ ἦρος
αἷμα πολὺ ἐκ τοῦ ἀριστεροῦ ἀγκῶνος
ἀφήρουν.   Opp. Alex. Tralliani,
p. 427, ed. Basil.

greater leechdom, for the want of might in the man, or for want of digestion, or for old age, or for youth, or for bad weather, or for diarrhœa, then wait till that thou may so do or dare. If heat, or *his* capacity to bear it, forbid it not, let him blood from the left arm from the upper vein ; if thou canst not find that, let *him blood* from the midmost vein ; if thou canst not find that, let *him blood* from the head vein. Further, if that cannot be found, let *him blood* from the left hand, near the little finger, from a vein. If *the blood* be very red or livid, then must it be let flow more plentifully ; if it be clean or clear, let it *flow* so much the less. *Blood* however is so to be taken *from the man* as that his vital power may not be unsettled.

xliii.

Thus shall the sick mens diet be administered in that disease ; juicy peas, and bread in hot water, and oxymel, of which we wrote before, *when speaking* of bladder disease, *the* southern acid drink ; marche *also* sodden in water, and such worts and diuretic drinks, and thin wine must be given them, and sheer *or clear;* that will better the power of the milt ; and shell fishes are to be taken, and fowls, those, *namely,* which are not *dwellers* in fens. This *that followeth* is to be foregone ; let them not partake of fen fishes, nor sea fishes which have hard flesh, and let them take the before named meats, oysters and periwinkles, not the meats which puff up a mans strength, nor let them take flesh of bullock, nor of swine, nor of sheep, nor of goat, nor of kid, nor let them drink thick wine, nor food either too extremely hot

blob bið ᵹob to lætanne ón foꞃan lenctene oꞅ þam
pinꞅtꞃan eaꞃme.

.XLIIII.

Eꞃt læcebom ꞃe þ yꞃel ut tihð oꞅ þam milte ⁊ ꞃe
beah to maneᵹum oꞃꞃum ablum · ᵹením ᵹꞃene ꞃuban
ane bæᵹe æꞃ ᵹeꞃomna ⁊ mebmicel piꞃoꞃeꞃ · oꞃeꞃ ꞅꞃilc
cymeueꞃ oðbe ma · bo þ cymen ane bæᵹe æꞃ oððc
tꞃam oꞃꞃe þꞃim ón eceb abꞃiᵹe ⁊ aᵹnib to buꞅte ealle
þaꞃ ꞃyꞃta · menᵹe pꞃð huniᵹ aꞅiꞃen · ᵹebo þonne ón
ᵹlæꞃene ampullan ⁊ ꞃele þonne cucleꞃ ꞃulne þeꞃ beah
piþ maᵹan ablapunᵹe ⁊ innoþa · hneꞃceþ þa pambe ·
þynnað þa omán bitꞃe hꞃæcetunᵹe aꞃeᵹ beþ ⁊ bꞃeoꞅt
coþe · ⁊ ꞃib pæꞃce · ⁊ liꞃeꞃ able · ⁊ lenben pæꞃce · ⁊
milte pæꞃce eal þ liht.

.XLV.

Læcebomaꞃ ⁊ ꞅpið bꞃenc piþ aꞅpollenum milte · acele
ðu pealbat iꞃen þonne hít ꞃuꞃþum ꞅie óꞅ ꞃyꞃe atoᵹen·
ón pine oꞃꞃe ón ecebe ꞃele þ bꞃincan þ þu meaht eác
ꞃellan þam þe habbaþ heaꞃbne lichoman · ne ꞃceal
món hꞃæþeꞃe þíꞃne bꞃincan ꞃellan ón ꞃoꞃeꞃeaꞃbne
þone ece ⁊ þa able ác ymb ꞃela nihta.

fol. 96 b.

.XLVI.[2]

Deꞃ ꞅinbon læcebomaꞃ piþ æᵹhpæþcꞃꞃe ꞅiban ꞃaꞃe ⁊
taꞇn hu ꞅio abl toꞃeaꞃb ꞅie · ⁊ hu þ mon ónᵹitan
mæᵹe · ⁊ hu hioꞃa[3] mon tilian ꞃcyle · þaꞃ læcebomaꞅ
ꞃceal mon bon piþ ꞅiban ꞃaꞃe · ⁊ þiꞃ ꞅinbon þæꞃe able

---

[1] Καὶ μὴν καὶ στομώματος λεκὶς,
ἣν ἐκεῖνο ἐν χαλκείοις πυρούμενόν τε
καὶ σφύρᾳ κοπτόμενον ἀποβάλλει, σὺν
ὕδατι ἀναμεμιγμένη ἐν ποτῷ συμφέρει.
Opp. Alex. Trall., lib. viii., 13,
p. 506, ed. Basil.

[2] Alexandros of Tralles, lib. vi.
chap. 1, treats of the diagnosis between pleurisy and disease of the
liver.

[3] This plural may refer to the tacn
or the ꞃiban.

or too cold. Again, it is good to let blood in early
lent *or spring* from the left arm.

xliv.

Again, a leechdom which draweth out the evil from
the milt, and which is efficacious for many other disorders. Take green rue one day before *it is used,*
collect it and a moderate quantity of pepper, so much
also of cummin, or more, put the cummin one day
beforehand, or two or three, into vinegar, dry it and
rub to dust all the worts, mingle *this* with honey
strained, then put them into a glass pitcher, and so
give *the man* a spoon full. This is good against upblowing of the maw and of the inwards; it maketh
nesh the wamb; it thinneth the corrupt gastric juices,
it doth away hreakings, and breast disease, and side
pain, and liver disorder, and loin pain, and milt pain :
all that it lighteneth.

xlv.

Leechdoms and strong drink for a swollen milt; cool
thou a fiercely hot iron, when it is just withdrawn from
the fire, in wine or in vinegar, give *the man* that to
drink. Thou mayest also give that to them who have
a hard body : notwithstanding, this drink shall not
be given in the early stage of the ache and the disease,
but after many days.

xlvi.

Here are leechdoms for sore of either side, and tokens
how the disease approaches, and how a man may understand that, and how a man shall treat it. These leechdoms shall be done for sore of side, and these are the

tacn[1] ȝelic lunȝen able tacnum Ᵹ liꝼeꞃ pæꞃceꝼ tacnum. þa men beoþ miÐ hꞃiþinȝum ſꞃiþe ſtꞃanȝum
pæcede · Ᵹ micel ſaꞃ on bam ſiÐum. Ðpilum cnyꞃꞃeþ
ꝥ ꞃaꞃ on þa ꞃib · hpilûm oꞃeꞃ ealle ſiÐan biþ ꝥ ꞃaꞃ ·
hpilûm becymÐ on þa peoþoban Ᵹ eꝼt ymib lytel ȝe
þa ȝeſculÐꞃu ȝe eſt þone nepeſeoþan ꝥ ꞃaꞃ ȝꞃet · Ᵹ
hpoꞃaÐ[2] ȝelome · hpilum bloÐe hꞃæcaþ · ꞃinȝale pæc-
cean þꞃopiaÐ · tunȝe biÐ dꞃiȝe · ne maȝon ȝeliczean
ón þæꞃe pineſtꞃan ſiÐan · ȝiꝼ ón þæꞃe ſpiÐꞃan ꝥ ꞃaꞃ

biÐ · ne maȝon eác eꝼt ón þa ſpiÐꞃan · ȝiꝼ on þa pin-
ſtꞃan ꝥ ꞃaꞃ biþ · ȝeꝼelaÐ ꝥ þa mnoþaꞃ hi penÐaþ miÐ
hioꞃa heꝼiȝneꞃꞃe Ᵹ on þa ꞃiÐan ꝼeallaÐ þe he on lic-
ȝeaÐ · æꞃ þæꞃe able þaꞃ tacn beoþ · biþ eác ȝeonÐ
ꝼinȝꞃaꞃ[3] cele Ᵹ cneopa unmeht eaȝan ꞃeaÐiaÐ ꞃeoÐ[4] Ᵹ
beoþ heop Ᵹ ꝼamiȝ utȝanȝ micȝe aȝeólpoÐ Ᵹ lytel biþ
þæꞃ mnoþeꞃ meltunȝ Ᵹ[5] æÐꞃa clæppetunȝ · eþunȝ biÐ
ꞃaꞃlic ȝehnycneÐ neb Ᵹ þaꞃa bꞃeoſta biþ Ðeapiȝ pætunȝ
ſpa ſpa ſie ȝeſpat · moÐeꞃ elhyȝÐ ceolan hꞃiſtunȝ Ᵹ
hꞃeounȝ · hlybenÐe ſpiþuſt mnan piſtlaÐ oꝼ þam dæle
þe ꝥ ꞃaꞃ biÐ hlinunȝe Ᵹ hliȝiunȝe piÐ piþeꞃꞃæc · ȝiꝼ
þaꞃ tacn lanȝe puniaÐ · þonne biþ ſeo abl to ꝼꞃecen-
lico Ᵹ ne mæȝ him món ȝetilian · ahꞃa hpæþꞃe þone
mannan þe þiꞃ þꞃopaÐ hpæþeꞃ he æꝼꞃe pæꞃe ꞃleȝen
on þa ꞃiÐan oÐÐe ȝeſtunȝen oþþe hpæþeꞃ he lenȝe æꞃ
aꝼeolle oÐÐe ȝebꞃocen puꞃÐe · ȝiꝼ hit ꝥ pæꞃe þonne
biÐ he þy eaÐlæcna·[6] ȝiꝼ hit biþ oꝼ cyle cumen oþþe oꝼ
yꝼelꞃe inꝑætan hit biÐ þe uneaþlæcꞃa.[7] Ȝiꝼ he þonne

biþ æꞃ on þæꞃe liꝼꞃe oþþe on þám lunȝenum ȝeſaꞃȝoÐ

---

[1] These symptoms are fully stated
in nearly the same words by Aretæos, Acut. I. x. Possibly the
diagnosis and the symptoms were
stated, as they are in the text, by
Philagrios.   The Saxon author
mentions mechanical causes for the
sore of the side, as well as nosolo-
gical ; he does not therefore confine
himself to pleurisy.

[2] Read hpoꞃtaÐ.

[3] Aretæos accompanies us no further.

[4] Read Ᵹ biþ heop ꞃeoÐ ?

[5] Ðeanb or some word to express
ΣκληρÓς is wanting.

[6] Read eaÐleacꞃꞃa.

[7] For uneaÐleacꞃꞃa.

tokens of the disease, like unto the tokens of lung disease, and the tokens of liver pain. The men are afflicted with very strong fevers, and mickle sore on both sides. At whiles the sore striketh[1] upon the ribs, at whiles the sore is over all the side; at whiles it cometh up on the collar bones, and again, after a little, the sore greeteth either the shoulders or the lower belly, and they cough frequently, at whiles they hreak up blood, they suffer a constant wakefulness, the tongue is dry, they cannot lie on the left side if the sore is on the right side, nor again can they lie on the right, if the sore is in the left; they feel that their viscera by their weight shift place, and fall upon the side on which they lie. These tokens are before the disease. There is also cold all through their fingers, and powerlessness of their knees, their eyes are red, and red is their hue, and their discharge[2] is foamy, their mie is turned yellow,[3] and the digestion of the inwards is little, and *hard* the pulsation of the veins, the breathing is sorelike, the face twitched, and there is a dewy wetting of the breast, as if it sweated, a delirium of the mind; a spasmodic action, and roughness of the throat, sounding chiefly from within, whistleth from the part on which the sore is; the disease is unfavourable to a leaning posture and to laughing. If these tokens continue long, then is the disease too dangerous, and one can do nothing for the man: notwithstanding, ask the man, who endureth this, whether he ever were stricken or stabbed in the side, or whether he long before had a fall, or got a breakage; if it were that, then will he be easier to cure. If it is come of cold or of inward evil humour, it is so much the harder to cure. If further the man have been before troubled with soreness in the liver, or in the lungs, and the

---

[1] Νύσσει, doubtless.
[2] Expectoration?

[3] Thus the Saxon.

ꞇ þanan cymeð fıo¹ roꝛæꞃc þonne bıþ ꝥ ſpıðe ꝼꞃecne.
ȝıꝼ hıꞇ on þam mılꞇe bıþ æꞃ þonne bıþ hıꞇ þy eaþ-
lacꞃe · ȝıꝼ he þonne bıþ æꞃ on þæꞃe lunȝene ȝepunðoð
ꞇ þanan cymð ſe roꝛæꞃc þonne bıþ ꝥ ſpıðe ꝼꞃecne ·
ȝıꝼ hıꞇ on þam mılꞇe bıð æꞃ · þonne cymð ꝥ ꞃaꞃ on
þa pınſꞇꞃan ſıðan · ȝe þa habbað² heꝛıȝe ꝼꞃecenneꝛꝛe ·
ahſa hıne hꞃæþeꞃ hı́m ſe mılꞇe ꞃaꞃ · ſıe oððe hꞃæþeꞃ
hı́m ſpeoꞃcoþu ſıe · ſpa þu meahꞇ onȝıꞇan ꝥ þæꞃ⸗ ſıðan
ꞃaꞃ cymð óꝼ yꝼelꞃe pæꞇan ꞇ bıþ ſpıðe ꝼꞃecne. ȝıꝼ hım
ſe uꞇȝanȝ ꝼoꞃſeꞇen ſıe oððe ȝemıȝan ne mæȝe mıð
ſıneþꞃe ónðounȝe pyꞃꞇðꞃenceꝛ þuꝛıh hoꞃn oððe pıꞃan
ſıo pamb bıþ ꞇo clænſıanne · ꝼꞃecne bıð eac þonne
þæꞃ ꞃeocan manneſ hꞃaca bıð manıȝeꝛ hıpeꝛ ꞇ bleo :³

be þıꞃum ꞇacnum þu meahꞇ hꞃæꞃ ſe ’man ꞇo lac-
nıanne ſıe ónȝıꞇau hꞃæꞃ ne ſıe · hꞃæꞃ món unſoꝛꞇe
ȝeꞇılað ón ꝼoꞃepeaꞃðe þa aðle þonne ꝥ ſaꞃ æꞃeſꞇ
ȝeſꞇıhð on þa ſculðꞃu ꞇ on þa bꞃeoſꞇ. Sona ꞃceal
món blob óꝼ æðꞃe læꞇan. Ȝıꝼ ꝥ ꞃaꞃ ȝepunıȝe ón þam
bꞃeoſꞇum anum oþþe on þam uꝼeꞃan hꞃıꝼe oþþe on
þam mıðhꞃıꝼe · þonne ꞃceal hı́m món pyꞃꞇðꞃenc ꞃellan
ꞇ nımán ſpeꞇe pæꞇeꞃ mıð ele ȝebon ón ſpıneꝛ blæðꞃan
ꞇ beþıan ꝥ ſaꞃ mıð.

.XLVII.

Læceðomaſ þa þe þynnunȝe mæȝen hæbben ꞇ ſmal-
unȝe · þam lıchoman þa ða hæꞇo meðmıcle oþþe ſꞇꞃanȝe
þꞃopıan ꞇ hu hım món ſcyle ſpıneſ blæðꞃan ónðon.
Ȝenım hunan ꞇ peax ꞇ ele ȝemenȝe oþþe ȝeȝnıð ꞇo-
ȝæðꞃe ealꞃa emꝼela ꝥ hıꞇ an ſıe ſmıꞃe mıð ꞇ ðo on
clæþ leȝe ón. Þıþ ſaꞃe ſıðan eꝼꞇ ȝenı́m puðan leaꝼ ꞇ

¹ Read ſe.
² hab, MS., at the end of a line,
the writer forgetting to complete
the word.

³ In I. xlv. 5, the genitive was
bleoꝛ. Bleo, by a zeugma, may be
genitive plural.

side pain cometh thence, then is that very dangerous ; if it has been ere that on the milt, then it is the easier to cure. Further, if *the man* have been before wounded in the lung, and thence cometh the side pain, then is that very dangerous. If it have been formerly in the spleen, then the sore cometh on the left side, yea, those *tokens* have heavy mischief; ask him whether the milt be sore, or whether he hath neck disease. So thou mayest understand that sore of the side cometh from evil humour and is very mischievous. If his anal discharge be stopped, or if he may not mie, the wamb must be cleansed by an always easy application of a wort drink, *in this case a clyster*, through a horn or pipe. There is danger also when the sick mans *expectoration or* hreak is of many a hue and complexion.[1]

2. By these tokens thou mayest understand in what case the man is curable, in what case he is not. In case one treateth *a man* unsoftly in the early stage of the disease, then the sore first mounteth into the shoulders and into the breast. Soon must one let blood from a vein, if the sore continue on the breast alone, or in the upper belly, or in the midriff; then must one give *the man* a wort drink, and take sweet water with oil put into a swines bladder, and warm the sore therewith.

xlvii.

Leechdoms which have the power of thinning and of making small, for the bodies which suffer the heat, *either* moderate or strong, and how one must apply a swines bladder to them. Take *hore*hound, and wax, and oil, mingle or rub together equal quantities of all, that it, *the mixture*, may be one ; smear therewith, and put *also* on a cloth *and* apply. For sore of side, again ;

---

[1] Πάντα ἀναπτύεται κεχρωσμένα. Alex. Trall.

launer cpoppan ʒebeat fmæle ꞃ feoð on hunıʒe leʒe
on cla $ð$ oþþe ón ꞃel þ̄ hıt ealle þa ſıðan ꞃ þ̄ ꞃaꞃ oꞃeꞃ-
lıoʒe leʒe ón ꞃ beþe mıð þy ꞃ beleʒe æꞃceꞃ þæꞃe
beþınʒe mıð hatte pulle · ꞃ bınð peaxhlaꞃ ón · ʒıꞃ þ̄
ꞃaꞃ þonne ne ſıe þe læꞃꞃe teoh þonne mıð ʒlæꞃe ón
þa ſculðꞃu · ꞃ ſceaꞃpa þæꞃ hıt ſaꞃ ſıe ſpıþuſt · ꞃ ſcꞃep
þ̄ blob oꞃ ſpıðe · ꞃ ʒıꞃ hīt þonne ʒıt ſpıþoꞃ ꞃaꞃ ſıe ·
ne ðo þu þonne mıð ſealte þa blæðꞃan ón · āc on ꞃoꞃe-
peaꞃðe þa aðle þenden þ̄ ꞃaꞃ læꞃt ſıe. Ruðan ʒeſeoð
on ele oððe on pıne · ꞃ ðıle ſmıꞃe þa ſıðan mıð þy

neoðlıce · ꞃ beþe mıð hneꞃcꞃe pulle ꞃ mıð þy ele ꞃ
ðo þonne þa blæðꞃan ón · ðo peaꞃm ꞃealt to ðo eāc
ſeoꞃoþa ón ꞃealt pıeteꞃ ðo on þa blæðꞃan aleʒe on þ̄
ꞃaꞃ ðo þıꞃ þꞃeo nıht.

.XLVIII.

Ʒıꞃ þaꞃ ꞃultumaſ ne ꞃyn helpe · læt [1] blod þonne
ón æðꞃe óꞃ eaꞃme næꞃ on þa healꞃe þe þ̄ ꞃaꞃ bıþ · ꞃ
þa pambe mán ꞃceal clænꞃıan [2] mıð ſmeþe pyꞃtðꞃence.
Eꞃt eoꞃoꞃſpıneꞃ [3] cpeað þ̄ món ꞃınt ón puða ʒemylte
ón pætꞃe aꞃeoh ðo on hıꞃ ðꞃıncan · oþþe ðꞃıʒe ʒemenʒ
ꞃ ʒeʒnıð on hıſ ðꞃıncan þ̄ hælþ þæꞃe ꞃıðan ꞃaꞃ. Eꞃt
celenðꞃeꞃ [4] ſæð ʒeʒnıð ꞃ ſeoþ on hunıʒe oþ þ̄ hıt ðıcce
ſıe · ʒenīm þæꞃ þonne ón moꞃʒenne ꞃ ón æꞃenne þꞃeo
cucleꞃ mæl ꞃele to þıcʒenne.

.XLVIIII.

Læceðomaꞃ ꞃ peaxꞃealꞃa ꞃ ꞃceaꞃpunʒa pıþ ſıðan ꞃaꞃe ·
ꞃ hpæt hım ſıe to þıcʒanne. Eāc þu ꞃcealt þonne þu
on þam ꞃculðꞃum tyhſt blod teon ſpıðe ón þæꞃe ꞃıðan

---

[1] Trallianus, p. 85, ed. Lutet, recommends φλεβοτομία and the κά-
θαρσιν τῆς κοιλίας, after Hippokratea.

[2] clæꞃnıan, MS.
[3] Marcellus, col. 351, B.
[4] Marcellus, col. 351, C.

take leaves of rue and bunches of laurel heads, beat
them small and seethe them in honey, lay on a cloth
or on a skin so that it may overlie all the side and
the sore; lay on and foment with that *mixture*, and
cover after the fomenting with hot wool, and bind on a
cake of wax. Then if the sore be not the less, then
draw with a *cupping* glass on the shoulders, and
scarify where the sore is most, and scrape the blood
off thoroughly; and if it then be still more sore, do
not thou then apply the bladder with salt, but *do this*
in the early period of the disease, while the sore is
least. Seethe rue in oil or in wine, and dill; anoint
the sore with that, of necessity, and foment with nesh
wool and with oil, and then apply the bladder: add
warm salt, put bran also into salt water; put it on the
bladder: lay it on the sore, do this for three nights.

xlviii.

If these remedies are no help, then let blood on a
vein from the arm, *but* not on the side on which the
sore is, and the wamb shall be cleansed with a smooth
wort drink. Again, melt in water the dropping of a
boar swine, which one findeth in a wood, strain it, put
it into his drink: or dry it, mingle and rub it into
his drink, that will heal the sore of the side. Again,
rub *small some* seed of coriander, and seethe it in
honey, till it be thick, then take of that, at morning
and at even, three spoon measures; give *the man* this
to swallow.

xlix.

Leechdoms and wax salves and scarifyings for sore
of side, and what *the sick* are to take for diet. Also
thou shalt when thou drawest blood on the shoulders,
draw it strongly on the side, and for about three days

ꞇ ymb .iii. niht ſceappian ꞇ peax ꞃealſe ꞇ ele on lec-
ȝean ꞇ ꞃellan ꝺꞃencaꞃ þa þu piꞇe ᵹᵽ piꝺ ꞃiꝺ pæꞃce
ſcylen · ȝiꝼ þe pyꞃꞇ ꝺꞃenc ne limpe ꞃele ſꞇꞃanȝꝺe ·

fol. 99 a. leohꞇe meꞇꞇaſ þicȝe ꞇ ȝeꞃeap bꞃoþu [1] ꞇ ȝeꞃeape pyꞃan
ꞇ ȝeꞃleȝen æȝꞃu ꞇ bꞃeaꝺ ȝebꞃocen on hᷓꞇ pæꞇeꞃ [2]
pincpinclan [3] aꝺon oꝼ ꞃcellum miꝺ pyꞃᷓm.

.L.

Eꝼꞇ piþ ꞃiꝺan ꞃaꞃe beꞇonican leaꝼ ȝeꞃcoꝺ ᷓn ele ꞇ
ȝebꞃyꞇe aleȝe ᷓn þa ꞃiꝺan.

.LI.

Deꞃ æꞃꞇeꞃ ſinꞇ lunȝen abla laꝺlicu ꞇacn ꞇ hꞃanan
ſio cume ꞇ hu mᷓn læcebomaſ piþ þon [4] pyꞃcean ꞃcyle ·
bꞃcoſꞇ ablapen ꞇ ꞃaꞃ þeoh ꞇ liꞃa · ꞇ hᷓim ſe maȝa
micla þinꝺeþ ꞇ ban ꞇ ꞃeꞇ ꞃela ſpellenꝺe yꞃele ſpilaꞃ
unꞃelenꝺc ꞇ hine ꝺꞃeceþ þyꞃꞃe hpoſꞇan ꞇ hᷓim ᷓn þam
hpoſꞇan hꞃilum loꞃaꝺ ſio ſꞇemn. Smiꞃe þone mannan
miꝺ ele · ꞇ eac miꝺ niꞃꞃe pulle beþe þa ſiꝺan ꞇ ꞃib ·
ꞇ beꞇꞃeox ſculꝺꞃum hpene æꞃ æꞃenne · læꞇ þonne on
peſan · æꞃꞇeꞃ þᷓn læꞇ him bloꝺ oꝼ þam halan haþoli-
þan In oꞃne þæꞃ him ne eȝle ꝼyꞃi · ȝiꝼ þu him ꞇo ꞃela
læꞇſꞇ ne biþ him þonne ꞃeoꞃeꞃ ꝼen. Pyꞃc hᷓim bꞃip
ᷓꝼ pealpyꞃꞇe moꞃan · ꞇ oꝼ ꞃleaþan pyꞃꞇe · ꞇ hunan
fol. 99 b. ꞇ ꝺile ꞃæꝺ ꞃeoþ þaꞃ on buꞇꞃan ꞃele eꞇan colne on
moꞃȝen ꞇ on niht bꞃip hiſ meꞇe piþ ele ꞇ eal hiꞃ
ꝺꞃinca ſie cealꝺ. Oaneȝum men lunȝen ꞃoꞇaꝺ on
ꝺꞃince · [5] he ſpipleꞃ ꝺꞃenceſ ꞇ ꞃela henne æȝꞃu ȝeꞃlea
on an ꞃæꞇ ſpa hꞃeap · ȝeþꞃeꞃe þonne ꞇ þicȝe ꞇ ȝemenȝe æꞃ piþ ꞃleꞇan ꞇ nan oþeꞃ molcen þicȝe. Leohꞇ
ꝺꞃenc · ȝenᷓim ȝaȝellan pyl ᷓn pyꞃꞇe læꞇ þonne hpon

---

[1] Πτισσάνη, Alex. Tr.

[2] ψίχες, crumbs, Alex. Trall., p. 87,
line 15, ed. Lutet.

[3] Marcellus, col. 351, b.

[4] þon, we expected a feminine.

[5] The stop is misplaced thus in
MS.

scarify and lay on cerote and oil, and give such drinks
as thou knowest are suitable for side pain. If a *mild*
wort drink do not suffice, give a strong one. Let *the
man* take light meats and juicy broths, and juicy peas,
and beaten eggs, and bread broken in hot water, *and*
periwinkles removed from the shells, with peas.

l.

Again, for sore of side, seethe in oil leaves of betony,
and bruise them, lay them on the side.

li.

1. Hereinafter are *set forth* the loathly tokens of
lung disease, and whence it cometh, and how one must
work leechdoms against it. The breast is upblown,
and the thigh and muscle is sore, and *the mans* maw
distendeth much, and his legs and his feet swell much
with evil unfeeling swellings, and a drier cough vexes him,
and in the cough at whiles his voice is gone. Smear
the man with oil, and also warm the sides and the
ribs with new wool, and between the shoulders, a little
before evening, then let *the oil* remain on him; and
after that let him blood from the sound elbow " in an
oven, where the fire cannot harm him;" if thou lettest
him too much blood, there will be no hope of his life.
Work him a brewit from roots of wall wort, and from
fleath wort, and *hore*hound, and dill seed; seethe these
in butter; give him *this brewit* to eat cold in a
morning; and at night dress his meat with oil, and
let all his drink be cold. In many a man the lung
decayeth. Let him drink some emetic drink, and
beat up many hens eggs into a vessel, all raw, then
let him curdle it and eat it, and previously mingle
with curds, and let him take no other milk diet.
A light drink; take gagel, *or sweet gale,* boil it in
wort *of beer,* then let it stand a little, remove the

ȝeſtanðan ðo oꝼ þa ȝaȝellan ðo þonne nipne ȝiſt ón
beꝼꝛeoh þonne ꝥ hıc ahebbe pell · ðo þonne eolenan ·
ꞇ peꝛmoð · ꞇ bekonıcan · ꞇ meꝛce · ꞇ ankꝛan ko ꝛele
ðꝛıncan.

Ȝepýꝛc beopyꝛc pıþ lunȝen punðe · ꞇ banpyꝛc ſeo
þe hæbbe cꝛoppan ȝecnua þa pyꝛca kꝛa pyl on bukꝛan. ðꝛenc pıð lunȝen aðle ȝením hınðheoloþan leaꝼ ·
ꞇ hınð beꝛȝean · ꞇ ȝaꝛclıꝛan heopbꝛemleꝛ[1] leaꝼ pyl
on pyꝛce læc ðꝛıncan.

Pıþ lunȝen aðle · hınð beꝛȝean leaꝼ ꞇ hꝛeobeſ ſpıꝛ
ꝛeaðe hóꝛan · bíꝛceoppyꝛc ðolhꝛunan · neꝛcan on clænum pæcꝛe ealle þaꝛ pyꝛca pylle ꞇ ðꝛınce. Pıþ lunȝen
aðle pyꝛc ꝛealꝼe on bucepan ꞇ þıȝe ón meolcum · nım
bꝛune pyꝛc meoðopyꝛc · beꝛc naȝo · neꝛce · ȝaꝛclıꝛe.

Pıþ lunȝen aðle bꝛune pyꝛc cneopholen · bekonıca ·
puðu meꝛce ſuꝛe · eoꝛoꝛ ꝛeaꝛn · acumba · ȝaꝛclıꝛe ·
kpeȝen bꝛemlaꝛ · uouelle · pað · pyꝛc ko ðꝛence ꞇ ko
ꝛealꝼe. Ȝenım eoꝛoꝛꝛeaꝛn ȝecnupa ꞇ apylle on bukꝛan
ðo þa ꝛealꝼe ón apyllebe ȝace meolúc ꞇ þıcȝe on neahc
neꝛcıȝ · ꞇ on uꝛan mece. Ðꝛenc pıþ ðꝛıȝꝛe lunȝenne · holen ꝛınðe · ꞇ .v. leaꝛan · ðıle · ꞇ ꝛeðıc ȝecnua ko ðuſce · ꞇ óꝼ ȝeóc mıð ealoð ꝛele ðꝛıncan
ȝelome. Eꝼc ðꝛenc · maꝛubıan · ꞇ bekonıcan · meꝛce
ꝛuðe · ſuꝛapulðꝛe ꝛınðe · ꝛlah þoꝛn ꝛınðe ðꝛınce ón
ealað. bꝛup pıþ lunȝen aðle · óncꝛan · eolonan · maꝛubıan · penpyꝛc · þa clıꝛıhcan · ꝛuðe · meꝛce · pıpoꝛ ·
hunıȝ. Pıþ ðꝛıȝꝛe lunȝenne · óꝼ pealpyꝛce moꝛan · ꞇ
óꝼ ꝛleoþan pyꝛce · hunan · ðıleꝛ ꝛæð · ſeoþ on bucꝛan
ꝛele ecan colne on moꝛȝenne · ꞇ on nıhc · ꞇ bꝛıp hıꝛ
mece pıþ ele. Eꝼc úím alꝛeꝛ ꝛınðe ſeoþ on pæcꝛe oþ
ꝥ þæꝛ pæceꝛeſ ꝛıe þꝛıðða ðæl onbepylleð ꝛele þonne

---

gagel, then add new yeast, then wrap it up that it may rise well, then add helenium, and wormwood, and betony, and marche, and ontre; give *the man this* to drink.

2. Work together beewort, for a lung wound, and that bonewort which hath bunches of flowers; pound the two worts, boil in butter. A drink for lung disease; take leaves of hindheal, and hind berries, *or raspberries,* and garclife, *or agrimony,* and leaves of the hip bramble, *or dogrose;* boil them in wort *of beer;* make *the man* drink.

3. For lung disease; leaves of hind berries, *or raspberries,* a spike of a reed, red hove, bishopwort, dolhrune, nepeta; let *the man* boil all these worts in clean water, and drink. For lung disease, work a salve in butter, and take *the same* in milk; take brownwort, meadwort, birch lichen, nepeta, garclife, *or agrimony.* For lung disease; brown wort, knee holly, betony, wild marche, sorrel, everfern, oakum (ashes), garclife, the two brambles, *the dogrose and blackberry,* wowelle, woad; work *these* into a drink and into a salve. Take everfern, pound it, boil it in butter, put "the salve" into boiled goats milk, and let *the man* take it at night fasting, and on the top of that *his* meat. A drink for a dry lung; pound to dust rind of holly and cinqfoil, dill and radish, and pour them all over with ale; give *the man that* to drink frequently. Again, a drink; let him drink in ale, marrubium and betony, marche, rue, rind of crab apple tree, aloe thorn rind. A brewit for lung disease; ontre, helenium, marrubium, wenwort, that *namely* which is bulbed, rue, marche, pepper, honey. For a dry lung; some root of wallwort, and of fleath wort, *hore*hound, seed of dill; seethe these in butter, give *the brewit to the man* to eat cold, in the morning and at night, and dress his meat with oil. Again, take rind of alder, seethe in water till a third part of the water be boiled away, then give *the*

cælic fulne to drincanne on þry siþas · læt simle dægþerne betƿeonum. Ƿiþ lungen ƿunde · þær blacan fol. 100 b. ifiges croppena ⁊ corna ærest þreo on dæg .v. on morgene seofan þy þriddan dæge þonne nigon · þonne .xi. þonne þreottyne · þonne fiftyne · þonne seofontyne · þonne nigantyne · þonne .xxi. sele sƿa æfter dagum drincan on ƿine. Eft ƿiþ lungen ƿunde betonican ƿyl on ƿine sele drincan. Ƿiþ þon ilcan genim mugcƿyrt niþeƿearde · ⁊ bruneƿyrt ƿyl on buteran. Ƿiþ lungen adle genim cƿican · ⁊ ac rinde · ⁊ garclifan gecnuƿa togædere · beƿylle þonne[1] þriddan dæl on hƿætene ƿyrte suƿe æfter amylte buteran.

Eft genim brune ƿyrt · ⁊ bisceop ƿyrt · ƿudu merec · ƿudu cerfillan · eofor fearn · lind hioloþe · acumba · attorlaþe · reade hofe · ⁊ mædere. Ƿiþ lungen adle · dolhrune · ⁊ æferþe nioþoƿeard · ⁊ brune ƿyrt · ⁊ reade hofe · ⁊ reade netlan aƿylle ōn hunige ⁊ ōn cubuteran sūp on meolcum. Eft genim rædices .iii. snæda · ⁊ brade leaces gelice ⁊ spices .iii. do ꝥ .iii. dagas oþþe nigon.

fol. 101 a.

.LII.

To spiƿ drence .vi. corn alƿan .xxx. lybcorna ⁊ þa greatan ƿyrt nioþoƿearde · hƿerƿe hatte drige þa on sunnan ⁊ ellen rinde niþeƿearde drige eác ⁊ getrifula sƿiþe smæle · do healfne bollan ealoð to · ⁊ sƿete mid hunige · do hƿon buteran · ⁊ piƿores hƿon · ⁊ gehæte ꝥ ealu ⁊ do hƿon sealtes to. Eft ƿermod ⁊ eolonan læsse læt standan tƿa niht ōn ealoþ drince þonne. Eft glædene · hofe fleotƿyrt cnuƿa ōn ealaþ ⁊ gesƿet drince þonne. Gif mōn hine brece ofer gemet to spiƿanne siþþan him spiƿ drenc of sie · genim fættes flæsces sele tƿa snæda. Ƿece drenc · elene þone læs-

[1] Insert oþ, as emendation.

man a chalice full to drink at three times ; leave always a days space between. For lung wound ; of the berry bunches of the black ivy and of its grains, at first three a day, five on the morrow, seven the third day, then nine, then eleven, then thirteen, then fifteen, then seventeen, then nineteen, then twenty-one ; give them so, according to the days, to be drunk in wine. Again, for lung wound, boil betony in wine, give it to be drunk. For the same ; take the netherward part of mugwort and brownwort, boil in butter. For lung disease ; take quitch, and oak rind, and agrimony ; pound them together, then boil to the third part in wheaten wort *of beer;* sip afterwards some melted butter.

4. Again, take brownwort, and bishopwort, wild marche, wood chervil, everfern, hindheal, oakum (ashes), attorlothe, red hove, and madder. For lung disease ; dolhrune, and the netherward part of æferth, and brownwort, and red hove, and red nettle ; boil them in honey and in cows butter ; sip this in milk. Again, take three slices of radish, and the like of broad leek, and of bacon three : do that for three days or nine.

lii.

1. For an emetic ; six grains of aloes, thirty of libcorns, and the netherward part of great wort, wherwe it hight, dry it in the sun, and elder rind, the netherward part, dry it also, and triturate it very small, add half a bowl of ale, and sweeten with honey, add a little butter, and a little pepper, and heat the ale, and add a little salt. Again, wormwood, and helenium, but less of it ; let them stand for two nights in ale, then let *the man* drink. Again, gladden, hove, float wort, pound these in ale, and sweeten it, then let *the man* drink. If a man strain himself overmuch to spew, after a spew drink is *past* off from him, take some fat flesh, give him two slices. A weak emetic drink ; helenium,

R 7 +

can dæl þunȝeſ · cámmóc pyl þ on ealaþ ꞃele þ lytlum ſupan þonne hit col ſie oþ þ he ſpipe. þ iſ hoꞃe
niþepeanð beſcꞃepen ꝡ ȝecnuað · ꝡ ellen pyꞃttꞃuman
ꞃinðe apæꞃc þa clæne ꝡ beſcꞃepene · aꞃenð þonne oꞃ
þam pyꞃttꞃuman · ꝡ ȝecnua ȝotꞃoþan · ꝡ penꝑyꞃt ſio
peaxeþ ón ealðum lanðe · ȝeot þonne hluttoȝ eala to ·

fol. 101 b. pylle ſpiþꞃe meðo ȝiꝼ hebbe beꞃꞃeo ꝡ læt ſtanðan nihteꞃne aꞃeoh bollan ꞃulne ȝeſpete þonne mið
huniȝe aꞃeoh þonne eꝼt · bebinðe þonne ȝenoh peaꞃme ·
læte þonne ſtanðan neahteꞃne. ðꞃince þonne on
moꞃȝen ꝡ hine pꞃéo peaꞃme ꝡ him ꞃlæp beoꞃȝe ſpiþe
ȝeoꞃne · lanȝe he mæȝ on þam pyꞃtum ſtanðan ꝡ
þonne hine món ðꞃincan ꝑille ónhꞃeꞃe eꝼt. Þyꞃce
þonne in þæꞃ bollan ꞃulne ſpa he æꞃ poꞃhte · ȝiꝼ he
ſie to unſpið ȝeȝniðe he ꞃiꝼtiȝ lyb coꞃna ȝeſpete
þonne. Þyꞃce ſpiðꞃan ȝiꝼ he ꝑille · abelꞃe þa ȝꞃeatan
pyꞃt aſcꞃep þa ȝꞃeatan ꞃinðe óꞃ ȝecnupa þonne ſmæle
ȝeót þonne hluttoꞃ eala ón. Se ðꞃenc biþ ſpa ꞃelꞃa
ſpa þ ealu ꞃelꞃe biþ. Spipe ðꞃenc · ȝenim ellenꞃinðe
niþepeaꞃðe · ꝡ hámpyꞃte ꝡ hunðteontiȝ lybcoꞃna ȝecnua ſpiþe ꝑel ealle þa pyꞃta ðo on ealo menȝe þonne ·
ȝenim þonne pah mela hæꞃleſ oþþe alꞃeſ aꞃiꞃt þonne
ꞃul clæne tela micle hanð ꞃulle ðo on ȝemanȝ læt

fol. 102 a. neahteꞃne ſtanðan ahlyttꞃa, ſpiþe ꝑel · ȝeſpet mið
huniȝe ȝeðꞃinc ſcenc ꞃulne tela micelne. Ȝiꝼ re ðꞃenc
nelle óꞃ ȝením óꞃꞃeð ꞃelle ón ealað ðꞃincan ſcenc ꞃulne
peaꞃmeſ ꞃona biþ ꞃel. Þyꞃc ſpiþðꞃenc. ȝenim lybcoꞃn
ꝡ ꝑipoꞃ coꞃn ꝡ hꞃit cpuðn ꝡ alꞃan ȝꞃinð to ðuſte
þa pyꞃta ſpiþe · ðo on beoꞃ ſpa on ꝑin ſpa on þeoꞃiꝼe

the least bit of thung *or aconite*, cammock *or peuce-danum;* boil that in ale; when it is cool, give *the man* that to sip little by little, till he spew. . . . that is, hove, the nether part of it scraped and pounded, and the rind of elder roots ; wash them clean, and *have them* scraped, then rend *the rind* away from the roots, and pound goutweed, and wenwort, that *namely* which waxeth in old land, then pour thereon clear ale, boil *it*, or strongish mead if thou have it, wrap it up and let it stand or the space of a night, strain out a bowl full, then sweeten with honey, then strain again, then bind it up warm enough, then let it stand for a nights space; then let him drink it the morning, and let him wrap himself up warm, and let him very earnestly beware of sleep. Long may *the drink* stand upon the worts, and when a man hath a mind to drink it, let him shake it up again : then let him work thereinto a bowl full, as he before wrought it ; if it be too weak let him rub small fifty libcorns,[1] *and* then sweeten it. Let him work it stronger if he will ; delve up the great wort, scrape away the great rind, then pound it small ; then pour clear ale upon it : the drink is the better according as the ale is better. An emetic ; take the netherward part of the rind of elder, and home-wort, and a hundred libcorns, pound them very well, put all the worts into ale, then mix; then take fine meal of the hazel or alder, then sift it full clean, put in a good large handful amidst *the rest,* let it stand for a nights space, clear it very thoroughly, sweeten with honey, drink a good mickle cup full. If the drink will not *be thrown* off, take onred, give in ale a cup full of it warm *ω the man* to drink; soon he will be well. Work a spew drink *thus;* take libcorns, and pepper-corns, and mastich, and aloes, grind the worts to dust thoroughly, put into beer, or into wine, or into skim

---

[1] Seeds of *Momordica elaterium.*

meolúc ȝiꝼ þu þaꞃa oþeꞃꞃa naþþeꞃ næbbe · ȝiꝼ þu on
ꝑine ꝑyꞃce oþþe on meolce ȝeꝼꝑeꞇ miꝺ huniȝe ꝺꞃince
ꞇela micelne ꝛcenc ꝛulne.

Spiꝑe ꝺꞃenc ꝑyꞃc óꝼ beoꝛe ꝺo coꝼꞇ to ꞇ alꝑan ꞇ
lybcoꞃna ꝼiꝼꞇyne þaꞃa oþeꞃa ȝelice.

Spiꝑe ꝺꞃenc hampyꞃꞇe .iii. ꝼnæba · ꞇ ellen ꞃinꝺe be-
ꞃenꝺe ȝelice micel .xxv. lybcoꞃna¹ ȝeȝniꝺ ꝺo huniȝeꝛ
ꝼꝑilce an ꝼnæb ꝼie on eꞇe þonne miꝺ cucleꞃe on ꝼuꝑ
haꞇeꝛ pæꞇeꞃeꝼ oððe cealꝺeꝛ. Ȝíꝼ ꝺꞃenc óꝼ men nelle ·
ȝenim meꞃce · ꞇ ceꞃꝼillan ꝼeoþ ꝼꝑiþe on pæꞇꝛe ꝺo ꝛealꞇ
to ꝺꞃince þonne. Ȝiꝼ hine innau pæꞃce · ȝením niȝeꝛ
ealaꝺ ambeꞃ ꝛulne ꝺo hanꝺ ꝛulle hampyꞃꞇe ón · læꞇ
on hebban ꝺꞃince oþ þ þu ꝼꝑiꝑe · ꝼꞇinȝ þonne ꝛeþꞃe

fol. 102 b.

ón muꝺ ꞇeoh þa ȝelleꝼꞇꝛan úꞇ ꝺꞃinc eꝛꞇ Sona:·

Ním ꝼcamoniam þ peniȝ ȝeꝑeȝe ꞇ ȝeȝniꝺ ꝼmæle ꞇ
hꞃeꞃ henne æȝ ꝼꝑiꝺe ꝛealꞇ ꝺo þa ꝑyꞃꞇ ón ne læꞇ ȝeyꞃ-
nan þ æȝ ac ꝛúp. Ƿyꞃꞇꝺꞃenc · ꝼcamonian ȝeceoꝛ þuꝛ
bꞃec on ꞇu ꝺo hꝑon ón þine ꞇunȝan ȝíꝼ hío hꝑiꞇe oꝛeꞃ-
bꞃeȝꝺeþ ꝼꝑa meluc þonne hio biþ ȝoꝺ · ȝeȝniꝺ þonne
on ꞇꝛeopenum ꝛæꞇe næꝛ on nanum oþꞃum miꝺ ꝼꞇiccan
oþþe miꝺ hæꝛꞇe ꝺo óꝼ þ món ȝeȝniban ne mæȝe þ
biþ ȝeuꞃnen · ꝺo caulicef ón .ii. ꝺꞃoꝛan oððe þꞃy ·
oþþe eleleaꝼeꝛ ꝼꞇelan ȝeꝑyl toꝛómne · ȝiꝼ hio biþ ȝoꝺ ·
ꝺꞃenc biꝺ ón peninȝe · ȝíꝼ mæꞇꞃa biꝺ on oðꞃum heal-
ꝛum oððe ón ꞇꝛam auuiꝛeþꞃimænemæ.² Spiꝑe ꝺꞃenc ·
hoꝛan ꞇ onꞃeꝺ · ꞇ ellen ꞃinꝺe ȝecnua to Somne ellen
læꝼꞇ · ꝺo þonne to .xxx. ꝑiꝛoꝛ coꞃna ȝeꝼꝑeꞇ miꝺ huniȝe
ꝛele ꝺꞃincan.

---

¹ cybcoꞃna, MS.
² Read anꝺ ȝiꝼ iꝛel þꞃim ac ne

ma? Yet the letters of the text
are quite legible and clear.

milk, if thou have neither of the others; if thou work it in wine or in milk, sweeten it with honey; let *the man* drink a good mickle cup full.

2. Work a spew drink of beer, add costmary, and aloes, and fifteen libcorns, of the others similarly.

3. An emetic; of homewort three pieces, and rend up elder rind, the same quantity, twenty-five libcorns, rub *them to dust*, and of honey as much as would be one piece *or proportion*, then eat thereof with a spoon, sip some water hot or cold. If *such* a draught will not *pass* from a man, take marche and chervil, seethe them thoroughly in water, add salt, then let *the man drink*. If there is inward pain, take a jug full of new ale, add a hand full of homewort, have *the jug* held up and drink till thou spew; then poke a feather into thy mouth; draw the bad matter out, drink again soon. Take scammony, so much as may weigh a penny, and rub it small, and half cook a hens egg, salt it thoroughly, put 'the wort into it, let not the egg coagulate, but sip it. A wort drink; choose scammony thus, break it in two, put a bit on thy tongue, if it bursteth out white as milk, then it is good; rub it then in a treen vessel, not in any other, with a spoon or with a handle, remove what cannot be rubbed down, that *part* is coagulated, add two or three drops of κωλικόν,[1] or boil together *with it* a stalk of olive leaf: if it be good the dose will be one pennyweight; if moderately good, one and a half or two pennyweights; if bad, three; no more than that. A spew drink; hove, and onred, and elder rind ; pound these together, *put least of* elder, then add thirty peppercorns, sweeten with honey, give *the man* to drink.

---

[1] " Eat etiam medicamentum . . . " quod *κωλικόν* nominatur... magis " prodest potui datum." Celsus, IV. xiv. See the mention of θηριακόν. Book II. lvi. 4.

274

.LIII.

To leohtum ꝺꝛence ælꝼþonan ȝyþꝛiꝼan · betonican
þa cluꝼyhtan penꝛyꝛt · eoꝛoꝛþꝛotan · heah hioloþan ·
ealehtꝛan · eolonan tꝛa ſnæꝺa · clatan · peȝbꝛæban ·
óntꝛe · cꝛopleſc to pætan healꝼ haliȝ pæteꝛ · healꝼ
ꝛie hluttoꝛ eala. To leohtum ꝺꝛence · biſceop pyꝛt

elehtꝛe · peꝛmoꝺ · pulꝼeꝛ camb pyl ón meolcum ſpiþe
apꝛinȝ þonne þuꝛh claꝺ ꝺꝛyp ealo ón oꝺꝺe ꝼín ꝛele
ſupan. Leoht ꝺꝛeno biꝛceop pyꝛt ontꝛe eolone ·
maꝛubie · ꝺꝛeoꝛȝe ꝺpoſtle · meꝛce · æꝛcꝛꝛotu · betonica ·
heah hioloꝺe · hinꝺ hioloþe · ȝaȝille · mínte · ꝺile · ꝛinul ·
cenꝛille · ꝺꝛinoe on ealuꝺ ȝepoꝛhte. Unſpiꝛol ꝺꝛenc
biſceop pyꝛt · peꝛmoꝺ · attoꝛlaꝺe · ſpꝛinȝ pyꝛt ȝyꝺ-
ꝛiꝼe · ꝺꝛeoꝛȝe ꝺpoſtle · ꝛinul · ȝebeaten piꝛoꝛ · ȝeꝺo þa
pyꝛta ealle on an ꝼæt ȝeꝺo þonne ealꝺ ꝼín hluttoꝛ
on ꝺone ꝺꝛenc oꝺꝺe ſꝛiꝺe ȝoꝺ meꝺo ꝺꝛince þonne þone
ꝺꝛenc neahtneꝛtiȝ · ꝺ ſpa beteꝛe him íꝛ ſpa he óꝛtoꝛ
ꝺꝛince ꝺ ete þone bꝛiꝛ þe heꝛ áꝛꝛiten iꝛ · byꝛiȝ eolonan ómpꝛan · ontꝛe · ȝotꝛoþe hꝛomȝeallan · ȝeſcab-
pyꝛt nioþoꝛeaꝛꝺe · ȝecnua þa pyꝛta ꝺo ſealt ón pyl on
butꝛan. Eꝼt unſpiꝛol ꝺꝛenc · biſceoppyꝛt · ȝyþꝛiꝼe ·
ſpꝛinȝ pyꝛt .v. baȝaſ ꝺꝛince ætſomne ſimle on moꝛȝne
ꝼoꝛlæte oþꝛe ꝼiꝼe .v. ꝺꝛince. Leoht ꝺꝛenc ȝením

peꝛmoꝺ · ꝺ betonican · ꝺ hioloþan[1] læſt ꝺ hinꝺ hioloþan
ꝺo on eala. Stille ꝺꝛenc · betonican · eolone · peꝛmoꝺ ·
ontꝛe · hune · elehtꝛe · penpyꝛt · ȝeaꝛꝛe · ꝺꝛeoꝛȝe
ꝺpoſtle · attoꝛlaꝺe ꝼelꝺmoꝛu.

.LIIII.

Þiþ inſtice · ȝením apꝛotanan · ꝺ attoꝛlaꝺan · biſceop
pyꝛt þa ſuþeꝛnan · ȝehæte on beoꝛe ꝺ ſupe. Ꝺíꝼ ſtice

---

[1] Read eh hioloþan.

liii.

For a light drink, *use* elfthon, githrife, betony, the cloved wenwort, everthroat, horse heal, lupins, two proportions of helenium, clote, waybroad, ontre, cropleek, for liquid let half be holy water, half clear ale. For a light drink; bishopwort, lupin, wormwood, wolfscomb, boil thoroughly in milk, then wring through a cloth, drop ale or·wine upon it, give it *the man* to sip. A light drink; bishopwort, ontre, helenium, marrubium, dwarf dwostle, marche, ashthroat, betony, horse heal, hind heal, gagel *or sweet gale*, mint, dill, fennel, chervil, let *the man* drink *them* wrought up in ale. A not emetic drink; bishopwort, wormwood, attorlothe, springwort, githrife, pennyroyal, fennel, beaten pepper, put all the worts into one vessel, then put clear old wine into the drink or very good mead, then let the man drink the draught after his nights fast, and it is the better for him according as he oftener drinketh, and let him eat the brewit which is here written ; borough-helenium, ompre *or sorrel*, ontre, goutweed, ramgall, the nether part of oxeye, pound the worts, add salt, boil in butter. Again, a not emetic drink ; bishopwort, githrife, springwort ; let *the man* drink for five days together, always in the morning, let him leave it alone for other five, and drink for five *more*. A light drink; take wormwood, and betony, and horse heal, the least *of this*, and hind heal, put them into ale. A quieting drink ; betony, helenium, wormwood, ontre, *horehound*, lupin, wenwort, ˈyarrow, dwarf dowstle, attorlothe, field-more *or carrot*.

liv.

For an inward stitch ; take abrotanon and attorlothe, the southern bishopwort, *that is, ammi*, let *the man* heat them in beer and sip. If there be a stitch, but

butan iunoðe fie · ʒenim þonne þa ɲeaðan netlan Ᵹ
ealbe ɲapan ʒebeat toSomne Ᵹ ſmiɲe miꝺ Ᵹ beþe miꝺ
to ꝼyɲe.

.LV.

Dɲenc ʒiꝼ món innan ɲoɲhæɲꝺ fie · ʒecnua eolonan
ꝼyl ón ealoð Ᵹ betonican · peɲmoꝺ Ᵹ þa cluɲihtan [1]
ꝼenꝼyɲt ɲele ꝺɲincan. Þiþ Incoþe coſteɲ ʒoðne bæl ·
Ᵹ ꝼinoleɲ ɲæbeɲ oþeɲ ſpilc ʒebeat ſmæle Ᵹ ʒeʒniꝺ to
buſte. Ʒeními þæɲ cucleɲ ꝼulne · ʒeꝺo ón ealꝺ ꝼin oþþe
cæɲen ꝺɲince þonne neahtneɲtiʒ þɲy baʒaɲ.

Þiþ ɲæɲcoþe biɲceoɲɲyɲt · peɲmoꝺ · betonica · ɲeꝺíc ·
meɲce · coſt · ɲuꝺan ɲæꝺ ꝼyɲc to ꝺɲence.

.LVI.

Ʒiꝼ món ne mæʒe útʒeʒan · ʒením uman · Ᵹ eac
ʒecɲyɲte hanꝺ ꝼulle · Ᵹ meꝺmicelne bollan ꝼulne ealað ·
beꝼyl þɲimme þ ealo on þæɲe ꝼyɲte ꝺɲince þonne
neahtneɲtiʒ. Eꝼt ʒiꝼ món ſyþ ʒaɲleſc on henne
bɲoþe Ᵹ ɲelð ꝺɲincan þonne to læt hio þ ɲaɲ. Eꝼt
ʒate meoluc Ᵹ eceꝺ ſeoþ ætʒæðeɲe ɲele ꝺɲincan. Eꝼt
ʒate meoluc Ᵹ huniʒ Ᵹ ɲealt ɲele ꝺɲincan. Eꝼt ꝼylle
ʒeaɲɲan on huniʒe Ᵹ ón butɲan ete þa ꝼyɲt miꝺ.

Þiþ útꝼæɲce eɲt eɲelaɲtan uɲepeaɲꝺe · peʒbɲæban
ellenɲinꝺe ɲealt ón ealo ʒeʒniꝺen.

Tácn [2] be utɲihtan ʒe on þam uɲeɲɲan hɲiɲe ʒe ón
þam niþeɲɲan. þa able món mæʒ onʒitan be þam
utʒanʒe hɲilc ɲe ón ónſyne fie. Sum biþ þynne ſum
miꝺ þiccum pætum ʒeonꝺ ʒoten. Sum miꝺ þæɲ in-
noþeɲ · Ᵹ miꝺ þaɲa ſmæl þeaɲma ʒebɲocum [3] ʒemenʒeð ·

---

[1] The MS. has a stop after cluɲ-
ihran.

[2] Nearly as Trallianus, book x.,

cap. i. p. 167, line 27, ed. Lutet. ;
book viii., p. 455, ed. Basil.

[3] ξύσματα, Trall.

not in the inwards, then take the red nettle and old soap, beat them together and smear therewith, and foment therewith at the fire.

lv.

1. A drink, if a man be costive within; pound helenium, boil in ale it and betony, *and* the cloved wenwort; give *the man* to drink. For inward disease; a good deal of costmary, and as much more of seed of fennel, beat small and rub to dust; take a spoon full of this, put it into old wine, or wine boiled down one third, let *the man* drink this after his nights fast for three days.

2. For sudden sickness; bishopwort, wormwood, betony, radish, marche, costmary, seed of rue; work *these* into a drink.

lvi.

1. If a man may not discharge his bowels; take "unan," and also a contracted hand full *of it*, and a moderately mickle bowl full of ale; boil strongly the ale on the wort, then let *the man* drink it after his nights fast. Again, if one seetheth garlic on chicken broth, and giveth it *the man* as a drink, then it removes the sore. Again, seethe together and give *him* to drink goats milk, and honey, and salt. Again, let him boil yarrow in honey and in butter, let him eat the wort with *those*.

2. For painful evacuation; the upper part of everlasting, waybroad, elder rind, salt, rubbed up into ale.

3. Tokens of dysentery either in the upper part of the belly or in the nether. One may understand the disease by the fæcal discharged, *observing* what like it is in appearance: some is thin; some is suffused with thick humours; some is mingled with fragments of the inwards, and of the small guts; some is much

ɼum ɼpiðe ȝeꝼylleð mið poɼmſe. Sum ſpiðe bloðiȝ.
Sum cymð oꝼ þam uꝼeɼpan hɼiꝼe. Sum oꝼ þam
niþeɼpan · þam þe óꝼ þam uꝼeɼpan hɼiꝼe cymð ɼe
ûtpæɲc þiſ tâcn bið · ꝥ ɼe man ɼap ȝeꝼelð æt hiſ
naꝼolan ꝫ on hiɼ ſculðpum heꝼiȝ ɼap · ꝫ þuɼſt ꝫ
unluſt ꝫ þuɼh bǽc þeaɲm lytel bloð ðɼopað;

fol. 104 b.

Sió utɼiht aðl cymð maneȝum æɲeſt oꝼ to miclum
ûtȝanȝe · ꝫ þonne lanȝe hɼile ne ȝymð mon þæſ oþ ꝥ
ɼe innoþ pyɲð ȝe onbuɲnea ȝe þuɼh ꝥ ȝepunðoð ·
hɼilum onȝinneð oꝼ þam miðhɼiꝼe ɼe iſ betpeox þæɲe
pambe ꝫ þæɲe liꝼɲe · ꝫ þa ɼeap þa ðe beoð ȝemenȝeðu
óꝼ mettum piþ bloð ꝫ piþ oman ȝeonðȝeotaþ þone
Innoþ pyɲceað yɼelne ûtȝánȝ ꝫ ꝼoɲ þæɲe ȝɲimneɼɼe
þaɲa omena ne mæȝ beón ȝehæɼð þy ſe mete âc beoþ
ɼomoð þa innoþaſ beðɲiɼen þonne pyɲð ꝥ to utpæɲce.
Ðu món þa utyɲnenðan men ɼcyle lácnian þam món
ſceal ɼellan þa mettaɼ þa ðe pambe neaɲpian ꝫ þam
maȝan ne ſceþþan · cauleɼ ſeap · hɼilum pyſena bɼioþ
ꝫ eceð · ꝫ poɲ mið peȝbɼæðan ȝeſoðen ꝫ ealðne cyſe
ȝeſoðenne ón ȝate meolce mið þy ſmeɲpe ȝate · hɼilum
bɼæðe þone cyſe ꝫ ðɼiȝne hlaꝼ ꝫ pæteɲ ꝥ ɼie ɲoſe on
ȝeſoðen hɼilum ɼ·ceaɲp piu ðɲince. Ðync him onleȝena
to clame ȝepoɲlit · beɲen melo oþþc hɼætcen mið huniȝe
ȝeSoðen · mið mebmicle   *   *   *   *   *

*   *   *   *   *   *   *   *   *

*Here many folios have been taken from the MS. In
the margin "hic lacuna eſt," now erased, may be read.*

filled with ratten; some is very bloody; some cometh
from the upper belly,[1] some from the lower: of that
in which the discharge cometh from the upper belly, this
is a token, that the man feeleth sore at his navel, and
heavy sore on his shoulders, and thirst, and loss of
appetite, and a little blood droppeth through the back
gut *or rectum*.

4. The disease dysenteria cometh to many first from
too mickle fæcal discharge, and then a man for a long
while attendeth not to this, till the inwards become
either inflamed, or through that neglect wounded.
At whiles it beginneth from the midriff, which is,
betwixt the wamb and the liver, and the juices from
meats which are mingled with blood and with bad humours, pour themselves through the inwards and cause
an evil fæcal discharge, and for the grimness of the
inflammatous matters the food cannot be contained,
but the inwards,[2] along with it, are driven down,
then that turneth to dysentery. *We say now*, how
one must cure the man thus afflicted; to him one must
give the meats which restrain the wamb and do not
scathe the maw, juice of colewort, at whiles peas broth,
and vinegar, and porrum *or leek* sodden with waybroad,
and old cheese sodden in goats milk, along with the
grease of goat. At whiles roast the cheese and dry
bread, and let him drink water which has been sodden
upon roses, at whiles sharp wine. Work him poultices
wrought to a clammy mass, barley or wheaten meal
sodden with honey, with a moderately mickle   *

* * * * * * * * * *

---

[1] 'Εξ ὑψηλῶν ἐντέρων, *bowels* correctly.
[2] That is ξύσματα, *abraded por-*
tions of the intestines, and τῶν
ἐντέρων ἡ φυσικὴ πιμελή, *the fat
naturally* adhering to them.

280   LÆCE BOC.

* * * ᴄ * * * * *

.LIX.

MS. Harl. 55., fol. 1 a.

Πάρεσις or
Παράλυσις.

Þið þæne healꝼ beaðan able ⁊ hpanon seo cume·
seo aðl cymð on þa ſpiðpan healꝼe þʉꝼ lichoman·
oððe on þa pýnſtpan· þæp þa ꝼína to�;upað ⁊ beoð
mið ꝼhpiꟇne ⁊ þíccepe pætan ýꝼelpe ⁊ ýꝼelpe þiccepe
⁊ mýcelpe.[1]

þā pætan man ꝵcæl mið bloðlæꝵum ⁊ ðpencum ⁊
læcebomum on peꟇ aðōn· þonne ꝵeo aðl cume æpeſt
on ðone mannan þonne ontýne þu his muð ꝵceapa hiꝵ
tunꟇan þonne bið heo on þa healꝼe hpittpe þe ꝵeo aðl
on beon pile· lacna hinc þonne þuꝵ· Geꝵepe þæne
mannan on ꝵpiðe ꝵæꝵtne cleoꝼan ⁊ peapmne Ꟈepeſte
him ꝵpiðe pel hleope þæp ⁊ peapme Ꟈleba bepe man
Ꟈelome īnn.

Onppeoh hine þonne ⁊ ꝵceapa his hanða Ꟈeojine· ⁊
ꝵpa hpæþepe ꝵpa ðu cealðe ꝼinðe læt him ꝵona bloð
on þæpe cealðan æðpe· æꝼtep þæpe bloðlæꝵe· huhpeꟇa
ýmb .iii. niht ſele him pýpt ðpenc ūtýpnenðe ðó
Ꟈiðcojina ſpa ꝼeala ꝵpa læcaꝵ piton þ to pýptðpence
ꝵculon ⁊ ꝵpa Ꟈepaðe pýpta.

Ꝺpilum alpan æꝼtep hipe pihte· him mon ſcæl ꝵellan
hpilum ſcamoniam· hpilum eꝼt æꝼtep pýptðpencum·
þonne he Ꟈepeſt ꝵý· læt eꝼt blob on æðpe ꝵpa þu on
ꝼpuman ðýbeꝵt· hpilum þu teoh mið Ꟈlæꝵe oððe mið
hopne blob oꝼ þam ꝵapan ſtopum abeaðoðum.

fol. 1 b.

Þiþ þæpe healꝼbeaban able· beþe hpilum þa ꝵapan
ſtope æt heopðe oððe be Ꟈlebum· ⁊ ꝵmepe mið ele·
⁊ mið halpenðum ꝵealꝼum· ⁊ Ꟈnið ꝵpýðe þ þa ꝵealꝼa

---

[1] The MS. thus.

* * * * * * * * * *

lix.

The MS. seems to have been written about A.D. 1040.

1. For the half dead disease and whence in cometh. Hemiplegia.
The disease cometh on the right side of the body, or
on the left, where the sinews are powerless, and are
afflicted with a slippery and thick humour, evil, thick,
and mickle.

2. The humour must be removed with bloodlettings,
and draughts, and leechdoms. When first the disease
cometh on the man, then open his mouth, look at his
tongue, then is it whiter on that side on which the
disease is about to be; then tend him thus: carry
the man to a very close and warm chamber, rest him
very well there in shelter, and let warm gledes be
often carried in.

3. Then unwrap him and view his hands carefully,
and whichsoever thou find cold, on that cold vein let
him blood. After the bloodletting, somewhere about
three nights, give him a purging wort drink, put in
as many githcorns[1] as leeches know must be put into
a wort drink, and suitable worts.

4. At whiles must be given him aloes after their
proper method, at whiles scammony; at whiles again
after wort drinks, when he is in repose, let blood
again on a vein as thou didst at first; at whiles draw
blood with a *cupping* glass or a horn from the
sore deadened places.

5. For the half dead disease. Warm at whiles the
sore place at the hearth or by gledes, and smear
with oil, and with healing salves, and rub smartly so

---

[1] Berries of the *Dafne laureola.*

ın beꞃıncen. Þýꞃc co ꞃealꝼe ealƀne ꞃýꞃle ꞃealcne heop-
ceꞃ meaꞃh · ȝoꞃe ꞃýꞃle · oððe hænna · ⁊ ƀó ȝoðe pýꞃca
có beðe þa saꞃan ꞅcope æc ꝼýꞃe.

Ðpılum onleȝe ⁊ onbınð píc · ⁊ peax · pıpoꞃ · ⁊
ꞅmeꞃu · ⁊ ele · coȝæðeꞃe ȝemılceð. Ðpılum on þa
ꞃaꞃan ꞃınua ⁊ aꞃpollenan leȝe ón ⁊ bınð on ȝace
cýꞃðelu ȝemenȝeð pıð hunıȝ · oððe on ecebe ȝeꞃoben ·
þonne þpınað þa aꞃlapenan ⁊ þa aꞃpollena [1] ꞃına.

Þýꞃc hım pýꞃc ðꞃenc þe ne bıð úcýꞃꞃnenðe · ꞃe
ꞃpıpol ác cobꞃıꞃð ⁊ lyclað þa ýꞃelan pæcan · on þaꞃn
ꞃeocum men þe bıþ ꞃpa ꞃpa hoꞃh oððe ꞃuꞃoða oððc
ȝıllıꞃcꞃe.
Genim hunıȝeꞃ þıꞃ [1] lýcle punð ƀó þonne co þan ȝe-
beacen ⁊ aꞃıꞃc pıpoꞃ · sýle þonne co þıcȝanue þaꞃn
uncꞃuma [1] men. Eꞃc ýmbe þꞃeo nıhc ꞃýle hım on
þam ılcan ȝemece oððe maꞃe · ⁊ ꞃpa ýmb ꝼeopeꞃ
nıhc.

Þıð þæꞃe healꝼ ðeaðan aƀle · ðo þu hpılum ꞃealceꞃ
cucleꞃ mæl có menȝe pıð hunıȝ ⁊ eꝼc pıpoꞃ · cunna
ꞅpa æȝþeꞃ ȝe on þıꞃum læcebome ȝe on oðꞃum þæın
þe ıc eac pꞃıce hu hıc on n´ıman polbe · ȝıꝼ þ̵ lıc
heaꞃð ꞃı ucan leȝe on þane læcebom þe þ̵ heaꞃð ꝼoꞃðı
lıpelıȝe ⁊ þæc ýꝼel úc ceo. ceoh hım blob óꝼ ȝıꝼ þæc
neb oððe þ̵ heaꞃob ꞃáꞃ ꞃı on þam hneꞃcan · ⁊ nıcca [2]
þaꞃa læceboma þe þane hoꞃh oꝼ þam heaꞃbe ceo · [1] oþþe
þuꞃh muð · oððe þuꞃh noꞃu · ⁊ þonne he þa mıhc
hæbbe ȝeðo þ̵ he ȝelome ȝeꝼneꞃe · sýle hım þa meccaꞃ
þe ꞃýn eaðmýlce · ⁊ ȝob ꞃeap hæbben ⁊ he ꞃꞃam þam
meccum mæȝe ꞃmalıȝan · þæc ꞃýn ȝeꞃobene pýꞃca ·
pýll · ȝeoce man þ̵ æꞃeꞃce póꞃ ⁊ þ̵ aꝼceꞃe onpeȝ · ƀó

---

[1] MS. thus.　　　　　[2] Corrected to nýcca, MS.

that the salves may sink in. Work into a salve some old salt grease, some horse marrow, some goose fat or hens, and add good worts, and warm the sore places at the fire.

6. At whiles lay on and bind on pitch, and wax, and pepper, and grease, and oil melted together. At whiles lay on and bind on the sore swollen sinews goats treadles, mingled with honey, or sodden in vinegar; then the paralyzed and swollen sinews dwindle *to their proper size.*

7. Work him a wort drink, which is not purging nor yet emetic, but which driveth off and diminishes the evil humour in the sick man, which is, as it were, foulness, or rheum, or mucus.

8. Take of honey this small pound,[1] then add to it beaten and sifted pepper; then give it to the infirm man to eat. Again, about three nights *after,* give it him in the same quantity, or more; and so about four nights *after that.*

9. For the half dead disease; at whiles, apply a spoon measure of salt; mingle with honey and pepper besides. Try both in this leechdom and in others, which I also write, how it will hold; if the body be hard on the outside, lay on the leechdom that the hard part by it may turn to ratten, and may draw out the mischief. Draw blood from him, if the face or the head he sore, in the tender place; and make use of the leechdoms, which may draw the foul matter from the head, either through the mouth or through the nose; and when he hath the power, cause him to sneeze often; give him the meats which are easy of digestion, and have a good succulence, and *that* he by means of the meats may grow slender; that is to say, *give him* sodden worts; boil them; let the first and the second

---

[1] That is, a pound by weight, not a pint by measure: see Leechbook, II. lxvii.

þonne ᵹob ƿúr tó · ꞇ ꞃýle to þýcᵹanne bo lýtel ꞃealꞇ ·
ꞇ ele · ꞇ meꞃce tó ꝡ póꞃꞃ · ꞇ þæm ᵹelice. healꝺ þonne
ᵹeoꞃne ꝥ ꞃe meꞇe ꞃí ᵹemýlꞇ æꞃ he him eꞃꞇ ᵹýꞃe ·
ꞃoꞃꝺan þe ꞃe unᵹemýlꞇa meꞇe him pýꞃcꝺ mýcel ýꞃel ·
ꞃaꞃeꞃ pineꞃ bꞃince æꞇ hꝥæᵹa ᵹiꞃ he má pille · bꞃince
háꞇ pæꞇeꞃ. healꝺe hine ᵹeoꞃne pꞃꝺ bæþ · ꞇ hꝥilum
þonne he hiꞇ ᵹeþꞃoꝥian mæᵹe læꞇe him blob on innan
eaꞃme ꞇ ꞃceaꞃpꞃᵹe þa ꞃcancan · æþele læcebom · ꞇ hu
ꞃeo healꞃ ꝺeabe aꝺl · æꞃ ꞃeopeꞃꞇiᵹum oꝺꝺe ꞃiꞃꞇiᵹum
pinꞇꞃa næꞃꞃe on men ne becume.

Sume béc læꞃaꝺ pꞃꝺ þæꞃe healꞃbeaꝺan aꝺle ꝥ man
pinꞇꞃeoꞃ bæꞃnᵹ to ᵹlebum ꞇ þonne þa ᵹleꝺa ꞃeꞇꞇe
toꞃoꞃan þam ꞃeocum men ꞇ ꝥ he þonne onꞇýnꝺum
eaᵹum ꞇ opene muþe þane ꞃéc ꞃpelᵹe þa þꞃaᵹe þe he
mæᵹe · ꞇ þonne he má ne mæᵹe onpenꝺe his neb
apéᵹ lýꞇhpon ꞇ eꞃꞇ penꝺe tó ꞇ onꞃó ꝺam ꞃꞇeme ꞇ ꞃpa
bú ælce ꝺæᵹe oꝺ ꝥ ꞃe bæl þæꞃ lichoman þe þæꞃ aꝺea-
boꝺ pæꞃ ꞇ ᵹelepeꝺ to þæꞃe æꞃꞃan hælo becume.

Soꝺlice ꞃeo aꝺl cýmꝺ on monnan æꞃꞇeꞃ ꞃeopeꞃꞇiᵹum
oꝺꝺe ꞃiꞃꞇiᵹum pinꞇꞃa ᵹiꞃ he biꝺ cealꝺꞃe ᵹecýnꝺo þonne
cýmꝺ æꞃꞇeꞃ ꞃeopeꞃꞇiᵹum elcoꞃ cýmꝺ æꞃꞇeꞃ ꞃiꞃꞇiᵹum
pinꞇꞃa his ᵹæꞃᵹeꞇaleꞃ · ᵹiꞃ hiꞇ ᵹinᵹꞃan men ᵹelimpe
þonne biꝺ ꝥ eaꝺlæcneꞃe · ꞇ ne biꝺ ꞃeo ýlce aꝺl
þeah þe unᵹleape lꝽcaꞃ penan ꝥ ꝥ ꞃeo ýlce healꞃbeaꝺe aꝺl ꞃí. hu ᵹelic aꝺl on man becume on ᵹeo-
ᵹoꝺe on ꞃumum lime ꞃpa ꞃpa ꞃeo healꞃbeaꝺc aꝺl on
ýlbo beꝺ. ne biꝺ hiꞇ ꞃeo healꞃ ꝺeabc aꝺl ac hꝥilc
æꞇhpeᵹa ýꞃel pæꞇc biꝺ ᵹeᵹoꞇen on ꝥ lim þe hiꞇ on
ᵹeꞃiꞇ · ac biꝺ eaꝺlæcneꞃe · ác ꞃeo ꞃoꝺe healꞃbeaꝺe aꝺl
cýmꝺ æꞃꞇeꞃ ꞃiꞃꞇiᵹum pinꞇꞃa.

Giꞃ mon ꞃý þæꞃe healꞃbæban aꝺle ꞃeoc · oꝺꝺe bꞃæc
ꞃeoc · pýnc him oxumelli ꞃuꝺeꞃne eceꝺ bꞃcnc ecebeꞃ ·
ꞇ huniᵹeꞃ · ꞇ pæꞇeꞃeꞃ ᵹemanᵹ.

infusion of them be poured away; then add some good decoction, and give it him to partake of; add a little salt, and oil, and marche, and leek, and such as those. Observe then carefully that the meat be digested, ere one give him *any* again; since the undigested meat worketh him much evil : let him drink some sheer wine; if he want more, let him drink hot water. Let him hold back carefully from the bath, and at whiles, when he may endure it, let him blood on the inner part of the arm, and scarify his shanks. A noble leechdom! And *now*, how the half dead disease never cometh on a man before forty or fifty years of age.

10. Some books teach for the half dead disease, that one should burn a pinetree to gledes, and then set the gledes before the sick man, and that he then, with eyes disclosed and open mouth, should swallow the reek, for what time he may ; and when he is no longer able, he should turn his face away a little, and again turn it to the *hot embers*, and accept the glow; and so do every day, till the part of the body which was deadened and injured come again to its former health.

11. Well, the disease cometh on a man after forty or fifty winters; if he be of a cold nature, then it cometh after forty; otherwise, it cometh after fifty winters of his tale of years; if it happen to a younger man, then it is easier to cure, and it is not the same disease, though unclever leeches ween that it is the same half dead disease. How can a like disease come on a man in youth in one limb, as the half dead disease doth in old age? It is not the half dead disease, but some mischievous humour is effused on the limb, on which the harm settles; but it is easier of cure; and the true half dead disease cometh after fifty years.

12. If a man be sick of the half dead disease, or epileptic, work him οξύμελι, a southern acid drink, a mixture of vinegar, and honey, and water.

Nim eceþeꞃ anne ðæl · huniȝeꞃ tƿeȝen ðælaꞃ pēl
ȝeclæꞃnoðeꞃ · þæteþeꞃ ꝼeoꞃðan · ꞃeoð þonne oð þ
þꞃibban ðæl þæꞃe þætan · oððe ꝼeoꞃðan · ꞃ ꝼleot
þ ꝼam ꞃ þ ꞃot ꞅýmle¹ óꝼ oðþæt hit ȝeꞃoben ꞃi ·
ȝiꝼ þu ƿille þone bꞃenc ꞃtꞃenȝꞃan pýꞃcan · þonne
ðó þu ꞃꝛa mýcel þæꞃ eceþeꞃ ꞃꝛa þæꞃ huniȝeꞃ ꞃ nýtta
þæꞃ læcebomaꞃ ȝe pið þiꞃꞃe able ȝe pið ælceꞃe ꝼul
neah. Nim ꞃimble þæꞃ eceðꞃenceꞃ ꞅꝛa ȝepoꞃhteꞃ
ꞃꝛa mýcel ꞃꝛa þe þince · ðó pið þiꞃꞃum ablum ꞃæbic

on þ ꞃeap þæꞃ bꞃinceꞃ læt beo nihteꞃne ón · ꞅýle
þonne on moꞃȝeꞃiie þam ꞃeocum men · neahtneꞅti-
ȝum þane ꞃæbic ꞅꝛá ȝeꞅeapꞃe to þicȝanne ꞅꝛa he
ꞅpýðuꞅt mæȝe · ꞃ þ þu þanne læꝼe þæꞃ ꞅeapeꞃ
ꞃýððan ꞃe ꞃæbic oꝛe² ꞃý · ȝeot hat þæteꞃi on ꞅýle
bꞃincan þam ꞅeocum men to ꝼýlle. And þonne ýmbe
aneꞃ bæȝeꞃ hꝛile ꞅtinȝe him mon ꝼeþeꞃe on muð
oððe ꝼinȝeꞃ nebe hine to ꞅpiꝛanne. Nim eꝛt eleꞃ
anne ðæl · peaꞃmeꞃ þæteþeꞃ tꝛeȝan · ꞃealteꞃ tꝛeȝan
cuceleꞃ³ ꝼulle menȝ toȝæbeꞃe ꞃýle to bꞃincanne ceac
ꝼulne ꞃ þanne ꞅtinȝe ꝼinȝeꞃ on muð bæbe to ꞅpi-
panne · læt þanne ꞅpipan on þane ýlcan ceac þe he
æꞃ óꝼ bꞃanc ȝeꞅceapa þonne hꝛæðeꞃi þe⁴ ꞅpipða ꞃý
ꞃꝛa micel ꞃꝛa he æꞃi ȝeðꞃanc · ȝiꝼ he maꞃa ꞃý týla
hiꞃ ꞃꝛa · ȝiꝼ he emmicel ꞃi þane⁵ þe he æꞃi ȝeðꞃanc
ꞃýle eꝛt on ða ilcan piꞃan oðþæt he ma ꞅpipe þanne
he ȝeðꞃince æꞃi · þiꞃ ꞃceal ꞅpiþuꞅt pið blæðꞃan able
ꞃ þæm ꞅtanum þe on blæðbꞃan ꞃýn.

Þið þæꞃe healꝼbeaban [able] · Nim þ þæteꞃ þe
pýoꞃan ꞃæꞃan on ȝeꞃobene oꝛeꞃ pilleba ꞃýle bꞃincan
ꞅpiðe þonne ꞃecð⁶ þ þone innoð ꞃ clænꞃað. Eꝛt ꞃýn-

---

¹ ꞅmýle, MS.

² Read oꞃ, for oꞃe.

³ Read cuclepaꞃ.

⁴ On this form, see St. Marharete,
p. 84.

⁵ Read þam.

⁶ Perhaps ꞃecð, *washeth*.

13. Take of vinegar, one part; of honey, well cleansed, two parts; of water, the fourth *part;* then seethe down to the third or fourth part of the liquid, and skim the foam and the refuse off continually, till the *mixture* be *fully* sodden. If thou wish to work the drink stronger, then put as much of the vinegar as of the honey, and use the leechdom either for this disorder, or for full nigh any one. Take always of the acid drink, so wrought, as much as may seem good to thee. For these disorders put a radish into the liquor of the drink; let it be in it for the space of a night; then give in the morning to the sick man, after his nights fast, the radish so liquored to eat, as he best may; and then, when the radish is gone, pour thou hot water on the remains of the liquor; give it to the sick man to drink to the full. And then, after about a days space, let some one poke a feather into his mouth, or a finger; let him compel him to spew. Again, take of oil, one part; of warm water, two; of salt, two spoons full; mingle them together; give to drink a jug full, and then poke a finger into his mouth; bid him spew; let him spew into the same jug from which he before drank; then examine whether the vomit be as much as he ere drank. If it be more, tend him then; if it be just as much as he before drank, give him again in the same wise, till he spew more than he drank before. This must be applied chiefly for disease of bladder, and for the stones which are in the bladder.

14. For the half dead [disease]. Take the water on which peas were sodden, *and* overboiled; give it *the man* to drink. That strongly waketh up and cleanseth

fullan leaf on ƿín gegníden ꝥ clænsað þane innoð. Ƿið þan ilcan eft · elleneſ blosman genim ⁊ gegnid ⁊ gemenge ƿið hunig ⁊ gedó on box · ⁊ þonne þearf si genim bollan fulne hluttres gesƿettes ƿínes gemenge ƿið ꝥ ⁊ afeohhe sýle drincan. Ƿið þan ilcan betan mid hire ƿýrtruman seoð on ƿætere butan sealte · sýle þonne þæs ƿæteres bollan fulne to gedrincanne.

* * * * * * * * *

.LXIV.

* * * * * * * * *

fol. 105 a. ꝥte oþerne healfne pening geƿege gegnid sƿiþe smale
do þonne on hluttor æg ⁊ sele þam men to sup-
anne · hió is sƿiþe god eác on þas ƿisan ƿið hƿostan
⁊ ƿiþ springe do þas ƿyrte on he biþ sona hal. Þis
is balzaman smyring ƿiþ eallum untrumnessum þe on
manneſ lichoman biþ · ƿiþ fefre · ⁊ ƿiþ feinlace ⁊ ƿið
eallum gedƿolþinge. Eal sƿa same se petra oleum he
is god ⁊ feald to drincanne ƿið innan tiedernesse ⁊
utan to smerƿanne on ƿintres dæge for þon þe he
hæfð sƿiðe micle hæte for ðy hine mon sceal drincan
on ƿintra · ⁊ he is god gif hƿam seó spræc oþfylð
nime þonne ⁊ ƿyrce cristes mæl under his tungan ⁊
his an lytel sƿelge · gif món eác of his geƿitte ƿeorðe
ª ælcum? þonne nime he his dæl ⁊ ƿyrce cristes mæl on ælcre[a]
lime butan cruc on þam heafde foran se sceal on
balzame beon ⁊ oþer on þam heafde ufan. Tyriaca
is god drenc ƿiþ eallum innoð tydernessum · ⁊ se
man se þe hine sƿa begæþ sƿa hit her on segð þonne
mæg he him miclum gehelpan. To þam dæge þe he
fol. 105 b. ƿille hine drincan he sceal fæstan oþ midne dæg ⁊ ne
læte hine ƿind beblaƿan þy dæge · ga him þonne ón

the inwards. Again, leaves of houseleek bruised in wine; that cleanseth the inwards. For the same again; take blossoms of elder, and rub them, and mix them with honey, and put them in a box, and when need be, take a bowl full of clear sweetened wine, mingle with that and strain: administer. For the same; seethe beet with its roots in water without salt; then administer a bowl full of the water to drink.

* * * * * * * * *

lxiv.

* * * * * * * * *

so much as may weigh a penny and a half, rub very small, then add the white of an egg, and give it to the man to sip. It (balsam) is also very good in this wise for cough and for carbuncle, apply this wort, soon shall the man be hole. This is smearing with balsam for all infirmities which are on a mans body, against fever, and against apparitions, and against all delusions. Similarly also petroleum is good to drink simple for inward tenderness, and to smear on outwardly on a winters day, since it hath very much heat; hence one shall drink it in winter: and it is good if for anyone his speech faileth, then let him take it, and make the mark of Christ under his tongue, and swallow a little of it. Also if a man become out of his wits, then let him take part of it, and make Christs mark on every limb, except the cross upon the forehead, that shall be of balsam, and the other also on the top of his head. Triacle (θηριακόν) is a good drink for all inward tendernesses, and the man, who so behaveth himself as is here said, he may much help himself. On the day on which he will drink triacle, he shall fast until midday, and not let wind blow on him that day: then let him go to the bath, let him sit there

bæþ ſitte þæn on oð ꝥ he ſpæte · nime þonne ane
cuppan bo an lytel peaƿmeſ pætſeſ on innán nime
þonne ane lytle ſnæb þæſ cyſiacan ꜽ ʒemenʒe¹ piþ ꝥ
pæteſ ꜽ ſeoh þuſh þynne hſæʒl bſince þonne · ꜽ ʒa
him þonne to hiſ ſeſte ꜽ beſſeo hine peaƿme · ꜽ licʒe
ſpa oþ he pel ſpæte · aſiſe þonne ꜽ ſitte him úp ꜽ
ſcinpe hine ꜽ þicʒe ſiþþan hiſ mete to noneſ ꜽ beoſʒe
him ʒeoſne piþ þone pinð þæſ bæʒeſ · þonne ʒelyſe
ic to ʒobe ꝥ hit þam men miclum ʒehelpe. Se hſita
ſtan mæʒ piþ ſtice ꜽ piþ ſleoʒenðum attſe · ꜽ piþ
eallum uncuþum bſocum · þu ſcealt hine ſcaſan on
pæteſ ꜽ bſincan tela micel ꜽ þæſe ſeaban eoſþan bæl
ſcaſe þæſ to ꜽ þa ſtanaſ ſint ealle ſpiðe ʒobe óſ to
bſincanne piþ eallum uncuþlicu þinʒ · ² þonne ꝥ ſyſ
óſ þam ſtane aſleʒen hít iſ ʒob pið liʒetta · ꜽ pið
þunoſſaba ꜽ pið ælceſ cynneſ ʒeðpol þinʒ · ꜽ ʒiſ mon
on hiſ peʒe biþ ʒeðpolob ſlea him anne ſpeaſcan
beſoſan biþ he ſona on ſihtan. þiſ eal het þuſ
fol. 106 a. ſécʒean ælſſebe cyninʒe bomne heliaſ patſiaſcha ón
ʒeſuſalem.

. LXV.

Ʒiſ hoſſ óſſcoten ſie · Nim þonne ꝥ ſeax þe þæt
hæſte ſie ſealo hſyþeſeſ hoſn ꜽ ſien . III. æſene
næʒlaſ ón · Þſit þonne þam hoſſe on þam heaſbe
ſoſan cſiſteſ mæl ꜽ on leoþa ʒehpilcum þe þu ætſeo-
lan mæʒe · Nim þonne ꝥ pineſtſe eaſe þuſh ſtinʒ
ſpiʒenbe · þiſ þu ſcealt bon · ʒenim ane ʒiſbe ſleah
on ꝥ bæc þonne biþ ꝥ hoſſ hal · ꜽ aſſit on þæſ
ſeaxeſ hoſne þaſ poſð · benebicite omnia opeſa
bomini bominum. Sy ꝥ ylſa þe him ſie þiſ him mæʒ
to bote. Þiþ utpæſce bſembel þe ſien beʒen enbaſ

---

¹ After ʒemenʒe, MS. has pe piþ. | ² Read ealle.

till he sweat; then let him take a cup, and put a
little warm water in it, then let him take a little bit
of the triacle, and mingle with the water, and drain
through some thin raiment, then drink it, and let him
then go to his bed and wrap himself up warm, and
so lie till he sweat well; then let him arise and sit
up and clothe himself, and then take his meat at noon,
three hours past midday, and protect himself earnestly
against the wind that day: then, I believe to God,
that it may help the man much. The white stone is
powerful against stitch, and against flying venom, and
against all strange calamities: thou shalt shave it into
water and drink a good mickle, and shave thereto a
portion of the red earth, and the stones are all very
good to drink of, against all strange uncouth things.
When the fire is struck out of the stone, it is good
against lightenings and against thunders, and against
delusion of every kind: and if a man in his way is
gone astray, let him strike himself a spark before him,
he will soon be in the right way. All this Dominus
Helias, patriarch at Jerusalem, ordered *one* to say to
king Alfred.

lxv.

If a horse is elf shot,[1] then take the knife of which
the haft is horn of a fallow ox, and on which are three
brass nails, then write upon the horses forehead Christs
mark, and on each of the limbs which thou may feel
at: then take the left ear, prick a hole in it in silence;
this thou shalt do; then take a yerd, strike *the horse*
on the back, then will it be hole. And write upon the
horn of the knife these words, "Benedicite omnia opera
domini, dominum." Be the elf[2] what it may, this is
mighty for him to amends. Against dysentery, a

---

[1] Elf shot in the Scottish phrase.
[2] The construction as in Ic hit
eom, *I am he*; combined with the

partitive, as Hpilc hæleða, *what
hero*.

292
LÆCE BOC.

on eonþan · ȝenim þone neoppan pynttpuman delf ūp
þpic niȝon fponaf on þa pinftpan hand ꞇ pinȝ þpipa
miSepeпe mei deuf · ꞇ niȝon fiþum paꞇep nopꞇep ·
ȝenim þonne mucȝpypꞇ · ꞇ efelaftan · pyl þaf þpeo [1] on
meolcum oþ þ hy peadian fupe þonne on neaht nepꞇiȝ
ȝode blede fulle hpile æp he oþepпe mete þicȝe · pefte

hine fopꞇe · ꞇ ppeo hine peapme · ȝif ma þeapf fie do
efꞇ fpa · ȝif þu þonne ȝiꞇ þupfe do þpidban piþe ne
þeapfꞇ þu ofꞇop. Ȝif uꞇȝanȝ fopfeꞇen fie ȝenim ȝid-
copпef leafa ȝode hand fulle ꞇ þa pupan peȝbpæban
пioþopeapde · ꞇ doccan þa þe fpimman pille · pyl þaf
þpeo on ealdum ealað fpiþe ꞇ do fealte buꞇepan on
pylle þicce læꞇ dpincan ȝode blede fulle hpile æp oðpum
mete ꞇ ppeoh hine peapme · ꞇ pefte ftille do þuf þpipa
ne þeapf ofꞇoȝ.

Þiþ lunȝen able læcedom dun tæhꞇe · faluie · pude be
healfan þæpe faluian · fefep fuȝian emmicel þapa ꞇpeȝea
pypꞇa þæпe faluian þpeo fpelc dpeopȝe dpoftlan hiepe þe
nu [2] ealпa pypꞇa fypmefꞇ on þa fealfe þe him þifef
læcedomef þeapf fie healde hine ȝeoppe piþ ȝefpeꞇ eala
dpince hluttop eala ꞇ on þæf hluttpan ealað pypꞇe
pylle ȝeonȝe ácpinde ꞇ dpince. Þiþ ūꞇpæпce ȝenim
unfmepiȝпe healfпe cyfe do enȝlifcef huniȝef . III.
fпæba to · pylle on pannan oþ þ hiꞇ bpuniȝe · ȝenim
þonne ȝeonȝpe acpinde hand fulle ꞇ fpa fpiȝende æꞇ
ham ȝebpinȝ ꞇ næfпe in on þone mon fceafe þ ȝpene

on uꞇan pylle þa fæp fpone on cu meolce ȝefpeꞇe mid
þpim fпædum huniȝef þone dpenc þicȝe þonne mid ðy
cyfe æfꞇep dpence . VII. niht eala fopȝa ꞇ meoloc
þicȝe unfupe. Þiþ unlybbum fupe cu buꞇepan . VIIII.

---

[1] Two herbs are named : the chips are third.　　[2] These words are scarcely without error.

bramble of which both ends are in the earth;[1] take the newer root, delve it up, cut up nine chips into the left hand, and sing three times the Miserere mei, deus, and nine times the pater noster; then take mugwort and everlasting, boil these three, *the worts and the chips*, in milk till they get red, then let *the man* sip at night fasting a good dish full, some while before he taketh other meat; let him rest himself soft, and wrap himself up warm; if more need be, let him do so again: if thou still need, do it a third time, thou wilt not need oftener. If the fæcal discharge be lodged, take of the leaves of githcorn a good hand full, and the nether part of the rough waybroad, and the dock which will swim; boil these three in old ale thoroughly and add salt butter, boil it thick, let *the man* drink a good dish full a while before other meat, and let him wrap himself up warm, and let him rest quiet; do this thrice, no need *to do it* oftener.

2. For lung disease, a leechdom; Dun taught it; sage, rue, half as much as of the sage ; feverfue as much as of the two worts ; of pennyroyal three times as much as of the sage ; take thee of it of all worts foremost *to put* into the salve. Let *the man*, who hath need of this leechdom, withhold himself earnestly from sweetened ale, let him drink clear ale, and in the wort of the clear ale let him boil young oak rind, and drink. For dysentery, take an ungreasy half cheese, and four parts of English honey, boil in a pan until it browneth, then take a hand full of young oak rind, and so in silence bring it home, and never *bring* it in to the mans presence, shave off the green outside *the house*, boil the sappy chips in cows milk, sweeten it with three parts of honey, let *the man* take the drink with the cheese, afterwards let him drink : for seven days let him forego ale and take milk not *turned* sour. For poisons; let him sip cows butter for nine mornings, for three,

---

[1] Frequently seen : spontaneous propagation

moɲȝnaɼ . III. ɼopan . VIII. moɲȝnaɼ ceɲɼillan ȝemetlice
on pine þɲubba ðæl pætɲeſ nime þonne hpeɲhpettan
nioþopeaɲðe ȝnið on pyliſc[1] ealo ſpete mið huniȝe
ðɲince þæɲe teoþan niht . to mete þone ðɲenc on þɲeo
þicȝe æt þam þɲim honcɲeðum.

Þiþ þæɲe ȝeolpan aðle . ȝenim nioþopeaɲðe eolenan
ȝeðo þ þu hæbbe on þam ɼoɲman ðæȝe þonne þu hiɲe
æ̃ɲeſt bɲuce on moɲȝen nim þɲeo ſnæða ꝼ þɲeo on niht
ꝼ hiɲe ɼculon beon on huniȝ ȝeſnæð . ꝼ þy æɼteɲan
meɲȝen . IIII. ſnæða ꝼ IIII. on niht . ꝼ þɲiððan meɲȝen . V. ſnæða ꝼ . V. on niht . ꝼ þy ꝼeoɲþan meɲȝen.
. VI. ꝼ VI. on niht.   þeɼ ðɲenc ɼceal piþ þon ilcan.
ȝenim alexanðɲian ꝼ ȝɲunðeſpelȝean cnua ſmale ꝼ bo
to ðɲence on hluttɲum ealað.   ȝiꝼ men ſie ɼæɲlicc
yꝼele pyɲce . III. cɲiſteɼ mæl an on þæɲe tunȝan oþeɲ
on þam heaɼðe . þɲiððe on þam bɲeoſtum ɼona bið ɼel.
To ȝehealðanne lichoman hælo mið ðɲihtneɼ ȝebeðe .
þiɼ iſ æþele læceðom . ȝenim myɲɲan ꝼ ȝeȝnið on ſín
ſpilce ſie tela micel ſteap ꝼul ꝼ þicȝe on niht neɼtiȝ .
ꝼ eꝼt þonne ɲeſtan pille þ ȝehealðeþ punðoɲlice líchoman hælo ꝼ hít eac ðeah piþ ꝼeonðeɼ coſtunȝûm
yꝼlum.

Þonne iſ eꝼt ſe æþeleſta læceðom to þon ilcan . ȝenim
myɲɲan ꝼ hɲit ɲecelſ ꝼ ſaɼman . ꝼ ſaluiam . ꝼ puɲman ꝼ
þæɼ ɲecelſeɼ ꝼ myɲɲan ſy mæɼt . ꝼ þa oþɲe ſyn âpeȝene
þaɲa ſien emɼela . ꝼ ætſomne on moɲteɲe ȝeȝnîðe to
ðuſte ɼette unðeɲ peoɼoð þonne cɲiſteɼ tîð ſie ꝼ
ȝeſinȝe môn . III. mæɼɼan oɼeɲ þa . III. ðaȝaſ on miðne
pinteɲ ꝼ æt ſteɼaneſ tîðe ꝼ Sce Iohanneɼ euanȝe-
liſta ꝼ þa þɲy baȝaɼ þicȝe on pine on neaht neɼtiȝ ꝼ
þ þæɲ to laɼe ſie þæɼ ðuſteɼ haɼa ꝼ ȝehealð ; hit

fol. 107. b.

soap, for eight mornings of chervil, a moderate quantity, in wine, a third part *also* of water; then let him take the netherward part of cucumber, rub it up into foreign ale, sweeten with honey, let *the man* drink *that* the tenth night, for meat let him take the drink at three *times* at the three cock crowings.

3. For the yellow disease; take the netherward part of helenium, contrive that thou mayest have it on the previous day; when first thou usest it, take three pieces in the morning and three at night, and they shall be *bits* of it sliced into honey; and the second morning four pieces, and four at night; and the third morning five pieces, and five at night; and the fourth morning six, and six at night. The following drink shall avail for the same; take alexanders and ground-sel, pound them small, and form them into a potion in clear ale. If a man have sudden ailments, make three marks of Christ, one on the tongue, the second on the head, the third upon the breast, soon he will be well. To keep the body in health with prayer to the Lord: this is a noble leechdom: take myrrh and rub it into wine, so much as may be a good stoup full, and let *the man* take it at night fasting, and again when he will rest; that wonderfully upholdeth the health of the body, and it also is efficacious against the evil temptings of the fiend.

4. This is the noblest leechdom for the same; take myrrh and white frankincense, and savine and sage, and dyeweed, and of the frankincense and of the myrrh let there be most, and let the others be weighed, of them let there be equal quantities; and have them rubbed to dust together in a mortar, have them set under the altar, when it is Christmas tide, and let one sing three masses over them, for three days in mid-winter, and at St. Stephens tide, and St. John the evangelists *day*, and for those three days let *the man* take the *leechdom* in wine at night fasting, and what there is left of the dust hold and keep; it is power-

mæȝ piþ eallum ꝼæn [1] untꞃymneꞃꞃum · ȝe piþ ꝼeꝼꞃe
ȝe piþ lencten able ȝe piþ atꞃe · ȝe piþ yꝼelꞃe lyꝼte.
Ȝeꝼꞃitu eac ꞃecȝeaþ ꞃe þe þone læcebom beȝa ꝥ he
hine mæȝe ȝehealban . XII. monaþ piþ ealꞃa untꞃym-
neꞃꞃa ꝼꞃeceneꞃꞃe.

Þonne eꝼt piꝺ ȝicþan ꝥ eal ꞃe lichoma ꞃy clane ꞃ
hiꝼeꞃ ⁊ ȝlaðeꞃ ⁊ beoꞃhteꞃ · ȝenim ele ⁊ ealðeꞃ pineꞃ
ðꞃærtan emꝼela ðo on moꞃteꞃe ȝemenȝ pel to ꞃomne
⁊ ꞃmiꞃe mib þy þone lichoman on ꞃunnan. Piꝺ ælꝼe
⁊ piþ uncuþum ꞃiðꞃan [2] ȝnið myꞃꞃan on ꝼin ⁊ hꞃiteꞃ
ꞃecelꞃeꞃ em micel · ⁊ ꞃceaꝼ ȝaȝateꞃ bæl þæꞃ ꞃtaneꞃ
on ꝥ ꝼin ðꞃunce . III. moꞃȝenaꞃ neaht neꞃtiȝ oþþe
. VIIII. oþþe . XII. Piþ lonb able pyl peꞃmob ꞃpa ðꞃuȝne
ꞃpa ȝꞃenne ꞃpa þeꞃ he hæbbe on oleo [inꝼiꞃmoꞃum] [3]
oþ ꝥ þæꞃ eleꞃ ꞃie þꞃibban ðæl bepylleb ⁊ ꞃmiꞃe mib
þone lichoman ealne æt ꞃyꞃe · ⁊ mæꞃꞃe pꞃeoꞃt ꞃceal
bon þone læcebom ȝiꝼ man hæꞃþ. Piþ ȝonȝel pꞃæꞃꞃan
bite ꞃmit on iꞃen ꞃpat. Piþ utꞃihte meꞃ ȝeallan ·
blæc ꞃneȝl pyl on meolcum ꞃup on æꝼenne ⁊ on
moꞃȝenne. Deaꞃob ꞃealꝼ muꞃꞃe ⁊ alpe libania ealꞃa
ȝelice ꝼela menȝ piþ eceb ꞃmiꞃe mib ꝥ heaꝼob. Piþ
þon ilcan ꞃpeꞃl ⁊ ꞃpeȝleꞃ æppel muꞃꞃe · ⁊ æȝhꝼilceꞃ
cynneꞃ ꞃecelꞃ niȝon pyꞃta enȝliꞃce · polleie · bꞃembel · æppel · elehtꞃe · biꞃceop pyꞃt · ꝼinul · ꞃuꞃe peȝ-
bꞃæbe · haꞃan ꞃpꞃecel · ꞃio haꞃe pyꞃt · liþ pyꞃt · ealꞃa
þiꞃꞃa emꝼela · oleum [inꝼiꞃmoꞃum] · [3] haliȝ pæteꞃ ·
haliȝ ꞃealt · oþeꞃ ele · ꞃmiꞃe þe mib þyꞃ uꞃan þonne
þu hi ȝnibe.

. LXVI.

Cf. Marbodæus. Be þam ꞃtane þe ȝaȝateꞃ hatte iꞃ ꞃæb ꝥ he . VIII.
mæȝen hæbbe. An iꞃ þonne þunoꞃꞃab biþ ne ꞃceþeꝺ

---

[1] Read ꞃæplicum.
[2] Perhaps miswritten.

[3] The letters have been paled
away purposely.

ful against all dangerous infirmities, either against fever, or against typhus, or against poison, or against evil air. Writings also say, that he who employs the leechdom is able to preserve himself for twelve months against peril of all infirmities.

5. Then again, against itch, and that all the body may be of a clean, and glad, and bright hue : take oil and dregs of old wine, equally much, put them into a mortar, mingle well together, and smear the body with this in the sun. Against an elf and against a strange visitor,¹ rub myrrh in wine and as mickle of white frankincense, and shave off a part of the stone *called* agate into the wine, let him drink *this* for three mornings after his nights fast, or for nine, or for twelve. For land disease *or nostalgia*, boil wormwood so dry (*or*) so green, as he hath there, in oleum infirmorum, *the oil of extreme unction*, till a third part of the oil is boiled away, and smear all the body at the fire with it, and a mass priest shall perform the leechdom, if a man hath means to get one. For a bite of gang-weaving spider, smudge hydromel ² on iron. For diarrhœa, boil in milk horse gall and black snail, sip in the morning and evening. A head salve ; myrrh and aloes, and libanum *or frankincense*, of all a like quantity, mingle with vinegar, smear the head therewith. For the same ; sulfur and swails apple, myrrh and frankincense of every sort ; nine English worts, pulegium, bramble, apple, lupin, bishopwort, fennel, rough waybroad, vipers bugloss, the hoar wort, lithewort, of all these equal quantities ; oil of unction, holy water, holy salt,³ common oil, smear thyself with this upwards *on the head*, when thou hast rubbed *them*.

lxvi.

Of the stone which hight agate. It is said that it hath eight virtues. One is when there is thunder, it

---

¹ Interpreted by Herbarium cxi. 3.
² Perhaps *Sweat*.
³ Salt which has had the formula of benediction pronounced over it.

þam men þe þone ſtan mið him hæfð. Oþeꞃ mæȝen
iſ on ſpa hpilcum huſe ſpa he bið ne mæȝ þæꞃ inne
feonð peſan. þꞃiðde mæȝen iſ þ nan attoꞃ þam men
fol. 108 b.   ne mæȝ ꝛceþþan þe þone ſtan mið him haꝼaþ. Feoꝛþe
mæȝen iſ þ ſe man ꝛe þe þone laþan feonð on him
beaȝollice hæꝼþ ȝiꝼ he þæꝛ ſtaneſ ȝeꝛceaꝛeneſ hpilcne
ðæl on pætan onꝛehð þonne bið ꝛona ſpeotol æteopoð
on him þ æꝛ beaȝol mað. Fiꝼte mæȝen iſ ꝛe þe
æniȝꝛe able ȝeðꝛeht bið ȝiꝼ he þone ſtan on pætan
þiȝeþ him bið ꝛona ꝛel. Syxte mæȝen iſ þ ðꝛycꝛeꝼt
þam men ne ðeꝛeþ ꝛe þe hine mið him hæfð. Seoꝛoþe
mæȝen iſ þ ꝛe þe þone ſtan on ðꝛince onꝛehð he hæꝼþ
þe ſmeþþan lichoman. Eahtoþe iſ þæꝛ ſtaneſ mæȝen
þ nan næðꝛan cynneſ bite þam ꝛceþþan ne mæȝ þe
þone ſtan on pætan byꝛiȝþ.

LXVII.

ðimitte.   Punð eleſ ȝepihð .xii. peneȝum læꝛꝛe þonne punð
pætꝛeſ · ꝛ punð ealoð ȝepihð .vi. peneȝum maꝛe þonne
punð pætꝛeſ · ꝛ .i. punð pineſ ȝepihð .xv. peneȝum
maꝛe þonne .i. punð pætꝛeſ · ꝛ punð huniȝeſ ȝepihð
.xxxiiii. peneȝum maꝛe þonne punð pætꝛeſ · ꝛ .i.
punð buteꝛan ȝepihð · lxxx. peneȝum læꝛꝛe þonne punð
pætꝛeſ · ꝛ punð beoꝛeſ ȝepihð .xxii. peneȝum læꝛꝛe
þonne punð pætꝛeſ · ꝛ i. punð meloꝛeſ ȝepihð .cxv.
peneȝum læꝛꝛe þonne punð pætꝛeſ · ꝛ i. punð beana
ȝepihð .lv. peneȝum læꝛꝛe þonne punð pætꝛeſ · ꝛ xv.
fol. 109 a.   punð[1] pætꝛeſ ȝaþ to ꝛeꝛtꝛe :·

balð habet hunc[2] libꝛum cilð quem conſcꝛibeꝛe iuſꝛit;
Ðic pꝛecoꝛ aꝛꝛibue cunctiſ in nomine cpiꝛti·
Quo[3] nulluſ tollat hunc libꝛum peꝛꝛibuſ a me·
Nec ui nec fuꝛto nec quodam ꝼamine ꝼalꝛo·
Cuꝛ quia[4] nulla mihi tam caꝛa eſt óptima ȝaza·
Quam caꝛi libꝛi quoꝛ cpiꝛti ȝꝛatia comit.

---

[1] An error, read yntꝛan, *ounces.*
[2] hunð, MS.
[3] Read Quod.
[4] Read as Cur? Quia.

doth not scathe the man who hath this stone with him. Another virtue is, on whatsoever house it is, therein a fiend *perhaps enemy* may not be. The third virtue is, that no venom may scathe the man who hath the stone with him. The fourth virtue is, that the man, who hath on him secretly the loathly fiend, if he taketh in liquid any portion of the shavings of this stone, then soon is exhibited manifestly in him, that which before secretly lay hid. The fifth virtue is, he who is afflicted with any disease, if he taketh the stone in liquid, it is soon well with him. The sixth virtue is, that sorcery hurteth not the man, who has *the stone* with him. The seventh virtue is, that he who taketh the stone in drink, will have so much the smoother body. The eighth virtue of the stone is, that no bite of any kind of snake may scathe him who tasteth the stone in liquid.

lxvii.

A pint of oil weigheth twelve pennies [1] less than a pint of water ; and a pint of ale weigheth six pennies more than a pint of water ; and a pint of wine weigheth fifteen pennies more than a pint of water ; and a pint of honey weigheth thirty-four pennies more than a pint of water ; and a pint of butter weigheth eighty pennies less than a pint of water ; and a pint of beer weigheth twenty-two pennies less than a pint of water ; and a pint of meal weigheth 115 pennies less than a pint of water ; and a pint of beans weigheth fifty-five pennies less than a pint of water ; and fifteen ounces of water go to the sextarius.[2]

---

[1] This is the Saxon silver penny of twenty-four grains, our penny-weight.

[2] " Sextarius medicinalis habet " uncias decem." Plin. Valer. Pref.

[*Book III.*]

Þɪþ heaɼoð ece · Ᵹ pɪþ ealðum heaɼoð ece · Ᵹ pɪþ
healɼeɼ heaɼðeɼ ece. II. Þɪþ aſpollenum eaȝum Ᵹ ȝoð
eah ɼealɼ · Ᵹ pɪð mɪſte on eaȝan Ᵹ pɪð ɼlɪe · Ᵹ pɪð pyp_mum on eaȝum Ᵹ pɪþ þæm ȝɪɼ ɼlæɼc on eaȝum peaxe ·
Ᵹ ȝɪ́ɼ on eaȝum peaxan ɲeaðe ſponȝe · Ᵹ ȝɪɼ eaȝan
typen Ᵹ ɼceaðe ɼealɼ to eaȝum · Ᵹ ſmeþe eah
ɼealɼ.
.III. Þɪþ eaɲpæɲce Ᵹ pɪþ þæm ȝɪɼ pypmaſ ɪɲyn on
eaɲan Ᵹ ȝoð eaɲ ɼealɼ. IIII. Þɪþ toþ ece Ᵹ ȝɪɼ teþ ſyn
hole.
.V. Þɪþ ɪnnan toðɲocenum muðe .VI. Þɪþ ceoc aðle
Ᵹ pɪþ ceol pæɲce. VII. Þɪþ healɼ pæɲce. VIII. Þɪþ
bɪte. VIIII. Þɪþ hpoſtan. X. Þɪþ þam þe mōn bloðe
hɲæce. XI. Þɪþ ɼeonðum ȝeallan. XII. Þɪþ þæɲe
ȝeolpan aðle. XIII. Þɪþ bɲeoſt pæɲce. XIIII. Þɪþ
hpoſtan Ᵹ pɪþ lunȝen aðle. XV. Þɪþ maȝan pæɲce Ᵹ
pɪþ aþunðeneɼɼe. XVI. Þɪð mɪlt pæɲce.

.XVII. Þɪþ lɪnðen pæɲce. XVIII. Þɪþ pambe pæɲce
Ᵹ ɲyɼel pæɲce. XVIIII. Þɪþ blæðbeɲ pæɲce.
.XX. Þɪþ þam ȝɪɼ man ne mæȝe ȝemɪȝan Ᵹ þam
men þe ſtanaſ peaxan oɲ þæɲe blæðɲan. XXI. Þɪþ
þam ȝɪɼ men ſie ſe utȝánȝ ɼoɲſeten. XXII. Þɪþ utɪɲɪht
aðle ðɲenc Ᵹ bɲɪp. XXIII. Þɪþ þam pyɲmum þe beoþ
on manneɼ ɪnnoþe. XXIIII. Þɪþ lɪð pæɲce. XXV. Þɪþ
peaɲtum. XXVI. Þɪð þam mɪclan lɪce ſmɪɲɪnȝ Ᵹ bæþ
Ᵹ ðɲenc Ᵹ bɲɪp. XXVII. Þɪþ ſinȝalum þuɲſte un-
tɲumɲa manna. XXVIII. Þɪþ ɪnnan ɼoɲtoȝe Ᵹ ſmæl
þeaɲma ece. XXVIIII. Þɪþ þam þe man ſie mɪð ɼyɲe
anum ɼoɲbæɲneð Ᵹ pɪþ þam þe man ſie mɪð pætan
ɼoɼbæɲneð · Ᵹ pɪþ ſunbɲyne. XXX. Þɪþ þeoɲe ðɲenc
Ᵹ eɼt pɪþ þæɲeᵃ Ᵹ ſceotenðum penne Ᵹ eɼt beþɪnȝ pɪþ
þam ȝɪɼ þeoɲ ȝepunɪȝe on anɲe ſtope. XXXI. Þɪþ
penne ɼealɼ. XXXII. Þɪþ ðolȝe ɼealɼ. XXXIII. Þɪþ þam

Book III.

ȝiꝼ man ſie uꝼan on heaꝼoð punð Ᵹ ſie ban ȝebꞃocen
Ᵹ ƿiþ þam ȝiꝼ ſio eaxl upſtiȝe . Ᵹ ȝoð ðolh ðꞃenc
Ᵹ ȝiꝼ ȝebꞃocen ban ſie on heaꝼðe Ᵹ oꝼ nelle. XXXIIII.
Ƿiþ hunðeꞃ ꞃlite Ᵹ ƿiþ þon ȝiꝼ ꞃinꝛe ꝼoꞃcoꞃꝼene Ᵹ ƿiþ

þam ȝiꝼ ſinꝛe ſien ȝeſcꞃuncene. XXXV. Ƿiþ ȝonȝe-
ꝛiꝼꞃan bite. XXXVI. Ƿiþ cancꞃe. XXXVII. Ƿiþ þam þe
ꝼiꝼ ne mæȝe beaꞃn acennan Ᵹ ȝiꝼ oꝼ ꝛiꝼe nelle ȝan
æꝼteꞃ þam beoꞃþꞃe Ᵹ ȝecynðelic ſie . Ᵹ ȝiꝼ oꝼ[1] ꝛiꝼe ſie
ðeað beaꞃn. Ᵹ ƿiþ þam ȝiꝼ ꝛiꝼ bleðe to ſꝛiþe æꝼteꞃ
þam beoꞃþꞃe. XXXVIII. Ƿiþ þam þe ꝛiꝼum ſie ꝼoꞃſtan-
ðen hiꞃa monað ȝecynð Ᵹ ƿiþ þam ȝiꝼ ꝛiꝼe to ſꝛiþe
oꝼꝼlope ſio monoþ ȝecynð. XXXVIIII. Ƿiþ ſmeaȝea
ꝛyꞃme ſmiꞃinȝ Ᵹ anleȝen. Ᵹ beþinȝ Ᵹ ꞃealꝼ. XL. Ƿiþ
þam þe man ſie monaþ ſeóc. [XLI.][2] Ƿiþ ealle ꞃeonðeꞃ
coꝼtunȝa ðꞃenc Ᵹ ꞃealꝼ. Ƿiþ þon ilcan Ᵹ hu man ꞃcyle
ȝeꝛitſeocne man lácnian. Ᵹ hu mon ꞃcyle ꝛyꞃcean
ſꝛiꝛðꞃenc utyꞃnenðum. XLII. Ƿiþ þam ȝiꝼ ſꝛiꝛðꞃenc on
men ȝeſittan[3] Ᵹ he nelle utȝan. XLIII. Ƿiþ attꞃeꞃ
ðꞃence. [XLIIII.][4] Ƿiþ luꞃum. XLV. Ƿiþ þam ȝiꝼ þoꞃn
ſtinȝe mon on ꝼót oððe hꞃeoð Ᵹ þonne nelle oꝼȝan.
XLVI. Ƿiþ æꞃmælum Ᵹ ƿiþ eallum eaȝna pæꞃce. XLVII.
Ƿiþ lyꝼt aðle ȝiꝼ ſe muþ ſie poh oþþe þon læcebom Ᵹ
beþinȝ Ᵹ bæþ ꞃealꝼ Ᵹ leah Ᵹ bloðeꞃ læꞃ. XLVIII. Ƿiþ
ꞃic aðle ðꞃenc Ᵹ beþinȝ. XLVIIII. Ƿiþ ſculðoꝗ pæꞃce

Ᵹ eaꞃma. L. Ƿiþ cneopa ꞃaꞃe. LI. Ƿiþ ꝼota ꞃaꞃe. LII.
Ƿiþ þam ȝiꝼ þu ne mæȝe bloð ðolȝ ꝼoꞃꞃꞃiþan. LIII.
Ƿiþ þam ȝiꝼ meolóc ſie ȝeꞃeꞃð. LIIII. Ƿiþ niht ȝenȝean
ꞃealꝼ. LV. Ƿiþ þam ȝiꝼ men beo ſio heaꝼoð panne
ȝehlenceð. LVI. Ƿið þam ȝiꝼ men nelle meltan hiꞃ
mete. LVII. Ƿiþ ꝼiꝼ ȝemæðlan. LVIII. Ƿiþ ꝼeonðeꞃ
coꝼtunȝa. LVIIII. Ƿiþ þeoꝗ penne ȝiꝼ he ſie men on
cneope oþþe on oꝙꞃum lime. LX. be þam hu món
ꞃcyle eaꞃ ꞃealꝼe ꝛyꞃcean.

. LXI. Ƿiþ ælꝼ cynne ꞃealꝼ Ᵹ ƿiþ niht ȝenȝan . Ᵹ

---

the head and bone be broken, and in case the shoulder rise *by dislocation*, and a good wound drink, and if a broken bone be in the head and will not come away. 34. For tear by a hound, and if sinews be cut through, and in case sinews be shrunken. 35. For the bite of the gangwayweaving spider. 36. For cancer. 37. In case a woman may not kindle a child, and if, after the birth, that which is natural will not come away from a woman; and in case there be a dead bairn in a woman, and in case a woman bleed too much after the birth. 38. In case womens natural catamenia be stopped, and in case the natural catamenia flow too freely. 39. A smearing, and an onlaying, and a fomentation, and a salve against a boring worm. 40. In case a man be a lunatic. 41. A drink and a salve for all temptations of the fiend. For the same, and how one must treat a deranged man; and how a man shall work a spew drink for those that have diarrhœa. 42. In case a strong dose lodge in a man and will not come away. 43. Against a drink of poison. 44. Against lice. 45. In case a thorn, or a reed, prick a man in the foot, and will not be got rid of. 46. Against imminutions and all pain of eyes. 47. Against palsy, if the mouth be awry or livid, a leechdom and a fomentation, and a bath salve, and ley and bloodletting. 48. Drink and fomentation for "fig" dieease. 49. For pain of shoulder blade and arms. 50. For sore of knees. 51. For sore of feet. 52. In case thou be not able to bind up a bloodletting incision. 53. In case milk is turned sour. 54. A salve against night comers, *incubi, etc.* 55. In case a mans skull is "linked," *or seems to feel bound round.* 56. In case a mans meat will not digest. 57. Against womens prating. 58. Against temptations of the fiend. 59. Against a "dry" wen, if a man hath it on his knee or on another limb. 60. Of this; how a man must work an earsalve. 61. A salve against the elfin race and night goblins, and for the *women,*

þam monnum þe ðeoꝼol miꝺ hæmð. LXII. Ƿiþ ælꝼ
able læceꝺom ⁊ eꝼt hu mōn ꞃceal on þa ƿyꞃte ꞃinᵹan
æꞃ hi mōn nime ⁊ eꝼt hu mon ꞃceal þa ƿyꞃta ꝺon
unꝺeꞃ peoꝼoꝺ ⁊ oꝼeꞃ ſinᵹan · ⁊ eꝼt tacnu be þam
hƿæþeꞃ hit ſie ælꝼ ꞃoᵹoþa ⁊ tacn hu þu onᵹitan
meaht hƿæþeꞃ hine mōn mæᵹ ᵹelacnian ⁊ ꝺꞃencaſ ⁊
ᵹebeꝺu ƿiþ ælcꞃe ꝼeonꝺeꞃ coſtunᵹe. LXIII. Tacnu hu
þu meaht onᵹitan hƿæþeꞃ mōn ſie on pæteꞃ ælꝼ able ·
⁊ læceꝺom ƿiþ þam ⁊ ᵹealꝺoꞃ on to ſinᵹanne ⁊ ꝥ ilce
mōn mæᵹ ſinᵹan on punꝺa. LXIIII. Ƿiꝺ ꝺeoꝼle liþe
ꝺꞃenc · ⁊ unᵹemynꝺe · ⁊ ƿiþ ꝺeoꝼleſ coſtunᵹa. LXV.

fol. 111 a.

Ƿiþ þon ᵹiꝼ mon ſie ᵹeᵹymeꝺ ⁊ tacnu hƿæþeꞃ he
libban mæᵹe. LXVI. ꝺꞃenc ƿiþ þam ᵹiꝼ þeoꞃ ſie on
men. LXVII. Ƿiþ ꝺeoꝼle ſeoce ⁊ ƿiþ ꝺeoꝼle. LXVIII.
Ƿiþ peꝺen heoꞃte leoht ꝺꞃenc. LVIIII. Ƿiþ þam¹ ᵹiꝼ
men ſie maᵹa aſuꞃoꝺ ⁊ ꝼoꞃþunꝺen · ⁊ ƿiþ maᵹan
pæꞃce · ⁊ ᵹiꝼ man biþ aþunꝺen. LXX. Ƿiþ pambe
pæꞃce · ⁊ ƿiþ maᵹan pæꞃce · ⁊ ƿiþ pambe heaꞃꝺneꞃꞃe.
LXXI. Ƿiꝺ ſpꞃinᵹe ſmiꞃinᵹ ⁊ ſealꝼ. LXXII. Ƿiþ attꞃe
ꝺꞃenc ⁊ ſmiꞃinᵹ. LXXIII. Ƿiþ þæꞃe ᵹeolpan able.
LXXIIII. Ƿiþ þam ᵹiꝼ innelꝼe ſi ute. LXXV. Ƿiþ
ælcꞃe innan untꞃymneꞃꞃe ⁊ ƿiþ heꞃiᵹneꞃꞃe ⁊ ƿiþ
hleoꞃblæce. LXXVI. be þam hu mān ſcyle haliᵹe
ꞃealꝼe ƿyꞃcean.

. I.

Ƿiþ þon þe mōn on heaꝼoꝺ ace · ᵹenim nioþo-
peaꞃꝺe pꞃætte ꝺo on ꞃeaꝺne pꞃæꝺ binꝺe ꝥ heaꝼoꝺ miꝺ.
Ƿiþ þon ilcan · nim ſeneꝼeꞃ ꞃæꝺ ⁊ ꞃuꝺun ᵹeᵹniꝺ on ele
ꝺo on hat pæteꞃ þpeah ᵹelome ꝥ heaꝼoꝺ on þam pætꞃe
he biþ hal. Ƿiþ ealꝺum heaꝼoꝺ ece ᵹenim ꝺꞃeoꞃᵹe

---

¹ Ƿiþũ, MS.

with whom the devil hath commerce. 62. Against elf disease, a leechdom; and again, how one must sing upon the worts, ere one take them; and again, how one must put the worts under the altar, and sing over them; and again tokens of this, whether it be elf hicket, and tokens how thou mayst understand, whether one may cure the man; and drinks and prayers against every temptation of the fiend. 63. Tokens how thou mayst understand whether a man be in the water elf disease, and a leechdom for that, and a charm to be sung upon it, and that ilk may be sung over wounds. 64. A lithe *or soft* drink against the devil, and want of memory, and against temptations of the devil. 65. In case a man be overlooked, and tokens whether he may live. 66. A drink in case the "dry" disease be on a man. 67. For the devil sick *or demoniac*, and against the devil. 68. A light drink against the wild heart. 69. In case a mans maw be soured and distended; and against pain of the maw, and if a man be inflated. 70. For pain of the wamb, and for pain of the maw, and for hardness of the wamb. 71. Against carbuncle; an ointment and a salve. 72. A drink and smearing against venom. 73. For the yellow disease, *jaundice.* 74. In case the bowels be out. 75. For every inward infirmity, and for heaviness, and for cheek blotch. 76. Of this, how a man must make a holy salve.

i.

In case a man ache in the head; take the netherward part of crosswort,[1] put it on a red fillet, let him bind the head therewith. For that ilk, take seed of mustard and rue, rub into oil, put into hot water, wash the head often in the water, *the man* will be hale. For an old head ache, take pennyroyal, boil in oil, or

---

[1] *Galium cruciatum.*

ðpoſtlan pyl on ele oððe on butpan ſmıpe mıð[1] þa
þunponȝan Ꝫ bupan þam eaȝum on upan ꝥ heapoð
þeah hım ſıe ȝemynð oncypped he bıþ hal. Þıþ ſpıþe

ealdum heapoð ece nım pealt Ꝫ puðan Ꝫ ıfıȝ cpop cnua
ealle to pomne[2] ðo on hunıȝ Ꝫ ſmıpe mıð þa þunpanȝan · Ꝫ þone hnıpel Ꝫ upan ꝥ heapoð. To þon ılcan
pec lytle ſtanaſ on ſpealpan bpıðða maȝan Ꝫ healð ꝥ
hıe ne hpınan eonþan ne pætpe · ne oþpum ſtanum
bepeopa hıpa . III. on þon þe þu pılle ðo on þone mon
þe hım þeapf ſıe hım bıþ pona pel · hı beoþ ȝobe pıþ
heapoð ece Ꝫ pıþ eaȝpænce Ꝫ pıþ feonðep coſtunȝa Ꝫ
nıhtȝenȝan · Ꝫ lencten aðle Ꝫ mapan Ꝫ pyptfopbope ·
Ꝫ malſcpa · Ꝫ yflum ȝealðoȝ cpæftum · hıt ſculon beon
mıcle bpıððap þe þu hıe pcealt on fınðan · ȝıf mon on
healf heapoð ace ȝecnua puðan ſpıþe ðo on ſtpanȝ eceð
Ꝫ ſmıpe mıð ꝥ heapoð upan pıhte. Þıþ þon ılcan aðelf
peȝbpæðan butan ıſene æp ſunnan upȝanȝe bınð þa
mopan ymb ꝥ heapoð mıð ppæte peaðe ppæðe pona
him bıð pel.

.II.

Þıþ aſpollenum eaȝum ȝenım cucune hpepn[3] aðo
þa eaȝan of Ꝫ eft cucune ȝebpınȝ on pætpe Ꝫ ðo þa
eaȝan þam men on ſpeopan þe hım þeapf pıe he bıþ
pona hal. Þypıc ȝoðe eaȝpealfe Nım celeþonıan Ꝫ
bıpceop pypt · pepmoð · puðu mepce · puðu bınðep
leap · ðo ealpa empela cnupa pel ðo on hunıȝ · Ꝫ on
pin · Ꝫ on æpen fæt oððe on cypepen ðo tpæðe þæp
pınep · Ꝫ þpıððan ðæl þæp hunıȝep ðo ꝥ pe pæta mæȝe
fupþum ofep ypnan þa pypta læt ſtanðan . VII. nıht
Ꝫ ppeoh mıð bpeðe aſeoh þuph clænne claþ ðone ðpenc
ðo eft on ꝥ ılce fæt nytta ſpa þe þeapf pıe. Se mon

---

[1] The MS. has a stop after mıð.　　[2] Nearly as Marcellus, col. 269 f.
[3] pome, MS.

in butter, smear therewith the temples, and over the
eyes, and on the top of the head; though his intellect
be deranged, he will be hale. For a very old head
ache; take salt and rue, and a bunch of ivy berries,
pound all at once, add honey, and therewith smear the
temples, and the forehead, and the top of the head.
For that ilk; seek in the maw of young swallows for
some little stones, and mind that they touch neither
earth, nor water, nor other stones; look out three of
them; put them on the man, on whom thou wilt, him
who hath the need, he will soon be well. They are
good for head ache, and for eye wark, and for the fiends
temptations, and for night *goblin* visitors, and for
typhus, and for the *night* mare, and for knot, and for
fascination, and for evil enchantments by song. It must
be big nestlings on which thou shalt find them. If a
man ache in half his head, pound rue thoroughly, put
it into strong vinegar, and smear therewith the head,
right on the top. For that ilk; delve up waybroad
without iron, ere the rising of the sun, bind the roots
about the head, with crosswort, by a red fillet, soon
he will be well.

ii.

For swollen eyes, take a live crab, put his eyes out,
and put him alive again into water, and put the eyes
upon the neck of the man, who hath need; he will soon
be well. Work a good eye salve *thus;* take celandine
and bishop wort, wormwood, wood marche, leaves of
woodbind; put equal quantities of all, pound them well,
put them into honey, and into wine, and into a brazen
vessel, or a copper one; put in of the wine two parts
in three, and a third part of the honey, order it so
that the liquor may just overrun the worts; let it
stand for seven nights, and wrap it up with a piece
of stuff; strain the drink through a clean cloth, put it
again into that ilk vessel, use as occasion may be.

ꞃe him ȝebeþ ymb .xxx. nihta ꝼoxeꞃ ȝelynbeꞃ bæl
on þa eaȝan he biþ ece hal;

ȝiꝼ miꞅt ꞃie ꝼoꞃe eaȝum nim cilbeꞃ hlonb ⁊ huniȝeꞃ
teaꞃ menȝ toꞃomne beȝea emꝼela ꞅmiꞃe mib þa eaȝan
Innan;

Eꝼt hꞃeꝼneꞃ ȝeallau ⁊ leaxeꞃ ⁊ eleꞃ ⁊ ꝼelb beon
huniȝ menȝ to ꞃomne ꞅmiꞃe mib þæꞃe ꞃealꝼe innan þa
eaȝan;

Þiþ ꝼlie ȝebæꝼneb ꞃealt ⁊ ꞅpeȝleꞃ æppel ⁊ attꞃum
ealꝼa emꝼela ȝnib to buꞅte ⁊ bo on þa eaȝan þꞃealh
leohtlice mib pylle pætꞃe ⁊ ꞅmiꞃe æꝼteꞃ mib piꝼeꞃ
meolce;

ȝiꝼ pyꞃmaꞅ ꞅien on eaȝum ꞃceaꞃpa þa bꞃæpaꞃ innan
bo on þa ꞃceaꞃpan celeþonian ꞃeap· þa pyꞃmaꞅ bioþ
beabe ⁊ þa eaȝan hale. ȝiꝼ ꝼlæꞃc on eaȝum peaxe
pꞃinȝ pyꞃm pyꞃte on þa eaȝan oþ þ him ꞃel ꞃie.

ȝiꝼ on eaȝan peaxen ꞃeabe ꞅponȝe bꞃype on hat
culꝼꞃan blob oþþe ꞅpealpan uððe piꝼeꞃ meoluc oþ þ þa
ꞅponȝe apeȝ ꞃynb. ȝiꝼ eaȝan tyꞃien nim bꞃiȝe ꞃuban
⁊ huniȝeꞃ teaꞃ menȝ toꞃomne læt ꞅtanban .iii. niht

apꞃinȝ þuꞃh þicne clað linenne ⁊ bo on þa eaȝan
ꞃiþþan. Þyꞃc ȝobe bꞃiȝe ꞅcabe ꞅealꝼe nim ꞅpeȝleꞃ
æppel ⁊ ȝebæꝼneb ꞃealt ⁊ piꞃoꞃ ⁊ attꞃum ⁊ liꞃt
cpubu ȝeȝnib to buꞅte aꞃiꞃt þuꞃh clað bo lytlum on.
Eꝼt hꞃit cpubu ⁊ ȝebæꝼneb ofteꞃ ꞃcyl ȝnib to buꞅte
⁊ nytta ꞅpa þe þeaꞃf ꞅie æȝþeꞃ mæȝ abon ꝼlie oꝼ
eaȝan. Þyꞃc ꞅmeþe eaȝꞃealꝼe nim buteꞃan pyl on
pannan aꝼleot þ ꝼam oꝼ ⁊ ahlyttꞃe þa buteꞃan on
blebe bo eꝼt þ hluttꞃe on pannan ȝecnua celeþonian

The man who putteth upon his eyes for about thirty nights, part of the suet of a fox, he will be for ever healthy.

2. If there be a mist before the eyes, take a childs urine and virgin honey, mingle together of both equal quantities, smear the eyes therewith on the inside.

3. Again, mingle together a crabs gall,[1] and a salmons, and an eels, and field bees honey, smear the eyes inwardly with the salve.

4. Against a white spot in the eye; rub to dust burnt salt, and swails apple, and olusatrum, of all equal quantities, rub to dust, and put on the eyes, wash lightly with spring water, smear afterwards with womans milk.

5. If there are worms in the eyes, scarify the lids within, apply to the scarifications the juice of celandine; the worms will be dead and the eyes healthy. If flesh wax on eyes, wring wormwort into the eyes, till they are well.

6. If red sponges wax on the eyes, drop on them hot culvers blood, or swallows, or womans milk, till the sponges be got rid of. If eyes are bleared, take dry rue and virgin honey, mingle together, let it stand for three nights, wring through a thick linen cloth, and afterwards apply to the eyes. Work a good dry salve for dim vision thus: take swails apple, and burnt salt, and pepper, and olusatrum, and mastich; rub to dust, sift through a cloth, apply by little and little. Again, reduce to dust mastich, and burnt oyster shell, and use as need be; either hath power to remove white spot from the eyes. Work a smooth eyesalve *thus*; take butter, boil in a pan, skim the foam off, and purify the butter in a dish; put the clear part again into a pan; pound celandine

---

[1] " Corvi marini fel." Marcellus, col. 277. F. If that passage were in view, this fish would be the mullet, *Mugil cefalus*: but I follow the passage in Wanley, p. 168 a. Hæÿepn is another spelling.

ꞇ biſceop pyꞃꞇ · puðu meꞃce · Ᵹyl ſpiþe aꞃeoh þuꞃh
cla𝛿 nyꞇꞇa ſpa þe þeaꞃꝼ ſie ;

.III.

Ꝥiþ eaꞃi pæꞃce ȝenim henne ȝelynðo ꞇ oſꞇeꞃ ꞃcylle
ꞃeꞇe on ȝleða ȝepyꞃm hꞃon ꞇ ðꞃyp on þa eaꞃan ſona
beo𝛿 hale; Eꝼꞇ celenðꞃan[1] ꞃeap ꞇ piꝼeꞃ meoluc ȝepӯꞃm
on ꞃcylle ꞇ ðꞃyp on þa eaꞃan · ȝiꝼ pyꞃmaſ ꞃien on
eaꞃan ðo belenan ꞃeap peaꞃm on þa pyꞃmaſ hie beoþ
ðeaðe ꞇ ꞃealla𝛿 oꝼ ꞇ þa eaꞃan hale.

Eꝼꞇ pꞃinȝ cuꞃmeallan ꞃeap on oþþe maꞃubian o𝛿𝛿e
peꞃmoð peaꞃmne Sona hîm bi𝛿 ꞃel. Pyꞃc ȝoðe eaꞃi
ꞃealꝼe · ȝenim baꞃeꞃ ȝeallan · ꞇ ꞃeaꞃꞃeſ · ꞇ ele ealꞃa
emꞃela læꞇ ðꞃypan peaꞃm on ꝥ eaꞃe.

.IIII.

Ꝥiþ ꞇoþ ece ceop piꞃoꞃi ȝelome mið þam ꞇoþum
him biþ ꞃona ꞃel. Eꝼꞇ ꞃeo𝛿 beolenan moꞃan on
ſꞇꞃanȝum eceðe oþþe on piꞃie ꞃeꞇe on þone ꞃaꞃan ꞇoþ
ꞇ hꞃilum ceope mið þy ꞃaꞃan ꞇoþe he bi𝛿 hal. ȝiꝼ þa
ꞇeþ ſynð hole ceop boþeneꞃ[2] moꞃan mið eceðe on þa
healꝼe.

.V.

Ꝥiþ innan ꞇobꞃocenum mu𝛿e nim plûm ꞇꞃeopeꞃ leaꝼ
Ᵹyl on piꞃie ꞇ ſpile mið þone muþ :·

.VI.

Vi𝛿 ceoc aðle nim þone hꝼeopꞃan þe ꝼiꝼ mið
ſpinna𝛿 binð on hiꞃ ſpeoꞃan mið pyllenan þꞃæðe ꞇ

_____

[1] Read celeþenian.
[2] boȝeneꞃ, with ȝe dotted, and þe written above, MS.

and bishopwort, wood marche, boil thoroughly, strain
through a cloth; use as need may be.

iii.

1. Against earwark; take a hens fat and oyster
shells, set them on gledes, warm a little, and drip into
the ears, soon they will be hale. Again, warm juice of
coriander (*celandine rather ?*) and womans milk in a
shell, and drop *them* into the ears. If worms be in
the ears ; apply juice of henbane warm, to the worms,
they will be dead and fall off, and the ears will be
well.

2. Again, wring juice of centaury upon them, or
marrubium, or wormwood warm ; soon they will be
well. Work a good earsalve *thus :* take a boars and
a bulls gall, and oil, of all equal quantities, have *this*
dropped warm into the ear.

iv.

For tooth ache ; chew pepper frequently with the
teeth, it will soon be well with them. Again, seethe
henbane roots in strong vinegar or in wine, set this
into the sore tooth, and at whiles chew with the sore
tooth ; it will be well. If the teeth are hollow, chew
rosemary roots with vinegar on that part.

v.

For a mouth troubled with eruption within ; take
leaves of plum tree, boil in wine, and swill the mouth
therewith.

vi.

For cheek disease, take the whorl, with which a
woman spinneth, bind on *the mans* neck with a
woollen thread, and swill him on the inside with hot

fpıle ınnan mıð haꞇe ȝaꞇe meolcc hım bıþ ꞅel. Pıð
ceol ꞃæpce aðelꝼ æp ꞅunnan úpȝanȝe peȝbꞃæðan bınð
on híꞅ ꞅpeopan. Eꝼꞇ bæpn ꞅpealpan ꞇo ðuꞅꞇe · ꟾ menȝ
pıþ ꝼelðbeon hunıȝ ꞅele hım eꞇan ȝelome.

.VII.

Pıþ healꞅ ꞃæpcc pyl neoþepeapðe ncꞇelan on oxan
ꞅmeppe ꟾ on buꞇepan þonne[1] þone healꞅpæꞃc ꞅmıpe ða
þeoh · ȝıꝼ þa þeoh ꞃæpce ꞅmıpe þonc healꞅ mıð þæpe
ꞅealꝼe. Eꝼꞇ pyl nıþepeapðe neꞇelan on ecebe ðo oxan
ȝeallan on ꝥ eceð ꟾ þa pypꞇe óꞅ ꞅmıpe mıð þone
healꞅ.

.VIII.

Vıþ bıꞇe pyꞃc ꞅealꝼe · nım þaꞅ pypꞇe ꞅaꞃenan ꟾ
meꞃꞅc mealpan ꟾ aꞇꞇoꞃlaþan ꟾ peoþobenð ꟾ hpeꞃhpeꞇ-
ꞇan ꟾ cluꝼpypꞇ ꟾ ꞅıȝel hþeopꞃan · hınð heoloþan ·
mucȝpypꞇ · puðu ꝼıllan · ȝapclıꞃan · pꞃæꞇꞇe · luꞅeꞅꞇıce ·
maȝeþan · ȝıþcopn · pað · ꞅınul · þeꞃan þopn · ꞅelꝼæꞇe ·
coꞃoꞃþꞃoꞇe · cıcena meꞇe · ðulhꞃune · pylıꞅc mopu ·
hnuꞇ beameꞅ leaꞅ · næp · ȝcappe · hoꞃe · hóc leaꞅ ·
alexanðꞃe · ꞅıca peꞃꞅıca ·[2] ꞅe ꞅula peꞃmoð · ꞅıo ȝꞃeaꞇe
banpypꞇ · acleaꞅ · peȝbꞃæðe · ȝꞃunðe ꞅpelȝe · ꞃeað
clæꞃꞃe · leahꞇꞃıc · þuꞃe þıꞅꞇel · ꞇapu · heȝe clıꞃe · cluꞅ
þunȝ · enȝlıꞃc mopu · ðynıȝe.

.VIIII.

Pıþ hpoꞅꞇan pyl maꞃubıan on pæꞇꞃe ȝoðne ðæl ȝeꞅpeꞇ hpon ꞅele bꞃıncan ꞃcenc ꝼul.[3] Eꝼꞇ maꞃubıan ꞅpıðe
pyl on hunıȝe ðo hpon buꞇepan on ꞅele .III. ꞅnæða
oþþe .IIII. eꞇan on neahꞇ neꞅꞇıȝ beꞅup ꞅcenc ꝼulne mıð
peaꞃmeꞅ þæꞅ æppan ðꞃenceꞅ.

LEECH BOOK. III. 313

goats milk; it will be well with him. For jowl pain;
delve up waybroad before the rising of the sun, bind
upon *the mans* neck. Again, burn a swallow to dust,
and mingle *him* with field bees honey; give the man Apis silvarum.
that to eat frequently.

vii.

For neck pain; boil the netherward part of nettle
in fat of ox and in butter, then for the hals wark,
smear the thighs; if the thighs be in pain, smear the
neck with the salve. Again, boil the netherward part
of nettle in vinegar, add ox gall to the vinegar and
remove the wort; smear the neck therewith.

viii.

For cancer, work a salve; take these worts, savine,
and marsh mallow, and attorlothe, and withywind,
and cucumber, and clovewort, *or ranunculus,* and
turnsol, hindheal, mugwort, wild chervil, agrimony,
crosswort, lovage, maythe, githcorn, woad, fennel, tufty
thorn, wildoat, everthroat, chickenmeat, pellitory, carot,
leaves of the nut tree, nepeta *cattaria,* yarrow, hove,
hollyhock, alexanders, vinca pervinca, *or periwinkle,*
the foul wormwood, the great bonewort, oak leaves,
waybroad, groundsel, red clover, lettuce, tufty thistle,
tar, hedge clivers, cloffing, wild parsnip, * * * *

ix.

For host *or cough*; boil marrubium in water, a good
deal *of it,* sweeten a little, give *the man* to drink a
cup full. Again, boil marrubium strongly in honey,
add a little butter, give three or four bits for *the man*
to eat; at night fasting let him sup up a cup full of
the former drink warm therewith.

.X.

Vıþ þon þe món bloðe hꝛæce Ᵹ ſpıꝛe · ᵹením ᵹoð
beꝛen mela · Ᵹ hꝛıꞇ ꝛealꞇ ðo on ꝛeam oþþe ᵹoðe ꝼleꞇe
hꝛeꝛ oð bleðe oþ ꝥ hıꞇ ſıe þıcce ſpa þynne bꝛıꝛ ꝛele

etan .VIIII. ꝛnæða .VIIII. moꝛᵹenaſ on[1] neahꞇ neꝛꞇıᵹ ·
ðo þæꝛ meluper ꞇpæðe Ᵹ þæꝛ ꝛealꞇeſ þꝛıðdan ðæl ꝛyꝛc
ælce ðæᵹe nıꝛne.

.XI.

Þıþ ſeonðum ᵹeallan eꞇe ꝛæðıc Ᵹ pıpoᵹ on neahꞇ
neꝛꞇıᵹ · Ᵹ apylleð hnꝛæð on meolce ſupe mıð[2] ðo þuꝛ
ᵹelome hım bıþ ꝛona ꝛel

.XII.

Vıð þæꝛe ᵹeolpan aðle ſıo cymð óꝼ ſeonðum ᵹeallan
ᵹenım þæꝛ ꝛceaꝛpan þıſꞇleꝛ moꝛan Ᵹ beꞇonıcan · Ᵹ aꞇꞇoꝛlaþan hanð ꝼulle · Ᵹ ᵹyþꝛıꝼan hanð ꝼulle Ᵹ .VIIIL
ſnæða nıoþoꝛeaꝛðe æꝛcþꝛoꞇan óꝼ ᵹeoꞇ mıð ſꞇꝛanᵹan
beoꝛe · oþþe mıð ſꞇꝛanᵹum ealað Ᵹ ðꝛınce ᵹelome ꝛele
hım eꞇan ᵹeꝛyꝛꞇoðne henꝼuᵹel Ᵹ ᵹeꝛoðenne capel on
ᵹoðum bꝛoðe ðo þuꝛ ᵹelome hım bıþ ſona ꝛel.

Pyꝛc ᵹoðne ðuſꞇ ðꝛenc ꝛıþ þæꝛe ᵹeolpan aðle · nım
meꝛceꝛ ꝛæð · Ᵹ ꝼınoleꝛ ꝛæð · ðıle ꝛæð · eoꝼoꝛþꝛoꞇan
ſæð · ꝼelðmoꝛan ſæð · ꝛæþeꝛıan ꝛæð · peꞇoꝛꝛılıan ꝛæð ·
alexanðꝛan ſæð luꝛeſꞇıceꝛ ꝛæð · beꞇonıcan ſæð · cauleꝛ
ꝛæð · coſꞇeꝛ ꝛæð · cymeneꝛ ꝛæð · Ᵹ pıpoꝛeꝛ mæꝛꞇ
þaꝛa oðeꝛꝛa emꝛela ᵹeᵹnıð ealle pel ꞇo ðuſꞇe nım þæꝛ
ðuſꞇeꝛ ᵹoðne cucleꝛ ꝼulne ðo on ſꞇꝛanᵹ hluꞇꞇoꝛ eala
ðꝛınce ſcenc ꝼulne on neahꞇ neꝛꞇıᵹ · he ıꝛ ᵹoð ꝛıþ
ælcꝛe hman unꞇꝛumneꝛꝛe Ᵹ ꝛıþ heaꝛoð ece Ᵹ ꝛıþ un-

fol. 114 a.
fol. 114 b.

[1] Unless moꝛᵹenaſ, *morrows*, can be taken in the sense of *successive days*, on must be omitted. Observe, a new page begins.
[2] In margin heꝛꞇo.

x.

In case a man hreak up and spew blood; take good
barley meal, and white salt, put it into cream or good
skimmings, agitate in a dish, till it be as thick as
thin brewit, give *the man* to eat, nine doses for nine
mornings after his nights fast : apply of the meal two
parts in three, and of the salt a third part ; prepare
it every day new.

xi.

For bile straining out ; let the patient eat radish
and pepper at night fasting, and let him sup besides
linseed boiled in milk ; do this frequently ; it will
soon be well with him.

xii.

1. For the yellow disease, *jaundice,* which cometh
of effusion of bile ; take roots of the sharp thistle, and
betony, and a handful of attorlothe, and a handful of
githrife, and nine bits of the netherward part of ashthroat, pour them over with strong beer, or with
strong ale, and let him drink *this* frequently : give
him to eat a pullet dressed with herbs, and colewort
sodden in good broth ; do this frequently, soon it will
be well with him.

2. Work *thus* a good dust drink for the yellow
disease. Take seed of marche, and seed of fennel, seed
of dill, seed of everthroat, seed of fieldmore, seed of
satureia, *savory,* seed of parsley, seed of alexanders,
seed of lovage, seed of betony, seed of colewort, seed
of costmary, 'seed of cummin, and of pepper most, of
the others equal quantities ; rub all well to dust, take a
good spoon full of the dust, put it into strong clear
ale, let *the man* drink a cup full at night fasting.
This *drink* is also good for every ailment of limb, and
for head ache, and for want of memory, and for eye

ȝemynde ꞃ ꝟiþ eaȝꝑænce ꞃ ꝟiþ unȝehypneꞃꞃe ꞃ bꞃeoꞅꞇ
pænce ꞃ lunȝen able ꞃ lenden pænce · ꞃ ꝟiþ ælcꝑe
ꝼeonbeꞃ coꞅꞇunȝa ȝepyꞃc þe buꞅꞇ ȝenoh on hæꝑꞃeꞅꞇe
þonne þu þa pyꞃꞇa hæbbe nyꞇꞇa þonne þe þeaꝛꝼ ꞅie.

.XIII.

Ƿið bꞃeoꞅꞇꝼænce maꝛubie · neꝛꞇe · onꞇꝛe biꞅceop
pyꞃꞇ · penpyꞃꞇ · pyl on huniȝe ꞃ buꞇeꞃan bo þæꞅ
huniȝeꞅ ꞇꝛæbe · ꞃ þæꝛe buꞇeꞃan þꞃibban bæl nyꞇꞇa
ꞅpa þe þeaꝛꝼ ꞅie.

.XIIII.

Ƿiþ hpoꞅꞇan ꞃ lunȝen able · ȝenim ꞅpeȝleꞅ æppel ꞃ
ꞅpeꞃl ꞃ ꝛeceiꞅ calꝑa emꝼela menȝ ꝟiþ peaxe leȝc on
haꞇne ꞅꞇan bꞃinc þuꝛih hoꝛn þone ꝛec ꞃ eꞇe æꝼꞇeꝛ
ealbeꞃ ꞅpiceꞃ ·III. ꞅnæba oððe buꞇꞃan ꞃ ꞅupe mid
ꝼleꞇum; Ƿiþ lunȝen able · ȝenim beꞇonican · ꞃ maꝛubian · aȝꝛimonian · ꝛeꞃmod · ꝼel ꞇeꝛꝛe · ꝛube. acꝛind ·
ȝaȝollan · pyl on pæꞇꝛe · bepyl þæꞃ pæꞇeꝛeꞅ þꞃibban
bæl · bo oꝼ þa pyꞃꞇe bꞃince on moꝛȝenne peaꝛmeꞅ
ꞅcenc ꝼulne eꞇe ·III. ꞅnæba mid þæꞅ bꞃiꝛeꞅ þe heꝛ
æꝼꞇeꝛ ꞅeȝþ :·

Ƿyꞃc bꞃiꝛ ꝟiþ lunȝen able nim beꞇonican · ꞃ maꝛubian · ꝛeꝛmod · hinbheoloþan · penpyꞃꞇ nioþoꝛeaꞃb ·
elehꞇꝛe · elene · ꝛæbic · eoꝼoꝛþꞃoꞇe · ꝼelbmoꝛe · ȝecnua
ealle ꞅpiþe ꝛel ꞃ pyl on buꞇeꞃan ꞃ apꝛinȝ þuꝛh cla ·
ꝛceað on þ póꞅ beꝛen mela hꝛeꝛ on blebe buꞇan ꝛyꝛe
oþ þ hiꞇ ꞅie ꞅpa þicce ꞅpa bꞃiꝛ eꞇe . III. ꞅnæba · mid
þy bꝛence peaꝛmeꞅ.

Eꝼꞇ ꝛyl on huniȝe aꝛum maꝛubian bo hꝛon beꝛen
mela ꞇo eꞇe on nealiꞇ neꞅꞇiȝ ꞃ þonne þu him ꞅelle

wark, and for dull hearing, and for breast wark, and lung disease, loin wark, and for every temptation of the fiend. Work thyself dust enough in harvest, when thou hast the worts, use it when thou hast need.

xiii.

For pain of breast; marrubium, nepeta, ontre, bishop-wort, wenwort, boil in honey and butter; put two parts in three of the honey, and of the butter a third part; use as need may be.

xiv.

For host, *or cough*, and lung disease; take swails apple, and brimstone, and frankincense, of all equally much, mingle with wax, lay on a hot stone, let *the man* swallow the reek through a horn, and afterwards eat three pieces of old lard or of butter, and sip *this* with cream. For lung disease; take betony, and marrubium, agrimony, wormwood, fel terræ *or centaury*, rue, oak rind, sweet gale; boil them in water, boil off a third part of the water, remove the worts; let *the man* drink in the morning of *this* warm a cup full, let him eat therewith three pieces of the brewit that is here afterwards mentioned.

2. Work *thus* a brewit for lung disease; take betony, and marrubium, wormwood, hind heal,[1] the lower part of wen wort, lupin, helenium, radish, everthroat, field-more; pound all thoroughly well, and boil in butter, and wring through a cloth; shed on the decoction barley meal, shake it in a dish without fire till it be as thick as brewit; let him eat three pieces, with the drink of the warm *liquor*.

3. Again, boil in honey alone, marrubium, add a little barley meal, let *the man* eat at night fasting; and when

---

[1] *Eupatorium cannabinum.*

ðrenc oððe brup rele him hatne ɇ læt ȝeneſtan þone
man æfter tibe[1] dæȝeſ on þa ſpiðran ſiðan ɇ haɼa þone
earm aþeneð.

.XV.

Þiþ maȝan þænce pyl píc on cu meolce abo ꝥ pic
óɼ rupe hpon pearm rona biþ ɼel. Þiþ aþunðeneɼɼe ɇ
[ȝiɼ][2] men nelle myltan hir mete pyl on pæteɼe
polleian ɇ leac cenſan rele ðrincan him biþ ſona
ɼel;

.XVI.

Viþ milte þænce cnua ȝɼene realbɼinbe ſeoð on
huniȝe anum rele him etan .III. ſnæða on neaht
neɼtiȝ.

.XVII.

Þiþ lenðen þænce maɼubie. neɼte. boȝen em ɼela
ealɼa ðo on ȝoð ealu pyɼc to ðɼence ſpet hþón rele
ðrincan licȝe uppeaɼð æfter þon ȝoðe hpile.

.XVIII.

Þiþ pambe þænce ɇ nyɼel þænce þæɼ þu ȝeſeo toɼð
piɼel on eoɼþan úp þeoɼɼan ymbɼo hine mið tɼam
hanðum mið hir ȝeþeoɼɼe paɼa mið þinum hanðum
ſpiþe ɇ cpeð þɼipa · Remeðium ɼacio að uentɼiſ ðoloɼem.
Þeoɼp þonne oɼeɼ bæc þone piɼel on þeȝebehealð ꝥ
þu ne lociȝe æfter · þonne monneſ pambe þænce oððe
ɼyɼle ymbɼoli mið þinúm hanðum þa pambe him biþ

_____

[1] Thus MS. | [2] ȝiɼ not in MS.

thou givest him drink or brewit, give it him hot; and
make the man rest after an hour, by day, on the right
side, and have the arm extended.

XV.

For pain in the maw; boil pitch in cow milk, remove the pitch, let him sip a little warm, soon *the
man* will be well. For distention, and if a mans
meat will not digest; boil in water pulegium and leek
cress,[1] give *this* to the man to drink, soon it will be
well with him.

xvi.

For milt pain; pound green sallow rind, seethe in
honey alone, give *the man* to eat three pieces at night
fasting.

xvii.

For loin wark; marrubium, nepeta, thyme, of all
equal quantities, put into good ale; work to a drink,
sweeten a little, give *to the man* to drink; let him
lie with face up afterwards for a good while.

xviii.

For wamb wark and pain in the fatty part of the
belly; when thou seest a dung beetle[2] in the earth
throwing up *mould*, catch him with thy two hands
along with his casting up, wave him strongly with
thy hands, and say thrice, "Remedium facio ad ventris
"dolorem;" then throw the beetle over thy back away;
take care thou look not after it. When a mans wamb
or belly fat is in pain, grasp the wamb with thine

---

[1] *Erysimum alliaria.*
[2] Our Saxon must have had Tal-
pam, or Ἀσπάλακα before him in

this sentence; but he names the
Scarabæus stercorarius.

ꝛona ꞃel · XII. monaþ þu mealht ꞃpa bon ꞃeꝼteþ þam
piꝼele

XVIIII.

Víþ blæbbeþ pæꞃ ce. Þudu mence · ꝺ leaccepꞃe pȳl
ꞃpiþe on ealað ꞃele ðꞃincan ꝺ etan ȝebꞃæbne ꞃtæꞃ.

.XX.

Ȝiꝼ man ne mæȝe ȝemiȝan ꝺ him peaxan ꞃtanaꞃ on
þæꞃe blæðꞃan pyl ꞃunðcoꞃn on ealað ꝺ peteꞃꞃilian ꞃele
him ðꞃincan.

.XXI.

Giꝼ men ꞃie ꞃe utȝanȝ ꞃoꞃꞃeten pyl peꞃmoð on
ꞃuꞃum ealaþ ꝺ bo buteꞃan þæꞃ to him biþ ꞃona ꞃel
ȝíꝼ he hit ðꞃincþ.

.XXII.

Þiþ útꞃiht aðle · v. leaꞃan · hleomoce · cuꞃmealle ·
elehtꞃe. ȝecnua þa pyꞃta · ꝺ pyl on meolce ꞃele him

ðꞃincan peaꞃm on moꞃȝenne ꝺ on æꞃen ; Þyꞃc bꞃiþ
to þon ilcan puðu cunellan · hleomóc · bepyl þaꞃa
meolce þꞃiðban ðæl þæꞃe pyꞃte oꝼ þam meolcum[1]
ꞃceað hpæten mela þæꞃ on ꝺ ete þone bꞃiþ cealðne ·
ꝺ ꞃupe þa meolúc him bið ꞃona ꞃel ȝíꝼ ꞃe bꞃiþ ꝺ ꞃe
ðꞃenc inne ȝepuniað þu meaht þone man ȝelácnian
ȝiꝼ him óꝼꞃleoȝeð him bið ꞃelꞃe þ þu hine na ne
ȝꞃete him biþ hiꞃ ꞃeoꞃh aðl ȝetenȝe.

. XXIII.

Ȝíꝼ pyꞃmaꞃ beoþ on manner innoðe pyl on buteꞃan
ȝꞃene þuðan ðꞃinc[2] on neaht neꞃtiȝ ꞃcenc ꝼulne hi

---

[1] Read as before bepyl on meolce oþ þꞃiðban ðæl · bo þa pyꞃta oꝼ
þam meolcum.
[2] Vowel dropped.

hands, it will soon be well with *the man;* for twelve months after the beetle thou shalt have power so to do.

xix.

For bladder pain; wood marche and sauce alone; boil *them* strongly in ale; administer to drink, and to eat a roasted starling.

xx.

If a man cannot mie, and stones wax in the bladder; boil sundcorns[1] in ale, and parsley; give *him* this to drink.

xxi.

If a mans excrement be lodged; boil wormwood in sour ale, and add butter thereto; it will soon be well with him, if he drinketh it.

xxii.

For diarrhœa; cinqfoil, brooklime, churmel, lupin; pound the worts, and boil them in milk; give *this* to the man to drink warm in the morning and in the evening. Work *thus* a brewit for the same: wild cunila, brooklime; boil in milk to a third part, remove the worts from the milk, shed wheaten meal thereon, and let him eat the brewit cold, and let him sip the milk, it will soon be well with him. If the brewit and the drink remain within him, thou mayst cure the man; if they flow away, it will be better for him, that thou should not meddle with him, his death sickness is upon him.

xxiii.

1. If worms be in a mans inwards; boil green rue in butter, let the man drink at night fasting a cup

---

[1] *Saxifragia granulata.* Prescribed because saxa frangit.

ȝepıcað ealle apeȝ mıð þy utȝanȝe Ꝫ he bıð ꞃona
hal ;

To þon ılcan ȝenım cymeneꞃ ðuſt menȝ to ȝate
ȝeallan Ꝫ ꝼeaꝛꝛeꞃ ȝnıð þone naꞃolan mıð ealle hı ȝepıcaþ
nıþeꝛ ; oꝼ þæm meɴ.

. XXIIII.

Þıþ lıð pæꝛce ſinȝ . VIIIL ſıþum þıꞃ ȝealðoꞃ þæꝛ
on · Ꝫ þın ſpatl ſpıp on · ꝏalıȝnuꞃ oblıȝauıt · anȝeluꞃ
cuꝛauıt · ðomınuꞃ Saluauıt · hım bıþ ꞃona ꞃel.

To þon ılcan ȝenım culꝼꝛan toꞃð · Ꝫ ȝate toꞃð ðꞃıȝe
ſpıðe Ꝫ ȝnıð to ðuſte menȝ pıþ hunıȝ Ꝫ pıþ butꝛan
ſmıꞃe mıð þa leoþu.

. XXV.

Þıþ peaꝛtum ȝenım hunðeꞃ mıcȝean Ꝫ muꞃe bloð
menȝ to ꞃomne ſmıꞃe mıð þa peaꝛtan hı ȝepıtaþ ſona
apeȝ   :·

fol. 116 b.   ### . XXVI.

Þıþ mıclan lıce ȝenım nıoþopeaꝛðe elenan Ꝫ þunȝ ·
Ꝫ ōmꝛꝛan þa þe ſpınman ꝛıle ealꝛa emꞃela · Ꝫ ȝecnua
ꝛel · Ꝫ ꝛyl on buteꝛan ðo ꝛel ꞃealteꞃ on Ꝫ ſmıꞃe mıð.
Þyꞃc bıð[1] pıþ þam mıclan lıce · elene · ælꝼþone ·
maꝛubıe · cuꝛmealle · ellen tanaſ · Ꝫ ac tanaꞃ ꝛyl ſpıðe
on pætꞃe Ꝫ beþe on ſpıðe hatum þ̶ lıc. Þyꞃc ðꞃenc
pıð þam mıclan lıce hınðhıoloþan · cuꝛmeallan · boȝen ·
neꝼte · aȝꞃımonıa · betonıca · ꞃınul · ðıle · ðo on ȝoð
ealo ꞃele ðꞃıncan on bæȝe . III. ꞃcencaſ ꝼulle. Þyꞃc
bꞃıp pıþ þon ılcan · ȝenım nıoþopeaꝛðe elenan · Ꝫ eoꞃoꝛ
þꞃotan · ꝛebıc · Ꝫ þa ꞃeaðan netlan nıoþopeaꝛðe ſceaꝛꝼa
ſmæle Ꝫ ȝecnua ꝛel · ꝛyl ꞃıþþan on buteꝛan ðo clæne
ıꞃıȝ taꝛan þæꝛ on ȝıꞃ þu hæbbe · Ꝫ hpon beꝛeneſ melꝛeꞃ
ðo on blebe mıð þam pyꞃtum Ꝫ hꝛeꝛ mıð ſtıccan oþ

---

[1] That is, bæð.

full; they will all depart away with the evacuation, and
he will soon be well.

2. For that ilk. Take dust of cummin, mingle it
with goats and bulls gall, rub the navel with them all,
the *worms* will all disappear from the man downwards.

xxiv.

1. For joint pain; sing nine times this incantation
thereon, and spit thy spittle on *the joint:* "Malignus
" obligavit; angelus curavit; dominus salvavit." It
will soon be well with him.

2. For that ilk. Take doves dung and a goats tord,
dry them thoroughly and rub to dust, mingle with
honey and with butter, smear the joints therewith.

xxv.

For warts; take hounds mie, and a mouses blood,
mingle together, smear the warts therewith, they will
soon depart away.

xxvi.

For elephantiasis, take the netherward part of helenium and aconite, and dock, that *namely* which will
swim, of all equal quantities, and pound well and boil
in butter, add a good spice of salt, and smear therewith. Work *thus* a bath against the mickle body
brought on by leprosy, helenium, enchanters nightshade, marrubium, churmel, elder twigs, and oak twigs;
boil strongly in water, and bathe the body in it very
hot. Work *thus* a drink against the mickle body; put
hindheal, churmel, thyme, nepeta, agrimony, betony,
fennel, dill, into good ale; administer to be drunk in
a day three cups full. Work a brewit for that ilk;
take the netherward part of helenium and everthroat,
radish, and the netherward part of the red nettle, scrape
them small, and pound them well. Afterwards boil
them in butter; add ivy tar besides if thou have it,
and a little barley meal; put this on a dish with the

þ hic col fie ꝼele etan on neahꞇ neꞃꞇiȝ . III. ſnæða
ꝼele þone bꞃiꝼ ꞇ þone ðꞃenc æꞃ þam bæþe þy læꞃ hiꞇ
inꞃlea æꝼꞇeꞃ þam baþe.

. XXVII.

Þiþ ꞃinȝalum þuꞃſꞇe [1] unꞇꞃumꞃa manna · Nim peꞃmoð ꞇ hinð hioloþan ꞇ ȝyþꞃiꝼan ꝑylle ón ealaþ ȝeſꝑeꞇe
hꝑon ꝼele him ðꞃincan híꞇ hælþ þone þuꞃſꞇ [2] pun-
ðoꞃliceꞇ

. XXVIII.

Þiþ innan ꝼoꞃꞇoȝe [3] ſmæl þeaꞃma ece · ȝenim beꞇonican · ꞇ peꞃmoð · meꞃce · ꞃæðic · ꝼinul · ȝecnua ealle ·
ꞇ ðo on eala ſeꞇe þonne ꞇ beꞃꞃeoh ðꞃinc on neahꞇ
neꞃꞇiȝ ꞃcenc ꝼulne.

. XXVIIII.

Viþ bꞃyne ȝiꝼ món ſie mið ꝼyꞃe ane ꝼoꞃbæꞃneð
nim puðuꞃoꝼan · ꞇ lilian · ꞇ hleomoc ꝑyl on buꞇeꞃan
ꞇ ſmiꞃe mið. ȝíꝼ mon ſie mið pæꞇan ꝼoꞃbæꞃneð nime
elm ꞃinðe · ꞇ lilian moꞃan ꝑyl on meolcum ſmiꞃe mið
þꞃiꞃa on ðæȝ. Þiþ ſunbꞃyne · meꞃꞃe iꝼiȝ ꞇꞃiȝu ꝑyl
on buꞇꞃan ſmiꞃe mið.

. XXX.

Þyꞃc ȝoðne ðeoꞃ ðꞃenc · peꞃmoð · boȝen · ȝaꞃcliꝼan ·
polleian · penꝑyꞃꞇ · þa ſmalan ꝼel ꞇeꞃꞃe · eaȝꝑyꞃꞇ ·
þeoꞃꝑyꞃꞇ · ceaſꞇeꞃ æꞃceſ . II. ſnæða · elenan . III. com-
muceſ [5] III. puðu peax án ȝoðne ðæl · cuꞃmeallan ·
ȝeꞃceaꞃꝼa þaſ ꝑyꞃꞇa on ȝoð hluꞇꞇoꞃ eala oþþe ꝑyliſc
ealu læꞇ ſꞇanðan . III. nihꞇ beꞃꞃiȝen ꝼele ðꞃincan
ꞃcenc ꝼulne ꞇiðe æꞃ oþꞃum meꞇe. Þiþ þeoꞃe ꞇ ꝑiþ
ꞃceoꞇenðum penne · nim boȝen · ꞇ ȝeaꞃꞃan ꞇ puðu peax

---

[1] ðuſꞇ, MS.
[2] þꞃſꞇ, MS.

[3] Read ꞃoꞃꞇoȝenneꞃꞇe ꞇ.

worts, and stir it about with a spoon till it be cool; give *the man* to eat at night fasting three bits of it; give the brewit and the drink before the bath; let it strike inwards after the bath.

xxvii.

For the constant thirst of ailing men; take worm-wood, and hind heal, and githrife, boil in ale, sweeten a little, give to the man to drink, it healeth the thirst wonderfully.

xxviii.

For inward griping and small guts ache; take betony, and wormwood, marche, radish, fennel; pound all and put into ale, then set it down and wrap it up; drink at night fasting a cup full.

xxix.

For a burn; if a man be burnt with fire only, take woodruff, and lily, and brooklime; boil in butter, and smear therewith. If a man be burnt with a liquid, let him take elm rind and roots of lily; boil them in milk, smear therewith thrice a day. For sunburn; boil in butter tender ivy twigs; smear therewith.

xxx.

Work a good "dry" drink *for the "dry" disease;* wormwood, thyme, agrimony, pennyroyal, wenwort, the small centaury, eyewort, inula conyza, two pro-portions of black hellebore, three of helenium, eight of cammock, wood wax, a good deal of it, churmel; scrape these worts into good clear ale, or foreign ale, let it stand wrapt up for three nights, give *the man* a cup full to drink an hour before other meat. Against the "dry disease" and against a shooting wen; take bothen, and yarrow, and wood wax, and ravens foot, put into

ꞇ hꞃeꞃneꞃ ꝼoꞇ ꝺo on ȝoꝺ ealu ꞃele ꝺꞃincan on ꝺæȝe
. III. ꞃcencaꞅ ꞃulle. Ȝiꞃ þeoꞃ ȝeꝑuniȝe on anꞃe ꞅꞇoꝑe
ꝑyꞃc beþinȝe nim ꝥ iꞃiȝ þe on ꞅꞇane ꝑeaxe · ꞇ ȝeaꞃꝑan ·
ꞇ ꝑuꝺu binꝺeꞃ leaꝼ ꞇ cuꞃlyppan ȝecnua ealle ꝑel leȝe
on haꞇne ꞅꞇan on ꞇꞃoȝe ȝeoꞇ hꝑon ꝑæꞇeꞃeꞅ on læꞇ
ꞃeocan on ꝥ lic þæꞃ þæꞃ him þeaꞃꞃ ꞃie þonne ꞃe col
ꞅie ꝺo oþeꞃne haꞇne on beþe ꞅꝑa ȝelome him biþ
ꞅona ꞃel.

. XXXI.

Ꝑyꞃc ȝoꝺe ꝑenꞃealꝼe nim ꝑuꝺu meꞃce · ꞇ hꞃeꞃneꞃ
ꝼoꞇ · ꞇ ꝑeꞃmoꝺ nioþoꝑeaꞃꝺne · cū ꞃlyppan · ꝯuꝺan ·
ꝑuꝺu binꝺeꞃ leaꝼ · iꞃiȝ leaꝼ þe on eoꞃþan ꝑixþ · þa clu-
ꞃihꞇan · ꝑenꝑyꞃꞇ · ȝecnua ealle · ꝑyl on ꞃammeꞃ ꞅmeꞃꝑe
oþþe on buccan ꝺo þꞃuꝺꝺan ꝺæl buꞇeꝲan apꞃinȝ þuꞃh
claþ ꝺo' þonne ȝoꝺne ꞅciꝲ ꞇaꞃan ꞇo ꞇ hꞃeꞃ oþ ꝥ hiꞇ
col ꞅie.

. XXXII.

Vyꞃc ȝoꝺe ꝺolh ꞃealꝼe nim ȝeaꞃꝑan · ꞇ ꝑuꝺu ꞃoꝼan
nioþoꝑeaꞃꝺe · ꞃelꝺ moꞃan · ꞇ nioþoꝑeaꞃꝺne ꞃiȝel hꝑeoꞃꞃan ꝑyl on ȝoꝺꞃe buꞇeꝲan apꞃinȝ þuꞃh claꝺ ꞇ læꞇ ȝe-
ꞅꞇanꝺan ꝑel ælc ꝺolh þu meahꞇ lacnian miꝺ.

. XXXIII.

Ȝiꞃ mon ꞅie uꝼan on heaꝼoꝺ ꝑunꝺ ꞇ ꞅie ban ȝebꞃocen nim ꞃiȝel hꝑeoꞃꞃan · ꞇ hꝑiꞇe clæꞃꞃan ꝑiꞅan ·
ꞇ ꝑuꝺuꞃoꝼan ꝺo on ȝoꝺe buꞇꞃan aꞃeoh þuꞃh claꝺ ꞇ
lacna ꞃiþþan.   :·

Ȝiꞃ ꞅio eaxl uꝼꞅꞇiȝe nim [1] þa ꞃealꝼe ꝺo hꝲon ꝑeaꞃme
miꝺ ꞃeþeꞃe him biꝺ ꞃona ꞃel. Ꝑyꞃc ȝoꝺne ꝺolh ꝺꞃenc
nim aȝꞃimonian ꞇ ꝑuꝺu ꞃoꝼan ꝺo on ȝoꝺ ealo ꞃele
ꝺꞃincan ȝoꝺne ꞃcenc ꞃulne on neahꞇ neꞃꞇiȝ. Ȝiꞃ ȝe-

fol. 118 a.

---

[1] ni ꝺo, MS.

good ale, give *the man* to drink three cups full a day: if the "dry disease" remain in one place, work a fomentation *thus;* take the ivy, which groweth on stone, and yarrow, and leaves of woodbind and cowslip; pound all *these* well, lay *them* on a hot stone in a trough, pour a little water upon *them,* let it reek upon the body, where need may be; when *the stone* is cool, put another hot one in, foment *the man* so frequently. It will soon be well with him.

xxxi.

Work a good wen salve *thus;* take wood marche, and ravens foot, and the netherward part of wormwood, cowslip, rue, leaves of woodbind, ivy leaves, that ivy which groweth on the earth, the cloved wenwort; pound *them* all, boil in rams grease, or in bucks grease, put a third part of butter, wring through a cloth, then add good ship tar, and shake till it be cool.

xxxii.

Work a good wound salve *thus;* take yarrow, and the nether part of woodruff, fieldmore, and the nether part of solwherf; boil in good butter, wring through a cloth, and let it stand. Pretty well every wound thou mayst cure therewith.

xxxiii.

1. If a man be wounded in his upper quarter, in his head, and *some* bone be broken; take solwherf, and white clover plants, and woodruff; put into good butter, strain through a cloth, and so treat *the patient.*

2. If the shoulder get up out of place, take the salve, apply a little warm with a feather: it will soon be well with the man. Work a good wound drink *thus;* take agrimony, and woodruff, put *them* into good ale, give *the man* to drink a good cup full, at

bꞃocen ban ſie on heaꞃðe Ᵹ óꝼ nelle cnua ꝷꞃene betonican Ᵹ leꝣe on ꝥ ðolh ꝣelome oþ ꝥ þa ban oꝼ ſyn Ᵹ
ꝥ ðolh ꝣebatoð.

.XXXIIII.

Þiþ hunðeꞃ ꞃlite cnupa ꞃibban leꝣe on ꝥ ðolh Ᵹ
ꞃuðan pyl on butꞃan lácna mið ꝥ ðolh. ꝣiꝼ ſinꞃe fyn
ꝼoꞃcoꞃꝼene nim ꞃenpyꞃmaꝼ ꝣecnupa ꝑel leꝣe on oþ ꝥ hi
hale ſynð. ꝣiꝼ ꞃinꞃe ꞃien ꝣeꞃcꞃuncene nime æmettan
mið hioꞃa beðꝣeꞃiðe ꝑyl on pætꞃe Ᵹ beþe mið Ᵹ ꞃece
þa ꞃinꞃe ꝣeoꞃnlice.

.XXXV.

Viþ ꝣoꝣeꞃiꝼꞃan bite nim henne æꝣ ꝣnið on ealu
hꞃeaꞃ Ᵹ ꞃceaꞃeꞃ toꞃð ꞃiꝑe ſpa he nyte ꞃele him ðꞃincan
ꝣoðne ſcenc ꝼulne.

.XXXVI.

Þiþ cancꞃe nim ꝣate ꝣeallan Ᵹ huniꝣ menꝣ to
ſomne · beꝣea emꝼela ðo on ꝥ ðolh. To þon ilcan niꝑe
hunðeꞃ heaꝼoð bæꞃn to ahꞃan ðo on ðolh · ꝣiꝼ hit
nelle ꝥ nim monneſ ðꞃoꝣan ðꞃiꝣ ſꝑiðe ꝣnið to ðuſte
ðo on ꝣiꝼ þu mið þyꞃ ne meaht ꝣelacnian ne meaht
þu him æꞃꞃe nahte.

.XXXVII.

Þiþ þon þe ꝼiꝼ ne mæꝣe beaꞃn acenuan · nim ꝼelð
moꞃan nioþoꞃeaꞃðe ꝑyl on meolcum Ᵹ on pætꞃe ðo
beꝣea emꝼela ꞃele etan þa moꞃan Ᵹ ꝥ ꝑoꞃ ſupan. To
þon ilcan binð on ꝥ ꞃinſtꞃe þeoh up ꝑið ꝥ cennenðe
lím nioþoꞃeaꞃðe beolonan oþþe .XII. coꞃn cellenðꞃan
ꞃæðeꞃ Ᵹ ꝥ ꞃceal ðon cniht oððe mæðen · ſpa ꝥ beaꞃn
ꞃie acenneð ðo þa pyꞃta aꝑeꝣ þy læꞃ ꝥ innelꝼe utꞃiꝣe.

fol. 118 b.

night fasting. If there be a broken bone in the head, and it will not come away, pound green betony and lay it on the wound frequently, till the bones come away and the wound is mended.

xxxiv.

For rending of hound ; pound ribwort, lay it on the wound, and boil rue in butter, tend the wound therewith. If sinews are cut through ; take worms, pound them well, lay on till *the sinews* be restored. If sinews be shrunken ; take emmets with their nest, boil them in water, and beathe therewith, and earnestly reek the sinews *with the vapour.*

xxxv.

Against bite of gangwayweaving spider ; take a hens egg, rub it up raw into ale, and a sheeps tord new, so that *the patient* wit it not, give him a good cup full to drink.

xxxvi.

Against cancer ; take goats gall and honey, mingle together of both equal quantities, apply to the wound. For that ilk ; burn a fresh hounds head to ashes, apply to the wound. If *the wound* will not *give way to* that, take a mans dung, dry it thoroughly, rub to dust, apply it. If with this thou art not able to cure him, thou mayst never do it by any means.

xxxvii.

In case that a woman may not kindle a bairn ; take of fieldmore the nether part, boil it in milk and in water, apply of both equal quantities, give the roots *to her* to eat and the wash to sip. For that ilk. Bind on her left thigh, up against the kindling limb, the netherward part of henbane, or twelve grains of coriander seed, and that shall give a boy a or maiden : when the bairn is kindled, remove the worts away, lest

ʒıꝼ óꝼ pıꝼe nelle ʒan æꝼꞇeꞃ þám beoꞃþꞃe þ ʒecynꝺelıc
ꝼıe · ꝼeoþe ealꝺ ꝼpıc on pæꞇꞃe beþe mıꝺ þone cꝛıþ oꝺꝺe
hleomóc oþþe hocceꞃ leaꝼ pyl on ealoþ ꞃele ꝺꞃıncan
hıꞇ haꞇ. ʒıꝼ on pıꝼe ꞃıe ꝺeaꝺ beaꞃn pyl on meolce ꝺ
on pæꞇꞃe hleomóc ꝺ polleıán ꞃele ꝺꞃıncan ón ꝺæʒ ꞇupa.
ʒeoꞃne ıꝼ ꞇo pyꞃnanne beaꞃneacnum pıꝼe þ hıo ahꞇ
ꝼealꞇeꞃ eꞇe oꝺꝺe ꝼpeꞇeꞃ oþþe beoꞃ ꝺꞃınce · ne ꝼpıneꝼ ꝼlæꞃc
eꞇe ne nahꞇ ꝼæꞇeꞃ · ne ꝺꞃuncen ʒeꝺꞃınce ne on peʒ ne
ꝼeꞃe · ne on hoꞃꝼe ꞇo ꝼꝛıꝺe ꞃıꝺe þy læꝼ þ beaꞃn óꝼ
hıꞃe ꝼıe æꞃ ꞃıhꞇ ꞇıꝺe. ʒıꝼ hıó[1] bleꝺe ꞇo ꝼpıþe æꝼꞇeꞃ
þam beoꞃþꞃe nıoþoꞃeaꞃꝺe claꞇan pyl on meolce ꞃele
eꞇan ꝺ ꝼupan þ poꞃ.

. XXXVIII.

Þıþ þon þe pıꝼum ꝼıe ꝼoꞃꝼꞇanꝺen hıꞃa monaþ ʒecynꝺ
pyl on ealaꝺ hleomóc ꝺ ꞇꝛa cuꞃmeallan ꞃele ꝺꞃıncan
ꝺ beþe þ ꝼíꝼ on haꞇum baþe ꝺ ꝺꞃınce þone ꝺꞃenc on
þam baþe haꝼa þe æꞃ ʒeꞃoꞃhꞇ clam óꝼ beoꞃ ꝺꞃæꞃꞇan
ꝺ óꝼ ʒꞃenꞃe mucʒꞃyꞃꞇe ꝺ meꞃce · ꝺ óꝼ beꞃene melpe
menʒ ealle ꞇoꝼómne ʒehꞃeꞃ on pannan clæm on þ
ʒecynꝺe lím ꝺ on þone cꝛıꝺ nıoþoꞃeaꞃóne þonne hıo
óꝼ þam baꝺe ʒæþ ꝺ ꝺꞃınce ꝼcenc ꝼulne þæꞃ ılcan
ꝺꞃenceꝼ[2] peaꞃmeꞃ ꝺ beꞃꞃeoh þ ꝼíꝼ pel ꝺ læꞇ beon ꝼpa
beclæmeꝺ lanʒe ꞇıꝺe þæꞃ ꝺæʒeꝼ ꝺo ꝼpa ꞇupa ꝼpa þꞃıpa
ꝼpæþeꞃ þu ꞃcyle · þu ꞃcealꞇ ꝼımle þam pıꝼe bæþ pyꞃcean ꝺ ꝺꞃenc ꞃellan on þa ılcan ꞇıꝺ · þe hıꞃe ꝼıo ʒecynꝺ
æꞇ pæꞃe ahꞃa þæꞃ æꞇ þam pıꝼe.

ʒıꝼ pıꝼe ꞇo ꝼpıþe óꝼꝼlope ꝼıo monaꝺ ʒecynꝺ · ʒenım
nıꝼe hoꞃꞃeꞃ ꞇoꞃꝺ leʒe on haꞇe ʒleꝺa læꞇ ꞃeocan ꝼpıþe

_____

[1] hıó in MS. follows þy læꝼ ; the scribe having copied from some
older writing in which it had been placed out of the line.
[2] ꝼcenceꝼ, MS

the matrix prolapse. If what is natural will not come away from a woman after the birth, seethe old lard in water, bathe the vulva therewith; or boil in ale brooklime or hollyhock, administer it to drink hot. If there be a dead bairn in a woman, boil in milk and in water brooklime and pulegium, give it *her* to drink twice a day. Earnestly must a pregnant woman be cautioned, that she eat naught salt or sweet, nor drink beer, nor eat swines flesh, nor aught fat, nor drink to drunkenness, nor fare by the way, nor ride too much on horse, lest the bairn come from her before the right time. If she bleed too much after the birth, boil in milk the netherward part of clote, give *it her* to eat, and the ooze to sip.

xxxviii.

1. In case mulieribus menstrua suppressa sunt; boil in ale brooklime, and the two centauries, give "*her*"[1] *this* to drink, and beathe "the woman" in a hot bath, and let her drink the draught in the bath; have ready prepared a poultice of beer dregs, and of green mugwort, and marche, and of barley meal; mix them all together; shake them up in a pan, apply to the natura, and to the netherward part of the vulva, when she goeth off the bath, and let her drink a cup full of the same drink warm, and wrap up the woman well, and leave her so poulticed for a long time of the day,[2] do so twice or thrice, whichever thou must. Thou shalt always prepare a bath and give the potion to the woman at that ilk tide, at which the catamenia were upon her; inquire of the woman about that.

2. Si muliebria nimis fluunt; take a fresh horses tord, lay it on hot gledes, make it reek strongly

---

[1] The Saxon text varies the numbers, plural and singular.
[2] By a transposition in the text, we should get "twice or thrice a day."

betpeoh þa þeoh ūp unðeɲ þæt hɲæȝl þ ɲe mōn
ſpæte ſpiþe.

. XXXVIIII.

Vıð ſmeapyɲme ſmıɲunȝ · nım ſpɲneſ ȝeallan ꝫ
ɲıɲceſ ȝeallan · ꝫ hɲeɼneſ ȝeallan · ꝫ haɲan ȝeallan
menȝ to ɲomne ſmıɲe þa ðolh mıð blap mıð hɲeobe on [1]
þ ɲeap on þ ðolh cnua þonne heoɲot bɲembel leáɼ leȝe
on þa ðolh. Þyɲc beþınȝe to þon ılcan nım æpſ ɲınðe ·
ꝫ pıɲ ɲınðe · cpıc ɲınðe · ɼlah þoɲn ɲınðe · pıɲɲınðe · [2]
beɲc ɲınðe · cnua ealle [3] þa ɲınða pyl on cyɲe hpæȝe
þþeah mıð ꝫ beþe þ līm þe ɲe pyɲm on ſie · ꝫ æɼteɲ
þæɲe beþınȝe aðɲıȝ ꝫ ſmıɲe mıð þæɲe ɲealɼe · ꝫ blap
þa ɲealɼe on þa ðolh ꝫ leȝe ða bɲembel leaɼ ōn ðo ſpa
on ðæȝe ðɲıpa on ſumeɲa ꝫ on ɲıntɲa tɲıpa.

Þyɲc þa blacan ɲealɼe ȝıſ þe þeaɲſ ſie · ȝeɲamna
þe tū ambɲu hɲyþɲa mıcȝean · ꝫ ambeɲ ɼulne holen
ɲınða · ꝫ æɼcɲınða · ꝫ þunȝeſ · pylle þonne on cetele
oþ þ ɲe pæta ſie tpæbe on bepylleð aðo ōɼ þa pyɲta
ꝫ þa ɲınða · pyl eɼt oþ þ hıt ɲie ſpa þıcce ſpa molten
ꝫ ſpa ſpeaɲt ſpa col ſmıɲe mıð ɲıþþan þ ðolh ꝫ haɼa
clám ȝeɲoɲht ōɼ mealteſ ſmeðmán ꝫ oſ hɲıtınȝ melpe ·
ꝫ elehtɲan cluɼa cnua ꝫ ȝnıð toɲomne pyɲc to clame

ȝıſ he ſie to ðɲıȝe ðo on bɲeopenðe pyɲt hɲon clænı
on þa ðolh ꝫ utan ymb · ɲıþþan hıe ȝeſmyɲeð ſynð
feo ɲealſ pıle æɲeſt þa ðolh ɲyman ꝫ þ ðeaðe ſlæɼc
ōɼetan ꝫ þone ſpıle aþþænan ꝫ þone pyɲm þæɲ on
ðeaðne ȝebeþ oþþe cɲıcne oɼðɲıſð ꝫ þa ðolh ȝelácnað. :·

---

[1] ō þ ɲeap, MS.   [3] elle, MS.
[2] pıɲɲınðe is thus repeated in MS.

between the thighs, up under the raiment, that the
woman may sweat much.

xxxix.

1. A smearing for a penetrating worm; take swines
gall, and fishes gall, and crabs gall, and hares gall ;
mingle them together, smear the wounds therewith;
blow with a reed the liquid into the wound ; then
pound hart bramble[1] leaves, lay them on the wounds.
Work up a fomentation for that ilk ; take aspen rind,
and myrtle rind, quickbeam rind, sloethorn rind, birch
rind; pound all the rinds together, boil them in cheese
whey, wash therewith and foment the limb on which
the wound is, and after the beathing dry and smear
with the salve, and blow the salve into the wounds,
and lay on the bramble leaves; do so thrice a day in
summer, and in winter twice.

2. Work up the black salve, if need be, *thus;* collect
two buckets of bullocks mie, and a bucket full of holly
rinds, and of ash rind, and of aconite; then boil in
a kettle till the liquor be boiled to two thirds, remove
the "worts" and the rinds ; boil again till it be as
thick as milk porridge and as swart as a coal; afterwards smear the wound therewith, and have a plaster
ready wrought of fine smede of malt, and of whiting
meal, and lupins; cleave, pound, and rub *them* together,
work them into a paste; if it be too dry, add brewing wort, a trifle *of it;* dab it on the wounds and
round about them. After they are smeared, the salve
will first enlarge the wounds, and eat off the dead
flesh, and soften the swelling, and it will do to
death the worm therein, or drive him away alive,
and will heal the wounds.

---

[1] *Rhamnus.*

.XL.

Ƿiþ þon þe mon ſie monaþ ƿeóc nim meþe ſpineꞃ ꝼel
ꝛyꞃc to ſꞃipan ſꝛinꝫ miꝺ þone man ꞃona biꝺ ꞃel .
amen.[1]

.XLI.

Vyꞃc[2] ꝫoꝺne ꝺꞃenc ꝛiþ eallum ꞃeonꝺeſ coſtunꝫum .
Nim betonican . biſceop ꝛyꞃt . elehtꞃan . ꝫyþꞃiꝼan .
attoꞃlaþan . ꝛulꝼeꞃ camb . ꝫeaꞃpan . leꝫe unꝺeꞃ peoꞃoꝺ
ꝫeſinꝫe .VIIII. mæꞃꞃan oꝛeꞃ ꝫeſceaꞃꝼa þa ꝛyꞃta on
haliꝫ pæteꞃ ꞃele ꝺꞃincan on neaht nejtiꝫ ꞃcenc ꝼulne .
ꝛ ꝺo þ haliꝫ pæteꞃ on ealne þone mete þe ꞃe man
þicꝫe. Ꝺyꞃc ꝫoꝺe ꞃealꝼe ꝛiþ ꞃeonꝺeꞃ coſtunꝫa . biſceop
ꝛyꞃt . elehtꞃe . haꞃan[3] ſꝛꞃecel . ſtꞃeaꝛbeꞃian ꝛiꞃe . ſio
cluꝛihte ꝛenꝛyꞃt eoꞃꝺꞃima . bꞃembel æppel . polleian .
peꞃmoꝺ . ꝫecnua þa ꝛyꞃta ealle apylle on ꝫoꝺꞃe
buteꞃan ꝛꞃinꝫ þuꞃh claꝺ ſete unꝺeꞃ peoꞃoꝺ ꞃinꝫe
.VIIII. mæꞃꞃan oꝛeꞃ . ſmiꞃe þone man miꝺ on þa þun-
ponꝫe . ꝛ buꝼan þam eaꝫum ꝛ uꝼan þ heaꝼoꝺ . ꝛ þa
bꞃeoſt ꝛ unꝺeꞃ þam eaꞃmum þa ſiban. þeoꞃ ꞃealꝼ
iꞃ ꝫoꝺ ꝛiþ ælcꞃe ꞃeonꝺeꞃ coſtunꝫa ꝛ ælꞃſibenne ꝛ
lencten able. ꝫiꞃ þu pilt lacnian ꝫeꞃitſeocne man
ꝫeꝺo byꝺene ꝼulle cealꝺeꞃ pætꞃeꞃ ꝺꞃyꝛ þꞃiꞃa on þæꞃ
ꝺꞃenceꞃ . beþe þone man on þam pætꞃe ꝛ ete ꞃe man
ꝫehalꝫoꝺne hlaꝼ . ꝛ cyꞃe . ꝛ ꝫaꞃleac . ꝛ cꞃopleác ꝛ
ꝺꞃince þæꞃ ꝺꞃenceꞃ ꞃcenc ꝼulne ꝛ þonne he ꞃie
bebaþoꝺ ſmiꞃe miꝺ þæꞃe ꞃealꝼe ſꝛiþe . ꝛ ꞃiþþan him
ꞃel ꞃie ꝛyꞃc him þonne ſꝛiꝺne ꝺꞃenc útyꞃꞃenꝺum.[4]
Ꝺyꞃc þuꞃ þone ꝺꞃenc nim lybcoꞃꞃeꞃ leaꝼ . ꝛ celeþonian moꞃan . ꝛ ꝫlæꝺenan moꞃan . ꝛ hooceꞃ moꞃan .
ꝛ elleneꞃ ꝛyꞃttꞃuman ꞃinꝺe pyl on ealaꝺ læt ſtanꝺan
neahteꞃne ahlyttꞃe þonne ꝛ ꝫeꝛyꞃm ꝺo buteꞃan to ꝛ

---

[1] amen is in a different hand.   [3] haꞃa, MS.
[2] Vꞃc, MS.   [4] Read utyꞃꞃenꝺe, for -ꝺne.

xl.

In case a man be lunatic; take skin of a mereswine *or porpoise*, work it into a whip, swinge the man therewith, soon he will be well. Amen.

xli.

Work *thus* a good drink against all temptations of the devil. Take betony, bishopwort, lupins, githrife, attorlothe, wolfscomb, yarrow; lay them under the altar, sing nine masses over them, scrape the worts into holy water, give *the man* to drink at night fasting a cup full, and put the holy water into all the meat which the man taketh. Work *thus* a good salve against temptations of the fiend. Bishopwort, lupin, vipers bugloss, strawberry plant, the cloved wenwort, earth rime, blackberry, pennyroyal, wormwood; pound all the worts, boil them in good butter, wring through a cloth, set them under the altar, sing nine masses over them; smear the man therewith on the temples, and above the eyes, and above the head, and the breast, and the sides under the arms. This salve is good for every temptation of the fiend, and for a man full of elfin tricks, and for typhus fever. If thou wilt cure a wit sick man, put a pail full of cold water, drop thrice into it some of the drink; bathe the man in the water, and let the man eat hallowed bread, and cheese, and garlic, and cropleek, and drink a cup full of the drink; and when he hath been bathed, smear with the salve thoroughly; and when it is better with him, then work him a strong purgative drink. Work the drink thus; take leaves of libcorn, and roots of celandine, and roots of gladden, and root of hollyhock, and rind of root of elder; boil in ale, let it stand for the space of a night, then clarify, and warm *it*, add butter and salt, ad-

ꞃealt ꞃele ꝺꞃincan. Ƿyꞃc ꞅpiꞃe ꝺꞃenc úꞇyꞃnenꝺne ním
ꞅeopeꞃꞇiᵹ lybcoꞃna beꞃenꝺ ꝑel ⁊ ᵹeᵹniꝺ on moꝥoꞃeaꞃꝺe
celeꝥonian ⁊ hócceꞃ moꞃan ⁊ ꞇꞃa cluꞃe ꝥæꞃe cluꞃehꞇan
penꞃyꞃꞇe ⁊ hꞃeꞃhꝑeꞇꞇe niꝥeꞃeaꞃꝺe an lyꞇel · ⁊ hampyꞃꞇe moꞃan meꝺmicel · ᵹeꝺo ealle ꝥa pyꞃꞇa ꞅpiꝥe ꝑel
clæne ⁊ ᵹecnua ꝺo on eala beꞃꞃeoh læꞇ ꞅꞇanꝺan neah-

ꞇeꞃne ꞃele ꝺꞃincan ꞃcenc ꞃulne.

.XLII.

Ᵹiꞃ ꞅpiꝺꝺꞃenc on man ᵹeꞃiꞇꞇe ⁊ he nelle óꞃᵹan
nim niꝥeꞃeaꞃꝺe celeꝥonian · ⁊ lybcoꞃneꞃ leaꞃ oꝥꝥe
aꞃoꝺ pyl on ealaꝺ ꝺo buꞇeꞃan ⁊ ꞃealꞇ ꞇo ꞃele ꝺꞃincan
peaꞃmeꞃ ꞃcenc ꞃulne.

.XLIII.

Ƿiꝥ aꞇꞇꞃeꞃ ꝺꞃince ꞅeoꝥ henne ⁊ hócceꞃ leaꞃ on
pæꞇꞃe aꝺo ꝥone ꞃuᵹel óꞃ ⁊ ꝥa pyꞃꞇa ꞃele ꞅupan ꝥ
bꞃoꝺ ꝑel ᵹebuꞇeꞃoꝺ ꞅpa he haꞇoꞅꞇ mæᵹe · ᵹiꞃ he æꞃ
hæꞃꝥ aꞇꞇoꞃ ᵹeꝺꞃuncen ne biꝥ him ahꞇe ꝥe pyꞃꞃ ᵹiꞃ
he ꝥ bꞃoꝺ ꝥonne æꞃ ꞅyꝥꝺ ne meahꞇ ꝥu him ꝥy ꝺæᵹe
aꞇꞇoꞃ ᵹeꞃellan;

.XLIIII.

Viꝥ luꞃum ꞃele him eꞇan ᵹeꞅoꝺenne capel on neahꞇ
neꞃꞇiᵹ ᵹelome he biꝥ luꞃûm beꞃeꞃeꝺ.

.XLV.

Ᵹiꞃ ꝥoꞃn ꞅꞇinᵹe man on ꝼóꞇ oꝥꝥe hꞃeoꝺ ⁊ nelle
óꞃᵹan nime niꞃe ᵹoꞃe ꞇoꞃꝺ · ⁊ ᵹꞃene ᵹeaꞃꞃan cnupiᵹe
ꞅpiꝥe ꞇoꞃomne clæm on ꝥ ꝺolh ꞅona biꝥ ꞃel ;

minister to drink. Work *thus* a purgative spew drink; take forty libcorns, rend them well, and rub them *small* upon the netherward part of celandine and mallow roots, and two cloves of the cloved wenwort, and a little of the netherward part of cucumber, and a moderate quantity of the root of homewort; make all the worts thoroughly well clean, and pound *them;* put them into ale, wrap up, let it stand for a nights space, give *the man* a cup full to drink.

xlii.

If a strong potion lodge in a man, and will not come away, take the netherward part of celandine, and leaves of libcorn or arod,[1] boil in ale, add butter and salt, give to drink a cup full of it warm.

xliii.

For drink of poison; seethe a hen and leaves of mallow in water, remove the fowl and the worts, give *the man* the broth to sip, well buttered, as hot as he can *take it.* If he hath drunken poison before, it will be none the worse with him. If he suppeth the broth beforehand thou mayst not that day give him poison (effectually).

xliv.

Against lice; give *the man* to eat sodden colewort at night fasting, frequently: he will be guarded against lice.

xlv.

If a thorn or a reed prick a man in the foot, and will not be gone; let him take a fresh goose tord and green yarrow, let him pound them thoroughly together, paste them on the wound, soon it will be well.

---

[1] Aron?

.XLVI.

Þiþ æꞃmælum · ⁊ piþ eallum eaᵹna pæꞃce · ceop
pulꝼeꞃ comb pꞃinᵹ þonne þuꞃh hæpenne cla𐌳 pyllenne
on þa eaᵹan ᵽ ꞃeap on niht þonne he ꞃeꞅtan pille ⁊
on moꞃᵹen 𐌳o æᵹeꞅ ᵽ hpite þæꞃ on.

.XLVII.

Viþ lyꝼt able ᵹiꝼ ꞅe mu𐌳 ꞃie poh oþþe pon · nim
cellenþꞃan ᵹnib on piꝼeꞅ meolce 𐌳o on ᵽ hale eaꞃe him
biþ ꞃona ꞅel. Eꝼt nim cellenþꞃan aðꞃuᵹ ᵹepyꞃc to
𐌳uꞅte ᵹemenᵹ ᵽ 𐌳uꞅt piþ piꝼeꞅ meolūc þe pæpne𐌳 ꞃebe
apꞃinᵹ þuꞃh hæpenne cla𐌳 ⁊ ꞅmiꞃe ᵽ hale ponᵹe mi𐌳
⁊ 𐌳ꞃype on ᵽ eaꞃe pæꞃlice. Þyꞃc þonne beþinᵹe ·
ᵹenim bꞃembel ꞃinðe ⁊ elm ꞃinðe · æꞃc ꞃinðe · ꞅlah-
þoꞃn ꞃinðe apulboꞃ ꞃinbe · iꝼiᵹ ꞃinbe · ealle þaꞃ
nioþopeaꞃðe ⁊ hpeꞃhpettan · ꞅmeꞃu pyꞃt · eoꝼoꞃ ꝼeaꞃn ·
elene · ælꝼþone · betonice · maꞃubie · ꞃeðic · aᵹꞃi-
monia ᵹeꞅceaꞃꝼa þa pyꞃta on cetel ⁊ pyl ꝼꞃiðe · þonne
hit ꞅie ꞅpiþe ᵹepylle𐌳 𐌳o oꝼ þam ꝼyꞃe ⁊ ꞅete ⁊ ᵹepyꞃc
þam men ꞅetl oꝼeꞃ þam citele ⁊ beꞃꞃeop 𐌳one man
mi𐌳 ᵽ ꞅe æþm ne mæᵹe ūt nahþæꞃ butan he mæᵹe
ᵹeeþian · beþe hine mi𐌳 þiꞅꞅe beþinᵹe þa hpile þa he
mæᵹe aꞃæꞃnan. Daꝼa him þonne oþeꞃ bæþ ᵹeaꞃa ·
ᵹenim æmet beð mi𐌳 ealle · þaꞃa þe hpilum ꝼleoᵹa𐌳
beoþ ꞃeaðe · pyl on pætꞃe beþe hine mi𐌳 · onᵹemet-
hatum. Þýꞃc him þonne ꞃealꝼe nim ælceꞃ þaꞃa
cynneꞅ pyꞃta pyl on buteꞃan ꞅmiꞃe mi𐌳 þa ꞃaꞃan
limu hie cꞃiciaþ ꞃona. Þyꞃc him leaᵹe ōꝼ ellen ahꞃan
þꞃeah hiꞅ heaꝼo𐌳 mi𐌳 colꞃe him biþ ꞃona bet · ⁊ ꞅe
man læte him blo𐌳 ælce monþe on · V · nihta ealðne
monan ⁊ on ꝼiꝼtyne ⁊ on · XX.

xlvi.

For imminutions,[1] and for all pain of the eyes; chew wolfscomb, then wring the ooze through a purple cloth upon the eyes, at night, when *the man* has a mind to rest, and in the morning apply the white of an egg.

xlvii.

For palsy, if the mouth be awry or livid, rub coriander in womans milk, put it into the sound ear, it will soon be well with *the man*. Again, take coriander, dry it, work it to dust, mingle the dust with milk of a woman, who brought forth a male, wring through a purple cloth, and smear the sound cheek therewith, and drip it on the ear warily. Then work a fomentation; take bramble rind, and elm rind, ash rind, sloethorn rind, appletree rind, ivy rind, all these from the nether part of the trees, and cucumber, smearwort, everfern, helenium, enchanters nightshade, betony, marrubium, radish, agrimony; scrape the worts into a kettle, and boil strongly. When it hath been strongly boiled, remove it off the fire and set *it down*, and get the man a seat over the kettle, and wrap the man up, that the vapour may get out nowhere, except only so that the man may breathe; beathe him with this fomentation as long as he can bear it. Then have another bath ready for him, take an emmet bed, all at once, *a bed* of those *male emmets* which at whiles fly, they are red ones, boil them in water, beathe him with it immoderately hot. Then make him a salve; take worts of each kind of those *above mentioned*, boil them in butter, smear the sore limbs therewith, they will soon quicken. Make him a ley of elder ashes, wash his head with this cold; it will soon be well with him: and let the man get bled every month, when the moon is five, and fifteen, and twenty nights old.

---

[1] Contraction of the pupil.

.XLVIII.

Ðƿenc ƿiþ ƒíc able nim buluc · ⁊ eoƒoꞃþꞃocan
nioþopeaꞃðe · ⁊ puðu ꞃillan · ⁊ ȝeaceƒ ꞃuꞃan · ⁊
æƒeꞃþan ȝeꞃceaꞃꞃa þaƒ pyꞃco coSomne ðo on ȝellec
innan læc ƒcanðan neahceꞃne æꞃ þu hine ðꞃince.
Ƿyꞃc beþinȝe nim ꝥ ꞃeaðe ꞃyðen ðo on cꞃiȝ hæc
þonne ƒcanaƒ ƒꞃiþe hace leȝe on ꝥ cꞃiȝ innan ⁊ he
ꞃicce on ƒcole oꞃeꞃ þæꞃe beþinȝe ꝥ hio hine mæȝe
cela ȝeꞃeocan þonne ƒeallað þa ƒíc pyꞃmaƒ on þa
beþinȝe him biþ ꞃona ꞃel · ðꞃince þone ðꞃenc æꞃ
þæꞃe beþinȝe · ȝíƒ he þonne þa beþinȝe þuꞃhceon ne
mæȝe ðꞃince þone ðꞃenc ælce ðæȝe oþ ꝥ him ꞃel ƒie.

.XLVIIII.

Viþ ꞃculboꞃ pæꞃce ⁊ eaꞃma · pyl becomican ón ealoð
ꞃele ðꞃincan ȝelome ⁊ ꞃimle ƒmiꞃe hine æc ƒyꞃe mið
peꞃpyꞃce.

.L.

Ȝiƒ cneoꞃ ꞃaꞃ ꞃie cnua beolenan ⁊ hemlic beþe mið
⁊ leȝe on.

.LI.

Giƒ ꞃe ƒóc ꞃaꞃ ꞃie ellen leaƒ · ⁊ peȝbꞃæðan ⁊
mucȝpyꞃc ȝecnua ⁊ leȝe on ⁊ ȝebinð hac þæꞃ on. :·

.LII.

Ȝiƒ þu ne mæȝe bloð ðolh ƒoꞃꞃꞃiþan nim niꞃe
hoꞃꞃeƒ coꞃð aðꞃiȝ on ƒunnan ȝeȝnið co ðuƒce ƒꞃiþe
pel leȝe ꝥ ðuƒc ƒꞃiþe þicce on hnenne claþ ꞃꞃiþ mið
þy ꝥ ðolh.

.LIII.

Ȝíƒ meoluc ƒie apyꞃð binð coSomne peȝbꞃæðan · ⁊
ȝiþꞃiƒan · ⁊ ceꞃƒan leȝe on þone ꞃilðcumb ⁊ ne ƒece ꝥ
ƒæc niþeꞃ on eoꞃþan ƒeoƒon nihcum.

xlviii.

A drink for the "fig" disease; take bulot, and the netherward part of everthroat, and wild chervil, and cuckoosour, and æferth; scrape these worts together, put them into a basin, let it stand for the space of a night, ere thou drink it. Work a fomentation *thus;* take the red ryden, put it in a trough, then heat stones very hot, lay them within the trough, and let *the man* sit on a stool over the fomentation, that it may reek him well, then the "fig" worms will fall on the beathing, and it will soon be well with him. Let him drink the drink before the beathing; if then he cannot pull through the beathing, let him drink the drink every day till it be all right with him.

xlix.

Against pain of shoulders and arms; boil betony in ale, give *it the man* to drink frequently, and always smear him at the fire with wenwort.

l.

If a knee be sore, pound henbane and hemlock, foment therewith and lay on.

li.

If the foot be sore, pound and lay on elder leaves, and waybroad, and mugwort; and bind hot upon *the foot.*

lii.

If thou be not able to stanch a bloodletting incision, take a new horses tord, dry it in the sun, rub it to dust thoroughly well, lay the dust very thick on a linen cloth; wrap up the wound with that.

liii.

If milk be spoilt; bind together waybroad, and githrife, and cress, lay them on the milk pail, and set not the vessel down on the earth for seven nights.

. LIIII.

Þýnc ꞃealꝼe pıð nıhtȝenȝan · pyl on buteꞃan
elehtꞃan · heȝeꞃıꞃan · bıſceop pynt · ꞃeaðe maȝþan ·
cꞃopleác · ꞃealt ſmıꞃe mıð hım bıð ꞃona ꞃel.

. LV.

Ȝıꝼ men ſıo heaꝼoð panne beô ȝehlenceð aleȝe þone
man ûppeaꞃð ðꞃıꝼ . II. ſtacan æt þam eaxlum leȝe
þonne bꞃeð þpeoꞃeꞃ oꞃeꞃ þa ꞃet ꞃleah þonne þꞃıpa on
mıð ꞃleȝe bytle hıo ȝæþ on ꞃıht Sona.

. LVI.

Gıꝼ men nelle myltan hıꞃ mete nıþepeaꞃð clate ꞇ
meꞃce ꞇ ſunðcoꞃneꞃ leáꞃ pyl on ealaþ ſele ðꞃıncan.

. LVII.

Vıþ ꝼıꝼ ȝemæblan ȝebeꞃȝe on neaht neꞃtıȝ ꞃæðıceꞃ
moꞃan þy dæȝe ne mæȝ þe ꞃe ȝemæbla ꞃceþþan.

. LVIII.

Þıþ ꞃeonðeꞃ coſtunȝe ꞃuð molın[1] hatte pynt peaxeþ
be yꞃnenðum pætꞃe · ȝıꝼ þu þa on þe haꝼaſt ꞇ unðeꞃ
þınum heaꝼoð bolſtꞃe · · ꞇ oꞃeꞃ þıneꞃ huꞃeꞃ ðuꞃum · ne
mæȝ þe ðeoꝼol ꞃceþþan Inne ne ute.

. LVII[II].

Þıþ þeoꞃ penne ȝıꝼ he ſıe men on cneoꞃe oþþe on
oþꞃım lıme pync clam ôꝼ ꞃuꞃꞃe ꞃıȝeꞃꞃe ȝꞃut oððe
ðaȝe ȝebo æȝeſ hꞃıt to ꞇ bꞃoc ceꞃſan leȝe on ꝥ lím
oþ ꝥ ꞃe clam hatıȝe ðo oꞃ þone leȝe oþeꞃꞃe þæꞃ on.

---

[1] Read niolın.

liv.

Work a salve against nocturnal *goblin* visitors ; boil in butter lupins, hedgerife, bishopwort, red maythe, cropleek, salt; smear *the man* therewith, it will soon be well with him.

lv.

If a mans head-pan, or skull, be *seemingly* iron-bound lay the man with face upward, drive two stakes into *the ground* at the armpits, then lay a plank across over his feet, then strike on it thrice with a sledge beetle, *the skull* will come right soon.

lvi.

If a mans meat will not digest, boil in ale the netherward part of clote, and marche, and leaves of saxifrage, give *him that* to drink.

lvii.

Against a womans chatter; taste at night fasting a root of radish, that day the chatter cannot harm thee.

lviii.

Against temptation of the fiend, a wort hight red niolin, *red stalk*, it waxeth by running water : if thou hast it on thee, and under thy head bolster, and over thy house doors, the devil may not scathe thee, within nor without.

lix.

For a " dry " wen; if it be on a man's knee, or on another limb, work a paste of sour rye groats or dough, add the white of an egg and brook cresses, lay on the limb till the paste gets hot, remove it then and lay another on.

.LX.

Vypc ʒoðe eaprealɼe hunðeɼ tunʒe nɪþepeapð ꝼ ſin-
ʒpene ꝼ ſinꝼulle · tunhoꝼe nɪoþopeapð · celeþonɪan leaꝼ ·
ʒapleác · cpopleác ðo on pɪn oððe on eceð ppɪnʒ þuph
hæpenne cla ð on þ eape læt ſtanðan .III. nɪht æp þu
hɪne on ðo. Eꝼt nɪm cpopleác ꝼ ſinꝼullan ʒecnua[1]
hpon pɪneɼ to ꝼ ppɪnʒ on þ eape hɪm bɪþ ɼona ſel　：·

.LXI.

Þype ɼealɼe pɪþ ælꝼcynne ꝼ nɪhtʒenʒan ꝼ þam
mannum þe ðeoꝼol mɪð hæmð · ʒenɪm eopohumelan ·
peɪ̣moð bɪrceoppynt · elehtpe · ærcþpote · beolone ·
haɪ̣e pynt · haɪ̣an ſppecel · hæþ benʒean pɪɼan · cpopleác · ʒapleác · heʒepɪꝼan copn · ʒyþpɪɼe · ꝼɪnul. ðo
þaɼ pypta on an ꝼæt ſete unðep peoꝼoð ɼɪnʒ oꝼep
.VIIII. mæɪɼan apyl ón butepan ꝼ on ɼceapeɼ ſmeppe
ðo halɪʒeɼ ɼealteɼ ꝼela on aɼeoh þuɪ̣h clað · peoɼp þa
pypta on ypnenðe pæteɼ. ʒɪꝼ men hpɪlc yꝼel coɼtunʒ
peoɼþe oþþe ælꝼ oþþe nɪht ʒenʒan · ſmɪpe hɪɼ ꝼplɪtan
mɪð þɪɼɼe ɼealɼe ꝼ on hɪɼ eaʒan ðo ꝼ þæp hɪm ɼe
lɪchoma ɼap ſɪe · ꝼ ɼecelſa hɪne ꝼ ſena ʒelome hɪɼ
þɪnʒ bɪþ ɼona ɼelpe.

.LXII.

Vɪð ælꝼable nɪm bɪɼceop pynt · ꝼɪnul · elehtpe ·
ælꝼþonan nɪoþopeapðe · ꝼ ʒehalʒoðeɼ cpɪſteɼ mæleɼ
ɼaʒu · ꝼ ſtoɪ̣ ðo ælcpe hanð ꝼulle · bebɪnð ealle þa
pypta on claþe beðyp on ꝼont pætpe ʒehalʒoðum

---

[1] ðo is to be added.

lx.

Work a good ear salve *thus* ; tho netherward part
of hounds tongue, and singreen, and sedum, the netherward part of garden hove, leaves of celandine, garlic,
cropleek ; put *them* into wine or vinegar, wring them
through a coloured cloth into the ear ; let *the liquor*
stand for three nights before thou apply it. Again,
take cropleek and sedum, pound them, add a little
wine, and wring into the ear, it will soon be well
with it.

lxi.

Work thus a salve against the elfin race and nocturnal *goblin* visitors, and for the women with whom the
devil hath carnal commerce ; take the ewe hop plant,
probably the female hop plant, wormwood, bishopwort,
lupin, ashthroat, henbane, harewort, vipers bugloss,
heathberry plants, cropleek, garlic, grains of hedgerife,
githrife, fennel ; put these worts into a vessel, set
them under the altar, sing over them nine masses,
boil *them* in butter and sheeps grease, add much holy
salt, strain through a cloth, throw the worts into running water. If any ill tempting occur to a man, or
an elf or *goblin* night visitors *come*, smear his forehead
with this salve, and put it on his eyes, and where his
body is sore, and cense him with incense, and sign
him frequently with the sign of the cross ; his condition will soon be better.

lxii.

Against elf disease ; take bishopwort, fennel, lupin,
the lower part of enchanters nightshade, and moss or
lichen from the hallowed sign of Christ, and incense,
of each a hand full ; bind all the worts in a cloth, dip
it thrice in hallowed font water, have sung over

þɲupa · læt ſinʒan oɟeɲ .III. mæɟɟan · ane omnibus
Scīɟ · oþɲe contɲa tɲibulatjonem · þɲiððan pɲo in-
piɲmiS · ðo þonne ʒleða an ʒlebɟæt ɟ leʒe þa pyɲta
on · ʒeɲec þone man mið þam pyɲtum æɲ unðeɲn ɟ
on niht ɟ ɲinʒ letania ɟ cɲeðan ɟ pateɲ noɟteɲ ɟ
pɲit him cɲiſteɟ mæl on ælcum lime ɟ nim lytle hanð
ɟulle þæɟ ilcan cynneɟ pyɲta ʒelice ʒehalʒoðe ɟ pyl on
meolce ðɲyp þɲupa ʒehalʒoðeɟ pætɲeɟ on ɟ ſupe æɲ
hiſ mete him biþ ɟona ɟel. Þiþ þon ilcan · ʒanʒ on
þunɲeɟ æɟen þonne ſunne on ɟetle ſie þæɲ þu pite
elenan ſtanðan ɲinʒ þonne beneðicite · ɟ pateɲ noɟteɲ ·
ɟ letanian · ɟ ſtinʒ þin ɟeax on þa pyɲte læt ſtician
þæɲ on ʒanʒ þe apeʒ ʒanʒ eɟt to þonne ðæʒ ɟ niht ɟuɲ-
þum ɟcaðe on þam ilcan uhte ʒanʒ æɲeſt to cɲiucean
ɟ þe ʒeɟena ɟ ʒoðe þe bebeoð ʒanʒ þonne ſpɲʒenðe
ɟ þeah þe hɲæt hɲeʒa eʒeſliceſ onʒean cume oþþe man
ne cɲeþ þu him æniʒ poɲð to æɲ þu cume to þæɲe
pyɲte þe þu on æɟen æɲ ʒemeaɲcobeſt ſinʒ þonne
beneðicite · ɟ pateɲ noɟteɲ · ɟ letania abelɟ þa pyɲt
læt ſtician þ ɟeax þæɲ on · ʒanʒ eɟt ſpa þu ɲaþoſt
mæʒe to cɲiucean ɟ leʒe unðeɲ peoɟoð mið þām ɟeaxe
læt licʒean oþ þ ſunne uppe ſie · apæɟc ſiþþan ðo to
ðɲence · ɟ biɟceop pyɲt ɟ cɲiſteɟ mæleſ ɲaʒu apyl
þɲipa on meolcum ʒeot þɲipa haliʒ pæteɲ on ſinʒ on
pateɲ noɟteɲ · ɟ cɲeðan · ɟ ʒloɲia in excelſiɟ ðeo · ɟ
ſinʒ on hine letania · ɟ hine eſc ymb pɲit mið ſpeoɲðe
on .IIII. healɟa on cɲuce · ɟ ðɲince þone ðɲenc ſiþþan
him biþ ɟona ɟel. Eɟt piþ þon leʒe unðeɲ peoɟoð þaɟ
pyɲte læt ʒeſinʒan oɟeɲ .VIIII. mæɟɟan · ɲecelſ ·
haliʒ ɟealt .III. heaɟoð cɲopleaceɟ ſalɟþonan nioþe-

it three masses, one "Omnibus sanctis," [1] another "Contra tribulationem," [2] a third "Pro infirmis." [1] Then put gledes in a glede pan, and lay the worts on: reek the man with the worts before nine in the morning, and at night, and sing a litany, and the credo, and the Pater noster, and write Christs mark on each of his limbs, and take a little hand full of worts of the same kind similarly hallowed, and boil in milk, drop thrice some hallowed water into it, and let him sip of it before his meat; it will soon be well with him. For that ilk. Go on Thursday evening, when the sun is set, where thou knowest that helenium stands, then sing the "Benedicite," and "Pater noster," and a litany, and stick thy knife into the wort, make it stick fast, and go away: go again, when day and night just divide;[3] at the same period go first to church and cross thyself, and commend thyself to God; then go in silence, and though anything soever of an awful sort or man a meet thee, say not thou to him any word, ere thou come to the wort, which on the evening before thou markedst; then sing the Benedicite, and the Pater noster, and a litany, delve up the wort, let the knife stick in it; go again as quick as thou art able to church, and lay it under the altar with the knife; let it lie till the sun be up, wash it afterwards, and make into a drink, and bishopwort, and lichen off a crucifix; boil in milk thrice, thrice pour holy water upon it, and sing over it the Paternoster, the Credo, and the Gloria in excelsis deo;[4] and sing upon it a litany, and score with a sword round about it on three sides a cross, and then after that let *the man* drink the wort; soon will it be well with him. Again for that; lay these worts under the altar, have nine masses sung over them, incense, holy salt, three heads of cropleek, the netherward part of enchanters nightshade,

---

[1] In the missal.
[2] The same as "Pro quacunque necessitate"?
[3] In early morning.
[4] Luke ii. 14.

peaþde · elenan · nim on morʒen fcenc fulne meoluce
ðryp þripa haliʒeɼ pætepeſ on ſupe ſpa he hatoſt
mæʒe · ete mið .IIL ſnæða ælɼþonan ⁊ þonne he neſtan pille hæbbe ʒleða þæp inne leʒe ſtop ⁊ ælɼþonan

fol. 124 b.

on þa ʒleða · ⁊ nec hine mið þ he ſpæte · ⁊ þ hūɼ
ʒeonð nēc ⁊ ʒeopne þone man ʒeɼena · ⁊ þonne he
on neſte ʒanʒe ete .III. ſnæða eolenan · ⁊ .III. opop-
leaceɼ · ⁊ .III. ɼealteɼ · ⁊ hæbbe him fcenc fulne
ealað ⁊ ðrype þripa haliʒ pætep on · befupe ælce
ſnæb · ʒepeſte hine riþþan · ðo þiɼ .VIIII. morʒenaſ · ⁊
.VIIII. niht him biþ ɼona ɼel. ʒiɼ him biþ ælɼfoʒoþa
him beoþ þa eaʒan ʒeolpe þæp hi neaðe beón fceolðon.
ʒiɼ þu þone món lacnian pille þænc hiſ ʒebæpa ⁊
pite hpilceſ haðeſ he fie · ʒiɼ hit biþ pæpneð man
⁊ locað úp þonne þu hine æpeſt ɼceapaſt ⁊ ɼe ⁊plita
biþ ʒeolpe blac · þone món þu mealht ʒelacnian æltæplice
ʒiɼ he ne biþ þæp on to lanʒe · ʒiɼ hit biþ píɼ ⁊ locað
niþep þonne þu hit æpeſt ɼceapaſt · ⁊ hipe ⁊plita biþ
neaðe pan þ þu miht eác ʒelácnian · ʒiɼ hit bið bæʒ-
þepne lenʒ on þonne .XII. monaþ ⁊ fio onfyn biþ
þyɼlicu þonne mealht þu hine betan to hpile · ⁊ ne
mealht hpæþepc æltæplice ʒelácnian. Þpit þiɼ ʒeppit ·
Scpiptum eSt pex peʒum et ðominuɼ ðominantjum ·
bypnice · bepomce · luplupe · iehe · aiuɼ · aiuɼ · aiuɼ ·
Scɼ · Scɼ · Scɼ · ðominuɼ ðeuɼ Sabaoth · amen · alleluiah.
Sinʒ þiɼ oɼep þam ðpence ⁊ þam ʒeppite · ðeuɼ om-

fol. 125 a.

nipotenſ patep ðomini noɼtpi iesu cpiɼti · pep Inpofi-
tjonem huiuſ ɼcpiptupa expelle a ɼamulo tuo N̄ ·[1] Omnem Impetum[2] caſtalıðum ·[3] ðe capite · ðe capilliſ · ðe

---

[1] nomen.
[2] impetuū, MS.
[2] Castalides, ðun elɼen, Gl. Somn.
p. 79 b. *Elves of the downs.*

helenium; take in the morning a cup full of milk,
drop thrice some holy water into it, let *the man* sup
it up as hot as he can: let him eat therewith three
bits of enchanters nightshade, and when he hath a
mind to rest, let him have in his chamber gledes, let
him lay on the gledes στύραξ and elfthone, and reek
him therewith till he sweat, and reek the house all
through; earnestly also sign the man with the sign of
the cross, and when he is going to bed, let him eat
three bits of helenium, and three of cropleek, and three
of salt, and let him have a cup full of ale, and thrice
drop holy water into it; let him sup up each bit, *and*
afterwards rest himself. Let him do this for nine
mornings and nine nights, it will soon be well with
him. If *a man* hath elf hicket, his eyes are yellow,
where they should be red. If thou have a will to
cure the man, observe his gestures, and consider of what
sex he be; if it be a man and looketh up, when thou
first seest him, and the countenance be yellowish black,
thou mayst cure the man thoroughly if he is not too
long in the disease; if it is a woman and looketh
down, when thou first seest her, and her countenance
is livid red, thou mayst also cure that; if it has been
upon *the man* longer than a twelvemonth and a day,
and the aspect be such as this, then mayst thou amend
it for a while, and notwithstanding mayst not entirely
cure it. Write this writing, "Scriptum est, rex regum
" et dominus dominantium Veronica,[1] Veronica, . . . IAO,[2]
" ἅγιος, ἅγιος, ἅγιος, sanctus, sanctus, sanctus, domi-
" nus, deus sabaoth, amen, alleluiah." Sing this over
the drink and the writing, "Deus omnipotens, pater
" domini nostri Iesu Christi, per impositionem huius
" scripturæ expelle a famulo tuo, *here insert the name,*
" omnem impetum castalidum de capite, de capillis, de

---

[1] The miraculous portrait on the kerchief of St. Veronica.

[2] יהוה

cerebro · de fronte · de lingua · de sublingua · de guttore · de faucibus · de dentibus · de oculis · de naribus · de auribus · de manibus · de collo · de brachiis · de corde · de anima · de genibus · de coxis · de pedibus · de compaginibus · omnium membrorum intus et foris · amen. Wyrc þonne drenc font wæter · rudan · Saluian · cassuc · dracongan · þa smeþan wegbrædan niþeweard feþer fugian · biles crop · garleaces .III. clufe · finul · wermod · lufestice · elehtre · ealra emfela · writ .III. crucem mid oleum infirmorum ⁊ cweð · pax tibi · Nim þonne þ gewrit writ crucem mid ofer þam drince ⁊ sing þis þær ofer. Deus omnipotens pater domini · nostri · iesu cristi per Inpositionem huius scripturæ[1] et per gustum huiuS expelle diabolum a famulo tuo · N̄ ·[2] ⁊ credo · ⁊ pater · noster · wæt þ gewrit on þam drence ⁊ writ crucem mid him on ælcum lime ⁊ cweð signum cruciS xp̄i conseruate In uitam eternam · amen. gif þe ne lyste hát hine selfne oþþe swa gesubne swa he gesibbost hæbbe ⁊ senige swa he selost cunne · þes cræft mæg wiþ ælcre feondes costunge.

.LXIII.

Gif mon biþ on wæter ælfadle þonne beoþ him þa hand næglas wonne ⁊ þa eagan tearige ⁊ wile locian
fol. 125 b. niþer · do him þis to læcedome · eofor þrote · cassuc · fone niopoweard · eowberge · elehtre · eolone · merscmealwan crop · fen minte · dile · lilie · attorlaþe · pollegie · marubie · docce · ellen · fel terre · wermod · streawberge leaf · consolde · ófgeot mid ealaþ · do haligwæter to sing þis gealdor ofer þriwa · Ic binne awrat[3] betest beado wræda swa benne ne burnon ne

---

[1] -ra, MS.
[2] *nomen.*
[3] From wriðan rather than writan.

" cerebro, defronte, de lingua, de sublingua, de gutture, de
" faucibus, de dentibus, de oculis, de naribus, de auribus,
" de manibus, de collo, de brachiis, de corde, de anima,
" de genibus, de coxis, de pedibus, de compaginibus
" omnium membrorum intus et foris. Amen." Then
work up a drink thus; font water, rue, sage, cassuck,
dragons, the netherward part of the smooth waybroad,
feverfue, a head of dill, three cloves of garlic, fennel,
wormwood, lovage, lupin, of all equal quantities; write
a cross three times with the oil of unction, and say,
"Pax tibi." Then take the writing, describe a cross
with it over the drink, and sing this over it, "Dominus
" omnipotens, pater domini nostri Iesu Christi, per im-
" positionem huius scripturæ et per gustum huius expelle
" diabolum a famulo tuo;" *here insert the name*, and the
Credo, and Paternoster. Wet the writing in the drink,
and write a cross with it on every limb, and say,
" Signum crucis Christi conservet te in vitam æter-
" nam. Amen." If it listeth thee not *to take this
trouble*, bid *the man* himself, or whomsoever he may
have nearest sib to him, *to do it*, and let him cross
him as well as he can. This craft is powerful against
. every temptation of the fiend.

lxiii.

If a man is in the water elf disease, then are
the nails of his hand livid, and the eyes tearful, and
he will look downwards. Give him this for a leechdom; everthroat, cassuck, the netherward part of fane,
a yew berry, lupin, helenium, a head of marsh mallow,
fen mint, dill, lily, attorlothe, pulegium, marrubium,
dock, elder, fel terræ, *or lesser centaury*, wormwood,
strawberry leaves, consolida; pour them over with ale,
add holy water, sing this charm over them thrice:—

I have wreathed round the wounds
the best of healing wreaths,

buꞃſton ne ꝼunðian ne ꝼeoloȝan · ne hoppetan ne
punð paco ſiau · ne ðolh ðiopian · ac him ꞃelꝼ healðe
hale pæȝe · ne ace þe þon mn þe eoꞃþan on eaꞃe ace ·
Sinȝ þiꞃ maneȝum ꞃiþum · eoꞃþe þe on beꞃe eallum
hiꞃe mihtum ⁊ mæȝenum · þaꞃ ȝalðoꞃ mon mæȝ ſinȝan
ón punðe.

.LXIIII.

Þiþ deoꝼle liþe ðꞃenc ⁊ unȝemynðe do on ealu
caꞃꝼuc · elehtꞃan moꞃan · ꝼinul ontꞃe · betonice · hinð
heoloþe · meꞃce ꞃuðe · peꞃmoð · neꝼte · elene · ælꝼþone ·
pulꝼeꞃ comb · ȝeſinȝ · XII. mæꞃꞃan oꝼeꞃ þam ðꞃence ⁊
ðꞃince him biþ ꞃona ꞃel. ðꞃenc ꝼiþ deoꝼleꞃ coſtunȝa ·
þeꞃan þoꞃn cꞃopleac · eletꞃe · ontꞃe · biſceop pyꞃt ·
ꝼinul · caꞃꞃuc · betonice · ȝehalȝa þaꞃ pyꞃta do on ealu
haliȝ pæteꞃ · ⁊ ſie ꞃe ðꞃenc þæꞃ inne þæꞃ ꞃe ſeoca mnn
inne ſie · ⁊ ſimle æꞃ þon þe he ðꞃince ſinȝ þꞃiꞃa
oꝼeꞃ þam ðꞃence · deuꞃ In nomine tuo ꝼaluum
me ꝼác.

.LXV.

Ȝiꞃ man ſie ȝeȝymeð ⁊ þu hine ȝelacnian ꞃcyle ·
ȝeſeoh þ he ſie toꞃeaꞃð þonne þu inȝanȝe þonne mæȝ
he libban · ȝiꞃ he þe ſie ꝼꞃampeaꞃð ne ȝꞃet þu hine
ahte · ȝiꞃ he libban mæȝe pyl on buteꞃan betonican ·

that the baneful sores may
neither burn nor burst,
nor find their way further,
nor turn foul and fallow,
nor thump and throb on,
nor be wicked wounds,
nor dig deeply down;
but he himself may hold
in a way to health.
Let it ache thee no more,
than ear in earth[1] acheth.

Sing *also* this many times, [2] " May earth bear on
" thee with all her might and main." These charms
a man may sing over a wound.

lxiv.

A lithe drink against a devil and dementedness.
Put into ale cassuck, roots of lupin, fennel, ontre,
betony, hindheal, marche, rue, wormwood, nepeta, helenium, elfthone, wolfs comb; sing twelve masses over
the drink, and let *the man* drink, it will soon be well
with him. A drink against temptations of the devil;
tuftythorn, cropleek, lupin, ontre, bishopwort, fennel,
cassuck, betony; hallow these worts,[3] put into some ale
some holy water, and let the drink be in the same
chamber as the sick man, and constantly before he
drinketh sing thrice over the drink, " Deus! In
" nomine tuo salvum me fac."

lxv.

If a man be overlooked, and thou must cure him,
see that his face be turned to thee when thou goest
in, then he may live; if his face be turned from thee,
have thou nothing to do with him. If he may live,

---

[1] In the grave.
[2] This seems intended to quell the
elf.

[3] By a formula of benediction.

ᵹyþpiꝼan · ᵹeappan · polleian · bolhpunan · appinᵹ þuph
claþ læt ſtanðan · ᵹehæt ſcenc ꝼulne cu peapmpe meolce
ðo þæpe pealꝼe .v. ſnæba þæp on ſupe on neaht nepᴅiᵹ
ꝼ ete pepſc ꝼlæpc þæp þæp hiᴅ pæᴅoſᴅ ſie · ꝼ þioᵹe on
niht þa pealꝼe ꝼ þ bolh pet mið ealðan ſpice oþþe mið
ꝼepſcpe buᴅepan þonne hiᴅ ſie clæne ꝼ pel peað · lacna
mið þa ilcan pealꝼa · ꝼ ne læt ᴅoSomne ᵹiꝼ hio ſie
clæne · læt piþþan ᴅoSomne. ᵹiꝼ hiᴅ nelle ꝼop þiſûm
læcebome baᴅian · pyl on meolcum þa peaðan ᵹeappan
ꝼ ꝼinul · linpypᴅ · ealpa ᵹelice læt apeallan .v. piþum
appinᵹ þuph cla̋ ᵹebjup pel ſpiþne bpip þæp on mið
hpæᴅe melpe ꝼ ᵹepceaꝼ ᵹobeſ peaxeſ ane ſnæðe þæp
on ꝼ hpep ᴅoſomne læt ᵹecolian · ᵹenim hapan pulle
lyᴅle ſnæðe .iii. bepinð mið þy bpipe uᴅan þ he mæᵹe
ꝼopſpelᵹan ꝼ beſupe mið cu peapmum.[1]

fol. 126 b.

. LXVI.

Dpenc ᵹiꝼ þeop pie on men nim þaſ pypᴅe nioþe-
peapðe · ꝼinol biſceop pypᴅ æpcþpoᴅan ealpa emꝼela
þiſſa ᴅpeᵹa mæſᴅ · uꝼepeapðe puðan · ꝼ beᴅonican ōꝼ-
ᵹeoᴅ mið hluᴅᴅpum ealaþ ꝼ ᵹeſinᵹe .iii. mæſſan oꝼep
ꝼ ðpince ymb .ii. niht þæſ þe he oꝼᵹoᴅen ſie æp
hiſ meᴅe ꝼ æꝼᴅep.

. LXVII.

Viþ ðeoꝼol ſeoce ðo on haliᵹ pæᴅep ꝼ on eala biſceop
pypᴅe hinðhioloþan · aᵹpimonian · alexanðpian · ᵹyþpiꝼan pele him ðpincan. Eꝼᴅ caſſuc · þeꝼan þopn · ſtan
cpop · elehᴅpe · ꝼinul · eoꝼopþpote cpopleāc oꝼᵹeoᴅ
ᵹelice. Eꝼᴅ ſpipe ðpenc pi̋ ðeoꝼle · nim micle hauð

---

[1] Supply meolcum.

boil in butter betony, githrife, yarrow, pulegium, pellitory; wring through a cloth, let it stand, heat a cup full in milk warm from the cow, put five pieces of the salve into it; let *the* man sup up that at night fasting, and let him eat fresh flesh in the part where it is fattest : and at night take the salve and comfort the wound with old lard or with fresh butter ; when it is clean, and a good red, leech with the same salve, and let it not unite, if it be clean; make it unite afterwards. If it will not for this leechdom get better, boil in milk the red yarrow, and fennel, and flaxwort, of all equal quantities, let them boil five times, wring through a cloth. Brew up a pretty strong brewit upon this, with wheat meal, shave a piece of good wax into it, and shake up together; let it cool, take three little bits of hares wool, wind them on the outside about with the brewit, that he may swallow them, and let him sup it up with milk warm from the cow.

lxvi.

A drink, if the " dry " disease be on a man ; take the netherward part of these worts, fennel, bishopwort, ashthroat, of all equal quantities; of these two *following* more than of the others, the upward part of rue, and betony ; pour them over with clear ale, and sing three masses over them, and let *the man* drink about two days from the time when it was poured over, before his meat and after.

lxvii.

For one devil sick ; put into holy water and into ale, bishopwort, hind heal, agrimony, alexanders, githrife ; give *to the man* to drink. Again, cassuck, tufty thorn, stonecrop, lupin, fennel, everthroat, cropleek ; pour over them similarly. Again, a spew drink against the devil ; take a mickle hand full of sedge, and gladden,

ꝼulle fecȝeſ · ⁊ ȝlædenan ðo on pannan · ȝeot micelne
bollan ꝼulne calaþ on bepyl healꝼ ȝeȝnıð. xx. lybcoꞃna ðo on þ̵ þıſ ıſ ȝoð ðꞃenc pıþ beoꝼle.

[LXVIII.]

Leoht ðꞃenc pıþ peðen heoꞃte elehtꞃe · bıſceop pyꞃt
ælꝼþone · elene · cꞃopleac · hınð hıoloþe · ontꞃe · clate ·
Nım þaſ pyꞃta þonne bæȝ ⁊ nıht ſcabe · ſınȝ æꞃeſt
on cıꞃıcean letanıa · ⁊ cꞃeðan · ⁊ pateꞃ noſteꞃ · ȝanȝ
mıð þy ſanȝe to þam pyꞃtum ymbȝa hıe þꞃıpa æꞃ þu
hıe nıme · ⁊ ȝa eꝼt to cıꞃıcean ȝeſınȝ . xıı. mæſſan
oꝼeꞃ þam pyꞃtum þonne þu hıe oꝼȝoten hæbbe.

. LXVIIII.

Ȝıꝼ men ſıe maȝa aſuꞃoð ⁊ ꝼoꞃþunðen · ȝenım holen
leaꝼa mıcle tꞃa hanð ꝼulla ȝeꞃceaꞃꝼa ſpıþe ſmale pyl ðn
meolcum oþ þ̵ hıe ſyn pel meaꞃupe puꞃla ſnæð mælum
ete þonne .vı. ſnæða · on moꞃȝen .ııı. ⁊ on æꝼen .ııı.
⁊ æꝼteꞃ hıſ mete · ðo þuſ .vıııı. nıht lenȝ ȝıꝼ hım
þeaꞃꝼ ſıe.   :·

Ȝıꝼ mon bıþ aþunðen ete ꞃuðan ⁊ ðꞃınce he bıþ
hal.   :·

Þıþ maȝan pæꞃce ꞃuðan ſæð ⁊ cꞃıc ſeolꝼoꞃ ⁊ eceð
beꞃȝen on neaht neꞃtıȝ. Eꝼt ȝnıð on eceð ⁊ on pæteꞃ
polleıan ſele ðꞃıncan ſona þ̵ ſaꞃ toȝlıt.

. LXX.

Vıþ pambe pæꞃce ðꝼȝeot polleıan ⁊ ðꞃınce ⁊ ꞃume
bınðe to þam naꝼolan · ⁊ pıte ȝeoꞃne þ̵ ſıo pyꞃt apeȝ
ne aȝlıðe ꞃona bıþ ꞃel.

put them into a pan, pour a mickle bowl full of ale upon them; boil half, rub *fine* twenty libcorns, put them into it; this is a good drink against the devil.

lxviii.

A light drink for the wood heart; lupin, bishop-wort, enchanters nightshade, helenium, cropleek, hind-heal, ontre, clote. Take these worts when day and night divide; sing first in church a litany, and a Credo, and a Pater noster, with the song go to the worts, go thrice around them, before thou touch them; and go again to church, sing twelve masses over the worts when thou hast poured —¹ over them.

lxix.

1. If a mans stomach be soured and swollen; take holly leaves, two mickle hands full, scrape them very small, boil them in milk till they be pretty tender, pick them out by a bit at a time; then let the man eat six bits, in a morning three, and in evening three, and after his meat. Thus do for nine days, longer if need be.

2. If a man be swollen, let him eat rue and drink it; he will be well.

3. For pain of maw; let the man taste at night fasting, seed of rue, and quicksilver, and vinegar. Again, rub pulegium into vinegar and into water, give *the man* to drink, soon the soreness glideth away.

lxx.

1. For wamb wark; drench in ——² pulegium, and let him drink it and bind some to his navel, and let him earnestly beware that the wort do not glide away. Soon he will be well.

---

¹ Not mentioned; to be supplied from above.   ² The liquid is not mentioned.

Þiþ maȝan pænce puðu þiſtleſ þone ȝnenan[1] meaṗh
þe biþ on þam heaꝼbe ꞃele him etan mið hatan ele.

Uiþ pambe heaꝺneꞃꞃe ȝeclænſa ȝiþcoꞃn ȝnið on
cealð pæteꞃ ꞃele him ꝺꞃuncan.

Þiþ ſpꞃinȝe ȝnið ꞃaluian piþ huniȝ ſmiꞃe mið Sona
biþ ꞃel. Eꝼt pyꞃc ꞃealꝼe nim hanð ꝼulle ſpꞃinȝ
pyꞃte · ꝼ hanð ꝼulle peȝbꞃæðan · ꝼ hanð ꝼulle maȝþan ·

ꝼ hanð ꝼulle niðepeaꞃðe ðoccan þæꞃc þe ſpimman
pille on butꞃan ahlyttꞃe þ ꞃealt oꝼ ꝼ þ ꞃám ðo hpon
huniȝeꞃ to enȝliꞃceꞃ · ðo oꝼeꞃ ꝼyꞃ apyl · þonne hit
pealle· ſinȝ . III. patꞃeꞃ noꞃteꞃ oꝼeꞃ ðo eꝼt oꝼ ſinȝ
þonne .VIIII. ſiþum patꞃeꞃ noꞃteꞃ ón ꝼ þꞃipa apyl ꝼ
ſpa ȝelome óꝼ aðo ꝼ lacna mið ꞃiþþan.

Viþ þæꞃe ȝeolpan aðle óꝼȝeot þaſ pyꞃte mið ſpiþe
beoꞃe · ꞃibban hanð ꝼulle · cꝑíc ꞃinða hanð ꝼulle .VIIII.
ſnæða niþepeaꞃðꞃe æꞃcþꞃotan · ꝼ .VIIII. niþepeaꞃðꞃe
eolenan.

Eꝼt ðilc · celenðꞃc · Saluian mæꞃt pyl ón ſpiþum
beoꞃe þ hit ſie þicce · ꝼ ȝꞃene · nim niþepeaꞃðe eolenan
ȝeſniþ on huniȝ ete ſpa maniȝe ſnæða ſpa he mæȝe
ȝeðꞃince þæꞃ ðꞃenceſ ꞃcenc ꝼulne æꝼteꞃ ꝼ eal þ ꝼæc
ete ꞃceapen ꝼlæꞃc ꝼ nan oþeꞃ.

Ȝiꝼ men ſie innelꝼe ute ȝecnua ȝallúc apꞃinȝ þuꞃh
claꝺ on cu peaꞃnme meolce · pæt þine hanða þæꞃ ón ꝼ
ȝeðo þ innelꝼe on þone man ȝeſeope mið ſeolce pyl him
þonne ȝallúc .VIIII. moꞃȝnaſ butan him lenȝ þeaꞃꝼ
ſie ꝼeð hine mið ꝼenſce hænne ꝼlæꞃc   *   *   *
         *   *   *   *

2. For maw pain ; give *the man* to eat the green marrow which is in the head of a wood thistle, with hot oil.

3. For hardness of wamb ; cleanse githcorns, rub them *fine* into cold water, give *to the man* to drink.

lxxi.

Against carbuncle ; rub sage with honey, smear therewith, soon he will be well. Again, work a salve, take a hand full of spring wort, and a hand full of way broad and a hand full of maythe, and a hand full of the netherward part of dock, that *namely* which will swim ; boil in butter, clear off the salt and the foam, add a little English honey, put over a fire, boil *it;* when it boileth sing three Pater nosters over *it,* remove it again, then sing nine Pater nosters, and boil it thrice, and so frequently ; remove it, and after that cure *with it.*

lxxii.

1. For the yellow disease ; souse these worts in strong beer, of ribwort a hand full, of quickbeam rind a hand full, nine bits of the netherward part of ashthroat, and nine of the lower part of helenium.

2. Again, boil dill, coriander, most of sage, in strong beer, that it may be thick and green ; take the netherward part of helenium, cut it up into honey, let the patient eat as many bits as he can ; let him drink after it a cup full of the drink, *as above;* and all the time let him eat sheep flesh and none other.

lxxiii.

If a mans bowel be out, pound galluc, wring through a cloth into milk warm from the cow, wet thy hands therein, and put *back* the bowel into the man, sew up with silk, then boil him for nine mornings galluc, *that is, comfrey,* except need be for a longer time, feed him with fresh hens flesh.

Perhaps one folio is missing.

There is some writing along the margin of the last page, the few readable syllables of which are unintelligible.

. . . .
ðıla ðɲa bınð þ . . . . . . poð þı . . . . ʌ Bẏp
ın ıp bɲen.

GLOSSARY.

GLOSSARY.

THE following glossary relies almost entirely upon
original authorities; upon a collation of the manuscript ancient extant glossaries with their printed
editions, which have been falsified by ignorant conjectures; and upon a careful examination of many
Saxon volumes never yet published. No reliance has
been placed on modern productions, in the way of
dictionaries; they will be found full of errors.[1] Every
article either supplies a deficiency or corrects an error;
but our limits will not admit of the insertion of every
correction prepared for the press. Corrections were, of
course, to be accompanied by their proofs, and this adds
to the length of the various articles. Some refer to
genders or declensions or terminations, for an exact
knowledge of our Oldest English is impossible, as long
as students are deceived on these elementary points.
The most important printed texts of Saxon works have
been collated from beginning to end, letter by letter,
with the original manuscripts. The modern editions in
particular are, sometimes, very faulty.

In the names of plants the reader will observe that
a name, however wrong, is within its own bounds, still

---

[1] See SHRINE (Williams and Norgate).

a name. Mistakes often thrive, and even overpower a true old tradition. Many decided spirits would have all error thrown over, but to do so, would render our collection less complete.

The order of the letters is so arranged that K goes with C, Y with I, and þorn is last of all.

TABLE OF CONTRACTIONS.

PRINTED BOOKS.

Æ.G. Ælfrics Grammar, ed. Somner,
quoted by pages and lines.

A.R. Adrian and Ritheus, ed. Kemble, by pages.

A.W. Ælfreds Will, reprint 1828, by pages.

Bw. Beowulf, ed. Grundtvig, collated with MS., by lines.

Cæd. Cædmon, if Cædmon, by the pages and lines of the original MS.

C.D. Codex Diplomaticus, by numbers.

C.E. Codex Exoniensis, by pages, ed. Thorpe.

Ch. Charms, Leechdoms, Vol. I.

DD. (Dooms) Laws and Institutes, ed. 1840, by pages.

Dief. Glossarium Diefenbachii.

D.R. Durham Ritual, by pages.

F.F. Fight at Finnesburg, ed. Thorpe.

G. Goodwins Andrew and Veronix.

Gð. Goodwins Guðlac.

Hh. Herbarium, Leechdoms, Vol. I., by articles.

Hom. Ælfrics Homilies, ed. Thorpe.

Lb. Leechbook, Leechdoms, Vol. II., by chapters.

M. Mones Glossaries in Quellen und Forschungen, von F. J. Mone, 1830.

M.Sp. Mannings Supplement to Lye, paged for the purpose, from Testamentum Elfhelmi, page 1.

N. Narratiunculæ, 1861. (Russell Smith.)

O.cl. O clerice, in preface to Leechdoms, Vol. I. p. lviii.

O.T. Orosius, ed. Thorpe, by pages and lines.

Quad. Medicina de Quadrupedibus, Leechdoms, Vol. I.

Runl. The Runlioð, or Runelay, quoted by articles.

SH. Shrine, where some Saxon pieces are printed.

S.S. Solomon and Saturn, ed. Kemble.

SSpp. Spoon and Sparrow, for etymology.

IN MANUSCRIPT.

Generally cited by folios.

---

xii.Ab. De xii. Abusivis. MS. C.C.C.

BL. Blooms, or Flores Soliloquiorum.

D.G. Dialogues of Gregorius, MS. C.C.C.

Διδαξ. The treatise περὶ διδάξεων, in Leechdoms, Vol. III.

F.D. De Falsis Dis. MS. C.C.C.

F.L. Fourth Leechdoms, for publication in Leechdoms, Vol. III.

G.D. Dialogues of Gregorius, MS. Cotton.

HID. Liber de Hida.

Lacn. Lacnunga, in Vol. III. of Leechdoms, by articles.

M.H. Minster Homilies of Ælfric, except Sigewulfi responsiones, de xii. Abusivis, and de Falsis Dis.

P.A. The Liber Pastoralis of King Ælfred, MS. Hatt.

R.M. Rule of Mynchens.

Sc. Liber Scintillarum.

SMD. Somniorum Diversitas.

GLOSSARIES.

Gl. Brux. A Brussels Glossary, printed by Mone, p. 314, by Thorpe, unpublished, p. 36, by Wright, p. 62.

Gl. C. An early Glossary in MS.

Gl. Dun. An old Glossary in the library of the cathedral at Durham. The compiler had used the Saxon Herbarium, as in Lactuca leporina.

Gl. E. Glossaries printed by Eckhart, in Commentarii de rebus Franciæ Orientalis, Wirceburgi, fol., 1729, 2 vols.

Gl. Hoffm. Althochdeutsche Glossen, von A. H. Hoffmann, 1826.

Gl. M. A manuscript on vellum, the property of Rev. W. D. Macray.

Gl. M.M. Glossary of Moyen Moutier, printed, but unpublished.

Mone. Glossaries printed by Mone, in Quellen und Forschungen, Aachen und Leipsig, 8vo., 1830. The herb glossary fetches from. IIb. Used MS. B.

N. Bakers Northamptonshire Gl.

Gl. Prud. Glossary on Prudentius, printed but unpublished.

Gl. R. Junius transcript of the Rubens MS. Glossary, MS.

Gl. Somn. The Glossaries printed by Somner, in Dictionarium Saxonico-Latino-Anglicum. Oxonii, fol., 1659, printed with errors from Gl. R.

Other manuscript Glossaries numbering about fifteen.

GLOSSARY.

A.

A, as prefix, is a shorter form of—1. And, as in abidan, for andbidan.

2. On, as in among, for onmang, and aweg, for onweg, both of which are occasionally parallel MS. readings. See MH. 115 a, with var. lect.

3. Un, as in atynan, open, for untynan.

4. Of, as in acalan for ofcalan. Hom. II. 248.

5. Embe, as in ymbutan, abutan, and by apokope buton.

6. Ge, as in alefed, for gelefed.

Acumba, -an, masc.? oakum, stupa. Cf. " Coarse fibres among wool are kemps," Gl. N. Putamina, acuman, æcumba, Gl. Mone, p. 398 a, p. 407 a, as consisting of coarse fibres. Νάφθα is an approximation only, explained in SH. p. 10. Similarly "Napta, genus fomenti, i.e. " tyndir," Gl. M.M. p. 159 b. Acumba in ashes seems administered as a substitute for Σπόδιον. Lib. I. i. 15 ; xxxiii. i ; xlvii. 3.

Æ, as a prefix, is commonly a shorter form of Æf, which answers to the Latin Ob, in the sense of annoyance, as in Officere and the like. Thus Æbylgan, Æcyrf. Bed. 552, l. 13 ; Æmod.

Æc, Ac, gen. -e, fem., oak, quercus robur. Sume ac astah, Hom. II. 150, got up into an oak. Of ðære óc, C.D. 570, p. 78. þeor ac, Æ.G. 7, 48. Gen. Ace,

Æc—cont.
Lb. I. xxxviii. 11. Vowels dropped, C.D. 588, 624, etc. Gen. pl. Acana, C.D. 126.

2. As a letter of the alphabet the same word is masc., gen. -es. Acap ʈpeᵹen hæᵹelaʈ ʈpa ʈome, C.E. 429, two As and two Hs along with them.

Æcelma, gen. an, masc.? a chilblain, mula. Gl. Mone, p. 359 b. " Mula est quædam " infirmitas in homine quæ uocatur " gybehos," Gl. Harl. 3388, that is, kihc of heel. In Italian, " mule, kibes, chil- " blanes " (Florio). In French, "mule, " a kibe "(Cotgrave). Palagra, æcilma, Gl. Cleop., where understand podagra and footsore. The word is compounded of Æ for Æʈ, signifying annoyance, cel, chill, and the participial man. SSpp., art. 943.

Ædre, vein, vena, gen. both -e, and -an, fem., Lb. L i. 13; II. xviii.; II. xxxii., etc. IIb. iv. 4. On oþrum monþe þa ædron beoð geworden, N. p. 49, in the second month the veins are formed. S.S. 148, 192.

2. pl. kidneys, renes. R.M. 69, a. Hb. lxxxvi. 3; cxix. 3. Paris Ps. cxxxviii. 11.

3. In the sense of water spring found neut. þæt wæteræddre, perhaps by attraction. Hom. II. 144. Ealle eorðan æddre onsprungon ongean þam heofonlican flode. MS. C.C.C. 419, p. 42.

Æferðe, gen. -an, fem.? an herb unknown. Lb. I. xxxiii. 2, etc.

Ægwyrt, gen. -e, fem., eggwort, dande-
lion, leontodon taraxacum ; like Germ.
Eyerblume, from the round form of the
pappus. Lacn. 40.

Ælfsibenne, from ælf, elf, and sido, masc.
manners, as Boet. p. 45, l. 21, p. 131, l. 10,
often taken in a good sense as morals.
Lb. I. lxiv. The termination -en, like
-wos, -inus, does not always relate to
metals and materials, but as in fyrlen,
distant, myrten, mortuary, is more general.
We may therefore take this word as the
accusative of an adjective. It is, however, possible that it may be a substantive. Lacn. 11.

Ælfsogoða. See Sogoða. Lb. III. lxii.

Ælfðone, gen. -an ; fem. ? probably cir-
cæa lutetiana, enchanters nightshade,
which in old Dutch is Alfrancke. Lb.
I. xxxii. 4; II. liii.

Æpening, masc., gen. -eʒ, a medlar, fruit of
mespilus germanica. Lb. II. ii. 2. See
the passage and the glossarial openæpʒ,
mespilum.

Æppel, gen. -ples, masc. in sing. pl. -pla,
apple, malum. Numb. xi. 5. P.A. 19 b.
Also a soft fruit, as fruit of the bramble.
Lb. I. lxiv.; III. xli. Fingeræpla, dates,
M.H. 131 b. A translation of Δακτυλοι.
Copðæppel, Numb. xi. 3, a cucumber.
Fic æppel, a fig (Lyc), pl. ƿcæppla,
Matth. vii. 16 ; Luke vi. 44. Palmæpla,
Gl. Cleop. fol. 66 d. Gl. Mone, p. 409 b.
Lb. II. i. ; II. xxxvi. SSpp. 543.

2. A dumpling. Hb. cxxxiv. 2.

3. The ball of the eye, with pl. masc.
On ðæʒ ʒpenlʒean eaʒum beoð ða
æpplaʒ hale. Ac ða bʒæpaʒ ʒpeatiʒeað,
P.A. 15, a. In the eyes of the bleareyed
the balls are healthy, but the lids swollen.
Se oðeʒ æppel pæʒ ʒeemtiʒob, M.H.
98 b, the ball of one eye was emptied
of its crystalline, aqueous, and vitreous
humours. Applied less exactly as a
translation of pupilla, Boet. p. 132, l. 25.

Æpse, gen. -an, fem. ? the aspen, populus
tremula. Lb. I. xxxvi. SH. 25. The
last syllable in the modern name represents the case endings. Æps, occurs in

Æpse—cont.
the glossaries, and Lb. III. xxxix ; it is
regarded by Ælfric in Gr. as Abies.

Æsc, gen. -es, masc. C.D. 461, the ash,
fraxinus excelsior. Se ʒophʒa æsc. C.E.
429.
Ceaster æsc, helleborus niger, black
hellebore, which has leaves like those of
the ash. " Eliforus (read Helleborus),
" pebe bepʒe (mad berry) vel ceafcep
" æʒc," Gl. Cleop. fol. 36 b. Lacn. 39.

Æsce, gen. -an, fem., ash, cinis. Lb. I.
xxxviii. 4. Quad. iii. 4. Axe þu eapt
ꞃ on axan leoʒa. Cinis es et in cinere
uine. Sc. 11, a. Æ.G. 11, 47. C.E. 213,
line 27. Cf. Aska, fem., old Dansk.

Æscþoꞃu, gen. -an, fem. 1. Verbena
officinalis. Hb. iv., with the drawing.
Verbenaca, in MS. Bodley 130, is drawn
and glossed Verbena, vervain. Also
Veruyn in MS. T. Verbenaca in
Dodoens is Vervain. " Verveyne,
" Veruena vocatur grece ierobotanum
" vel peristerion et dicitur verbena
" quia virtutibus plena," MS. Douce,
290. MS. G. has a gl. " Taubencropf,"
which, as I learn from Adelung, is
Verbena. " Hiera quam Latini Ber-
" benam uocant ideo a grecis hoc
" nomen accepit quod sacerdotes eam
" purificationibus adhibere consueve-
" runt." MS. Harl. 5264, fol. 56, b.
" Verbena, æscwert," Gl. Mone, p. 442 a.
" Berbenaces, eascvyrt," Gl. Dun. Lb.
III. 72.

2. Annuosa, which is found in a few
glossaries, is a mere blunder for anchusa,
translated in Hb. ci. 3, by ashthroat.

3. Goutweed, ægopodium podagraria.
Ashweed is this in Mylnes Indigenous
Botany. This plant I take to be meant
by the Ferula of Gl. M.M., Gl. Dun.,
Somner Lex., Gl. Brux. The Ferula
communis, or fennel giant, is not a
native of England, and under all cir-
cumstances, would either not have an
English name or one extended to plants
of a similar aspect, even if smaller.
This ægopodium is often called Angelica,

Æscþrotu—*cont.*
even down to Ray, and the angelicas
are also large and hollow. Throat seems
to imply hollowness, and Ash either size
or similar leaves.
The fennel giant is, however, mentioned in the life of St. Godric as
affording walking staves for pilgrims,
(A.D. 1159), p. 163.
Æsmœlum, dat. pl., a disease of the eye,
*contraction of the pupil, oculorum immi-
nutio.* "Evenit etiam ut oculi, vel ambo
" vel singuli, minores fiant quam esse
" naturaliter debeant." Celsus, VI. vi.
14. " Pupillœ malum est, quum an-
" gustior ac obscurior rugosiorque effi-
" citur." Actuarius, 184, c. Lb. I. 2,
and contents. A comp. of Æ, for Æf,
implying mischief, and Smæl.
Æþelfepʼðingpýpt, fem., gen. -e, *stichwort,
stellaria holostea,* with *s. graminea.*
Æþelfepʼðincpypt in Hb. lxiii. 7, translates "agrimoniam," and lxxviii. 1,
"argemonitis." *See* Plinius, xxvi. 59.
" Agrimonia alpha, eathelferthing vyrt
" vel glofvyrt," Gl. Dun. " Alfa, œðel-
" fepʼðingpýpt," Gl. Somn., p. 64 b, 7.
Some supposed agrimonia to be stichwort, though as the translator of the Herbarium had called it fapchfe, a very
appropriate name, we should not have
expected this uncertainty from him.
" Agrimonia, fticpýpt," Gl. Somn. p.
64 a, 65. In Lacn. 29, œþelfepʼðing-
pypt is glossed "auis lingua." " Lingua
" avis. i. pigle, stichwort," Gl. M. " Lin-
" gua auis. i. pigle," Gl. Rawl. C. 607.
" Lingua auis, stichewort," Gl. Sloane, 5.
The name describes the leaves.
Afreoðan, *to froth.* Lb. I. xlvii. 2.
Ahwænan, præt. ede, p.p. ed, *to trouble,
contristare.* Hb. xx. 7, where Lat. con-
tristatus. "Herofþe lauedies to me
meneþ, Au wel sore me ahweneþ, Wel
neh min heorte wulé tochine, Hwon ich
beholde hire pine. Owl and Nightingale,
1562. *Of this the ladies to me moan, and
pretty sorely distress me; well nigh my*

Ahwænan—*cont.*
heart will break (tocinan), *when I behold
their pain.* Vtan fpeppian ahpænebe ꞇ
hyptan opmobe, MS. C.C.C. 419, p. 246.
*Let us comfort the distressed and encou-
rage the despairing.* Cf. DD. 139, xlvii.
Aleþpan, *to lather.* Lb. I. liv. *See* Leaðor.
It is for Geleþpan.
Alor, Alr, gen. -es, masc., *the alder, alnus
glutinosa.* Lb. I. ii. 14 ; alres, Lb. II. li.
3 ; masc. C.D. 376.
Ananbeam, gen. -es, masc., *the spindle
tree, euonymus Europæus.* Lb. I. xxxii.
4. Germ. anisbaum. " ꝼanabeam, fusa-
" num, *spindle tree, prichtimber.*" Somner Lex. " Fusarius, uuananbeam," Gl.
M.M.
Anapypm, *Ons worm,* masc. Lb. I. xlvi. 1.
In the Ynglinga Saga, Anasott is said to
have taken its name from On, a king of
Sweden, who prolonged his own life by
sacrificing from time to time one of his
sons to Woden. Siðan andæʼðist ꝋn
konúngr, ok er hann heygʼðr at Uppse-
lum. Þat er siðan kellut Anasott er
maʼðr deyr verklaus af elli. Heims-
kringla, Ynglinga S. xxix. *Then ex-
pired king On, and was buried at Upsal.
It was afterwards called On-sickness,
when a man dies from old age, without
agony.* That the former element in
Anapypm, Anasott, is the same cannot
be doubtful.
Anfpilbe, *unique* (*unicus, singularis*).
Lb. I. ii. 9. Cf. Zwispild, geminus,
biformis. (Graff.)
Antre. *See* Ontre. Lb. II. li.
Arendan. Lb. II. lii.
Argesweorf, gen. -es, *brass filings.* Lb. I.
xxxiv. 1. *See* Gesweorf.
Arod, an herb, probably *arum,* Ἄρον. Lb.
III. xlii. Lacn. 2. Thus Cymed for
Cymen.
Ap ðm, *copperas.* The reading of the
MS. in Lb. II. xv. is sap ðm, translating
μετὰ χαλκάνθου λείου (καὶ μέλιτι ὀλίγῳ
ἀναλαβών). Χάλκανθος is *green vitriol.*
But it is also *brass rust, ærugo,* and the

Aꞃ óm—*cont.*
true reading may be aꞃ óm. The word
copperas is commonly used for either the
green rust of copper, or the green vitriol
with which the kitchenmaid cleans brass
pans; from its ambiguity it was con-
venient. Aꞓlou points to the levigated
rust.

Aꞅaꞃu, *asarabacca, asarum Europæum.*
Lb. II. xiv. Foles foot is Tussilago far-
fara.

Aꞅiftan, *to sift.* Lb. I. ii. 20.

Aꞅlawen, *struck, stricken,* from aꞃlean, for
† aꞃlaꞃan, a collateral form. Contents,
Lb. I. lvi.=aꞃlaꞃen in text. So cnuoan
becomes cnupan, cnuan.

Aꞅprindlad, *ripped up and spanned open
with tenter hooks.* Lb. II. xxiv. From
sprindel, *tenticum,* Gl. C., *a tenter hook.*
Cf. Spreisseln, Schmeller, Bayerisches
Wörterbuch, IV. p. 593.

Aꞇpum, a Latin word, *Smyrnium olusatrum.* Lb. I. ii. 20, etc.

Aꞇꞇoꞃlaꞃe, gen. –an; "venom-loather,"
panicum crus galli. In Hb. xlv. aꞇꞇoꞃlaꞃe is galli crus, and were there doubt,
it seems removed by MSS. G. T. A.,
which draw the *p. sanguinale, Linn.,* now
called *digitaria sanguinalis.* These two
grasses are included together in the
"cockaleg," hahnenbein of the Germans.
The corresponding article in MS. Bodley, 130, gives the name˙sanguinaria, and
the old gloss is Blobwrt, with a later of
the 14th century, "Blodwerte." San-
guinaria is often glossed as shepherds
purse, thlaspi or capsella bursa pastoris,
or as tormentilla, these being esteemed
stanchers of blood, or as polygonum;
but in this instance it must be as above,
d. sanguinalis. With these testimonies
it is vain to consider how such virtue
was attributed to a grass. Did they
confuse panicum with panacea? The
glossaries give no real help. "Atrilla,
" attorlathe," Gl. Dun., where atrilla
seems to be aꞇꞇoꞃlaꞃe with a Latin termination. "Astrilla," Gl. Sloane, 146.

Aꞇꞇoꞃlaꞃe—*cont.*
"Cyclaminos, attorlathe," id., but cyclamen is in Herbarium "slite." "Galli
" crus, attorlathe," id., a quotation from
our book. "Fenifuga, attorlathe," id., understand venenifuga, a translation of the
Saxon word. "Venenifuga, aꞇꞇeꞃlaꞃe,"
Gl. Somner, p. 66 [63] b. 27. "Morella,
" atterloꞃe," Gl. Harl. 978, but morella
is atropa belladonna, and poisonous itself.
Aꞇeꞃlaꞅe, betonica, Lye, from a Gl.;
but betony and attorlothe are separately
named in Lb. I. i. 15. The claims of
asclepias vincetoxicum are set aside by
its being a foreign plant. The heal all
of the old Dansk, Laukr, has no support
from our authorities. Lye prints, by
some error, sattorlaꞃe also. The small
attorlothe occurs in Lb. I. xlv. 6.

Auꞃuꞃo is interpreted by Du Cange *la
jaunisse, the jaundice.* This rendering is
supported by the etymon aurum, *gold,*
and by authority; aurugo, *color in auro,
sicut in pedibus accipitris,* i. *gelesouch,*
Gl. E. vol. ii. p. 992 a, *the colour one
sees in gold, as in a hawks feet, the
yellow sickness.* Gelesuhtiger, *ictericus,*
auruginosus, Graff. vol. vi. col. 142.
Our text, however, interprets aurugo, as
a tugging or drawing of the sinews, Hb.
Perhaps this may be explained by observing that auriginosus is glossed arcuatus, Du Cange; auruginosus, arcuatus, Gl. Isid. Not very differently
from our text; "Artuatus, ꞃybmyole
" abl," Gl. R. p. 11, ult., read arcuatus
and it may be, ꞃeole, or muscle;
whence] it might well be supposed
that ὀπισθότονος was meant, a term applied to bows, bent back the opposite
way to their natural curvature, especially
true of horn bows, Gortynia cornua, and
to persons suffering under that extreme
form of tetanus, in which the feet and
head are drawn back till they touch.
Aurigo is also,'in Apul. lxxxvii., *morbus
regius,* which was another mediæval
name for the jaundice; Graff. vol. vi.,

Aurugo—cont.

141. Graffs mark of interrogation at the word Gelbsucht, would be removed by the publication of our texts.

Aþþepan, † -þþeap, -þupen, *turn, coagulate.* See þpepan. Lb. I. xlv. 5.

Aþyn, *press.* Lb. I. viii. 2. His eyes æp pæpon utaðyðe oy þam eahbpingum, MH. 98 b, *were before thrust out of their sockets.* See þyn.

B.

Ban—1. *A bone.*

2. *A leg,* neut., pl. ban. Lb. I. i. 15; I. xxvi.; II. li., where it is *leg,* so Cædm.? Daniel, MS. p. 195, 5. Pseudo Cædm. H.H. MS. p. 223, 20, *their legs failed them.* " Tibialis, banpyʒt," Gl. M.M.

Banpýʒt, fem., gen. in -e. 1. *bonewort, viola,* not blue voilet, but *viola lactea, white violet,* and *v. lutea, Heartsease.* In Hb. clii. 1, bonewort is in the Latin version of Dioskorides, (not existing in the Hellenic) " viola alba :" in Hb. clxv. it is also distinguished from viola purpurea in art. clxvi. Lb. I. i. 15.

2. *Bellis perennis, daisy,* bæʒey eaʒe ; but at a period latʋeʒþan our text ; and perhaps by error. " Consolida minor, " daysey, venwort, idem bonewort," Gl. Harl. 3388. " Consolida minor . i. bon-" wert," Gl. M. "Consolida minor, days-" yʒe," Gl. Bodley, 178. " Consolida " minor. Daysei is an herbe þat sum " men callet hembrisworte oþer bone-" wort," Gl. Douce, 290. " Consolida " minor . i . petit comferi.anglice dayis-" hege . habet florem album," Gl. Rawlinson, c. 607. Benwort, daisy, (Dickinsons Cumberland Gl. in add.)

3. *Erythræa centaureum,* if we trust " centaurea minor, banpýʒt," Gl. Somn., p. 64 b, 18. The wort is said to have cpoppan, *bunches,* either racemes or

Banpýʒt—cont.

umbels or cimes, which applies better to this lesser centaury than to heartsease or to daisy. Lb. II. li. 2.

4. " Filia aurea, banpyʒt." Gl. Cleop. *Filia aurea, Solidago virgaurea, Bot.,* sometimes called consolida Saracenica.

Baðian, *to bathe,* is to be distinguished from Beðian, *to beathe* or *warm.* In the Lb. MS. fol. 92 a, the penman first had written e, but this he erased to put a. But as the old idea of a bath did not include cold water, the words are nearly allied.

Belene, beolene, gen. -an, fem. ? *henbane, hyoscyamus niger.* Hb. v. Lb. I. ii. 22 ; I. iii. 3. Another name is henne belle, from its bell shaped capsules, which are drawn in MS. V., and from them the name belene, seems derived ; belle, *a bell;* bellen, *furnished with bells ;* and the final e is the usual final distinctive form of names of worts. The modern name henbane is independent, and derived from its poisonous qualities; another is hennepol, with the same sense.

Beopc, *bark, latratus.* Hb. lxvii. 2. Gebeopc, Sc. 55 b. Æ.G. 2, 44.

Beorðor, byrðor, gen. -res. 1. *the embryo, fœtus.* Quad. iv. 4 ; Bed. 493, 40. " Fœtu, cuðpe vel mið beopþpe," Gl. Cleop. 40 b. N. 50.

2. *Childbirth, partus,* Quad. iv. 6. Beopðopcpelmay, *abortivi,* Lye. Lb. III. xxxvii. Cf. Mone, p. 411 a.

Beopýʒt, fem., beewort, sweet flag, *acorus calamus.* Hb. vii. " Marubium, hune " vel beopyʒt," Gl. Cleop. fol. 61 a, wrong. In Hb. vii. a synonym in the Latin is Veneria, and the mediæval marginal annotations on Dioskorides give on Ἄκορον˳ (not Acorus), οἱ δὲ, χόρος, Ἀφροδισίας, Ῥωμαῖοι βενέρεα, οἱ δὲ, ναυτικὰ ῥάδιξ, Γάλλοι τεπεραπιουμ; that is, Acorum is called in Latin Veneria, and by the Gauls peper apium (for apum), *bees pepper :* (for the Celtic use of kappa instead of pi, see SSpp. art. 20). What our text says about bees, is to be under-

Beopýpc—*cont.*

stood, as that the wort will induce an
•unsettled swarm of bees to reconcile
themselves to an offered hive ; hence it
was reasonably called beewort : and so
Dioskorides, of Acorum says, that the
roots are not in smell unpleasant ; τῇ
ὀσμῇ οὐκ ἀηδεῖς. In MS. V. the root
chiefly is drawn, and the figure corresponds minutely with the description in
Dioskorides, that they,for he uses a plural,
are not straight grown, but oblique and
superficial, divided by knots ; οὐκ εἰς εὐθὺ
πεφυκυίας ἀλλὰ πλαγίας καὶ ἐξ ἐπιπολῆς,
γόνασι διειλημμένας. That he adds
ὑπολεύκους, whitish, while the English
drawing has a strong red, may be set
down to the artistic tastes of the painter.
The drawing in MS. A. is very similar.
Somners Gl. p. 63 a, line 59, translates
apiago by beowyrt. In MS. Bodley,
130, veneria is drawn as acorum, with a
large creeping root, and glossed "lemre"
for the English name. Dorsten calls the
roots of acorus "rubicundas," as coloured in MS. V., and on this ground
several glossaries make acorus=madder.
The χόρος of the margin of Dioskorides
is another form of acoros, and 'Αφροδισίας
has the same sense as veneria. MS. G.
figures a crow foot, with gl. "honefus."
2. *Acanthe.* Hb. cliv. figured as *stellaria holostea.*

Besengian, *to singe.* Lb. I. li. *See* Sengian.

Besoreadan, *to empurple.* Lb. I. xlvii. 1;
from baso, *purple,* and read, *red.*

Byben, gen. -e, fem., *a bucket:* used in
Lb. I. xxxii. 2, with a perforated stool,
and thus evidently the modern bidet.

Bingrpypc, fem., gen. in -e, *a rush,* a *iuncus*
or *carex* or *butomus umbellatus,* as in
German.

Bypigbepge, fem., gen. -an, -ean, *a mulberry.* Lb. II. xxx. 2. Moros, *mulberry
trees,* Ps. lxxvii. 52, is translated by
bypig and by mapbeamaf. Spelm.
Bepigbpenc, *dlamoron,* Gl. in Lye, a
drink made from mulberries with honey.

Bypla, masc., gen. -an, *the barrel,* in the
horse keepers sense ; Lb. I. lxxxviii. 3,
from the context and the modern word.
As, however, there is but this known
example, it may be *perineum,* like bœre,
in Molbech. Cf. "Burlings, the tails
" and other parts,.which are taken from
" lambs when sheared. Burl, to take such
" wool from lambs as is dirtied, or liable
" to additional deterioration from their
" laxity of body." Salopia antiqua Gl.

Bipceoppypc, fem. gen. in -e, *bishopswort,
ammi maius.* (Skinner, Nemnich, Florio,
Cotgrave, Lovell, Culpeper.) This is
medicinal, but foreign, and must be
taken as cultivated by our " herborists,"
as Lyte says of it. Bishops weed=ammi.
Skinner. So we read "the southern "
bishopwort, Lb. II. liv.
2. *Verbena officinalis?* if we trust Gl.
Somn. p. 64 a, 1, with p. 66 [63] b, 32.
3. "Hibiscus?" *tree mallow.* Gl. Cleop.
Gl. M.M. *Vitex* "*Agnus castus,*" Gl.
Arund. 42, fol. 92. " Puleium mon-
" tanum," Gl. Arund. 42.

Bipceoppypc peo lærpe, *the lesser
bishopswort, betonica officinalis.* "Beto-
" nica," Gl. Somn. p. 64 a, 49 ; Gl. Arund.
42; Gl. Dun. ; Gl. Mone, p. 320 b ; Gl.
Faust; Hb. i. ; but Skinner says " be-
" tonica aquatica," which is *scrophularia
aquatica, Bot.*; and Culpeper says,
"water betony, in Yorkshire bishops
" leaves."

Bipe, gen. -ep, masc. 1. *a bite.* 2. *a
cancer.* 1. pl. bicaf, Quadr. xiii. 7; Isl.
bit, *a bite,* is neuter (B.H.). Biz, ohg.,
biss in Germ., are masc. The word is
followed by heo, Quadr. xi. 7, but that
will be an error. Slice also and others
have final e. Lb. I. xliv. 1.

Blæc, gen. -ep? *a blotch.* Lb. Contents,
I. xxxii., with article þam. "Vitiligo,
" blec," Gl. M.M. p. 154 b, 39, where
is added þpuppel, *leprosy,* the same as
Goth. þrutsfill, λέπρα. Similarly id. p.
164 b, 3, but bleccb.
2. *Ink, encaustum,* DD. 395.

Blopan, præt. † bleop, pp. blopen, *to blow, bloom, blossom, florere.* Tpeopa he beþ
þæplice blopan, M.Sp. p. 16, Trees he shall *cause suddenly to bloom.* Mid
blowendum wyrtum, Hom. II. 352, *with blooming worts.* Oð þ hi becomon
tó þumum þcinenbum þelba þægþe ᵹeblopen, M.H. 99 b, *Till they came
to a shining plain, fair and blooming* ("fairly blown"). C.E. 199, 200, etc.

Boᵹen. *See* Boðen, convertible, Lb. p. 310, note. Lb. III. iv. xxvi. xxx. lxii. 1.

Box, neut. ? Lb. II. lix. 14. tobþocenum þealþboxe, Mark xiv. 3. Buxus, box
tþeop. Buxum, þopcaþuen box, ÆG. 5, ult. It is therefore direct from the
late Latin, and seems to follow its gender.

Boðen, gen. -eþ; probably *wild thyme, thymus serpyllum.* Boþeneþ, Lb. III. iv. In
Hb. lxxxi. boðen is rosemary, which is a native of the south of Europe. In
Hb. cxlix. it is employed to translate *thyme,* and this is native to England.
"Lolium, boþen," Gl. Somn., p. 77 a, but darnel is not to the unskilled eye
at all like thyme and rosemary; it seems however to be considered only
as a mean herb by the glossator. The drawing in MS. V., fol. 39 d,
has not simple leaves as for either rosemary or thyme it should have (H.), but
it may be the artists view of either. "Rosmarinus, sundeav vel bothen vel
"feld medere," Gl. Dun. "Rosmarinus, "sundeaw," Gl. Mone, p. 322 b.; this
is a failure to translate ros marinus as sea dew; our sundew or *drosera* is wholly
different. In MS. Bodley, 130, there is no drawing of rosmarinus, but a hand of
the 14th century has glossed the article "feld modere;" this seems to come of
very careless observation. "Rosmari-"num, feld mædere," Gl. Mone, p. 322 a.
White bothen is great daisie, says Gerarde.

Bþeað, *brittle.* Hb. cxl. 1. εὔθραυστος.

Bþecan, verb reflexive, bþecan hine, *make an effort to spew.* Lb. II. lii. 1.

Bþecan—*cont.*
"Brakyn or castyn or spewe, *vomo* "*evomo,*" Prompt. Parv. "Brakynge or
"parbrakynge, *vomitus, evomitus,*" id.

Bþebe? *a particolour ed cloth*; mið bþebe. Lb. III. ii. 1. Cf. Bþæbelþ, *stragulum,*
Gl. in Lye. Cf. Bþ.fᵹð, C.E. 218, line 9. Breᵹben, C.E. 219, line 13.

Bþeᵹban, præt. bþæb, p. part. bþoᵹben, *to do anything with a sudden jerk or start.*
Lb. II. li. 3. etc.

Bþyþepypt, fem., gen. -e, *pimpernel, anagallis.* "Anagallis, brisewort," Gl. Rawlinson, c. 506. Gl. Harl. 3388. Leechdoms, vol. I. p. 374.

2. *Bellis perennis,* MS. Laud. 553, fol. 9. Plainly for Hembriswyrt. *See* Banþýpt, 2.

Bþiþan, *to brew,* præt. bþeop, p. part. bþopen. Lb. I. xlvii. 3, *make a brewit,
a lomentum, dress.* Lb. I. xxxvi. Bþiþ his mete þiþ ele. Lb. II. li. 1, 3. O.T.
254, 9. Hom. I. 352.

Bþyþen, neut., *what has been brewed.* Lb. I. lxvii. 2. C.E. p. 161, 4 = MS. fol. 47 a,
8, where the use of barm is mentioned. He ᵹeann . . . an bþyþen mealtes; *one
brewing of malt*; malt for one brewing. Wulfgeats Will, unpublished.

Bþocminte, -an, fem., *mentha hirsuta, Bot.* Hb. cvi. "Sisymbrium, an herbe,
"wherof bee two kyndes, the one is "called Sisymbrium alone, whiche is also
"called Thymbrea, in englishe water "mynte." Elyots Dict. by T. Cooper.
See the synonyms from mediæval sources in the Flora Britannica, with the words
"In aquosis vulgaris."

Bþom, gen. -eþ, masc. ? *broom, cytisus scoparius,* (Hooker). Lb. I. ii. 14.

Bþoþeþpypt, fem., gen. -e, *penny royal, mentha pulegium,* Gl. Brux.

Bþuneþan, a dative : Lb. I. iv. 6, a disease, *brunella*; as I conclude from the
following ; "oris vitium cum linguæ "tumore, exasperatione, siccitate et
"nigredine ; unde et nomen teutonice "habet, vulgo brunella." Kilian in

Bᵽuneþan—*cont.*

bruᵹne. Album Græcum, prescribed in
Lb. for this disease, is said by Salmon
(Engl. Phys. p. 753) to cure "Diseases
" of the Throat and Quinsies : for a sore
" throat called *Pruna*, you may use it."
Bᵽunᵽypᵹ, fem., gen. in -e, *brown wort*,
scrofularia aquatica, *water betony*.
(Skinner, Lyte, Nemnich, Culpeper.) So
braunwurtz in Dodoens. I suppose " the
" broad leaved brownwort which waxeth
" in woods," Lb. I. xxxviii. 4, to be
scrofularia nodosa.

2. Hb. art. lvii. makes bᵽunᵽypᵹ the
fern called splenium or asplenium, and
Gl. Dun. copies that. *Ceterach officina-
rum* is meant. It has a brown under
surface, but the drawing in MS. V. is
not a fern at all. Spimon vel reverion,
Gl. Brux., where spimon is a misreading
of splenion.

3. Also the vaccinium or bilberry
shrub, Gl. Somn. p. 66 [63] b, 12, where
bᵽanᵽypᵹ is printed. Gl. Dun.

4. *Prunella vulgaris*, where prun is
brown. So the Mæstricht Gl. in Mone,
p. 285 a. Nemnich. *See also* Bruyne
in Kilian.

Bulenᵽᵱe, a wort. Lb. I. xlvii. 2. There
must have been more than one of the
name, as the passage mentions the small
sort.

Buloᵹ, Lb. I. lviii. 2 ; Buluᵹ, Lb. III.
xlviii. ; *the root of lychnis flos cuculi?*
See Plinius xxi. 97 = 26. *Ballota*, Βαλ-
λώτη, *nigra?* Boletus?

C.

Cæᵽen, neut.? a Latin word, *carenum*,
wine boiled down one third and sweetened.
" Cyᵽen, i.e. apilleþ pin . dulcisapa," Gl.
in Lye. Miþ þam ceᵽenum þæᵽe ᵹob-
ᵱpellican ᵱᵽecnyᵱᵱe, St.Guðlac, cap. xvii.
= p. 72, l. 7. Gen. -eᵱ. Lb. I. i. 17.

Cæᵽᵱe, gen. -an, fem. ? *cress, water cress,
nasturtium officinale.* The drawings in
V. A. have opposite leaves and a stout
tripartite terminal fruit or inflorescence,
so that they are " most like caper spurge,
" euphorbia lathyris," (H.) But the opposite leaves with a racemose arrange-
ment of the flowers, which latter may be
seen in MS. T., is sufficient for us, with
the synonym in Hb. xxi. "Nasturtium."
In MS. G. is a gloss, "Cart chresse,"
where the former word may stand for
κάρδαμον, *cress.* The drawing in MS. G.
is a good deal like the herb, and that in
MS. T. is meant for it. "Cardamon,
" cearse," Gl. Dun. Tun cæᵽᵱe, *garden
cress, lepidium sativum;* Dutch, Tuinkers.
Camecon, *cammock?* which see. Lb. I.
xlvii. 3. Cf. Illeomoc, Hleomocan.
Cammoc, Commuc, gen. -eᵱ. 1. *Sulfur
wort, harestrang, peucedanum officinale,*
Hb. art. xcvi., and so drawn MS. V. fol.
45 a. Peucedanum, gl. dogge fenell,
MS. Bodley, 130, adding " or balde-
" monie," which is gentian. "Peuce-
" danum, cammok," Gl. M. ; Gl. Dun.,
dog fenell (Grete Herbal). The fine
linear leaves are meant in a bad drawing
in MS. Harl. 5294, where is gl. band
fenell. Peucedanum is harstrang in
Hollands Plinius (index, vol. ii.), and
in Dutch and German, and in Cotgrave.
Harestrong is *peucedanum officinale* in
Mylnes Indigenous Botany, 1793. Peu-
kedanum was also rightly read as *hogs
fennel,* in a Welsh Gl. of the 13th century (Meddygon Myddfai, p. 291). The
name fennel is derived from its linear
leaves. The genitive. Lb. III. xxx.

2. *Anonis, rest harrow,* Gl. Harl. 3388.
Gl. Arundel, 42. Gerarde. Gl. Sloane,
405. Gl. Dorsetshire, Culpeper. *See*
Cammoc whin, which is the correct word.

3. *Hypericum,* also *pulicaria dysenterica,*
also *senecio Iacobæa;* Gl. New Forest.
Cammoc whin, *rest harrow, anonis,* MS.
Laud. 553, fol. 18. The leaves are ternate like those of the true cammock.

Carruc, gen. in -er, masc., *hassock, aira cæspitosa*. Lb. III. lxii., lxiii., lxiv. Hassuc, masc., C.D. 655. Cf. Nemnich. A confirmation in Lacn. 79.

Caulic, gen. -er, a medicine of which two or three drops are prescribed, Lb. II. lii. 3, perhaps κωλικόν, κολικόν.

Capel, masc., *colewort, brassica oleracea*, Lb. III. xii.; xliv.

Ceac, gen. -es, masc., *a jug, urna:* pl. ceacar. Bed. p. 520, l. 6, with Smiths note, p. 97. Lb. I. ii. 11. Hom. I. 428.
2. *Laver* of the temple of Solomon ; luter, λουτήρ. P.A. 21 b.

Cealpe, ceolpe, ceolbpe, acc. -e, nom. pl. -as, masc., *pressed curds, curds crumbled and pressed into a cake.* " Calmaria, " cealpe ; Caluiale, cealepbpip," Gl. Cleop. "Muluctra, ceolbpe," Gl. C. The dat. occurs, Lb. I. xxxix., acc. I. xliv. 1. Lacn. 57, pl. Διδαξ. 51. Compare Germ. Gallerte, fem., *jelly*.

Cearcep erc. *See* Æpc.

Cearcep pypt, fem., gen. -e, *black hellebore, helleborus niger*. Lb. I. xxxix. 2.

Cebelc, *Mercurialis perennis*. Hb. lxxxiv. from the text and drawings. " Mercuri- " alis, cedelc vel merce," Gl. Dun., where the insertion of marche or celery arose from its similarity to the first syllable in mercurialis. " Mercurialis, cebelc. " cyphc," Gl. Mone, p. 320 b ; but the tradition of our people forbids us to believe that mercury is charlock.

Celenbpe, fem., gen. -an, *coriander, coriandrum sativum*. Lb. I. iii. 9. Also celenbep, Lb. I. iv. 2, probably after the Latin and neuter ; dat. -bpe, Lb. I. xxxv.

Celebenie, celebonie, cylebenie, fem., gen. -an, *celandine, chelidonium maius*, by English tradition. But Glaucium luteum is the χελιδόνιον μέγα of Dioskorides, according to Sprengel. The drawing in MS. V. fol. 38 a, is meant perhaps for *chelidonium maius* (H.) Hb. lxxv. Lb. I. ii. 2, and often.

Ceppnlle, cyppnlle, fem., gen. -an ; *garden chervil, anthriscus cerefolium, Bot.*

Ceppnlle—*cont.*
Fubuceppnlle, *wild chervil, anthriscus silvestris*, Lb. II. li. 4. Lacn. 62. Seo peabe pubu pnlle, Lacn. 68. Fubu ceppnlle, Hb. lxxxvi., is in both places *sparagia agrestis, wild asparagus, or asparagus acutifolius, Linn. Asparagus agrestis*, becomes eopönapola, Hb. cxxvi. 2, by neglecting *agrestis*. Sparagia grestis, vude cearfille. Sparago, nefle, Gl. Dun.

Cicel, masc., *a cake.* Germ. Kuchen, masc., *a cake.* Quadr. ix. 17. Lb. I. xlvi. 2. " Buccella," Gl. in Lye ; masc. Lacn. 44. Διδαξ. 63, 21. A word still in use ; Moores Suffolk words, Bakers Northants Gl. Kersey. " *A flat triangular cake.*" Moore.

Cicena mete, masc.. gen. -er, *chickenmeat, chickweed, stellaria media*, formerly called alsine media, Linn. Hippia minor, etc. " Ispia minor, [*read Hippia*], chyken- " mete," Gl. Rawl. c. 607. " Ipia minor, " chykynmete album florem [habet]." Gl. Harl. 3388. Similarly, Gl. M., Gl. Sl., 1571. "Modera," Gl. Dun. Muronis, Gl. Brux.

Cymeb for Cymen? N and D being kindred dentals. Lb. I. xxxix. 2. Lye conjectured for chamædrys, *germander*.

Cymen, neut. (as Lb. II. xliv.), *cummin*, κύμινον, *cuminum cyminum*, a foreign plant.

Kincean, Lb. I. xvi. 1. I find " Kinnock, " the artichoke, cynara scolymos," (Nemnich). " Cariscus, kinhbeam," Gl. Sloane, 146. "Cariscus, cpicbeam," Gl. Somner, p. 64 b, 54, all agree that the quickbeam is the (sorbus or) *pirus aucuparia*. The reader will suspect I should have read kuihbeam, but the MS. marks the i. " Virecta, cincae," Gl. M.M. In these times virecta are green shoots, as in Vita Godrici, p. 43, line 1, applying well to the parts of the artichoke that are eaten. Kinphen, gremsich, Gl. Mone, p. 289 a, and Grensing,

Kıncean—*cont.*
nymphæa, Graff. Gl. Mone, p. 290 b, 6, corrected.

The spelling qınce in Lacn. 4, makes us suspect *quince*.

Cyꞃnel, masc., gen. -eꞅ, *kernel* of a nut. "Nucli, cyꞃnlaꞅ," Gl. Cleop. fol. 66 a, read *nuclei*.

Cyꞃnel, neut., pl. cyꞃnelu, *kernel, hard glandular swelling, churnel, grumus*. Hb. iv. 2, 3; xiv. 2; lxxv. 5.

Cyꞅlybb, neuter? *rennet*, Quad. iv. 14. *See* Lıb. Rennet is the substance which turns milk to curd, for which purpose is often used a calfs stomach; haꞃan cyꞅlyb implies that the stomach of a hare or leveret would have the same effect. Otherwise cyꞅᵹeꞃunn, Colloquium, p. 28; not *caseus*, nor yet *a cheese*, but *rennet*. Unlıbban is otherwise declined, Hom. II. 504; lyb is in Gl. C.C.C. Cf. Lacn. 18.

Clæꞅꞃe, gen. -an, fem.? *clover, trifolium pratense*, Lb. I. xxi. Amid a wilderness of confusion, the ternate leaves of the figure in MS. Bodley, 130, at Hb. lxx.; the close relationship between hares foot and clover in the old herbals, as Lytes, the similarity of the drawings in MS. V. at art. lxx. and art. lxii.; a comparison of the drawings of clover, art. lxx., and hart clover, art. xxv., have convinced me that I have rightly determined the worts meant by Ꝥaꞃan hıᵹe and Clæꞅꞃe. Κίρσιον to which clæꞅꞃe is equivalent, Hb. lxx., was in Dioskorides a pappose plant, *carduus parviflorus* (Sprengel). Lindley makes cirsium a cynaraceous genus. The *trifolium pratense* or purple clover is in German Kleber, Klever, Kleve, and -klee, Rothe-, Gemeiner- and Brauner-Wiesen-klee; in Dutch Roode klaver, etc.; in Dansk Röd-klever, etc.; in Swedish Klöfver, etc. The drawing in MS. V. Hb. lxx. by itself "won't do for "Trifolium; corresponds as far as it "goes with Thymus serpyllum," (H.) J. Grimm makes clæꞅꞃe *clover*.

Claꞇe, fem., gen. -an; 1. The greater, *the burdock, arctium lappa*. "Blitum vel "lappa, claꞇe," Gl. Somn. p. 66 [63] b, 30. "Bardane la grande, the burrdock, "slote [*read* clote] burr, great burr," Cotgrave. "Bardona.i.cletes.vel burres "secundum aliquos," Gl. Rawl. c. 607. "Elixis.i.lappa bardana.i.clote," Gl. Harl. 3388. "Lappa maior.i.bardana, clote," Gl. Harl. 3388.

2. The lesser; *clivers, goosegrass, catchweed, little bur, galium aparine*. "Amorfolia, claꞇe," Gl. Somn. p. 66 [63] b, 44, that is, *love leaves*, from cleaving to passengers; so Gl. Dun. Hb. clxxiv. MS. O. The drawing, MS. V. fol. 64, is "a very neat representation of aspe-"rula odorata," (H.), but the asperula is not a burr plant, and the nearly akin G. Aparine must have been in the draughtsmans intention. It is called φιλάνθρωπος, as sticking to men and women. "Philantropium, lappa, claꞇe," Gl. R. 41.

Lappa, *the catcher*, from λαβέσθαι, *lay hold of*, is applied like clote to both these herbs, in other particulars unlike. Clote itself must have the same sense, and with exceptional vocalisation is a derivative of cleoꞃan, and for † cleoꞅꞇe, as slıꞇe for † ꞅlıhꞇe, is from slean, † ꞅleᵹan.

Clıꞅe, fem., gen. -an; *clivers*. The greater is *burdock, arctium lappa*. The lesser is *galium aparine*, Lb. I. l. 2. The same as clıꞅꞃyꞃꞇ. "Apparine, cliue." Gl. Dun.

Clıꞅꞃyꞃꞇ, fem., gen. in -e, *burdock, arctium lappa*. Assuming the syllable clıꞅ to signify *cleaving*, the Xanthium strumarium and the Asperugo procumbens are too rare; the Galiums or the Arctium lappa are common; the equivalent ꞅoxeꞅ clıꞅe (Lacn. 112), seems to suit better the burdock, which will grow in the wet shore of a river, and so be eaꞃyꞃꞇ. "Blitum vel lappa, claꞇe vel clıꞅꞃyꞃꞇ," Gl. Somn. p. 66 [63] b, 30. Lb. I. xv. 3.

2. *Galium aparine*, written clıꝺꞃyꞃꞇ, Lacn. 69, where occurs a gloss, Rubea minor.

Cluꝼe? fem., pl. in -e, *a clove*, the bulb or tuber of a plant. Lb. III. xli., etc.
Cluꞃhꞇ, cluꞃehꞇ, *cloved, having a clove, bulbed, tuberous.* Lb. III. xli., etc.
Cluꝼþunȝ, cluꝼþunȝe, fem., gen. in -e, also -an, *cloffing, ranunculus sceleratus,* Hb. ix. In MS. G. the true herb is drawn; in MS. A. the flowers are at least yellow, with five petals; but in MS. V. fol. 21 a, all likeness is lost. þunȝ is *poison*, cluꝼ- is *clove*, the tuberous root; as of some of this tribe. Cluꝼþunȝan, Hb. cx. 3, where the Latin again makes the wort a ranunculus. " Mortali veneno, mid ættrigere cluf- " þunȝe," Gl. Mone, p. 349 b, an erroneous version; but an example of the feminine. " Scelerata herba vel apium " risus, anglice cloftong," Gl. Sloane, 405. " Scelerata, gl. cloftunge," MS. Bodley, 130. " As yellow as a claut," that is, marsh ranunculus (Wilts.). " Batra- " chium," Gl. Brux. " Cicuta, cloftunke," Gl. Harl. 3388, an error, cicuta is hemlock; the poisonous quality misled the writer. " Cloffing, the plant hellebore." Halliwell and the English Macer, MS. in Prompt. Parv., vol. i. p. 198; a similar error occurs, Lb. I. i. 7.
Cluꝼpypꞇ, *clovewort*, fem., gen. -e, *ranunculus acris.* In MS. G. the figure is that of ranunculus as in " scelerata," but here the root is tuberous, so MS. T., but less well; MS. A. preserves a resemblance, which is almost lost in MS. V. Hb. x. " Batrocum," Gl. Dun., that is βατρόχιον.
Cneopholen, masc., *knee holly, knee holm, -holn, -hulver, butchers broom, Ruscus aculeatus,* Hb. lix. The gender is determined by C.E. p. 437, 19, where the translation "alder," is an unfortunate blot. Two kinds are mentioned, Lb. I. xlvii., but one only is native to England. The second may be presumed to be R. Alexandrina of the middle ages, which included *R. hypoglossum, R. hypofyllum, R. racemosus,* of the Bot.

Coꞃc, gen. -eꞇ, *costmary, alecost, tanacetum balsamita.* Lb. II. lv. 1, etc.
Crawleac. *See* Leac.
Cꞃimman, prmꞇ. cꞃam, p. part. cꞃumen, *to reduce to crumbs,* to *crumble.* Cꞃim. Lb. I. lxi. 1.
Cropleac. *See* Leac.
Cꞃuc, masc., *a cross.* Lb. II. lvi. 4.
Cu, gen. cue, fem., *cow, vacca.* The declension is often contracted; gen. Lb. I. xxxviii. 11, by contr. cu; Sæꞇ an beoꝼol on þæꞃe cu hꞃycȝe, M.H. 194 a, *There sat a devil on the cows back.* Dat. cȳ. Feꞃbe oꝼ ꝺæꞃe cȳ, ibid., *the devil went off from the cow;* gen. pl. cuna; ꝼeopeꞃꞇiȝ cuna, Gen. xxxii. 15; dat. pl. cum; unꝺeꞃ ꝼolcum, Par. Ps. lxvii. 27, for ꝼolc cum, as Grein suggests; acc. pl. cȳ; ic hæbbe . . . ȝecelꝼe cȳ, Gen. xxxiii. 13, where ȝe is con; SSpp. 261, *cows with their calves.*
Culmillan, for cupmellan? Lb. I. xvi. 1.
Cumb, masc., gen. -eꞃ, *a vessel,* " *dolium,*" MS. St. Joh. Oxon. 154; SSpp. art. 1026. Lacn. 37. Cf. ꞃlbcumb. Lb. III. liii.
Cumulu, pl., *glandular swellings,* translates σκιρρώματα. Hb. clvii.
Cunelle, fem., gen. -an, a Latin word, cunila, a thymiaceous plant, say *Thymus vulgaris,* a garden herb, but it is not rue, as the glossator of the Lindisfarne Gospels, Luke xi. 42, says, nor chervil, as another Gl. says.
ꝼubu cunelle, *thymus serpyllum, wild thyme.* Lb. III. xxii.
Cupmelle ꝼeo mæpe, *Chlora perfoliata, Bot.* ; Cupmelle ꝼeo læꝼꝼe, *Erythræa centaureum, Bot.* Hb. xxxv. xxxvi. All the MSS., V., A., G., T. figure in both these articles, the same wort, and in all they are the *Erythræa centaureum.* The mediæval glossaries make no difficulty of the lesser, but they had lost the clue to the greater. The tradition is from Plinius, xxv. 30, 31. Though some of the continental botanists make no hesitation in identifying the greater centaurion of Plinius, with centaurea, yet his

Cupmelle—*cont.*

expression, "caules geniculati," seems irreconcileable with the genus. The interpreter of our MS., however, and the draughtsman did not know what plant to name for the greater, nor did Fuchsius, the botanic reformer. Of the less, Plinius says, " Hoc (*minus*) centaurion nostri " fel terræ vocant propter amaritudinem " summam." " The whole plant is ex- " tremely bitter, and when dried is used " in country places as a substitute for " gentian root," (Lindley). Lyte (p. 375) describes Eryth. c., and mentions (p. 436) its bitterness, calling it " the small cen- " torie." " Centaurea minor, horse galle," Gl. Sloane, 5, where " horse " means *wild.* " C. maior, cristes ladder," Gl. Sloane, 5, but minor, Gl. Sloane, 135; Christs ladder cannot be polemonium cæruleum, which is nowise to the purpose. " C. þe more is not well knowen," Gl. Sloane, 5, fol. 18 b. " Centaurea " maior, anglice more centori or yrthe " galle, it hathe leuys like lasse centori " whytt, with on [*one*] stalk and yolow " flowrys and he flowryth nott in þe " topp," Gl. Sloane, 135; and so Harl. 3840, this is *chlora perfoliata.* Centaurea maior coniungit folia iuxta stipitem, florem habet croceum, MS. T., fol. 63 a. " Centaurea minor, anglice lasse centori, " with lasse leuys and grener þen þe more " centori, and hath mony branches com- " yng out of on, with flowre some dele " redde," Gl. Sloane, 135, plainly *erythræa c.* The [H]ortus Sanitatis figures for centaurea, the *erythræum c.* Sibthorp in the Flora Græca sustains the assertion. Centaurea, erthegalle, is drawn in Grete Herbal as *C. cyanus.* Dorsten says the greater centaury is unknown, yet draws it as C. cyanus.

Cuślyppan, obl. case, *cowslip, primula veris;* fem. ? is a compound of cu, perhaps in the genitive, and slyppan. *See* Oxanŗlyppan, Lb. III. xxx. Slyppan is probably the sloppy dropping of a cow.

Cpæb, neut., *dung.* Lb. I. l. 2 ; II. xlviii. þynne is also neuter.

Cpelbehr, *full of evil matter, of pestilence.* Lb. I. liv. The termination as in cæpŗihr, *cressy;* cluŗihr, *cloved;* cneoehr, *kneed;* hæpihr, *hairy;* hæþihr, *heathy;* hpeodihr, *reedy;* helmihr, *leafy;* stænihr, *stony;* þoŗnihr, *thorny.* For cpylb, see Lye.

Cwicbeam, gen. –es, masc. 1. By tradition the *rowan tree, Pirus aucuparia.* 2. *Iuniperus communis,* many glossaries. 3. *Furze,* or *gorse, Vlex Europæus,* Lb. I. xxxi. 3. Prompt. Parvul. *See* Hb. cxlii. 4. The aspen, *Populus tremula,* Pref. vol. I. p. lxxxvi.

Cpið, gen. in –eŗ, masc., *the matrix, uterus, vulva.* Lb. III. xxxvii. xxxviii.

Cpið, Lb. I. xlvii. 3, *Matricaria ?* Read cpice ?

D.

Dæl, gen. –es, neut. *a dale, vallis, "barath- " rum."* C.E. p. 93, l. 26, p. 94, l. 18. Cædm. if Cædm., p. 16, line 11, p. 22, l. 10.

Dæl, gen. –es, mostly masc., sometimes neut., like Germ. Theil, *part, pars.* The masc. occ. everywhere. Exx. of neut. Διδαξ. 52, unless nominatival apposition is there used ; as is perhaps the case in Lb. II. xxx. Heo næniᵹ bæl leohteŗ ŗciman ᵹeŗeon mihte, Bed. 578, 20. Sum bæl oðŗeŗ peoŗcef to pyŗcanne, D.G. 23 b.

Deaŗe, gen. –e, fem. ? *deafness, surditas,* Lb. I. iii. 2, 5. Cf. Isl. Deyfa, fem. id. (B.H.)

Dile, gen. –es, masc., *dill, anethum graveolens.* Lib. I. i. 8 ; II. xxxiii. Leechd. vol. I. p. 374, where hæpene is for hæpenne by suppression of consonant; Pref. vol. I. p. c. ci.

Dile—cont.

Hæpen dile ; perhaps *Achillea tomentosa* ; for Cotgrave explains Anet as secondly, " little or yellow harrow," for which I read yarrow, the finely divided leaves of which might obtain it this name.

Dylæta ? *mucus*; pl. dylæran. Lb. I. xxxi. 5. Cf. II. xxix.

Dylæriht, *mucous, slimy.* Lb. I. xxix. 1.

Dynige, it seems, an herb. Lb. III. viii. Read pynige ?

Dyþhomap, *papyrus.* Gl. Somn. p. 64 a, 39. Lb. I. xli.

Docce, gen. -an, fem., *dock, rumex*; commonly *R. obtusifolius*, but often in medicine for 8uþbocce. Lb. I. xxxviii. 9, probably also *R. pulcer*, which is drawn in MS. T. ; fem. in Gl. Cleop. fol. 71 c.

Fallow dock. Lb. I. xlix. ; perhaps *R. maritimus*, and *R. palustris.*

Red dock. Lb. I. xlix. *R. sanguineus*, and perhaps for Suþbocce.

The dock that will swim frequently occurs. Lb. II. lxv. 1 ; L. xxxvi ; also the Ompre that will swim, which is the same plant. Lb. III. xxvi. Gerarde calls " swimming herbe," duckes meat = *Duckweed* = *Lemna*, which is doubtful.

Suþbocce, *sorrel, Rumex Acetosa* is the gl. in MS. T. Hb. art. xxxiv., and a bad sorrel is drawn.

The Saxons did not botanize on modern principles, and it easily follows that their genus Dock is not of the same reach as the modern Rumex. Thus Crousope, which is Saponaria officinalis, is glossed fomedok, Gl. Harl. 3388. The word " foam " shows that the writer knew his plant, which he calls a dock. As in this instance, and in Cammock whin, and many others, similarity of leaves seems to have been the chief guide to Saxon nomenclature. I cannot therefore believe that Eabocce (spelt bocca) is Nymphæa, Gl. Somn. p. 64 a, 61. The word Nymphæa, like many others, must have been misunderstood ; I therefore believe that,

Docce—cont.

Eabocce is the great *water dock, rumex uquaticus* of Smith, and *R. hydrolapathum* of Hudson.

Dockenkraut in German is *Arctium lappa*, and dockcresses are *Lapsana communis.*

Dolh, gen. -es, mostly neuter, rarely masc., *wound, scar, vulnus, cicatrix.* Hb. x. 3. Lb. I. xxxi. 7, xxxviii. 9, 10; III. xxxiii. xxxiv. C.E. p. 68, 24, p. 89, 10. Syð-ðan ɼe dolh pæɼ ȝeopenod. M.H. 93 b.

Dolhpune, gen. -an, fem.? *pellitory, parietaria officinalis.* Hb. lxxxiii., as perdicalis, which is the same herb ; Lb. often.

Dopa, masc., gen. -an, *the humble bee, bumble bee, dumble dore*, bombus generically. The mediæval glosses Burdo, Fucus, Attacus, mean this insect or some nearly allied. The commonest is *Bombus terrestris*, which stores honey. "Bourdon, " a drone or dorr bee," Cotgrave. Lb. often.

Dɼacenrɼe, gen. -an, fem.?. Dragons, *arum dracunculus*, Hb. xv. Dragons was a name applied by English herbalists, 1. to *Polygonum bistorta*, which is, I think, the herb figured in the Latin Apuleius, MS. Bodley, 130, as dracontea ; 2. to *ofioglossum vulgatum*, Hb. art. vi. ; and 3. to *arum maculatum.* All these three have a resemblance to a snakes erected head and neck. The figure in MS. V., art. xv. is intended for *arum dracunculus*, and, this being so, it is impossible not to concede the name. That plant is not of English birth, but neither is the name.

Dɼaconɼjan, *gum dragon*; Lb. II. lxiv. contents.

Dɼige, bɼyȝe, *dry, siccus, aridus*, Bed. 478, 14. Andreas, 1581. Lb. II. xlvi. (In C.E. 426, 22, ɼoɼum bɼiȝe is ɼ. bɼiȝum).

Dɼince, gen. -an, fem., *a drink, potus.* Lb. I. li. 1. ; I. xlii. Hom. II. 180.

Dɼopa, -an, masc., *palsy of a limb.* Lacn. 9. The Saxon interpreter was wide of his original in Hb. lix. 1, where "Ad " hecmata intercidenda," in cxxiv. "tussi

Dɲopa—*cont.*

" medendo " (so). Drop, droppe, *para-*
lysis (Kilian); Troppf, *gout* (Wachter).
The original sense remains in the "drop-
" ped hands," " wrist drop " of painters,
paralysis of the extensor muscles of the
wrist. Root Drapan, *to strike,* p. part.
Dropen, Bw. 5955, MS.

2. *A drop, gutta.* Lb. I. ii. 21. Hence
" colera " meaning lymph, in Sc. 30 b.
Duɟc, neut., *dust,* pulvis, powder. Neuter
everywhere ; Mark vi. 11, Luke x. 11,
Psalm i. 5, Matth. x. 14.

Dpeopʒe bpoɟcle, bpeopɪʒe bpoɟle, *penny*
royal, mentha pulegium. Hb. xciv. clvi. 2,
as pulegium. So GL Dun. So Διδaʒ.
30, 51. " Pulegium regule, puliole
" reale," GL Harl. 3388. " Pulegio,
" peniroyall," Florio ; so Cotgrave.
" The smallest of its genus," Sir J. E.
Smith, and therefore well called "dwarf."
" Much used in medicine," (All). Penny
royal is only puliole royale. Flea bane
is not this plant, nor is the reading
bpeopʒeɟ.

Mentha ƿulegium is called, Hb. xciv. a
male and female plant, but this has no
reference to the sexual system of Linné,
which make it didynamous not diœcous.
Some notion of strength influenced Theofrastos and Dioskorides in giving these
names. The drawing in MS. V. is like
the herb intended. The flowers are sometimes white.

Dpoɟle seems in the German glossaries to be Origanum.

E.

Eaʒpyɲc, fem., gen. -e, *eyebright, eufrasia*
officinalis. Lb. III. xxx. Germ., au-
gentrost ; Dutch, oogentrost ; Dansk,
" oientrost;" Swed., "ogontröst."

Eala̋ð, ealőð, ealo, ealu, eala, neut. unde-
clined in sing., *ale, cerevisia;* gen. eala̋ð,

Eala̋ð—*cont.*

DD. 63; O.T. 256, 5; Lb. I. xiv. and often;
dat. eala̋ð, DD. 357 d; Lb. often; gen.
pl. eale̋ða, DD. 487, where it is used of
fermented liquor generally. Gen. Al̋ðes,
D.R. 116, but the forms of D.R. are ab-
normal, or late.

Some interesting information on ale
and beer is collected by that learned and
accurate antiquary, Mr. Albert Way, in
the Prompt. Parv. p. 245. The frequent
mention of Wort (as I. xxxvi), that is, the
warm malt infusion in the mash tub,
prepared for fermentation, shows plainly
enough that the Saxons brewed for themselves. The Alevat (I. lxvii.) is the vessel
in which the ale was left to ferment.
Double brewed ale (I. xlvii. 3.) was
brewed on ale, instead of on water, and
gave them then a very Strong ale (III.
xii. p. 314, twice). Even without hops
such ale would keep till it became Old
ale (II. lxv. 1, p. 292, line 12). Keeping
and careful treatment would secure its
being Clear (I. lxiii.; II. lxv. 2, etc.).
Sweet ale is opposed to the clear (II.
lxv. 2), and so was thick. ɣiɫɟc ealu,
foreign ale, is often mentioned (I. lxx.,
etc.). Ale is much more frequently
named than beer ; strong beer is opposed
to strong ale (III. xii.). Hopping drinks
is mentioned, Hb. lxviii.; further, *see*
Ɗymele.

Ealɪɟeɲ, *eileber, alliaria, sauce alone*
(Gerarde). *Erysimum alliaria.* Lb. II.
xxiv., etc. But Callitrichum, Gl. Dun.

Ealla, *gall, fel.* Cf. Gealla. So Euang.
Nicod., xxvi.

Eaɲban, pl. *tares, ervum* and *orobus.* Well
made out by Somner. " Rolon," in Gl.
Mone, is doubtless a corruption of orobus,
ὄροβος, which, though divided by Bot.,
is every way the same as ervum. Lb. I.
xxvi.

Eaɲɲɪcʒa, –an, masc., *earwig, forficula au-*
ricularis. Lb. I. iii. 2, followed by he.

Eɟelaɟce, fem., gen. in -an, *Gnaphalium.*
Somner found some authority for " Mer-

Crelarce—cont.

" curialis, the herb mercury, D.," and so
Gl. Harl. 978, yet all the gnaphaliums
have very lasting blooms, retaining their
colour when dry ; the G. margaritaceum
is specially our modern Everlasting, and
found "near Bocking, on the banks of
" the Rhymney, in Wire forest, and near
" Lichfield." Skinner also, Gnaphalium
Americanum, which is a misnomer by
Ray. The genus is in Dausk, Evigheds-
blomster.

Croprreapn, neut., gen. -er, polypody, polypodium vulgare. Hb. lxxxvi., where it
= Radiolus ; " Alii filicinam dicunt,
" similis est filici, quæ fere in lapidetis
" nascitur vel in parietinis, habens in
" foliis singulis binos ordines puncto-
" rum aureorum," Lat. In MS. Bodley,
130, a fern, as polypodium is drawn and
a Gloss. in a hand of the 12th century
gives "wilde brake." "Felix (read
" Filix) quercina pollipodium . i. ewer-
" wan," Gl. M. "þe iii.d is ouerfern,
" and þat groys on walles," MS. Bodley,
536. "Polypodyn . i. ouerferne ꝉ it
" grewiþ on okys þis is lest," id. "Poly-
" podium murale, euerfern," MS. Rawlinson, c. 506. To the entry, "Polypo-
" dium arborale, pollipodie ; Pollipodium
" murale, euerferne," MS. Harl. 3388, has
been added a cross, so as to invert the in-
terpretations. " Polypodium rubeas ma-
" culas habet et uocatur filix quercina .
" i . euerferne," id. " fiilex quercina pol-
" lopodium, euerferne idem (sunt)," id.
" Filix a[r]boratica, eropreapn," Gl.
Somn. p. 64 a, 14. Culpeper, under
polypody of the oak, describes at length
and cleverly, pol. vulg. (H.), and his
mention is one link in a long medicinal
tradition. "And why, I pray, must
" polypodium of the oak only be used,
" gentle college of physicians? Can
" you give me but a glimpse of reason
" for it ? It is only because it is
" dearest." Culpeper. Polypodium vulgare is "very frequent on the tops of

Eropreapn—cont.

" walls, old thatched roofs, shady banks
" and the mossy trunks of rotten trees."
(Sir J. E. Smith.) Its fructification
forms a double row of golden spots on
each frondlet. See also his allusion to
tradition in English Botany, 1149. The
older names were, "polypodium quer-
" cinum; filix arborum; filicula; herba
" radioli." (Nemnich.) Italian, felce-
quercina. The figure in MS. V. "would
" do very well for plantago lanceolata,
" (H.), it is not a fern at all." The
gender neuter, Boet. p. 48, l. 31 ; Lb.
I. lvi.

Chheolope, heahheolope, gen. -an, fem. ?
elecampane, inula helenium; from eh,
horse, equus, = heah, horse, ꞇꞃꞃoꞅ. "Ele-
" campana ys an erbe þat som men
" calleþ horshele, he beryth grene levis
" and longe stalkys and berith yelowe
" floures." Gl. Sloane, 5, fol. 22 c ; so
Gl. Bodley, 178. Lb. I. xxxii. 2 ; I. i.
5, etc.

Elena, latter, comp. adj. Lb. II. i. 1, related to Elcian, be late ; Elcung, late-
ness ; Elcop, later, adverb.

Elehtpe, gen. -an, lupin, the cultivated
sort of course, lupinus albus; so translated, Hb. cii. 3. Given for diarrhœa,
Lb. III. xxii. " Electrum multos habet
" stipites folia virid[i]a et flores cro-
" ceos," Gl. Harl. 3388. "Syluestres
" lupini candida habent folia. Sativi
" foliis non adeo albicant," Dorsten.
"Lypinus . i. lyponys, þis erbe has
" leuys lyke to þe v. levyd grass, bote
" þe erbe fore the more party has v.
" leues and a whyt floure, etc.," MS.
Bodley, 536. "Elehtpe, maura," MS.
in Somner. "Walupia, electre," Gl.
Dun.

Elhyzð, strange thought, distraction. Lb.
II. xlvi. Þyzð is found fem. neut.

Elm, masc., gen -er, elm, ulmus campestris;
perhaps also u. sativa. Gen. elmer, Lb.
I. vi. 8, therefore like old Dansk, Almr,
elm, masc.

Eoɲoɲþþotu, also -e, fem., gen. in -an;
carlina acaulis, Eberwurtz. carlina acaulis (Adelung). "The Carline thistle,
" formerly used in medicine, is not this
" (carlina vulgaris), but carlina acaulis
" of Linnæus. It was reported to have
" been pointed out by an angel to Charle-
" magne, to cure his army of the plague.
" His name is the origin of the generic
" one." (Sir J. E. Smith, English Botany,
plate 1144). Everwortel, chamæleon,
Kilian; that is χαμαιλίων (λευκύς), which
was identified, rightly or not, by Sprengel, as carlina acaulis. "Eberwurz,
" cardo [read carduus] rotunda. Euer-
" wurz, cardo pana, al. chamæleon," Gl.
Hoffm. "Scissa," a gl. in Lye, perhaps
a genuine name. "Scasa, eboɲþþotœ,"
Gl. M.M. p. 162 b. "Colucus," Gl. Brux.
"Colicus," Gl. Cleop. "Colitus vel Colo-
" cus," Gl. Dun.; which I take to be mis-
readings of Cō, for Cardo, and that for
Carduus, λευκός. "Scasa vel scafa vel
" sisca," further, Gl. Dun.; these are
attempts to read a crabbed MS. Also
"Anta," also "Borotium," Gl. Dun.,
the last being the English word eoɲɲp,
boar, with a Latin termination. Lb.
I. i. 6; xxxviii. 10.

The χαμαιλίων, which, by its name
must have hugged the ground, is wrongly
interpreted in Hb. xxvi., cliii., as a teazle,
which has a strong long stem.

Eolone, Elene, gen. -an; fem., elecampane,
inula helenium. Lb. I. xxxiv. 2, and
everywhere.

Colone læɲɲe, flea bane, pulicaria dysenterica, doubtless. Lb. II. lii. 1.

Eoɲnlice, earnestly, "diligenter." Hb.
lxxxvii. 2.

Coɲ̃ogealla, masc., gen. -an, Erythræa
centaureum, Bot. This is made the
same as Centaurea maior, Hb. xxxv.,
and the drawings in MSS. V. G. T. A.
represent Erythræa centaureum, which
is "intensely bitter." It is, however,
C. minor, not maior. In the pictorial
Apuleius, MS. Bodley, 130, Se maɲe

Coɲ̃ogealla—cont.
curmelle, is intended for feverfue,
Pyrethrum Parthenium, which is "herba
" amara, aromatica," Flor. Brit. "Cen-
" taurya maior. i . þe more centore or
" erthe galle, his flowrs ben ȝolow in þe
" tope, etc." MS. Bodley, 536. Dorsten
agrees with us. He figures Eryth. cent.,
and says the greater centaury has leaves
like the walnut, green as the cabbage,
and serrated. "Fel terræ. centaurea.
" idem. muliebria educit. habet in sum-
" mitate plures flores rubros," MS.
Rawlinson, c. 607, which describes
Erythræa. "Centauris, eoɲ̃ ȝealle [a],
Gl. Somn. p. 64 a, 5. Lb. II. viii., etc.

Coɲ̃onaɲola, masc., gen. -an, earth navel,
asparagus officinalis. Hb. xcvii. 1,
"asparagi." So cxxvi. 2, masc. Oros.
iv. 1 = p. 380, 30.

Coɲ̃oɲima, gen. -an? masc. Lb. III. xli.
conjecturally potentilla reptans, since ɲima
stands for ɲeoma masc., as in toɲ̃ɲima,
gl. for toɲ̃ɲeoma, cf. Germ. Riem, masc.,
a thong, a strap. The signification is
therefore "Earth cord;" this is not applicable to the dodder, which does not
touch the earth, and has its own Saxon
name boðbeɲ, Mone, 287 a; the strawberry, which is almost a potentilla, has
also its old English name; the common potentilla reptans is therefore most
likely.

Coɲ̃o yɲɲ, neut., gen. -eɲ, ground ivy, glechoma hederacea, the equivalent is Hedera
nigra, Hb. c., according to our botanists,
our common climbing ivy is Hedera
helix, which name, however, in Plinius,
lib. xvi. 62, is given to a sort which has
no berries, "fructum non gignit." The
plant eoɲ̃ yɲɲ would not be ground
ivy, for its eɲoppaɲ or corymbi are
mentioned, Hb. c. 3, but there is no
getting over the common voice of
England, which calls by the name
ground ivy, what is not ivy at all.
Hedera is of constant occurrence as iɲɲ,
and to be correct, the interpreter should

Eopð yŋʒ—cont.

have added nothing. Glechoma is German Erd epheu ; French, le lierre terrestre ; Italian, ellera terrestre ; Spanish, hiedra terrestre ; Portuguese, hera terrestre. The errors lie perhaps in our misunderstanding of the words κισσός, Hedera, when used for that which is not ivy.

Eop, Ip, masc., gen. –eɲ, *the yew, taxus baccata.* Masc., C.E. p. 437, line 18. " Ornus eop," Gl. Somner, p. 65 a, 40, only proves that the glossator did not understand the word ornus as we do ; whether current notions are correct appears questionable ; but at any rate the old folk of England know the yew out of which they made their victory giving bows. Cf. ohg. Iwa ; mod. g. Eibe, fem., *the yew*; Fr. If, masc. ; Ip is masc., C.D. 652.

Eop beɲʒe, *yew berry.* Lb. III. lxiii.

Eopohumele. Lb. III. lx., *the female hop plant. See* Ƿymele.

F.

Fæp, Feɲ, gen. –es, masc., *fever, febris,* Lb. I. contents, lxii., a contraction of ɲeɲoɲ.

Fætelɲian, –obe, –ob, *put into a vessel, bottle off.* Quad. i. 3.

Feaɲn, neut., *fern,* Boet. p. 48, line 31.

Ƿæt micle ɲeaɲn, *the mickle fern, bracken, aspidium filix.* Lb. I. lvi.

Feap, Lb. I. xxxv., as opposed to micel, is *paucus,pauculus, paullus, little,* like Goth. Faws, 1 Timoth. iv. 8. Hence, perhaps, its construction with a genitive, Feapa ɲixa, Matth. xv. 34, a few of fishes, like a Few of us.

Feban, Lb. I. lxiii., see Pref. vol. I. p. xl. Matter for conjecture. Se beopa ɲeað , bpeoɲʒe ɲebeð, C.E. 94, 25, *the deep pit feedeth* or *keepeth them dreary.*

Feɲeɲɲuʒe, gen. –ean ; fem. ? *erythræa centaureum.* Hb. xxxvi. Gl. Harl. 585. Any wholesome bitter might be called feverfue, serving the purpose now served by quinine.

Felðmoɲu, " fieldmore," *carrot* or *parsnep, daucus cariota,* or *pastinaca sativa.* Though pastinaca, Hb. lxxxii., is now decided to be a parsnep, yet the weight of nearly cotemporary authority stands for carot. In MS. Bodley, 130, the glosses are " a carott," "ffeldmore." " Daucus, wildmoren," Hortus Sanitatis, and figures a carot. The Gl. Somn. p. 64 a, 32, distinguishes "pastinaca, " ɲelbmoɲa," (read –ɲu, as Gl. Dun.), " Daucus, pealmoɲa [-ɲu] cariota ɲalb- " moɲa ;" but the distinction between a field root and a weald root is over fine. " Pastinaca, uuallimoɲae," Gl. M.M. The words should include both. " Pastinaca domestica . i . parsnep." Gl. Bodl. 536. The p. silvatica has been improved by cultivation into *p. sativa.*

Felðpyɲt, gen. –e, fem., *gentian, gentiana,* Hb. xvii., where the marginal note, erythræa pulcella, describes the drawing in MS. V. The reading ɲelpyɲt of Skinner and others, from Fel, gall, gives us a hybrid word. Probably, as in Esthonian, the earliest name was ɲelb- hymele, *field hop,* the plant being employed as a substitute for hops in embittering ale. Then as the appearance and leaves negatived this name, it was exchanged for ɲelbpyɲt.

Fellepæpe, ɲyllepæɲc, masc., *epileptic convulsions.* Lb. II. i. 1. The word must be interpreted in harmony with ɲylleseoc, ɲylleseocnyɲ. I had written so much before I detected the equivalent ἀρχομένας ἐπιληψίας in Alex. Trallianus.

Feltpyɲt, fem., gen. in –e, feltwort, *verbascum thapsus.* Hb. lxxiii. The reading ɲelbpyɲt is a mistake, the felty leaves give it the name, whence it is also called in German Wollkraut ; mullein also is supposed to be woollen. Felt

Felcpypc—*cont.*

was Latinised (Gl. Somn. p. 59 a, 58)
as feltrum, filtrum (John de Garlond,
p. 124); Dansk, filt, *felt*; Swedish, filt,
masc. *felt*; Germ., filz, masc. felt. The
drawing in MS. V. fol. 37 d, represents
the plant. "Filtrum terre, anglice felt-
" wort vel molayn idem." Gl. Rawl.
c. 607. " Thapsus barbastus [*read bar-*
" *batus*], G. moleyn, A. felwort." Gl.
Sloane, 5; so Gl. Sloane, 405. In Gl.
Somn. 63 b, 38, read Anadonia, relc-
pypc. Feltwort vel hegetaper, Gl.
Arund. 42.

Fepbpypc, fem., gen. in -e. Lb. I.
lxxxvii.

Fepþe, masc., *sound part?* Lb. I. i. 15.
" Probus ferth," Gl. M.M. p. 160 b, 20.
Leasrepŏnes, *false probity*, P.A. 59 b.
See repe, Chron. 1016, and Layamon,
1052, 1075, 1055. But there is also a
syllable repŏ in "reolurepŏ, *torax*." Gl.
C., that is, θώραξ, from perhaps Lorica,
p. lxxii. Cf. Gl. Cleop. fol. 85 b, and
relu-repŏ, *centumpellio*, Gl. Cleop. fol.
26 b, which appears to be an altered
form of centipedem. In these two words
it is possible that repŏe may signify
ring, which would suit Lb. well. So,
Fleocenbpa repŏ, C.E. 289, line 26, a
ring of floating ones.

Fıc, Gepg, masc., a disease known as ficus,
Συκῆ, Σῦκον, Σύκωμα, Σύκωσις. In the
Lb. I. ii. 22, the disease "fig " is said to
be χύμωσις, *a moisture in the skin en-*
closing the eyes (Florio), but without
exactly negativing that statement we
must bend to an overwhelming weight
of testimony, and accept it as *an excre-*
scence like a fig with an ulcer, so called
from a fig bursting with fatness, "ficus
" hians præ pinguedine." It affects all
parts of the body which have hair, especially the eyebrows, beard, head, and
anus; and it was sometimes called
marisca. Dioskor. i. 100; Pollux from
Apsyrtus, iv. 203; Celsus, vi. 3; Paulus
Ægineta, iii. 3; Psellus in Ideleri Phys.,

Fıc—*cont.*

vol. i. p. 223, 704; Pollux, iv. 200;
Aetius; Martialis; Hippokrates, p. 1085
H.; Oribasius ap. Phot., p. 176, 3;
Schol. Aristoph. Ran., 1247. These
references I have taken from the Paris
ed. of Etienne. The name was in constant technical use among mediæval
medical writers. " Contra ficum arden-
" tem," "Contra ficum sanguinolen-
" tum," "Contra ficum corrodentem,"
" Contra ficum uomere facientem." MS.
Sloane, 146, fol. 28. Hæmorrhoids are
ficblattern in the [H]ortus Sanitatis. In
Florios time (1611) fico in Italian had
been reduced to "a disease in a horses
" foot." Cotgrave (1673) has "fic, a
" certain scab, or hard, round, and red
" sore, in the fundament." " Fijck,
" tuberculum acutum cum dolore et
" inflammatione," (Kilian). It was a
running sore, Lb. I. xxxix.; it was
equivalent to þeopabl, Lb. I. ii. 22.
Written Uic, and masc., Lacn. 6; 44,
following the Latin usage.

" Dicemus ficus quas scimus in arbore
" nasci,
" Dicemus ficos, Cæciliane, tuos."
                    Martialis, I. 66.
Hic fygus, *the fyge.* Wrights Gl. p. 224.

Fılb, Lb. I. lxvii., with Fılbcnmb, Lb. IIL
liii., may be taken to mean *the milk*
drawn at one milking from how many cows
soever; commonly called *the mornings*
milk, the evenings milk. In a dairy every
several milking is kept separate.

Fılle, an apocopate form of cepplle, *chervil*,
anthriscus cerefolium, as clearly appears
from a comparison of the poetical names,
Lacn. 46, with the same in prose. " Cer-
" folium . i . cerfoil. i . villen," Gl. Harl.
978 (A.D. 1240).

Fleaþe, rleoþe, fem., gen. -an, *water lily*,
Nymphæa alba, N. lutea. Lb. II. li. i. 3.
" Nimfea, i . fleaperc," MS. Ashmole,
1431, fol. 19. " Nympha, fleathorvyrt,"
Gl. Dun. But " flatter dock, pondweed,
" potamogeiton," Gl. Chesh.

Fleoᵹan, *flow*, not "fly." Lb. III. xxii.

Fleotpypr, fem., gen. -e, "floatwort," Lb. II. lii. 1. " Algea, flotvyrt," Gl. Dun. " Alga," Gl. M. I fear the description is too vague, *Potamogeiton fluitans?* *Sparganium natans? Lemna?*

Fletan, ꝛlietan. 1. Found only in pl., *fleetings, hasty curds,* skimmed, but yet not cream, Lb. III. x. ; I. ii. 23. " After the " curd for making new milk cheese is " separated from the whey, it is set over " the fire, and when it almost boils, a " quantity of sour butter milk is poured " into the pan, and the mixture is gently " stirred. In a few minutes the curd " rises to the surface, and is carefully " skimmed off with a fleeting dish into " a scive, to drain." (Carrs Craven Gl.) " Sarrasson, fleetings or hasty curds, " scumd from the whey of a new milk " cheese," (Cotgrave.) Cf. Wilbraham and Mr. Ways Promptorium. 2. In singular, *cream,* as Lye ; used in this sense, Lb. I. xliv. 2. The common notion of these two senses, is *skimmings.*

Fnærꝼtiaᵹ, Lib. II. xxxvi. If the passage be without error, which is hardly to be supposed, ꝛnæꝛtiaᵹ must be a plural. Fnæst is masc., and makes acc. þonc ꝛnæst, Διᵹaᵹ. 28, 51 ; therefore we should perhaps read ꝛnæstas.

Foꝛbeꝼan, præt. bæꝛ, p. part. boꝛen, *restrain, cohibere, continere.* Hb. iv. 9. Lib. I. xlv. 6, in a special sense, *continere, render continent, tie with a knot of poison.* See preface, on knots. To this binding down the instincts by herbs, allude the glosses, "obligamentum, lyb-" lyꝛefn ;" "Obligamentum, lyb," Gl. Cleop. fol. 69 a, fol. 71 b; Gl. M.M. p. 160 a, 22, where lib is φάρμακον and liꝛesn, φυλακτήριον, *an amulet;* ᵹalboꝛ oᵹᵹe liꝛeꝛne, Beda, p. 604, 9. In the Njal saga, Una, virgin wife of Hrut, thus tells her tale, attributing the misfortune to something that had poisoned him :

VOL. II.

Foꝛbeꝼan—*cont.*
Vist hefir hringa hristir
Hrutr likama þrutinn
eitra þa en linbeᵹs leitar
lundygr munnᵹ dryia.
Known has Hrut,
the ring bestower,
his body bloat
with venom vile,
when he would, with all goodwill,
in linen white,
in bleached bed,
the bliss enjoy
of loves delights
with me the lass
he wooed and wed.
Cf. pyꝛtꝛoꝛboꝛe. Lb. III. i. Foꝛbeꝼan is *restrain,* Bw. 3748.

Foꝛcuuolftan, *to swallow.* Lb. I. iv. 6. Cf. Qvolk, *gullet, throat* (Molbech).

Foꝛneteꝛ ꝛolm, " Fornjots palm," some herb ; Lb. I. lxx. lxxi. Gl. Cleop. fol. 65 b, which gl. only translates ꝛolm, *manus.* Cf. Gorfærs nægler, Ƴihꝛtmæꝛeꝛ pyꝛt, Sigmærts cruyt = Sigmunds kraut.

Foꝛpeaxen ; that this word has been rightly read *overgrown,* appears by Hb. ii. 4, and by ᵹy læꝛ hie to ᵹæm ꝛoꝛpeoxen ᵹæt hie ꝛoꝛꝛeaꝛoben ꞇ ᵹy unpæꝛᵹmbæꝛꝛan pæꝛen, P.A. 54 b, *Lest they overgrew to that degree that they withered and were thus less fertile.*

Foꝛþylmian. See þelma.

Foꞇ, masc., *foot,* pl. ꝛeꞇ, as Mark ix. 45 ; but ꝛoꞇas, Gᵹ. 114. Lb.

Foxeꝛ claꞇe, fem., gen. -an, " fox clote," *Arctium lappa.* Lb. I. lxix. See Claꞇe.

Foxeꝛ ꝛoꞇ, *bur reed, Sparganium simplex.* In Hb. xlvii. is ξίφιον. By the drawing in MS. G. this seems to have been understood as the German Schwertelried = *Sparganium simplex,* the burn on which may account for the name foxes foot. Hares foot is a name similarly given. The drawing in MS. V. is much eaten out. " Xifion, foxes fot," Gl. Dun., copied from Hb. So Gl. Laud. 567.

B B

Foþopn, masc., gen. -eʝ, *tenaculum*, in a
surgeons case of instruments. Lb. I.
vi. 7. Taken as a compound of ꝼon, *to
catch*, and þopn.

Fꝛampeaꞃbeʝ, *in a direction away from*,
Lb. I. lxviii. 1.

Fulbeam, fulanbeam, masc., gen. -eʝ, *the
black alder, rhamnus frangula*. Lb. I.
xxxii. 4.

G.

Gaᵹel, Lb. I. xxxvi. ; Gaᵹelle, Gaᵹille,
fem. ? gen. -an. Lb. II. li. 1 ; II. liii.;
III. xiv., *sweet gale, Myrica Gale*.
But ᵹaᵹelen, Laen. 4.

Galluc, masc., *comfrey, symphytum officinale.* "Simphitone, the hearbe Alo,
" Confrey or wallwort of the rocke,"
(Florio). So Hb. lx., Gl. Dun. copy-
ing Hb. "Cumfiria," Gl. Harl. 978
(A.D. 1240). "Adriatica vel malum
" terræ, galluc," Gl. Somn. p. 66 [63],
l. 9. If this means that the earth apple,
whether Cyclamen or Bunium, is galluc,
the statements above must be preferred.
Copied into Gl. Dun. Occ. Lb. I.
xxvii. 1, masc.

Gaꞃcliʝe, *agrimony, agrimonia eupatoria.*
IIb. xxxii. Gaꞃcliʝe is also the gloss of
Agrimonia in Gl. Dun. and Lb. II. viii.
Gl. Sloane, 146. MS. G. draws a rude
likeness of agrimony, and MS. T. attempts ἀργεμώνη, *papaver argemone.*
The word Agrimonia is said to be a
corruption of Argemone, Plinius,
xxvi. 59, but those who choose to enter
into the subject of the Latin names had
better compare Dioskor. 4i. 108, who
speaks of a poppy. Gaꞃ, *a spear*, is
evidently the first element in the name
of the plant, the spike of which rises
like a narrow dagger above the grass :
cliʝe is, perhaps, connected with our
Cliff, and with Hlꞇꝛan, *to tower.*

Gaꞇeꞇpeoꝅ, neut., gen. -eʝ, *the nettle tree,
the tree lotus, celtis australis.* Lb. I.
xxxvi. Somners conjecture is wholly
an error, his tree is the Gattridge tree.
" Geiꞇꝅoum, lothon ; [λωτός, genus
" arboris, latine mella]," Gl. Hoffm.

Geaceꝛ ꝛuꝅe, gen. -an, *cuckoo sorrel, wood
sorrel, oxalis Acetosella.* Proofs abound.
Lb. I. ii. 13, 22.; III. xlviii.

Geaᵹl, neut. and masc, gen. -eʝ, *the jowl,
the fleshy parts attached below the lower
jaw.* Lb. I. i. 16, 17.; iv. 3.

Gealla, masc., gen. -an. 1. *Gall, bile.* 2. *A
gall, a fretted place on the skin, intertrigo.*
Lb. I. lxxxviii.

Geaꞃuꝅe, ᵹæꝅuꝅe, ᵹaꝅꝅe, fem., gen. -an,
yarrow, Achillea millefolium.

Seo ꝛeaþe ᵹaꝅꝅe, *red yarrow, Achillea
tomentosa.* Lb. III. lxv.

Gebꞃæceo, *cough, tussis*, Hb. cxxiv., cxxvi.
Gl. in MS. H. Hoꞇꞇ, *cough*, SII. p. 26.

Gebꞃocum, *with fragments*, Lb. II. lvi. 3.
Cf. Scꝛgebꞃoc, Lye.

Geceꝛꝛnaþ, *granulated*, Lb. I. lxxv. Cf.
ohg. Kirnjan, *nucleare ;* Isl. at Kyrna, *to
granulate.*

Gecꝛꝛpan, præt. -pꝛe, p.p. -pꞇ, *contract* =
Old Dansk Kreppa, *contrahere.* Lb. II.
lvi. Hence Cripple.

Geꝛoᵹ, Geꝛeh, neut. 1. *a joining, a joint,
commissura, compago.* (Lye, etc., ÆG.
often.)

2. *glue.* Lb. I. ii. 2. Cf. Umbifangida,
glutinum, in Graff., and Kauahsa (=
gefahsa), *purgamenta*, the parings of
hides and hoofs from which glue is
made, id. III. 421. Cf. also many entries
in 422.

Geꝛꝛꝛþeþ, *dense with boughs*, from ꝛꝛð,
forest, opacus, Hb. i. 1, where the
Saxon made no error. Þa ꝅæꝛ an pꝛn-
ꞇꝛeoꝅ pꝛð þ ꞇempl ᵹeꝛꝛꝛðeð, M.H. 183
b. *There was then a pine tree opposite
the temple thick with foliage.*

Geᵹyman, præt. -eðe, p. part. -eð, *to over-
look*, Lb. III. lxv. A man is overlooked
when one having the power of witch-

Gegyman—*cont.*
craft has set designs against him. An approach to this sense of the Saxon word is found in De eode on rumes Fariſea ealdres hus on ræſtedæge þ he hlaf æte. ⁊ hig begymdon hyne. Luke xiv. 1. Warlock hatred has a blasting effect. This faith is strong in Devonshire; they say that the witch has no power over the firstborn.

Gehepian, *to extol, laudibus ampliare.* Hb. lvii. 2. Simple vb. in dictt.

Gehlenced, *linked,* Lb. III. lv. *See* the passage. Hlencan, *links,* found as yet in pl. only; Elene, 47, Cædm.? MS., p. 154, line 9, but probably masc., as old Dansk, Hlekkr, *a chain,* masc.; Dansk, Lænke, not neuter; Swed., Lænk, masc. Translate in Cædm.? *have their linked mail coats.*

Gehnæcan, præt. -te, p. part. -gd, *to twitch.* Hb. cxlviii. 1., clxiii. 6. Paris Ps. ci. 8, *allidere.* Cf. Hnykkja in Egilsson, prose sense, *vellere.*

Gehpeorf, gen. -es, *a turning,* also *a vertebra.* Lb. II. xxxvi., so Laws of Æþelstan, 10, var. lect. Cf. Hrioprban, Lorica, lxxl.

Gelered, *corrupted.* Lb. II. xxxvi. p. 244. Root Ler, *mischief.*

Gelic, *proper, consentaneus.* Lb. II. xvi. 1.

Gelodpyrt, fem., gen. -e, *silverweed, potentilla anserina.* Its leaves resemble the human spine, gelodpe, with the ribs. "Heptaphyllon," Gl. in Lye. Gl. Dun. Lb I. xxxii. 3; xxxviii. 11.

Gemædla, masc., gen. -an, *talk.* Lb. III. lvii., from mædlan, *to talk,* C.E. 82, 14, MS. reading.

Genæða, pl. *ephippia, a packsaddle.* O clerice, p. lx. Visibly related to ohg. Ginait, *consutus.* That Ge signifies and is identical with Con, *together, see* SSpp. art. 261, a large induction. The German Nähen, *to sew,* exhibits the remainder of the root. But, as Wachter truly says, it is sufficiently manifest, that the word

Genæða—*cont.*
has suffered sincopation, and that in its original form it had a D or T, as Neten, or Neden. So that it is related to Nædel, *needle.* "Ouh sih tharzua ni nahit | "uuiht thes ist ginait." *Et se ad hoc non approximat quicquam eius, quod est netum.* Otfrid Euangel. IV. xxix. 17, ed. Schilter; "ioh' unginaten redinon; *et inconsutili arte.* Ibid. 64.

Geopman leaf, all the gll. interpret *mallow,* but gl. C. writes geappan leaf, *yarrow-leaf,* or *leaves;* explaining the word geopman, but rendering the tradition doubtful, for no mallow has leaves like yarrow. Ld. vol. I. p. 380. Lb. I. xxvii. I.; xxxiii. 1., etc.

Gescadpyrt, fem., gen. -e, an herb uncertain. "Berbescum [*read Verbascum*], "gescadvyrt," Gl. Dun., Gl. Sloane, 146. "Herbescum," id. "Talumbus, gescald-"pyrt," Gl. Cleop.; gescadpyrt, Gl. M.M., p. 164 a, 4., read *βούφθαλμον,* gescadpyrt, that is to say, Oxeye, whether *Anthemis tinctoria,* as in Hb. clxi., or *Chrysanthemum leucanthemum,* not distinguished from the other by our folk. Lb. II. liii.

Gesceorf, neut., *abrasion,* Lb. II. i. xxxv.

Geseap, *juicy,* Lb. II. xliii., as gedeap, *dewy.*

Gespæt, *see* Spæt, Lb. I. i. 15.

Gespat, *sweaty,* Lb. I. xxvi. Cf. Geseap.

Gespeorf, gespyrf, gen. -es, *filings, limatura,* Hb. ci. 3. *See* Spyrfan, *also* Ap-.

Gespogung, fem., gen. -e, *swooning,* Lb. II. i. 1, in Trallianus *συγκοπή,* the syncope of modern medical phraseology, Lb. II. xvi. 1. Geswogen betwux ðam ofslegenum, Hom. II. 356, *in a swoon among the slain.* From this form comes SWOON.

Getapa, pl. only (as yet), *tools, instruments,* DD. p. 470, 2. Lb. I. xxix., where it is *instrumenta virilia.*

Getead, *prepared, paratus.* Lb. II. xxix. *See* Teagan.

Getenge, *incident*, CONTINGENT, which is of the same component parts ; so also Tυγχάνειν, where the NO sound is radical.

Getpiꞃulan, *to rub down, triturare*, Lb. I. i. 9, etc. Cf. Τρίβειν.

Gepealꞇ, neut., *the natura, inguen*, Hb. civ. 2, pl., Hb. v. 5 ; Gl. Prud. p. 140 b. The devil got a horn of an ox, ꞇ mıꞇ þam hoꝑne hıne þẏꞇe on þ ȝepealꞇ ꞅpꞃıꝺe, MII. 190 a, *and with it struck* a monk of St. Martins *in the private part severely.*

Gepune, as a pl. adj., *customary*. Hb. lxviii.

Geþeꝑan, præt. ȝeþeop, p. part. ȝeþopen, ȝeþupen, *to turn*, as cream to butter, milk to curd, *to alter, convertere*, Lb. I. xliv. 2. Buteꞃȝeþꝑeop translates "butyrum" in the Colloquium M., p. 28, but not quite correctly. Hameꝑe ȝeþupen, Beowulf, 2564, poetically *consolidated by the hammer.* C.E. 497, 16.

Gıcþa, masc. ? *hicket, hiccup*, Lb. contents, I. xviii., answering to ȝeocꞅa, ȝeohꞅa, in the text ; ꝛoxing for hicketing is frequent in English, in a later stage. Hick, hickse, *singultus, convulsio ventriculi* (Kilian).

2. Musc., *itch, prurigo*, Lb. II. xli. ult. ; II. lxv. 5 ; Hom. I. 86, where the true translation is ascertainable from the original passage of Josephus, κνησμός. Translates *prurigo*. P.A. 15 b.

Gılhꞃtep, ȝeolbꞃtoꝑ, neut., *ratten, pus, matter, sanies*, Lb. I. i. 17 ; Beda, p. 589, line 3, var. lect. Virus, ȝeolteꝑ (*so*), Gl. Mone, p. 430 a. Dansk, Qualster, *thick moist slime.* þa ȝılꞅtꞃe. Lacn. 1.

Gılhꞃtꝑe, fem., gen. -an, *ratten*, etc. Lb. I. i. 3. Virus, ȝeolꞇꞃꝑe, Gl. Mone, p. 432 b. "Pituita," Gl. M.M.

Gıꞃt, masc., *yeast, fermentum* ex cerevisia. Lb. II. li. 1. Hb. xxi. 6.

Gıtꝑıꞃe, ȝẏꝺhꝑoꞃe, fem., gen. -an, *cockle*, *Agrostemma githago.* The syllable pıꞃe, as in Hedgeriffe, refers to the roughness of the plant. "The whole is rough, "with hoary upright bristles," (Sir J. E. Smith). "Gith, cokkell," Gl.

Gıtꝑıꞃe, ȝẏꝺhꝑoꞃe—*cont.*

Harl. 3388. But in Gl. Cleop. Lassar vel æsdre ; where Laser is *Ferula assafœtida.* Lb. I. i. 5 ; xxxviii. 4, 5, etc.

Gıtte, an herb, probably Gıꝺ. Lb. II. xxxix.

Gıꝺcoꝑn, tho seeds of *daphne laureola, the spurge laurel.* Hb. cxiii. ; Plinius, xiii. 35. They are taken medicinally, and are like poppy seeds (Theofrastos, ix. 24). They are so hot they were wrapped in fat or crumb, Ibid. More exactly the seeds of *D. Gnidium ;* see the Latin of Apuleius ; but that is not English, and I have not supposed it imported. The name κόκκοι Κνίδιοι refers to their employment as purgatives by the early Knidian school of medicine.

2. *Agrostemma githago*, drawn to Hb. cxiii. in MS. V. fol. 49 a, and in MS. A. A plant is mentioned, Lb. II. lxv., not a grain. MS. Bodley, 130, glosses "Lathyris, febecorn," *sieve corn.*

Glæꝺene, gen. -an, *gladden, Iris pseudacorus.* As a Latinism I would have passed by this word ; but Sir J. E. Smith in Flora Britannica has made "Gladwyn" *Iris fœtidissima :* hence I quote. "Gladiolus . i . . . . habet croceum florem . yris . purpureum florem "gerit . alia alba. Gladiolus croceum "sed spatula fætida nullum," MS. Rawlinson, c. 607. "Gladiolus florem habet "croceum spatula fœtida nullum," MS. Harl. 3388. "Gladiolus Acorus . gla"dene," id. I observe, however, that if we take Sir J. E. Smiths words, "stinking iris or gladwyn," as the same words were understood in the old herbals, they mean *stinking iris* or *stinking gladden.*

Glappan, perhaps from ȝlappe, as herbs commonly are feminine in the an declension : perhaps *buckbean, menyanthes trifoliata*, Germ. Klappen, vol. I., p. 399, where the construction may be plural. Cf. ȝlæppan, C.D. 657. Thorpe compared Lappa, but that is clare, everywhere.

Glorpypc, fem., gen, -e ; 1. *convallaria
maialis, lily of the valley* : drawn, but
without the blooms, at Hb. art. xxiii., in
MSS. A., G., T. glossed "clofwort" in
a hand of the 14th century, MS. Harl.
1585, a copy of Apuleius. The blooms
are drawn MS. Bodley, 130, and glossed
"foxes glove," but it is *convallaria*, not
digitalis, that is drawn. "Apollinaris,
"goldwort," Gl. Rawl. c. 506. "Apol-
"linaris, golewort," Gl. Harl. 3388.
"Apollinaris, glofwert," Gl. M.
2. *Buglossa,* IIb. xlii. 1, the same as
"houndstongue," *cynoglossum officinale*,
or perhaps *lycopsis arvensis.*
Goman, pl. 1. *the fauces, the back of the
mouth :* it translates φάρυγγα, Hb. clxxxi.
2. Paris Ps. lxviii. 3, cxviii. 103. C.E. p.
363, 31 ; p. 364, 26. Luporum faucibus,
pulpa ξomum, Reg. Concord. Fauces,
ξoman, Gl. Cleop.
2. *the gums ; see* Lye. The gums are
mostly toðpeoman, *tooth straps.*
Gonξepæpne, gen. -an, *a gangway weaver,
a spider, aranea viatica.* Lb. III. xxxv.
Gpeaзepypc, fem., gen. -e, *meadow saffron,
colchicum autumnale.* In IIb. xxii. Hieribulbus, which according to Zedler is
colchicum ; and this plant is drawn in
MS. G. ; with broader leaves in MSS.
V. T. : the artist in MS. A. has taken
the liberty of turning the bulb into a
costly flower pot. "Hieribulbum, greate
"výrt. Hierebulbum, cusloppe," that is,
cowslip! Gl. Dun. "Hierobulbus, col-
"chicum," Humelberg, an editor of Apuleius. If the Saxon translator put the
name on the sight of the drawing only,
he may have meant by greatwort, man-
gold würzel. Some make Hieribulbus,
allium Ascalonicum, eschallot, but that
will not pass for greatwort. *See also*
Hpeppe.
In Lb. II. lii. 1, greatwort has a rind
to be scraped off: it is to be dug up too.
Gpunðerpylige, fem., gen. -an, *groundsel,
senecio vulgaris,* Lb. I. ii. 13 ; I. xxii.
Hb. lxxvii. etc.

Gpuc, fem. neut., Boeth., p. 94, 3, indecl.;
*grout, the wet residuary materials of malt
liquor, condimentum cerevisiæ.* Dutch,
grauwt (Kilian). Lb. III. lix. The term
is now applied also to the settlings in a
tea or coffee cup. "Wort of the last
"running," Carr.
Gunb, masc., *ratten, virus, virulent mutter.*
Lb. I. iv. 2, 3.

H.

Ꝺæpepn, Ꝺæbepn, masc., gen. -er, *a crab
(cancer),* masc. Lb. I. iv. 2.
Hæpce, neut., *a haft, manubrium,* Lb. II.
lxv. Somner cited it right.
Ꝺæpirceapð, neut., *hairlip.* Lb. I. xiii.
Hæsel, gen. -es, -les, masc., *the hazle,
corylus,* C.D. 624. Lb. I. xxxviii. 8 ;
II. lii. = p. 270.
Hæslen, *of hazle, colurnus ;* Lb. I. xxxix. 3.
Hæpen hybele ; Hb. xxx. The various
reading is instructive ; Huybele, which
is close akin, apparently, to Netele, and
Κάνναβις : and the Brittanica of the
Vienna drawings (*See* pref. Vol. I., p.
lxxxi.) is so much like *Lamium purpu-
reum, the red dead nettle,* that there arises
a fair presumption this is the true identi-
fication. Lacn. 2. The gll. support
Cochlearia Anglica. (Lyte, index)
Flora Britannica, by Sir J. E. Smith.
Florio. Fig. in MS. V. There were
other Brittanicas. Sprengel holds that
the Βρετοννική of Dioskorides is *Rumex
aquaticus.*
Ꝺæþbepgean pipe, gen. -an, fem., *heath
berry plant, bilberry plant, vaccinium.*
Lb. III. lxi.
Ꝺapocpypc, fem., gen. -e ; perhaps *hawk-
weed, Hieracium.* Lb. I. xiv. In all
Teutonic languages.
Ꝺalan, "secundæ," secundinæ, the after-
birth. Quad. vi. 25. The analogies
require Ꝺamlan. "Inluvies secundarum,
"hama," Gl. C. "Hamme, *secundæ,*"
(Kilian). "Heam, *secundinæ,*" Nemnich.
Germ. Hamen : etc., etc.

Þalrpyrc must have been *Campanula truchelium*, which in Dansk is Halsurt; in German, Halswurz, Halskraut ; in Dutch, Halskruid. It is said to have obtained these names from being used for inflammations in the throat. In English it is Throatwort.

2. *Bupleurum tenuissimum*, Haresear, " auris leporis, halrpyrc," Gl. Somn. p. 63 b, line 48. "Auricula leporina, " halswort," Gl. Harl. 3388. "Auri- " cula leporina, halswort," MS. M. So Gl. Dun.

3. *Scilla autumnalis*, MS. G. figure, fol. 18 b. = Narcissus, Herb. lvi. = Bulbus, text of Hb. cix. Narcissus, Gl. Dun., probably from Hb.

4. Symphytum album, Hb. cxxviii., seems unsupported. Epicosium, Gl. Dun.

The figure in MS. V. lvi. to my sense is C. Trachelium, with the bell flowers spoiled ; to Dr. II. "a boraginaceous " plant."

Þamoppÿpc, fem., gen. -e, *parietaria officinalis ?* as appears by a gl. in MS. II. on Herb. art lxxxiii. So Gl. Brux., and Gerarde. Grimm Mythol. speculates (126), thinking that perhaps Thors hammer is alluded to in the name. Lb. I. xxxi. 9. Since hamoppyrc and bolχpune are mentioned together in Lb. I. xxv. 1, there is much doubt in the interpretation. Leechdoms, Vol. I. p. 374. Lacn. 1, 2, 6.

Is not hamoppyrc the same as Hembriswort, *bellis perennis*, and derived from Hamop, a bird, such as the Yellowhammer, Emberiza? *See* Secχ.

Þanbpypm, masc., gen. -er, *an insect supposed to produce disease in the hand;* [*cirio*], *curio, cirus.* Wrights vocab. p. 177, p. 190., from χelp. "Surio vel brien- " sis vel sirineus, hanbpypm," Gl. Somn. p. 60 a, 25, which is to read by the preceding, the hissing sound being given to the letter C. So Gl. Harl. 1002. Prompt. Parv., vol. I. p. 225.

Þapan hyχe, "*haresfoot*" (trefoil), *Trifolium arvense.* In Hb. lxii.,. Leporis pes, haresfoot; the connexion of hyχe with the verb "to hie" is plain. Gl. Dun. copies. The artist in V. has omitted, as was the manner, the third leaflet of the trefoil, and the heads are eaten up. MS. A. has clover heads. MS. G. draws *Geum urbanum*, another harefoot, and glosses it, "Hasin uuobh " "Benedicta," *herb bennet.* The later hand in B. also glosses Avens. But Fuchsius, the link between us and the middle ages, is clear as to the trefoil both by name and figure.

Þapanrpecel, -rppecel, *vipers bugloss, Echium vulgare.* Speckle in our usage, the verb frequentative, in this case the frequentative adjective of speck, rpecca, masc. (as MS.) is very applicable to this herb : hare only means that where hares live, it lives. Lb. I. xxxii. 2, 4 ; lxxxvii. Spreckle is now a Scotch and Suffolk form for Speckle. "Eicios, haran- " speccel," Gl. Mone, p. 321 a. "Echius, " Echium," Gl. in Lye. "Ecios, haran- " svecoel," Gl. Dun. Eicios, hapan rpeccel, Gl. Brux.

Þapanpypc, Þapepypc, fem., gen. -e. The little harewort oftenest groweth in gardens, and hath a white flower. Lb. I. lxi. 1 ; L lxxxviii. ; IIL lx. ; II. lxv. 5.

Þapbbeam, masc., gen. -er, *sycomore, acer pseudoplatanus.* The translation of sycomore in the Lindisfarne Gospels, Luke xix. 4. The true sycomore is not English. Vol. I., p. 398, where the separation of the elements makes no difference.

Hares lettuce, *Prenanthes muralis.* IIb. cxiv. Lactuca or Lactuca siluatica. MS. T. The prenanthes m. is drawn in MS. T., and it is equivalent in German to Hasenlattich, in Dansk to Vild latuk. It is also drawn in MS. Bodley, 130, and glossed "slepwert." "Lactuca leporina " i . wyld letys, and he has leues like

Hares lettuce—*cont.*

" sow thestyll," MS. Bodley, 536. The figures in MSS. V., G., Λ. are of no account.

Haꞇian, translates *gravari*, Lb. II. xxv.

Ɖaþoliþe ? fem. ? declined in -an ; probably *elbow joint.* The word is compounded of the syllable haþ, which is found in Ɖeaᵭepian, *cohibere* (Boet. xxxix. 5 ; Beda, iv. 27 ; C.E. p. 401, 17, where the fac simile of the MS. reads mec not me, p. 482, 5, and in Umbehathlichiu, *nexilis*, in Graff. iv. 805,) and of Liþ, *a joint ;* it signifies, therefore, the *nexile joint,* or *the fast tied joint.* The patient was to be bled on it. The fastest tied joint on which a patient can well be bled is the elbow. Somner conjectured, probably from knowledge of the Latin, *vena axillaris;* that is the same vein, τὴν ἐν ἀγκῶνι, τὴν ὑπὸ μασχάλην, says Trallianus (p. 127, ed. 1548).

Ɖeahhealeþe, Ɖeahhioloþe, *inula helenium ; See* Ch. Lb. I. xxxix. 2, etc. " Hinnula " campana, hoꝛfellen," Gl. Laud, 567, *i.e.,* Horse Helenium.

Ɖealebe, *belly bursted, herniosus,* Gl. Somn. p. 71 b, 60. Hb. lxxviii. 2, where *ad ramicem pueri,* Lat. ; " Ponderosus," in Lye, which means not "weighty," but *bursted ;* " Ponderosus, hernia laborans " (verba improbata in Bailey) ; Haull, masc., *hernia* (Islandic) ; þ cilb biᵭ hoꞃoꝺobe ꝺ healebe (MS. Cott. Tiber. Λ. iii. fol. 41), *the child shall be humpbacked and bursted.* SH. 23.

Ɖealꝼ, neut., *the half, dimidium, pars dimidiu,* Lb. II. ii. 2. Ɖealꝼ, *side, quarter* is fem.

Healꝼ heaꝺob, *half head;* Æ.G. 14, line 24, distinctly defines as the *sinciput, the forward half;* (hoc sinciput), healꝼ heaꝺob ; hoc occiput, ꝼe mꝛtꝺa bæl þær heaꝺbeꝛ.

Ɖealꝼ puþu, masc., gen. -beꝛ, *field balm, calamintha nepeta,* Lb. I. xlvii. 2.

" Ꝺidebalme . i. halue pude," Gl. Harl. 978. This plant was placed by Linnæus as Melissa ; it is perennial.

Ɖealm, neut., *halm, calamus.* Gabꝺꞁon himꝛýlꝼe þ healm. Exod. v. 7. Lb. I. lxxii.

Heaꝺ, Lb. I. ii. 21, *austere.* Cf. Heoꝺo, *sword,* C.E. 346, and its senses as a prefix.

Hebclaᵭ, *a coarse upper garment,* Quad. iv. 17. " Heben, casla," gl. C., *that is, a chasuble.* " Heben gunna," gl. C. *gunny cloth.* Ne hæbbe he on heben ne cæppan, DD. 348, ix. *Let him have on neither chasuble nor cope ;* the English rite. Cf. Heᵭinn, *a kirtle or cape of skin,* in Islandic. (Jonsson.)

Ɖeꝼeclꝼe, fem., gen. -an, *hedge clivers, cleavers, clivers, Galium aparine,* Lb. I. ix.

Ɖeꝼepiꝼe, gen. -an, fem. ? " hedgeruff," " hayreve," *Galium uparine.* " Rubia " minor, Hayreff oþer aron [*read* Hay- " renn ?] is like to wodruff, and þe sed " tuchid will honge in oneis cloþis," MS. Sloane, 5, fol. 29 a. "Rubia minor " cleuer heyreue," Gl. Harl. 3388. Lb. L xxxii. 4 ; I. lxiv.

Ɖelbe, *tansy, tanacetum vulyare,* " Tana- " ceta," Gl. Somn. p. 66 [68] b, 22. So Gl. Jul., Gl. Dun., Gl. Harl. 978 (A.D. 1240) ; Tenedisse, Gl. Brux., also " Arti- " mesia hilde," Gl. Dun., but the tansy is generically akin to the mugwort. Lb. I. xxvi. Διδαξ. 58.

Ɖemlic, gen. -e, also -an ; *hemlock, conium maculatum.* Other plants may be sometimes called hemlock, for the umbellate herbs require educated eyes, but this is the starting point for English notions. *Cicuta virosa* is water hemlock (Sir J. E. Smith) ; " Cicuta," Gl. Somn. p. 64 a, 47, classically right, though botanically wrong ; for it follows from Plinius, xxv. 95, that Κώνειον =cicuta. Acc. Hymlican. Lb. I. i. 6. Has a masc. adj. Lacn. 71 ; dat. hymlice. Lb. I. lviii. 1.

Ɖeoꝺoꝛbþembel, masc., gen. -eꝛ, *the buckthorn, rhamnus.* " Ranno, Christs thorne, " Harts thorne, Way thorne, Bucke " thorne, or Rainberry thorne," Florio

Ɖeoporbɲembel—*cont.*

Lb. III. xxix. 1. The berries are exceed-
ingly loved by stags, Cotgrave, v. Bour-
daine. Gerarde.

Ɖeoprot cɲop, Lb. I. vi. 3, probably a
bunch of the flowers of hart wort, or
seseli. (Nemnich, Cotgrave.)

Ɖeoprt clæɲɲe, *hart clover or medic, medi-
cago maculata*. In Hb. xxv. Hart clover
is made germander, *teucrium chamædrys*,
and there is no doubt about the identity
of germander with the chamædrys
of the Latin ; the name germander is a
gradual alteration from the Hellenic
word, and in MS. G. the plant is drawn.
In MSS. V. and A. we see something
more like anagallis arvensis, but we must
make concessions to these old artists.
There is, however, no doubt but that
clæɲɲe is *clover*, " trifillon [*trefoil*], clú-
" ɲɲe," Gl. Somn. p. 64a, 3. " Trifo-
" lium rubrum, reade cleaure," Gl. Dun.
" Calesta vel calcesta, hvit cleaure," Gl.
Dun. That we find " trifolium, ᵹeace-
" ruɲe," Gl. Somn. p. 66 [63] b, line 11,
may be satisfactorily explained by look-
ing at the *Oxalis Acetosella*, which
is a trefoil sorrel, abounding in groves
and thickets in the spring. The same
wort is meant by " Calcitulium, geaces
" swre," Gl. Dun.; for calta is *clover*
with the Saxons ; " Calta siluatica, vude
" cleaure," Gl. Dun. ; " wood sorrel "
is a frequent name of it at this day ; it
was panis cuculi, Fr. pain de cocu (Lyte).
The tradition of the word "hart" is
sufficient for us ; probably, however,
m. falcata and *m. sativa* were embraced
under the name. These were once known
as " horned clauer," or clover (Lyte);
and since the melilot *m. officinalis*, was
called hart clauer in Yorkshire (Gerarde),
that also may have been set down for a
variety. Culpeper calls melilot, kings
claver. " Cenocephaleon [*read* Cyno-],
" heort cleaure," Gl. Dun., may be a
misreading of a drawing, since toadflax
and melilot hang their heads in the same

Ɖeoprt clæɲɲe—*cont.*

manner. " Camedus," Gl. Brux., that
is, chamædrys, germander.

Ɖyɼ ? gen. -e, fem., *hive*. Hb. vii. 2. Lye.
Leechd. Vol. I. p. 397.

Ɖillpyprt, fem., gen. in -e, " hillwort,
calamintha nepeta. Hillwort is pulegium
montanum in the glossaries, to be distinguished by name and habitat from
pulegium regale or penny royal. Now
the Bergpoly of the Germans, Teucrium
polium, is not a native of England,
we must then select, as above, a plant
which grows on " dry banks and way
" sides on a chalky soil," with " odour
" strong resembling mentha pulegium,"
(Hooker). But if the words be of the
savour of a version from the Latin, then
hillwort will be *teucrium polium*. See
Hb. lviii. ; Promp. Parv. p. 399.

Ɖymele, gen. -an, *the hop plant, humulus
lupulus*=humle (Dansk) =humall, masc.
(Islandic). Hb. lxviii. The female plant
is evidently meant by the ewehymele,
eopohumelan, Lb. III. lx.

The statement that men mix hymele
with their ordinary drinks, shows what
plant the writer of Hb. had in his mind.
That he identifies it with bryony is an
error in his Greek. Lovells Herball
(1659) thus, "Hops, *lupulus*. In fat
" and fruitfull ground, the wild among
" thornes. The flowers are gathered in
" August and September. Βρύον καὶ
" βρυωνία, lupus salictarius et reptitius."
Most of the early glossaries translate
however, bryonia by Wilde nep, and
Dioskorides (iv. 184, 185) describes what
is certainly not the hop plant. Columella
is charged with having confused the
bryony with the hop, Lib. x. p. 350.

" Quæque tuas audax imitatur Nysic
" uites,
" Nec metuit sentes, nam uepribus
" improba surgens
" Achradas indomitasque Bryonias
" alligat alnos."

The lines hardly support the charge.

Dymele—cont.

According to the present usage of those who speak rural English, the hop is the fructification of the female plant, and the plant itself has no name but hop plant. It is quite incorrect according to the country folk to speak of the plant as the hop. No such name as Humble seems to be known.

The contrasted Dezehýmele, hedge-humble, affords presumption that there was a cultivated kind, and other proofs exist that the Saxons grew this plant.

Dymele, *hop trefoil, trifolium procumbens*. In Hb. lii. we had a problem to solve; polytrichum was hair moss, and hymele was hop, and yet the two plants must be the same. The trefoil leaves of poly-trichum in MS. G. suggested a solution; it is hoped the right one. The text in IIb. lii. speaks plainly of hair moss; but the drawing in the MS. has nothing of the sort; in this difficulty the interpreter solved not the Hellenic word, but the drawing, and named it hymele; as it has no resemblance to the hop, nor to geum rivale. Jordhumle in Swedish is trifolium agrarium (Nemnich). The name Humble was not confined to the hop, *see* pelɔpypꞇ; and in Islandic Val-humall is Achillea millefolium. (Olaf Olafsens Urtagards Bok, p. 88.)

Dınbhæleþe,-heoloþe, -an, *water agrimony, liverwort, Eupatorium cannabinum*. "Ambrosia." Hb. lxiii. 7; so Lacn. 69. Gl. Sloane, 146. Our gll. make this ambrosia maior to be widely distinguished from chenopodium botrys, which is also ambrosia, but not an English plant. Hindheal is Hirsch-wundkraut in Germ. "stag-wound-wort." "Eupatorium lilifagus [*understand* ἐλελίσφακος], ambrosia maior, wyldc "sauge, hyndhale," Gl. Harl. 3388. "Ambrosia, hindhelethe," Gl. Dun. "Ambrose . salgia agrestis [*read salvia*], "lilifagus . eupatorium . idem," Gl. Rawl. c. 607. So Gl. M. "Hintloipha,

Dınbhæleþe—cont.

"ambrosia," Gl. Hoff. "Euperatorium, "ambrose, is an erbe that som men "calliþ wilde aauge oþer wode merche "oþer hyndale," Gl. Sloane, 5, fol. 15 a. Similarly Gl. M.

2. *Sanicle, Sanicula Europæa*, as above; the plants have very similar foliation.

Dypbepypꞇ, fem., gen. -e, *herd-* (shepherd) *wort, Erythræa centaureum*, Lb. II. viii., etc.

IIıp, gen. -es, neut., *hue, complexion, color*. IIb. cxli. 2. Hom. II. 390. Hpy íp ꝺıp zolb abeopcab . ꝸ ꝺæꞇ æꝺelefꞇe hıeþ hpy þeaþꝺ hıꞇ onhpoþꝛen, P.A. 26 a, *Why is this gold darkened, and why is its noble colour changed ?* Lamentations iv. 1. See N. p. 71. Δıꝺaꝼ. 58.

Dleomoce, Dleomoc, fem. gen., -an; *brooklime* (where lime is the Saxon name in decay), *Veronica beccabunga*, with *V. anagallis*. Lb. I. ii. 22. "It waxeth in "brooks," Lb. I. xxxviii. 4. Both sorts Lemmike, Dansk. They were the greater and the less "brokelemke," Gl. Bodley, 536. "Fabaria domestica . i . lemeke. "Fabaria agrestis similis est nasturtio "aquatico et habet florem indum [*blue*] . "i . faucrole et crescit iuxta aquas," Gl. Rawl. c. 607. In those words the *v.* anagallis is described. The following agree more or less, Gl. in Lye; Gl. Dun.; Gl. Cleop.; Gl. Harl. 978; Gl. Harl. 3388; Gl. Mone, p. 288 a, 27: *read lemicke;* Islandic, Lemiki.

Dlypꞇ, masc., gen. -eꝛ, *hearing;* masc. DD. 41, xlvi. Lb. I. iii. 7; Hom. II. 374; also fem., gen. -e, Lb. I. iii., contents; and in old Dansk.

Dluꞇꞇoþ bþenc, masc., gen. -es, "clear "drink," *claret, made of wine, honey, aromatic herbs, and spices*. "Accipe "ergo hirtzunge [*hartstongue*] et eam "in vino fortiter coque, et tunc purum "mel adde, et ita iterum; tunc fac semel "fervere, deinde longum piper et bis "tantum cynamomi pulverisa, et ita

Þlurroþ bþenc—*cont.*

" cum prædicto vino fac iterum semel
" fervere, et per pannum cola et sic fac
" LUTER DRANCK." St. Hildegard. Phys.
xxx., and similarly ciii.

Þnıɾel, masc., *forehead*, Lb. III. i.
Hoc, gen. hocces, *one of the mallows, malva.*
Lb. III. xxxvii., xli. Many gll.

Þoɾe, gen. –an, fem., *alehoof, hove, ground
ivy, glechoma hederacea.* Lb. I. ii. 19.
Seo þeabe hoɾe, the same.

2. Meþɾc hoɾe, *stachys palustris!*
Lb. I. xxxviii. 5.

Iloɾþec, hoɾþæc, neut., *hoof nick, hoof track.*
Vol. I. p. 392. A parallel charm has
ɾorspoþ.

Þolcæþɾe, fem., gen. –an, *field gentian,
gentiana campestris.* Lb. I. ii. 17. The
same as the Holgræss of Œder, Icones
Plantarum, vol. 3, where he gives the
local Norwegian names.

Þomoþɾecʒ, masc. Lb. I. lxxvi. 2. *See*
Secʒ.

Þoþb, Þoþ, gen. –eɾ, also Þoþepes, masc.;
foulness, filth, foul humour, flegma, pituita,
is masc., Lb. II. xvi. 2 ; xxviii. and in
hoþaɾ, *pituita,* Gl. in Lye. Gl. Somn.
p. 72 a, 55. Written Oþaɾ, Quadr. viii.
6. *See* corrections, Vol. I. Neuter, Lb.
II. xvi. 1.

Flegmata, hoþh, Gl. M.M., p. 156 b,
5. Gl. Cleop. fol. 39 d. Horewes, Gl.
Mone, p. 404 b.

Iloþuʒ, *mucous, purulent.* Gl. Prud. p.
146 b.

Þoþn aðl, *a disease of foul humours in the
stomach.* Lb. II. xxvii. From hoþh,
filth.

Iĺþacn, gen. –an, fem., *throat, guttur.* Þæþ
ʒynube on ðaþe hþacan ɾþýlce þæþ
hþýlc ɾeað pæþe. G.D. 226 b. *There
yawned in the throat as if there had been
a sort of pit.* Lb. I. i. 17. K. prints a
masc. SS. p. 148, line 32.

Iĺþæ·ɑn, acc., *hreaking, exscreatio*, Lb. I.
i. 16.

Þþæccunʒe, *the uvula*, Lorica, lxx. Lb.
I. v. 4. Hþacan, *fauces*, Gl. in Lye.

Þþæccunʒe—*cont.*

+ rɑnʒe, tongue. Hþæccunʒ is different,
Lb. II. viii. Hþæcɑn, *to clear the throat,*
screaɾe, + er frequentative, + unʒ, participial termination.

Þþæþneɾ ɾor, masc., "ravens foot," *pilewort,
ranunculus ficaria, Bot.* In Hb. xxviii.
made Chamædafne, which, literally
translated, is " ground laurel or bay,"
and determined by Sprengel to be *ruscus racemosus.*" That it is indeed a
ruscus is quite evident by the words of
Dioskorides ; καρπὸν δὲ περιφερῆ ἐρυθρόν,
τοῖς φύλλοις ἐπιπεφυκότα, nor can we doubt
from the rest of the description but that
the species is correctly determined.
Plinius, however, having more knowledge of words than things, while citing
the description ; " semen rubens an-
" nexum foliis" (xxiv. 81), which makes
the chamædafne a ruscus, yet has misled
many of the later inquirers by declaring
it to be periwinkle ; " vinca pervinca
" sive chamædafne," (xxi. 99.) In this
error he is followed by many, as a Welsh
gl. of plants in Meddygon Myddfai,
(p. 283 a.), and Coopers Thesaurus.
The Latin Apuleius, MS. G. draws, I
think, a periwinkle. The species R.
racemosus, is a native not of England,
but of the Archipelago. 'Our concern,
however, being with Ravens foot, it will
soon appear that it is neither Ruscus nor
Vinca. Ravens foot, like crowfoot, was
a name probably given from the shape of
the leaves ; whence it will follow at
once that ravens foot is neither chamædafne nor vinca maior. The old interpreter had before him a wholly different
drawing, having a resemblance in its
folded leaves to Alchemilla vulgaris.
The unfolded leaves are deeply cut, and
so " Pentaphilon, refnes fot," Gl. Dun.
Quinquefila. Gl. Brux. So Gl. M.M.
p. 161 b, 34, showing that the leaves were
like those of cinqfoil. MS. T. has a gl.
" Rauen fote, crowfote," to the same effect,
with a drawing which I take to intend

Ꝺpæꞃneꞃ ꞃox—*cont.*
periwinkle, " quinquefolium, bꞁaeꞃnaeꞃ
" ꞃooꞇ," Gl. Moyen Moutier, p. 164 b;
so p. 161 b. " Pes corui apium moroi-
" darum, raveoys feete," MS. Bodley,
178. " Apium emoroidarum vel pes
" corui idem ravnys fete," MS. Harl,
3388. " Apium emoroidarum, pes corui
" idem," MS. Rawlinson, c. 607. The
tubers at the root of this plant were
compared to piles, hæmorrhoids, fici,
whence the names Pilewort, Apium
hæmorrhoidarum, Ficaria. " Pes pulli,
" Gallice pepol, Anglice remuies fote,"
Gl. Sloane, 146. " Pied poul, the
" round rooted or onion rooted crow-
" foot." Cotgrave. Similarly Gl. Harl.
3388. Thus authority and early tradition
run strongly for ranunculus ficaria ; at
the same time we cannot but feel a
difficulty in observing that the leaves of
this species are not crowfoot in shape,
and the plant is so unlike most of the
crowfoots, that on ancient principles it
should hardly be called by a similar name.

Ꝺpean, acc., Lb. II. xli, I suppose to be
= Isl. Ilrai, masc., *cruditas*, as perhaps
not *rawness*, but *indigestion.* Somner,
however, may have had authority for
φθίσις.

Ꝺpeoꞃol, fem., gen. -le, *roughness of the
body, leprosy.* Lb. I. lxxxviii.

Ꝺpieꞃca, gen. pl., Lb. I. xxxi. 5, from
some nom. s. signifying it seems *a crick*,
which is a small *wrench*, a *twist*, accompanied usually with a small sound ; a
little crack, a crick, produced by the
overstraining of some articulation. *See*
Lye in Ꝺpꞃcian.

Ꝺpiꞃ, neut., *the abdomen.* Lb. II. xxviii. ;
II. xxxii.

Ꝺpiꞃing, fem., gen. -e, *scab, crust of a
healing wound.* Lb. I. xxxv. at end,
the context requires this sense. Cf.
Ꝺpieꞃbo, *scabies.*

Ꝺpiꞃcung, fem., gen. -e, *spasmodic action.*
Isl. at Hrista *quatere*, in the reflexive,
contremiscere. Lb. II. xlvi.

Ꝺpyc, *febricitat.* Lb. II. xxv.
Ꝺpyꝺepen, *bovinus.* Lb. II. viii.
Ꝺpoꞇ, neut., *moisture, mucus, thick fluid.*
Lb. II. xxviii. ; obg. Roz, *mucus, in-
rheuma.*

Ꝺpuꝺ. Lb. II. xxiv.
Ꝺunbeꞃheaꞃob, " hounds head," *snapdragon,
antirrhinum orontium, Bot.* In IIb.
lxxxviii., Canis caput. The German
Hundskopf is *A. orontium*, and according
to Kilian in kalfs-snuyte, canis caput is
antirrhinum. The drawings in MSS.
V. and T. represent, I hold, this plant.
" Cynocephaleon, heopcclæꞃpe," Gl.
Somn. p. 63 b, 56, *hart clover*, melilot,
which might be made in a drawing to
cluster its flowers as snapdragon.

Ꝺunbeꞃ ꞇunꝛe, fem., gen. -an, *houndstongue, cynoglossum officinale.* In IIb.
xlii. this is made = bugloss ; in MS. V.,
allowing for conventional and incorrect
drawing, the figure (fol. 30 c.) seems
intended for *lycopsis arvensis, Bot.*, or
small bugloss ; similarly MS. A., fol.
24 b. MS. G. draws *echium vulgare*, or
vipers bugloss. MS. T. has given us,
instead of bugloss, a picture of houseleek. The houndstongue family of plants
is akin to the bugloss race, and our
Saxon interpreter was, perhaps, unable
to discriminate. " Buglossan, glosvyrt
" vel hundes tunga. Canis lingua, hun-
" des tunga," Gl. Dun. " Lingua bobule
" (*bubula*) oxan tunge," id., " buglossa
" hertestunge, ossentunge," Gl. in Mone,
p. 283 a. " Bugilla, hundestunge," id.
p. 285 b. (*bugle, aiuga reptans, Bot.*),
" lingua cervina, huntzenge," id. p. 289,
(a mistake, read *hertszunge*). " Buglosse,
" foxes glofa," id. p. 320 a ; " canis
" lingua, hundestunge," id. ibid. That
cynoglossum officinale is houndstongue in
German, Dutch, Dansk, Swedish, may
have arisen from translation and instruction ; but why not so also with the
Saxons ? The drawing in V. is more like
borage (II., from a pen and ink sketch),
but the blooms have no blue colour.

Ðune, gen. -an, *horehound, marrubium vulgare.* Lb. I. iii. 11., etc.

Þunixteaþ, gen. -es, masc., *destillation from the comb,* without squeezing, *virgin honey,* mel purissimum, e favo sponte quod effluxit. " Mell stillativum," Lb. I. ii. 1. " Nectareum, hunixteapenne," Gl. Prud. p. 140 b. " Nectaris, hunixteaþer," Gl. Mone, p. 384 b, 4. " Favum nectaris, " hunix camb teaper," Regularis Concordia.

Þpeoþra, masc., *a whorl, verticillus.* Lb. III. vi.

Þpeppe, fem.? gen. -an? Lb. lii. 1, is a " great wort;" the radical syllable implies roundness, as in Þpep, *a kettle,* Þpeppette (*a gourd, a calabash,* and then) *a cucumber.* See Hb. xxii. Is it then the bulb, *colchicum autumnale?*

Þpopyban, neut., *knee cap, patella.* In the Lorica, Vol. I. lxxi., the gloss of poples, which is an error. See Þeoh hpeoþra.

Þptcubu, -cpeobu, gen. hptcer cþibuer, *mastich,* the gum of the *pistacia lentiscus.* So the Gll. Lb. II. iii., Gl. Dun., etc.

Þptcinx, *whiting, chalk and size.* Lb. III. xxxix.

I.

Ipix, neut., gen. -er, *ivy; hedera helix* is the only species native to England; neut., Lb. III. xxx. Graff also marks the ohg. Ebah, *ivy,* neuter. Iper, gen. Lb. I. ii. 10 ; I. iii. 7, etc.

Iptxtapo, masc., gen. -an, *ivy tar.* Lb. III. xxvi. ; masc., Cf. Lb. III. xxxt. " It is " produced from the Body of the larger " Ivy, being cut or wounded, and some- " times dropping forth of it self." Salmons English Physician, 1693, p. 991. " Oleum cyfinum (*read κισσινον*) idem " de bagis (*read baccis*) hederæ confi- " citur sic. Sumis in ianuario mense " cum ceperunt hederæ grana crescere, " etc." MS. Harl. 4896, fol. 70 a.

Innoþapan, pl. *viscera.* Lb. II. xxxvi. Inþiran, pl., *flavouring, condimentum,* Lb. II. vi., from piran, *herbs.*

L.

Læcepypt, 1. generally *a herb of healing, herba medicinalis,* M.H. 137 a.
2. *Campions,* or *ragged robin,* or one of that kindred, Hb. cxxxiii. ; but, I fear, only from the syllables Læc- and Lych-.
3. *Plantago lanceolata,* " læcepypt, " quinquenervia," Gl. Cleop. fol. 83 a. Gl. M.M. Läkeblad, *plantago maior,* in West Gothland (Nemnich). The plaintain was famed for healing power. Lb. I. xxxii. 3.

Læs, *a letting, missio,* Lb. III. cont. xlvii. fem. ? Cf. þa blobloese, Lb. II. xxiii. ; blobloespu, Beda, 616, 12, on ðæpe blobloespe, 616, 5.

Lamber cæppe, gen. -an, is said, Lb. I. i. 17. to be the same as Cress.

Laþep, labeþ, *laver,* Hb. cxxxvi., is called Sium by Lyte also ; the botanists now call sium water parsnep, and the eaten laver, porphyra laciniata. Laver is a Latin word.

Leac, gen. -es, neut. 1. Originally *a wort, herba, olus,* whence are derived leacceppe, leactun, " hortus olitorius," leacpepe, *a gardener.* Houseleek and holleac are not alliaceous. Aarons leek is arum maculatum, Gl. Sloane, 5.
2. *A leek, allium porrum,* Lb. II. xxxii. vol. I. p. 376, where I cannot now find a verification for the masculine gender, unless by resorting to the old Dansk, Laukr, masc. Þer, in Æ.G. is a misprint.

Bpabeleac, probably *leek, Allium porrum,* from the breadth of its leaves. Lb. II. li. 4. Lacn. 12.

Leac—cont.

Cnapleac, *crow garlic, allium ursinum,*
or *vineale,* vol. I. p. 376. "Centum ca-
" pita, asfodillus, ramese, crowe garlek,"
Gl. Rawl. c. 506.

Cnopleac, *allium sativum.* A gl. gives
" serpyllum," but that is an inadmis-
sible tale, for cnop means *bunch,* as of
berries, and leac means *leek;* we must
therefore make our choice among asfodelaceous plants; and as those which
answer the description best are open to
objection, for allium ampeloprasum is
by far too rare, and allium vineale is
crowleek, we fix on a common foreign
but cultivated species. Lb. I. ii. 13, 15;
I. iii. 11; I. xxxix. 2; III. lxviii. The
German Knoblauch has the same sense,
and is this plant.

Gapleac, *allium oleraceum?* See Lb. I.
ii. 16; III. lx. lxi.

Holleac, " hollow wort," *fumaria bul-
bosa,* the " radix cava " of the herborists;
Runde Hohlwurzel, Germ.; Ilnulroed,
Dansk; Holwortel (Kilian); Hällrot,
Swed. Lacn. 23, 61. Lb. ――. It
is not corydalis, the root of which is not
hollow. *See* English Botany, 1471.

Secgleac, Lb. I. lviii. 1, Lacn. 37, is
of course *chive garlic, allium schœnopra-
sum,* the English and Hellenic names
having the same sense.

Leac cepse, fem., gen. -an. Lb. III. xv.
Erysimum alliaria is both leek and cress.

Leah, gen. leaxe, fem., *ley, lixivium.* Quad.
ix. 14. Leechd. vol. I. p. 378. Lb. III.
xlvii. Læx, Gl. C.

Leaþop, neut.? *lather, spuma suponacea;*
see Lyþpan, not fem. Lacn. 1. Islandic
Löðr, neut. *lather.* Cf. Lyþpan, Alyþ-
pan. St. Marharete.

Leaþoppypt, fem., gen. -e, *latherwort, soap-
wort, saponaria officinalis.* " Borith
" herba fullonum, leaðoppypt," Gl.
Cleop. The plant yields lather freely.
Lb. I. iii. 11.

Leonpot, masc., gen. -ep, *lion foot, alchemilla vulgaris,* Hb. viii. This name is

Leonpot—cont.

foreign, and a translation of λεοντοπόδιον
in Dioskorides. Leontopodion is *alchemilla vulgaris* in Dorsten, in Lyte, in
Dansk; " Alchemilla vulgo appellatur et
" pes leonis," Cæsalpinus xiv. 249. Sibthorp says, alchemilla alpina is to this
day called Λεοντοπόδιον. Sprengel says,
that the Leontopodium of Dioscorides
is " Gnafalium leontopodium," and the
figures in V. G. T. Bodley, 130 (lxii.)
agree.

Lib, lyb, neut.? *something medicinal and
potent, a harmful or powerful drug,*
φάρμακον. Cf. lib-lac, *sorcery;* oxna-
lib, " *medicine of oxen,*" *black hellebore;*
libcopn, *cathartic grains.* " Luppi, neut.
" *venenum,* succus lethiferus, etc.," Graff.
Onglappi, *eye lib,* collyrium, *eye salve,* id.
Goluppeten pfil, *venenata sagitta,* Gl.
Schilter. " Coagulum, lap," a gl. in
Mone, p. 287 a. Congulo, cyrhbbu, Gl.
Prud. 141 a, as if τυροφάρμακον; it is the
runnet to turn milk to curd.

Libcopn, neut., gen. -ep, *a grain of
purgative effect, especially* the seeds of
various *euforbias,* probably also the seeds
of some of the gourds, as *momordica elaterium, cucumis colocynthis.* Lb. I. ii. 22;
II. lii. 1, 2, 3.

Carthamo, also citocasia, also lacte-
rida, also catharticum, Gl. Dun.; lacy-
ride, Gl. Brux.; these are the milky
spurges.

Lim, mostly neut., but also fem., *a limb,*
artus; fem., Lb. II. lxiv. p. 288; fem.
also in Islandic. Cf. Lb. I. xxv. 2, xxvii.
1, xxxi. 7, lxxiii.; III. xxxvii.

Limung, fem., gen. -e, *an attachment, car-
tilago.* Lb. II. xxxvi.

Lið, neuter and masc., *joint, articulus.* I.b.
I. lxi. 1; II. xxxvi. In old Dansk,
Llðr, masc.

Lið, *drink,* gen. -es, neut. Lb. I. xix.
Boet. 110, 33. Cpt ða him ðæt lið
gefcipeð pæp, P.A. 55 a, *when the drink
was gone from him.*

Líð ꝼyꝛꞇ, fem., gen. -e, lithewort, *dwarf elder, sambucus ebulus.* Hb. xxix. This is made Ostriago. *See* Pref. vol. I. p. lxxxv. : from the drawings, nothing can be learnt. " Ostriago, lith výrt. " Chamedafne, leoth výrt," Gl. Dun., read χαμαιδϰϛη, that is, *ground elder.* " Ebulus, wall wort," in later hand " lyþe " wort," MS. Harl. 3388. In Hb. cxxvii. líþꝼyꝛꞇ is erifia, which is unknown, and from the drawing probably nothing but dwarf elder was understood. Viburnum lantana was never known by this name.

Lyþꝩan ? *to lather, spumam e sapone con- ficere, aut ex quovis eiusmodi.* Lyþꝩe, imperat., Lb. I. l. 2. Alyþꝩe, Lb. I. xxii. 2. Aleþꝩe, Lb. I. liv.

Lꞇꝩule, Lb , I. lxi. 2. Somner said *fistula,* which is a disease ; Lye, *fistula, enema*; it has been translated in connexion with the foregoing leechdoms, as if líð-ele, *joint oil, synovia.*

Lonꝺ abl, fem., gen. -e, *nostalgia,* Lb. II. lxv. 5.

Lunᵹenpyꝩꞇ, fem., gen. -e, *lungwort, pulmonaria officinalis.* Germ., Lungen- wurz; Dansk, Lungurt; Swed. Lungört.

   2. A sort mentioned, Lb. I. xxxviii. 4, " yellow upwards," *hieracium murorum* and *pulmonarium, golden lung wort.*

Luscmoce, fem., gen. -an, not in the gll., possibly by corruption of syllables, *Ladys smock, cardamine pratensis,* Lb. I. xxxviii. 3. 10. A kind with a cropp or bunchy head, Lb. I. xxxix. 2 ; I. xxxviii. 3.

M.

(Dœl, gen. -eꝼ, neut., *measure.* Orientis Mir. ix. Chron. p. 354, line 31, anno 1085. Lb. I. ii. 1 ; II. vii. " Circinum, " mælcanᵹe," Gl. Somn. p. 65 b, 4, *a pair of compasses, measure tongs.* Where bæᵹmœlaꝼ is printed, the MS. has dæᵹmœl uꝼ.

(Daᵹeþe, (Daᵹoþe, fem., gen. -an, *maythe, Anthemis nobilis.* 2. pilbe maᵹeþe, *maythe, Matricaria chamomilla.* 3. *maythe, maythen, Anthemis cotula.*

   1. Chamœmelon is translated maᵹeþe, Hb. xxiv. " Camemelon, magethe." Gl. Dun. " Beneolentem," Gl. Brux. p. 41 a, the distinctive mark of true chamomille. " Chomomilla, megede " blomen," a Gl. in Mone, 286 b.

   2. Þilbe maᵹþe, Lb. II. xxii., *wild maythe,* must be wild chamomille, for I do not find that No. 3 was ever supposed to possess medicinal properties; it is therefore *matricaria chamomilla.*

   3. The *anthemis cotula* is now called maythen, the final being, to speak after our grammars, derived from the termi- nation of the oblique cases ; country folk say it may be always distinguished from the true camomille by its bad smell. The glossaries agree, " Camomilla " i . camamille similis est amarusce [*read* " -æ] sed camomilla herba breuis est et " redolens et amarusca i . maythe fetit " [fœtet], MS. Rawlinson, c. 707. " Herba " putida, mæᵹða," Gl. Somn. p. 64 a, line 11. " Mathers, May weed, Dogs " cammomill, Stinking cammomill, and " Dog fenel." Lyte (A.D. 1595).

   Perhaps the Saxons included *pyreth- rum parthenium.* These plants are so much alike that it requires much tech- nicality to distinguish them ; the artist in MS. V. took the liberty of making the flowers blue. Calmia, mayþe, MS. Sloane, 146, with i marked. " Culmia, " magethe," Gl. Dun., whence correct Somner. Gl. p. 66 [63] b, line 6. Calmia is calamine, ore of zinc, and these glosses are blunders.

   Reabe maᵹeþe, *anthemis tinctoria.* Lb. I. lxiv.

   White maythe, *pyrethrum inodorum.* " Bucstalmum [*read* βούφθαλμον], hvit " megethe," Gl. Dun.; printed bucstal- inum, Gl. Brux. p. 41 a.

Ɯaɲe, Lb. I. xxxi. 7, perhaps *potentilla* as Mara, in Iceland now (Olaf Olafsens Urtagards Bok) ; the cottony potentilla will be *silverweed, p. anserina,* with *argentea.*

Ɯaɲcɲyɲc, max-, fem., *mashwort, the wort in the mash tub,* Lacn. 111. Lb. II. xxiv. On the malt boiling water is poured, and allowed to stand three quarters of an hour ; the liquid is wort, or mashwort. Braxivium atque bulita cum braseo nondum cerevisia, *vert* ; a Belgic Gl. in Mone, p. 304 a.

Ɯeaɲh, meapᵹ, masc. and neut., *marrow* ; masc., old Dansk Margr, Lb. III. lxx. ; neut., Germ. Mark, Lb. I. ii. 22.

Ɯeaɲɲc meaɲɪ ᵹealla, masc., gen. -an, belongs, from its bitterness implied in " gall," to gentianaceous plants, and from its habitat in marshes may be, *gentiana pneumonanthe.* Lb. I. xxxix. 2 ; I. l. 2.

Ɯebo, gen. mebeɲeɲ, neut., *mead.* Lb. II. lii. 1 ; II. liii. In old German, Mete, and in old Danish, Miö̈r, are masc. Gen. Gl. Mone, p. 395 b.

Ɯeboɲyɲc, fem., gen. -e ; 1. *Meadow sweet, spiræa ulmaria.* " Regina prati, Germ. " Wiesenkönigin ; Dansk, Miödurt " (Nemnich). " Melissa, medwort, regina " prati." Gl. Harl. 3388. So Gl. Bodley, 178. " Melletina," Gl. Somn. 63 b, 53. " Regina medɲurt," Gl. Harl. 978 (A.D. 1240). " Mellanna," Gl. Dun. Lb. I. xxxviii. 10.
2. *Melissa officinalis, balm.* " Nas- " turtium [h]ortolan[um] medwort," Gl. Harl. 3388.

Ɯen, masc. ? *a part, a proportional part* = Swedish, Mån, masc. *a part.* Lb. I. l. 2. The construction with a numeral admits either a plural or a singular.

Meox, Meohs, neuter, *muck, dung, fimus, stercus.* Ðæt meox is þæt ᵹemynb his ɲulan bæba. Hom. II. 408, *The dung* of the parable *is the memory of his foul deeds.*

Ɯepce, gen. -eɲ, masc., *marche, apium.* Hb. xcvii., cxx. ; Gl. Somn. p. 64 a, 11 ; Hb. cxxix. Stan meɲce, *parsley,* Apium petroselinum. Gl. Brux. Ƿubu meɲce, *wood marche, sanicle,* Sanicula Europæa, a gloss in Lacn. 4, also Gl. Laud. 553, fol. 18. Gl. Harl. 978, which was overlooked, so that note 9, p. 35, requires correction. It is a suitable name. Lb. I. i. 15 ; I. xxxix. 2 ; I. lxi. 2 ; III. ii. 6.

Ɯeɲ ? = miɲc, *a mess, dung.* Lb. I. xxxviii. 11. Mes, *stercus, fimus* (Kilian). Micel lic, *elephantiasis.* Sona puɲbon ö́uɲhɲleᵹene mib þaɲe able þæɲ myclan liceɲ, G.D. 210 a, *Soon were smitten with "elephantinus morbus."*

Mylsc ? or Mylsce ? *mild, mitis.* Lb. I. xlii. ; II. xvi., p. 194. Gemilsceb, Lb. II. xix. xx.

Ɯilce, masc., gen. -eɲ, also -an, *the milt, the spleen.* Lb. II. xxxvi. with gen.-eɲ ; but gen. -an, Lacn. 110 ; Quad. ii. 8 ; IIb. xxxii. 6 ; and fem., IIb. xxxii. 6 ; lvii. 1.

Mynec, neut., *money, moneta.* Bed. 532, 1. Lb. II. xv.

Ɯince, fem., gen. -an, *mint, mentha.* Fenmince, *mentha silvestris.* Lb. I. iii. 2.

Sæmince. Lb. I. xv. 4.

Tunminre, *mentha sativa.* Lb. I. ii. 23.

Ɯiɲcel, masc. ? *basil.* 1. *Clinopodium vulgare.* In Hb. cxix., cxxxvii. equivalent to ὄκιμον, *basil.* " Ocimum, mistel," Gl. Mone, p. 321 b, is a repetition not a support. " Ocimus, mistel," Gl. Dun., another echo. " Mistil, basilice," MS. Bodley, 130, on Ocimum : an independent statement. Ɯiɲcel is a derivative of Ɯiɲc, *much,* and the *clinop. vulg.* is called in German, Kleiner dost, from Doste ; old high g. Dosto, *marjoram,* and that may be compared with Dost *cænum, dirt.* Ɵopð miƿcel, Lb. xxxvi., seems to distinguish this from the mistletoe ; a few lines lower is Acmiƿcel.

ꞮꞮꞮꞮ—*cont.*

2. *Misteltoe, viscum album.* Germ.
Swed. Mistel, masc ; Dansk, Mistel (en).
"Viscarago, mιꞃcιlꞇan," Gl. Somner,
p. 64 a, line 56. "Mιꞃcelꞇa, chamæleon,
" viscus, Cot. 175, 210." Lye. Cha-
meleon is ꝥιꞃcel, not mιꞃcel. " Mistil,
" viscus," Graff. ohg. Lb. I. xxxvi.
The mistle or mistletoe is propagated
by being carried in the dung of birds.
ꞮꞮyxenplanꞇe, fem. ? gen. -an ? Lb. I.
lviii. 4. "Morella," Gl. Sloane, 146 ;
so MS. T., fol. 62 b, that is, *atropa
belladonna.*

ꞮꞮoꞥob, ꞮꞮoꞥaꞝ, a *decoction*, the ζέμα of the
medical writers ; glossed *carenum*, Gl.
Somn. p. 62 a, 11, which is *must boiled
down to one third part of its bulk and
sweetened.* But this gloss is not quite
appropriate in the first example in Lb. I.
xxxv., which requires τὰ ἐκ ζέματος, like
ἰχθῦς ἀπὸ ζέματος in Trallianus. Occ.
Lb. I. xlviii. 2. Moraz in the Nibelunge
Not., 1750, is interpreted by the Germans
mulberry wine, Do schancte man den
gesten . . . . mete môraz unte win ;
*then was poured out for the guests mead,
moraz and wine.*

ꞮꞮoꞥu, fem., gen. -an ; 1, *a root.* 2, the
root, the edible root, namely, *carrot*,
δαῦκον. Lb. I. xviii. ; I. ii. 23. Cf.
Felbmoꞥu, Germ. Möhre, fem. " ꝥis erbe
" [squill] haꝥ a rounde more lyk to an
" onyon." MS. Bodley, 536.
" Ne beoꝥ heo nowt alle forlore,
" That stumpeꝥ at ꝥe flesches more."
          Owl and Nightingale, 1389.
Єnꝥlιꞃe moꞥu, *parsnep, pastinaca
sativa*, Lb. I. ii. 23 ; III. viii.
Ᵽylιꞃe moꞥu, pealmoꞥu, *carrot, daucus
cariota*, Lb. III. viii. Gl. Somn. p. 64 a,
33.

ꞮꞮoꞥꞥyꞥꞇ, fem., gen. -e, "moor wort ;"
the small moor wort occurs Lb. I.
lviii. 1. Somner says, Moor grasse is
ros solis, that is, sundew, drosera, which
grows on moist heaths. " Silver weed,

ꞮꞮoꞥꞥyꞥꞇ—*cont.*

" or cotton grass " (Nemnich), that is,
potentilla anserina or erioforum.
The German interpreters of St. Hildegard make it the *Parnassia palustris.*
Mucꝣꞥyꞥꞇ, Hb. art. xiii., *artemisia Pontica.*
See Anzeiger für Kunde teutscher Vorzeit, 1835.
ꞮꞮuꞥꞥa, fem., gen. -an ? *cicely, myrrhis
odorata.* Lb. I. i. Μυῤῤίς, οἱ δὲ μύῤῥαν
καλοῦσιν, Dioskor. lib. iv. c. 116, which
is " scandix odorata " (Sprengel), now
named as above.

N.

Næꝥꞥe ꞥyꞥꞇ, fem., gen. in -e, *adderwort,
polygonum bistorta.* In Hb. vi. næꝥꞥe-
ꞥyꞥꞇ = *viperina.* Our adderworts are
those plants which resemble an irritated
snake raising its head, the *ofioglossum
vulgatum*, the *arum maculatum*, the *polygonum bistorta.* In MS. G., the German
gloss is " Naterwurc," and the German
Natterwurz may be *polygonum bistorta*,
or provincially *sedum*, or again provincially *echium vulgare.* (Adelung). We
are therefore to conclude that the two
glossators, agreeing, made the herb
p. bistorta. The figures in MSS. V.,
A., G., T. have much the appearance of
alisma plantago. In MS. Bodley, 130,
the figure and gloss are " Sowethistell."
From MS. G. fol. 8 a, the Germans
called the Satirion orchis " Natarwurc,"
which must be applied to enlarge
Adelung.

Næꞃe, a *fawn skin*; a *piece of fawn skin*,
Lb. I. ii. 20 ; I. xxxix. 3. " Nebris,"
Gl. Cleop., that is, νεβρίς, and support
is had from Gl. Somn., p. 61 a, line 27.
So Gl. Jul. If we take nebris for a
piece of soft leather, as a " tripskin,"
a " rybskin," it comes to the same at
last. Næꞃe in the Lib. Med. corresponds
to " Phœnicium " in Marcellus.

Napa, *never*, Lb. II. xli. Ne, *not* + Apa, *ever*.

Neahτ neρçιϡ, *fasting for a night, with fast unbroken; see* Lb. II. lxv. 5, and II. vii. at beginning.

Neτle, fem., gen. -an, *nettle, urtica.* ſio mιcle popþιϡ neτle, *u. dioica.* Lb. I. xlvii.

Neuпιρne, acc., a *disease.* Lb. I. lix. and contents.

Nepeρeoþa, Nu-, masc., gen. -an, *that part of the belly which lies between the navel and the share* or pubes, *the pit of the belly.* Lb. II. xxxvi., xxxi., xvii. and contents, xlvi. "Ilium," Gl. M.M., p. 137 b, 15.

O.

Oρepρyllo, neut., *overflow, overfilling, spuma vas coronans.* Lb. I. li.

Oρepρæpιρc, *from over sea, transmarinus.* Lb. I. vi. 6. M.H. 100 a. The reading Oρepρæpιρc is not in the MS. nor agreeable to analogy.

Oρneτ, (gen. prob. -eρ), *a close vessel.* In Lb. I. ii. 11, oρneτe translates "vas- "culo clauso vel operto." The word may be connected with oρen, *oven;* the κλίβανος was a close vessel covered up in the hot embers, and an oven at the same time.

Oρcoτen, properly *badly wounded by a shot,* but specially used, Lb. I. lxxxviii. 2., II. lxv. i., for *elf shot,* the Scottish term, that is, *dangerously distended by greedy devouring of green food.* It is spoken of cattle; sheep are very subject to it, if they get into a clover field at full freedom. "The disease consists in "an overdistension of the first stomach, "from the swelling up of clover and "grass, when eaten with the morning "dew on it."

VOL. II.

Oρcoτen—*cont.*
Next you'll a warlock turn, in air you'll ride,
Upon a broom, and travel on the tide ;
Or on a black cat mid the tempests prance
In stormy nights beyond the sea to France ;
Drive down the barns and byars, prevent our sleep,
Elfshoot our ky, and smoor mang drift our sheep. Falls of Clyde, p. 120.
"The approved cure is to chafe the parts "affected with a blue bonnet. The bas- "ting is performed for an hour without "intermission, by means of blue bonnets. "The herds of Clydesdale, I am assured, "would not trust to any other instru- "ment in chafing the animal." Jamie- son in Elfshot, and Suppl. "When "cattle are swollen they are said to be "degbowed. I have frequently known "a farmer strike a sharp knife through "the skin, between the ribs and the "hips, when the cow felt immediate "relief from the escape of air through "the orifice, so that the distended car- "case instantly collapsed, and the ex- "crements blown with great violence "to the roof of the cow house." Carrs Craven Gl. "Deggbound, mightily "swelled in the belly." Yorkshire dialogue, Gl. 1697, A.D.

Ome ? -an ; fem. ? *corrupt humour,* es- pecially *gastric,* the *pituita* of the medical and classical authors ; also *Erysipelas,* the external symptom of such a humour. Lb. I. xxxv. Dat. pl. Omum ; gen. pl. Omena. The analogy of the Islandic suggests a feminine form.

Ompρe, fem., gen. -an, *dock, rumex;* the German Ampfer, masc., *dock, rumex.* "Rodinaps, ompre, docce," Gl. Mone, p. 322 a. "Cocilus,' Gl. Cleop. If κaυκaλίς, not likely. Of the Ompρe, that will swim, *see* Docce. Lb. I. viii. 2 ; III. xxvi. Lacn. 23.

C C

Onꝛealle, *fellon*. Lb. I. xxxix., xli., obl.
cas., from the contents.

Onꝑed, gen. –es, some wort ; herba quædam. Lb. I. xl. i.; II. lii. 1.

Onꝛppenᵹan, *to administer a clyster*. Lb.
I. iv. 6. From Spꝛınᵹ, *a gush of water*,
hence, *a lavement, a sousing, a washing*,
a κλυσμός.

Onꝑwꝛı ? *unripe*. Lb. I. ii. 14.

Oꝑaꝛ, Quad. viii. 6, plural of Hoph.

Oxanꝛlyppe? fem. ? gen. –an, *oxlip*,
primula elatior. Lb. I. il. 15.

Oxnalıb, neut. ? *oxheal, Helleborus fœtidus*
and *H. viridis* (Cotgrave in Ellebore).
Oleotropius, Gl. Dun. Lb. I. xxxii.
2. ; I. x.

P.

Pıc, gen. –es, neut., *pitch, pix*. Lb. I.
xxxviii. 9 ; II. xli. ; III. xv.

Pıpoꝑ, gen. –es, masc., *pepper, piper;*
Lb. II. vii.

Poc, gen. pocces, masc., *a pock, pustula* ut
in variola. Lb. I. xl.

Punb, gen. –es, neut.; 1. *a pound*, as Lexx.
2. *a pint.* Lb. II. lxvii. So " Norma,
" pꝫteꝑ punb," Gl. Somn. p. 68 b, 11.,
that is, a pound of water is a pint of
water, and a pint of water is a pint for
all liquids.

Puꝛlıan, *to pick out the best bits, optima
quæque legere.* Lb. III. lxix. " Peuse-
" len, (among kindred senses) *summis
" digitis varia cibaria carpere,*" (Kilian).

R.

Rꝫᵹeꝑeofe, fem., Lb. II. xxxi. ; also
Rꝫᵹeꝑeosa, masc., Lb. I. lxxi. ; pl. –an ;
*the two ridges of muscles on either side of
the spine up and down the back.* " Pisali,

Rꝫᵹeꝑeofen—*cont.*

" reosan," Gl. Mone, p. 321 b. ult.
Pisali is a contraction of Paxilli ; similarly " Peysel, *pieu, échalas*," Roque-
fort. But, as we know from Cicero,
Paxillus was also contracted into Palus,
and these muscles were called Palæ,
like Pala, *stipes, palus*, in Du Cange.
" Rugge—bratun, *palæ*, sunt dorsi dex-
" tra lævaque eminentia membra," Gl.
Hoffmann. " Palæ Ugutioni 'Dorsi
" ' dextra lævaque eminentia membra,
" ' dicta sic, quia in luctando eas pre-
" ' mimus, quia luctari vel luctam
" ' Græci dicunt Palim.' ' Palæ sunt
" ' dorsi dextra lævaque eminentia
" ' membra ; dicta quod in luctando
" ' eas premimus, quod Græci ταλαίειν
" ' dicunt.' Isidorus," and so on (Du
Cange). The sense suits the passages
where pꝫᵹeꝑeoꝛan occurs, Lb. I.
lxxi., lxxxi. ; II. xxxi. " Palæ,
ᵹeꝛculbꝛe," Gl. Somn. p. 71 a, 44, *the
shoulder blades*, and in this sense the
dictionary to Cœlius Aurelianus, who
often uses the word, understands it.
" Palæ, ricgrible," Gl. Mone, p. 317 b.

Rꝫp ? *row, ordo, series:* dat. ꝛꝫpe, C.D.
vol. iii. p. xxv. ; acc. ꝛꝫpe. Lb. II.
xxxiii ; also Gl. in Lꝛe.

Raᵹu, Raᵹe, *lichen,* λειχήν. Lb. I.
xxxviii. 8 ; I. lxviii.

Raᵹu ꝛ meoꝛ, Deuteron. xxviii. 42,
neither word is used there with precision.
The Gl. give Massiclum, Mossidum,
which are formatives of our Moss,
lichen being considered a sort of moss.

Ramᶜealla, masc., gen. –an, " *ramgall.*"
From the name gall, no doubt a gentianaceous plant ; said Lb. I. li. to be par-
ticoloured. This description answers to
Menyanthes trifoliata, which is very
bitter and much administered by herb
doctors. (Sir J. E. Smith.)

Renbꝛıan, I presume to be the still current
Render, applied to suet. Suet is full of
films, thin membranes, with some other

Renbpnan —*cont.*
not fatty substances ; to render it, is to
make it homogeneous by melting. The
word may be a derivative of Hrein,
clean. Gepenðpian is applied to elm-
rind, Lb. I. xxv. 2. ; to the black alder,
I. xv. 4.

Renʒpypm, Ren-p., Rænʒ-p. *See* Pypm.
Rib, neut., *a rib.* Lb. II. xlvi. 8.S.
p. 198, 11.
Ribbe, gen. -an, fem.? *ribwort, plantago
lanceolata.* Hb. xxviii. Lb. I. ii. 22.
Ryben ; Þ peabe pyben. Lb. III. xlviii.
Rinb, gen. -e, fem. ; *rind, cortex.* Lb. I.
xxxviii. 5, 6.; II. lxv. 2, and often.
Hom. II. 8 and 114. Lyes quotation
was false, Lb. I. xlv. 5, and the more
recent deduction from him.
Riroba, *rheum,* ῥευματισμός, *a flowing.*
Lb. lix. 7. *See* Brem. Worth. p. 502. 4.
Rop, masc., gen. poppeƧ, *the colon, wide
intestine.* Lb. II. xxxi. often.
Rot, neut., *scum, spuma, reiectamentum.*
Lb. II. xx. as Hpot.
Rube, fem., gen. -an, *rue, Ruta graveolens.* Foreign, but adopted. Pilbe
pube, Lb. I. ii. 1, is foreign, but a
garden herb, *Peganum harmala.*
Rubmolin, read Rubniolin, Lb. III. lviii.,
a Norse word signifying *Red stalked,*
from poð, *red,* nioli *stalk.* It is said, to
grow by running water ; and it is *Polygonum hydropiper,* called Redshanks or
Water pepper in Bailey's dictionary.
Run, gen. -e, *secret, heathen mystery,
arcanum quid,* Bw. 363.
Leob pune, gen. -an, fem., *the same,
idem.* Lb. I. lxiv.

S.

Smþepie, Suðepiʒe, fem., gen. -an, *savory,
satureia hortensis.* The interpretation,
" Satirion," Gl. Somn., p. 64 b, 16, is
an evident error. Savory is in England
a garden plant, and retains its foreign

Smþepie—*cont.*
name. All the orchis tribe are "bal-
"loc" worts. Lb. III. xii. 2.
Sap, gen. -es, neut. everywhere : *See* acc.
Sapan, Lb. II. xxviii. It is also, as
Sio sap, sometimes put for Sio soph ;
Bw. 49, 29. So G.D. 201 b. C.E. 134,
line 23.
Sapcpen, *disposed to soreness.* Lb. II. i. 1.
There is no corresponding word in
the Hellenic text ; this is epexegetical,
and must be interpreted accordingly.
Scapu, fem., gen. -e, *the share, that is,
the pubes.* Lb. II. xxxi, xxxii. It is a
word well known to those who have
heard pure English spoken, and is neither
" Ilium " nor " Penis " nor " Alvus,"
but something near each of those. The
books generally make a confusion, but
Sharebone is always, I think, Os pubis.
See a quotation in Halliwell, but strike
out " of a man." Compare also Penil,
pubes, with Penul, a schare, in Garlande
and Biblesworth, p. 121, p. 148.
Sceaban, præt. Sceab, p. part. Sceaben, *to
shed, let fall ;* also intransitively *fall ;
infundere, inspergere.* Lb. I. ii. 23.;
I. lxi. 2.; II. iii. Hb. ii. 6. Cf. Lye,
Sceban. Ærceba, *migma,* Gl. in Lye,
which is doubtless to be understood
as the substantive of Ἀπομύττεσθας,
Emungi.
Sceapen, adj., *of sheep, ovinus.* Lb. I. lviii.
Sceapplan, *to scrape, radere.* Hb. lxxxi.
5. The L is frequentative.
† Sceappan, præt. † Sceapp, *scrape,* es-
pecially scrape herbs fine. Gepceapp,
Hb. lvii. 1. The same in substance as
Sceapnan, Hb. i. 2.
Sceappe, fem., gen. -an, *a scarification,
incisura in cute.* Lb. I. lvi.; I. xxxv.
Sceappian, *to scarify, in superficie cædere.*
Lb. I. xxxii. 2.
Sceopran, *to scarify, rodere, mordere.*
Scyprð, Scyprenbum, Lb. I. xviii. Þa
ʒæpicrðar ꝺ þa pyptpuman pceoppenbe
pmpon, O.T. 270, line 32, *began gnawing
the grass sprouts and the roots.*

Scınlac, gen. -es, neut., *an apparition, visum;* gen. Gl. Monc, p. 402 b. ; peaꝼlaces, Matth. xxiii. 25. Boet. p. 55, 7 ; accus. ꞏenıꝥ ꝛcınlac, Quad. x. 1 ; plur. -lacu, SMD. 27 b ; constr. neuter, DD. 437 foot, M.Sp. 8, plur. Scınlac, Quad. ix. 1. But *see* lyblacas, DD. 344. Scyꞇel, *dung,* from Scıꞇan. Quadr. iii. 14, xi. 13. *See* the passages, where Somners notion of testiculus would require some drying process not mentioned.

Scꝛımman, *to shrink,* a synonym of Scꝛıncan. Lb. I. xxvi., contents. " Skrim- " pen, adj. som vrider eller undslaaer " sig for Arbeide, som er megꞇt kiælen " eller ꞌemtaalig," Molbech, *one who flinches from work,* etc. Cf. Shrammed, *chilled* (pinched with cold, O.C.) Wilts. Scrimd ; Devon, (heard by myself).

Scꝛuꝼ, Geꝛceopꝛ, neut., *scurf.* Lb. II. xxxv. Hb. clxxxi. 3.

Seaꝺan, Seaꝺan, *a feeling as if the cavity of the body were full of water swaying about,* κλύδωνες, *undulationes,* Lb. I. xiv.

Sealh, Sealh, masc., gen. -eꝛ, *the sallow, salic-em, salix,* of which seventy English sorts are reckoned. The termination of the gen. shows the word is not fem., and few names of trees are neuter.
　　Red Sallow, Lacn. 89, *Salix rubra. See* also *S. repens,* of Smith.

Seaꝛ, neut., gen. -eꝛ, *juice.* Hb. v. 2. Lb. I. ii. 14, and frequently.

Secꝼ, masc., gen. -eꝛ, *sedge;* " carex, " gladiolus," Gl. in Lye ; masc., Lb. I. xxiii. ; gen. I. xxxix.
　　Ꝺomoꝛꝛecꝼ, " hammer sedge." Lb. I. lvi. 2. Homoꝛ is probably a bird, as in yellow hammer. " Scorellus, omeꝛ," Gl. C. Emberiza. Cf. clobhameꝛ, Gl. Mone, 315 a ; also Gl. Dief.
　　Reaꝺ secꝼ, " red sedge," Lb. I. xxxix.

Selꝛꝛꞇe, gen. -an, *avena fatua? wild oat?* Lb. I. xxxiii. 2 ; III. viii., and perhaps by emendation for ꝛealꝛ æꞇan, Lb. I. xlvii. 2.

† Sengıan, *singe ; see* Beꝛengıan ; ohg. Sengjan, Bısengjan, and Bıꝛenꝥ is what grammarians would have end in a vowel. Sybe, masc., *decoction,* ἀφέψημα, Hb. cliii. 4, from Seoꝺan.

Sıꝺsam, Lb. II. lxv. 5.

Sıꝛe, *sieve,* constr. as neut. Lb.'I xxxviii. 5, as Germ. Sieb, neut. Yet Dutch Zeef is fem.

Syꝛeꝺan, Sıꝛeꝺan, Sıoꝛeꝺan, pl. *bran, furfures.* Boet. p. 91, line 23. Gl. Cleop. In Hb. clv. 1, it translates ὠμὴ λύσις, which is said to be flour ; but here is a tradition that it is *bran.*

Sıꝥelhpeopꝛa, gen. -an, masc. 1. *Yellow milfoil, Achillea tomentosa,* masc., as Lb. III. xxxii. In Hb. l. = Heliotropion. All plants turn to the sun, which of them is meant ? In MS. V. " Achillea ser- " rata " (H.) seems to be drawn ; the other drawings do not at all resemble this. " Eliotropia, sigelhverpha. Elio- " trophus, sigel hveorfa. Nimphea, collon " croh vel sigelhveorua. Solsequia, si- " gel hveorua. Achillea, collon croch," Gl. Dun. Most of these are translations, and so equivalents : nymphea is the yellow water lily, and croh is crocus, yellow also. The testimony of the drawing fails in so well with that of the old glossary, that we must accept Achillea ; and as we must also attend to the hints for yellowness, it must be *A. tomentosa.*

2. *Scorpiurus heliotropion,* for Hb. cxxxvii. is founded on Dioskorides, ἡλιοτρόπιον τὸ μέγα, ὃ ἔνιοι ἐκάλεσαν σκορπίουρον. The figure in MS. T. for art. 1. agrees. The drawing in MS. V. art. cxxxvii. is nearly destroyed, what remains looks like " Polygonum convol- " vulus." (H.) The " round seed " forbids us to think of sunflower, Helianthus, which is also Mexican.

3. *Cichorium intybus?* Often Turnsol and Heliotrope in glossaries. Só Germ. Sonnen wendel (Adelung).

4. *Euphorbia helioscopia.* A small Sıꝥelhpeopꝛe, Lb. I. xliv. 2.

Sıȝronte, a wort, herba quædam ignota. Lb. I. xxxi. 7.

Sinebe, *ever easy*; ɲn-ebꝑe, Lb. II. xlvi.

Sınɲulle, gen. -an, *houselcek, Sempervivum tectorum*. The syllable sın like sem in Semper, means *always*; as also in Sın-ȝꝑene. Sınɲulle is Sempervivum, Hb. cxxv. That herb is drawn in MS. V., explained, as the green pigment has left only the external cast in the vellum, by MS. A., and in MS. G., where it is glossed "hufwurc," that is, Hauswurz, and in MS. T. These all point the same way. Singreen seems only a more generic term, in later times, but "The mickle "sinfulle," Lb. II. xxxiv., shows that this term also in early times would include Sedums, as *S. Telephium*, Lb. I. iii. 11.

Sınȝꝑene, fem., gen. -an, *singreen*, any sort of Sedum, with *sempervivum tectorum*, literally *always green*. Hb. lxxxvi. "Sedo magno, Houseleeke or Sen-"greene," Florio. "Joubarbe, House-"leek, Sengreen, Aygreen, etc." Cot-grave. In Hb. xlix. = Temolus, that is, Moly, the Homeric μῶλυ, a garlic, *Allium moly*. In Dansk. the evergreen periwinkle, *Vinca*. Þa ɲmalan ɲınȝꝑenan, Lb. I. viii. 2, shows that Singreen was a gene-ric name. "Colatidis," also "Temolus "vel titemallos," Gl. Dun. "Temolus," IIb. xlix., saying the root is bulbous, drawing it large, and with leaves and stem in MS. V., like Pinguicula vulgaris (H.), with no resemblance to Vinca.

Sıntrꝑænbel, masc.? *a bolus*, "*turundula*," Lat. IIb. xiv. 2. Sın, as in Sınepealt, *round*; Tɲenbel has a masc. termina-tion.

Slaꝑıe? gen. -an, *Salvia sclarea*, Lb. I. xv. 5.

Slecȝeran, *palpitate with strong beats*, Lb. II. xxvii ; from Slecȝe, *a sledge* hammer, and the frequentative termination -ecan, -eccan.

Slȳpe? gen. -an, *a viscid or sloppy sub-stance*. Masc. Lb. L i. 6. Fem. Laen.

Slȳpe—*cont.* 46. Cf. Slıpıȝ. Cf. Cu slyppan, Oxan slȳppan.

Smeȝaɲyꝑm, Smoeȝa-, Smea-, masc., gen -eɲ, Lb. I. liii. ; III. xxxix., *a worm or insect that penetrates, that eats its way, a burrowing insect*; cf. Norse, Smjúga, 1. *irrepere*, 2. *penetrare*, E. Smuȝan, *to crcep*, Smyȝelaɲ, *cuniculi, conies or their burrows*. Somn. Gl. M.M.

Smeꝑopȳꝑt, 1. *Aristolochia rotunda*, for-eign, and *A. clematitis*,English. Hb. xx., Lb. III. xlvii., with several glossaries and MSS., Gl. Dun., Gl. HarL 3388, Gl. Sloane, 5. *A. longa*, Gl. Sloane, 405. 2. *Mercurialis*, Gl. Rawl. C. 607. Gl. HarL 3388 in margin. G. de Bibles-worth, p. 162. Gl. Sloane, 5, fol. 34. Gl. Sloane, 135. 3. From the qualities, *Pinguicula*, *butterwort*.

Smıtan, *to smudge, illinere*, Lb. I. xxxi. 3 ; related to modern Smut ; in Lye Smıtta.

Snæb, fem. gen. -e, *a bolus, a morsel*, Laen. 81. Lb. I. xv. 6 ; I. lii. 3 ; II. lxiv. ; III. lxii. p. 348 ; III. lxv. Seo snæb, Hom. II. 272. S.S. p. 169, line 809. But ठa snæbas, C.D. 207.

Soȝoठa, gen. -an, *corrupt humour, pituita* with *hiccup, hicket, sobbing*, λυγμός, *sin-gultus*, Hb. xc. 11 ; Lb. I. ii. 1 ; II. xxxix., where the original is μετὰ δὲ ταῦτα λύζουσι. Alex. Trall. p. 480, ed. Basil. From Suȝan. Ælɲoȝoठa, *elvish hiccup*, the same thing gone to a frightful extreme. Thus πάντα γὰρ ἐποίησα ταῦτα καὶ ἐπὶ μεγάλου λυγμοῦ τοσοῦτον, ὡς ὑπονοεῖν ἐκτὸς κλίνης ἐξάλλεσθαι τὸν κάμνοντα. Alex. Trall. p. 121, ed. Paris.=lib. viii. 15, *in as instance of so strong a hiccup that we supposed the patient was springing out of bed*, Lb. III. lxii. p. 348.

Soloɲece, *Heliotropium Europæum*. IIb. lxxxvi. Sprengel says that by Solse-quium, Charlemagne understood II.E. as above.

Soppiȝan, *to sop, to dip in liquid.* Lb. II. xxx. 1. Cf. Soppcuppe, fem., C.D. 593, 685, 721.

Spæran, *to syringe, spout, aquam proiicere;* Lb. II. xxii. p. 208 ult., where the sense hardly admits *spuere.* "Spoyts, sprützen, " sprenken, so auch Süddän." Outzen. Spepb pypc, 1. *Ranunculus flammula.* " Flamula . i. sper wortt or launsele, this " erbe is schapyn as hit wer a sper all " so. and in the crope of þe stalk " commys aut mony smale branches ꝛ " hit has a whyte floure, ꝛ hit groys in " waters." MS. Bodl. 536. The flower is yellow. " Flammula, anglice spere- "wort," MS. Rawl. C. 607, similarly C. 506, Harl. 3388, and again adding " lanceola," id. " fflamula minor. Las " sper wort hauith leuis shapid like a " spere," Gl. Sloane, 5, fol. 32 c. Gl. Sloane, 405.

2. *Inula Helenium,* Hb. xcvii. and Gl. Harl. 978, make spearwort Inula campana = *Inula Helenium, Bot.* Gl. Dun. perhaps copies Hb. Gl. Brux. agrees. MSS. V., G., A. draw spears springing from a root. In MS. Bodl. 130, is an explanation, Centaurea, and a gloss in a hand of the 14th century, "Sperewert." The Centaurea Cyanus is so far like Inula II., that it may be mistaken in a drawing. " Policaria minor," Gl. Harl. 3388.

3. *Carex acuta,* Germ. Spiessgras, is probably meant in the following, " Fla- " mula mynor. i. sperworte thys erbe " has smale leuys lyke to grase, bot hit " (*omit hit*) schape as hit were a speyr. " and growes in feldys," MS. Bodl. 536.

4. † *Brassica rapa, turnep,* "Nap " silvatica [*read Napus silvaticus*] rpepe- " pypc," Gl. Somn. p. 64 a, 16. This must be rejected.

Spican, *spices,* Latinism ? species. Lb. II. lxiv., contents.

Sppacen, neut. ? *berry bearing alder, Rhamnus frangula.* Lb. I. xv. 4., xxiii.

Sppacen—*cont.*
Germ., Spreckenholz, Sporkenholz ; Dutch, Sporkenhout ; Dansk., Spregner; Swed. dial., Sprakved. "Apeletum," Gl. Cleop. for alnetum, misunderstood as alnus nigra.

Sppinȝ pypc, fem., gen. in -e, "spring- "wort," *Euphorbia lathyris.* "Sprincwrz, " *lactaridia.* al. *lactariola* vel. citocasia," Gl. Hoffm. Graff. vol. i. col. 1051. "Cra- "pucia [*read catapatia*] springwort," a Gl. in Mone, p. 287 a. Lb. I. xxxix. 2.

Stæppypc, fem. gen. -e, "staithwort ; " if we choose the commonest of the sea- shore plants it will be *Statice,* compre- hending *thrift* and *sea lavender.* Lb. I. xxxii. 3. "Aster atticus," Somner, but why?

Stanbæþ, neut., *a vapour bath,* contrived by heating "stones" that would not fly, and pouring on water. Lb. I. xli.

Stebe, masc., *strangury,* "stranguria," Lat. of Quad. ii. 15., viii. 11. Radically; *the being stationary, still standing;* as in Sunnstebe, *solstice.* So Næpon þine heopba rcebiȝe, Gen. xxxi. 38., *thine herds were not barren.*

Stemp, *stamp,* Leechd. vol. I. p. 378.

Sticce, neut., *sticky stuff, viscid fluid;* Lb. I. xxxix. 2.

Stice, fem., gen. -e, *a pricking sensation, a stitch, a stab;* Quad. xiii. 10. Instice, Lb. II. liv. lxiv. contents. All cited passages have this declension.

Stpælpypc, fem., gen. -e, the commonest *club moss, Lycopodium clavatum.* "Cal- "litrichon," MS. ap. Somn., but in this term were included the club mosses. Stpæl as *arrow,* may have given name to this moss, as the stems look like arrows with the feathers up and the heads in the ground. Were it not for this gl. we might interpret *Galium verum,* from Stpæl, *bed; our ladys bed straw.*

Stpeap, Stpeop, *straw,* neuter in Lb. I. iii. 12. Rushw. Matth. vii. 3. (streu), is masc. Διδαξ. 46.

Suȝan, *to moisten, macerare, madefacere,*
Syȝð, Hb. xxxv. 3 ; p. part. Soȝen, as
appears by Soȝoða, Foproȝen; cf. Socian
in Lexx.; also Isl. Söggr, *madidus,* Lb. II.
xv. Ða popporeban punbe puȝe ꝺ clæn-
pȝe, P.A. 24 b. *Moisten and cleanse the
putrified wound.* Asoȝen. C.E. 373. l. 19.
Sunbcopn, gen. -ep, neut., *Saxifraga granulata.* Sunbcopn, Hb. xcix. is saxifraga,
and the statement is accompanied by a
remarkable drawing, represented in the
fac simile to Leechdoms, vol. I.; *see* pref.
lxxix. The word copn itself, as signifying *grain,* assists our determination of the
herb. In the Latin Apuleius, MS. Bodley,
130, a gloss is " Sundcorn." MS. A. fol.
45 b, has also a portion of earths surface,
but figures the herb above ground, not
quite correctly. " Saxifrigia, sundcorn,"
Gl. Dun. The same gl. in the MS.
Lacn. 18, where fifteen grains are mentioned in the text. So Gl. Mone, p.
442 a.

2. Lithospermon officinale, Hb. clxxx.
It appears by a glossary in Anzeiger für
Kunde der teutscher Vorzeit. 1835, col.
247, that the false readings meant funnan
copn, Milium solis, which must be taken
as an emendation of the text.

Supe, fem., gen. -an, sorrel, *Rumex Acetosa,* also *Oxalis.*

Geacep pupe, *cuckoos sorrel, Oxalis
Acetosella.*

Monnep pupe, *Rumex Acetosa.* Lb.
I. li.

Supmelpc, *sourish, sour sweet.* Lb. II. i.
" Malus matranus, pupmelpc apulbep,"
Gl. Somn., p. 64 b, 48 ; correct *Malus*
matiana, pupmelpc apulbpe ; *the crab
tree.* " Maciana . i . mala siluestria,"
Gl. Harl. 3388. " Mala maciana, po-
" mum siluestre, wode crabbis," id.
So Dornsten, Gl. Mone, p. 290 a. Melpc
is a separate word, " Melarium, mulpc
" apulbp." Gl. M.M. p. 159 a, 27, probably for mel-ipc, formed on Mel, *honey,*
which therefore appears genuine English,
as in Melpeocel, Melbeap, St. Marh. Gl.,

Supmelpc—*cont.*
not hibrid words ; related to Mebu, *mead,*
SSpp. art. 511.

Spane pypt, fem., gen. -e. Lb. I. xxxi. 7.
Spat, gen. -es. 1. *sweat.* 2. *blood.* 3.
hydromel. Hɪᴅ. 22 a. The gender has
been given only from other Teutonic
languages, as masc. ; but in Lacn. 111,
spa ða spat beoð mippenhcu, *as the
sweats are various,* the form makes it
neuter. Dutch Zweet, neut; Isl. Sveiti ;
Germ. Schweiss ; Swedish Svett, masc.

Speȝlep æppel ; Lfb. I. ii. 12, also 21 ; I.
xiv., I. xxiii. The receipt Lb. I. ii. 12,
pepper, salt, wine, and swails apple,
corresponds with the following words of
Alex. Trall., p. 48, line 4, ed. 1548.
Ἁλὸς ἀμμωνιακοῦ (our author often solves
his difficulties by omission) Γο d, φύλλων
Γο γ, τεπέρεως Γο s', ποιήσας ξηρίον
ὑπάλειφε καὶ ποιεῖ πρὸς ξηροφθαλμίας.
Φύλλα are the leaves of the malobathrum.
Plinius, xxiii. 43, also prescribes malobathrum for the eyes.

† Speðan, *to swathe,* not yet found, whence
Spaðil and Speðunȝ, *a swathing,* Lb. I.
xxxi. 7, and Beppeþan, id. I. i. 2 ; II.
xlii. C.E. p. 100, 19. Weak conjuga-
tion.

Spiȝan, Speȝan, præt. speoȝ, spoȝen, *to
invade, pervade, penetrate.* Read Spi-
ȝende, Lb. II. xxiii. Sette hine
pȳlpne onȝean þone (so) ppeȝenban pȳp,
M.H. 184 b. St. Martin *set himself in
opposition to the invading fire.* Ealle ða
pullnerpa ðæp ðȳptpan opnep ðe me æp
ðuphȝpeoȝh on peȝ aplȳmebe, Beda,
629, 21. *Put to flight all the foulnesses
of the darksome furnace, which previously
had scorched me.* Þ næniȝ bipceop oþpep
bipceoppcipe onppoȝe, Beda, 575, 32,
*that no bishop invade another bishops
diocese.* Cf. Inppoȝennyp, *invasion,* Beda,
507.

Spȳle, masc., gen. -ep, *a swelling.* Hb. ix.
3. On mȳcelpe spȳle, Bed. 616, 6, is
some error ; *see* 616, 38.

Spýpran, præt. Speopr, p. part. Spoppen, *to file, to grind away, whether by a file or a grindstone; and so to polish.* "Spypiþ *limat*," Gl. Prud., p. 144 b. " Appoppen *expolitus*," *id.* p. 142 a. Spoppen C.E., p. 410, 24; p. 497, 18, also notes. Cf. Gothic Swairban; ohg. Swerban, Fars-werban. Appeppeopr, *brass filings.* Lb. I. xxxiv. 1. Geppypr, gen. -ep, *filings.* Hb. ci. 3. Sppman, *swarm,* dc apibus, *examen ex alveari educere.* Leechd. vol. I., p. 384. Cf. " Coalaissent, suopnabun." Gl. C. read suopmabun for speopmabon? Spopan, *to swoon, see* peppopung, swowe in Will. and Werwolf, p. 4.

T.

-range, -renge, -tinge, as a termination occurs in Getenge, *accidental to, quod accidit alicui,* in Intinga, *occasion,* in Geaboptenge, *adjacent,* in Samtenger, *continually*; the same syllable is seen in contingit, contigit, Τυγχάνειν, Τύχη, Tangere, Θιγεῖν, Touch.

Teagan, *to prepare, parare.* þ lanð mib to reagenne :· Ða þ lanð ða geteað pær. Beda, 605, 33. Cuðbertht requested some husbandry tools wherewith *to till the land; so when the land was prepared.* præt. teobe, CE. 335, l. 16, 336, l. 4.

Tapu, Teapo, neut., gen. -op; *tar, gum, distillation from a tree; wax in the ear;* neut., Lb. I. xlv. 3, I. liv., I. lxi. 1, also makes tapan, masc., Lb. III. xxvi., xxxi. þone teap, Lacn. 3. Geclæm ealle þa seamas mid tyrwan, Hom. l. 20, *calk all the seams with tar.* So Gen. vi.14. Týppan rop peallum, Gen. xi. 3. Gepopht op tigelan .] op eopðtypiepan, OT. 304, 12, *wrought of tiles,* thin bricks, such as the Romans made, *and bitumen.*

Telgna, masc., gen. -an, *branch, ramus,* Quad. i. 7. Sume þonne sneddun telgran of treowum, Matth. xxi. 8, Rushworth, ed K.

Teon, præt . teah, p.p. togen, *draw, ducere.* The translation of getogen, Quad. vi. 11, *as tightened,* is justified by the context and by the following example. A monk calls on the devil to untie his sandals, and the devil does so : then the monk is frightened and backs out, but ða gepuneðon ða þpangay on micelum bæle ontogene] onliðobe ; GD. 217 a., *the thongs remained in great part untightened and eased.*

Tetpa, Lb. II. xxx., appears to be an error for Tetep, masc., *tetter, impetigo.* Hæjð tetep on his lichoman, P.A. 15 b., *hath tetter on his body.* Se tetep butan pape he opepgæð ealne ðone lichoman, ibid., "Impetigo quippe sine dolore corpus " occupat." So Sc. 46 a. The gll., Quad. ii. 10, Hb. xlvi. 6, cxxii.

Tipe, fem? *bitch;* Isl. Tik, *bitch,* fem. Dansk. Tæve, *bitch.* Lb. II. lx. contents.

Typðelu, Typðlu, pl., *little tords, tredles;* the droppings of sheep are called sheeps tredles in Somerset, trattles in Suffolk. See Moor Gl.; further. Tridline: Craven Gl. Lb. I. xxxi. 4, II. lix. 6, etc.

Togetteð, *there are tuggings, spasms.* Lb. I. xxv.

Top begete, *hard gotten,* Lb. I. xlv. 5. The expression goes to mark a Dansk admixture in the Lb. Cf. Torpenginn, *hard to get,* in the Laws of Magnus the law mender ; Nú ap því at vinno menn ero miök torfengnir í heraði, oc allir vilia nú í kaupferdir fara. Kaupa Bólkr. 23, *Now since men for labour are very hard to get in the country, and all will now go a trading.* Tor, with o long, is frequent in later English, "It were tor for " to telle al here atyr riche," William and Werwolf, fol. 21 ; "It were toor for " to telle treuli al þe soþe," id. fol. 75, with the notes.

Toþb, *a piece of dung, stercus conformatum*; neat, Lb. I. xlviii. 2 ; I. lxxii. ; III. xxxviii. Quad. vi. 14, 18, 19, 20, 21, 24, Lacn.

Topnıȝe, *blear eyed*, with eyes inflamed and full of acrid tears. Hb. xvi. 3, " ad " lippitudinem oculorum," Lat. Hb. liv. 1, "ad epiphoras oculorum," Lat., that is, *excess of lacrymose humour*. A compound of ʒypan, and eaȝe.

Toð, *tooth, dens*, makes dat. sing. roþe, Lb. III. iv., but reþ, Exod xxi. 24, and nom. pl. reþ, Lb. III. iv., but roþas, Gð. 34, SS. 141, acc. pl. reð, Lb. I. vi. 5.

Toþȝap, *a tooth pick*. Lb. I. ii. 22. Gap is not a weapon originally, but αἰχμή, something at an acute angle, as in the Gore of a gown. *See* ȝapıa, Cod. Dipl. vol. iii.

Trıȝ, neut., *a trough*, Lb. III. xlviii. Þpuh, another form of the same word, is fem. in all the examples cited by Lye ; is neut. in C. D. 118, A.D. 770. Bıbbenbe anep lýtlep ʒpoȝep, OT. 312, 32, *Begging for a little boat*.

Tulȝe, *root of tongue*, Lb. I. xlii., there is no notion of flesh, or muscle, or hypoglottis. It is Gothic, Tulgus, ἑδραῖος, στερεός. Gothic, Tulgiða, fem. ὀχύρωμα, ἀσφάλεια, ἑδραίωμα.

Tunȝılpınpypr,fem., gen. -e, *white hellebore?* Veratrum album, for it seems probable enough, that Tunpnȝpypr, Hb. cxl. and Gl. Dun., is a contraction of this older form. Lb. I. xlvii. 3.

Tpæbe, *two parts in three*; Lb. III. ii. 1. ; III. x., xiii., xxxix.

Tpınıht, *downy*; from Tpın *byssus*, Gl. Lb. I. xxxi. 7.

Ƿ.

Ƿæpc, masc., gen. -ey, *wark, pain*. Wark, in compounds at least, is in most of the modern gl. Dansk. Wærk, *pain*. Isl. Verkr., masc. Occurs masc. Lb. I. iv. 2 ; II. xlvi. 1. Also Ƿeopce, Ƿeopc, Ƿpæc.

Ƿæpc—*cont*, *See* Pref. vol. I. p. xcvi. Not to be confounded with Ƿeopc, *work*, neuter. The feminine article in Lb. II. xlvi. 1, for *sidewark*, is an error, it is masc. in the next four lines ; such errors occurred by attraction, for pbe is feminine.

Ƿæpcan, *be in pain*. Lb. III. xviii.

Ƿæceþbolla, masc., gen.-an, *dropsy, dropsical humour*, ὕδρωψ ὕδερος, Lb. I. xxxix. ὑδερική παρέγχυσις, Lb. II. xxi., occ. I. xliii.

Ƿæceppypr, fem., gen. in -e, *waterwort*, Callitriche verna. In Hb. xlviii. waterwort is made Callitriche, and we may perhaps trust our botanists in their own science for this herb. The figure in MS. V. is such that it resembles Raphanus raphanistrum stripped of leaves (H). " Waterwort Callitriche verna " (Nemnich). Sir W. Hooker says Water star wort.

Ƿæcla, masc., gen. -an, *a cloth*. Lb. II. xxii.

Ƿapıan, *wave, iactare*. Lb. III. xviii.

Ƿah, in pahmela, Lb. II. lii. *finc*, ohg. Wahi, mhg, Waeke, *subtilis, expolitus, venustus*, künstlich, fem. schön.

Ƿealpypr, fem., gen. -e, *wallwort, dwarf elder, Sambucus ebulus*, Hb. xciii. ; but *Intuba, endive, intubus*, Gl. Cleop. fol. 53 d.

Ƿeap, masc., *bowl*; Lb. II. xxiv., the same as Þþepı = Norse Hverr, masc. It translates *uter*, a waterskin, Paris Psalter, Ps. cxviii. 83.

Ƿeap, masc., pl. peappas, *a hard pimple on the face*; *a hardened callosity*; varus. " Vari parvi ac duri sunt circa faciem " tumores." Paul. Ægin., col. 444 Λ. Lb. I. lxxiv.

Ƿeapȝ,—Ƿeaphbpæbe, gen. -an, fem ?, *a wide spread warty eruption*, Hb. ii. 18, " ulcus," Lat. xx. 8; " carcinoma," Lat. Lb. I. xxxiv.

Ƿece, *weak, debilis*, Lb. II. lii. 1 ; Ƿace, DD. p. 425 vi. Without the final vowel, Gl. R. 115 ; Sc. 10 b ; Boet. p. 176 a ; Cædm. (if Cædm.), 154, 20 MS.

Ƿebe, *mad, furious, phreniticus,* indeclinable in Hb. i. 25, in contents *see* var. lect. ii. 21, contents iv. 10, xxxvii. 5, etc. Lb. I. lxix.

Ƿeʒbpæbe, fem., gen. -an, properly " way- " broad," but called *waybread*; 1. *Plantago maior*; 2. ʒeo pupe peʒbpæbe, *plantago media,* it it hoary, hirsute. Hb. ii., Lb. II. lxv., etc.

Ƿenʒe, Ƿænʒe, Ƿanʒe, neut., gen. -an, *cheek, bucca*; Matth. v. 39 ; Luke v. 29 ; Lb. I. i. 8, 10 ; III. xlvii. ; Hom. II. 180. And him ða ponʒan bpiceð, S.S. 140.

Ƿenn, Ƿen, *a wen,* masc., pl. pennas. Lb. I. lviii, ; III. xxx. ; Lacn. 12.

Ƿenpypt, fem., gen. -e ; " wenwort," is of sorts:— 1. cluphc, or cloved ; Lb. I. lviii., II. li. 3. 2. cneoehte, kneed ; id. L lxvi. Wenwort must be so called from curing wens ; for wens are good, says Salmon, " Alexander, Archangel, Asarabacca, " Celandine, Chickweed, Coriander, " Crow foot, Cresses, Darnel, Endive, " Figwort, Laser wort, Lentils, Melilot, " Purslane, Thorowwax, Turnsole, " Wound wort." Among these, for 1, *Ranunculus acris,* as crow foot, *Ranunculus ficaria,* as the lesser celandine, and for 2, Darnel, *Lolium temulentum,* are the most likely.

Ƿepmob, gen. -es, masc., *wormwood, Artemisia absinthium.* Lb. II. xxii., lxv. 5 ; III. iii. 2, xxxi.

Se pula pepmob, *Anthemis cotula ?* Lb. III. viii.

Ƿice, *wych elm, Ulmus montana,* occ. Lb. I. xxxvi. Declension and gender unascertained.

Ƿipel, masc., *a beetle.* Lb. III. xviii. Topbpipel, *Scarabæus stercorarius,* Linn. *Geotrupes,* others Lb. III. xviii. It feeds on and lays its eggs in dung.

Ƿilbe (with final vowel), *wild, silvestris.* Ƿilbe appa. Gl. R. 21. (Lye inexact). Ƿilbe bap. Gl. R. 20. (Lye inexact). Ƿilbe oxa. Gl. R. 19, which has also pilbe cynner hopp, 20. Ƿilbe cypper.

Ƿilbe—*cont.*
Gl. R. 39, but pilb, 44. Ƿilbo popiʒ. Gl. R. 41. Hpit pilbe pinʒeapb. Gl. R. 39. Ƿilbe lactuce. Gl. R. 44. (Lye inexact). Ƿilbe næp. Gl. R. 42 and 44. (Lye inexact). Ƿilbe pinʒepb. Gl. R. 39. Ƿilbe pyp. Gl. R. 11. (Lye inexact). To some of Lyes quotations are attached no references. Ƿilbbeop is a compound, sometimes written pilbeop, and the genitive plural is pilbbeopa. The separate words are found Nan pilbe beop. Hom. I. 486. Ðapað pilbe mob. S.S. 168, line 755, where mob is neuter. Lib. I. xxxvii. 2. Probably more examples of e dropped, than as above, may appear.

Ƿylpen ? or –ne ? gen. -e, *a she wolf, lupa.* Quad. ix. 7. Germ. Wölfinn. Cf. Mynecenu.

Ƿyllecæppe, -cypre, fem., gen. -an, *fenugreek, Trigonella fœnum græcum,* from Gl. Brux. Gl. Dun.

Ƿinbelytpeap, neut., gen. -ep, *windle straw, cynosurus cristatus.* Lb. I. iii. 12. Jamieson. Nemnich. The expression " two edged" belongs perhaps to the spike. But Mylne (Indigenous Botany) did, and the author of the name, Parkinson, must have understood *Agrostis spica venti.*

Ƿypm, masc., gen, -ep, *any creeping thing, worm, snake, dragon, mite, insect, acarus, vermin.* Lat. Vermis and Vermiculus. So multipedæ are " many foot wormes," in Hollands Plinius. The numerous worms mentioned in the Saxon text are not all lumbrici.

Anapypm. *See* Ana.

Ðanbpypm, *hand worm,* perhaps translating Κειρίαι as if from Χείρ. Κειρίαι occurs as *lumbrici lati* in Aetios, 492 e Lb. I. 1. " Teredo, urcius, surio, Gl. in Lye. Surio, or Sirio, which is the name of the itch mite in many European languages, seems to me to be only Cirio from χείρ ; but at the same time an error for Κειρία. The lumbricus latus is *Tænia solium* or *Bothriocefalos latus.*

GLOSSARY. 411

Ƿyꝑm—cont.

In Cod. Exon. p. 427, 24, it is said to be
"delved," whence the translation "earth
" worm " seemed justified.

Smoeȝapyꝑm, see letter S.

Deappyꝑm, dew worm, in Lb. L 1.,
infests the feet.

Renȝpyꝑm, Ren-, ringed worm, a kind
of belly worm. Alex. Trallianus divides
the worms which infest the human body
into three, of which this is one. Πρῶτον
τοίνυν ἡμᾶς εἰδέναι δεῖ, ὡς τριττόν εἰρήκα-
σιν οἱ παλαιοὶ τῶν ἐλμίνθων εἶδος, ἐν μὲν
τὸ μικρὸν πάνυ καὶ λεπτόν, ὃ καλεῶ
εἰώθασιν ἀσκάριδας, δεύτερον δὲ τούτων
στρόγγυλον, καὶ τρίτον ἄλλο τὸ τῶν
πλατειῶν. Ed. Ideler, p. 315. To the
same effect M. Psellus in the same
vol. p. 241. The moderns have more
sorts. Hb. lxv. See Lb. L xlviii. xlix.
They seem to derive their name from
the rings of some of them. An earthworm is Anȝeltpiece.

Ƿyꝑmpyꝛc, wormwort, Sedum album or
villosum. Wilde Prick madame. (Lyte)
Lb. I. xxxix.; I. lvii.; III. ii. 6.
Chenopodium anthelminticum is American.

Ƿyꝑp, gen. -e, fem., recovery, valetudo in
melius conversa. Lb. I. iv. 5. Nu ɪꝼ
þæt bæꝑn cymen apæcneþ co pyꝑpe
peopcum ebꝑea, C.E. 5, line 8, now is
that bairn come, raised up for the recovery
of the Hebrews from their miseries. The
passage is congratulatory. C.E. 336,
line 5.

Ƿyꝑcunȝ, fem., gen. -e, a preparation of
worts. Quad. iv. 5.

Ƿicmæꝑeꝼ pyꝑc, pihcmæꝑeꝼ pyꝑc, " Wiht-
" mars wort." Lb. I, ii. 13. " Britta-
" nica Vihtmeres vyrt vel heaven hin-
" dele," Gl. Dun. It may therefore be
spoonwort, scurvy grass, Cochlearia
Anglica. See Dæpen hybele.

Ƿiðe- Ƿiðopinbe, gen. -an, fem. ?, withywind, convolvulus, both Conv. sepium and
arvensis. Lb. L ii. 20; I. vi. 7; I. xlix.

Ƿiðiȝ, masc., gen. piðieꝼ, a withy, a willow,
salix. Lb. I. lxxiv. ÆG. 13, line 54.

Ƿonꝛceaꝛca and þa ponꝛceaꝛcan, Lb. II.
xxxviii. and contents, may be taken either
as lividness or meagreness. The passage
of Philagrios, does not exhibit the word.

Ƿꝑæcce, gen. -eꝼ, crosswort, galium cruciatum. Lb. III. i., viii. Lacn. 12, 29. Wa-
rantia ꝑꝑec, gl. Leechd. vol. L p. 376.
" Vermiculum. i. parance. i. protte,"
Gl. Harl. 978, with " cruciata maior
" warence," Gl. M. The Galium tribe
were often called by names which mark
their relationship to the Madder, thus
Vermiculus, properly the cochineal insect
used to get a red dye, transfers its name
to Madder, Rubia tinctorum, and Madder gives its appellations to the Galiums
its relatives. " Cruciata maior. i.
" warence. anglice madir," Gl. Harl.
3388.

Ƿububenb, -binb, gen. -es, masc. ?, woodbind. Hb. clxxii.; Lb. L ii. 21; III. ii. 1;
III. xxxi., convolvulus, from the leaves of
the drawing, the likeness to the caper
plant, and modern usage ; which, besides
convolvulus, applies the name also to the
honeysuckle.

Ƿubu cepuille, wood chervil, cow parsley,
Anthriscus silvestris. Cepuille being an
English adaptation of Cerefolium, Χαιρέ-
φυλλον (Columella), and pubu being
taken in the sense of our wild, we ascertain at once, that we have here the
Chærophyllum silvestre, which Koch
and Hooker now name Anthriscus silv.
Nemnich agrees, and Lytes description.
In Hb. lxxxvi. wood chervil is made to
be Asparagus agrestis, and the drawings
in MSS. V., T., A. have clearly the
characteristics of Asparagus officinalis.
If our Saxon interpreter held his opinion
with deliberation, he differs from the
rest of our English world. Asparagus
in MS. Bodl. 130, is drawn like the
mature plant.

Ƿubu lecꝛpic, masc., wood lettuce, wild
sleepwort, Lactuca scariola is Hb. xxxi.

Ƿubu lecꞇᵖıc—*cont.*

Lactuca sylvatica. Masc. G.D. 11 a. The
gloss in H. Scariola must be accepted ;
Sir J. E. Smith turns it Prickly Lettuce;
Sir W. Hooker says it is found on waste
ground in Cambridgeshire, at Southend,
Essex, and formerly near Islington. He
adds that the garden lettuce, L. sativa, is
not a native of this country. " Lactuca,
" letuse, slepewort, idem ; domestica et
" campestris." Also " Lactuca agrestis,
" rostrum porcinum . mylk thistell." MS.
Harl. 3388. " Lactuca silvatica idem
" wild letys, þis erbe has leuys like to a
" thystell, and they ben scharpe ꞇ ken ꞇ
" hit has a floure of purpure colour, ꞇ
" hit groys in feldes ꞇ in whet," MS.
Bodl. 536, fol. 17. The word purpure
was in early times an exact repetition
of purpureus, which the Romans applied
to any bright colour. The flower of
Lactuca scariola is yellow. Lactuca silvatica has yellow rays in MS. Bodl. 130,
but the leaves are too like sword blades.
It is there glossed Suge þhıſtel, that is,
sow thistle. " Scarola . endiua . txᵒnna
(?) lactuca agrestis," Gl. M. The
drawing in MS. T is an exact representation of *L. scariola*, glossed Branca vrsina,
to which there is resemblance.

Ƿubu ꞁoꝛe, hꞁoꝛe, gen. -an: 1. *Asfodelus
ramosus.* In Hb. xxxiii., liii. Woodroffe
is astula regia, that is hastula regia, the
royal sceptre, and all accounts agree that
it is a kind of onion, an asfodelaceous
plant, with a vast number of bulbs,
" LXXX. simul acervatis sæpe bulbis,"
" Plinius, xxi. 68 ; and though it has
" transferred its name to the daffodil,
" yet not that plant, *Narcissus pseudo-
" narcissus,* is its equivalent. The As-
phodelus is figured in MS. V. fol. 28 a,
but the flower is gone ; the drawing, as
much as remains, matches that in Fuchsius, p. 121. " Asphodellus, wode houe"
(*so*), MS. Harl. 3388. " Astula regia.i.
" wode rove," MS. Rawl. C. 607. " Has-
" tyca regia.i. woderofe." MS. Bodl. 536.

Ƿubu ꞁoꝛe—*cont.*
" Affodillus vude hofe," (*so*), Gl. Dun.
So Gl. M. Fuchsius makes his goldwurz,
asfodelus luteus, Gl. R. 40. Lacn. 69.
2. *Asperula odorata,* modern usage.
In MS. Bodl. 130 ; for hastula regia is
drawn a true *Asperula,* with gloss in
14th century hand " woodrofe." "Rubea
" minor woodroff," MS. Bodl. 178.

Ƿubuꞁoꝛe, gen. -an, fem., *wild rose, dogrose, hedgerose, rosa canina.* Lb. I.
xxxvii. 1.

Ƿubu ꞁeaxe, gen. -an, fem ? *wood wax,
wood waxen, Genista tinctoria.* Lb. I.
xlvii. 2 ; III. xxx.

Ƿulꝛes camb, masc., gen. -es, " wolfs-
" comb," *wild teazle, Dipsacus silvestris.*
In Hb. cliii. translates χαμαιλίων, which
in clvi. is turned by pulꝛeꞃ ꞇæꞃl ; as the
teazing wool is combing it, this has no
surprise. The figure in MS. V. art. xxvi.
is a teazle, so MS. T. The equivalent
χαμαιέλαια was misunderstood by our
interpreter. However χαμαιλίων is no
teazle at all, but a stemless thistle, the
Carlina acaulis, *see* eoꞁoꝛþꞃoꞇu, Masc.
Lacn. 3.

Ƿullıan, *wipe with wool, lana detergere,*
Quad. vii. 4.

Ƿunbel ? *a wound,* pl. ꞁunbela, Hb. i. 11,
cont., iv. 10, ix. 2. Ƿunbelan, DD. 417,
xxiii.

Ƿuꞁme?, fem.?, gen. -an, *woad, Isatis
tinctoria.* Somn. in Lex. has a gloss,
" Lutum," which is *woad.* Lb. II. lxv. 4.
Ƿuꞁme being properly any thing having
the power of dying, not blue, but vermilion ; and representing the vermiculi
or cochineal insects.

Þ.

Þeaꝛꝛ, Þeoꝛꝛ, *wanting in something, ἐνδεής,
cui quid opus est,* as they interpret the
Norse þarfi. Whence 1, *poor.* 2, *un-
leavened,* of bread. 3, *skimmed,* of milk.
Lb. II. lii. 1.

Þeapm, *gut*, pl. -maʃ, *guts, intestina.* But Þ smælþeapme, Lb. II. xxxi. Da ðybbe ærneþ hine mið hinbeþenðe fceaʒte on ðæt ſmælðeapme, P.A. 55. a, *Then Abner stabbed him with the hinder end of his spearshaft in the small gut.* Gl. R. has both ſmælþeapmaʃ and æmæle þeapmaʃ, 74.

Þeʃeþopn, þeʃanþopn, masc., gen. -eʃ, "*tufty thorn*," *buckthorn, Rhamnus catharticus and R. frangula,* Lb. I. lxiv. "Ramni. i. þeſeþorn," Gl. Harl. 978. So Gl. Arundel, 42, Gl. Dun., Gl. M. M. p. 162 a, 24.

Þeʒan for þiʒan, *press, pierce,* by contraction þyn, which see. Lb. I. xvii. 1. Þupſte ʒeþeʒeðe, C.E., p. 92, line 17. Lacn. 114.

Þelma, masc., gen. by analogy in -an; Lb. I. xxxv. Foþþylman in the Lambeth Psalter is *obscurare.* Foʃðon þe þeoʃtpu ne beoð ʃopþylmoðe *vel* ʃopʃpoþcene to þe : ꝺ niht ʃpa ʃpa dæʒ bið onlihteð. Quia tenebræ non obscurabuntur a te, et nox sicut dies illuminabitur, Ps. cxxxviii. 11. Ne þeapʃ he hopian no · þyʃtʃpum ʃopþylmeð · þ he þonan mote, Judith x. = p. 23, line 12, Thwaites. Combined with burning brands of fire in Cod. Exon. p. 217, line 23 = MS. fol. 60 a, line 4. Compare Διὰ τὸ ἐπιφέρειν τοὺς κατὰ πνιγμὸν κινδύνους καὶ καίειν τὴν φάρυγγα, Dioskor. iv. 156, with IIb. clxxxi. 2, last words. Þelma and heat go together in the Lb. In Hb. cxl. 1, I do not find the words the Saxon had before him, but translate as guided by clxxxi.

Þeoh hpeopʃa, masc., *kneecap, Lorica,* Gl. Harl., *genusculum.* So "Whirl booan, *the round bone of the knee, the patella,*" Gl. to Tim Bobbin. The bone has some similarity to lumbar and caudal vertebræ.

Þeop, *the dry disease,* fem., gen. -e. See þeopabl. Fem. Lb. III. xxx., contents ; if þæpe be correct.

Þeopabl, fem., *the dry disease or wasting away.* Lb. II. lxiii. A different signifi-

þeopabl—*cont.*
cation was assigned by Somner, whose words are "Ðeop, ðeope, morbus qui-" dam, fortasse, inflammatio, phlegmone, " an inflammation, a blistering heat of " the blood or a swelling against nature " being hot and red." Probably this conjecture of Somners was founded partly on the etymological considerations which follow. Þeop seems to have for its kindred words þyn *dry,* þypʃt *thirst,* that is, *dryness,* the German dorre, *dry,* and a large number of other words, for which *see* Spoon and Sparrow, arts 478, 592, etc. In the German Dürrsucht (*dry sickness*) *atrophy, meagreness, consumption,* the withering effects of dryness have produced the expression. The Latin equivalent for these ideas would be Tabes, which is treated of by Celsus (iii. 22) as having for its species ἀτροφία, *atrophy,* καχεξία, *corrupt habit of body,* and φθίσις, consumption. Þeopabl appearing in the feet, Lb. xlvii., is Tabes in pedibus, such a wasting away of the feet as arises from ulceration produced by an over long journey on foot. That the disease is spoken of as local sometimes follows from the teaching of Celsus : " Huic (scil. cachexiæ) præter " tabem, illud quoque nonnunquam ac-" cidere solet, ut per assiduas pustulas " aut ulcera, summa cutis exasperetur, " vel aliquæ corporis partes intumes-" cant." That worms belong to the disease is paralleled in German, which has its Dürrmäden, worms which cause a meagre habit and atrophy.

Þeopþypt, ðyoþþypt, fem., gen. -e, *ploughman's spikenard, Inula conyza,* formerly called C. squarrosa, Germ. Durrwurz, Doorkraut ; which is as above. Lb. III. xxx. Lacn. 40.

Þymel, *a thumbstall.* Lb. I. lxxv. Thimble is the same word, the material is not in the syllables. Cf. Germ. Däumling, *a thumbstall;* Dutch, Duymelinck, *tegmen sive munimen pollicis, theca pollicis*

þymel—*cont.*

(Kilian). Þymel seems to have been
originally an adjective, hence its use in
Laws of Ine. xlix. Duymelinck in
Kilian is also a wren, *a bird as big as
ones thumb.*

þýn, præt. þýbe, p. part. þyb ; *squeeze,
press, stab.* Lb. II. iii. v., Quadr. vi. 15.
Norse at þjá. The infinitive þýban of
dictionaries has no existence. Geþýn,
squeeze, Solom. and Sat. p. 150, line 34.
Geþýð, id. p. 162, line 607. *See* Aþyn.
It is a contraction of þiȝan. Beda, 611,
41. The present Ic þi, *fodio,* ÆG. 32,
line 45.

þinan, *grow moist;* the intransitive to
þænan, *moisten,* as Lb. I. ii. 21.

þure þiftel, masc.,gen. -les ; "tufty thistle,"
sow thistle, sonchus oleraceus, Bot. Also
þuþirtel, Germ. Dudistel, Lb. III. viii.

þunopclaþre, fem., gen. -an ; *bugle, aiuga
reptans,* if we may rely on a gl. Leechdoms, vol. I. p. 374. " Consolida media,
" þundre clouere," Gl. Harl. 978. On
consolida media, *see* Fuchsius, p. 386.

þunoppyþr, fem., gen. -e, *houseleek, sempervivum tectorum,* so called from its
averting thunderbolts ; Grimm. Mythol.
clxi.: an allusion to this is found in some
copies of Dioskorides, iv. 189.

þunranȝe, -penȝe, gen. -an, neut. as penȝe,
temple, timpus. Lb. I. i. 8 ; III. 1.

þunranȝe—*cont.*
Plural in -ȝe. Lb. III. xli. Geyloh þa
mid anum býtle buȝan hir þunpenȝan,
Judges iv. 21, where, I presume, buȝan
is not for beȝen, but rather begeonb.
ÆG. 12, line 16.

þpænan, *make to dwindle, minuere,* it appears
Hb. ii. 7, compared with Dpinan, Hb.
ii. 4. So Lb. L. xxxi. 1. This signification now seems too conjectural.

2. *To soften, mollire.* Tiloben hir
læcar ꝸ ðone rpile mid realrum ꝸ mid
beþenum ȝeþpænan polbon, Bed., 611, 19,
*Curabant medici hunc adpositis pigmen-
torum fomentis emollire.* Done unȝe-
þpænan rpýle mid ðyȝbe ꝸ ðpenbe, ibid.
line 40, *Tumorem illum infestum horum
adpositione comprimere ac mollire curabat.*

3. *Irrigate.* Foþ þam ȝir þ pæteþ hi
ne ȝeþpænbe, ðonne bruȝobe hio, etc.
Boet. p. 78, line 27. *If the water had
not irrigated her,* the earth, *she would
have got dry, etc.* Ða abþuȝoban heoptan ȝeðpænan mid ðæm rlopenban yðon
hir lapre, P.A. 14 a, *Corda arentia
doctrinæ fluentis irrigare.* Donne rio
milðheoptneþ ðæy lareopeþ ȝeðpænð
ꝸ ȝelecð ða bþeoft ðæþ ȝehiepenbeþ,
P.A. 27 a, *Quando hoc in audientis pec-
tore pietas prædicantis rigat.* Cf. þænan.

þrepan, *turn. See* ȝeþþepan.

INDEX OF PROPER NAMES.

LONDON :

Printed by GEORGE E. EYRE and WILLIAM SPOTTISWOODE,
Printers to the Queen's most Excellent Majesty.

For Her Majesty's Stationery Office.

[2508.—1000.—1/65.]

LIST OF WORKS

By the late Record and State Paper Commissioners,
or under the Direction of the Right Honourable
the Master of the Rolls, which may be pur-
chased of Messrs. Longman and Co., London;
Messrs. J. H. and J. Parker, Oxford and London; Messrs. Macmillan and Co., Cambridge and
London; Messrs. A. and C. Black, Edinburgh;
and Mr. A. Thom, Dublin.

PUBLIC RECORDS AND STATE PAPERS.

ROTULORUM ORIGINALIUM IN CURIA SCACCARII ABBREVIATIO. Henry
III.—Edward III. *Edited by* HENRY PLAYFORD, Esq. 2 vols
folio (1805—1810). *Price 25s.* boards, or 12s. 6d. each.

CALENDARIUM INQUISITIONUM POST MORTEM SIVE ESCAETARUM.
Henry III.—Richard III. *Edited by* JOHN CALEY and JOHN
BAYLEY, Esqrs. Vols. 2, 3, and 4, folio (1806—1808; 1821—1828),
boards : vols. 2 and 3, *price 21s.* each; vol. 4, *price 24s.*

LIBRORUM MANUSCRIPTORUM BIBLIOTHECÆ HARLEIANÆ CATALOGUS.
Vol. 4. *Edited by* The Rev. T. HARTWELL HORNE. (1812), folio,
boards. *Price 18s.*

ABBREVIATIO PLACITORUM, Richard I.—Edward II. *Edited by* The
Right Hon. GEORGE ROSE and W. ILLINGWORTH, Esq. 1 vol.
folio (1811), boards. *Price 18s.*

LIBRI CENSUALIS vocati DOMESDAY-BOOK, INDICES. *Edited by* Sir
HENRY ELLIS. Folio (1816), boards (Domesday-Book, vol. 3).
Price 21s.

LIBRI CENSUALIS vocati DOMESDAY-BOOK, ADDITAMENTA EX CODIC.
ANTIQUISS. *Edited by* Sir HENRY ELLIS. Folio (1816), boards
(Domesday-Book, vol. 4). *Price 21s.*

[LEECHD. II.]   D D

STATUTES OF THE REALM, large folio. Vols. 4 (in 2 parts), 7, 8, 9, 10, and 11, including 2 vols. of Indices (1819—1828). *Edited by* Sir T. E. TOMLINS, JOHN RAITHBY, JOHN CALEY, and WM. ELLIOTT, Esqrs. *Price* 31s. 6d. each; except the Alphabetical and Chronological Indices, *price* 30s. each.

VALOR ECCLESIASTICUS, temp. Henry VIII., Auctoritate Regia institutus. *Edited by* JOHN CALEY, Esq., and the Rev. JOSEPH HUNTER. Vols. 3 to 6, folio (1810, &c.), boards. *Price* 25s. each.

₊ The Introduction is also published in 8vo., cloth. *Price* 2s. 6d.

ROTULI SCOTIÆ IN TURRI LONDINENSI ET IN DOMO CAPITULARI WESTMONASTERIENSI ASSERVATI. 19 Edward I.—Henry VIII. *Edited by* DAVID MACPHERSON, JOHN CALEY, and W. ILLINGWORTH, Esqrs., and the Rev. T. HARTWELL HORNE. 2 vols. folio (1814 —1819), boards. *Price* 42s.

" FŒDERA, CONVENTIONES, LITTERÆ," &c. ; or, Rymer's Fœdera, New Edition, 1066—1377. Vol. 2, Part 2, and Vol. 3, Parts 1 and 2, folio (1821—1830). *Edited by* JOHN CALEY and FRED. HOLBROOKE, Esqrs. *Price* 21s. each Part.

DUCATUS LANCASTRIÆ CALENDARIUM INQUISITIONUM POST MORTEM, &c. Part 3, Calendar to the Pleadings, &c., Henry VII.—Ph. and Mary ; and Calendar to the Pleadings, 1—13 Elizabeth. Part 4, Calendar to the Pleadings to end of Elizabeth. (1827— 1834.) *Edited by* R. J. HARPER, JOHN CALEY, and WM. MINCHIN, Esqrs. Folio, boards, Part 3 (or Vol. 2), *price* 31s. 6d. ; and Part 4 (or Vol. 3), *price* 21s.

CALENDARS OF THE PROCEEDINGS IN CHANCERY, IN THE REIGN OF QUEEN ELIZABETH; to which are prefixed, Examples of earlier Proceedings in that Court from Richard II. to Elizabeth, from the Originals in the Tower. *Edited by* JOHN BAYLEY, Esq. Vols. 2 and 3 (1830—1832), folio, boards, *price* 21s. each.

PARLIAMENTARY WRITS AND WRITS OF MILITARY SUMMONS, together with the Records and Muniments relating to the Suit and Service due and performed to the King's High Court of Parliament and the Councils of the Realm. Edward I., II. *Edited by* Sir FRANCIS PALGRAVE. (1830—1834.) Folio, boards, Vol. 2, Division 1, Edward II., *price* 21s. ; Vol. 2, Division 2, *price* 21s.; Vol. 2, Division 3, *price* 42s.

ROTULI LITTERARUM CLAUSARUM IN TURRI LONDINENSI ASSERVATI. 2 vols. folio (1833—1844). The first volume, 1204—1224. The second volume, 1224—1227. *Edited by* THOMAS DUFFUS HARDY, Esq. *Price* 81s., cloth ; or separately, Vol. 1, *price* 63s.; Vol. 2, *price* 18s.

PROCEEDINGS AND ORDINANCES OF THE PRIVY COUNCIL OF ENG-
LAND, 10 Richard II.—33 Henry VIII. *Edited by* Sir N. HARRIS
NICOLAS. 7 vols. royal 8vo. (1834—1837), cloth. *Price 98s.* ; or
separately, 14s. each.

ROTULI LITTERARUM PATENTIUM IN TURRI LONDINENSI ASSERVATI,
1201—1216. *Edited by* THOMAS DUFFUS HARDY, Esq. 1 vol.
folio (1835), cloth. *Price 31s. 6d.*
** The Introduction is also published in 8vo., cloth. *Price 9s.*

ROTULI CURIÆ REGIS. Rolls and Records of the Court held before
the King's Justiciars or Justices. 6 Richard I.—1 John. *Edited
by* Sir FRANCIS PALGRAVE. 2 vols. royal 8vo. (1835), cloth.
Price 28s.

ROTULI NORMANNIÆ IN TURRI LONDINENSI ASSERVATI, 1200—1205 ;
also, 1417 to 1418. *Edited by* THOMAS DUFFUS HARDY, Esq.
1 vol. royal 8vo. (1835), cloth. *Price 12s. 6d.*

ROTULI DE OBLATIS ET FINIBUS IN TURRI LONDINENSI ASSERVATI,
tempore Regis Johannis. *Edited by* THOMAS DUFFUS HARDY,
Esq. 1 vol. royal 8vo. (1835), cloth. *Price 18s.*

EXCERPTA E ROTULIS FINIUM IN TURRI LONDINENSI ASSERVATIS.
Henry III., 1216—1272. *Edited by* CHARLES ROBERTS, Esq.
2 vols. royal 8vo. (1835, 1836), cloth, *price 32s.* ; or separately,
Vol. 1, *price 14s.* ; Vol. 2, *price 18s.*

FINES, SIVE PEDES FINIUM ; SIVE FINALES CONCORDIÆ IN CURIÂ
DOMINI REGIS. 7 Richard I.—16 John (1195—1214). *Edited by*
the Rev. JOSEPH HUNTER. In Counties. 2 vols. royal 8vo.
(1835—1844), cloth, *price 11s.*; or separately, Vol. 1, *price 8s. 6d.*;
Vol. 2, *price 2s. 6d.*

ANCIENT KALENDARS AND INVENTORIES OF THE TREASURY OF HIS
MAJESTY'S EXCHEQUER ; together with Documents illustrating
the History of that Repository. *Edited by* Sir FRANCIS PAL-
GRAVE. 3 vols. royal 8vo. (1836), cloth. *Price 42s.*

DOCUMENTS AND RECORDS illustrating the History of Scotland. and the
Transactions between the Crowns of Scotland and England ;
preserved in the Treasury of Her Majesty's Exchequer. *Edited
by* Sir FRANCIS PALGRAVE. 1 vol. royal 8vo. (1837), cloth.
Price 18s.

ROTULI CHARTARUM IN TURRI LONDINENSI ASSERVATI, 1199—1216.
Edited by THOMAS DUFFUS HARDY, Esq. 1 vol. folio (1837),
cloth. *Price 30s.*

REPORT OF THE PROCEEDINGS OF THE RECORD COMMISSIONERS.
1831 to 1837. 1 vol. folio, boards. *Price 8s.*

REGISTRUM vulgariter nuncupatum "The Record of Caernarvon," e codice MS. Harleiano, 696, descriptum. *Edited by* Sir HENRY ELLIS. 1 vol. folio (1838), cloth. *Price* 31s. 6d.

ANCIENT LAWS AND INSTITUTES OF ENGLAND ; comprising Laws enacted under the Anglo-Saxon Kings, from Æthelbirht to Cnut, with an English Translation of the Saxon ; the Laws called Edward the Confessor's ; the Laws of William the Conqueror, and those ascribed to Henry the First ; also, Monumenta Ecclesiastica Anglicana, from the 7th to the 10th century ; and the Ancient Latin Version of the Anglo-Saxon Laws ; with a compendious Glossary, &c. *Edited by* BENJAMIN THORPE, Esq. 1 vol. folio (1840), cloth. *Price* 40s. Or, in 2 vols. royal 8vo. cloth. *Price* 30s.

ANCIENT LAWS AND INSTITUTES OF WALES; comprising Laws supposed to be enacted by Hewel the Good ; modified by subsequent Regulations under the Native Princes, prior to the Conquest by Edward the First ; and anomalous Laws, consisting principally of Institutions which, by the Statute of Ruddlan, were admitted to continue in force. With an English Translation of the Welsh Text. To which are added, a few Latin Transcripts, containing Digests of the Welsh Laws, principally of the Dimetian Code. With Indices and Glossary. *Edited by* ANEURIN OWEN, Esq. 1 vol. folio (1841), cloth. *Price* 44s. Or, in 2 vols. royal 8vo. cloth. *Price* 36s.

ROTULI DE LIBERATE AC DE MISIS ET PRÆSTITIS, Regnante Johanne. *Edited by* THOMAS DUFFUS HARDY, Esq. 1 vol. royal 8vo. (1844), cloth. *Price* 6s.

THE GREAT ROLLS OF THE PIPE FOR THE SECOND, THIRD, AND FOURTH YEARS OF THE REIGN OF KING HENRY THE SECOND, 1155—1158. *Edited by* the Rev. JOSEPH HUNTER. 1 vol. royal 8vo. (1844), cloth. *Price* 4s. 6d.

THE GREAT ROLL OF THE PIPE FOR THE FIRST YEAR OF THE REIGN OF KING RICHARD THE FIRST, 1189—1190. *Edited by* the Rev. JOSEPH HUNTER. 1 vol. royal 8vo. (1844), cloth. *Price* 6s.

DOCUMENTS ILLUSTRATIVE OF ENGLISH HISTORY in the 13th and 14th centuries, selected from the Records in the Exchequer. *Edited by* HENRY COLE, Esq. 1 vol. fcp. folio (1844), cloth. *Price* 45s. 6d.

MODUS TENENDI PARLIAMENTUM. An Ancient Treatise on the Mode of holding the Parliament in England. *Edited by* THOMAS DUFFUS HARDY, Esq. 1 vol. 8vo. (1846), cloth. *Price* 2s. 6d.

MONUMENTA HISTORICA BRITANNICA, or, Materials for the History of
Britain from the earliest period. Vol. 1, extending to the Norman
Conquest. Prepared, and illustrated with Notes, by the late
HENRY PETRIE, Esq., F.S.A., Keeper of the Records in the Tower
of London, assisted by the Rev. JOHN SHARPE, Rector of Castle
Eaton, Wilts. Finally completed for publication, and with an
Introduction, by THOMAS DUFFUS HARDY, Esq., Assistant Keeper
of Records. (Printed by command of Her Majesty.) Folio
(1848). *Price 42s.*

REGISTRUM MAGNI SIGILLI REGUM SCOTORUM in Archivis Publicis
asservatum. 1306—1424. *Edited by* THOMAS THOMSON, Esq.
Folio (1814). *Price 15s.*

THE ACTS OF THE PARLIAMENTS OF SCOTLAND. 11 vols. folio (1814—
1844). Vol. I. *Edited by* THOMAS THOMSON and COSMO INNES,
Esqrs. *Price 42s.* Also, Vols. 4, 7, 8, 9, 10, 11 ; *price 10s. 6d.*
each.

THE ACTS OF THE LORDS AUDITORS OF CAUSES AND COMPLAINTS.
1466—1494. *Edited by* THOMAS THOMSON, Esq. Folio (1839).
Price 10s. 6d.

THE ACTS OF THE LORDS OF COUNCIL IN CIVIL CAUSES. 1478—
1495. *Edited by* THOMAS THOMSON, Esq. Folio (1839). *Price
10s. 6d.*

ISSUE ROLL OF THOMAS DE BRANTINGHAM, Bishop of Exeter, Lord
High Treasurer of England, containing Payments out of His
Majesty's Revenue, 44 Edward III., 1370. *Edited by* FREDERICK
DEVON, Esq. 1 vol. 4to. (1835), cloth. *Price 35s.* Or, in royal
8vo. cloth. *Price 25s.*

ISSUES OF THE EXCHEQUER, containing similar matter to the above;
James I.; extracted from the Pell Records. *Edited by* FREDERICK
DEVON, Esq. 1 vol. 4to. (1836), cloth. *Price 30s.* Or, in
royal 8vo. cloth. *Price 21s.*

ISSUES OF THE EXCHEQUER, containing similar matter to the above ;
Henry III.—Henry VI. ; extracted from the Pell Records. *Edited
by* FREDERICK DEVON, Esq. 1 vol. 4to. (1837), cloth. *Price 40s.*
Or, in royal 8vo. cloth. *Price 30s.*

NOTES OF MATERIALS FOR THE HISTORY OF PUBLIC DEPARTMENTS.
By F. S. THOMAS, Esq., Secretary of the Public Record Office.
Demy folio (1846), cloth. *Price 10s.*

HANDBOOK TO THE PUBLIC RECORDS. *By* F. S. THOMAS, Esq. Royal
8vo. (1853), cloth. *Price 12s.*

STATE PAPERS DURING THE REIGN OF HENRY THE EIGHTH. 11 vols.
4to., cloth, (1830—1852), with Indices of Persons and Places.
Price 5l. 15s. 6d. ; or separately, *price 10s. 6d.* each.

Vol. I.—Domestic Correspondence.
Vols. II. & III.—Correspondence relating to Ireland.
Vols. IV. & V.—Correspondence relating to Scotland.
Vols. VI. to XI.—Correspondence between England and Foreign
Courts.

HISTORICAL NOTES RELATIVE TO THE HISTORY OF ENGLAND; from
the Accession of Henry VIII. to the Death of Queen Anne (1509
—1714). Designed as a Book of instant Reference for ascertaining
the Dates of Events mentioned in History and Manuscripts. The
Name of every Person and Event mentioned in History within
the above period is placed in Alphabetical and Chronological Order,
and the Authority whence taken is given in each case, whether
from Printed History or from Manuscripts. *By* F. S. THOMAS,
Esq. 3 vols. 8vo. (1856), cloth. *Price 40s.*

In the Press.

CALENDARIUM GENEALOGICUM ; for the Reigns of Henry III. and
Edward I. *Edited by* CHARLES ROBERTS, Esq.

CALENDARS OF STATE PAPERS.

[IMPERIAL 8vo. *Price 15s.* each Volume or Part.]

CALENDAR OF STATE PAPERS, DOMESTIC SERIES, OF THE REIGNS OF
EDWARD VI., MARY, and ELIZABETH, preserved in Her Majesty's
Public Record Office. *Edited by* ROBERT LEMON, Esq., F.S.A.
1856.
Vol. I.—1547–1580.

CALENDAR OF STATE PAPERS, DOMESTIC SERIES, OF THE REIGN OF
JAMES I., preserved in Her Majesty's Public Record Office.
Edited by MARY ANNE EVERETT GREEN. 1857–1859.
Vol. I.—1603–1610.
Vol. II.—1611–1618.
Vol. III.—1619–1623.
Vol. IV.—1623–1625, with Addenda.

CALENDAR OF STATE PAPERS, DOMESTIC SERIES, OF THE REIGN OF
CHARLES I., preserved in Her Majesty's Public Record Office.
Edited by JOHN BRUCE, Esq., V.P.S.A. 1858–1864.
Vol. I.—1625–1626.
Vol. II.—1627–1628.
Vol. III.—1628–1629.
Vol. IV.—1629–1631.
Vol. V.—1631–1633.
Vol. VI.—1633–1634.
Vol. VII.—1634–1635.

CALENDAR OF STATE PAPERS, DOMESTIC SERIES, OF THE REIGN OF
CHARLES II., preserved in Her Majesty's Public Record Office.
Edited by MARY ANNE EVERETT GREEN. 1860–1864.
Vol. I.—1660–1661.
Vol. II.—1661–1662.
Vol. III.—1663–1664.
Vol. IV.—1664–1665.
Vol. V.—1665–1666.
Vol. VI.—1666–1667.

CALENDAR OF STATE PAPERS relating to SCOTLAND, preserved in
Her Majesty's Public Record Office. *Edited by* MARKHAM JOHN
THORPE, Esq., of St. Edmund Hall, Oxford. 1858.
Vol. I., the Scottish Series, of the Reigns of Henry VIII.,
Edward VI., Mary, and Elizabeth, 1509–1589.
Vol. II., the Scottish Series, of the Reign of Elizabeth,
1589–1603 ; an Appendix to the Scottish Series, 1543–
1592 ; and the State Papers relating to Mary Queen of
Scots during her Detention in England, 1568–1587.

CALENDAR OF STATE PAPERS relating to IRELAND, preserved in Her
Majesty's Public Record Office. *Edited by* HANS CLAUDE
HAMILTON, Esq., F.S.A. 1860.
    Vol. I.—1509–1573.

CALENDAR OF STATE PAPERS, COLONIAL SERIES, preserved in Her
Majesty's Public Record Office, and elsewhere. *Edited by* W.
NOEL SAINSBURY, Esq. 1860–1862.
    Vol. I.—America and West Indies, 1574–1660.
    Vol. II.—East Indies, China, and Japan, 1513–1616.

CALENDAR OF LETTERS AND PAPERS, FOREIGN AND DOMESTIC, OF THE
REIGN OF HENRY VIII., preserved in the Public Record Office,
the British Museum, &c. *Edited by* J. S. BREWER, M.A., Professor of English Literature, King's College, London. 1862–1864.
    Vol. I.—1509–1514.
    Vol. II. (in Two Parts),—1515–1518.

CALENDAR OF STATE PAPERS, FOREIGN SERIES, OF THE REIGN OF
EDWARD VI. *Edited by* W. B. TURNBULL, Esq., of Lincoln's Inn,
Barrister-at-Law, and Correspondant du Comité Impérial des
Travaux Historiques et des Sociétés Savantes de France. 1861.

CALENDAR OF STATE PAPERS, FOREIGN SERIES, OF THE REIGN OF
MARY. *Edited by* W. B. TURNBULL, Esq., of Lincoln's Inn,
Barrister-at-Law, and Correspondant du Comité Impérial des
Travaux Historiques et des Sociétés Savantes de France. 1861.

CALENDAR OF STATE PAPERS, FOREIGN SERIES, OF THE REIGN OF
ELIZABETH. *Edited by* the Rev. JOSEPH STEVENSON, M.A., of
University College, Durham. 1863.
    Vol. I.—1558–1559.

CALENDAR OF LETTERS, DESPATCHES, AND STATE PAPERS relating to
the Negotiations between England and Spain, preserved in
the Archives at Simancas, and elsewhere. *Edited by* G. A.
BERGENROTH. 1862.
    Vol. I.--Hen. VII.—1485–1509.

CALENDAR OF STATE PAPERS AND MANUSCRIPTS, relating to ENGLISH
AFFAIRS, preserved in the Archives of Venice, &c. *Edited by*
RAWDON BROWN, Esq. 1864.
    Vol. I.—1202–1509.

In the Press.

CALENDAR OF STATE PAPERS relating to IRELAND, preserved in
Her Majesty's Public Record Office. *Edited by* HANS CLAUDE
HAMILTON, Esq., F.S.A. Vol. II.—1574–1585.

CALENDAR OF STATE PAPERS, DOMESTIC SERIES, OF THE REIGN OF ELIZABETH (continued), preserved in Her Majesty's Public Record Office. *Edited by* ROBERT LEMON, Esq., F.S.A. 1580–1590.

CALENDAR OF STATE PAPERS, FOREIGN SERIES, OF THE REIGN OF ELIZABETH. *Edited by* the Rev. JOSEPH STEVENSON, M.A., of University College, Durham. Vol. II.—1559–1560.

CALENDAR OF STATE PAPERS, DOMESTIC SERIES, OF THE REIGN OF CHARLES I., preserved in Her Majesty's Public Record Office. *Edited by* JOHN BRUCE, Esq., F.S.A. Vol. VIII.

CALENDAR OF LETTERS AND PAPERS, FOREIGN AND DOMESTIC, OF THE REIGN OF HENRY VIII., preserved in Her Majesty's Public Record Office, the British Museum, &c. *Edited by* J. S. BREWER, M.A., Professor of English Literature, King's College, London. Vol. III.—1519, &c.

CALENDAR OF STATE PAPERS, DOMESTIC SERIES, OF THE REIGN OF CHARLES II., preserved in Her Majesty's Public Record Office. *Edited by* MARY ANNE EVERETT GREEN. Vol. VII.—1667–1668.

CALENDAR OF STATE PAPERS AND MANUSCRIPTS, relating to ENGLISH AFFAIRS, preserved in the Archives of Venice, &c. *Edited by* RAWDON BROWN, Esq. Vol. II.

In Progress.

CALENDAR OF LETTERS, DESPATCHES, AND STATE PAPERS relating to the Negotiations between England and Spain, preserved in the Archives at Simancas, and elsewhere. *Edited by* G. A. BERGENROTH. Vol. II.—Henry VIII.

CALENDAR OF STATE PAPERS, COLONIAL SERIES, preserved in Her Majesty's Public Record Office, and elsewhere. *Edited by* W. NOËL SAINSBURY, Esq. Vol. III.—East Indies, China, and Japan.

THE CHRONICLES AND MEMORIALS OF GREAT BRITAIN AND IRELAND DURING THE MIDDLE AGES.

[ROYAL 8vo. *Price* 10*s.* each Volume or Part.]

1. THE CHRONICLE OF ENGLAND, by JOHN CAPGRAVE. *Edited by* the Rev. F. C. HINGESTON, M.A., of Exeter College, Oxford. 1858.
2. CHRONICON MONASTERII DE ABINGDON. Vols. I. and II. *Edited by* the Rev. JOSEPH STEVENSON, M.A., of University College, Durham, and Vicar of Leighton Buzzard. 1858.
3. LIVES OF EDWARD THE CONFESSOR. I.—La Estoire de Seint Aedward le Rei. II.—Vita Beati Edvardi Regis et Confessoris. III.—Vita Ædnuardi Regis qui apud Westmonasterium requiescit. *Edited by* HENRY RICHARDS LUARD, M.A., Fellow and Assistant Tutor of Trinity College, Cambridge. 1858.
4. MONUMENTA FRANCISCANA ; scilicet, I.—Thomas de Eccleston de Adventu Fratrum Minorum in Angliam. II.—Adæ de Marisco Epistolæ. III.—Registrum Fratrum Minorum Londoniæ. *Edited by* J. S. BREWER, M.A., Professor of English Literature, King's College, London. 1858.
5. FASCICULI ZIZANIORUM MAGISTRI JOHANNIS WYCLIF CUM TRITICO. Ascribed to THOMAS NETTER, of WALDEN, Provincial of the Carmelite Order in England, and Confessor to King Henry the Fifth. *Edited by* the Rev. W. W. SHIRLEY, M.A., Tutor and late Fellow of Wadham College, Oxford. 1858.
6. THE BUIK OF THE CRONICLIS OF SCOTLAND ; or, A Metrical Version of the History of Hector Boece ; by WILLIAM STEWART. Vols. I., II., and III. *Edited by* W. B. TURNBULL, Esq., of Lincoln's Inn, Barrister-at-Law. 1858.
7. JOHANNIS CAPGRAVE LIBER DE ILLUSTRIBUS HENRICIS. *Edited by* the Rev. F. C. HINGESTON, M.A., of Exeter College, Oxford. 1858.
8. HISTORIA MONASTERII S. AUGUSTINI CANTUARIENSIS, by THOMAS OF ELMHAM, formerly Monk and Treasurer of that Foundation. *Edited by* CHARLES HARDWICK, M.A., Fellow of St. Catharine's Hall, and Christian Advocate in the University of Cambridge. 1858.

9. EULOGIUM (HISTORIARUM SIVE TEMPORIS) : Chronicon ab Orbe condito usque ad Annum Domini 1366 ; a Monacho quodam Malmesbiriensi exaratum. Vols. I., II., and III. *Edited by* F. S. HAYDON, Esq., B.A. 1858–1863.

10. MEMORIALS OF HENRY THE SEVENTH : Bernardi Andreæ Tholosatis Vita Regis Henrici Septimi ; necnon alia quædam ad eundem Regem spectantia. *Edited by* JAMES GAIRDNER, Esq. 1858.

11. MEMORIALS OF HENRY THE FIFTH. I.—Vita Henrici Quinti, Roberto Redmanno auctore. II.—Versus Rhythmici in laudem Regis Henrici Quinti. III.—Elmhami Liber Metricus de Henrico V. *Edited by* C. A. COLE, Esq. 1858.

12. MUNIMENTA GILDHALLÆ LONDONIENSIS ; Liber Albus, Liber Custumarum, et Liber Horn, in archivis Gildhallæ asservati. Vol. I., Liber Albus. Vol. II. (in Two Parts), Liber Custumarum. Vol. III., Translation of the Anglo-Norman Passages in Liber Albus, Glossaries, Appendices, and Index. *Edited by* HENRY THOMAS RILEY, Esq., M.A., Barrister-at-Law. 1859–1860.

13. CHRONICA JOHANNIS DE OXENEDES. *Edited by* Sir HENRY ELLIS, K.H. 1859.

14. A COLLECTION OF POLITICAL POEMS AND SONGS RELATING TO ENGLISH HISTORY, FROM THE ACCESSION OF EDWARD III. TO THE REIGN OF HENRY VIII. Vols. I. and II. *Edited by* THOMAS WRIGHT, Esq., M.A. 1859–1861.

15. The "OPUS TERTIUM," "OPUS MINUS," &c., of ROGER BACON. *Edited by* J. S. BREWER, M.A., Professor of English Literature, King's College, London. 1859.

16. BARTHOLOMÆI DE COTTON, MONACHI NORWICENSIS, HISTORIA ANGLICANA (A.D. 449—1298). *Edited by* HENRY RICHARDS LUARD, M.A., Fellow and Assistant Tutor of Trinity College, Cambridge. 1859.

17. BRUT Y TYWYSOGION ; or, The Chronicle of the Princes of Wales. *Edited by* the Rev. J. WILLIAMS AB ITHEL. 1860.

18. A COLLECTION OF ROYAL AND HISTORICAL LETTERS DURING THE REIGN OF HENRY IV. Vol. I. *Edited by* the Rev. F. C. HINGESTON, M.A., of Exeter College, Oxford. 1860.

19. THE REPRESSOR OF OVER MUCH BLAMING OF THE CLERGY. By REGINALD PECOCK, sometime Bishop of Chichester. Vols. I. and II. *Edited by* CHURCHILL BABINGTON, B.D., Fellow of St. John's College, Cambridge. 1860.

20. ANNALES CAMBRIÆ.   *Edited by* the Rev. J. WILLIAMS AB ITHEL. 1860.

21. THE WORKS OF GIRALDUS CAMBRENSIS.   Vols. I., II., and III. *Edited by* J. S. BREWER, M.A., Professor of English Literature, King's College, London.   1861–1863.

22. LETTERS AND PAPERS ILLUSTRATIVE OF THE WARS OF THE ENGLISH IN FRANCE DURING THE REIGN OF HENRY THE SIXTH, KING OF-ENGLAND.   Vol. I., and Vol. II. (in Two Parts).   *Edited by* the Rev. JOSEPH STEVENSON, M.A., of University College, Durham, and Vicar of Leighton Buzzard.   1861–1864.

23. THE ANGLO-SAXON CHRONICLE, ACCORDING TO THE SEVERAL ORIGINAL AUTHORITIES.   Vol. I., Original Texts.   Vol. II., Translation.   *Edited by* BENJAMIN THORPE, Esq., Member of the Royal Academy of Sciences at Munich, and of the Society of Netherlandish Literature at Leyden.   1861.

24. LETTERS AND PAPERS ILLUSTRATIVE OF THE REIGNS OF RICHARD III. AND HENRY VII.   Vols. I. and II.   *Edited by* JAMES GAIRDNER, Esq.   1861–1863.

25. LETTERS OF BISHOP GROSSETESTE, illustrative of the Social Condition of his Time.   *Edited by* HENRY RICHARDS LUARD, M.A., Fellow and Assistant Tutor of Trinity College, Cambridge. 1861.

26. DESCRIPTIVE CATALOGUE OF MANUSCRIPTS RELATING TO THE HISTORY OF GREAT BRITAIN AND IRELAND.   Vol. I. (in Two Parts) ; Anterior to the Norman Invasion.   *By* THOMAS DUFFUS HARDY, Esq., Deputy Keeper of the Public Records. 1862.

27. ROYAL AND OTHER HISTORICAL LETTERS ILLUSTRATIVE OF THE REIGN OF HENRY III.   From the Originals in the Public Record Office.   Vol. I., 1216–1235.   *Selected and edited by* the Rev. W. W. SHIRLEY, Tutor and late Fellow of Wadham College, Oxford.   1862.

28. THE SAINT ALBAN'S CHRONICLES :—THE ENGLISH HISTORY OF THOMAS WALSINGHAM, MONK OF SAINT ALBAN'S.   Vol. I., 1272– 1381.   Vol. II., 1381–1422.   *Edited by* HENRY THOMAS RILEY, Esq., M.A., Barrister-at-Law.   1863–1864.

29. CHRONICON ABBATIÆ EVESHAMENSIS, AUCTORIBUS DOMINICO PRIORE EVESHAMIÆ ET THOMA DE MARLEBERGE ABBATE, A FUNDATIONE AD ANNUM 1213, UNA CUM CONTINUATIONE AD ANNUM 1418.   *Edited by* the Rev. W. D. MACRAY, M.A., Bodleian Library, Oxford.   1863.

30. RICARDI DE CIRENCESTRIA SPECULUM HISTORIALE DE GESTIS REGUM ANGLIÆ.   Vol. I., 447–871.   *Edited by* JOHN E. B. MAYOR, M.A., Fellow and Assistant Tutor of St. John's College, Cambridge.   1863.

31. YEAR BOOKS OF THE REIGN OF EDWARD THE FIRST. Years 30–31, and 32–33. *Edited and translated by* ALFRED JOHN HORWOOD, Esq., of the Middle Temple, Barrister-at-Law. 1863–1864.

32. NARRATIVES OF THE EXPULSION OF THE ENGLISH FROM NORMANDY, 1449-1450.—Robertus Blondelli de Reductione Normanniæ: Le Recouvrement de Normendie, par Berry, Herault du Roy: Conferences between the Ambassadors of France and England. *Edited, from MSS. in the Imperial Library at Paris, by* the Rev. JOSEPH STEVENSON, M.A., of University College, Durham. 1863.

33. HISTORIA ET CARTULARIUM MONASTERII S. PETRI GLOUCESTRIÆ. Vol. I. *Edited by* W. H. HART, Esq., F.S.A.; Membre correspondant de la Société des Antiquaires de Normandie. 1863.

34. ALEXANDRI NECKAM DE NATURIS RERUM LIBRI DUO; with NECKAM'S POEM, DE LAUDIBUS DIVINÆ SAPIENTIÆ. *Edited by* THOMAS WRIGHT, Esq., M.A. 1863.

35. LEECHDOMS, WORTCUNNING, AND STARCRAFT OF EARLY ENGLAND; being a Collection of Documents illustrating the History of Science in this Country before the Norman Conquest. Vols. I. and II. *Collected and edited by* the Rev. T. OSWALD COCKAYNE, M.A., of St. John's College, Cambridge. 1864-1865.

36. ANNALES MONASTICI. Vol. I.:—Annales de Margan, 1066-1232; Annales de Theokesberia,1066-1263; Annales de Burton, 1004-1263. *Edited by* HENRY RICHARDS LUARD, M.A., Fellow and Assistant Tutor of Trinity College, and Registrary of the University, Cambridge. 1864.

37. MAGNA VITA S. HUGONIS EPISCOPI LINCOLNIENSIS. From Manuscripts in the Bodleian Library, Oxford, and the Imperial Library, Paris. *Edited by* the Rev. JAMES F. DIMOCK, M.A., Rector of Barnburgh, Yorkshire. 1864.

38. CHRONICLES AND MEMORIALS OF THE REIGN OF RICHARD THE FIRST. Vol. I. ITINERARIUM PEREGRINORUM ET GESTA REGIS RICARDI. *Edited by* WILLIAM STUBBS, M.A., Vicar of Navestock, Essex, and Lambeth Librarian. 1864.

39. RECUEIL DES CRONIQUES ET ANCHIENNES ISTORIES DE LA GRANT BRETAIGNE A PRESENT NOMME ENGLETERRE, par JEHAN DE WAURIN. From Albina to 688. *Edited by* WILLIAM HARDY, Esq., F.S.A. 1864.

40. A COLLECTION OF THE CHRONICLES AND ANCIENT HISTORIES OF GREAT BRITAIN, NOW CALLED ENGLAND, BY JOHN DE WAVRIN. From Albina to 688. (Translation of the preceding.) *Edited and translated by* WILLIAM HARDY, Esq., F.S.A. 1864.

14

In the Press.

LE LIVERE DE REIS DE BRITTANIE. *Edited by* J. GLOVER, M.A., Vicar of Brading, Isle of Wight.

THE WARS OF THE DANES IN IRELAND : written in the Irish language. *Edited by* the Rev. J. H. TODD, D.D., Librarian of the University of Dublin.

A COLLECTION OF SAGAS AND OTHER HISTORICAL DOCUMENTS relating to the Settlements and Descents of the Northmen on the British Isles. *Edited by* GEORGE W. DASENT, Esq., D.C.L. Oxon.

A COLLECTION OF ROYAL AND HISTORICAL LETTERS DURING THE REIGN OF HENRY IV. Vol. II. *Edited by* the Rev. F. C. HINGESTON, M.A., of Exeter College, Oxford.

POLYCHRONICON RANULPHI HIGDENI, with Trevisa's Translation. *Edited by* CHURCHILL BABINGTON, B.D., Fellow of St. John's College, Cambridge.

OFFICIAL CORRESPONDENCE OF THOMAS BEKYNTON, SECRETARY TO HENRY VI., with other LETTERS and DOCUMENTS. *Edited by* the Rev. GEORGE WILLIAMS, B.D., Senior Fellow of King's College, Cambridge.

ROYAL AND OTHER HISTORICAL LETTERS ILLUSTRATIVE OF THE REIGN OF HENRY III. From the Originals in the Public Record Office. Vol. II. *Selected and edited by* the Rev. W. W. SHIRLEY, D.D., Regius Professor in Ecclesiastical History, and Canon of Christ Church, Oxford.

ORIGINAL DOCUMENTS ILLUSTRATIVE OF ACADEMICAL AND CLERICAL LIFE AND STUDIES AT OXFORD BETWEEN THE REIGNS OF HENRY III. AND HENRY VII. *Edited by* the Rev. H. ANSTEY, M.A.

ROLL OF THE PRIVY COUNCIL OF IRELAND, 16 RICHARD II. *Edited by* the Rev. JAMES GRAVES, A.B., Treasurer of St. Canice, Ireland.

RICARDI DE CIRENCESTRIA SPECULUM HISTORIALE DE GESTIS REGUM ANGLIÆ. Vol. II., 872-1066. *Edited by* JOHN E. B. MAYOR, M.A., Fellow and Assistant Tutor of St. John's College, and Librarian of the University, Cambridge.

THE WORKS OF GIRALDUS CAMBRENSIS. Vol. IV. *Edited by* J. S. BREWER, M.A., Professor of English Literature, King's College, London.

HISTORIA ET CARTULARIUM MONASTERII S. PETRI GLOUCESTRIÆ. Vol. II. *Edited by* W. H. HART, Esq., F.S.A. ; Membre correspondant de la Société des Antiquaires de Normandie.

HISTORIA MINOR MATTHÆI PARIS. *Edited by* Sir FREDERICK MADDEN, K.H., Keeper of the Department of Manuscripts, British Museum.

ANNALES MONASTICI. Vol. II. *Edited by* HENRY RICHARDS LUARD, M.A., Fellow and Assistant Tutor of Trinity College, and Registrary of the University, Cambridge.

CHRONICON RADULPHI ABBATIS COGGESHALENSIS MAJUS; and, CHRONICON TERRÆ SANCTÆ ET DE CAPTIS A SALADINO HIEROSOLYMIS. *Edited by* the Rev. JOSEPH STEVENSON, M.A., of University College, Durham.

THE SAINT ALBAN'S CHRONICLES :—Vol. III., THE CHRONICLES OF RISHANGER, TROKELOWE, BLANEFORD, AND OTHERS. *Edited by* HENRY THOMAS RILEY, Esq., M.A., Barrister-at-Law.

CHRONICLES AND MEMORIALS OF THE REIGN OF RICHARD THE FIRST. Vol. II. *Edited by* WILLIAM STUBBS, M.A., Vicar of Navestock, Essex, and Lambeth Librarian.

YEAR BOOKS OF THE REIGN OF EDWARD THE FIRST. 20th, 21st, and 22nd Years. *Edited and translated by* ALFRED JOHN HORWOOD, Esq., of the Middle Temple, Barrister-at-Law.

RECUEIL DES CRONIQUES ET ANCHIENNES ISTORIES DE LA GRANT BRETAIGNE A PRESENT NOMME ENGLETERRE, par JEHAN DE WAURIN (continued). *Edited by* WILLIAM HARDY, Esq., F.S.A.

DESCRIPTIVE CATALOGUE OF MANUSCRIPTS RELATING TO THE HISTORY OF GREAT BRITAIN AND IRELAND. Vol. II. *By* THOMAS DUFFUS HARDY, Esq., Deputy Keeper of the Public Records.

In Progress.

CHRONICA MONASTERII DE MELSA, AB ANNO 1150 USQUE AD ANNUM 1400. *Edited by* EDWARD AUGUSTUS BOND, Esq., Assistant Keeper of the Department of Manuscripts, and Egerton Librarian, British Museum.

DOCUMENTS RELATING TO ENGLAND AND SCOTLAND, FROM THE NORTHERN REGISTERS. *Edited by* the Rev. JAMES RAINE, M.A., of Durham University.

WILLIELMI MALMESBIRIENSIS DE GESTIS PONTIFICUM ANGLORUM, LIBRI V. *Edited by* N. E. S. A. HAMILTON, Esq., of the Department of Manuscripts, British Museum.

January 1865.

www.ingramcontent.com/pod-product-compliance
Lightning Source LLC
Chambersburg PA
CBHW031820270326
41932CB00008B/476